The Global Practice of Forensic Science

The Global Practice of Forensic Science

EDITED BY

Douglas H. Ubelaker

Former President, American Academy of Forensic Sciences
Senior Scientist, Smithsonian Institution
Department of Anthropology, National Museum of Natural History
Smithsonian Institution, Washington, D.C.

FOREWORD BY DANIEL A. MARTELL

WILEY Blackwell

This edition first published 2015 © 2015 by John Wiley & Sons Ltd

Registered office: John Wiley & Sons, Ltd, The Atrium, Southern Gate, Chichester
West Sussex, PO19 8SQ, UK

Editorial offices: 9600 Garsington Road, Oxford, OX4 2DQ, UK
The Atrium, Southern Gate, Chichester, West Sussex, PO19 8SQ, UK
111 River Street, Hoboken, NJ 07030-5774, USA

For details of our global editorial offices, for customer services and for information about how to apply for
permission to reuse the copyright material in this book please see our website at
www.wiley.com/wiley-blackwell.

Library of Congress Cataloging-in-Publication Data

The global practice of forensic science / Douglas H. Ubelaker, editor.
    pages cm. – (Forensic science in focus)
 Includes index.
 ISBN 978-1-118-72416-3 (hardback)
 1. Forensic sciences.   I. Ubelaker, Douglas H.
 HV8073.G568 2015
 363.25–dc23   2014035953

A catalogue record for this book is available from the British Library.

ISBN: 9781118724163

Wiley also publishes its books in a variety of electronic formats. Some content that appears in print may not
be available in electronic books.

Set in 8.5/12pt Meridien by Aptara Inc., New Delhi, India

Printed in Singapore by C.O.S. Printers Pte Ltd

1   2015

Disclaimer: The opinions expressed in this volume are those of the identified authors and do not necessarily
reflect the policy or position of the American Academy of Forensic Sciences.

Contents

About the editor

Douglas H. Ubelaker, PhD, is a curator and senior scientist at the Smithsonian Institution's National Museum of Natural History in Washington, DC, where he has been employed for nearly four decades. Since 1978, he has served as a consultant in forensic anthropology. In this capacity he has served as an expert witness, reporting on more than 900 cases, and has testified in numerous legal proceedings.

He is a Professorial Lecturer with the Departments of Anatomy and Anthropology at The George Washington University, Washington, DC, and is an Adjunct Professor with the Department of Anthropology, Michigan State University, East Lansing, Michigan.

Dr. Ubelaker has published extensively in the general field of human skeletal biology with an emphasis on forensic applications. He has served on the editorial boards of numerous leading scientific publications, including the *Journal of Forensic Sciences, The Open Forensic Science Journal, International Journal of Legal Medicine, Human Evolution, Homo, Journal of Comparative Human Biology, Anthropologie, International Journal of the Science of Man, Forensic Science Communications, Human Evolution, International Journal of Anthropology* and *Global Bioethics.*

Dr. Ubelaker received a Bachelor of Arts Degree and a Doctor of Philosophy from the University of Kansas. He has been a Member of the American Academy of Forensic Sciences since 1974 and achieved the status of Fellow in 1987 in the Physical Anthropology Section. He served as the 2011–2012 President of the AAFS. He is a Fellow of the Washington Academy of Sciences and is a Diplomate of the American Board of Forensic Anthropology. He is a member of the American Association of Physical Anthropology and the Paleopathology Association.

Dr. Ubelaker has received numerous honors including the Memorial Medal of Dr. Aleš Hrdlička, Humpolec, Czech Republic; the Anthropology Award of the Washington Academy of Sciences; the T. Dale Stewart Award by the Physical Anthropology Section of the American Academy of Forensic Sciences; the FBI Director's Award for Exceptional Public Service; the Federal Highway Administration Pennsylvania Division Historic Preservation Excellence Award; a special recognition award from the FBI; and was elected Miembro Honorario of the Sociedad de Odontoestomatólogos Forenses Ibero Americanos.

List of contributors

Hugo Rodríguez Almada MD is the Director of the Legal Medicine Department (School of Medicine in the University of the Republic, in Montevideo city, Uruguay). He has worked since 1993 in Legal Medicine as a forensic doctor, professor and researcher. He is currently employed by the public University of Uruguay and is head of the Department of Legal Medicine, where Uruguayan experts in forensic medicine are educated and trained. Dr Rodríguez Almada has also been a visiting professor of other Latin American universities and has been Adjunct Director of the virtual Master in Forensic Medicine of the University of Valencia, Spain, since 2002. He has published several scientific papers and books on various topics of forensic sciences, especially in the field he calls "Legal Medicine of women and children". Much of his research is focused on sudden unexpected infant death. He has also served broadly as an editor or scientific adviser of several local and international journals and has been a member of their editorial boards or a peer reviewer. He is currently the editor in chief of the *Uruguayan Medical Journal* (RMU), the most widely spread biomedical journal in his country. Although he is not presently employed in the judicial system he is continually participating actively in several complex forensic investigations when requested by prosecutors or judges. Many of these cases are related to violations of human rights in the recent past committed during the civic–military dictatorship (1973–1985), some serial murders and several cases of medical malpractice. He is an honorary adviser of the National Institution of Human Rights and Uruguayan Ombudsman. He has been a representative of Uruguay in the Iberoamerican Network of Legal Medicine and Forensic Science Institutions since its beginnings in 2007. He has held several positions in national and international medical institutions. In 2000 he founded the Iberoamerican Society of Medical Law (SIDEME). In 2003, he was elected President of the Latin American and Caribbean Medical Confederation (CONFEMEL). More recently, he was elected by his colleagues as a member of the first Ethics Tribunal of the Medical Association of Uruguay (CMU), created by law in 2009.

Mario Alva-Rodríguez obtained his MD from the Military Medical School of Mexico and was a Postgraduate in Human Morphology at the Anatomical Institute in Münster, Westphalia, Germany. He has been Chief of the Department of Anatomy at the Military Medical School, Chief of the Department of Anatomy at the School of Medicine of the Anahuac University, General Subdirector of the Medical Services of Mexico City, Director of the El Rosario General Hospital in Mexico City, Subdirector of the Medical Military School, Chief of the Criminalistics Laboratory of the Attorney General Office in Mexico City, Subdirector of the Postgraduate Military Medical School, Founder and Chief of the Mastership in Forensic Medicine at the Postgraduate Military Medical School, Director of the School of Medicine at the Anahuac University, Chief of Forensic Medicine at the Attorney General Office of the Mexican Republic, General Director of the Medical Examiner Office of Mexico City, Founder and Chief of the Specialty in Forensic Medicine at the Medical Examiner Office of Mexico City, General Director of the Forensic Sciences Department at the Attorney General Office of the Mexican Republic, Director of Behavior Promotion at the National Institute of Drugs Enforcement, Coordinator of Criminalistics and Forensic Medicine at the National Institute of Penal Sciences, Director of the Educational Department at the National Institute of Penal Sciences, Coordinator of the Academic Committee of Legal Medicine at the Postgraduate Division of the Medicine Faculty of the National Autonomous University of Mexico and a Fellow of the Mexican Society of Criminology, Mexican Academy of Penal Sciences, Mexican Academy of Surgery, Mexican Academy of Bioethics, Mexican Council of Legal and Forensic Medicine, and the American Academy of Forensic Sciences.He participated in many Courses, Congresses and Symposia as organizer, teacher, lecturer or adviser for undergraduate and postgraduate personnel of medicine, law, criminalistics and police. He had a number of articles and books published: *Basic Forensic Medicine, Atlas of Forensic Medicine* and *Compendium of Forensic Medicine*.

Philip Beh MD graduated from the Faculty of Medicine at the University of Hong Kong in 1981. He has worked in the area of forensic medicine ever since. He is currently a Clinical Associate Professor at the Department of Pathology, the University of Hong Kong. He works with many professional bodies including the ICRC and UNODC. He is an Honorary Advisor to Rain-Lily, Hong Kong's first multidisciplinary rape crisis center. He is also a member of the Editorial Board on several international forensic medical journals. He was Vice-President of the International Association of Forensic Sciences (2002–2005) and President of World Police Medical Officers (2005–2008).

Fawzi Benomran MB ChB, DCH, MSc, MD is the director of Forensic Medicine and Senior Forensic Consultant at the Department of Forensic Medicine in Dubai Police General Headquarters in Dubai, UAE, where he has been employed for the past 16 years. His experience in Forensic Medicine and Forensic Pathology goes back to 1980 when he started his training in the Department of Forensic Medicine in Glasgow University. After he had finished his training in Glasgow, he returned to his home country, Libya, where he worked in Benghazi from 1983 to 1997. In August 1997 he joined the Dubai Police and started to develop the department in a progressive manner. He also has extensive teaching experience though teaching medical students as well as lawyers and policemen from 1983 till now. During his time in Libya, and in addition to his job with the Justice Department, he held the post of Head of the Department of Forensic Medicine and Toxicology and an Associate Professor of Forensic Medicine. In Dubai, he teaches at the Dubai Medical College where he is currently a full Professor of Forensic Medicine and also teaches at the Dubai Police Academy. He is an adjunct Professor with the Faculty of Medicine and the Faculty of Dentistry in Sharja and Ajman Universities, and a Visiting Professor and external examiner in several medical schools in Libya. Dr Benomran has written four books in the Arabic language, one about forensic medicine, two about medical ethics and responsibility and the fourth was a general knowledge book, a translation of its title from Arabic being *Book of the Dead*. He has had 22 scientific articles published in peer reviewed journals in forensic medicine and science. He has also written extensively for Arabic journals on general knowledge and literature, which, put together, exceed 300 articles. In addition, his work has been published extensively on many Arabic websites. Dr Benomran received his Bachelors degree in Medicine (MB ChB) from the University of Benghazi, his DCH degree from the University College of Dublin (Ireland), his MSc (Forensic Medicine) from the University of Glasgow and his doctorate degree (MD) in Forensic Medicine from the University of Colombo. He is also a member of several local and international professional societies and organizations.

Herman Bernitz is a private dental practitioner and Senior Stomatologist in the Department of Oral Pathology and Oral Biology in the School of Dentistry, University of Pretoria, South Africa. Professor Bernitz completed his BChD in 1978, his MSc (Odont) *cum laude* in Oral Pathology in 1996, a Dip Odont *cum laude* in Forensic Odontology in 1998 and a PhD in Forensic Dentistry in 2004. He lectures in both Oral Pathology and Forensic Dentistry and is the manager of Forensic Dental Research. He was the International President of IOFOS (International Organisation for Forensic Odonto-Stomatology) from 2005 to 2011. He is presently the Vice-President of IOFOS. He is a member of the scientific committee of the International Academy of Legal Medicine. He was the Chairman of the "bite mark" working group in Lillihamer, Norway, where international standards were set for bite mark analysis. Since 1998 he has acted as forensic consultant during which time he has been involved in all aspects of Forensic Dentistry, which have included the Air Kenya disaster in Douala, Cameroon, Sundance mining air disaster in Brazzaville, Congo, and the ammunition explosion in Maputo, Mozambique. He has acted as an expert witness in both the Pretoria and Johannesburg Supreme Courts as well as circuit courts around South Africa in bite mark, identification and age estimation cases. He has lectured extensively on four continents on forensic odontology related subjects. He is a member of the Editorial Board of the *Journal of Forensic Odonto-Stomatology* and online *Forensic Journal*.

Luis Bosio MD of the Forensic Medical Corps, Buenos Aires, Argentina, is a forensic doctor, who spent 20 years as a forensic doctor at the Cuerpo Medico Forense (CMF) de la Corte Suprema de Justicia de la Nación, Argentina. He was head of the CMF (2008–2010) and is now retired and is an independent consultant. He teaches at the Faculty of Medicine of the University of Buenos Aires.

Angel Carracedo is a Professor at the University of Santiago de Compostela, Spain, Director of the Institute of Forensic Science (USC), Director of the Galician Foundation of Genomic Medicine (SERGAS, Galician Service of Health), Director of the Spanish National Genotyping Center and a Member of the Centre for Biomedical Network Research on Rare Diseases (CIBERER). In a first step of his career his activity was mainly devoted to population and forensic genetics. His group leads scientific production in the SCI area of legal and forensic science worldwide (http://sciencewatch.com/ana/fea/11julaugFea). He was a Director of the Institute of Legal Medicine (USC) from 1995 and from 2002 has also been working in the clinical genetics area, where he has set up the Galician Foundation of Genomic Medicine. Most of his recent research is now mainly concentrated in forensic genetics and genetics of complex traits (particularly sudden cardiac death, cancer, psychiatric diseases and pharmacogenomics). He has had 12 books and over 480 papers published in SCI journals, including papers in *Nature, Nature Genetics, Science, PNAS, American Journal of Human Genetics, Gene, European Journal of Human Genetics* and especially in Forensic Science journals. He is a highly cited researcher in Molecular Biology and Clinical Medicine and a Board member and external adviser of different national and international institutions, foundations and societies on Forensic Science (IALM, ISFG, MAFS), Genetics and Pharmacogenomics. He is a Director of 70 PhDs, all with the highest qualifications and 18 with University or National Awards. He is also a representative of Spain in the European Medicine Agency (Pharmacogenetics Working Group) and different regulatory boards (i.e. IRDiRC, ICRC, CNUFADN), the Editor of *Forensic Science International Genetics* and a member of the editorial board of a number of the international and national journals on genetics, cancer and forensic science. Prizes and distinctions include the Jaime I Award, Adelaide Medal, Galien Medal, Medal Castelao, Medal of Galicia, Medal to the Police Merit, Galician Prize of Research, Fernandez Latorre Award, Prismas Award and various prizes from foundations

and scientific societies. He is a Doctor Honoris Causa for different universities in Europe and the Americas.

Cristina Cattaneo, a forensic pathologist and anthropologist, received a BSc in Biomedical Sciences at McGill University, Canada, an MA in Osteology, Funerary Archaeology and Palaeopathology and a PhD in Pure Sciences at the University of Sheffield, UK, and then moved to Italy where she graduated in Medicine and went on to specialize in Legal Medicine. She is currently Associate Professor of Legal Medicine at the Faculty of Medicine of the Università degli Studi di Milano (Italy), founder and director of LABANOF, Laboratorio di Antropologia e Odontologia Forense at the Institute of Legal Medicine of the Dipartimento di Scienze Biomediche per la Salute and teaches Anthropology at the Faculty of Sciences and Arts at the same University. She is author and co-author of books and scientific articles concerning anthropology and forensic pathology in general, identification, trauma and clinical forensic medicine, as well as a legal expert in forensic pathology, anthropology and clinical forensic medicine for various courts in Italy and occasionally in Europe. She is co-founder and vice-president of FASE (Forensic Anthropology Society of Europe), a subsection of IALM (International Academy of Legal Medicine) and a member of the Swiss DVI (Disaster Victim Identification) team. She is associate editor for the journal *Forensic Science International*. Since 2007 she has been actively involved with the Italian Ministry of Internal Affairs in the creation of a national database for unidentified human remains and has recently been involved in the development of a forensic humanitarian service for asylum seekers in the city of Milano.

P.K. Chattopadhyay, formerly Professor and Founder Head of the Department of Forensic Science, Punjabi University, Patiala, did his MSc and PhD in Anthropology at the University of Delhi. He started his teaching career as Lecturer in Forensic Science, Delhi University in 1968 before moving to Patiala to set up the first fully fledged Department of Forensic Science in the world. Professor Chattopadhyay has delivered Key Note and Plenary Addresses and Chaired Sessions at several International Congresses in India and abroad, including the International Meeting of Forensic Sciences (he Chaired the Session on Forensic Anthropology at Zurich, Switzerland, in 1975, the only Indian to have been so honoured; he also Chaired the Session on Forensic Education at the International Meeting of Forensic Sciences at Hong Kong in 2005), the World Congress on Medical Law at Gent, Belgium, in 1991, the International Symposium on Advances in Legal Medicine, Osaka, Japan, in 1995, and the International Congress of Anthropological and Ethnological Sciences in 1978 at Delhi. He has had more than 100 original research papers on various aspects of forensic sciences published, including ones on the determination of sex, blood groups and enzyme types from hair, bones, teeth, muscles, stains of blood, semen, saliva, urine, genetics of the dermal ridges and hair keratin, drugs from hair, insecticides in mothers' milk, salivary agglutinins, determination of hand and finger from a single fingerprint, effect of alcohol on hand rriting, determination of sex from hand writing, pattern of suicides, autosomal and Y-STR types from blood stains (DNA profiling), membrane associated transfer protein (MATP), gene and the founder's effect, etc. Several students have worked with him for their PhD Degree (18) and MD in Forensic Medicine (2). Two students are working with him for their PhD now. A Visiting Fellow of the Indian Council for Medical Research in 1973, Dr Chattopadhyay has received extensive training on various aspects of Forensic Sciences at the Central Forensic Institute, Calcutta, and in Forensic Medicine at the Calcutta Medical College. He has been a Visiting Professor with the Department of Anthropology, Manipur University, Imphal, Manipur, in 1987, Institüt für Rechtsmedizin, Christian Abrechts University, Kiel, Germany, in 1994, the Departments of Forensic Medicine, Nagasaki and Akita University Medical Schools in 1993, 1995, 2002 and 2008 and the University of Kebangsaan, Malaysia, in 2009, and a Visiting Scientist to the United Kingdom, the United States, Germany, France, Belgium, Australia, Singapore, the Czech Republic, Switzerland, Yugoslavia, Nepal, Thailand, Bangladesh, Hong Kong, Indonesia, Egypt, Sri Lanka and several other countries of the developed world in 1972,1973,1975, 1982, 1984, 1986, 1988, 1990, 1991, 1992, 1993, 1994, 1995, 1996, 1998, 1999, 2001, 2002, 2004, 2005, 2007, 2008, 2009, 2010, 2011, 2012 and 2013 and lectured extensively on various aspects of Forensic Science, Forensic Medicine, Genetics and Anthropology. A member of several national and international societies (he has been a Vice-President of the Indo-Pacific Association of Law, Medicine and Science) and the Editorial Board of a number of journals, including the *Legal Medicine*, an Elsevier publication. A Fellow of the Indian Academy of Forensic Sciences, Indian Academy of Forensic Medicine and the Indian Association of Medico-Legal Experts, Dr Chattopadhyay has won several Prizes and honours such as the Dr S.S.Sarkar Oration Award in Anthropology in 2000, Best Researcher Award of the Indian Academy of Forensic Medicine in 1997, Best Teacher and Forensic Scientist of the Decade of the Medico-legal Society of India in 1998, Forensic Scientist of the Millenium Award of the Medico-Legal Society of India in 2002 and a Special Award from the Indo-Pacific Association of Law, Medicine and Science at Manila, Philippines, in 2004 for his contributions to knowledge and development of Forensic Science in the region. Professor Chattopadhyay has been the Congress Chairman of the 10th Indo-Pacific Congress on Legal Medicine and Forensic Science, 2010, and President of the Indo-Pacific association of Law, Medicine and Science for the years 2010–2013. Professor Chattopadhyay has just been invited by the Kwame Nkrumah University of Science and Technology, Ghana, to join the Department of Biochemistry and Biotechnology as a Visiting Professor of Forensic Science for the year 2014–2015 and joined the Amity in April 2004 as Director (2004–2013) and Advisor (February 2013–January 2014) of the Amity Institute of Forensic Science, NOIDA–201303, UP, India.

Paul Chui is a qualified practicing Senior Consultant forensic pathologist, accredited as a specialist in pathology by the Specialist Accreditation Board of the Ministry of Health, Singapore. He is also a gazetted forensic pathologist under the Coroner's Act 2010.

After graduating with an MBBS in 1983 from the National University of Singapore, he subsequently trained in forensic pathology from 1986 and spent 2 years in the United Kingdom from 1989 to 1991, where he attained both the Diploma in Medical Jurisprudence (DMJ) and Membership of the Royal College of Pathologists (Forensic) in 1991 and Masters in Business Administration (NUS) in the mid-1990s. In 1996, under an HMDP Fellowship, Dr Chui spent 3 months at the Coroner's/Medical Examiner's offices in Pittsburgh, Chicago and Los Angeles.

Over the years, Dr Chui has been involved in numerous Coroner cases and homicides, including a number of notable court cases, such as *Public Prosecutor vs Chee Cheong Hin Constance (Sindee Neo case)* and *Public Prosecutor vs. Tok Leng How* (*Huang Na Case*). He has also provided consultancy and technical assistance to overseas clients regionally. He testified on the forensic autopsy evidence before the Saket Court (Delhi, India) in the high profile gang-rape murder trial in February 2013, and was closely involved in the Coroner's Inquiry into the high profile case of *Shane Todd Truman* in May 2013.

Dr Chui took on the Directorship of the Centre of Forensic Medicine (CFM, later renamed the Forensic Medicine Division in 2008) when the Health Sciences Authority (HSA) was formed in 2001. Computerized tomography (CT) scanning capability was added in 2010 to support the work of FMD, and a forensic anthropology laboratory was established in 2011. In April 2013, Dr Chui was appointed Chief, Forensic Medicine. The Division successfully attained accreditation from the National Association of Medical Examiners (NAME) in 2005 and has been successfully reaccredited by NAME in 2011 for another five years.

In 2003, during the SARS outbreak, Dr Chui was personally involved in autopsy examination of deaths suspected as being due to SARS. He was involved in developing the world's first mobile containerized biosafety level 4 autopsy facility, which was commissioned in 2005 and is still operational. The experience from SARS had also led to a major revamp of biosafety procedures and workplace practices in the mortuary.

Dr Chui is a Fellow of the American Academy of Forensic Sciences and a full member of the National Association of Medical Examiners (NAME). He has been a long-time serving member of the International Ad-hoc Committee under NAME, and a certified NAME Accreditation Inspector from 2011 to 2016.

Since 2001, Dr Chui had also served in various concurrent corporate capacities such as Director (Corporate Management), Director (Office for Innovation and Enterprise), Chief Information Officer (CIO), etc., within the HSA. He had also been directly involved in leading the implementation of key IT operational Systems (LISA and FIONA) supporting the work in the Applied Sciences Group. Both LISA and FIONA won regional awards in IT excellence. Dr Chui served as the Group Director of the Applied Sciences Group (ASG) of HSA from July 2006 to January 2011. In 2011, Dr Chui received the Becton–Dickinson Award in Pathology, awarded by the Singapore Society of Pathology. He is one of the founding members in the forerunner group that spearheaded the formation of the Asian Forensic Sciences Network (AFSN), a regional professional association of forensic institutes in Asia, and was its President from October 2008 to May 2011. Presently, Dr Chui is also serving as the current Chairman of the DSO–SAF Institution Review Board, as well as a member of the Singapore Armed Forces Medical Advisory Board.

Heesun Chung PhD is a Dean and Professor of the Graduate School of Analytical Science and Technology, Chungnam National University, South Korea. She obtained her PhD in Pharmacy from Sookmyung Women's University, South Korea, in 1987 and subsequently was awarded a Foreign Commonwealth Office Scholarship to do further postdoctoral study at King's College, London. She was the Director General of the National Forensic Service (formally the National Institute of Scientific Investigation), South Korea from 2008 to 2012. She had also held many top forensic related posts in South Korea such as Head of Department of Forensic Science, Director of Narcotics Analysis Division, Director of Drug and Toxicology at the National Institute of Scientific Investigation and many more. She lectures at Sookmyung Women's University, Korean National Police University, Korean Police Investigation Academy, Central Officials Training Institute and Dongguk University. She is the current president of the International Association of Forensic Sciences (IAFS) and is also the President-elect for the International Association of Forensic Toxicologists (TIAFT). These are just two of her many involvements with forensic professional bodies. She is also on the Editorial Board of *Forensic Toxicologists and Forensic Science International*. Dr Chung is a licensed Pharmacist and Toxicologist and has presented findings at numerous international meetings and symposia. Her research has resulted in the publication of over 100 scientific articles. For the last five years, 40 articles have been published in international and national journals. She is the holder of several patents and the writer of books. Her research interests are the analysis of abused drugs in biological fluids and other alternative specimens including hair and impurity profiling of illicit methamphetamine. Dr Chung has been awarded many medals and awards, including a medal for distinguished service by the Korean Government, a medal for excellence in Forensic Science from the Mongolian Government and an award as a reviewer in Pharmacy and Medicine by the Medical News Agency. She received the most outstanding Woman Scientist award from the Ministry of

Science and Technology and the Bichumi Award from the Samsung Life Insurance Company. She has also received awards from the Ministry of Home Affairs, the Ministry of Health, Seoul Pharmaceutical Association, Korean Pharmaceutical Association and Seoul Daily Newspaper.

Luis Concheiro was Emeritus Professor at the University of Santiago de Compostela, Spain, Ex-Director of the Institute of Forensic Science (USC), Professor of Legal Medicine of the University of Santiago de Compostela from 1975. He was Director of the Institute of Legal Medicine from 1990 to 1998 and has had different academic positions including Vice-Rector of the University of Santiago de Compostela (1994–1998) and had Pregraduate formation under the direction of Professor Arsenio Nunes (Institute of Legal Medicine Lisbon, Portugal) in 1967–1968. He has had 6 books and over 150 papers in journals published, all of them related to forensic science. With reference to the subject of this book, his *Medicina Legal en la Historia* (Academia de Medicina, 2006), *De las Relaciones de la Medicina y el Derecho* (Universidad de Santiago de Compostela, 2010) and *Los Pecados Capitales de la Medicina Legal Rspañola, Revista Ciencia Forense* (2011) should be highlighted, and he was one of the authors of *Libro Blanco de La Medicina Legal* (Ministerio de Justicia, 1985). He is regularly invited as a keynote speaker at meetings, workshops and symposia in virtually all continents and prizes and distinctions include Gold Medal USC, Medal of Gold and Brilliants Real Medical Order, Medal to the Guardia Civil Merit, Medal San Raimundo de Peñafor Doctor Honoris Causa by the University of Coimbra (Portugal) and Universidad Nacional San Luis Gonzaga de ICA (Perú).

Aída Elena Constantín MD is a Physician of Universidad Nacional de Colombia, lawyer of Universidad Santo Tomas de Aquino, Specialist in Health Audit Universidad del Rosario, and Penal and Criminological Sciences in Universidad Externado de Colombia. She has worked for 24 years at the National Institute of Legal Medicine and Forensic Sciences of Colombia. She has served as an expert in Clinical Forensic Medicine and chief of the following areas: Medical Division, Division Clinical and Forensic Psychiatry, Division of Forensic Services, Forensic Science Research Division and National Reference of Violence Center, and is currently the Director of

Scientific Research. In performing her duties she has led and/or participated in the development of several guidelines and regulations in clinical forensic medicine and as a lecturer for many programs of medicine, law and odontology.

Stephen Cordner is Professor of Forensic Medicine at Monash University (Foundation Chair), Head of the International Program at the Victorian Institute of Forensic Medicine (VIFM), Forensic Advisor on the International Committee of the Red Cross and Patron of the African Society of Forensic Medicine. He has a particular interest in mass casualty management, disaster victim identification and international forensic medical capacity development. Professor Cordner has worked for the International Committee of the Red Cross and has undertaken forensic medical investigative work in Kosovo, East Timor, Fiji and Bali as well as his case work in Australia. He is particularly committed to teaching and has undertaken or organized training in Indonesia, Sri Lanka, the Middle East, Botswana and Uganda. Most recently Professor Cordner was deployed by the WHO to the Philippines for a month in late 2013 to provide advice on mass casualty management following the devastation wreaked by Typhoon Haiyan and by the ICRC to Liberia to provide advice on body management for the Ebola epidemic.

Agnes Dósa MD, JD, PhD is Assistant Professor and Vice-Director of the Institute of Forensic and Insurance Medicine, Semmelweis University, Budapest. She graduated from Semmelweis University in 1989 (MD) and from Eötvös Lóránd University in 1993 (JD). She earned her PhD degree in 2004; the title of her thesis was: Medical malpractice – analysis of Hungarian case law from a comparative perspective. She teaches forensic medicine and medical law. Being a proponent of integration of medical law and forensic medicine, she has introduced a new curriculum of medical law for medical students. She has served as secretary and member of the Board of Forensic Medicine Experts of the Health Scientific Council since 2006. She is a member of the Human Reproduction Committee of the Health Scientific Council and has served as a member and secretary of various research ethics committees. Dr Dósa's work has been published extensively in the field of medical law with an emphasis on medical malpractice and is the author of three books and more than 100 articles.

W. Eisenmenger is employed by the Institute of Forensic Medicine, Ludwig Maximilians University, Munich, Germany. He was head of the Munich Institute of Forensic Medicine from 1989 to 2009.

Luis Fondebrider (Lic) is a forensic anthropologist who graduated from the University of Buenos Aires. He is the current President of the Argentine Forensic Anthropology Team (EAAF), a scientific nonprofit organization that for the last 30 years has been using forensic anthropology as well as other disciplines to investigate cases of political, ethnic and religious violence around the world. As a member of EAAF, Mr Fondebrider has worked in 40 countries in Latin America, Africa, Europe, Asia and the Pacific region, exhuming and analyzing human remains. He worked as an expert witness and consultant for the International Tribunal for the former Yugoslavia, Truth Commissions of several countries, United Nations commissions of inquiry, Inter American Court of Human Rights, Prosecutors offices, medicolegal institutes and organizations composed of relatives of the victims. Mr Fondebrider teaches at the Faculty of Medicine of the University of Buenos Aires and is a Doctor Honoris Causa for the University of Buenos Aires.

Zeno Geradts has worked since 1991 at the Netherlands Forensic Institute as a forensic scientist. He is an expert witness in image analysis and biometrics (e.g. facial comparison) as well as R&D coordinator in digital evidence. In 2002 he received a PhD from the University of Utrecht based on research on computational matching of images from shoeprints, toolmarks, drugs, pills and cartridge cases. At the American Academy of Forensic Sciences he has been Chairman of the Engineering Section and since 2008 he has been Chairman of the section Digital Evidence and Multimedia and from 2010 to 2013 the Director of the section. He is Chairman of the European Network of Forensic Science Institutes Forensic IT working group. He authored and co-authored in many publications and presented a wide variety of papers and workshops, and is active in casework as an expert witness and in projects in digital evidence and multimedia (such as camera identification, repairing video streams, image analysis and heart beat detection from CCTV).

Antonio Grande is a Specialist in Legal Medicine and Forensic pathology, as well as Head of Medicolegal Services and Psychology applied to Criminalistics at the Scientific Police Service, Polizia Scientifica and Anti-Crime Central Direction – Rome. He is Contract Professor for the University of L'Aquila, Faculty of Psychology, in the postgraduate course in Psychology Applied to Criminal Analysis. He teaches Legal Medicine at the Faculty of Medicine and Dentistry at the Università la Sapienza, Rome, and several other postgraduate courses in forensic sciences at the Universities of La Sapienza, Rome, Tor Vergata, Rome, Pavia, Università Cattolica del Sacro Cuore, Rome, LUMSA, Rome, and for the Superior School of Police. He is author of several articles and book chapters on forensic medicine and sciences.

Mete Korkut Gulmen was born at Adana–Turkiye in 1957. He had been an International–Intercultural Scholar to the United States during High School years and had graduated from Mission Viejo High School, California in 1975. He graduated from Medical School and worked as a general practitioner for two years. He performed his Anatomo–Pathology licensure education at Cukurova University and served for the Turkish Military at the Gulhane Military Medical Academy of the Anatomo–Surgical Pathology department as a consultant pathologist as well as a lecturer. He later started to work at the Forensic Medicine Department of the School of Medicine. He gained his doctorate degree on Forensic Medicine and Forensic Pathology at the Health Sciences Institute of Cukurova University and worked as a Fellow in the summer of 1995 at the Department of Forensic Medicine of Dundee University, Scotland. Dr Gulmen became a full Professor of the field in 2005. He had been working as the chief forensic pathologist at Cukurova University as well as the Morgue Department of the Adana branch of the Legal Medicine Council and also worked as a lecturer and researcher at Cukurova University since 1992. He continues to teach Forensic Medicine and Forensic Pathology to the fifth year Medical School students. He has been on the Editorial Board of The Council of Forensic Medicine *Journal of Forensic Medicine*, Turkish Clinics (Türkiye Klinikleri) *Journal of Forensic Medicine* and *Bulletin of Legal Medicine* as well as the Editorial Board of the *Journal of Cukurova Medical School* since 1999 and the *Post Graduate Medical Journal* of the British Medical Association since 2004. He has worked as a committee member of the postgraduate education of the School of Medicine, Cukurova University from 1999 till 2003 and as a board member of the Cukurova University Health Sciences Institute from 1998 to 2004. He is a member of the Turkish Medical Association,

Turkish Forensic Medicine Specialists, Turkish Pathology Federation and Ethic Committee of the Pathology Federation, Turkish Cancer Research Association and Cukurova Pathology Association. He is one of the founders and presidents of the Adana Development Alliance Foundation and Adana Swimming–Diving Sports Club, which has built an educational village in Adana. He is also a member of the Turkish Cultural Foundation and AFS Volunteers Association and is one of the Presidents of the Turkish National Forensic Medicine Specialists Association and also the Chairperson of the Board of the Forensic Medicine Specialists. He was the 2007–2009 President of Tthe Mediterranean Academy of Forensic Sciences (MAFS)and organized the MAFS 2009 Congress at Antalya–Turkiye. He organized the last, 22nd IALM Meeting in 2012 at Istanbul–Turkiye and will be organizing the Fifth Congress of AIDC on "Standardization of Medical Expertise" in Istanbul on 3rd to 5th of September 2014. Professor Dr Gulmen has had numerous studies published in various journals of the world and organized several symposia and congresses. He has also participated in numerous conferences, panels, lectures, TV and radio programs as well as many workshops. He is also a founding member of several foundations and associations. He is serving as a volunteer for AFS International/Intercultural Scholarship programs on behalf of the Turkish Cultural Foundation as well as the International AFS. He is a member of the Turkish Medical Association and a founding member of the Forensic Medicine Specialists Association and past President of the Forensic Medicine Specialists Board. He is also a member of the European Cardiovascular Pathology Association and also the American Academy of Forensic Sciences. He has carried out many studies in various fields of Forensic Sciences, but mostly in Forensic Pathology and Sudden Deaths and Cardiac Pathologies in particular. He has been working as a full Professor and the Chairperson of the Forensic Medicine and Forensic Pathology Department since 2005 and has held the Forensic Pathology section Chair for the last 16 years. He has been happily married for 28 years and has a daughter and a son aged respectively 26 and 22.

Sheilah Hamilton PhD has been a forensic scientist for more than four decades. In 1965 she received her BSc (Hons) degree in Chemistry from the University of Glasgow, her MSocSc in 1994 and her PhD in 1999, both from the University of Hong Kong. Between 1968 and 1988 she worked as a forensic scientist in the Forensic Science Division of the Hong Kong Government Laboratory, then at the State Forensic Science Laboratory in Adelaide, South Australia, before establishing *Forensic Focus* in 1989, at that time the first independent forensic science consultancy in Hong Kong. In addition to having taught forensic science and fire investigation at universities in Hong Kong and the United Kingdom, she has written extensively about both subjects.

Steen Holger Hansen is a forensic pathologist at the Department of Forensic Medicine, Faculty of Health Sciences, University of Copenhagen, where he has worked since 1998. Steen Holger Hansen is an MD from the University of Copenhagen. He has been a specialist in Pathology and Histopathology from 1995 and a specialist in Forensic Medicine from 2008. He is also the Deputy Chief forensic pathologist at the Department of Forensic Medicine, which performs forensic autopsies, crime scene investigations and clinical forensic medicine. The section is accredited by international standards and Steen Holger Hansen is Chief of the quality assurance. Aside from teaching at the University of Copenhagen, he teaches doctors in training to become specialists in Forensic Medicine and police investigators. He has participated as a lecturer at international courses in forensic medicine. Steen Holger Hansen is an author and co-author of several journal articles and book chapters, focusing both on forensic pathology and clinical forensic medicine.

Matthew Hickman PhD is an Associate Professor in the Department of Criminal Justice at Seattle University. His general research interests include issues in law enforcement, quantitative methods and the impact of forensic sciences on the administration of justice. He received his PhD degree in 2005 from Temple University and was previously a statistician at the Bureau of Justice Statistics, US Department of Justice. His work has appeared in a wide variety of journals, including *Criminology, Criminology and Public Policy, Journal of Quantitative Criminology* and the *Journal of Forensic Sciences*. He is a member of the American Academy of Forensic Sciences, American Society of Criminology and the International Association of Crime Analysts.

Cengiz Haluk İnce was born on 12 August 1966 and is currently living in Istanbul. He is currently a Professor in the Istanbul University Medical Faculty Forensic Medicine Department. He is also an Adjuct Professor with the Law Faculty at Dogus University, Istanbul. He is married and has two children. Professor İnce graduated from the Uludag University Faculty of Medicine in 1990. He completed his residence training in 1995 at the Istanbul University Medical Faculty, Department of Forensic Medicine. He became an Associate Professor in 2006 and a full Professor in 2013. He also obtained his PhD degree in Public Health in 2005 and then his Master's degree in Business Administration in 2009. He served as President of the Turkish Forensic Medicine and Science Institution between the years 2009 and 2013. İnce's research is mainly based on clinical forensic medicine with medical malpractice and forensic applications. He has served on editorial boards of numerous leading scientific publications, including the *Journal of Trauma*, *Turkish Clinics Journal Medical Science*, *International Nursing Review* and *Archives of Neuropsychiatry*, as well as the American Board of Independent Medical Examiners (ABIME). He also served as a Member or President for several societies such as the National Society for the Prevention of Occupational Accidents (President), American Board of Independent Medical Examiners (ABIME), American Academy of Forensic Sciences, International Association of Personal Injury (AIDC) and EurAsia Forensic Medicine and Science.

Takaki Ishikawa MD,PhD is Professor and Chair of the Division of Legal Medicine, Faculty of Medicine, at Tottori University, where he has been since 2013. He received the degree of Doctor of Medicine from Okayama University in 2003. From 2004 to 2013, he worked at Osaka City University Medical School, eventually as a forensic pathologist. He was a guest researcher at the Institute of Legal Medicine, University Hospital Freiburg, Freiburg, Germany, in 2009. He works as an expert in forensic pathology and toxicology with primary specialties in clinical forensic pathology. His current researches focus on forensic endocrinology and forensic pathological evaluation of various stress responses.

Graham R. Jones PhD, DABFT is Chief Toxicologist for the Alberta Office of the Chief Medical Examiner, in Edmonton, Alberta, Canada. He originally qualified as a Pharmacist in the United Kingdom and later earned his PhD degree in Pharmaceutical Chemistry (Drug Metabolism) from the Chelsea College at the University of London. Dr Jones subsequently moved to Canada to take up a fellowship at the University of Alberta, later joining the University of Alberta Hospital as a Clinical Toxicologist. In 1981 he joined the Alberta Office of the Chief Medical Examiner as Director of the new forensic toxicology laboratory. Dr Jones has been very active in his profession and is a member of several professional organizations in Canada, the United Kingdom and the United States. He is a past-President of the American Academy of Forensic Sciences (AAFS), past-President of the Society of Forensic Toxicologists, past-President of the Forensic Specialties Accreditation Board and Chair of the Laboratory Accreditation Program of the American Board of Forensic Toxicology. He is also a member of the editorial boards of the *Journal of Analytical Toxicology* and the *Journal of Forensic Sciences*. Dr Jones is the recipient of the Alexander O. Gettler Award and the Distinguished Fellow Award from the AAFS and has been granted the Doug Lucas Award from the Canadian Society of Forensic Science. Dr Jones has been a leader in the development of professional standards for the forensic toxicology profession for over 25 years. In addition, he has been a toxicology laboratory inspector with the National Laboratory Certification Program for workplace drug testing in the United States, for the Standards Council of Canada and the American Board of Forensic Toxicology. Dr Jones has served as a consultant and expert witness in several toxicology-related murder trials in both Canada and the United States.

Eva Keller is a full Professor at the Semmelweis University Department of Forensic and Insurance Medicine, in Budapest, Hungary, where she has been employed for 33 years. Dr Keller received her medical degree at the Semmelweis University in 1981 and has specialized in anatomic pathology and forensic and insurance medicine. She is a Board Member of the European Council of Legal Medicine, International Academy of Legal Medicine. Dr Keller is a lecturer of international repute and has given several professional lectures and presentations, some as far afield as America, Hungary, Germany, Finland and Sweden. She was an invited lecturer at the Eye to Eye Conference: The Global Conference on Cultural Relations. Dr Keller gained her PhD in cardiac pathology and her scientific interest later turned to drug abuse. Recently she has carried out a joint research with Professor Yasmin Hurd (USA, Mt Sinai

Hospital) on molecular and pathologic changes on drug related death and has published extensively on the field of drug abuse. Dr Keller is a well-known forensic expert whose specialty is insurance fraud related cases. She is President of the Medical and Scientific Board/Forensic Expert Section (ETT/ISZT), the Hungarian Medical Association, Forensic Medicine Devision and the Hungarian Forensic Medical Association.

Michael Kenyhercz MS is currently a graduate student at the University of Alaska, Fairbanks. He completed his master's degree in 2010 at Mercyhurst University, focusing on biological and forensic anthropology. He then worked on two NIJ grants through Mercyhurst University focusing on fatal fire recoveries and mass disaster recoveries. In 2012 he completed a fellowship through JPAC-CIL's Forensic Science Academy. He has published mainly on the estimation of sex and ancestry, focusing on modern US populations and modern South African populations.

Burgert Kloppers MSc is the Technical Manager of the Ballistics Section of the Forensic Science Laboratory, South African Police Services and holds the rank of Colonel. He was appointed to the Forensic Science Laboratory in 1986. He is a firearms and toolmark specialist with a special interest in terminal ballistics.

Toshikazu Kondo MD, PhD graduated and received the degree of Doctor of Medicine from Kanazawa University, Medical School. He has been Chairman and Professor of the Department of Forensic Medicine, Wakayama Medical University, Japan, since 2003. He is a specialist in forensic autopsy. In addition, his specialist research activity has been in molecular forensic pathology.

Ericka Nöelle L'Abbé PhD was appointed in 2012 as Associate Professor, Department of Anatomy, University of Pretoria, South Africa. She received her PhD degree in 2005 from the University of Pretoria. She is a certified diplomat with the American Board of Forensic Anthropology (D-ABFA) and has published extensively in the field of forensic anthropology with a special interest in skeletal biology, bioarchaeology, estimation of ancestry and trauma analysis.

Gérard Nicholas Labuschagne PhD is a licensed Clinical Psychologist with the Health Professions Council of South Africa. He was appointed in 2013 as Extraordinary Professor, Department of Police Practice, University of South Africa and as an Honorary Associate Professor at the Division of Forensic Medicine and Pathology at the University of the Witwatersrand. He is currently Section Head of the Investigative Psychology Unit of the South African Police Service (SAPS) with the rank of Brigadier. He has published extensively on all aspects of forensic psychology with special interest in multi-murders, serial rapists, criminal profiling and child sexual offenders.

Üllar Lanno has been Director of the Estonian Forensic Science Institute since 2006 and was the Chairman of the Baltic Network of Forensic Science Institutions in 2009. He is a Member of the ENFSI Scene of the Crime Working Group and currently acts as the Chairman of the European Network of Forensic Science Institutes.

Soong Deok Lee MD, PhD is a Professor at the Seoul National University College of Medicine in South Korea. He graduated from the SNU College of Medicine in 1987 and received a PhD degree in 1994. The theme of his doctoral degree was about DNA fingerprinting, which was a newly introduced area at that time. He has served as a Professor in the Department of Forensic Medicine at the same university since 1995. As a researcher on forensic genetics, he has done a lot of work on DNA fingerprinting. As a member of leading persons in the field of forensic genetics in South Korea, he also contributed greatly for the establishment of the forensic lab and for launching criminal DB in South Korea. He is now a Board Member of the Administrative Committee for Criminal DB in Korea. As a practitioner in forensics he has worked as a medical examiner and has handled many socially well known cases. He is now also actively participating as an expert for the court. As an educator, he has lectured about forensic medicine, forensic genetics and forensics as a whole for medical students, biologists and field members of forensics including police and prosecutors. He established KAPO (Korean Association of Paleopathology and Osteoarcheology) in Korea and had been the first Dean of KAPO. He is now Vice-Dean of the Korean Society of Law and Medicine and a member of the National Academy of Medicine of Korea.

Marisol Intriago-Leiva from Chile has been a Forensic Anthropologist, Head of the Special Unit of Forensic Identification, under the Legal Medical Service of Chile since 2011, and has been in charge of coordinating the forensic analysis field and laboratory aimed at the identification and determination of injury in human rights cases and criminals in addition to the implementation of the National System of Forensic Identification Forensic Service. From 2003 to 2010 she served as an expert in this Service, participating in over 600 investigations related primarily to human rights cases.

Sikeun Lim PhD is a senior forensic DNA specialist at the National Forensic Service in South Korea where he has been employed since 1997. He has dealt with tens of thousands of crime cases including the Kang Ho-Soon serial killer case. He is an Adjunct Professor with the Graduate School of Forensic Science at Soon Chun Hyang University and is a specialist of KOSEN (Korea Science and Engineering Network) in KISTI (Korea Institute of Science and Technology Information). He was a visiting scientist at the Wellcome Trust Sanger Institute, Cambridge, United Kingdom, in 2004. Dr Lim has published many articles, columns and books in the field of forensic DNA analysis and human genetics. He received a Bachelor of Science Degree (Biology), Master of Science Degree (Biology) and a Doctor of Philosophy (Microbiology) from the Korea University and has received numerous honors including the Prime Minister's Award in 2012 and the Ministry of Safety and Public Administration Award in 2010. In 2006 he received the National Police Agency Award for participating in the French Frozen Baby case of Seorae village.

Bertrand Ludes is a French citizen born in 1959 and is married with two children. He has been Professor of Legal Medicine at the Medical School of Paris Descartes since 2013, Director of the Institut Medico-légal of Paris since 2013, Professor of Legal Medicine at the Medical School of Strasbourg from 1996 to 2013, Director of the Institut de Médecine Légale of Strasbourg from 1996 to 2013 and Dean of the Medical School of Strasbourg from 2001 to 2011. He gained the title of Medical Doctor obtained in 1985, a PhD in Molecular Pharmacology in 1990 at the University Louis Pasteur in Strasbourg, Research Habilitation at the same university in 1993, Specialization as a Forensic Pathologist in 1988, Assistant Professor at the Medical School of Strasbourg from 1991 to 1996, Doctor Honoris Causa of the Medical College of Kunming, PR China in 2003 and Member of the Deutsche Akademie der Naturforscher

LEOPOLDINA in 2000. He is a Member of Ehrenmitglied der deutsche Gesellschaft für Rechtsmedizin (23/09/2009), Vice President of the French Society of Legal Medicine since 2006, Vice President of the International Academy of Legal Medicine since 2006, Member of the International Society for Forensic Genetics, Member of the German Society for Legal Medicine, Co-founder of the genetic identification laboratory of the Institut de Médecine Légale de Strasbourg,Forensic Expert at the French "Cour de Cassation", Professorem Honorificum Senatus of the University POPA, IASI, Romania (27/04/2003) and an Honorary member of the Hungary Society for Legal Medicine. His main research subjects are human DNA profiling (mitochondrial and chromosomal STRs, SNP technology) and diatom research and analyses in drowning cases. He has written numerous book chapters and articles for international and national publications, given many oral scientific presentations and produced posters.

Niels Lynnerup is a Professor with special duties at the Department of Forensic Medicine, Faculty of Health Sciences, University of Copenhagen, where he has worked since 1990. Niels Lynnerup has an MD from the University of Copenhagen and his PhD thesis was based on an analysis of skeletal remains of the Norse Vikings in Greenland. Since then he has worked with forensic anthropology, becoming Head of the Unit of Forensic Anthropology at the Department of Forensic Medicine. Aside from working with human remains, the Unit also works with identification of the living, based on CCTV material, for example matching perpetrators as seen on CCTV with suspects. This work also includes the application of novel photogrammetric methods. He is also Head of the Laboratory of Biological Anthropology, which curates an extensive skeletal collection from Danish pre-history and history. His research in biological anthropology mostly focuses on the analysis of human skeletal remains and mummies and bog bodies in an archaeological setting. He works extensively with CT scanning and advanced three-dimensional visualization. Current projects also include stable isotope analyses and involvement in DNA extraction from Danish and Greenlandic skeletal material. He has also worked on paleodemographic issues, including mathematical modelling, Aside from teaching at the University of Copenhagen, Niels Lynnerup is regularly asked to participate as a lecturer at international courses in forensic and biological anthropology. He is the author and co-author of more than 200 journal articles and book chapters, focusing both on forensic anthropology and biological anthropology. Since 2012 he has also been Editor-in-Chief of the *Scandinavian Journal of Forensic Science*.

Hitoshi Maeda MD, PhD graduated and received the degree of Doctor of Medicine from Wakayama Medical University. Professor Maeda has been Director of the Department of Legal Medicine, Osaka City University Medical School, Japan, since 1990 and works as a board-certified specialist and supervisor of forensic/legal medicine. His practical and research activities extensively cover the fields related to forensic/legal medicine. He primarily studies collaborative organization of forensic autopsy laboratory systems for pathophysiological analysis of fatal insults in connection with clinical concepts, mainly involving pathology, toxicology, biochemistry, molecular pathology and radiology.

Patrice Mangin Prof. Dr Med. graduated from the Faculty of Medicine Broussais-Hôtel-Dieu, University René Descartes Paris VI (1967–1973). He obtained his MD thesis at the Faculty of Medicine, University Louis Pasteur – Strasbourg I (1978) and Board Certification in Legal Medicine in France (1980) and Switzerland (FMH 1996). He wrote his PhD thesis in toxicology with Professor G. Dirrheimer, Faculty of Pharmacy, University Louis Pasteur – Strasbourg I (1985). His professional activities include work as an intern and resident in different French hospitals (Besançon, Strasbourg). He was subsequently appointed "Assistant des Universités – Assistant des Hôpitaux", Institute of Legal and Social Medicine, Faculty of Medicine, University Louis Pasteur – Strasbourg I (1 March 1981–30 September 1986) and "Maître de Conférences – Praticien Hospitalier", Institute of Legal and Social Medicine, Faculty of Medicine, University Louis Pasteur – Strasbourg I (1 October 1986–30 September 1990). In 1990, he was appointed "Professeur des Universités – Praticien Hospitalier", Director of the Institute of Legal and Social Medicine, Faculty of Medicine, University Louis Pasteur – Strasbourg I and since 1 September 1996, he has been the Ordinarius Professor of Legal Medicine and Director of the Institute of Legal Medicine of the Faculty of Biology and Medicine, University of Lausanne. From 1999 to 2006 he was selected to become subsequently Vice-Dean of the Faculty of Medicine, University of Lausanne and then Dean of the Faculty of Biology and

Medicine, University of Lausanne (1 September 2003–31 August 2006). Since 2007, he has been the Director of the new University Center of Legal Medicine, Lausanne-Geneva, as Ordinarius Professor of Legal Medicine at the Universities of Lausanne and Geneva. In 2011, he was appointed Head of the Department of Health and Community Medicine of CHUV. Professor Patrice Mangin is a Member of the Presidium of the International Academy of Legal Medicine (since 1991) and Vice-President and Treasurer (1997–2012) and Vice-President again since 2012. He was President of the XVI Congress of the International Academy of Legal Medicine, Strasbourg, France (31 May–2 June 1994) and President of the Swiss Society of Legal Medicine (1999–2002). He is also a Member of the Board of the European Council of Legal Medicine (since 1996). His memberships on professional organizations include numerous institutions such as the International Academy of Legal Medicine, the American Academy of Forensic Sciences and the International Association of Forensic Toxicologists. He is the author or co-author of more than 250 international papers, 200 national papers, 350 oral presentations and 151 posters.

Pierre Margot fell early into the cauldron of forensic science by obtaining a combined degree in forensic science and criminology at Lausanne University, Switzerland, a long time ago. A short spell in the United Kingdom attracted him to pursue an MSc degree in forensic science at Strathclyde University, followed by a PhD degree, also at Strathclyde, and also in forensic science. Postdoctoral research led him from Salt Lake City (USA) in forensic toxicology, the Federal Institute of Technology in Lausanne (research in chromatography) and to ANU in Canberra (Australia) to pursue research and development in fingerprints. He was then called to take the professorial position in 1986 in Lausanne. He is the fourth professor to occupy the first academic chair in forensic science, created in 1909. One of his major contributions is to have created a research centre where over 60 PhD theses have been completed in the last 20 years and a full commitment to develop further this discipline as a key actor of forensic intelligence, investigative science and in providing solid and measurable evidence in court. His group has published over 220 peer-reviewed papers in forensic science within the last 10 years.

Jolandie Myburgh MSc is currently a laboratory and maceration manager for the Forensic Anthropology Research Centre, Department of Anatomy, Faculty of

Health Sciences at the University of Pretoria, South Africa. Her research interest focuses on trends in decomposition and body limb proportions.

Rolando Neri-Vela MD was born in 1953 in Mexico. He is a medical doctor, ophthalmologist and Master in History at the National Autonomous University of Mexico. He has a Diploma in Bioethics and teaches History of Medicine, Bioethics and Medical Anthropology at the Faculty of Medicine, National Autonomous University of Mexico. He belongs to the National Academy of Medicine of Mexico, Mexican Academy of Surgery, Mexican Society of Ophthalmology, Mexican Council of Ophthalmology, International Society for the History of Medicine, International Society of the History of Islamic Medicine, Mexican Society for the History and Philosophy of Medicine, among others. He works at the Department for the History and Philosophy of Medicine, Faculty of Medicine, National Autonomous University in Mexico and is now the Chief of the Department. He is the author of many articles and chapters in books in the field of the history of medicine.

Wim Neuteboom was born in 1949 and raised in The Hague (The Netherlands). He studied analytical chemistry at the Delft Technical University. During the final stage of his study, he developed an HPLC application for the identification of opiates in poppies. After a short working period in the oil piping industry, Wim joined the Netherlands Forensic Institute (NFI) in 1978. His first forensic discipline was "drunk driving", which included topics like alcohol and drug analyses in body fluids, physiological and pharmacokinetic processes, breath analyses, drunk driving legislations, etc. In the late 1980s, he was appointed as the (first) quality assurance manager of the NFI and became a member of the NFI management team. Under his supervision the NFI achieved ISO 17025 accreditation in 1994. After this QA period, Wim was appointed as the Head of the Supporting Division, a position he held till 2002. In the early 1990s Wim Neuteboom was intensively involved in the initiative by the NFI to create a network of forensic laboratories in Europe. He attended the 10th Interpol Symposium on Forensic Science in Lyon, November 1992, where most of the forensic science laboratory directors were present. This occasion was used to lobby amongst the West European colleagues about the idea for a European equivalent of the American Society of Crime Laboratory Directors (ASCLD). This was the start of ENFSI birth process, which was finalized in 1995 (Founding Meeting in Rijswijk). After this milestone, Wim focused on other activities outside ENFSI, but in 1997 he returned as a Member (later the Chairman) of the EAFS Standing Committee. Due to its prosperous development, ENFSI established a permanent secretariat at the beginning of the 21st century. As of 2002, Wim Neuteboom became the (first) ENFSI Secretary, a post he held for over 10 years. One of the first things he did was to prepare the historical and successful Noordwijkerhout sessions in 2003, where the membership discussed extensively the Future of ENFSI. In the years after, he formulated many ENFSI bylaws, set up a financial and book keeping system for ENFSI, explored the legal status of ENFSI (leading to the establishment of the Stichting ENFSI Secretariat), etc. As the ENFSI Secretary, he was among other things, involved in many activities:

- 2004: Organizer of the OOS "Education and Training: Quo Vadis?"
- 2005: Organizer of the ENFSI Annual Meeting 2005 in The Hague
- 2006–2007: moderator of courses on forensic science at CEPOL Budapest
- 2007: Organizer of the OOS "Forensic Research and Development"
- 2008: Author (with Kimmo Himberg) of the UNODC Criminal Justice Assessment Toolkit for Forensic Services and Infrastructure
- 2009–2010: Editor of the ENFSI Annual Reports
- 2009–2012: Organizer of the Triennial Conference EAFS2012 (with Jo Puts)
- 2010–2012: Member of the Future of the ENFSI Project Group (FEPG)
- 2010–2013: Manager of the EMFA-2 program (with Christina Bertler)
- 2011: Co-organizer of the Joint Meeting 2011 (with Peter de Bruyn)

Wim Neuteboom has an extensive personal network all over the world with forensic networks and legal agencies (e.g. European Commission, Europol, Eurojust, AICEF, ASCLD, SMANZFL, IFSA, CEPOL, Interpol and UNODC). He was successful as one of the ENFSI lobbyists introducing ENFSI in the complex EU structure, which led in the end to the recognition of ENFSI as monopolist, being "the sole voice of the forensic community in Europe". Finally, Wim has directed a number of quality assurance projects in various European countries, for example Croatia, Latvia, Macedonia, Slovenia and Turkey. He is (co-)author of about 35 (semi-)scientific articles and book contributions.

Antonel Olckers founded DNAbiotec (Pty) Ltd in 2001 and has served as its CEO since then. She holds a PhD degree in molecular human genetics from the University of Pretoria, South Africa, for which she performed research at the Johns Hopkins Medical Institution in Baltimore, Maryland, USA. Dr Olckers has acted as an independent forensic expert witness in DNA evidence since the late 1990s and has testified in multiple criminal cases in the High Courts of South Africa. Her view is that the expert witness is there to assist the court. She is often asked to evaluate DNA evidence to determine whether it is scientifically valid. Dr Olckers is a strong advocate for regulation of the forensic science profession, the accreditation of forensic science laboratories and the ethical practise of forensic science. She trains legal professionals to appropriately deal with DNA evidence in court, and to this end has presented the Essential DNA Evidence™ short course to legal professionals involved in prosecution as well as defence in the South African legal system. Dr Olckers is a member of the American Academy for Forensic Science (AAFS) and the International Society for Forensic Genetics (ISFG). She is currently appointed as an Extra-ordinary Professor in the Department of Immunology and the Department of Forensic Medicine at the University of Pretoria and has supervised more than 30 post-graduate students during her academic career.

George Paul is a Senior Consultant Forensic Pathologist and a two Branch Director of Forensic Medicine Division (FMD) and Health Sciences Authority (HSA), Singapore. He is also Senior Lecturer in Forensic Pathology at the Yong Loo Lin School of Medicine, Singapore. Dr Paul was born in Bombay, India, and after schooling in different cities of north, west and east India, graduated in Medicine (MBBS) from the Maulana Azad Medical College (MAMC), New Delhi, under the University of Delhi, India, in 1908, and subsequently did his MD (Doctor of Medicine) in Forensic Medicine at the Department of Forensic Medicine, Maulana Azad Medical College in 1984. After completing his senior registrarship in the same department, he was selected as Assistant Professor in Forensic Medicine in 1997 by the Ministry of Health and Family Welfare and served at MAMC, as well as Associate Professor from 1990. Subsequently he was on Foreign Assignment to lecture as a Forensic Pathologist at the University of Malaya, Kuala Lumpur, Malaysia, from 1996 to 2002. He subsequently also attained the Diploma in Jurisprudence (Forensic Pathology) from the Society of Apothecaries, London, and was awarded Fellow of the Academy of Medicine of Singapore, with membership to the College of Pathologists, Singapore. In 2002 he resigned his service with the Ministry of Health and Family Welfare, India, and joined the Centre for Forensic Medicine, Health Sciences Authority, starting as a Consultant and later Senior Consultant. Later HSA restructured the divisions with the Centre for Forensic Medicine, which was re-named the Forensic Medicine Division. Dr Paul's post-MD experience started with the mass casualty of so-called "genocide" of Sikhs in response to the assassination of the then Prime Minister of India, Mrs Indira Gandhi, in 1984, followed by a few other mass disasters, the most recent being the Christchurch earthquake of 2011 where he assisted as part of the Disaster Victim Identification five member team sent under the Singapore Armed Forces. He is the recipient of a WHO Fellowship in Analytical and Clinical Toxicology – Investigative in 1983 and the Health Manpower Development Program (HMDP) fellowship in Forensic Anthropology at Mercyhurst, Pennsylvania, the United States, in 2007. His special area of interest has been clinical age estimation (in the living), comparing various radiological exposures with dental radiological development, and he has conducted comparative studies of north and south Indians of Delhi versus the three dominant races of Malaysia. He continues research on this topic and has presented papers on this subject at various international meetings. Dr Paul has a large number of publications in international journals as well as presentations in conferences. He was involved in the autopsy for detection of the organism causing sudden death in toddlers in Malaysia, which was EV71, in 1997, and the death of pig farmers in Malaysia from a hitherto unknown new emergent virus, subsequently named the NIPAH virus. He is the recipient of Sijil Merit Sempena Penemuan Virus NIPAH (Certificate of Merit for Research on NIPAH Virus) on 28 July 1999, given by the Education Minister, Government of Malaysia, as well as a certificate of appreciation from the New Zealand High Commissioner on behalf of the Mayor of Christchurch, for assisting them in DVI, as well as medals from them, and also various other certificates and medals of appreciation through the years. His area of interest and involvement besides academic work is in choral arrangements, playing stringed and keyboard instruments and orchestration, and Aikido.

O. Peschel is employed by the Institute of Forensic Medicine, Ludwig Maximilians University, Munich, Germany.

Joseph Peterson DCrim. has been a member of the General Section of the American Academy of Forensic Sciences since 1975. He received his Doctor of Criminology degree from the University of California, Berkeley, in 1971 and is Professor of Criminal Justice (ret.) at California State University, Los Angeles. His research and publications have focused on the effects of scientific evidence on criminal justice decision making, the proficiency of crime laboratory results, and the resource and management needs of forensic laboratories. He received the Distinguished Fellow Award from the American Academy of Forensic Sciences in 2008.

Ivar Prits is Deputy Director of the Estonian Forensic Science Institute.

Luigi Ripani is a forensic chemist and is Commander of the RIS, Reparto Investigazioni Scientifiche, the main section of scientific investigations of the Carabinieri, in Rome, Italy. As head of the Department of Chemicals, Explosives and Inflammable Materials, he led scientific investigations in the area of drugs, explosives and merchandise studies, and later went on to lead the Department of Scientific Investigations of all areas of Criminalistics, initially in Messina and currently in Rome. He has recently led main national investigations on cases of common as well as organized crime. He is frequently an invited speaker in main forensic events and is author and co-author of several articles published in both national and international journals.

Alastair Ross is currently the Director of the National Institute of Forensic Science (NIFS), within the Australia and New Zealand Policing Advisory Agency (ANZPAA). He also held this position as the inaugural Director from 1992 to 2003. From 2003 to 2008 Alastair was Director of the Victoria Police Forensic Services Department, a full service forensic facility with over 300 staff. He holds

a Graduate Diploma in Business Administration and a Master of Applied Science (Research) from the University of South Australia. Alastair received the Adelaide Medal from the International Association of Forensic Sciences for international contributions to forensic science in 2002 and is a Member of the Order of Australia (AM).

Gert Saayman MBChB, MMed (MedForens) (*cum laude*) was appointed in 1998 as Professor and Head of Department of Forensic Medicine, University of Pretoria (South Africa) and as Chief Specialist of the Forensic Pathology Service (Pretoria). He is responsible for the organization, supervision and rendering of forensic pathology services in the Pretoria Metropolitan area as well as for the teaching and training programs in forensic medicine and pathology for under- and postgraduate students in medicine, science and law. He was awarded the Fellowship of the College of Forensic Pathologists of the Colleges of Medicine of South Africa in 2001.

Pekka Saukko MD, PhD is Professor of Forensic Medicine and Head of the Department of Forensic Medicine of the University of Turku, Finland, where he has been employed since 1992. Dr Saukko received a Dr University Medical degree from the University of Vienna, Austria, in 1975 and was certified as Specialist in Forensic Medicine in 1981 by the National Board of Health, Finland. In 1983 he received a Doctorate in Medical Science by a thesis in Forensic Pathology by the University of Oulu and was appointed Adjunct Professor of Forensic Medicine of the same University in 1986. From 1978 to 1989 he held the position of Provincial Medical Officer, Medico-legal Expert, Provincial Government of Oulu, Finland. In 1989 he was appointed Professor of Forensic Medicine of the University of Tampere, Finland. He has published widely as the author and co-author in scientific journals, books and encyclopedia chapters and is co-author of the *Atlas of Forensic Medicine* (CD-ROM) (Elsevier Science, 2003) and *Knight's Forensic Pathology* (Arnold, 2004), co-Editor of the *Encyclopedia of Forensic Sciences* (Academic Press, 2000) and co-Editor-in-Chief of the *Encyclopedia of Forensic Sciences* (Academic Press, 2013). Since 1993, he has been the Editor-in-Chief of the journal *Forensic Science International*, by Elsevier, and has served on the editorial boards of numerous scientific publications, including *Legal Medicine, Scandinavian Journal of Forensic Science, Archives* of *Forensic Medicine and Criminology – Archiwum Medycyny Sadowej i Kryminologii-Krakow, Cuadernos de Medicina Forense, Journal of Forensic and Legal Medicine, Adli Tip Bülteni – The Bulletin of Legal Medicine, Türkiye Klinikleri Journal of Medical Sciences, French Review of Forensic Science – La Revue de Médecine Légale, Law and Justice Review, Egyptian Journal of Forensic Sciences* and *Archiv für Kriminologie/Archives of Criminology*. Dr Saukko is a Member of the German National Academy of Sciences Leopoldina and an Honorary Member of the Hungarian Forensic Science Society, the Royal Belgium Society of Forensic Medicine, the German Society of Legal Medicine and the Japanese Society of Legal Medicine and a Founding and Honorary Fellow of the Faculty of Forensic and Legal Medicine at the Royal College of Physicians (London).

Anny Sauvageau MD, MSc is the Chief Medical Examiner for the province of Alberta, Canada. She started her career as a forensic pathologist in Montreal in 2002. In 2009, she moved to Alberta as Assistant Chief Medical Examiner and was named Deputy Chief Medical Examiner in 2010 and Chief Medical Examiner in 2011. She is an Associate Clinical Professor at the University of Alberta and the University of Calgary, and was previously Clinical Assistant Professor at the University McGill and the University of Montreal. She is the founder and program director of the forensic pathology residency program at the University of Alberta. Dr Sauvageau received her medical degree from the University of Montreal in 1996 and was board certified in anatomical pathology in 2002. She has a founder designation in forensic pathology from the Royal College of Physicians and Surgeons of Canada in recognition of her significant contribution to the development of this new specialty in Canada. From 2007 to 2012, she has been Vice-President of the Forensic Pathology Examination Board of the Royal College of Physicians and Surgeons of Canada. Dr Sauvageau is a well-known world expert on asphyxia. She is the author of more than 75 papers in peer-reviewed forensic journals and a much sought-after international speaker. Anny Sauvageau is also a co-author of *Autoerotic Deaths: Practical Forensic and Investigative Perspectives*. She is the founder of the Working Group on Human Asphyxia and the co-founder of the International Network for Forensic Research. Her innovative approach towards forensic research has significantly improved the understanding

of the pathophysiology of hanging and other types of strangulation.

Dina A. Shokry MBBCh, MSc, MD is a Professor and the Former Chair of the Department of Forensic Medicine and Clinical Toxicology – Faculty of Medicine, Cairo University, Egypt, and President of the New Mediterranean Academy of Forensic Sciences (nMAFS). She is the Secretary General of the Arab Union of Forensics and Toxicology (AUFT), which is a branch of the Arab Medical Union. Professor Shokry joined the Scientific Advisory Board of the Office of the Prosecutor of the International Criminal Court (OTP) in February 2014. She is a Board Member of the International Association of Body Damage (AIDC) representative of North Africa and the Middle East. Professor Shokry is also a Board Member of the National Committee of Organ Donation. She is a Director and Instructor of the training program for Gaza Forensic Doctors and crime scene investigators, Palestine via Arab Medical Union. From 2004 till now she has been the Editor-in-Chief of the *Egyptian Journal of Forensic Sciences and Applied Toxicology* (cited), a Board Member of Research Ethics and Clinical Research, WHO, Cairo, the Executive Director of the Research Ethics Committee, MUST, and a Board Member of the Middle East Clinical Research Association (MECRA), Lebanon. She is the contact for the DAAD academic activities in Egypt and the UN forensic consultant in Egypt. Professor Shokry has had more than 50 researches published in national and international journals and is the author of the following textbooks: *Forensic Medicine: A Guide to Principals*, 2006, *Clinical Toxicology: A Guide to Principals*, 2006, *Colored Atlas; Forensics and Toxicology*, 2007, *Medical Ethics: An Introduction for Medical Students*, 2008, *Medical Ethics, Law and Medical Responsibility*, 2009, and *Good Practice, Communication Skills* for *Medical Practitioners*, 2011.

Erkki Sippola has a PhD in analytical chemistry. He has 19 years of experience in forensic science and is currently the Director of the NBI Forensic Laboratory in Finland. Previously he has worked as a Deputy Director, as an R&D Director, as the Head of the Chemistry Department and as a leader of the Drugs Unit of the Forensic Laboratory. He has been Chairman of the Drugs Working Group of the European Network of Forensic Science institutes between 2002 and 2006 and also a Member of the American SWGDRUG Organization between 2002 and 2006. He was President of the European Academy of Forensic Science Conference held in June 2006.

Peter Sótonyi was born in Budapest. He studied medicine at the Semmelweis University where he received his MD in 1963. Since 1963 he was an assistant at the Institute of Forensic Medicine at the Semmelweis University. In 1989 he was appointed Professor and was head of the Department of Forensic Medicine from 1992 till 2003. He has certified qualification in forensic medicine, pathology–histopathology and insurance medicine. He was one of the most successful members of the Ökrös and Somogyi School. His basic pathology training determined his activities and attitude. He was extensively involved in studies on heart pathology and the biological effects of electricity. He made significant contributions to our knowledge on the pathomechanism of fine tissue damage developing from the effect of electricity. From his scientific activities is it worth mentioning his studies on the cytochemical analysis of the localization of heart glycosides as well as on the cell model of isolated cardiac muscle. He showed particular interest towards the introduction of new morphological research techniques as well as histo- and cytochemistry, scanning electromicroscopy with chemical analysis. He had great knowledge about the morphological identification of biological and nonbiological material. He improved the department with new laboratories (DNA, scanning electromicroscopy and cytochemistry). His fruitful scientific work is denoted by 350 publications and 25 books and book chapters. His textbook *Forensic Medicine* had four editions. Five lecture notes was founded in the English and German languages for foreign students at the Semmelweis University. He was Dean of the Medical Faculty (1997–2000) and Rector (2000–2003) of the University. He conducted the PhD school program law at the Semmelweis University and had an independent PhD program. Later he became Rector Emeritus (2009) and Professor Emeritus (2008). He became a Member of the Hungarian Academy of Sciences and is a Member of the European Academy of Sciences and Arts. He was Director of the National Institute of Forensic Medicine till 2003. He established widespread international connections and successful collaboration with Germany, Finland, Sweden and Poland. He had various academic degrees: PhD (1977), DSc (1990) and Member of the Hungarian Academy of Sciences (2004). He had memberships in many professional Hungarian and foreign

societies: Deutsche Geselschaft für Rechtsmedizin, Polish Academy of Medicine, Royal Microscopical Society, International Academy of Legal Medicine, etc. Several universities appointed him Doctor Honoris Causa, honorary senator and various university awards.

Maryna Steyn MBChB, PhD is director of the Forensic Anthropology Research Centre, Department of Anatomy, University of Pretoria, South Africa. She has published extensively in the fields of forensic anthropology and bioarchaeology, and has specific interests in craniofacial identification and assessment of sex from skeletal remains.

Patricio Bustos-Streeter MD is a Chilean physician and has been the National Director of the Legal Medical Service of Chile since 2007. He studied medicine at the University of Concepción and the State University of Milan, Italy. He has studied Planning and Management Programs STDs and AIDS in Latin America (Dominican Republic), Epidemiology (University of South Florida, USA) and Directive Leadership and Management (Faculty of Management and Economics at the University of Santiago in Chile). He is a Member of the Chilean Society of Health and has a long history in the public sphere, specializing in Public Health. He was Regional Secretary of Health and Government in Antofagasta and also Director of the Health Service of Iquique, as well as CONASIDA project manager and in charge of comprehensive care, among other responsibilities. Dr Streeter worked on the design and implementation of the Boards of assistance to victims of sexual abuse and chain of custody, among other aspects of the criminal procedure reform. He also worked in the Prison Hospital as a doctor of Gendarmerie of Chile.

Kyra Stull PhD is currently a collaborative researcher of the Forensic Anthropology Research Centre, Department of Anatomy, Faculty of Health Sciences at the University of Pretoria, South Africa. The majority of her research focuses on human growth and development and modern human variations and its applications in forensic anthropology.

Marika Väli has been Professor of Forensic Medicine of the University of Tartu, Estonia, since 2004, Head of the Institute of Pathological Anatomy and Forensic Medicine of the University of Tartu and Deputy Director of the Estonian Forensic Science Institute. She is the chief forensic medical expert of Estonia and a Member of the Executive Board of the European Council of Legal Medicine.

Arian van Asten studied analytical chemistry at the University of Amsterdam, The Netherlands. He obtained his PhD from the same University in 1995 on thermal field flow fractionation of synthetic polymers. From 1996 until 2000 he worked at Akzo Nobel R&D in Arnhem where he was heading the gas chromatography laboratory. From 2000 until 2006 he was employed by Unilever in Vlaardingen in various roles. In 2006 Arian van Asten transferred to The Netherlands Forensic Institute and became involved in forensic investigations and forensic science. He has been working at the NFI as a member of the management team and as head of the department for physical and chemical technology. Within the NFI he has coordinated the international forensic program and is also a member of a small team that coordinates the NFI contribution in urgent, high profile and/or complex cases. Since the start of 2011 he has become the head of a new department named WISK. This department aims at creating a world class forensic science program within the NFI and The Netherlands and developing forensic statistics and interdisciplinary investigations as novel forensic expertise areas. In June 2012 Arian van Asten was appointed Professor at the University of Amsterdam on a special Chair in Forensic Analytical Chemistry. He was the Chairman of the Scientific Committee of the EAFS 2012 conference, which was held in August 2012 in The Hague. He is author/co-author of 18 peer reviewed scientific articles and co-holder of three patent applications.

Sijtze Wiersma graduated in law at the University of Groningen, The Netherlands in 1973. Since then he has worked at the Ministry of Justice, The Hague, The Netherlands. Till 1997 he worked at the Child Care and Protection Board in several management functions. Between 1997 and July 2013 he was employed by the Netherlands Forensic Institute (NFI). He has been Secretary of the Advice Counsel of this institute, policy adviser and finally senior legal adviser.

Andrés Rodríguez Zorro MD, MSc is a forensic pathologist at the National Institute of Legal Medicine and Forensic Sciences in Bogotá, Colombia, where he has been employed for 15 years. Currently, he works at the National Group of Forensic Pathology as a consultant in pathology for the Division of Forensic Sciences. He is a professorial lecturer of the Department of Pathology at Universidad Nacional de Colombia and an invited lecturer in forensic medicine at Pontificia Universidad Javeriana, Universidad El Rosario, Universidad El Bosque and Fundaciòn Universitaria de Ciencias de la Salud. Dr Rodríguez Zorro received his medical degree and specialist title in Forensic Medicine from Universidad Nacional de Colombia. He received the title of Specialist in Hospital Management from Pontificia Universidad Javeriana. He also received a Masters degree in Forensic Medical Sciences from Queen Mary University of London. He is a fellow candidate of the Academy of Forensic Medical Sciences in London.

Foreword

Publication of this volume inaugurates the Forensic Science in Focus Book Project, a collaborative effort between the American Academy of Forensic Sciences and Wiley-Blackwell. This project seeks to publish a select number of books that relate closely to the activities and objectives of the American Academy of Forensic Sciences.

The book series reflects the goals of the AAFS to encourage quality scholarship and publication in the forensic sciences. Proposals for potential books in this project are reviewed carefully by a committee established for that purpose by the AAFS and directed by AAFS Past President Doug Ubelaker. Proposals are also reviewed independently by Wiley-Blackwell once they have been approved and forwarded by the AAFS. Authors who contribute to this book project generously donate their royalties to selected activities of the AAFS.

The global focus of this volume appropriately highlights the international nature of the forensic sciences and of the AAFS. We expect that this first volume will be followed by many more that enrich our knowledge and communication in the forensic sciences.

Daniel A. Martell
President, American Academy of Forensic Sciences

Series preface

Forensic Science in Focus

The forensic sciences represent diverse, dynamic fields that seek to utilize the very best techniques available to address legal issues. Fueled by advances in technology, research and methodology, as well as new case applications, the forensic sciences continue to evolve. Forensic scientists strive to improve their analyses and interpretations of evidence and to remain cognizant of the latest advancements. This series results from a collaborative effort between the American Academy of Forensic Sciences and Wiley-Blackwell to publish a select number of books that relate closely to the activities and objectives of the American Academy of Forensic Sciences. The book series reflects the goals of the AAFS to encourage quality scholarship and publication in the forensic sciences. Proposals for publication in the series are reviewed by a committee established for that purpose by the AAFS and also reviewed by Wiley-Blackwell.

The American Academy of Forensic Sciences was founded in 1948 and represents a multidisciplinary professional organization that provides leadership to advance science and its application to the legal system. The eleven sections of the AAFS consist of Criminalistics, Digital and Multimedia Sciences, Engineering Sciences, General, Pathology/Biology, Questioned Documents, Jurisprudence, Anthropology, Toxicology, Odontology and Psychiatry and Behavioral Science. There are over 6000 members of the AAFS, originating from all 50 States of the United States and many countries beyond. This series reflects global AAFS membership interest in new research, scholarship and publication in the forensic sciences.

Douglas H. Ubelaker
Senior Scientist
Smithsonian Institution
Washington, DC, USA
Series Editor

CHAPTER 1

Introduction

Douglas H. Ubelaker

Department of Anthropology, National Museum of Natural History, Smithsonian Institution, Washington, D.C., USA

In August 2012, I had the pleasure to serve as an invited speaker at the 16th Congreso Nacional de Medicina Legal y Ciencias Forenses in Bogotá, Colombia. This scientific gathering brought together forensic scientists for several days of workshops, lectures and discussions on recent developments in the forensic sciences. While attending this conference, I was invited to tour the Instituto Nacional de Medicina Legal Y Ciencias Forenses in Bogotá and discuss the work conducted there. On this visit, I found most of the major areas of practice within the forensic sciences integrated together within this single organization. I was struck that practitioners of very different areas of the forensic sciences were located within close proximity of each other, offering opportunities for consultation, cooperation and integration. This structure contrasted with my own forensic experience and what I had observed in other areas of the world. Although I had impressions of such global variation from my travels and international contacts, I realized that very little was known and published on the issue.

At the time of the visit to the Colombian Instituto, my thoughts also concentrated on our newly formed AAFS book project "Forensic Science in Focus." A volume on the global variation in forensic practice seemed to be an ideal candidate to inaugurate the project. Such a volume also represented a logical sequitur to our 2011–2012 AAFS meeting theme "Global Research, The Forensic Science Edge" and the many international elements highlighted at our Atlanta meeting in February 2012. While most of us were aware of the global nature of the forensic sciences, relatively little was known on international variations in the structure and practice of the forensic sciences. During my visit to the Instituto, I approached colleagues there, seeking their impressions of my new idea. Their positive feedback inspired me to continue discussion at the Congreso, where many colleagues also liked the idea and quickly responded with suggestions regarding countries, authors and issues that should be considered for inclusion.

The plan that emerged from this consultation and discussion consisted of invited chapters from authors relating to forensic practice in 30 individual countries. The 30 chapter limit enabled inclusion of sufficient countries to provide a sense of the patterns of global variation and yet provide the authors of each chapter a sufficient word count to cover the broad and varied themes involved. The selection of countries was made to provide a meaningful sample of the variation involved and to represent diverse geographical areas of the world. From the inception of the project, I realized that many countries with much to write about the practice of forensic science could not be included for reasons of limitations of space. Hopefully, those included provide a sense of the variation involved and reveal patterns that promote understanding. Authors were selected based on their scholarly reputations and the expectation that they could provide overviews of the forensic science issues examined in this volume. Since the volume seeks to cover most areas of the forensic sciences and most authors are specialists, all were encouraged to include co-authors as needed.

The authors who were contacted responded positively and enthusiastically. Many not only agreed to participate but offered helpful suggestions on volume coverage and thematic content. Once the lead author and country list was nearly complete, the proposal was reviewed and approved by our Forensic Science in Focus book project committee and the American Academy of Forensic Sciences (AAFS) Board of Directors was informed. With AAFS support, the proposal was submitted to Wiley-Blackwell for their peer review. Based on the reviews, the proposal and author/country list was adjusted, approved by Wiley-Blackwell and the writing/editing process was initiated.

Authors were given the following instructions (in addition to format information) in preparing their 9000 word chapters. These suggestions were offered to provide some uniformity in chapter structure and topics covered but with the expectation that authors would vary significantly in their approaches.

1.1 Chapter organization and information

- The title of each chapter should include the name of the country being discussed. For example, "The practice of forensic science in Argentina" or "History and current status of forensic science in Argentina." The chapters will be presented in the volume in alphabetical order by country.
- Each chapter should contain information on all of the forensic sciences, to include:

    Criminalistics, Digital and Multimedia Sciences, Engineering Sciences, Odontology, Pathology/Biology (including DNA and entomology), Anthropology/Archaeology, Psychiatry and Behavioral Science, Questioned Documents and Toxicology.
- Each chapter should address the following topics:

    History within the country. This section can include history of key organizations within the country as appropriate.

    Types of cases. Some information would be helpful on the variation of types of cases examined with statistical summaries as available.

    Structure. How are forensic science initiatives organized within the country? Are they centralized within a particular institution or agency or more diversely organized?

    Integration of forensic science. How is integration of forensic science achieved in crime scene investigation, case analysis, report writing and legal presentation? Are teams organized of the various specialties or are separate reports generated for integration later?

    Recruitment. By what process are new forensic scientists hired or encouraged to enter the field?

Training. How do forensic scientists acquire the necessary education? Do universities within the country offer courses/training/degrees in the forensic sciences? Are training programs conducted by forensic institutions?

Funding. A brief discussion of funding issues would be useful. Are funding sources through the national government or through other channels? What factors impact funding for forensic science? Who decides on the budgets for forensic science and prioritizes the use of funds?

Political influences. How does the political climate and shifts in political orientations affect the practice of forensic science?

Certification. What certification programs exist for individual forensic scientists? By what process are the qualifications of forensic practitioners evaluated?

Laboratory accreditation/quality control. What procedures are in place for accreditation of laboratories and quality control? How do these vary within disciplines?

Technology. What are the key technology issues that affect the practice of forensic science?

Disaster preparedness. What plans are in place for disaster preparedness?

Legal issues. How does forensic perspective enter the legal arena? What court procedures affect presentations of forensic science?

Research. What key research is being conducted and by what process?

Future directions. What do you see as the key challenges facing forensic science in the country and what trends are apparent?

An additional suggestion was made by Dr. Stephen Cordner, co-author for the Australia chapter and passed on to all authors with encouragement for inclusion. This suggestion was "Most countries have big cases which go wrong involving forensic medicine and science. A good heading might be a very brief summary of 2–3 such cases, the main problems in forensic medicine and science which contributed to the cases going wrong, and the state's response."

To some extent, this volume represents a research project; gathering global data and perspective on the practice of the forensic sciences. The patterns and perspectives that emerge from this work result from the commitment and hard work of each of the authors involved and their support teams. I thank all of them for embracing the concept of this volume from its inception and for accepting the challenge of attempting to synthesize so much information in such a limited format. I also extend my deepest appreciation to Rachel Ballard of Wiley-Blackwell for her encouragement to attempt this volume, our AAFS leadership and the Forensic Science in Focus book project committee for their support and my team at the Smithsonian Institution, Keitlyn Alcantara, Kristin Montaperto, Christian Thomas and Marcia Bakry, who worked with me on the editorial effort to produce this volume.

CHAPTER 2
The practice of forensic sciences in Argentina

Luis Fondebrider[1] & Luis Bosio[2]

[1] Argentine Forensic Anthropology Team (EAAF), Buenos Aires, Argentina
[2] Forensic Medical Corps, Buenos Aires, Argentina

Argentina

2.1 Introduction: the Argentine nation

The advent and development of forensic and criminalistic practice in Argentina is deeply rooted in the history of the country – its colonial origins under the Spanish rule, its political/legal organization following its independence and the various political circumstances faced by the country since 1930, when the Armed Forces first interrupted the democratic life of this young nation with a *coup d'état*.

The political organization of Argentina took place from 1810 (May Revolution, uprising against the Spanish colonial power) until 1952 (enactment of the National Constitution). The political model adopted as a result of this process had the following features: representative (the country shall be governed by the people's representatives), republican (such representatives shall be elected by the vote of the people) and federal (the provinces shall keep their autonomy, though under a common government, that is the National or Central Government).

The Global Practice of Forensic Science, First Edition. Edited by Douglas H. Ubelaker.
© 2015 John Wiley & Sons, Ltd. Published 2015 by John Wiley & Sons, Ltd.

The division of powers (Executive, Legislative and Judicial) was also established, and a written Constitution was adopted in 1853 and modified on several occasions later on.

The Argentine Republic is a federal state made up of 23 provinces and the Autonomous City of Buenos Aires. Each province chooses its own government leaders and legislators by direct vote; furthermore, each provincial state organizes and supports its own administration of justice.

Regarding this federal organization, it is important to understand that, from the perspective of the forensic services (state areas providing forensic and criminalistic – i.e. crime scene – expertise), there is not a single criterion guiding their practice. Instead, each province dictates its own form of organization following some common practices. To be more explicit, there is not one medico legal institute for all the country, but each province has its own forensic expert service. The same holds for criminalistics-related services, usually reporting to the police force of the province concerned.

2.2 The Judiciary: administration of justice

The Judiciary is independent from the other State powers, and this holds for both the provincial and national levels. The institutional role of the Judiciary is to control the other public powers as well as the individuals exercising such powers. Furthermore, it fulfills a jurisdictional role by administering justice in all the proceedings submitted to it for its decision. It enforces and interprets the law, and issues its decisions according to it, as well as to the evidence gathered in each case.

It can be stated that Argentina has a dual judicial system. On the one hand, there is a national system reaching out to the entire national territory in dealing with federal cases (i.e. drugs, kidnappings); on the other hand, there is a provincial judicial system hearing local cases and acting through the judicial bodies created and organized by each province.

The National Supreme Court of Justice (CSJN, in Spanish) is the highest court in the Republic, whereas the lower courts are made up of different kinds of trial and other courts. In this context, forensic and criminalistic services support the requests from judges and prosecutors, reporting to them at the national or provincial levels.

On the other hand, the Attorney General's Office, which is not within the purview of the Judiciary, is an autonomous body. Its role is to promote judicial actions in defense of the law and in the general interest of society.

Finally, as far as the laws are concerned, legislation (civil, commercial, criminal, labor, social security) is uniform and consistently enforceable in the entire country.

The legal system applied in Argentina has recently shifted from an inquisitorial model to a mixed, semi-adversarial system.

2.3 Law enforcement agencies: auxiliary bodies in support of the Judiciary

Each province organizes its own police with the purpose of fulfilling preventive and criminal investigation roles within its territory. Similarly, each province organizes its own judicial power and prison system. Along with this, there is a federal jurisdiction, of an exceptional nature, in such matters and areas of special interest to the National State.

The police forces are organized into the Federal Police, the Airport Security Police and the provincial police (in each of the 23 provinces and in the city of Buenos Aires).

There are two security forces: (a) the National Border Guard and (b) the National Coast Guard (rivers and seas).

The police (except for the Airport Security Police) and the two security forces also have their own expert services, which are summoned by judges and courts throughout the country.

To sum up, the practice of forensic sciences and criminalistics in Argentina takes place basically at two levels: (a) experts under the purview of the Judiciary (mainly forensic doctors) and (b) experts reporting to the police and security forces (some forensic doctors but mainly criminalistics), under the purview of the National Security Ministry.

There is a third level, made up of private experts who can be summoned by any individual to participate in a legal proceeding as an *ex parte* expert witness. These interventions are regulated by the code of proceedings.

2.4 A brief history of legal medicine in Argentina

The University of Buenos Aires (UBA) was created on August 9, 1821, giving birth to various scientific disciplines that started to be regulated, one of which was medicine. There are references from that time of the medical–legal advisory service rendered by police physicians to judges. During those years of development and restructuring, the discipline made progress at both the academic and practical levels.

On May 3, 1826, President Rivadavia established the Chair of "Theory and Practice of Deliveries, Child Diseases, and Legal Medicine." There is no accurate information as to the curricular contents of this course, but its first lecturer was Dr. Francisco Cosme Argerich, later replaced by Francisco Xavier Concepción Muñiz, who also stood out as a police physician. In 1899, Dr. Francisco de Veyga was appointed to the Chair, leaving behind as a legacy his book *Estudios medicolegales sobre el Codigo Civil*. At the same time, Veyga introduced some important courses such as criminal anthropology and forensic psychiatry.

On January 30, 1882, Dr. Julián M. Fernández was appointed by the National Executive Power as court physician and referendum of the law organizing the Federal Capital courts, which under the number 1893 was promulgated on November 12, 1882. In 1889, Dr. Adolfo Puebla was also appointed as court physician and on July 3, 1896, Law 3356 established that the position be occupied by six members, thus creating a specific body. The 1882 law provided that the person in charge was to be appointed by the President of the Republic, and the role as an advisor to judges was laid down in the following terms: "… is to issue reports and perform examinations as required and requested by magistrates for the better performance of their duties" (http://www.csjn.gov.ar/cmfcs/index.htm).

The Judicial Morgue of the city of Buenos Aires was created by National Law 3379 on August 18, 1896. This law had been drafted by Dr. Eliseo Cantón, Dean of the UBA School of Medicine. It was inaugurated on July 5, 1908, during the Presidency of José Figueroa Alcorta, under the direction of Dr. Guillermo Achával. This is where autopsies ordered by the judicial system have been done until today. In the police news section of *La Prensa* newspaper dated July 9, 1908, it read: "In the small hours of yesterday, injured Manuel

Monsalvo, a defendant before judge Dr. Lambí, ceased to exist at the Teodoro Álvarez Hospital. The Hospital authorities informed investigating judge Dr. Constanzo, who ordered the autopsy of the corpse at the recently inaugurated Judicial Morgue, for which purpose court physicians Acuña and Pacheco were designated."

In 1924, the Chair of Legal Medicine at the UBA School of Medicine was held by Dr. Nerio Rojas, who has been considered the first outstanding forensic physician of Argentina. His pioneering work extended up to 1946, when he resigned his Chair due to the country's political climate. His book *Legal Medicine*, published in 1936 and used as a textbook in several Latin American countries, is worthy of mention.

Among his students, Emilio Bonnet stood out. Bonnet started his teaching activity in 1935 and was granted the tenure in 1961. His textbook *Legal Medicine*, published in 1967, was another reference book in the teaching of this discipline in Argentina.

In relation to forensic doctors from outside Argentine, probably the most important influence had been the textbook of Dr. Calabuig, a Spanish forensic doctor (Gisbert Calabuig, 2008).

Outside Buenos Aires, other cities of the country underwent a similar development, led by Córdoba (its Legal Medicine course was established in 1874) and followed by Rosario (1921) and Mendoza (1957).

To specialize in legal medicine, medical doctors have to take a postgraduate course, which in the case of UBA lasts three years. After passing the course, they may submit their applications for the vacancies open in the forensic services already mentioned, positions to be filled by competition. It is not necessary to be a pathologist to be a forensic doctor.

The Chair of Legal Medicine at the UBA School of Medicine is the academic sphere in the city of Buenos Aires where such courses are given and where research should be encouraged. Medicine students attend the course as part of their curriculum.

Every year, new graduates who have completed the course are eligible to apply for a Legal Medicine vacancy within the Judiciary or in the police/security forces.

2.5 The Forensic Medical Corps

The Forensic Medical Corps (CMF, in Spanish) is the team of forensic physicians of different specializations that assist the Judiciary in cases of deaths in the city of Buenos Aires within federal proceedings (i.e. where the State is one of the parties to the case). It reports to the CSJN, and even though each province has a similar body, this is somehow regarded as the governing entity as far as Legal Medicine issues are concerned. Its experts are summoned from different regions of the country whenever a judge is not satisfied with the work performed by the local forensic doctors or when the case is very complex or has a high public profile. It is on account of its weight, therefore, that its development and current situation will be described here, as we believe it somehow reflects the current status of forensic sciences in the country. This paper, however, does not purport to be a thoroughgoing analysis, and it should be borne in mind that each of the 23 provinces has developed its own local conditions.

Until the position of court physician within the Judiciary was created, forensic expert reports were made by different official bodies, such as the council of medicine or the police.

It was not until 1886 that the law provided that "… a court physician shall issue reports and perform examinations as required and requested by magistrates for the better performance of their duties" (Bonnet, 1967).

Thus, a forensic corps with its own structure and regulation started to develop gradually. Among its roles, as provided for in Article 56 of Executive Order 1285 entitled "The Organization of the National Justice" and dated 1958, the following are mentioned: "… technical and expert witnesses shall: (a) conduct examinations, tests and analyses on people, objects and places; (b) assist in any judicial act or procedure; (c) issue expert reports; (d) act upon the request of judges."

The historical evolution of the CMF has not been written yet, but its course is marked by a continuing process of gradual administrative organization and functional technical specialization. Some of its members produced most of the few books existing on forensic sciences in Argentina (Achával, 1996; Patitó, 2003, 2008; Raffo, 1993, 2006; Vázquez Fanego, 2000, 2003).

However, it was not until the end of 2009 that the CSJN adopted the general rules of the CMF (CSJN Decision No. 47/09), the first set of organic regulations since its creation. In accordance with its provisions, this "… body is of a technical nature and will be exclusively devoted to providing expert opinions," the purpose of which "is to specifically assist the jurisdictional bodies within the national and federal system of justice," in

the context of which it shall "be the highest-ranking expert witness body in medical, psychological, dental, chemical and legal matters.

"From 1958 onwards, the Judicial Morgue, which had been created in 1908, legally became "… a body of the Forensic Medical Corps under the authority of its dean and the direction of a physician, who is to comply with the same requirements as the ones established for members of the Forensic Medical Corps" (Article 57, Executive Order 1285/58).

Professionals working at the Judicial Morgue include forensic doctors and technical assistants. The former, having different medical specializations, provide different specific services. Basically, there is a team exclusively devoted to autopsies and another one engaged in the examination of living patients. Furthermore, there is a team of forensic psychologists and psychiatrists.

The CMF also has a Forensic Anthropology service, made up of a forensic physician, as well as a Forensic Dentistry service.

The CMF forensic medical staff seldom go to the place where a corpse is found, unless they are so requested by the authority investigating the case. This task is in the hands of the scientific/criminal police, which include forensic doctors. Unfortunately, the link between the facts recorded and analyzed at the finding site and the subsequent autopsy is weak due to the lack of ongoing coordination and dialogue between both sectors.

2.6 Interaction with the police and the security forces

As mentioned above, in addition to the forensic doctors reporting to the Judiciary, there are forensic doctors and other specialists who form part of the "legal medicine" or "scientific police" areas of the police/security forces. Their major role is to visit the site where a dead body is found, conduct a preliminary investigation and send the corpse to the Judicial Morgue for its analysis by the forensic physicians within the Judiciary.

All the evidence associated with a corpse (bullets, weapons, blood samples, etc.) is documented and collected by experts in criminalistics from the police and the security forces and taken to their labs. In other words, there is a clear separation between the tasks carried out by the forensic doctors of the Judiciary (the CMF) and those of the police/security forces.

The different tasks usually grouped under the term "criminalistics" are mainly carried out by the police and the security forces. Each one of these forces has a "scientific police" or "legal medicine" area concerned with fingerprints, ballistics, documents, IT and accidents.

These areas are quite developed in the country. Usual reference is made of Juan Vucetich, a Serbo-Croatian criminalistics expert who settled in Argentina in 1882 and created the fingerprint identification system named after him.

As for which forensic expert team takes part in each case, judges or prosecutors may decide, for example, that a team other than the police – say the Border Guard – should analyze the evidence when the police are suspected of being involved in the crime.

2.7 Types of cases

The Argentine Republic has an estimated population of 40 million people, about a third of whom live in the province of Buenos Aires. This large territory comprises the city of Buenos Aires, where nearly three million people live. However, hundreds of thousands of people come into the city on a daily basis. Being in such a big city, forensic doctors take part in all kinds of cases.

Some figures regarding the most common types of cases are shown in Table 2.1 for illustrative purposes.

Table 2.2 shows the number of autopsies carried out at the Judicial Morgue in the last 14 years.

2.8 Training

The significant advances experienced in all branches of medicine in Argentina have not, however, produced a similar development in forensic sciences.

It is still commonly believed that forensic physicians work in isolation from other specialists and, to put it bluntly, that they only deal with the dead.

Initiatives to overcome this situation of stagnation and lack of update in this field have been mostly undertaken by individual forensic doctors, aware of the need to establish work protocols, quality controls, report reviews and ongoing training programs. In this regard, forensic medicine in Argentina is, in our opinion, lagging behind other countries of the region, such as Colombia and Chile.

As for the specific training in forensic sciences, there are almost no refreshment or update courses offered beyond those that are more trendy than academically serious.

The same holds in relation to the incorporation of nontraditional disciplines into the forensic field, such as anthropology and entomology, which started to be used out of curiosity of an individual physician or investigation policeman rather than as a result of an organic decision by the CMF.

In line with this, the relationship between the judicial/police expert witness services and the universities is weak. Little scientific research on matters of forensic interest is conducted.

2.9 Financial support to the development of forensic sciences

As with other aspects related with the State, the financial support given to the development of forensic sciences in Argentina, considering human resources and infrastructure, has been erratic, more associated with personal initiatives rather than State policies.

A good example is the CMF, which despite being the most important forensic medical body in the country,

Table 2.1 Autopsies by cause of death

Year	Accidents			Homicides			Suicides		
	Men	Women	Total	Men	Women	Total	Men	Women	Total
2008	513	231	744	210	44	254	190	103	293
2009	386	169	555	213	44	257	197	77	274
2010	349	114	463	180	19	199	170	67	237
2011	334	128	462	188	30	218	137	63	200
2012	362	139	501	158	23	181	138	62	200

Source: www.csjn.gov.ar/documentos/index.htlm.

Table 2.2 Autopsies carried out in the last 14 years

Year	Number of autopsies
1999	2856
2000	2963
2001	2915
2002	2947
2003	3479
2004	3476
2005	3434
2006	3094
2007	3396
2008	3118
2009	3026
2010	3108
2011	3224
2012	3374

Source: www.csjn.gov.ar/documentos/index.htlm.

has no forensic genetics lab of its own; therefore it has to outsource the service to private labs or universities. Another example is the Judicial Morgue, in charge of the most important autopsies carried out in the country; its building is more than 100 years old, and it has biosecurity deficiencies and contamination problems.

In the rest of the country, the situation varies depending on the province. In some places, morgues are located at cemeteries or hospitals, where work is carried out under very precarious conditions; in other cases, interesting projects have been designed to provide adequate facilities, in line with international standards.

Therefore, policies in support of the forensic field can be said to have been totally erratic. Sometimes, they have been adopted exclusively after some specific events. (In 1992, a terrorist attack against a building of the Jewish community caused 85 casualties. This situation brought to light the deficiencies of the Judicial Morgue at the organization and infrastructure levels, as a result of which special funds were allocated for its refurbishment.)

The decision to have ongoing training programs in place and to improve building facilities is the exclusive responsibility of the CSJN (in the case of the CMF) and of the security ministries (in the case of the police/security forces). Unfortunately, however, forensic work is regarded as a minor activity, and judges, prosecutors and lawyers in general are unaware of the weight carried by scientific evidence in any investigation process.

2.10 Certification/accreditation of professionals and abs – quality controls

Even though scientific development in Argentina is important, as already mentioned, at the forensic level there is no certification or accreditation process in place yet. For example, once a physician completes the three-year course to become a forensic doctor and is offered a position, there is no quality control (QC) or qualification requirement of any kind for him/her to meet until retirement.

At the laboratory level, i.e. in the Toxicology and Chemistry fields, the situation is almost the same.

In Argentina, there has been no such initiative as the one in the USA that gave birth to the 2009 report known as *Strengthening Forensic Science in the United States: A Path Forward*. Moreover, this report is almost unknown in the country. Discussions on the admissibility of scientific evidence, the value of DNA or probability issues are almost unknown to lawyers, judges, prosecutors and forensic experts.

2.11 Getting ready for mass disasters

Unlike other regions in the world, Argentina is not prone to frequent mass disasters, such as tsunamis or earthquakes. Nor is it likely to suffer a terrorist attack (only two in the last 30 years) or any other man-made disaster. Nevertheless, there have been episodes with mass victims, from 30 to 200, which have called for an efficient response from the forensic services.

In this regard, the city of Buenos Aires has an Emergency Master Plan, pursuant to Decree 695/09, which specifies the duties to be fulfilled by each area in the case of a natural, anthropic or technological threat. This plan is the result of an interjurisdictional agreement entered into by the National State and the Government of the city of Buenos Aires aimed at giving a coordinated response in the event of a major incident in the city (Bosio, Muro and Cohen, 2011).

2.12 The political context

Since 1930, Argentina's democratic system has been interrupted on six occasions by military *coups d'état*, the most tragic period taking place between 1976 and 1983. During such periods, the independence of the Judiciary was seriously constrained, and no doubt this had an impact on the forensic activity and its development.

Specifically concerning the victims of enforced disappearance during the period above mentioned, some forensic doctors, particularly those working for the police, issued and signed false death certificates while failing to report signs of torture, or carried out incomplete autopsies.

In 1984, in order to address the issue of the disappeared from a forensic point of view, the Argentine Forensic Anthropology Team (EAAF, in Spanish) was created, which was a private, scientific and nonprofit organization that could offer confidence and transparency to the relatives of the disappeared who did not trust the official forensic doctors. Under the initial guidance of Dr. Clyde C. Snow, EAAF, as an independent alternative to the official system, specialized in the exhumation and recovery of the remains of disappeared people who were buried as "John Does" in cemeteries and army/police former detention centers.

Finally, it is important to mention that Argentina is still a country where people with official positions in any of the three State powers are frequently more "important" than the institutions they represent. That is to say, if the head of the Security Ministry, the Federal Police or the CMF is replaced, the policies previously adopted are very likely to change, sometimes even radically. This lack of institutional continuity does affect the implementation of any medium- or long-term plan to encourage forensic practice and its development.

2.13 The future

There is a dire need to carry out a comprehensive assessment of the status of forensic sciences in Argentina, ranging from the degree of satisfaction of judges and prosecutors regarding expert witness reports to infrastructure issues, operational procedures, the training of professionals and the status of research.

Today there are no policies designed to promote forensic sciences and the initiatives to change the current situation depend more on individual efforts rather than on State policies.

Furthermore, justice administrators, particularly judges and prosecutors, should understand the value of scientific evidence and the need to streamline and adjust the system to international standards. Surprisingly, this has taken place in the field of medicine but not in the field of forensic medicine.

References

Achával, A. (1996) *Manual de Medicina Legal. Práctica Forense* (3rd ed.). Abeledo-Perrot, Buenos Aires.

Bonnet, E. (1967) *Medicina Legal* (2nd ed.). López, Buenos Aires.

Bosio, L., Muro, M., Cohen, R. (2011) *Manejo de Cadáveres. Desastres, Cólera y otras Infecciones* (1st ed.). Ministerio de Salud, Buenos Aires.

Gisbert Calabuig, J. (2008) *Medicina Legal y Toxicología* (6th ed.). Masson-Salvat, Barcelona, Spain.

Patitó, J. (2003) *Tratado de Medicina Legal y Elementos de Patología Forense*. Quorum, Buenos Aires.

Patitó, J. (2008) *Manual de Medicina Legal* (1st ed.). Akadia, Buenos Aires.

Raffo, O. (1993) *La Muerte Violenta* (1st ed.). Universidad de Buenos Aires, Buenos Aires.

Raffo, O. (2006) *Tanatología. Investigación de Homicidios* (1st ed.). Universidad de Buenos Aires, Buenos Aires.

Rojas, N. (1936) *Medicina Legal* (1st ed.). El Ateneo, Buenos Aires).

Vázquez Fanego, O. (2000) *Autopsias Médico-Legales* (1st ed.). Depalma, Buenos Aires.

Vázquez Fanego, O. (2003) *Investigación Medicolegal de la Muerte. Tanatología Forense* (1st ed.). Astrea, Buenos Aires.

CHAPTER 3
Australia

Stephen Cordner[1] & Alastair Ross[2]

[1] The Victorian Institute of Forensic Medicine, Monash University, Southbank, Victoria, Australia
[2] The Australia and New Zealand Policing Advisory Agency National Institute of Forensic Science, Docklands, Victoria, Australia

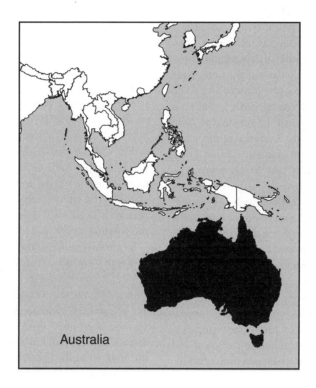

Australia

3.1 Introduction

When the First Fleet brought European settlement to Australia in 1788, it also brought English law, including that relating to crime and coroners. Arthur Phillip, the first governor of the Colony of New South Wales, was authorized to appoint officials necessary for the administration of justice, including coroners. The first inquiry in the nature of a coronial inquest was conducted on 14 December 1788. This was presided over by Augustus Alt, one of the first justices of the peace appointed by Governor Phillip.

For the purposes of this piece, forensic medicine is regarded as the application of the principles and practice of medicine to the needs of the law. Forensic science is similarly defined. For practical purposes, when discussing forensic medicine, we have not included forensic psychiatry.

The Global Practice of Forensic Science, First Edition. Edited by Douglas H. Ubelaker.
© 2015 John Wiley & Sons, Ltd. Published 2015 by John Wiley & Sons, Ltd.

3.2 History

The development of both forensic science and forensic medicine in Australia has been significantly influenced by a number of major cases and inquiries over the years.

3.2.1 The Gun Alley Murder (Lack and Morgan, 2005)

An early case relying heavily on what we now call forensic science was the 'Gun Alley Murder' of twelve-year-old Alma Tirtschke in Melbourne on 30 December 1921. Colin Ross ran a bar in the vicinity of where Alma Tirtschke was last seen. In addition to circumstantial evidence, including an alleged confession by Colin Ross to a cell mate while on remand, the prosecution relied on hairs from the deceased being allegedly found on a blanket in his possession in which he was said to have wrapped Alma Tirtschke's body. Evidence to this effect was given by the Government Analyst, Charles Price. Colin Ross strenuously denied any involvement. The defence sought access to the hairs pre-trial, for the purposes of undertaking its own analysis, and was refused. Colin Ross was convicted and hanged on 24 April 1922. In recent years, the actual samples were retrieved from storage and reviewed. It was concluded by Australia's pre-eminent expert in hair comparison that the samples on the blanket could not have been Alma Tirtschke's. At the request of the Attorney General, the conviction was reviewed by the Victorian Court of Appeal (Attorney General's Reference, 2007) and effectively quashed. Colin Ross was posthumously pardoned and the Attorney General publicly apologised to the family.

3.2.2 Wrongful conviction of Edward Splatt (Shannon, 1984)

In 1978, Mr Splatt was convicted of the murder of 77-year-old Rosa Simper who was found in her bedroom badly beaten, sexually assaulted and strangled. The evidence tying Mr Splatt to the crime scene was all scientific and based on the discovery in the bedroom of traces of paint, wood, birdseed and confectionary particles. Following a two-year campaign by the *Adelaide Advertiser*, the government established a Royal Commission, which led to a pardon for Mr Splatt in 1984.

Judge Shannon, the Royal Commissioner, said that some of the scientists appeared to have a dual role: both an investigative police role and a scientific analytical one. Furthermore, he said that a system that did not distinguish between scientific observations and deductions by police in their investigatory capacity was an unacceptable forensic system (Shannon, 1984, p. 47).

The Commissioner said of the lead police investigator, "I do not understand how he (the investigator) was allowed to express the opinions and theories in his evidence. There was no objection on the part of any person to it. I am bemused that such categorical assertions could have been allowed. One could not determine whether (the investigator) was speaking in the role of police investigator or scientist. The confusion of roles continued throughout his evidence."

He said that in a trial where the evidence is of such a scientific nature, a very serious obligation lies not only on the *scientists* who give evidence but on the representatives of the legal system who are responsible for the conduct of the trial. The vital obligation of the scientists is that they spell out in nonambiguous and precisely clear terms the weight and significance of the tests and analysis. The critical responsibility that rests upon legal persons is to ask such detailed and probing questions of the scientists as are likely to elicit the proper evidence.

As a consequence of the Splatt case, the Government of South Australia created the State Forensic Science Centre. It was independent of the police force and the various forensic sciences, previously provided by a number of agencies, came together in the Centre. Dr W.J. Tilstone, the newly appointed Director of the Forensic Science Division, said in a public awareness forum that the doors would be open "equally to the defence and the prosecution".

3.2.3 The Royal Commission into the Chamberlain Convictions, (Morling, 1987)

On the evening of 17 August 1980, a dingo entered the Chamberlain's tent at a camping ground near Uluru (better known at the time as Ayers Rock) in central Australia. In the tent was their 9-week-old baby girl, Azaria, who had just been placed in her bassinette by her mother, Lindy. Lindy had then returned to the barbecue area which was being shared by a number of families. Having heard her baby cry, she returned to the tent and was heard (by Mrs West, one of the other campers) to cry out: "My God. My God. A dingo has got my baby." Despite an immediate hue and cry, Azaria was never found. On 19 August, the Chamberlains left and returned home to New South Wales. Most of the baby's clothes (including the jump suit, singlet and nappy) were recovered 7 days later about 4 kilometres away from the camping ground.

This event triggered huge media interest in Australia and internationally – interest which was framed by bias, fanciful rumours, cartoons and misinformation generally directed at characterising the baby's parents, and particularly Lindy, as bad, even evil people. The finding of the first inquest, delivered on national television on 20 February 1981, concluded that Azaria likely died as a result of a dingo attack, but that there was human involvement subsequently. The coroner was particularly critical of the police investigation. The police were stung into action and within a fairly short period had gathered "evidence" to justify a second inquest, which in turn led to the trial which concluded in October 1982. Lindy was convicted of her daughter's murder and Michael, the father, was convicted of being an accessory after the fact. They were sentenced to life (with hard labour) and three years' imprisonment respectively.

The Crown case was that Lindy Chamberlain left the barbecue area with Azaria and her son Aidan (almost 7 years old) for a total of about 5–10 minutes. She returned to the barbecue area, having placed Azaria in the bassinette, with Aidan, and also carrying a can of baked beans as Aidan had said he was still hungry. During this absence, the Crown case was that "Mrs Chamberlain took Azaria from the tent into the car (adjacent to the tent), sat in the front passenger seat and cut the baby's throat…that Azaria's dead body was probably initially left in the car (possibly in a camera bag) and later the same evening buried in the vicinity of the barbecue area by Mr or Mrs Chamberlain" (Morling, 1987, p. 20). Having returned to the barbecue area, a cry was heard by one of the campers who was positive it was the cry of a small baby (who was at this point, on the prosecution case, dead). Mr Chamberlain said to his wife: "Was that the baby? She went back to check and when she was 5 yards from the tent she was heard by Mr Lowe to cry out: "That dog's got my baby." A hue and cry was immediately raised involving many of the campers. As mentioned above, the body was never found and the jump suit, singlet and nappy were found a week later.

The elements of scientific evidence at the trial included:

- Blood was found in and around the front seat of the car, including in the camera case and on a pair of scissors, purporting to have within it foetal haemoglobin indicating it was baby's blood.
- The blood under the dashboard was allegedly in a spray pattern, indicating an arterial spurt, indicating that it was the site of the murder.
- Blood found in the tent was transferred there by, or from the clothing of, Mrs Chamberlain.
- Professor Cameron from the London Hospital gave expert evidence that he could see the handprint in blood of a small adult hand on the baby's jumpsuit.
- The damage to the baby's clothing could not have been caused by a dingo and was caused by a knife or scissors to simulate dingo damage.
- No saliva was detected on the jumpsuit meaning that a dingo could not have carried the baby.
- Some hairs found on the jumpsuit were cat hairs.

The Crown addressed the jury on the basis that the claim that a dingo took the baby was "preposterous and not capable of belief".

Following conviction, the Chamberlains mounted two unsuccessful appeals. In the background a small group of scientists formed a Chamberlain Innocence Committee. Their work concluded a number of things, including (Chamberlain Innocence Committee, 1982):

- The spray material beneath the dashboard of the car was sound deadening synthetic material and not blood at all. It arrived there during manufacture of the car.
- The hairs found on the jumpsuit were canine or dingo hairs.
- Dingo teeth could cause the sort of damage sustained by the jumpsuit.

On 2 February 1986 Azaria's matinee jacket was found. The Crown case had been that the matinee jacket was another invention of Mrs Chamberlain's. It was found near a series of dingo lairs at the base of Uluru. This accidental finding of an item of Azaria's clothing, in an environment of increasing scepticism about the safety of the conviction, removed a significant foundation of the prosecution case. The existence of the jacket had been important for the defence to explain the lack of saliva and dog or dingo hairs on the jumpsuit. Five days later, a Royal Commission to inquire into the safety of the convictions was announced by the Northern Territory Government.

Amongst the findings of the Royal Commission were:

1. Examination of the 'spray' microscopically by a number of forensic pathologists and biologists who all agreed it did not look like blood in either the shape of the droplets or the pattern of the spray. Paint was present over the droplets.

2. The droplets were made of "bitumenous sound deadener" (Morling, 1987, p. 101).

3. Negative testing before the trial to the very sensitive "orthotolidine test" for blood had been overlooked.

4. Original testing using anti-adult haemoglobin antiserum was weak or negative. The anti-foetal haemoglobin testing was claimed to be strongly positive. The reason for the difference was said to be slower denaturation of the HbF molecule. Post-trial testing showed that both denatured at much the same rate. Thus the claimed results were anomalous.

5. The result book for the testing showed 12 occasions where the results of testing on three samples from under the dashboard were crossed out or changed.

6. Proper controls were not used, which if they had been would have demonstrated the nonspecific nature of the apparent results.

7. Negative and nonspecific test results on these samples were not mentioned in work notes produced for the trial, notes that were represented to be a complete record, and the negative and nonspecific results were not mentioned during oral evidence when there was an opportunity to do so.

For these reasons, I do not consider that the presence of baby's blood, or any blood, has been established upon the area under the dashboard....the strong probability is...that the spray pattern...was sound deadening compound and contained no blood at all (Morling, 1987, p. 106).

The Commission found that there was no evidence that the scissors, found when the car was examined in September 1981, were in the car in August 1980, but that in any event the material on it produced weak ortho-tolidine reactions and nonspecific immune chemical reactions, which did not allow the Commission to conclude that there was blood on them. The Commission found that it could not conclude that there was baby's blood on any of the items for which this was contended at the trial. The forensic biologist relied upon at the trial lacked the experience necessary for the testing conducted and reported on. One consequence of this

was a failure to use adequate controls. In respect of a number of places in the car, "the evidence falls far short of proving that there was any blood in the car for which there was not an innocent explanation" (Morling, 1987, p. 326). There was no blood of foetal kind in the car. This meant that there was no factual basis to say that the blood in the tent had arrived there by transfer from Mrs Chamberlain who, it was alleged, had killed the baby in the car. Virtually all of the Prosecution's scientific evidence was found to be flawed. There was no handprint that any one other than Professor Cameron could see. The matinee jacket was a good reason why there may have been no saliva on the jumpsuit, as the Defence contended at the trial.

The Royal Commission was scathing of the scientific evidence at the trial, concluding as follows:

The question may well be asked how it came about that the evidence at the trial differed in such important respects from the evidence before the Commission. I am unable to state with certainty why this was so. However, with the benefit of hindsight it can be seen that some experts who gave evidence at the trial were over confident of their ability to form reliable opinions on matters that lay on the outer margins of their fields of expertise. Some of their opinions were based on unreliable or inadequate data. It was not until more research work had been done after the trial that some of these opinions were found to be of doubtful validity or wrong. Other evidence was given at the trial by experts who did not have the experience, facilities or resources necessary to enable them to express reliable opinions on some of the novel and complex scientific issues which arose for consideration (Morling, 1987, p. 340).

Although expressed judiciously, this represents a serious and comprehensive rejection of the expert evidence given at the trial, evidence that led to the wrongful conviction of the Chamberlains.

On 12 June 2012, almost 32 years after her death, the fourth inquest into the death of Azaria Chamberlain announced its finding.

The findings are: The name of the deceased was Azaria Chantel Loren Chamberlain, born in Mt Isa, Queensland on 11 June 1980..... died at Uluru...on 17 August 1980. The cause of her death was as the result of being attacked and taken by a dingo (Northern Territory Magistrates Court, 2012).

Thus, the most extraordinary criminal case in Australian legal history ends up where it began: a terrible accident and tragedy. Along the way, many lives, principally those of the Chamberlain family, were irretrievably damaged.

The Royal Commission observed that there should be closer links between forensic science centres and universities and other appropriate institutions so as to ensure the former have the advantage of the research conducted by the latter. Setting appropriate standards in matters of forensic science would not be easy but was the type of issue a National Institute of Forensic Science could address so as to establish a uniform reliable practice throughout Australia. Such an Institute might also be a centre for the exchange of information and the location of reliable experts in unusual fields of expertise. The risk of an injustice occurring would be diminished if an accused person, in common with the Crown, had access to a National Institute of Forensic Science and its staff of experts.

A National Institute of Forensic Science was established in 1991 and further information about the Institute is provided in this paper under the heading 'Structure'.

3.2.4 The Royal Commission into Aboriginal Deaths in Custody (Johnston, 1991)

The Royal Commission into Aboriginal Deaths in Custody was established in October 1987 in response to *growing public concern that deaths in custody of Aboriginal people were too common and public explanations were too evasive to discount the possibility that foul play was a factor in many of them* (Johnston, 1991, para. 1.1.2).

Ninety-nine Aboriginal and Torres Strait Islander people died in prison, police or juvenile detention institutions between 1 January 1980 and 31 May 1989. (So weak was national coronial information gathering that the Royal Commission was actually established in the belief that there had been only 44 such deaths; Cordner, 1991.) The inadequacy of the investigations of the deaths led the Commissioners to undertake full-scale reviews in all cases. In 12 of the 99 cases there was no inquest held. In 41 cases, the autopsy was performed by a person other than a forensic pathologist, on 24 occasions by a general practitioner. A review for the Commission of the forensic pathology in 27 cases found a number of other deficiencies.

Misunderstanding of the nature and purpose of an autopsy lay at the root of many of those autopsies considered to be inadequate. In many cases it was obvious that the person undertaking the autopsy regarded the provision of the cause of death to be the beginning and end of the exercise. Most commonly, the identification of the cause of death is reasonably straightforward. The challenge for forensic pathology lies in its contribution to the reconstruction of the circumstances of death, and the onerous and more mundane tasks of recording, not only the positive but – often more importantly in the context of deaths in custody – the negative findings, so that another pathologist at another time is able to reach her/his own conclusions.

It was noted that a number of components of the forensic investigation of a death in custody must be of a suitable standard if the investigation is to be regarded as having been properly conducted. In addition to the qualifications and experience of the pathologist, mentioned above, and the forensic team, these include the

- Investigation of the scene
- Scene photography
- Autopsy
- Autopsy photography
- Histology and
- Toxicology.

A number of these elements were missing from some of the cases reviewed. On six of the 27 cases, no toxicology or inadequate toxicology was performed. Samples for histology were not taken in seven cases. Photographs of autopsy findings were available in only five cases. While the sample size was very small, these were cases of the highest importance, covered all jurisdictions and provided a snapshot of the state of forensic pathology in Australia at the time.

In 1991, the Commission made 339 recommendations to Australian governments, which aimed to reduce the rate of Aboriginal deaths, especially in police custody. The Commission found that the high number of Aboriginal deaths in custody reflected a "glaring overrepresentation of Aborigines in custody". Despite forming only 1.5% of the total population, indigenous Australians comprised 14.8% of the prison population and 28.6% of those held in police custody (Cordner, 1991). A number of the Commission's recommendations concerned the practice of forensic pathology and coronial inquests. These recommendations included the following:

- The scene of death should be subject to a thorough examination including the seizure of exhibits for forensic science examination and the recording of the scene of death by means of high quality colour photography.

- Investigations into deaths in custody should be structured to provide a thorough evidentiary base for consideration by the Coroner on inquest into the cause and circumstances of the death and the quality of the care, treatment and supervision of the deceased prior to death.
- All postmortem examinations of the deceased be conducted by a specialist forensic pathologist wherever possible or, if a specialist forensic pathologist is not available, by a specialist pathologist qualified by experience or training to conduct such postmortems.

Subsequently, as also recommended by the Commission, all jurisdictions followed the Victorian example and implemented state based coroner systems. By 2013, there is only one jurisdiction to replicate this with a state wide forensic pathology service: New South Wales, which has three separate forensic pathology services.

Unfortunately, 10 years following the report of the Royal Commission, the situation leading to its creation had not improved, with the number of Aboriginal deaths in custody actually increasing (Loff and Cordner, 2001).

3.2.5 Inquiries into the use of tissue removed at autopsy

In the late 1990s, following the Bristol and Alder Hay postmortem organ and tissue scandals in the UK, public concern about the possibility of similar practices in Australia developed. This resulted in inquiries in Western Australia, South Australia and New South Wales. While there was evidence of organs and tissues being retained without next of kin consultation or consent following coronial autopsies, generally speaking this was not illegal, unlike in the UK where it was. In addition, the Royal College of Pathologists of Australasia had published a position statement on autopsies and the proper use of tissues removed at autopsy. While its implementation was not uniform, it was evidence that the organized pathology profession was aware of the issues and had developed the appropriate policy position. The above inquiries did result in legislation in those states to regulate more strictly the retention of organs and tissues following autopsy.

3.2.6 Inquiry into the circumstances that led to the conviction of Mr Farah Jama (Vincent, 2010)

The most recent inquiry affecting the development of forensic medicine and science in Australia was in 2009 into the wrongful conviction of Mr Farah Jama. This 19-year-old of Somalian background was convicted of the penile/vaginal rape of a 48 year old Caucasian woman (M) at an over 40s night club on 15 July 2006. She was found unconscious in a toilet cubicle locked from the inside at about 10.50 pm. She had entered the club at about 10.20 pm, recalled speaking to some people, buying two glasses of a liqueur and lighting a cigarette at a table, but recalled nothing thereafter. She was taken to a hospital, and because she did not feel that the alcohol she had consumed accounted for her condition it occurred to her that she could have been surreptitiously given a drug of some kind and then sexually assaulted. Arrangements were thus made for a forensic examination, which duly occurred at 10.50 the next morning, and sexual assault samples were taken.

DNA extracted from the vaginal swab was profiled and compared to the DNA database and "matched" that of Farah Jama. What was never understood by investigators, or discovered at the trial, was that Farah Jama's DNA had been in the hospital examination suite the day prior to the above events. He had been involved in an interaction with a woman (B), resulting in his semen being in her hair, which was complained about to police but which did not result in charges. The complaint led to B being examined in the same suite where M was examined the following day. The suite was probably not cleaned between these two consecutive uses. Any discussion of the possibility of contamination was limited to the possibilities at the forensic science laboratory, and these were effectively discounted.

Mr Jama was convicted and spent 15 months in prison, until, in the course of preparing for his appeal, the prosecution realized the true course of events and the high probability of a contamination event having occurred in the examination suite at the hospital. Mr Jama was rapidly released and the inquiry instituted.

This was a case of a 'DNA-only' conviction. There was no other evidence. In addition, it was DNA which established that a crime had occurred, as well as establishing the identity of the culprit. In reality, of course, there was no sexual assault and Mr Jama was incarcerated not only for something he did not do, but for something that never happened. This case led to a number of improvements including in sample collection procedures and facilities, and prosecutorial guidelines requiring evidence other than simply DNA to be present before prosecutions will be launched. The inquiry was also critical of "those involved in the legal processes. There were ample warning signs along the way that suggested something was amiss, but they were simply not read."

3.3 Establishment of Forensic Service Provision in each Jurisdiction

3.3.1 States and Territories

Australia is a Commonwealth, a federation of six States and two Territories, the latter being very similar to states (see Figure 3.1). The Commonwealth itself is the ninth jurisdiction. There is a population of 21 million concentrated in the cities. Victoria and New South Wales are home to half the population. At the other end of the spectrum, the Northern Territory, which is larger in area than France, has a population of 240,000. The development of forensic medicine and forensic science services in each of the nine jurisdictions has been ad-hoc and the governance and infrastructure differs. In general, police in all jurisdictions have the responsibility for the "field sciences" such as crime scene investigation,

fingerprint identification, ballistics examination and impressions (e.g. shoes, tyres and tools).

The "laboratory sciences" such as biology (DNA), criminalistics, digital and multimedia, documents, drugs and toxicology are provided by a mix of Government Agencies including Health, Justice and Police, with some states having centralized comprehensive models of service provision.

Similarly, the "medical sciences", such as pathology, forensic medicine, anthropology, odontology, entomology and psychiatry/psychology, are provided by Justice and Health Departments.

Service provision is generally centred in the capital city of each State/Territory (see Figure 3.1). However, most States and Territories have regional facilities for crime scene investigation and fingerprint identification.

3.3.2 National

The Australian Federal Police (AFP) has jurisdiction for facilities such as airports and work closely with agencies including the Department of Customs and the National Measurement Institute for illegal drug and firearms

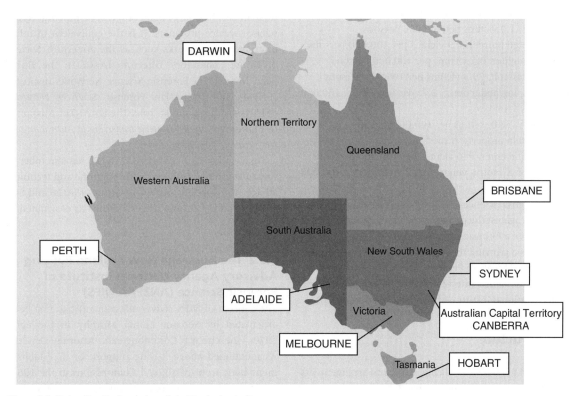

Figure 3.1 States, Territories and capital cities in Australia.

importation. AFP also has responsibility for community policing and forensic science service provision in the Australian Capital Territory.

3.4 Types of cases

3.4.1 Capability

In general, each State and Territory has a full forensic service capability albeit provided by a combination of agencies. Some of the smaller (population wise) jurisdictions do contract out some services to facilities in the larger jurisdictions.

3.4.2 Case types

All jurisdictions cover a broad scope of forensic science cases including crimes against the person (e.g. homicide and rape) and property crime (break and enter and theft of a motor vehicle). Overall, the crime rate in Australia is dropping but certain crimes such as alcohol fuelled violence are on the increase.

In 2010/2011, the Australian victimisation rates recorded by police for selected person offence categories were (Australian Bureau of Statistics, 2012):

- Murder, 1.0 victims per 100,000 persons
- Attempted murder, 0.9 victims per 100,000 persons
- Manslaughter, 0.1 victims per 100,000 persons
- Sexual assault, 79.5 victims per 100,000 persons
- Kidnapping/abduction, 2.7 victims per 100,000 persons
- Robbery, 56.0 victims per 100,000 persons.

For certain property crimes they were:

- Break and enter, 940 victims per 100,000 persons
- Theft of a motor vehicle, 235 victims per 100,000 persons.

The forensic science case load will reflect the statistics for crimes against the person as the vast majority of these will involve a forensic examination.

There is a growing tendency for crime scene examiners to attend break and enter scenes with approximately a 70% attendance rate of those cases reported to the police (National Institute of Forensic Science, 2013).

3.5 Structure

In relation to forensic medicine, structural arrangements vary between jurisdictions. Table 3.1 sets out some of the forensic pathology and clinical forensic medicine arrangements and related information in three of the eight jurisdictions.

The structure of forensic science service provision is (as previously stated) different in each jurisdiction based on historical grounds. However, there are agencies with a national focus which impact on the forensic sciences. These include:

- The Senior Managers of Australian and New Zealand Forensic Laboratories (SMANZFL)
- The Australia New Zealand Policing Advisory Agency National Institute of Forensic Science (ANZPAA NIFS)
- The Australian and New Zealand Forensic Science Society (ANZFSS)
- CrimTrac
- The National Association of Testing Authorities (NATA).

3.5.1 The Senior Managers of Australian and New Zealand Forensic Laboratories (SMANZFL)

SMANZFL (www.anzpaa.org.au/forensicscience/10606) was established in 1988 and consists of the Directors/Officers in Charge of all of the government forensic science service providers. It is the equivalent of other international networks such as the American Society of Crime Laboratory Directors (ASCLD), the European Network of Forensic Science Networks Institutes (ENFSI) and the Asian Forensic Sciences Network (AFSN) and has a similar role. The SMANZFL Mission is to *Provide coordinated strategic leadership to Australian and New Zealand forensic laboratories.*

Similar to other networks SMANZFL has a number of specialist groups, which provide scientific and technical advice. The Specialist Advisory Groups (SAGs) and Scientific Working Groups are established as designated in Table 3.2.

3.5.2 The Australia New Zealand Policing Advisory Agency National Institute of Forensic Science (ANZPAA NIFS)

The concept of NIFS (www.nifs.com.au) had first been articulated by Senator Lionel Murphy in the early 1970s when he was Commonwealth Attorney General. As mentioned above, strong support for its establishment came from two Royal Commissions in the 1980s into wrongful convictions. By agreement of the then

Table 3.1 Forensic pathology arrangements in NSW (Sydney), Victoria and South Australia

	New South Wales – Sydney (Glebe)	Victoria	South Australia
Name of department	Department of Forensic Medicine, Sydney, NSW Health Pathology	Victorian Institute of Forensic Medicine (VIFM), a statutory authority within the Justice Portfolio reporting to the Attorney General	Forensic Science, South Australia, Attorney General's Department
Number of cases or bodies received in the last 12 month reporting period	3229	4954	1150
Number of full autopsies in that period	1873	2440	1140
Full time equivalent consultant pathologists	6 forensic pathologists, 1 neuropathologist	11	5.3
% bodies with a CT scan	<1%	100%	13%
Any major inquiries in forensic pathology	Walker Inquiry into tissue retention and other matters	Nil	Splatt (see above)
Clinical forensic medicine/sexual assault/traffic medicine arrangements	Clinical and traffic: through medical staff employed by NSW police. Sexual assault: individual contracted practitioners, paid fee for service by Local Health Districts	All undertaken by staff forensic physicians employed by the VIFM, or by contracted doctors accountable to the VIFM	Sexual Assault Referral Centre. No formal forensic medicine arrangements

Australasian Police Ministers' Council, NIFS came into existence in 1991. It became a Directorate within ANZPAA in 2008. The functions of ANZPAA NIFS are to:

- Sponsor and support research in forensic science
- Assist with the development and coordination of forensic science services between jurisdictions
- Facilitate information exchange between relevant parties
- Support, coordinate and conduct training programs in forensic science
- Coordinate the delivery of relevant forensic science quality assurance programs.

In effect, ANZPAA NIFS has a national facilitation and coordination role for the forensic sciences. It maintains a small Directorate and works very closely with the wider forensic science community to enhance individual and jurisdictional capacity.

ANZPAA NIFS also has a very productive working relationship with SMANZFL and the SAGs and SWGs where with the latter, ANZPAA NIFS and SMANZFL, are involved in mutually beneficial projects.

ANZPAA NIFS oversees other specialist groups including the Chemical Warfare Agent Laboratory Network (CWALN) and the ANZPAA Disaster Victim Identification Committee (ADVIC).

In its 22 years of operation, the Institute has worked very closely with the forensic science community in all of its functional areas in order to address the concerns raised in the preceding Royal Commissions. The work has included:

- The establishment of a national forensic science accreditation program in conjunction with the National Association of Testing Authorities (NATA)
- The development and delivery of national training and certification programs, particularly in the field sciences
- The development of national forensic science standards in conjunction with Standards Australia (SA)
- The development and implementation of uniform practice methods across all forensic science disciplines in conjunction with the Senior Managers of Australian and New Zealand Forensic Laboratories

Table 3.2 SMANZEL groups

Specialist advisory groups	Scientific working groups
Biology	Statistics and interpretation
Chemical criminalistics	
Document examination	
Electronic evidence	Audio/video analysis
	Digital imaging
	Computer forensics
Field and identification sciences	Blood pattern analysis
	Crime scene investigation
	Fingerprint identification
	Firearms examination
	Impressions
Illicit drugs	
Medical sciences	Anthropology
	Entomology
	Mortuary sciences
	Odontology (Pathology)

(SMANZFL) and their Specialist Advisory Groups (SAGs)

• The establishment of partnerships with universities for joint research and development projects
• The development and delivery of an annual, national practitioner workshop program for the purposes of knowledge and technology transfer.

3.5.3 The Australian and New Zealand Forensic Science Society (ANZFSS)

The ANZFSS (www.anzfss.org) is a learned society with branches in all jurisdictions. It is managed by an Executive. The Australian Forensic Science Society was formed in 1971 with the aim of bringing together scientists, police, criminalists, pathologists, and members of the legal profession actively involved with the forensic sciences. It became ANZFSS in 1988 with the recognition of New Zealand membership.

The Society's objectives are to enhance the quality of forensic science by providing symposia, lectures, discussions and demonstrations encompassing the various disciplines within the science. Each Branch organizes regular meetings for its members and every second year a Branch, in conjunction with the Executive, takes responsibility for convening an International Symposium on the Forensic Sciences. These Symposia are world class with delegate numbers upwards of 800.

3.5.4 CrimTrac

CrimTrac (www.crimtrac.gov.au) was established in 2000 under an Inter-Governmental Agreement (IGA) between the Commonwealth of Australia and each of Australia's police agencies. The goal of CrimTrac is to enhance Australian policing and law enforcement with an emphasis on information based policing facilitated through rapid access to detailed, current and accurate police and law enforcement information.

From a forensic science perspective, CrimTrac supports and manages the national fingerprint database (NAFIS) and the national DNA database (NCIDD).

3.5.5 The National Association of Testing Authorities (NATA)

Established in 1947, NATA (www.nata.asn.au) is the world's first comprehensive laboratory accreditation body. It is the authority responsible for the accreditation of laboratories, inspection bodies, calibration services, producers of certified reference materials and proficiency testing scheme providers throughout Australia. It is also Australia's compliance monitoring authority for the OECD Principles of GLP.

NATA provides, amongst other programs, a forensic science accreditation program whereby participating facilities are accredited to ISO/IEC Standard 17025. The Forensic Science Accreditation Advisory Committee (FSAAC), which includes a number of very experienced forensic science practitioners, provides technical advice to NATA from a forensic science perspective.

The vast majority of government forensic science service providers, including the "field sciences" service providers are accredited through the NATA program.

3.6 Integration of forensic science

Mention has already been made about the fragmented approach in a number of jurisdictions. This results in different service providers providing reports for different forensic science disciplines in the one case. Other jurisdictions have a much more integrated system although "silos" do exist between the different disciplines, even where there is greater integration.

For homicide cases in most jurisdictions there will be case conferences involving different forensic disciplines (e.g. pathology, crime scene, biology and criminalistics) and police investigators. These conferences are designed to determine the most efficient form of forensic investigation. For other case types such conferences would occur rarely if at all.

Meaningful communication between science, medicine, law and law enforcement with respect to the investigation of criminal cases is limited in most jurisdictions.

3.7 Recruitment

To some extent, the recruitment method will be dependent on the forensic discipline. Traditionally practitioners in disciplines such as crime scene investigation, fingerprints and ballistics are recruited from within policing. This is changing in that in a limited number of jurisdictions, civilian university graduates are being recruited for these disciplines.

For the laboratory sciences, recruits require the minimum of a bachelor of science (BSc) but many recruits have higher degrees.

It is similar for the medical sciences with science or medical degrees, depending on the discipline, being the minimum requirement for employment.

3.8 Training

In relation to forensic medicine the following applies:

Forensic pathology. This is a subspecialty of pathology, with practitioners almost always having some training in anatomical pathology as well as forensic pathology. Five years of supervised training in institutions accredited for the purpose and a specified curriculum are accompanied by examinations and various requirements in terms of experience. Success in the various examinations and completion of the required periods of experience earns Fellowship of the Royal College of Pathologists of Australasia, which represents achievement of specialty status. In recent years, the College has established a faculty for oromaxillary pathologists (a pathway to which exists from dentistry), a subgroup of which is for forensic odontologists, a discipline now also recognized by the Australian Health Practitioner Regulation Agency.

Clinical Forensic Medicine. In Australia, this service area covers different fields in different states.

These fields include forensic aspects of the response to sexual assault; adult and paediatric physical assault; alcohol, drugs and driving; medical fitness to drive; fitness to be detained and/or interviewed by police; fitness to give evidence in court. In Victoria these services (with the exception of paediatric assault) are provided by forensic physicians at the VIFM. In other states they are provided from a mix of sexual assault physicians, general practice, emergency physicians and in NSW a small group of doctors employed by the police force. As with forensic odontology, the Royal College of Pathologists of Australasia is in the process of implementing a policy decision to create a faculty for clinical forensic medicine. This will lead to a structured postgraduate training program with assessment in accordance with a comprehensive curriculum.

In forensic science, training is to some extent discipline specific.

There are national training programs either in place or in development for the disciplines of crime scene investigation, blood pattern analysis, fingerprint identification, firearms examination and document examination. These programs are currently delivered outside the university sector. However, they are under review and are likely to be recognized as equivalent to a university degree.

There are a number of universities that offer forensic science programs. The undergraduate programs generally have a heavy focus on science and include forensic science related units. The postgraduate programs such as Masters Degrees are more heavily focused on forensic science. In some universities, the forensic science programs have reached a stage of maturity where PhD studies and postdoctoral positions are offered.

Following recruitment, irrespective of new recruits' qualifications, in-house training is also part of the education and training process. In most facilities the in-house training programs are well structured and involve assessment prior to endorsement for each new skill or competency.

Training records are kept for each practitioner as part of the accreditation process.

3.9 Funding

Funding for forensic science service provision is the responsibility of the government in each jurisdiction. In a minority of jurisdictions, police pay for some services (e.g. DNA) albeit provided through another government department. A very limited amount of forensic work is outsourced to private companies by government laboratories.

Infrastructure funding such as expensive equipment, building additions/renovations or new buildings are subject to a separate funding submission to government over and above annual budgets.

There is no dedicated commonwealth government funding for routine forensic services within the States and Territories with the exception of the Australian Capital Territory. However, there have been occasions where commonwealth funding has been available for forensic science projects. A recent example of this was the development of a central core of forensic science standards for collection, analysis, interpretation and reporting.

3.10 Political influences

Political influence on forensic science service provision is generally limited. However, there have been occasions where forensic failures, some of which are set out above, have led to enquiries and Royal Commissions with the outcome of these resulting in political decisions for change.

Government priorities, particularly during election campaigns, can also have an impact. For example, a political platform on law reform may result in additional funding for the forensic sciences.

Law reform is another example. Changes in legislation related to DNA or fingerprint databases often occur as a result of political policies.

3.11 Certification

There is a national certification program for the disciplines of crime scene investigation, fingerprint identification and firearms examination. The program is administered by the Australasian Forensic Field Science Accreditation Board (AFFSAB) under the auspices of ANZPAA NIFS.

A prerequisite for certification is the national qualification or its equivalent. Following completion of that qualification, practitioners are assessed within their jurisdiction as to whether or not they have the required skills and knowledge for certification.

The certification process consists of a series of written, practical and oral examinations (including moot courts), which are assessed by both internal and external (from another jurisdiction) assessors.

Re-certification is on an annual basis and determined by the performance of the practitioner in proficiency tests, assessment by the supervisor and endorsement by the director/OIC of the facility. Every fifth year there is a more rigorous re-certification process based on a points system.

There is no certification program in place for other disciplines at this time.

3.12 Laboratory accreditation/quality control

With only one exception, all of the primary government forensic science service providers are accredited to the Standard ISO/IEC 17025. The accreditation provider is NATA. The program is voluntary with full re-assessments every third year and a quality systems assessment every eighteen months.

In addition to the ISO/IEC 17025 Standard, there are also the NATA supplementary requirements for accreditation, which are taken into consideration at assessment. Most recently, in conjunction with Standards Australia, the forensic community has developed a set of four core forensic science standards; AS 5388 Forensic Analysis comprising:

- Recognition, recording, recovery and storage of material
- Analysis and examination of material
- Interpretation
- Reporting.

A comparative analysis of ISO/IEC 17025, the NATA supplementary requirements and AS 5388 has been undertaken to identify any duplication for both compliance and assessment purposes.

3.13 Technology

One of the key issues related to technology is that of information technology(IT) and, in particular, item and data management. While forensic facilities have some form of information management system they are often different to the main system of the larger organization. At present, there are also significant differences between the jurisdictions with respect to IT systems although a project to examine this situation has just begun.

As mentioned previously, the procurement of large items of equipment are generally the subject of separate budget submissions, but, in general, Australian laboratories are well equipped. Also, because of national discussion within the SAGs and SWGs there is some uniformity in the technology used. This is particularly so with DNA profiling.

There is a trend towards miniaturisation and mobility of technology with a view to undertaking more at-scene testing and with fingerprints, for example, electronic capture, transport and analysis of latent prints located in the field.

3.14 Disaster preparedness

As mentioned previously, ADVIC (ANZPAA Disaster Victim Identification Committee) is a group that is overseen by ANZPAA NIFS. It has a good history of promoting disaster preparedness in all jurisdictions. ADVIC consists of the DVI Commander (police officer) from each jurisdiction, scientific representatives from the disciplines of biology (DNA), anthropology, odontology and mortuary sciences, and a representative of the military.

National training courses have resulted in practitioners across the country having common knowledge and skills related to DVI and a depth of experience in the Asia Pacific region from instances of bombings, tsunamis, earthquakes and bush fires. ADVIC works very closely with Interpol and has had significant input to, and adopted, the Interpol guidelines for DVI.

CWALN (Chemical Warfare Agent Laboratory Network) also meets under the auspices of ANZPAA NIFS. One of the key roles of CWALN is to develop and maintain knowledge, skills and readiness for a potential chemical attack. As with ADVIC, they are also involved in training on a national basis to ensure complementary skills.

3.15 Legal issues

Because of its British heritage, Australia has an adversarial legal system although the range and level of courts vary between jurisdictions.

In the vast majority of instances, the government forensic science facilities will be engaged by the police early in an investigation and are generally called by the prosecution if they are required to present evidence in court.

While most forensic scientists would prefer to confer with the prosecutor and defence counsel prior to court, particularly in more complex cases, this rarely happens.

Increasingly courts are permitting the use of electronic aids in the court room to support expert testimony and there are provisions in some courts for presentation by video link. However, this is not generally encouraged by legal counsel.

3.16 Research

ANZPAA NIFS recently completed a survey of directors and those in charge of forensic facilities. One purpose was to learn what the key road blocks were to R&D in forensic science. The common points were:
• Limited funding
• Limited time
• Lack of research experience
• Difficulties in operationalizing outcomes.

In the development of an R&D strategy, NIFS reported three categories of research (Kirkbride, 2001):
• Technology adoption (e.g. validation of new methods)
• Technology extension (e.g. bringing technology from other areas of science into forensic science)
• Technology (and knowledge) creation (e.g. invention of new technology and discovery of knowledge).

To some extent, forensic science agencies are able to successfully engage in the first two categories, perhaps in partnership with academia at least for the second category. However, engagement with academia is all but essential for the final category.

The cooperation between forensic science service providers and academia in Australia is very productive. One of the funding sources provided by the Australian Research Council (ARC) is through Linkage Grants, which stipulate industry/academic partnerships, and forensic science has been successful in securing a significant number of these. They provide leverage for any funding forensic science agencies have available.

These grants not only apply to "hard science" but also to social science, and the forensic science community has engaged with social scientists in a number of linkage grants with plans for future grant applications.

Current areas of research interest include:
- Next generation sequencing and rapid DNA technology
- Fingerprint enhancement
- Pre- and post-blast explosive detection
- Cognitive processes and fingerprint identification
- Validation studies.

Forensic medicine research has been strongest in areas overlapping with clinical medicine and health care generally. A strong research based contribution has come from forensic toxicology based on a steady stream of doctoral students. Productive collaborations with the National Coronial Information System have been forged. The NCIS now has over 200,000 coronial cases in its database from all Australian jurisdictions since 2000, with New Zealand joining in 2010. This system, accessible by any recognized academic or law enforcement institution after formal application is made, is a powerful resource whose significance and potential is gradually becoming more recognized (www.ncis.org.au). In forensic pathology, research and development has focused on defining and understanding the application of new imaging technologies, molecular autopsy and ethics. More is needed, but inherent limitations in much forensic pathology research, reliant as it is on descriptive retrospective studies, need to be overcome.

3.17 Future directions:

The bottom line is simple: In a number of forensic science disciplines, forensic science professionals have yet to establish either the validity of their approach or the accuracy of their conclusions, and the courts have been utterly ineffective in addressing this problem. For a variety of reasons—including the rules governing the admissibility of forensic evidence, the applicable standards governing appellate review of trial court decisions, the limitations of the adversary process, and the common lack of scientific expertise among judges and lawyers who must try to comprehend and evaluate forensic evidence—the legal system is ill-equipped to correct the problems of the forensic science community (National Research Council, 2009).

This quote from the US National Research Council will echo through forensic science, forensic medicine and the courts all through the developed world for the foreseeable future. Our disciplines need to be paying heed – the future is not going to be the same as the past, and nor should it be.

The close association of forensic science with political law and order agendas offers some protection from an overall more constrained public budgetary environment that is developing. Keeping budgets in robust shape will be an important basis for dealing with the inevitably fast developing technological environment. This will involve:
- More, faster and cheaper at-scene testing
- The need for more validation and understanding of error rates
- Developing stronger forensic contributions to intelligence-led policing
- Strengthening forensic discipline specific responses to the various hazards in the provision of expert advice and evidence such as cognitive bias.

In forensic medicine, some developments will mirror trends in clinical medicine. So expensive is specialist medical expertise, streamlining its use is likely to become an emphasis. This means greater reliance on paramedical skills and processes, and on technologies such as CT and MRI to reduce dependence on the apparently expensive autopsy. Notwithstanding this, it is unlikely that easy access to these technologies will become ubiquitous and more traditional levels of reliance on autopsy will remain in many services. Molecular autopsy will flourish, following in the footsteps of the myriad discoveries in clinical medicine. Consolidation of the disciplines of clinical forensic medicine and forensic odontology, with each developing the recognized infrastructure of a medical and dental specialty respectively, will strengthen the contribution of these areas of practice to the justice system.

Acknowledgements

Associate Professor Johannes Du Flou and Associate Professor Neil Langlois are thanked for contributing forensic pathology figures from New South Wales and South Australia respectively.

References

Attorney-General's Reference to the Victorian Court of Appeal concerning the conviction of Colin Campbell Ross (2007) https://assets.justice.vic.gov.au/scv/resources/adeda430-db22-4e27-b96b-477c6a5c7e06/opinion+-+colin+campbell+ross.pdf.

Australian Bureau of Statistics (2012) Crime Victimisation in Australia 2010–11.

Chamberlain Innocence Committee (1982) http://www.lindychamberlain.com/files/Blue_Book.pdf.

Cordner, S. (1991) The Royal Commission into Aboriginal Deaths in Custody. Aspects of medical interest. *MJA* 155: 812–818, December 1991.

Johnston, E. (1991) Royal Commission into Aboriginal Deaths in Custody. Available at: http://www.austlii.edu.au/au/other/IndigLRes/rciadic/#national.

Kirkbride, K. (2001) The National Institute of Forensic Science Innovation Strategy: "The advancement of science for justice" (Unpublished. Available from NIFS).

Lack, J., Morgan, K. (2005) Ross, Colin Campbell Eadie (1892–1922) In: *Australian Dictionary of Biography*, Supplementary Volume, Melbourne University Press.

Loff, B., Cordner, S. (2001) Death rate of Aborigines in prison is increasing. *Lancet* 357 (9265): 1348.

Morling, J. (1987) *Report of the Commissioner. Royal Commission of Inquiry into Chamberlain Convictions*, ISBN 0 7245 1298 5, Government Printer of the Northern Territory.

National Institute of Forensic Science (2013) End to End Forensic Investigation Process Project (Unpublished. Available from NIFS).

National Research Council (2009) Identifying the needs of the forensic science community. In: *Strengthening Forensic Science in the United States: A Path Forward*, National Academies Press, Washington, DC, p. 53.

Northern Territory Magistrates Court (2012) Inquest into the death of Azaria Chantel Loren Chamberlain (2012), NTMC 020.

Shannon, C. (1984) *Royal Commission of Inquiry in Respect to the Case of Edward Charles Splatt*, Government Printer, Adelaide.

Vincent, F. (2010) Report on the Conviction of Mr Farah Abdulkadir Jama. http://www.justice.vic.gov.au/home/justice+system/laws+and+regulation/criminal+law/report+on+the+conviction+of+mr+farah+abdulkadir+jama.

CHAPTER 4
Forensic sciences in Canada

Anny Sauvageau & Graham R. Jones

Office of the Chief Medical Examiner, Edmonton, Alberta, Canada

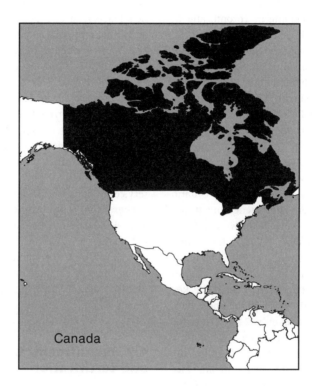

Canada

4.1 History of forensic science in Canada

The history of forensic science in Canada is a distinguished one, boasting the first forensic laboratory in North America and only the third in the world, after the laboratories in Paris and Lyon in France. The Laboratoire de Recherches Médico-legales was opened in Montreal in 1913. It pre-dated the Chicago Forensic Laboratory and the FBI Laboratory (opened in 1932). The first director was Dr. Wilfrid Derome, who served until his death in 1931, and was succeeded by Dr. Rosario Fontaine. In 1978 the laboratory was divided into two units, the Laboratoire de Police Scientifique, which encompasses the most of the traditional "crime lab" areas and the Laboratoire de Médicine Légale, which includes forensic pathology and forensic toxicology.

The Global Practice of Forensic Science, First Edition. Edited by Douglas H. Ubelaker.
© 2015 John Wiley & Sons, Ltd. Published 2015 by John Wiley & Sons, Ltd.

The second forensic laboratory in Canada was the laboratory of the Attorney General of Ontario, in Toronto, opened in 1932 with Dr. Edgar Frankish as head. In 1951 the laboratory was reorganized under the leadership of Dr. H. Ward Smith. The laboratory was renamed the Centre of Forensic Sciences in 1966. After Dr. Smith's untimely death in 1967, Doug Lucas took over and served as the laboratory's director until his retirement 27 years later. In 1975, the Centre moved to a much larger 70,000 square foot building in Toronto and in 1992, in recognition of the huge tract of land that the Toronto laboratory had to cover, the Northern Regional Forensic Laboratory was opened in Sault Ste. Marie. In 2013 the Toronto forensic laboratory moved into a large, modern facility that is shared with the Ontario Forensic Pathology Service and the Office of the Chief Coroner.

The first Royal Canadian Mounted Police forensic laboratory was opened at the training center in Regina, Saskatchewan, in 1937. The first director was Dr. (Surgeon) Maurice Powers. Because the forensic services had to cover most of Canada except for Ontario and Quebec, laboratories were later opened in Ottawa, Ontario (1942), Sackville, New Brunswick (1957), Vancouver, British Columbia (1963), Edmonton, Alberta (1967), Winnipeg, Manitoba (1970) and Halifax, Nova Scotia (1978). Originally most of the laboratories were "full service" in that they each covered the key forensic science disciplines. However, in the mid-1990s, services were regionalized and only 2 or 3 forensic disciplines were covered in any given laboratory. That reorganization of services included closure of the Sackville laboratory. As of 2013, plans are in place to further streamline forensic services by closing the Halifax, Winnipeg and Regina laboratories. By 2015 the RCMP Forensic Laboratory Services will be consolidated in Vancouver, Edmonton and Ottawa.

4.2 Structure and funding of Canadian forensic science

In Canada, death investigation and forensic science is largely the responsibility of the ten provinces and three territories, encompassing about 35.2 million population covering 9.984 million km². Although Canada has a national police force (Royal Canadian Mounted Police), provision of forensic science laboratory services is based on policing agreements with each province or territory. The two largest provinces, Ontario and Quebec, have their own forensic laboratories, the Centre of Forensic Sciences in Toronto and Sault Ste. Marie, and the Laboratoire de Sciences Judiciaires et de Médecine Légale in Montreal, respectively. All other provinces and territories have policing agreements that allow the Royal Canadian Mounted Police and city or local police forces to access the core Forensic Services of the Royal Canadian Mounted Police. As such, funding for forensic science services is largely provincial (either directly or through provincial policing agreements with the Federal Government). The Royal Canadian Mounted Police, individual provinces or territories and local police forces will decide how funds are allocated to forensic services, based on demand and local budget realities. Some coroner/medical examiner systems have dedicated forensic toxicology laboratories, whereas others do not. Some specialty services are provided by local universities or other professionals (e.g. anthropology, odontology, entomology), although generally forensic services in Canada are not university based.

There is no central source of funding for conducting forensic research in Canada. The majority of research publications are casework based and resources are typically drawn from operational funds. In some cases, grant money may be obtained on an ad hoc basis, most commonly when the research or discipline tends to be university based (e.g. anthropology).

4.3 Recruitment, training and certification

Recruitment and training is a responsibility of the individual agencies and is rarely carried out at a national level, with the possible exception of Royal Canadian Mounted Police forensic scientists and technicians. Most forensic scientists are recruited and trained locally, supplemented in some cases by additional training at a fellowship level, as occurs for many forensic pathologists. Some training or further specialization may occur through coursework or workshops, most often in the United States. Forensic scientists in Canada are not required to be certified in a specialty, except where required by their primary qualification (e.g. physicians, engineers, dentists). However, a small number of Canadian forensic scientists may voluntarily choose to seek certification through US-based certifying bodies.

4.4 Forensic education in Canada

For the main forensic sciences, graduates in a bachelor of science program most suited to the particular specialty are still preferred (e.g. chemistry based for toxicology, drug chemistry or forensic chemistry; a biology or genetics degree for a DNA specialist). While some universities in Canada do offer forensic technology or forensic science degree programs, these are often very broad in scope and may lack an adequate foundation in basic science for the core forensic science disciplines. Other programs may be more general in nature and focused more on criminal justice or crime scene criminalistics.

4.5 Laboratory accreditation

Canada does not currently require any of its forensic services to be accredited. However, the Royal Canadian Mounted Police forensic laboratories and the Laboratoire de Sciences Judiciaires et de Médecine Légale are accredited under ISO/IEC 17025 by the Standards Council of Canada. The Centre of Forensic Sciences is accredited by the American Society of Crime Laboratory Directors/Laboratory Accreditation Program (ASCLD/ LAB–ISO/IEC 17025-based) and two additional forensic toxicology laboratories accredited through the American Board of Forensic Toxicology (ABFT – the Alberta Office of the Chief Medical Examiner Toxicology Laboratory and the St. Boniface Hospital Toxicology Laboratory in Winnipeg, Manitoba). Only one private laboratory in Canada is currently offering a workplace drug testing service that is accredited by the US agency SAMHSA through the National Laboratory Certification Program. Some private laboratories offering DNA services are also accredited by the Standards Council of Canada under ISO/IEC 17025.

4.6 Death investigation systems in Canada

Two death investigation systems coexist in Canada: the Coroner and the Medical Examiner System. The vast majority of the provinces and territories of Canada operates under a Coroner system: British Columbia, Saskatchewan, Ontario, Quebec, Prince Edward Island, New Brunswick, Yukon, Northwest Territories and

Nunavut. In Ontario and Prince Edward Island, coroners are physicians. In Quebec, coroners are physicians or lawyers. In the other provinces with a coroner system, the system is based on lay coroners.

A medical examiner system is present in four Canadian provinces: Alberta, Manitoba, Nova Scotia and Newfoundland. In Alberta, Nova Scotia and Newfoundland, all medical examiners are forensic pathologists. In Manitoba, forensic pathologists act as the main medical examiners, with the use of nonforensic pathologists as local medical examiners outside the main urban areas.

In provinces with a coroner system, autopsies are performed at the request of the coroner. In British Columbia, Saskatchewan, Ontario and Quebec, forensic pathologists are available to assist the coroners by performing autopsies. In the other provinces and territories with a coroner system (Prince Edward Island, New Brunswick, Yukon, Northwest Territories and Nunavut), the bodies can be sent to a neighboring province for forensic pathology autopsies (several different agreements of services are in place to this effect).

Considering the vastness of Canadian lands and the scarcity of the population in several areas it is not possible to have forensic pathologists in every province or territory (90% of Canada's population is concentrated in a narrow band in the southern regions near the USA border, with only 10% of the population inhabiting the vast lands of the north). A medical examiner system composed exclusively of forensic pathologists or even a physician coroner system is not a realistic option in most provinces or territories of Canada.

There is currently no accreditation system in Canada and no standards of practice for death investigation. The Canadian Association of the Chief Coroners and Chief Medical Examiners has set up a working group to develop such standards and explore the feasibility of a Canadian accreditation system.

4.7 Forensic pathology

The Royal College of Physicians and Surgeons of Canada defines forensic pathology as a subspecialty of Anatomical Pathology and General Pathology that applies basic pathology principles and methodologies of these specialties to support the medicolegal and judicial systems in determining causes and manners of death, supporting the investigation of circumstances surrounding deaths and assisting in the interpretation of postmortem find-ings of medical legal significance.

The Royal College of Physicians and Surgeons of Canada recognized forensic pathology as a subspecialty of Anatomical or General Pathology in 2003. In 2004, a working group was mandated to work on the develop-ment of the new subspecialty. The working group met from 2004 to 2007, at which point the specialty became a reality and the first program was developed in 2008. Currently, there are three accredited programs of foren-sic pathology in Canada: the training program is offered at the University of Toronto, the University of Alberta and McMaster University.

Prior to this official recognition of forensic pathol-ogy by the Royal College of Physicians and Surgeons of Canada, many Canadians were working in the field of forensic pathology and had gained qualifications and recognition of their expertise through other mechanisms such as training in other countries or training in Canada combined with years of experience.

Since 2009, all new forensic pathologists in Canada must be trained in an accredited institution and pass the board examination of the Royal College of Physicians and Surgeons of Canada. For forensic pathologists who trained before 2009, the Royal College of Physicians and Surgeons of Canada is offering an option to challenge the board examination through a peer evaluation route. The Royal College of Physicians and Surgeons of Canada also offered a Founder designation to the members of the first subspecialty committee and examination board, in recognition of their work in the development of the new subspecialty.

Forensic pathologists are present in most provinces of Canada (British Columbia, Alberta, Saskatchewan, Manitoba, Ontario, Quebec, Nova Scotia and Newfou-ndland) with the exception of Prince Edward Island, New Brunswick and the Territories. Forensic pathol-ogists work in different settings depending on the provinces: full time forensic pathologists, combined forensic and anatomical pathology practice (autopsy and surgical pathology), leaders of the death investigation system, with a small number of private consultants (mainly to be found in the retired population). The num-ber of forensic pathologists is insufficient to meet the needs, and international recruitment (mainly the USA and the UK) is not rare. However, with the recent cre-ation of three training programs, it is most likely that Canada will be able to train the future generation of

forensic pathologists and will be able to produce enough forensic pathologists to fill the market need.

4.8 Forensic anthropology

In Canada, there are no recognized dedicated training programs or certification in forensic anthropology. Since academic anthropology does not recognize foren-sic anthropology as a subsection, the presence of forensic anthropologists in universities is limited and research suffers from a lack of funding.

Forensic anthropologists played a major role in Canada in developing the earliest undergraduate pro-grams in forensic sciences. However, it remains impos-sible at this time to obtain a graduate degree in the field.

Most forensic anthropologists working in Canada are part-time consultants offering their services to police agencies, coroner/medical examiner services or forensic pathology services. The only full time forensic anthro-pologist is working in Ontario; in all other provinces, forensic anthropologists, if available, are consulted on a case-by-case basis, usually as fee-for-service. The work will be conducted either directly at the scene or in morgue facilities shared with pathologists (hospital based or in forensic centers). Three provinces have built dedicated forensic anthropology spaces: Ontario, British Columbia and Quebec.

In Canada, forensic anthropology still suffers from a lack of official recognition as a subspecialty of anthro-pology. There is no national professional organization, no accreditation, and no professional standards. To com-pensate, several forensic anthropologists will turn to US standards.

Because of a lack of recognition and standardization, the education and qualification of anthropologists pre-senting themselves as forensic anthropologists varies greatly. In most cases, they are physical or biological anthropologists and/or archeologists who have full time positions as academics, with a Masters or PhD degree in a nonforensic discipline (anthropology or archeol-ogy). The forensic training varies from extensive edu-cation and experience from hands-on work in local or international settings, to very little practical experience and a learn-as-you-go situation.

In many parts of Canada, a great part of the tradi-tional forensic anthropology work is provided directly by forensic pathologists: determination of animal versus human bones, determination of whether human remains are of historical or forensic interest, recovery and interpretation of human remains at the scene, and documentation and interpretation of injuries and tool marks on bone. Even in provinces where forensic anthropologists are available, the work most often will be initiated by a forensic pathologist and a forensic anthropologist will be consulted if needed at a later stage in more complex cases.

4.9 Forensic odontology

In Canada, the Royal College of Dentists of Canada does not recognize forensic odontology as a subspecialty, and therefore there is no official accreditation or national standards. To address this lack of Canadian standards, several forensic odontologists have sought US board certification.

The expertise of forensic odontologists in Canada is requested by coroners or medical examiners, forensic pathologists or police agencies mainly to identify remains through dental records or for the identification of bite marks. Forensic odontologists in Canada are usually part time fee-for-service consultants who will offer their services after hours from their main professional activity as private practice dentists. The training and experience of Canadian forensic odontologists varies widely, from forensic odontologists with training in the USA and board certification, to dentists having attended only a few days of courses and with limited practical experience.

In British Columbia, there is a team of forensic odontologists called the B.C. Forensic Odontology Response Team (BC-FORT). This team is composed of approximately 50 dentists and 40 allied dental staff. Alberta has a team of five forensic odontologists providing fee-for-service consultation. About ten forensic odontologists are part of the Province of Ontario Dental Identification Team (PODIT). Forensic odontologists are also working in Quebec, Manitoba and Nova Scotia.

Apart for the provincial presence of forensic odontologists, forensic odontologists are also to be found at the national level in the Canadian Armed Forces. The expertise of forensic odontologists in the military setting is mainly focused towards disaster victim identification.

Because of the lack of official recognition of forensic odontology in Canada by the regulatory board (the Royal College of Dentists of Canada), there is no graduate program in the field. The forensic dentistry laboratory at McGill University offers a forensic dentistry distance learning course primarily focused on human bite-marks.

4.10 Forensic entomology

Only two forensic entomology facilities exist in Canada: one in British Columbia at the Simon Fraser University and one in Ontario at the University of Windsor.

Forensic entomologists are university professors contracted on a fee-for-service by police agencies, coroners, medical examiners or forensic pathologists. There is no Canadian board certification or national standards. To obtain certification, two forensic entomologists have chosen to go south of the border to the American Board of Forensic Entomology. Outside of these two recognized forensic entomologists, one in British Columbia and one in Ontario, expertise in forensic entomology is extremely limited in the rest of Canada.

The lack of graduate forensic programs, of certified forensic entomologists and of funded forensic research, is seriously jeopardizing the development of the field in Canada. Forensic entomologists are rarely used to their full capacity. In most provinces, forensic entomology is completely absent from death investigation. When called, it is often too late – well after the scene has been processed and the autopsy performed.

4.11 Forensic psychiatry

The Royal College of Physicians and Surgeons of Canada defines forensic psychiatry as a psychiatric subspecialty in which scientific and clinical expertise are applied to issues in legal contexts embracing civil, criminal, correctional and legislative matters. Forensic psychiatrists also have specialized expertise in the assessment and treatment of special populations, including young offenders, sexual offenders and violent offenders.

The Royal College of Physicians and Surgeons of Canada recognized forensic psychiatry as a subspecialty of psychiatry in 2009. A strong community of forensic psychiatrists was working in Canada before 2009, but their expertise was not officially recognized as a subspecialty of general psychiatry.

The first program was developed in 2012. Nowadays, accredited training programs are available in four centers: University of Alberta, University of British Columbia, University of Toronto and University of Ottawa. After the completion of a postgraduate general psychiatry residency program (five years), the trainees complete one additional year in forensic psychiatry to qualify for challenging the board examination.

It is estimated that Canada currently has an adequate numbers of trained forensic psychiatrists. The work of forensic psychiatrists includes treatment and assessment, with the majority of forensic psychiatrists in Canada spending most of their time in performing assessment and rehabilitation. One of the most important tasks of the forensic psychiatrist is to present opinions on the presence or absence of mental disorder and on the individual's ability to stand trial, along with assessment of criminal responsibility and risk mitigations strategies.

Forensic psychiatrists may work in various environments, from inpatient in a hospital setting, outpatient clinics outside of hospitals or correctional facilities. Forensic psychiatry in Canada functions in a particular legal framework, as there is a Federal Criminal Code but also Provincial Mental Health Acts. This means that while the criminal code is standard across the country, the work under the Mental Health Acts can vary between provinces. Nevertheless, the work between provinces is overall more similar than different.

4.12 Forensic psychology and behavioral science

Forensic psychology is considered a branch of clinical psychology. Three Canadian universities are offering degrees in forensic psychology: two universities in British Columbia (University of British Columbia and Simon Fraser University) and one in Ontario (Carleton University). Students are usually trained as clinical psychologists with a focus on the prison population. Very few are working as profilers.

The Royal Canadian Mounted Police and a few other police agencies have behavioral units. These specialists provide investigative behavioral tools such as criminal profiling, geographic profiling, truth verification and identification of serial criminals through analyses of reports on violent crimes. These specialists are most often police officers who have later been trained and gained experience in this particular field.

4.13 Forensic toxicology

As for most forensic services in Canada, toxicology is largely provided by the Royal Canadian Mounted Police and the provincial laboratories in Ontario (Center of Forensic Sciences) and Quebec (Laboratoire de Sciences Judiciaires et de Médecine Légale). The Center of Forensic Sciences provides virtually all forensic toxicology services in Ontario, including coroner cases, impaired driving toxicology (alcohol and drugs – so called driving under the influence) and toxicology related to drug facilitated crime. In Quebec, the Laboratoire de Sciences Judiciaires et de Médecine Légale (translation: Forensic Sciences and Legal Medicine Laboratory) handles virtually all toxicology related to criminal offences, although the Centre de Toxicologie du Québec (translation: Toxicology Center of Quebec) in Quebec City provides service for most noncriminal medicolegal cases. Across the rest of Canada, the Royal Canadian Mounted Police Forensic Laboratory Service has a mandate to provide crime-related toxicology, including driving under the influence, drug facilitated crime and, in most jurisdictions except Alberta, toxicology on homicide victims. The Royal Canadian Mounted Police currently has toxicology laboratories in Vancouver (province of British Columbia), Edmonton (province of Alberta) and Ottawa (province of Ontario). Provision of a routine medical examiner or coroner toxicology services in provinces outside of Ontario and Quebec varies considerably. In British Columbia, services are provided by the Provincial Toxicology Center, under contract to the British Columbia Coroner's Service. In Alberta, the Office of the Chief Medical Examiner has its own toxicology laboratory as part of global funding from Alberta Justice and Solicitor General. The Saskatchewan Coroner's Service toxicology is provided largely by the Saskatchewan Disease Control Laboratory as a provincially funded service. Toxicology for the Manitoba Office of the Chief Medical Examiner is provided under contract by the St. Boniface Hospital Clinical Laboratory. A toxicology service across the maritime provinces of New Brunswick, Nova Scotia, Prince Edward Island and Newfoundland is provided by a mix of clinical laboratories and testing referred out to private laboratories (mainly in the USA).

Toxicology for the northern territories (Yukon, North-west Territories and Nunavut) is mostly provided by one of the laboratories in British Columbia or Alberta.

4.14 Questioned documents

Questioned document examiners in Canada are employed in private practice, or in one of the three major forensic laboratories (Royal Canadian Mounted Police, Center of Forensic Sciences in Ontario or the Laboratoire de Sciences Judiciaires et de Médecine Légale in Quebec). Due to the long period of training required to become generally recognized or certified as a questioned document examiner, most practitioners train and work for many years in one of the government laboratories. A significant number of private practitioners will have previously trained during government service and later resigned to enter private practice. As for most forensic scientists, questioned document examiners in Canada establish their professional credibility via membership and affiliation with questioned document sections of one of the forensic membership organizations (Canadian Society of Forensic Science, American Academy of Forensic Sciences) or the American Society of Questioned Document Examiners, or certification by the US-based American Board of Questioned Document Examiners. Training is typically through peer-based mentorship and attendance at specialized workshops hosted by one of the forensic membership organizations.

4.15 Criminalistics

In the USA, traditional "crime laboratory" forensic testing, excluding toxicology, is clustered under the heading of "criminalistics". However, in Canada, the term is not generally used and the various areas are identified separately as forensic biology (mostly DNA-related testing), forensic chemistry, forensic physical sciences (including firearms, impression analysis, blood pattern analysis) and analysis of seized drugs.

4.16 Forensic biology

Forensic biology in Canada predominantly involves DNA testing of some type such as STR DNA, nuclear

DNA and mitochondrial DNA. Virtually all human crime-related DNA testing is performed by the Royal Canadian Mounted Police, Centre of Forensic Sciences or Laboratoire de Sciences Judiciaires et de Médecine Légale. Forensic scientists from Canada worked with their colleagues from the USA in the late 1980s and early 1990s to develop guidelines and standards of practice for forensic DNA analysis, ultimately culminating in the Scientific Working Group on DNA Analysis Methods (SWGDAM). SWGDAM has become the standard for forensic DNA analysis for laboratories throughout North America. Canada has developed a National DNA Data Bank that all public sector laboratories contribute to. The databank supports police investigations across Canada and internationally through a sharing agreement with Interpol.

In addition to public sector laboratories, a small number of accredited private laboratories also provide specialized forensic DNA services, including mitochondrial DNA and SNP-phenotype services. Specialized wildlife forensic DNA services are provided by laboratories of the Alberta Government in Edmonton, as well as Trent University in Ontario.

Forensic DNA laboratories in Canada are all accredited, either by the Standards Council of Canada or American Society of Crime Laboratory Directors/Laboratory Accreditation Board, both of which incorporate critical elements of the SWGDAM guidelines.

4.17 Forensic chemistry

As for forensic biology, forensic chemistry is primarily conducted by the three main laboratory systems, the Royal Canadian Mounted Police, Centre of Forensic Sciences and Laboratoire de Sciences Judiciaires et de Médecine Légale. Forensic chemistry includes such tasks as the analysis of accelerants in arson investigations, paint chip analysis involving such crimes as hit-and-run, and other miscellaneous physical and chemical testing that does not involve drugs, such as of the analysis of glass, fibres and other physical evidence.

4.18 Firearms and toolmark analysis

Firearm and toolmark testing is carried out by the three major forensic laboratory systems (Royal Canadian

Mounted Police, Centre of Forensic Sciences, Laboratoire de Sciences Judiciaires et de Médecine Légale), but may also be conducted by the forensic services of some major police forces. The requirement to have a specialized test firing range and such equipment as an electron microscope necessarily limits the type of testing that can be performed by smaller forensic facilities.

4.19 Crime scene investigation

Throughout most of Canada, crime scene investigation and associated evidence collection, including fingerprint and latent print evidence, is the responsibility of the investigating police force. Most medium to large police forces have a forensic investigation unit, as necessary supported by the Royal Canadian Mounted Police or the two major provincial police forces in Ontario and Quebec. The identification ("ident") officers staffing these units may also be responsible for the examination of physical and impression evidence such are boot or tire impressions.

Blood pattern analysts may be employees of the major Canadian laboratories or a major police force.

4.20 Drug chemistry

The identification, and as necessary the quantification, of controlled drugs in Canada falls under the jurisdiction of the Health Canada Drug Analysis Service (DAS). These drug chemists are appointed and certified to issue legal certificates that document their findings. While some police forces may employ chemical field tests to aid their investigation, authority to issue legally binding certificates of analysis for drug seizures rests with the DAS chemists. Health Canada operates the DAS in British Columbia, Winnipeg, Toronto and Montreal. DAS chemists also provide expertise to police regarding the hazards of illicit drug labs, and the type of drugs that may be synthesized in them, based on the precursors and reagents found.

4.21 Engineering sciences

There is no special requirement to practice forensic engineering in Canada beyond the usual education and professional requirements to practice as an engineer in the local jurisdiction. Usually that requires a minimum 4-year degree in a basic engineering specialty (e.g. electrical, mechanical), followed by 4 years of engineering practice under the supervision of a registered engineer and subsequent registration as a Professional Engineer in the province of practice. There is no requirement for specific certification as a forensic engineer in Canada, although some forensic engineers may be a member of the Canadian Society of Forensic Science.

4.22 Digital and multimedia sciences

The area of "digital and multimedia sciences" is relatively new as a forensic specialty, although so-called "computer forensics" has been recognized for many years, but has been expanded to include a broader range of digital media and information technology areas. Canadian forensic experts in this area may reside within universities, the major forensic laboratories, forensic units of large police forces, or within the private domain. Expertise is usually recognized by virtue of appropriate college or university education in information technology or computer sciences and extensive experience in the specific field of expertise.

4.23 Boards of inquiry

4.23.1 Kaufman Inquiry
This was a judicial inquiry called to examine the circumstances in which Guy Paul Morin was falsely convicted and jailed for the murder of a 9-year-old girl who lived next door to him. The young girl was murdered on or after October 3, 1984 and after investigation by police and examination of trace evidence, Mr. Morin was charged. He was tried and acquitted in 1986, but a new trial was ordered and Mr. Morin was subsequently found guilty of first degree murder. He appealed, and on January 23, 1995, on the basis of fresh DNA evidence, he was acquitted of the charge. Scientific evidence tendered in the original trial involved hair and fiber comparisons and the reported finding of an "indication" of blood. The inquiry judge, the Honorable Fred Kaufman, was critical of the vague way the forensic results were expressed and communicated to the investigating police, and the fact

that the strength and weakness of the forensic findings was not properly explained to them. At the conclusion of the 146-day inquiry in 1997, Judge Kaufman made 119 recommendations, 35 of which concerned the forensic evidence.

4.23.2 Goudge Inquiry

The Goudge Inquiry was an inquiry into pediatric forensic pathology in Ontario held by Justice Stephen T. Goudge from November 2007 to the early months of 2008, with the release of the report on October 1, 2008. The inquiry looked at systemic problems in the handling of criminally suspicious deaths of children in Ontario following the discovery of a large number of wrongful convictions based mainly on the work of Dr. Charles Randal Smith, a pathologist from The Hospital for Sick Children in Toronto. At the end of the inquiry, 169 recommendations were made to improve the death investigation system in Ontario.

Further reading

1. History of Forensic Science in Canada, in Virtual Museum of Canada. http://www.museevirtuel-virtualmuseum.ca/edu/ ViewLoitCollection.do;jsessionid=F9D756595EADE75794 CA03225F316ECB?method=preview&lang=EN&id=3491 (accessed February 28, 2014).

2. The Centre of Forensic Sciences (Ontario). http://www.csfs. ca/eng/history/the-centre-of-forensic-sciences-ontario (accessed February 28, 2014).

3. Ontario Forensic Service and Coroners Complex.http:// www.mcscs.jus.gov.on.ca/english/ForensicServicesandCoro nersComplex/Photos/FSCC_photos.html (accessed February 28, 2014).

4. History of the Royal Canadian Mounted Police Laboratory System. http://www.csfs.ca/eng/history/the-rcmp-labs (accessed February 28, 2014).

5. All you wanted to know about forensic science in Canada but didn't know who to ask! http://www.csfs.ca/contentad min/UserFiles/File/Booklet2007.pdf (accessed February 28, 2014).

6. Forensic Science in Canada. A Report of Multidisciplinary Discussion. http://www.forensics.utoronto.ca/Assets/LMPF +Digital+Assets/Forensic+Science+in+Canada.pdf (accessed February 28, 2014).

7. Report of the Kaufman Commission on Proceedings Involving Guy Paul Morin. http://www.attorneygeneral.jus. gov.on.ca/english/about/pubs/morin/ (accessed February 28, 2014).

8. Inquiry into Pediatric Forensic Pathology in Ontario. http:// www.attorneygeneral.jus.gov.on.ca/inquiries/goudge/ report/index.html (accessed February 28, 2014).

CHAPTER 5
The Chilean Forensic Medical Service

Patricio Bustos Streeter & Marisol Intriago Leiva

Servicio Médico Legal, Santiago, Chile

Chile

5.1 Introduction

The Forensic Medical Service is a public body that reports to the Ministry of Justice, with the objective of giving technical and scientific advice to Chile's Public Prosecutor's Office and the Law Courts in forensic medical issues, forensic sciences and other areas specific to its expertise.

Its vision and mission are to be the main scientific and technical State institution of reference in legal and forensic medical matters, working to ensure quality, efficiency, timeliness and objectivity, and providing a highly qualified service, both to justice administration bodies and the general public.

Furthermore, the institution is involved in scientific research, educational and extra-curricular activities in the areas related to its competencies (Servicio Médico Legal, 2013).

This body is governed by Law 20,065 on the Modernization, Charter Regulation and Personnel Composition

The Global Practice of Forensic Science, First Edition. Edited by Douglas H. Ubelaker.
© 2015 John Wiley & Sons, Ltd. Published 2015 by John Wiley & Sons, Ltd.

of the Forensic Medical Service, which establishes its functions, organization, powers and the general provisions that regulate its functions.

At present, this forensic body has almost one thousand officials in 38 offices throughout Chile, 15 in regional capitals and 23 in provinces. All are part of a nationwide forensic network, promoted and strengthened by the Forensic Medical Service by the creation of policies to foster decentralization. This may be seen in the development of Reference Centers in the north, center and south of Chile, which have a role as area headquarters to cover the demand for services throughout the country.

As an advisory body to the Ministry of Justice, this institution's work consists of carrying out forensic medical investigations in its different departments and specialized areas. Its work focuses on four main areas: Thanatology, Clinical Issues, Laboratories and Mental Health.

It also responds to specific issues such as forensic identification in older corpses, in cases associated with the victims of human rights violations, in emergency situations and large-scale disasters, as well as complex criminal matters (Servicio Médico Legal, 2013). This work is done jointly and in cooperation with other assisting bodies from the justice system, such as *Carabineros* (Chilean Police) and the Chilean Investigative Police.

5.2 History

The origins of forensic work in Chile date back to the first half of the 19th century, when the University of Chile Medical Faculty was created, which included a theoretical course on forensic medicine in its curriculum. However, this was a solely theoretical course.

Until then, and from a practical point of view, "city doctors" took charge of carrying out thanatological investigations, whether in morgues – in Santiago in the center of the city, alongside the Public Prison – or in public venues for autopsies, exhibition and recognition of bodies.

In 1901, the Ministry of Public Education named Dr. Carlos Ybar de la Sierra Professor of Forensic Medicine at the University of Chile. Ybar was an important character in Chilean forensic medicine, as under his leadership, which lasted until 1928, a new era in the teaching and practice of this specialization began.

5.2.1 The crime at the German Legation

This was a mysterious police case at the beginning of the 20th century with a great impact on the development of forensic sciences in Chile – particularly dentistry – beginning a chain of events that led to the creation of the Forensic Medical Service that we know today.

In February 1909, a huge fire broke out at the seat of the German Imperial Legation, in the downtown of Santiago. Once the fire was put out, among the ruins a body was found dressed in the clothes and alongside some personnel belongings of the Chancellor of the German Legation at the time, William Beckert, who was presumed to be the victim.

At the Santiago Morgue, the doctors who carried out the forensic medical autopsy reported that the death had been caused by a complete live incineration.

A second autopsy, handled by University of Chile professors Max Westenhoffer and Otto Aichel, of German nationality, and Dr. Aureliano Oyarzún, concluded that "the death likely took place due to a hemorrhage in the thoracic aorta caused by stabbing. The wound in the brain, due to its seriousness, would have been sufficient to cause death. All the alterations caused to the cadaver by fire occurred after the victim's death." That is, William Beckert was probably murdered (Ciocca Gómez, 2009, p. 33).

Until then, the doorman, Exequiel Tapia, had been suspected, who disappeared after the fire. The motive was robbery, as 25,000 pesos were missing from the German Legation's safe. All this led to suspicions that Tapia had probably been caught by Beckert while he committed the robbery, murdered him and burnt down the building while fleeing (Ciocca Gómez, 2009). However, the local press reported that a witness had vouched for William Beckert the same night the tragedy occurred.

These doubts led to the presiding judge to order the director of the University of Chile School of Dentistry, Dr. German Valenzuela Basterrica, to examine the cadaver's oral cavity. The report established that the teeth examined were almost complete, with only one cavity. Given the absence of decay, they belonged to a young person, which did not match the dental background of the supposed victim, who had had, according to his dentist, five extractions, eight fillings with different metals and a gold crown. The document concluded that the cadaver could not belong to William Beckert. A search began concluding with his detention as he tried to escape the country. The legal investigation established

Figure 5.1 Construction of the Medical Legal Institute, the area that housed the autopsy room, 1922.

that he had assassinated Exequiel Tapia, put his own clothes on him, and left objects near the cadaver to arouse suspicion that Beckert was the deceased. Then he had caused the fire in the Legation – all in order to cover up the robbery from the safe. Beckert was sentenced to death and executed on July 5, 1910.

These events created an intense public debate on the weaknesses of forensic practice, which led the Government to request a report from the University of Chile, where university leaders requested 100,000 pesos to review the procedures of the morgue. Dr. Carlos Ybar travelled to Europe to learn how institutions in Paris, Berne, Vienna, Berlin and Copenhagen operated, taking notes and even drafting plans that could be useful and necessary for the construction of Chile's first Forensic Medical Institute.

According to Dr. Ybar, this Forensic Medical Institute should have at least one morgue with all the related facilities, a toxicology laboratory, a room for autopsies, another for blood tests and microscopic cultures, an area for a library, a room for classes and a museum. Driven by the urgency to create new infrastructure, he oversaw the State's acquisition of land a few meters from the General Cemetery, on Avenida La Paz, in Independencia district.

The transfer of the Santiago Morgue to its new installations was ordered by Regulatory Decree No. 1851 of August 30, 1915. Furthermore, the management of the Forensic Medical Institute was given to the professor for forensic medicine course at the University of Chile. This structure ensured continuity between the teaching, research and investigating roles (Figure 5.1).

The importance of practical medical education was also laid down in this decree, stating that "it is important… to provide facilities not only in accordance with the technical rules for this type of establishment but also to make the most of its existence in the teaching of forensic medicine."

In turn, it was that this body should be able to carry out exams on people with mental disturbances that had previously been done by forensic doctors at the *Casa de Orates*.

The document that created the Forensic Medical Institute is Decree Law No. 646 of the Ministry of Public Education, dated October 17, 1925 whose 1st article states that "the Forensic Medical Institute has two fundamental purposes: to serve Justice with all the means necessary and to teach forensic medicine at the Medical Faculty."

With regards to teaching, it states that all units "shall take part in teaching of Forensic Medicine," and in its 6th article that "All medical staff, including those who work outside the central establishment, shall be considered teaching assistants of the professor of Forensic Medicine."

The charter of the "Dr. Carlos Ybar" Forensic Medical Institute and Forensic Medical Services of 1943, states in its 1st article that "the Dr. Carlos Ybar Forensic Medicine Institute shall be the central establishment for all Forensic Medical Services in Chile, and consequently, all forensic doctors, morgues and their personnel, shall report to it." As well as establishing responsibility for all investigatory matters, it also describes teaching tasks, as its 2nd article states: "The Forensic Medical Institute shall participate in forensic medicine lectures at forensic science, medical science and legal and social science faculties using all the elements applicable for teaching forensic medicine."

In 1930 the Forensic Medicine Institute left the purview of the University of Chile to become dependent on the Ministry of Justice under Decree Law No. 2175 of August 21, on the reorganization of the Forensic Medicine Institute and the services that report to it.

Decree No. 196 of March 25, 1960 lays down the text of the organic law of the current Forensic Medical Service (SML, in Spanish), confirming its teaching role and adding promotion of scientific investigation in forensic medical matters and establishing and maintaining museums and collections of pieces and items related with forensic medicine (articles 2 and 3). Therefore, in addition to its investigatory work, training and scientific research is deeply rooted in the institution's identity.

5.2.2 Military coup

It is impossible to refer to the development of any aspect of public institutions in Chile without referring to the violent and abrupt break in democracy that occurred on September 11, 1973. The military coup by the Armed Forces with the support of significant economic groups in our country ended the expansion of civil rights that had been taking place in Chile until then. The assassination and massive disappearance of supporters of Salvador Allende's socialist regime, and the civil population, was followed by organized terror which still divides Chilean society today, where illegal detentions, torture and forced disappearance and exile became institutionalized. From a social and economic process encouraging participation and justice for traditionally excluded members of society, Chile moved to a liberal economic philosophy, focused on self-regulation by the market and the weakening of the State and public services, widening gaps and social and economic inequalities.

After a plebiscite in 1988, the return to democracy revealed the horror experienced by thousands of families, albeit timidly and under military tutelage. Despite their fear and the dangers involved, these families organized a search for their disappeared family members and for truth and justice.

From the beginning of the 1990s, archeologists and anthropologists have joined this effort, voluntarily and with very little legal support, collaborating in the search for and recovery of the skeletal remains of victims illegally buried in cemeteries, gorges, mining shafts, ovens, military terrains and desert plains, among other sites. Degree Memorandum "Disappeared Detainees in Chile – the Archeology of a Denied Death". Iván Cáceres Roque, 2011. In www.cybertesis.uchile.d/tesis/uchile/2011/cs-caceres_i/pdfAmont/cs-caceres_i.pdf.

The Forensic Medical Service is responsible for recovering and analyzing these remains, demanding a methodological and technical skill, due to the scarce development of forensic sciences in Chile and the complexity of the cases.

5.2.3 Patio 29

This is one of the most emblematic cases of the criminal investigations associated with human rights violations. As mentioned above, in the first few weeks after the military coup, the civilian population in Santiago, the capital of Chile, lived under siege. Anyone who did not follow the orders of the military or uniformed police was likely to be murdered and his or her body abandoned in the street, thrown into the Mapocho River, at cemetery gates or at the doors of the Forensic Medical Service.

Bodies accumulated in the latter's facilities, barely leaving time for autopsies and identifying them. In many cases, they could not be delivered to their families and were sent for burial at the General Cemetery, one of Chile's largest and oldest.

On many occasions they were buried with only a number assigned to the unidentified body in the so-called patios – large spaces where people without economic resources for family tombs were temporarily interred. Around 400 of these victims were buried in the so-called Patio 29 according to the listing of Patio 29 issued by the General Cemetery of Santiago, June 24, 1991. Due to being temporary tombs, in 1979 the Cemetery began to remove their bodies to reuse the space.

In response, an Outreach Program by the Catholic Church created to assist victims of the dictatorship reported this situation to the Law Courts, achieving a halt in this operation, which was only partially achieved: a mere 108 graves belonging to nonidentified people were respected.

In 1991, between September 2 and 14, a team of voluntary archeologists and anthropologists, who formed the Forensic Anthropology Group (GAF, in Spanish), carried out the exhumation of 107 tombs, where 125 bodies were found (in 1997 tomb 108 was exhumed, reaching a total of 126 bodies). They were taken to SML facilities, but it was not until 1992 and the dissolution of the GAF that this institution could begin analyses to identify victims and the determination of the cause and form of their death. In 2002, 96 people had been identified, using "traditional" anthropological methods, including the use of cranial-facial superimposition. However, since 1994 doubts have arisen on the quality of the processes and methodologies used for these identifications, which were expressed and gathered by minister Sergio Muñoz who ordered that the forensic body carry out genetic analyses (of mitochondrial DNA) to verify the identifications made.

In April, 2006, the results showed that, of 94 cases analyzed, 48 were exclusionary, 38 were uncertain and the others had not given useful results for comparison.

Groups of families of victims of political violence demanded of the Chilean State a set of concrete actions to face this crisis, a radical response, leading to a scientific audit of the Forensic Medical Service. At that time, the precarious status of the institution's resources was revealed and the scarce support for technical and methodological development required to address highly complex human rights cases and other areas. The Chilean Government called an internationally recognized Expert Panel in diverse areas related to human identification, which presented a proposal for the SML, which was accepted by the State, leading to increased budgets and staff, better infrastructure, creation of new offices, development of accreditation and certification programs, and the creation of a Human Rights Program.

The Human Rights Program was run over the 2007–2010 period, and created a multidisciplinary investigatory technique, in order to ensure an integrated forensic approach; implemented a communications policy for families; created a Blood Sampling Center and a DNA profile bank of families of disappeared detainees and victims of political execution not returned to their families, among other advances.

This working model is currently still being implemented by the Special Forensic Identification Unit, using the same standards of quality, both in the case of victims of human rights violations, other complex criminal situations and cases of massive disasters.

5.2.4 The Criminal Process Reform

One of the most important areas where social modernization was needed had to do with the modification of the criminal process, which was still inquisitive in Chile. From 2000, the Criminal Proceedings Code was drafted, laying down rules regulating criminal trials. This legislation began the Criminal Proceedings Reform, aiming to modernize the administration of justice and enforce human rights standards in this area. It consists of an accusatory, oral and public proceedings system, in which functions are separated. On the one hand, in one body prosecutors investigate the supposed criminal deed, under the purview of the Public Prosecutor, while on the other hand, a Criminal Trials Judge ensures respect for constitutional guarantees throughout the procedure and a sentencing judge, the Oral Judge, lays down the sentence after the trial.

In turn, a Public Criminal Defense body was created, composed of qualified State lawyers who defend a person during the investigatory stage, guaranteeing the constitutional right of access to justice by citizens.

The process has the following stages. The Investigation is a nonjudicial stage carried out by investigators with

the collaboration of auxiliary justice bodies, such as the police and the Forensic Medicine Service, to investigate a criminal act. Then there is a Hearing to prepare for the oral trial (an oral hearing before the criminal trials judge where the crime to be judged and the responsibility of the accused are established, and where the prosecutor and defendant provide the evidence that will be given to the oral judge in a trial as such). Finally, the Oral Trial (a hearing with three oral judges who lay down a sentence, on the basis of the evidence and allegations both of the prosecutor and the defendant). In this context, the value of tests and testimony of expert witnesses are presented to the parties, representing an extensive challenge to the abilities of the Forensic Medical Service, considering that the justice reform process did not include structural or financial modifications.

This reform was gradually applied in Chile, in different regions, ending in the Metropolitan Region in 2005. From then on, any crime that is committed is governed by the Criminal Proceedings Code, except cases before this reform came into effect, which are governed by the old criminal procedure.

5.2.5 Teaching and academic background

SML's professionals come from the widest range of technical and scientific knowledge. Doctors, dentists, biochemists, psychologists, anthropologists, archeologists and other professionals use the knowledge they have acquired at the different Chilean academic institutions that offer these degrees in the service of judicial investigation. However, in Chile, only the degree of Medicine, taught in 2005 in 19 public and private academic bodies, offered the Forensic Medicine course, and only the University of Chile offers it also as a specialization (González *et al.*, 2005).

In this scenario, even though forensic investigations in Chile may be done by anyone named by the judicial authority, only the Forensic Medical Service and crime laboratories of both the Civil and Uniformed Police have professionals with the specific experience and academic backgrounds, and it is mainly in these institutions where most of the research and development applied to the forensic area takes place.

5.3 The modernization of the SML

Law 20,065, passed on October 4, 2005, which modernizes the Forensic Medical Service, establishes that the position of national director shall be decided by means of a contest by the Senior Public Administration, underlining the importance of experience and technical knowledge in the forensic area and in public administration.

Another relevant issue has been growth towards the regions, especially with the creation of the Reference Centers, which have contributed to the decentralization of the national headquarters. In 2007, the Northern Area Reference Center was opened, which responds to requests from courts from the Arica and Parinacota region to the Coquimbo region, in which blood alcohol, toxicology, biochemistry, criminal DNA, simple cases and filiation tests are carried out. In 2009, the Southern Zone Reference Center was opened, covering the areas from Maule to Magallanes, which carries out anthropological, toxicological and molecular biological investigations. In turn, the Valparaíso forensic office is responsible for the demand for its own and the Maule region.

Among the Forensic Medical Service's strategic objectives is to respond effectively to requests made by the bodies that administer justice and citizenship, emphasizing the modernization of institutional management at the national level, reduction of response times, quality of expert reports and service to citizens.

In this framework, it has been proposed to validate their procedures by implementing a Quality Management System, in order to certify and accredit their areas under ISO Standard 9001: 2008: "Quality Management Systems. Requirements," implemented for operational management processes and for the Clinical Units (Certification) and ISO Standard 17025: 2005: "General Requirements for the Competence of Testing and Calibration Laboratories," implemented only in Laboratories (Accreditation).

As a result of this initiative, 12 technical forensic processes have been certified as of the present date in addition to 7 cross-cutting management support processes. In turn, the processes for filiation exams at the Forensic Genetics Laboratory are accredited, where the work is ongoing.

5.4 SML technical areas

Thanatology, Clinical, Laboratories and Mental Health are the four investigation departments in which the Forensic Medical Service works. There are also other special units created for specific and complementary tasks, and an extra-curricular, investigation and teaching department.

The Thanatology Department is responsible for carrying out medical-legal autopsies to establish the cause of death and identity of a deceased person. All the investigations carried out by this department are ordered by the prosecutors in charge of the cases, who may also instruct the release of the body and delivery to family members. This department is present at all offices throughout the country, where around 12 thousand autopsies are carried out at a nationwide level. The Histopathology Unit comes under its purview, and collaborates in the search for the information to clarify a cause of death by analyzing tissue at the microscopic level, while the Identification and Presumed Death Unit is designed to corroborate the identity of the deceased when he or she enters without a name or with a presumed identity.

The Thanatology Department is also responsible for exhumation of remains with prior autopsy or no autopsy, and for supervising the removal of tissue and organs that are performed in health centers (in accordance with the Organ Donation Law) when an autopsy is required for the deceased. This is to ensure that the procedures do not affect later investigations.

The Clinical Department is responsible for carrying out clinical inspections of legal importance requested by the law courts as background for the legal process. This department consists of four specific units: the Injury Studies Unit, in charge of confirming the presence of injuries, their nature, seriousness and level of incapacity; the Forensic Sexology Unit, in charge of confirming sexual crimes; the Medical Responsibility Unit, which investigates the responsibility of a medical action, by SML and also third parties; and the Transit Unit, in the framework of an appeal to those whose driver's license had not been renewed.

The Laboratories Department is where the largest number of investigations carried out by the SML take place, being 78% of the total number of inspections at the national level. It is in charge of carrying out inspections of judicial interest by applying scientific, biological, chemical and physical methodss, which give the administration of justice technical principles to apply the law in complex situations. It has highly technological instruments and a qualified professional team, including pharmaceutical chemists, biochemists, chemists and medical technologists, responsible for caring for samples, analysis and the interpretation of the results obtained.

This department consists of the Sampling and Reception Units, which carry out, receive, encode, care for and distribute samples and/or evidence; Forensic Genetics, responsible for carrying out biological filiation tests, and identification and analysis of sexual crimes or criminal acts; the Blood Alcohol Laboratory, which determines the presence of alcohol and volatile substances in the blood and other biological fluids; the Biochemical and Crime Laboratory, which carries out analysis of body fluids to be used in investigations of sexual aggression, among others; the Toxicology Laboratory, to detect the presence of drugs or abuse of medications and toxic substances in general; and the Instrumentation Laboratory, where the quantity of chemical substances found is confirmed and quantified.

The Mental Health Department of the Forensic Medical Service consists of the Adult Psychiatry and Child Psychiatry Units. The psychiatrists, psychologists and social assistants that work therein carry out psychological and psychiatric examinations of the involved parties, which are necessary to verify the competencies of a witness and the validity of their testimony in a trial, as well as the emotional damage, interdiction and/or declaration of the legal responsibility of the accused among others. These examinations are carried out at the facilities of the Forensic Medical Service or residences or hospitals when necessary.

The development of the forensic sciences and the needs of judicial investigation have led to the creation of other units such as the Special Forensic Identification Unit, created in 2010, bringing together the professional experience and installed working capacity created over three years by the Human Rights Program (2007–2010), which aimed to identify disappeared detainees and those executed for political reasons whose remains were not delivered, as well as victims of violations of human rights (1973–1990). Its work is aimed at analyzing skeletal remains that date back significantly in time, both in human rights and criminal situations. It has carried out a multidisciplinary forensic intervention, with the participation of archeologists, anthropologists, doctors, dentists and geneticists, in addition to intervention strategies that ensure their participation from as soon as the site where the events occurred is found, through the investigations themselves and their historical contextualization. This system also guarantees the chain of custody, protecting evidence and systematizing records that show skeletal, cultural, blood evidence and associated documentation.

As a result of this approach, a model Integrated Investigation Report has been created, and is recognized as a vanguard at the worldwide level, contributing to a better understanding of a case, avoiding the dispersion of the results delivered by each specific intervening discipline and becoming a tool that is able to encompass all the results of the investigation.

This Unit is in charge of implementing a National Forensic Identification System, which aims to coordinate scientific and administrative actions throughout the SML, developing a local and nationwide capacity under scientific quality and excellence standards. The aim is to ensure that different forensic disciplines participate in a timely and effective fashion in human identification, with nationwide coverage and under a multidisciplinary and integrative approach, in reasonable timelines. With regards to areas for future development, the focus is on quality management and standardization of procedures, regulations, centralized antemortem and postmortem data bases, and providing attention and information to families of victims (carried out under Exempt Resolution No. 004743 dated April 15, 2011).

The National DNA Records Unit (CODIS) is a technical investigation unit that aims to consolidate a DNA record of convicts, accused persons, victims, evidence, disappeared persons and their families, whose genetic profiles may be compared with different samples taken in the context of criminal acts and identification of lost persons or in cases of massive disasters, under strict principles of observing the confidentiality, privacy, intimacy and dignity of these people. Currently it incorporates biochemistry professionals, pharmaceutical chemists, administrative personnel, and juridical and IT support personnel (Figure 5.2).

This digital DNA data base is possible through a computer software named CODIS (for its acronym in English, Combined DNA Index System), originally developed by the FBI to bring together genetics and IT. It was donated to our country by this North American organization, in a collaboration agreement with the Chilean Ministry of Justice, signed in November 2002.

This laboratory has cutting edge technology, and uses extraction systems and automated electrophoretic testing equivalent to that in the most modern international DNA data base laboratories. All stages of genetic testing are carried out using equipment validated at the forensic level, which was created for laboratories with a high volume of sample processing. The technology applied in

Figure 5.2 CODIS Laboratory (2012), genetic database of convicted defendants, evidence and missing persons and family, a pioneer in Latin America.

this laboratory has led to a significant increase in productivity due to the automation of its processes, and it is estimated that from 18 thousand to 20 thousand samples can be processed annually.

In order to consolidate this system, interinstitutional work is required, in which samples are taken by the Prison Guards Service, in the case of enclosed convicts, and by the Forensic Medical Service, in cases of convicts serving their sentence outside enclosures. Additionally, the forensic body works on-line with the Civil Registry and Identification Service, which is the body in charge of protecting this data base.

The Dr. Carlos Ybar Institute (ICY) is the area of the Forensic Medical Service in charge of teaching, extra-curricular activities and investigation. The policy and objectives of ICY are in accordance with Law No. 20,065 on the Modernization, Charter Regulation and Personnel Composition of the Forensic Medical Service, the Service's mission, and the priority given by the institution to teaching, investigation and extra-curricular activities.

The challenges of judicial reform demand investigators with high professional quality standards, and highlight the importance of fostering different forensic disciplines. In this regard, the Dr. Carlos Ybar Institute has the mission of "contributing to the quality of investigation by training professionals, incentivizing investigation, teaching in universities and other likeminded institutions, and through extra-curricular activities." Currently, it has 25 mutual collaboration agreements

with different universities that have Medicine or Science faculties.

In addition to shaping, training and contributing to the growth of SML professionals, students, applicants and officials from the Judicial Branch, Public Prosecutor's Office and Public Criminal Defense Office, the ICY aims to lead and ensure proper coordination in scientific development inside the service, to create and maintain museums and to collect items and objects related to forensic medicine and sciences.

Among its other activities it may be highlighted that, since 2011, the Dr. Carlos Ybar Competition for Unpublished Research Works of Distinction has been held to promote the study and analysis of the forensic sciences. Furthermore, in 2013, a travelling exposition named "The beginnings of the Forensic Medical Institute" was created, showing material from the Museum in order to bring the work of SML from its very beginning closer to citizens.

5.5 Gaps and challenges

One of the Forensic Medical Service's greatest challenges, as a centralized institution, is to develop the autonomy and management of regional and provincial offices, in order to respond to specific local needs and support other offices in cases of urgency and/or disasters, in coordination with police and judicial bodies. The relationship between the Central Headquarters and regional leadership, as well as managers of the different technical departments, intra-institutional communication and the creation of service protocols suitable for different local realities, all form an intricate web in an ongoing process of evaluation, modification and improvement.

One initiative implemented by the Forensic Medical Service has been the creation of an efficient, coordinated National Forensic Identification System that reflects the modernization of Chile's justice system, making it possible to deliver a multidisciplinary perspective at the national level, ensuring quality standards, proper attention to victims and their families, and a timely and reliable answer to the bodies in charge of enforcing justice. The responsibility for implementing this system today falls to the Special Forensic Identification Unit, but its effective development is actually the responsibility of each and every one of its seats (headquarters) and officials.

One issue that has attained importance in the Chilean justice system and that directly impacts on the operations and responsiveness of the SML is the increase in reported child abuse cases. Both physical examination and interviewing affected children has had to incorporate significant changes, considering the age and level of maturity of the victims, the harshness of the crime affecting them and the fact that the legal system as a whole lacks adequate tools to prevent secondary victimization, the manipulation of third parties and finally the impunity of the attacker and the permanent trauma resulting from the whole experience. In this regard, the SML is in the process of developing the protocols and procedures necessary to ensure better attention for victims as well as coordinating different levels of the police and judicial hierarchy, taking into account financial difficulties, the absence of sufficient professionals available and a growing demand not only for quality and timely investigations, but also for a humanitarian and respectful service to the victims and their families.

Ninety-eight years on from its creation, the Forensic Medical Service continues to seek to improve its technical and scientific response to the demand for justice of the citizens of our country. However, it does not only do so by improving the equipment and quality of its investigations but mainly through the professional growth of its officials, professionals and administrative staff, and, above all, in the quality of the service to users who require its services, who are undergoing a traumatic and difficult experience. Likewise, this nearly hundred-year-old institution is committed to continue improving its coordination and collaboration with the other technical bodies and professionals with whom it shares its forensic investigatory work, to thereby provide judicial bodies with reliable and timely products. Finally, it is also committed to support Chile's international partners when they experience disasters, such as the case of the Comayagua prison fire in Honduras in 2012 when a multidisciplinary team among many others supported the recovery work and identification of the more than 350 victims who died in these painful circumstances.

SML has been through difficult circumstances associated with Chile's history and the obstacles it has overcome. It has undergone many reviews, changes and interventions, but these have all led to the setting of new goals, and the development, growth and strengthening of our strong points and the identification of our weaknesses, in order to deliver a quality service that responds to the need for justice in accordance with the social and cultural changes that Chile has experienced, which impact on the whole structure of the State. However, this will always be guided by the ideal that the access to justice is a right, not a privilege, and that we all have a duty to work to guarantee it on a daily basis.

References

Ciocca Gómez, L. (2009) *Odontologia Médico-Legal,* Ediciones Jurídicas de Santiago.

González, L., Insunza, J. A., Bustos, L., Vallejos, C., Gutiérrez, R. (2005) Teaching and investigation in forensic medicine: the current situation and challenges for medicine faculties in Chile. *Rev. Med. Chile* 133: 805–812.

Servico Médico Legal (2013) Available from: www.sml.cl [March 17, 2014].

CHAPTER 6
Forensic science in Colombia

Andrés Rodríguez Zorro[1] & Aída Elena Constantín[2]

[1] *Grupo Nacional de Patologia Forense, Instituto Nacional de Medicina Legal y Ciencias Forenses, Bogotá, Colombia*
[2] *Subdireccion de Investigaciòn Cientifica, Instituto Nacional de Medicina Legal y Ciencias Forenses, Bogotá, Colombia*

Colombia

6.1 History

In 1914 (October 29) Law 53 was enacted giving birth to the Central Bureau of Legal Medicine in Bogotá to provide services in the areas of forensic medicine, pathology and toxicology. The law also created legal medical offices in the capital cities of different Departments, thus giving rise to scientific forensic practice as a public institution in Colombia. Dr. José María Lombana Barreneche, an illustrious physician and father of Internal Medicine in Colombia, was appointed to the position of Director of the Central Bureau. At the time the Bureau established its offices in the cities of Bogotá, Barranquilla, Santa Marta, Cartagena, Medellin, Bucaramanga, Manizales, Ibague, Neiva, Cali, Cúcuta, Popayán, Pasto and Tunja.

Years later Law 101 of 1937 was sanctioned; all offices in the departmental capitals and services were integrated and nationalized, thus unifying them to establish national coordination from a Central Office, in Bogotá, under supervision and authority of one head who was to be a doctor and chief scientist of legal medicine for the entire Republic. Under the same law departmental

The Global Practice of Forensic Science, First Edition. Edited by Douglas H. Ubelaker.
© 2015 John Wiley & Sons, Ltd. Published 2015 by John Wiley & Sons, Ltd.

assemblies were empowered to create their own legal medical services.

The Central Office of Legal Medicine under the direction of Dr. Guillermo Uribe Cualla first published the *Revista de Medicina Legal de Colombia* in 1935. It provided a forum for papers, cases and statistics on forensic activity carried out by the Bureau. The journal is still being printed.

As director of the institution, Dr. Cualla participated in the enactment of Act 94 of 1940 and Law 42 of 1945. The former provided for the construction of a building in the city of Bogotá to house the Bureau and the latter decreed the founding of the school of forensic pathologists.

The building was inaugurated in 1948. It facilitated the development of Forensic Sciences because it put under one roof the areas for clinical pathology and psychiatry, bacteriology, hematology and seminology; the area of chemistry and toxicology; the ballistics area with a shooting range, a radiology lab, a photography section and an identification office.

Using the extraordinary powers that Law 27 of 1963 gave the National Government, it created the Division of Legal Medicine through Decree 1700 of the same year by which the Section of Legal Medicine was to incorporate into one body the Clinic for Legal Medical Services, Forensic Pathology, Psychiatry and Psychology, and a Section of Forensic Laboratories with the services of Ballistics, Chemistry and Physics, Hematology, General Biology, Microbiology, Serology and Seminology, Toxicology, Radiology, Histopathology, Photography and Micrography.

It was also in the 1960s that Dr. Julio Ortiz, in the city of Medellin, warranted that "there are cases in which medical graduates, true scientific eminences of general medicine, render concepts which only serve to cast doubt in the minds of officials hindering investigations …," thus arguing for the need to recruit the first medical specialists in pathology and psychiatry with an emphasis on forensic work (Analisis de la Ley de Justicia y Paz, available at: www. fiscalia.gov.co).

In the early 1970s, drug laboratories, graphology, questioned documents, fingerprinting and Kenyeres mapping emerged, thus completing the portfolio of institutional services.

Decree 055 of 1987 provided for the consolidation of these services under the direction of Director Dr. Egon Lichtenberger. Once this was done, regional and sectional directories were created to operate as divisions in Forensic Medicine and Criminalistics.

Finally, transitional article of the Constitution No. 27 provided for ascribing the National Directorate of the Ministry of Justice Legal Medicine as a government office, with its dependencies, to the Attorney General. Decree 2699 of November 1991 provided the regulatory norms by which the Institute incorporated as a government dependency at the national level, having its own legal framework, social capital and administrative autonomy, thereinafter to be called the National Institute of Legal Medicine and Forensic Sciences (INMLCF for Instituto Nacional de Medicina Legal y Ciencias Forenses).

Correspondingly, the school of Specialization in Forensic Medicine at the National University of Colombia by Agreement No. 109 1996 of the Board of Directors of the University was founded and the first class took place in 2000.

At present the Institute provides services in 123 locations throughout Colombia, with supporting structures that include basic and mobile units, sectional and regional directorates, and a central level that sets policy and services to be deployed in convergence with the different disciplines. These areas include medical, clinical and forensic pathology, and the laboratories of Biology, Botany, Entomology, Trace Evidence, Narcotics, Toxicology, DNA, Physics, Graphology, Ballistics, Photography, Topography, Geology, Fingerprinting and Anthropology; all of these together giving a total of 1850 employees.

6.2 Types of cases

The practice of medicolegal autopsies in Colombia is regulated by Decree 786 of 1990, with the full weight of the law, which stipulates when they are to be performed:

- Homicide or suspected homicide
- Suicide or suspected suicide
- Accident or suspected accident
- Sudden deaths
- Deaths while in custody
- Death caused by accident or illness
- Maternal death or the product of conception by non-spontaneous abortion
- Suspected death caused by neglect or child abuse
- Suspected use of biological, chemical or physical agents to cause death
- Deaths caused by medical procedure.

The National Institute of Legal Medicine and Forensic Science carries out medicolegal autopsies only within its facilities and physicians working on mandatory social service, according to the guidelines set forth by the Institute. The mission of the Institute is to organize and direct the System of Legal Medicine and Forensic Sciences and control its operation in the Colombian territory.

6.2.1 Violent deaths in Colombia

The Center of National Reference on Violence is an office within the National Institute of Legal Medicine and Forensic Sciences, aided by the Information System Network for Missing and Dead Bodies and the National Statistics System, which registered 28,496 violent deaths in Colombia during 2012 (Forensis, 2012). Of these 13.2% (3717) were female and 86.8 % (24,745) male. According to figures of the same year the most likely ages to suffer violent death are those aged between 20 and 29, followed by those between 30 and 39. Those less vulnerable to violent deaths are between 0 and 9 years.

Homicides for both men and women were the manner of death most common in violent deaths in Colombia during this period. They accounted for 55.7% (15,727) of such deaths, while traffic accidents represented 21.55% (6152), accidental deaths 10.3 % (2952), suicides 6.6% (1901) and indeterminate violent deaths 6.1% (1764). For all deaths the most vulnerable are those aged between 20 and 29. However, there is a high incidence of accidental deaths among the elderly, i.e., those 60 and older. Also, accidental deaths are the most common manner of violent death among children between 0 and 10 years of age.

In accidental, violent undetermined and traffic deaths the main mechanism of death was a blunt instrument or fall. Accidental death represented 47% (1390), indeterminate 33.7%, while the percentage of those due to traffic accounted for 94.9% of all accidental and violent undetermined deaths. Moreover, firearms caused 77.6% (12,208) of all homicides in 2012, stressing the serious problem in the country as these are due to the ease with which these weapons are acquired and used. In the case of suicide, the mechanism that caused more deaths was hanging: 52.3% (995), distributed equally among men and women.

6.2.2 Nonfatal injuries

In 2012, 311,514 people were examined for nonfatal injuries. The highest percentage, 45.1% (155,507), of those injuries surveyed was classified within the framework of interpersonal violence: 26.9% (83,898) were evaluated as domestic violence, 12.6% (39,440) for a transportation accident, 6.9 (21,506) for an alleged sexual offense and 3.5% (11,163) for accidental injury.

Of those evaluated by the INMLCF 48.8% (151,806) were women and 51.2% (159,708) were men. There are clear differences in the violence that led to each of these genres. While men accounted for 63.5% of unintentional injuries examined, 64.2% of those evaluated were by traffic accident and 67.6% were caused by interpersonal violence; women accounted for 84.2% of those examined for alleged sexual offense and 77.7% of those evaluated were due to domestic violence. This behavior has been consistent over the years, evidencing the vulnerability of women in their role within the family, where they can be easily abused, and their role in Colombian society, which far from protecting them sees women as objects for sexual satisfaction.

When analyzing these types of violence according to the ages at which they occur, we found similarities in the behavior causing fatal injuries. That is, the most vulnerable to interpersonal violence, domestic violence, traffic accidents and accidental injuries are those between 20 and 29 years of age, while people 75 and older are the least vulnerable to these types of violence. This applies to both men and women.

Sexual offense behavior is different. The most vulnerable age for this type of violence is between 5 and 14. Of the 21,506 cases recorded in the INMLCF in 2012, 25% were children between 5 and 9 years of age and 37.8% were between 10 and 14 years.

Blunt mechanisms or falls caused of 57.2% (178,171) nonfatal injuries among those examined by INMLCF. In second place, 12.4% (38,733) injuries were in the category of Other and in third place were those due to Short Blunt at 10.8% (33,686). This behavior is common for men and women in lesions caused by accident, traffic accident and within the contexts of domestic and interpersonal violence.

The mechanism could not be recorded in 92.8% (19,954) of those tested for alleged sexual offense.

6.3 Structure

Forensic initiatives in Colombia are mainly centralized in the National Institute of Legal Medicine and Forensic Sciences, although there are forensic laboratories directly dependent on the Attorney General's Office and the National Police, which all fall under the control and verification of the Institute.

The main objective of the Institute is to provide forensic services to the scientific community as technical support to the administration of justice. Its mission has the following functions (Plataforma, 2013):

1. Organize and direct the system of Legal Medicine and Forensic Sciences and control its operation.
2. Provide legal services and forensic medical sciences that are requested by prosecutors, judges, judicial police, the Ombudsman and other competent authorities in the country.
3. Develop assistance, scientific and social functions in the field of legal medicine and forensic science.
4. Provide advice and answering inquiries on legal medicine and forensic sciences to prosecutors, courts and other competent authorities.
5. Define technical regulations to be met by other agencies and individuals to perform functions associated with expert forensic medicine, forensic science and exercise control over its development and implementation.
6. Serve as body of verification and control of expert evidence and forensic examinations carried out by the state police and other agencies at the request of the competent authority.
7. Serve as a national scientific reference center on issues related to forensic medicine and forensic science.
8. Accredit and certify laboratories, forensic evidence and experts in legal medicine and forensic science, when practiced by public and private entities.
9. Coordinate and advance the promotion and implementation of scientific research, graduate and undergraduate programs, continuing education and educational programs in the area of forensic medicine and forensic science.
10. Coordinate and promote under pre-existing agreements the practices of teaching at educational entities approved by the Colombian Institute for the Promotion of Higher Education (ICFES).
11. Disseminate research results, scientific advances, development of forensic practices and other information deemed relevant by the Institute to the community at large.
12. Delegate or hire natural or legal persons to perform some activities of expertise and to supervise their implementation.

To comply with the above the Institute has two subdivisions: the Division of Forensic Services and the Division of Scientific Research. Through the first it monitors and controls the practice of forensic pathology (dead people), forensic clinical and forensic psychiatry (living people), the Center of National Reference on Violence and all forensic laboratories. The second controls the School of Legal Medicine and Forensic Sciences, the Division of Forensic Research and Forensic Rules Division.

6.4 Forensic pathology

The National Forensic Pathology Group is in the Office of the National Institute of Legal Medicine and Forensic Sciences dedicated to ensuring the quality of forensic pathology in the country and is under the control of the Division of Forensic Services.

One of the main tools of Pathology is necropsy, an external and internal examination of the body after death using surgical techniques, performed by a medical doctor specially trained in that procedure, able to recognize and document the effects of the disease and trauma on the body. He studies the morphological appearance of a human body or parts of it within the context of a history or narrative of facts. It can be done by simple observation of the body with the naked eye or with the aid of microscopy methods and protocols.

The personnel at the National Institute of Legal Medicine and Forensic Sciences of the Republic de Colombia comprises forensic experts working as Medical Specialists, general practitioners and specialists in Pathology who have received special training or have experience in forensic pathology. The National Forensic Pathology Group helps those who actively work in the investigation of deaths and practice of medicolegal autopsies.

By means of this kind of scientific research the cause and manner of death is established. As part of the official investigation into deaths, the evolution of lesions is correlated with the findings in order to use the resulting data as a tool in the administration of justice carried out by the State to protect the innocent and punish culprits.

Because of the importance of identifying people within the judicial investigations and because the scientific technical data are taken from the human body with the aim to confirm or establish the identity of the victims, the National Forensic Pathology Group works closely with dental and anthropology professionals.

The functions of the National Forensic Pathology Group are:

1. To increase competencies in expertise of doctors or the Forensic Pathologist in relation to forensic autopsy in order to improve their participation in judicial and scientific research, and its impact on public health through training programs and monitoring the quality of Forensic Pathology.
2. Divulge important information to pathologists and Coroners and the community of forensic scientists in general.
3. Review, analyze and recommend legislative and regulatory issues that may have an impact in Forensic Pathology.
4. Coordinate all activities related to examination of corpses that originate from the Justice and Peace process or those in which violations to Human Rights or International Humanitarian Law violations are suspected.
5. Conduct studies and write expert reports of Forensic Pathology when requested by the competent authorities or directives of the Institute for one reason or another.
6. Help establish the identity of people by analyzing the information provided by matching antemortem information with postmortem information through joint analysis with other forensic areas such as the Forensic Anthropology Laboratory of Genetics, Dental, Fingerprinting and Photography.
7. Advise and support local groups in mass deaths caused by major national disasters and ensure training of experts and various officials regarding this issue.

Services include:

1. Practical training (rotations or internships to conduct autopsies).
2. Theoretical training (courses, workshops, seminars).
3. Scientific publications (scientific journals, articles containing data collected or case studies).
4. Postmortem examination of dead bodies in skeletonized or within complex cases including exhumations and secondary autopsies.
5. Technical concepts and/or consultancy (reviews grounded on objective data, references or expert criteria regarding decision-making based on data

and scientific knowledge in the area of Forensic Pathology).

6. Consult and provide support for management of cases involving Mass Disaster.
7. Expert examinations and reports in forensic dental anthropology.
8. Cross-reference identification information for identification and expert reports.
9. Expert reports on investigation of second instance for violent deaths and/or professional liability cases.
10. Criteria and/or procedural guidelines for the practice of autopsies and identification.
11. Monitor cases in Forensic Pathology.
12. Criteria and/or procedural guidelines for handling collective deaths.

6.5 Forensic anthropology

Within the overall framework of the provision of the National Institute of Legal Medicine and Forensic Sciences and the development of expert assistance, the Laboratory of Forensic Anthropology applies methods and techniques of biological anthropology, archeology and taphonomy, supporting medicine, in particular to study forensic pathology in cases of medicolegal death investigation when the state of the bodies limits the practice of autopsy in cases such as those where the bodies are in advanced states of decomposition, carbonization, dismemberment, fragmentation and skeletonization. The applied methods contribute in establishing the cause and manner of death, diagnosing skeletal abnormalities (bone and osteopathological traumas), supporting interdisciplinary processes of identification of bodies and body parts (determination of sex, racial standard, age, height, individualizing characteristics, laterality, etc.) and estimating the interval between death of an individual and the discovery of the body.

Following the implementation of Act 975 of 2005, the *Ley de Justicia y Paz* (Justice and Peace Law), recovery of complex bodies — mostly skeletonized — has increased (Analisis de la Ley de Justicia y Paz, n.d.), prompting the need to create new laboratories of both INMLCF and CTI as well as in the related area belonging to DIJIN (National Police), so that by 2013 the country had twelve forensic anthropology laboratories located in different major cities, five in the INMLCF, six in the CTI and one in the DIJIN.

Forty-eight forensic anthropologists are working in the above laboratories distributed as follows: 17 in the INMLCF, 28 in the CTI and 3 in the DIJIN. With these figures Colombia may rank as the country that has the most forensic anthropologists working in state institutions.

During its 23 years of existence in the country, forensic anthropology has faced significant challenges in conjunction with doctors, dentists and other forensic science professionals. They have been instrumental in the outcome of many lawsuits associated with violation of human rights and breaches of International Humanitarian Law in cases where bodies have been found of people who have died in the midst of an armed conflict and other violent contexts. As a result of these law suits the State has had to give comprehensive compensation to the victims within the provisions contemplated in the Law of Victims.

6.6 Forensic clinical medicine

The forensic team at The National Institute of Legal Medicine and Forensic Sciences consists of 300 doctors and 41 dentists (both men and women) who provide clinical and forensic dentistry services throughout the national territory.

During 2012, 440,153 clinical forensic expert reports were issued in Colombia. Of these 72.28% (318,125) were reports documenting injuries in various contexts (interpersonal/communal violence, domestic violence, child abuse, elderly abuse, accidental injuries including traffic events, mistreatment or torture, etc.). Domestic violence corresponded to 10.76% (47,366); reports documenting cases of sexual violence constituted 4.32% (18,996); reports to determine intoxication, 5.23% (23,012) and the remaining 7.42 % (32,654) were clinical cases to determine the age, health status and other forensic evaluations.

Expert reports issued by clinical forensic services include:

1. Injury documentation. Documentation of the presence of bodily injury in connection with the investigation of crimes against life and personal integrity. Cruel, inhuman or degrading treatment (Istanbul Protocol) is also used in the implementation of international protocols to document torture.
2. Documentation of cases of domestic violence. Documentation of injury in the context of domestic violence (whether or not of the same sex).
3. Evaluation of sexual violence. Documenting findings and interpretation of lesions in cases of sexual violence as well as recovering biological evidence, ensuring that victims get adequate attention in terms of emergency contraception, treatment of sexually transmitted diseases, HIV prophylaxis or abortion.
4. DWI documentation. Establishes clinically the state of intoxication in a living person, in the context of criminal, administrative, traffic or disciplinary investigations.
5. Determination of clinical age: assessment of chronological age of a person based on their characteristics of biological maturation. These reports are issued in connection with criminal, civil or administrative proceedings. It is done with interdisciplinary health teams and dentist.
6. Coroner determining health status of detainees: establishes whether a person deprived of liberty, detained or sentenced, presents any serious illness that is incompatible with life in formal detention. To this end it is necessary to consider the nature of the disease and its evolution according to the context in which it develops.
7. There are other forensic evaluations in response to the requirements of national authorities, such as case studies of alleged professional responsibility in health. In 2013 the Institute began working on concepts of physical dependence within the framework of tax law.

As of 2009 under the joint program "Comprehensive Strategy for the Prevention, Care and Eradication of all forms of gender violence in Colombia," the Institute developed the Model of Care for Gender Based Violence Clinic for Forensic, which began to be implemented in April 2012. With this model a transition begins where a service is performed on rights-based criteria and gender differential.

6.7 Forensic odontology

Forensic dentistry services apply specialized knowledge of the stomatognathic system in cases of personal injury, domestic violence, child abuse, common violence, sexual crime, professional liability and age identification. Forensic dental expert investigation is articulated in four areas corresponding to: 1. Identification, 2. Clinical and Forensic Odontology, 3. Forensic Pathology, 4. Forensic Anthropology.

1. Identification: performance of dental charts to unidentified corpses for inclusion within the SIRDEC information system, thus optimizing comparative ontological processes. Practice of dental charts in mass disasters and deaths in conflict for identification purposes.

2. Clinical and Forensic Odontology: integrated approach to lesions in the oral cavity as a result of violent acts in the context of interpersonal and domestic violence, political violence, traffic accident, sexual violence and dental procedures.

3. Forensic Pathology: based on the information provided by the oral autopsy within the framework of a criminal investigation. Support in cases of trauma that compromises oral and perioral anatomic areas, taking samples from the oral cavity when a sexual offense is suspected, documentation of oral lesions in child abuse, violation of human rights and estimating age on unidentified bodies.

4. Forensic Anthropology: valuations performed on skeletonized bodies in which the morphological and topographical description of dental structures, traumatic injuries to maxillofacial level and age estimate are recorded. Expert reports are integrated to those made by anthropologists and medical groups.

6.8 Forensic psychiatry

In 2011 a total of 16,586 applications for assessment by forensic psychology and psychiatry were received across the country and 8498 reports (3490 to 5008 forensic psychology and forensic psychiatry) were issued. In 2012 a total of 6753 reports (4241 and 2512 forensic psychiatry and forensic psychology) were issued. At present we have a total of 37 psychiatrists and 36 psychologists throughout the national territory.

The psychiatry and forensic psychology service performs 13 forensic psychiatric expertise determinations, 10 forensic psychiatric or psychological assessments and 2 interdisciplinary expertise evaluations. These assessments consist of the following areas of expertise.

6.8.1 Forensic psychiatric expertise

1. Capacity to reason and self-determination: nonimputability.
2. Changing, lifting or reaffirming security measures in cases of nonimputability.

3. Mental health status of detainees.
4. Mental capacity to declare, negotiate preliminary agreements and give depositions in inquiries.
5. Ability to manage assets and dispose of them in cases of judicial interdiction.
6. Alleged liability in the performance of health care in psychiatry.
7. Theoretical concepts about treatments in psychiatry to guide the authority in decision-making within guardianships.
8. Alteration of the integrity, unity and family harmony in domestic violence due to mental illness.
9. Children and adolescents or adult victims of sexual offences.
10. Mental capacity for legal action in the life of a deceased subject.
11. Mental ability in a subject, victim of abuse in conditions of disadvantage and others.
12. Mental Illness present in a parent for purposes of consent in cases of adoption.
13. Dependence due to disability under the tax statutes.

6.8.2 Forensic psychiatric or psychological expertise

1. Adult victims of sexual offences.
2. Children and adolescent victims of sexual offences.
3. Psychic disturbance in personal injury victims and others (extent for criminal purposes).
4. Psychic damage for compensation purposes, conciliation or repair (victims of sociopolitical violence).
5. Substance addiction.
6. Custody (or parental authority).
7. Visitor's guidelines and regulation of food.
8. Psychological autopsy in determining the manner of death (suicide, homicide or accident).
9. Mental impairment in domestic violence.
10. Procedures of amplification, clarification or addition of a diagnosis and evaluation in objection to incidents.

6.8.3 Forensic interdisciplinary expertise

1. Risk assessment in individuals convicted of domestic violence
2. Implementation of the Istanbul Protocol in cases where torture, cruel or inhuman treatment is suspected.

6.9 DNA laboratory

The National Institute of Legal Medicine and Forensic Sciences currently has four forensic genetics laboratories located in Regional Directories in Bogota and elsewhere in northwest (Medellin), southwest (Cali) and east (Villavicencio) to provide scientific support to the administration of justice throughout the country.

Also, the Institute through an interagency agreement with the Colombian Family Welfare Institute (ICBF for *Instituto de Bienestar Familiar*) performs tests with DNA genetic markers to establish paternity or maternity of an individual in cases of genetic parentage. These are done only in Bogotá.

Currently the laboratory of Genetics Bogotá is:

1. Accredited under Colombian technical standard NTC-ISO-IEC-17025: 2005 Certificate of Accreditation No. 10-LAB-010 2011-09-28 issued by the National Accreditation ONAC.
2. Certificate under ISO 9001: 2008 Certificate No. CO230612 of May 15, 2009 and under the rule NTCGP 1000: 2009 Certified No. GP 0050 May 15, 2009 by Bureau Veritas.

Among the services provided by our laboratories are:

1. Biological sampling references in living individuals (blood, hair, saliva).

   This service is only for sampling blood, saliva and hair on live people by request of the administration of justice for genetic studies.

   Determining genetic profiles

   These analyses are required for

   - Identification of human remains.
   - Individualization or determination of what person (i.e., suspects, defendants, victims and/or individuals associated with the investigation) could have been the origin of evidence or material elements for evidence retrieved from a scene where a crime is under investigation.
   - Determination of biological parentage (parenthood research).
   - Among biological samples that can be subjected to these tests are:
     Blood
     Semen
     Saliva
     Epithelial cells
     Bones

   Dental pulp
   Soft tissue
   Hair
   Urine
   Paraffin embedded tissue
   Any other human sample containing biological cells.

These analyses require genetic material or DNA to be removed or extracted from existing cells using standard techniques common to the forensic community (Chelex, FTA, differential extraction, organic extraction or silica). Depending on the case, certain regions of DNA may be studied – some located in the nucleus of all cells except the sex chromosomes, known as autosomal DNA, others localized exclusively on the sex chromosomes, known as DNA Chromosome X and Y and other regions localized in mitochondria the cytoplasm of cells, known as DNA or mitochondrial genome.

Genetic analyses are generally performed on autosomal DNA. Only in some special cases or situations is it essential to analyze other regions of the DNA.

Chromosome Y DNA analysis. This analysis is performed when required to establish filiation between patrilineal male individuals and applies in cases of criminal investigation as well as in those where affiliation and identification of missing persons need complementation.

Mitochondrial DNA analysis. This analysis is performed when required to establish matrilineal descent among both female and male individuals, given that mitochondrial DNA is identically inherited from the mother to her children (both men and women), but only women retransmit it to their offspring. These analyses are conducted primarily in hair samples and in very degraded or damaged remains or in cases where identification results for analysis by nuclear markers were negative or inconclusive, or in matrilineal families.

Storage, search and comparison of genetic profiles in CODIS, the database – National Genetic Database Profiles Applied to Judicial Research

This database holds information collected by the Laboratories Forensic Genetics Institute pertaining to entry, storage and search of genetic profiles obtained from the analyses of biological samples. It serves as a tool for the investigation of crimes that have a high rate of recurrence such as sex crimes or killings committed by serial offenders. To perform genetic search and comparisons in this database strict compliance is required, as stated in Articles 244 and 245 of the CPP and Case C-334/10.

Concepts of second opinions on genetic testing in other laboratories.

The DNA lab Bogotá receives an average of 1500 to 1600 cases per year.

6.10 Forensic biology

The analyses carried out in this laboratory are given below.

6.10.1 Blood search and identification of human blood
6.10.1.1 Orientation tests for detection of blood
The Thevenon and Roland technique, also called the Piramidon technique, is based on chemical redox reactions that allow the detection of peroxidases, catalases oxide and/or reducing agents such as iron in the HEM of hemoglobin.

6.10.1.2 Confirmatory tests for the detection of human blood
The presence of hemoglobin, which is a component of higher primate blood through human monoclonal anti-hemoglobin antibodies is qualitatively detected through an immunoassay used in the forensic field.

6.10.2 Analysis for the search of semen stains in forensic interest
6.10.2.1 Sperm analysis
In contrast coloration, used by the Biology Laboratories, saturated picric acid solution stains the sperm cell nuclei pale pink and the core that constitutes the remaining area of the head is stained in bright red highlights so that their morphology is visible against the glycogen background as these and other artifacts take on a green coloration, thus giving this procedure its characteristic name of "Christmas Tree Stain."

6.10.2.2 Test for prostate specific antigen in samples of forensic interest
Prostate Specific Antigen protein testing is performed through immunochromatographic tests that work basically like any valid immunoassay test in the forensic field

for the qualitative detection of this protein in semen so that the presence or absence of the fluid in the sample can be confirmed.

6.10.3 Macroscopic analysis and microscopic elements in hair
Concepts of the anatomical region to which a hair sample belongs are given and referenced as their origin, whether human or animal, dyed or not, or whether it is a fiber.

6.10.4 Analysis of clinical laboratory
6.10.4.1 Methods of analysis
- Analysis of electrolyte through the ion-selective method for analysis of sodium, potassium and chloride in serum and vitreous humor.
- Colorimetric method for detection of glucose, urea, BUN and creatinine in vitreous humor, serum and plasma.
- Dipstick is a qualitative method for detection of ketones and pH in urine and vitreous humor.

Immunochromatographic tests are used for detection of HIV1 and HIV2 antibody virus surface antigens of hepatitis B, pregnancy testing and serology tests.

6.11 Forensic toxicology

The Forensic Toxicology Laboratory supports the administration of justice by analyzing toxic substances in body fluids and tissues obtained from a medical examination, necropsy and nonbiological samples related to an event under investigation.

6.11.1 Samples used for analysis
The main samples collected for analysis are: peripheral blood vessel, urine, gastric contents, vitreous humor, liver, biliary tract, injection site, hair and nasal smears. Other samples include kidney, muscle, brain, spleen and purge fluid.

6.11.2 Analytical techniques
Two types of techniques are used in toxicological analysis: those called screening and confirmatory techniques, which give way to elaborate analysis methodologies, subsequently standardized and validated by the laboratory.

Table 6.1 Most frequent toxicology analysis in Colombia

Analysis	Technique
Ethyl alcohol, methanol, acetaldehyde, acetone, 2 propanol and other alcohols	CG/HS/FID
Carboxyhemoglobine	Cooximetry
Cyanide	CG/NPD – CG/SM
Cocaine and metabolites	Inmnunoassay – GC/SM
Opium derivatives and opioids	GC/SM – LC/SM
Cannabinoids	Inmnunoassay – GC/SM
Benzodiacepines	Inmnunoassay – LC/SM
Amphetamines	Inmnunoassay – LC/SM – GC/SM
Phenothiazines	LC/SM
Tryciclic antidepressants	LC/SM
Plaguicides: organophosphates, carbamates, organochlorates, Piretroids, propanil, Amitraz	GC/SM
Dimetyltriptamine, harmine and harmaline	GC/SM
Cumarin derivatives	LC/SM
Solvents: chloroform, toluene, dichloromethane, hexane	CG/HS/FID
Anticonvulsivants and barbiturates	Inmnunoassay – LC/SM
Other prescripted medications	Inmnunoassay – LC/SM

The most common analysis and the techniques used are given in Table 6.1.

The Toxicology Laboratory, Regional Bogotá, receives an annual average of about 10,000 cases. In 2012 there were 11,331 analyses performed. Disaggregated analysis was: ethyl alcohol: 5237, drug abuse: 3755, depressants, benzodiazepines, phenothiazines, tricyclic antidepressants: 933, pesticides and cyanide: 403, drugs and others (carboxyhemoglobin, solvents): 983.

6.12 Grafology and questioned documents

The laboratory has offices in the cities of Bogotá, Medellin, Cali, Bucaramanga, Pereira and Barranquilla. The services provided are:
- Authenticity of documents: identity cards, alien IDs, residence permits, transit permits, permission to leave the country, visas, passports and military service IDs.
- Authenticity and/or provenance of documents: invoices, receipts, money orders, purchase orders, release orders, contracts, public deeds, minutes, real estate contracts, debit and credit cards and tickets.
- Authenticity and/or forgeries: in bills of exchange, checks, promissory notes, savings bonds, bonds, time deposits, stocks, driving licenses, subpoenas, transportation permits for freight and livestock, mandatory transit accident insurance, certificates of gas emission

analysis, car insurance policies, car tax forms, national mobilization permits, lottery tickets, chance and raffles, tickets for concerts and shows, bingos, medical records, authorizations for medical procedures, medical formulas, permission to carry guns (CLP), imprints, posters, voting ballots, packaging, leaflets, faxes, photocopies, acetates, diplomas, report cards, other certificates and licenses, tags and labels on commercial products (liquor, drugs, etc.).
- Authenticity of domestic or foreign paper currency: Colombian pesos, dollars, euros and bolivar.
- Printed stamps.
- Provenance of typed texts.
- Manuscripts and signatures (handwriting comparison).
- Integration of forensic science.

6.13 Integration

Crime scene investigation is a direct responsibility of the authorities in the Judicial Police. In Colombia this entity is composed of the Technical Investigation Corps (CTI) ascribed to the Attorney General's Office and the Criminal Investigation Branch ascribed to the National Police. Today the Attorney General's Office has a service based on field Criminalistics Units immediate reaction, which handles or processes the crime scene, collects and packages and starts the chain of custody of evidence (documents, bullets, weapons, controlled substances, bodies, etc.) to be delivered to the various forensic laboratories of the Technical Investigation or the National Institute of Legal Medicine and Forensic Sciences.

Field technology includes the latest advances in photography and topography as well as the search for trace evidence and scans with forensic lights. Other advances in field technology include reconstruction of the scene using initial information management or through the testimony of those involved, to monitor versions and other expertise to be debated in court. All activity of body recovery, evidence handling and recovery stage is supervised and coordinated by an agent of the Attorney General's Office.

The information recovered in the crime scene by the authorities of the Judicial Police is consolidated in a document called the Certificate of Technical Inspection of the Body, which is forwarded in the chain of custody to the National Institute of Legal Medicine and Forensic Sciences. It is then delivered to the expert assigned to do the medicolegal autopsy. The doctor who performs the autopsy carries out the appropriate interdepartmental consultations with forensic laboratories ascribed to the National Institute of Legal Medicine and Forensic Sciences.

The same physician writes an expert report to document all findings and conclusions expressed in terms of the cause and manner of death and includes the results from the different laboratories considered in his/her analysis. The report is sent to the prosecutor assigned to the case. Simultaneously, the laboratory results are sent separately to the same prosecutor who may request additions or clarifications from the expert who performed the autopsy or at his/her discretion to any of the experts in the laboratories where the tests were performed. Finally, the prosecutor coordinates, manages and integrates the information of the case. If the cause of death is murder, he/she may summon the doctor or any of the laboratory experts to testify on their findings and conclusions and sustain them at trial. The technicians who participated in the preparation of the minutes of the inspection body at the scene of the crime or who performed some expertise in laboratories that do not belong to the National Institute of Legal Medicine and Forensic Sciences conduct their opinions separately. It is then the prosecutor's responsibility to integrate and interpret the information within the context of the case. These conclusions may also be susceptible to expansion or clarification by the prosecutor or any other party. In homicide

cases, findings may be cited by either of the intervening parties to support their findings and conclusions at a trial in court.

6.14 Recruitment

Through various media channels, the Institute seeks out candidates who meet the minimum requirements for the position. One means is through the Institute's page at www.medicinalegal.gov.co, where vacancies are published and resumes collected. Resumes may also be presented by staff in the Institute or received from professionals who developed academic and scientific activities within the Institute and show interest or skills in any practice of forensic science.

6.14.1 Testing

After receiving the resumes, suitability tests are performed. Suitability tests are tools for assessing compatibility between candidate and job requirements. The tests consist of psychological tests; others are exercises that simulate working conditions. Results are computed, averages obtained and scored.

- Psychological testing: focus on the personality and disposition for teamwork.
- Testing for knowledge: specific to each work area.
- Interviews: focused on determining an applicant's true motivation, understand their expectations and achievements and goals.

6.14.2 Verification of data and references

Once candidates have been selected, all information provided by the candidates is thoroughly verified, that is, of criminal and disciplinary history, if any, full resume, references of previous employers, authenticity of the high school, graduate or postgraduate diplomas, publications, participation in scientific organizations, certification of origin of income, among others.

6.15 Training

The forensic scientist staff receive training through formal education programs and through continuing education programs.

6.15.1 Formal education

There is a surgical medical specialization of three years in forensic medicine offered by the National University of Colombia. An important number of legal professionals who practice medical autopsies receive training in anatomic and surgical pathology; doctors specializing in psychiatry in collaboration with professional psychologists perform psychiatric evaluations. The General Santander Police Academy offers two master's degrees: one in criminal investigation and another in traffic accident investigation. In past years there were majors in forensic odontology at Universidad Javeriana, forensic anthropology at National University and a Master of Forensic Psychiatry at Universidad El Bosque.

6.15.2 Continuing education

With the support of the Institute's School of Legal Medicine and Forensic Sciences, the School of the Attorney General's Office and the School of National Police many nondegree seeking forensic sciences courses are given as well as workshops and seminars through teacher assistance agreements with other scientific institutions and universities. The School and the National Pathology Group have retraining programs for older officers. The Colombian Association of Legal Medicine and Forensic Sciences professional body of forensic scientists, a private entity, offers continuing education courses on various topics of interest, including a training course on forensic technical embalming for necropsy room attendants.

In Colombia the Chair of Legal Medicine is mandatory for all medical schools in the country, given that legal medical functions in small municipalities (medicolegal autopsies and forensic clinical evaluations) are performed by physicians during their year of required social service, which corresponds to the last year of student medical training before receiving the medical license. The School of Legal Medicine coordinates educational agreements with universities and provides guidelines for the practical and theoretical modules that students receive during rotation (internships). All teaching activities of the Chairs in Legal Medicine for medical students are carried out in the facilities of the Institute. Similarly, most professionals who teach theory are associated to the Institute.

6.16 Funding

The National Institute of Legal Medicine and Forensic Sciences has two sources of income.

6.16.1 Government funds

They are included in the General Budget of the Nation and are appropriated by the Government through the Ministry of Finance and the National Planning Department as established in the Annual Budget Law and Settlement Decree. They come from national income taxes, fees, fines and taxes.

6.16.2 Own resources

These depend on the income projection by the Institute at the stage of preparation of the draft budget derived from agreements signed by the entity with entities that are part of the general budget of the nation and territorial entities and their implementation depends on the progress of the collection.

The name is given to those generated and managed by the national public institutions and for the fulfillment of its objects in accordance with the law. They come from the signing of agreements, fines, photocopying, paternity testing and selling worthless financial returns, among others.

6.17 Political influence

Although Colombia is known for being the oldest democracy in Latin America, the political reality is far from stable. In 1991 a new Constitution was drawn up to replace the one enacted in 1886. Until January 2013, the 1991 Constitution has been amended 37 times, which gives an idea of the instability of the Colombian political system. On some occasions these constitutional reforms have been motivated by the changing needs of Colombian society, but in most cases changes have been driven by political interests of private sectors.

In addition to this political culture where the concept of the public and the common good is quite diffuse, it must be pointed out that Colombia has suffered an armed conflict for over 50 years in which political practices have also been seriously affected. Guerrillas, paramilitaries and drug traffickers and the armed forces appear as the main actors in the conflict. Many times each of these groups and their interests are clearly differentiated, but not in many others. Partnerships between drug traffickers and government, between government and paramilitaries, drug traffickers and guerrillas, among or between guerrillas and paramilitaries have been common during the years of civil war. In this context, it has become a high-risk affair for the political exercise of those who are not tied to either side or who challenge in one way or another their interests, and has become a very risky endeavor, but, as in every war, the real victim ends up being civil society. In figures from the Center for Historical Memory, between 1958 and 2012 the armed conflict has left 220,000 dead, 177,307 of them civilians, and 25,000 missing (Centro de Memoria Histórica, 2013). Violations of human rights are perhaps the greatest challenge of the Colombian judicial system and in this context the role of the National Institute of Legal Medicine and Forensic Sciences (INMLCF) is fundamental.

With the Constitution of 1991 the Institute became part of the Attorney General's Office. Although this implied a loss of administrative autonomy and perhaps because of its origin and scientific mission nature as long as its existence, the INMLCF has been able to maintain a remarkable independence in fulfilling its mission.

During a time when officials were denying the existence of missing persons, the Institute was diligently documenting the phenomena. The Institute's conclusions also have been instrumental in lawsuits against members of the armed forces in extrajudicial executions, among others. It is in the face of some of these events that one must understand the enormous pressure placed upon the forensic tasks of having to work in a political context of corruption and armed conflict, where information reported to the Forensic Institute often goes against the interests of certain groups. So it must be openly stated that while the INMLCF is committed to gathering and researching evidence on a scientific basis to forward the administration of justice, there are constraints to its labor due to the complexity of the context in which the work must be done.

State presence in Colombia is not uniform throughout the country and the afore-mentioned dynamics of corruption and the armed conflict are exacerbated in peripheral regions of the nation. Thus, coroners must often work in areas where security conditions are really risky and a necropsy report can be a matter of life or death. Fear is part of everyday life for many professionals in the INMLCF and this sets more or less limits on their professional autonomy.

6.18 Certification

6.18.1 Background

Act 938 of 2004, in Article 36, paragraph 8, contemplates the need to certify forensic experts in Colombia. It states that as part of the mission of the INMLCF its function is " ...to accredit and to certify laboratories, forensic evidence and expertise in legal medicine and forensic science, where practiced by public and private entities."

Thus in 2007 the first certification processes in the areas of pathology and forensic odontology began, and continued certifying forensic medical experts in 2008. During this period of time and until 2010, the Institute has certified approximately 7% (about 4000) of the total of forensic experts from institutions nationwide.

In 2012 the National Forensic Certification Group was created by Resolution 000513 of 31 July 2012 as an administrative and functional unit of the Directorate General, whose functions included: to advise, formulate, develop and control plans, programs and projects involved in forensic certification; to grant, maintain, renew, extend and reduce the scope of certification, and suspend or cancel it.

6.18.2 Purpose of certification

According to the regulatory framework already stated, the certification processes of forensic experts provides the Colombian justice system with a reliable assessment tool for forensic experts who can evidence mastery of a standard of competence in forensic expertise in order to facilitate the assessment of the evidence as to the scientific, technical and moral adequacy of the expert (Article 420, Law 906 of 2004).

6.18.3 Process description

The certification of forensic experts projected by the GNCF is based on the Colombian Technical Standard NTC/ISO IEC 17024: 2012, which establishes the set of rules for the certification of persons; its applications, issuance, suspension and repeal as well as the regulations regarding legal, academic, technical, security and confidentiality issues.

In this regard the steps that make up the certification process are: the application submitted to the Competency Assessment Body (CAB) once positions are posted; the evaluation composed of three continuous processes (a standardized test, an oral test of competencies and a practical exam); the decision taken by the OEC to certify or not the expert according to test results, and continued monitoring by which the OEC confirms the continuing competence of the expert certified.

The areas of expertise to be certified in 2014 include:

- Forensic pathology
- Forensic clinic
- Forensic anthropology – analysis of forensic-bioanthropology
- Forensic dentistry – dental age clinic
- Forensic dentistry – cases related to interpersonal, familial, sexual, child violence, torture and professional responsibility
- Forensic dentistry – forensic dentistry analysis in cases of lethal violence
- Forensic dentistry – forensic analysis of dental and cranial bones for identification purposes.

6.19 Laboratory accreditation and quality control

The Superintendence of Industry and Commerce was the accrediting agency of forensic laboratories in Colombia until the year 2008. As of 2013 the National Accreditation Agency of Colombia – ONAC – took over. According to the figures on ONAC's Web page (Directorio Official de Acreditaciones, n.d.), there are 165 testing laboratories – 80 accredited by the Superintendence of Industry and Commerce and 85 by ONAC. Of these 165, 17 correspond to laboratories performing forensic work permanently and 8 exclusively that perform genetic analysis because of the legal requirements to be accredited to perform this kind of analysis.

The global scientific community and specifically the forensic one established through ISO/IEC 17025 mandates that laboratories must demonstrate a management system, technical competency and the capability to generate valid technical results. This is done through an accreditation process defined by Decree 2669 of 1993 as a "process whereby the technical competence and the adequacy of certification and inspection agencies, testing laboratories and metrology is recognized for

Table 6.2 Accredited laboratories at the National Institute of Legal Medicine and Forensic Science, Colombia (www.medicinalegal.gov.co)

Laboratory	City
Toxicology	Bogotá
Toxicology	Medellin
Toxicology	Pereira
Toxicology	Barranquilla
Toxicology	Cali
Toxicology	Tunja
Narcotics	Bogotá
Metrology	Bogotá
Toxicology	Bucaramanga
Toxicology	Ibague
Narcotics	Bucaramanga
DNA	Bogotá
DNA	Cali
Trace Evidence	Bogotá
Biology	Bogotá
Biology	Bucaramanga
Biology	Tunja

carrying out the activities referred to in this decree...." The model used for this purpose is established by the Colombian Technical Standard 17025: 2005 NTC-ISO/IEC that establishes the "general requirements for the competence of testing and calibration laboratories."

Currently, in our Institute there are 17 accredited laboratories, shown in Table 6.2.

Forensic laboratories performing genetic testing to establish paternity or maternity shall, in addition to accreditation, have certification in the ISO 9001 management system. Moreover, state agencies are required to implement the Technical Standard on Quality Management NTCGP 1000, which corresponds to the latest 2009 version.

6.20 Technology

As described previously, the National Institute of Legal Medicine has advanced technology for forensic pathology services and clinical practices as well as each of their laboratories. The autopsy rooms in major cities of our country allow the practice of autopsies with high quality standards. Our Institute has forensic lights techniques for use in forensic autopsy rooms and a trace evidence laboratory. In the field of Criminalistics, the Technical Investigation Corps (CTI), which is dependent on the General Attorney's Office and the laboratories of the National Police, has technology as forensic lights, special recovery techniques, latent fingerprint analysis and retrieval spots blood and scene reconstruction.

Colombia is very strong in forensic identification through fingerprints. Our AFIS (Automated Fingerprint Identification System) provides online connection with the National Civil Registry Office (Registraduria Nacional del Estado Civil) and allows positive identification of people in minutes. Our application SIRDEC allows effective forensic identification for missing people based in odontology, anthropology and autopsy findings. We have other information systems such as IBIS (Integrated Ballistics Information System) and CODIS (Combined DNA Index System). There are areas that could be improved in our toxicology laboratories, especially in terms of the number of substances studied and response times. Another of our limitations is related to the concentration of best technological resources, mostly in the capital and major cities. Many of our basic units are very small and do not have X-ray equipment or have technical limitations in photography, among other problems. To solve this problem our Institute will implement projects such as mobile morgues and mobile X-ray equipment with a displacement capacity through the country. In special situations we have the possibility of referring bodies to the capital or another major city with adequate logistics for an expert professional approach or move teams to the location with all equipment required.

Within our strategic medium-term projects we will incorporate technology like virtual autopsy and other postmortem images for road traffic deaths in the city of Bogotá and molecular autopsy for specific cases of sudden death in adults.

6.21 Disaster preparedness

The disaster preparedness model in Colombia is decentralized. Each of the eight Regional Directorates of the Institute develop a regional disaster plan of their own, their own budget, infrastructure and human resources to practice autopsies in accordance with the characteristics and status of their territorial entity.

At the central level, the National Pathology Group is dependent on the Forensic Services Branch and is responsible for the validation of compliance of all these local plans with the National Disaster Plan. Among the functions of the National Pathology Group is to issue quality standards for addressing collective deaths through Standardized Guidelines and Protocols to be implemented in training rescue groups, monitoring the modus operandi, consolidating statistics and using them in planning future methods to deal with these deaths.

As part of its training program the National Pathology Group conducts periodic disaster drills involving forensic multidisciplinary teams and the active participation of local police and administrative authorities. From an operational point of view the National Pathology Group has the capacity to move teams of experts anywhere in the country to provide logistics and forensic specialized support to regional teams in complex high impact situations that affect national security.

The Institute has a lot of experience in disaster management because of the particular geographical features of the country and of the high number of cases related to deaths due to terrorism and the armed conflict. In terms of logistical, administrative and scientific disciplines, these deaths are seen and handled by the institute as disasters. The National Pathology Group has a substantial photographic and documentary archive of all such cases as well as documents that consolidate lessons learned in each of these situations.

6.22 Legal issues

Law 906 of 2004 is the norm, which issues the Code of Criminal Procedure for the oral adversarial criminal justice system in Colombia. It introduces a fundamental change in transforming expert evidence provided by independent evidence, as it were, to evidence collateral to testimonial evidence. Consequently, it has no probative value unless the expert is subjected to questioning and cross-examination by the parties at the hearing where the expert's testimony is heard. Whether this is admitted as evidence or not depends on the judge's conviction and this aspect is still being discussed.

Expert evidence is admissible when the process requires scientific, technical, artistic or expert support. Official experts, including, of course, the experts at the

National Institute of Medicine Legal and Forensic Sciences, the Judicial Police and public entities, regardless of their expertise in science, art or technology, are *eligible* to give expert testimony, but it is mandatory that the Prosecutor accepts them to be admitted as a judicial *expert*.

The expert presents a report sufficiently supported, which is to be investigated before the parties at the hearing. Contents must be known no less than five days before the public hearing is to take place and where the expert's opinion will be presented.

If the parties agree on the content and conclusions, the report many be accepted as evidence. That is, the report or events covered in it, as well as the expert's suitability will be admitted as proof of the appropriateness of the expert. In such a case, the appearance of the expert at the trial will not be required.

Conversely, if no there is no consensus, the parties will ask the judge to summon the expert at the trail to be questioned and cross-examined.

At the preliminary hearing, the judge will decide the admission of the expertise *report* and shall summon the expert to the hearing where his/her admission as expert will be decided (the above if the expert has not already been admitted at an earlier hearing within the process). The expert's testimony must be preceded by a summary report where the basis of the expert's opinion is expressed. As an expert witness the expert is allowed to give his/her qualified opinion on the subject of expertise.

The law establishes the criteria for the assessment of expert evidence. The suitability of both technical and moral proficiency, clarity and attitude when answering questions and the acceptance of technical, scientific or artistic principles on which it rests should be *considered*. It is possible to introduce demonstrative, pertinent and relevant evidence to facilitate understanding of the *concepts presented*.

The National Institute of Legal Medicine and Forensic Sciences is the scientific technical body of the system in accordance with the law, and provides scientific and technical support to both the prosecution and the accused or his *counsel*.

Arguably, much has been achieved in the implementation and use of expert evidence in the current judicial system, but there is still a long way to go.

In "Terminal crisis of accusatory penal system" (Gómez, 2013), published in *Sentido Común* (Common Sense), Dr. Fernando Gómez Jiménez argues that the funding of the National Institute of Legal Medicine and Forensic Sciences regarding the system of scientific technical support is inadequate. It is necessary to improve the judicial assessment of expert evidence. There are still cases where it is a decision privilege to give oral evidence, even when expert evidence is clearly contrary.

The challenge of meeting the needs for training judicial officers and those involved in the criminal process on issues related to the origin, relevance, understanding and interpretation of the expert evidence is yet to be met. Similarly, there is a need to improve the education, training and updating of forensic experts

6.23 Research

The Research Branch of Scientific Research, which depends on The National Institute of Legal Medicine and Forensic Sciences Division, is responsible for project evaluation and budget approval. The research budget is allocated by the State through the National Planning Office and on presentation of a specific investment project.

Researchers can conduct research at the school by means of one of the following:
- Officer of the Institution, who should have a project approved by the Research Division and approval from their immediate supervisor.
- As a student of a school having a valid agreement with the institute. In which case the student must have an institutional co-investigator who must demonstrate a clear standing association to the Institute and whose career is directly related to the research.
- As a member of a public or private, national or international entity in partnership with the Institute.

There are three distinct stages to managing proposals:

Preliminary phase. This begins when a research proposal is received, compliance with all rules and prerequisites checked, all assessments are approved and ends when the project number is given and the letter of commitment signed with investigators.

Development phase. This starts when the letter of commitment is signed with investigators and the investigation is carried out.

Closing phase. This starts when the researcher delivers the final report of the investigation in accordance with the parameters of the Research Division and ends with the delivery of the products committed to in the minutes at initiation.

All projects require a methodological assessment, a technical review (by academic peers) and a bioethical review.

The lines of research the institute handles today are:

1. Forensic clinical diagnostics
2. Basic research in forensic science
3. Cadaveric phenomenon
4. Human rights and international humanitarian law
5. Identification and population studies (population genetic studies)
6. Validation of analytical methods in laboratories
7. Forensic psychiatric diagnosis
8. Forensic art

The Research Division consolidates the final investigations reports in the institutional magazine called *Colombian Journal of Legal Medicine and Forensic Sciences*, which was founded 80 years ago and has been a benchmark for Colombian and Latin American training in forensic science. The magazine is in the process of requesting international indexing. The level of institutional science has been instrumental in allowing our professionals and their papers to be accepted in international conferences and leading publications mainly in the field of forensic laboratories and forensic pathology. Also a significant number of our specialists have participated as consultants in developing guidelines and protocols, as well as trainers in institutions in other countries in DNA, forensic identification, sexual crime, deaths by gunfire, disaster management and asphyxia, among other areas.

6.24 Future directions

The National Institute of Legal Medicine and Forensic Sciences has many challenges within the complex social and political context of Colombia. The Institute has played a key role in the investigation of deaths related to the Colombian armed conflict and within the Law Justice and Peace (*Ley de Justicia y Paz*), the legal framework by which legal benefits were granted to groups outside the law in exchange for confession crimes against humanity and the location of the bodies, which number in the thousands in Colombia. Much of the recent history as the country has been written in our autopsy rooms. However, given the progress in the peace talks our Institute must prepare for a different scenario: the postconflict and ensuing peace.

To this end, the Institute has undertaken humanization policies that will affect the procurement of services closer to the community and society. Consequently, the Institute launched a new policy of "legal medicine for a diverse Colombia," which aims to embrace cultural, racial, religious and gender diversity in the country. Thus clinical forensic services are developing treatment protocols for victims based on gender, with a strong awareness for minorities such as the LGBTI community. This year we successfully launched a project with mobile morgues with logistical capacity to travel to remote areas of our country, especially focusing on areas with high indigenous and Afro-descendant populations. Likewise the Institute will work to strengthen existing spaces and opportunities for attention to children and women within the context of domestic violence and sexual crime. A protocol to care for victims of femicide has been drawn up within the pathology group, as it is a cultural phenomenon that has become strongly visible in the last decade. The Institute will strengthen its participation in traffic, burn and fireworks prevention plans as well as in disaster management.

In 2014 the Institute will celebrate its 100th anniversary of having been established and recognized as a scientific institute within the Colombian legal system. Among the challenges for the future are to advance technologically into the field of virtual autopsy and other postmortem imaging techniques that will allow optimization of human resources to achieve the best results in the investigation of deaths. Concepts such as molecular autopsy will allow us to take the lead in research and approaches to sudden deaths. The Institute continues to strive to accredit all forensic laboratories and to implement its certification system of experts in various forensic areas with a view to becoming the certification center for other national and international entities. Research projects such as smart classrooms and telemedicine, bone collection and indexing our journal will make our Institute an obligatory reference in teaching and research in forensic science and other medical and social sciences.

Acknowledgments

Special thanks are due to the Colombian Association of Legal Medicine and Forensic Sciences (ASOMEF), sponsor of our 17th National Congress of Legal Medicine and Forensic Science (celebrating 100 years of our Institute), for their unconditional support for this project. Editorial overview was provided by Andrés Rodríguez Zorro. The authors would also like to acknowledge the following for their contributions to various sections of the chapter: history, Jorge Arturo Jimenez Pajaro; types of cases, Sandra Lucia Moreno; forensic anthropology, Cesar Sanabria; forensic clinical medicine, Martha Elena Pataquiva; forensic psychiatry, Luisa Fernanda Alarcón Rivera; DNA laboratory, Rosa Elena Romero Martínez; biology, Luz Adriana Londoño Vargas; toxicology, Patricia Heredia Marroquín; recruitment, Ruth Yolanda Pabon; funding, Yaneth Cuestas Gomez; politics, Natalia Lozano Mancera; certification, John Alexander Vergel; accreditation, Miguel Arturo Velasquez Acevedo; and legal issues, Aída Elena Constantín. Finally, special acknowledgment is given to Mario Alberto Hernández Rubio, President of the Colombian Association of Legal Medicine and Forensic Sciences, who sponsored the translation of this chapter.

Note

The authors would like to clarify that this chapter describes only the operation of the National Institute of Legal Medicine and Forensic Sciences (which is the organization that coordinates and regulates the practice of forensic science in the country), but there are other forensic laboratories run by other state organizations.

References

Analisis de la Ley de Justicia y Paz. Available at: www. fiscalia. gov.co.

Centro de Memoria Histórica (2013) Informe Basta Ya: Memorias de Guerra y Dignidad, Bogotá. Available at: www. centrodememoriahistorica.gov.co. Accessed November 2013.

Directorio Oficial de Acreditaciones. Organismo Nacional de Acreditaciones Colombia. Available at: www.onac.org.co.

Forensis (2012) Datos para la Vida. Available at: www. medicinalegal.gov.co. Accessed November 2013.

Gómez, F. (2013) *Crisis Terminal del Sistema Penal Acusatorio* (3rd ed.). Lex Asesores, pp. 28–38.

Plataforma Estrategica Servicio Forense Efectivo (2013) Available at: www.medicinalegal.gov.co. Accessed November 2013.

CHAPTER 7

Forensic science in Denmark

Niels Lynnerup & Steen Holger Hansen

Department of Forensic Medicine, University of Copenhagen, Copenhagen, Denmark

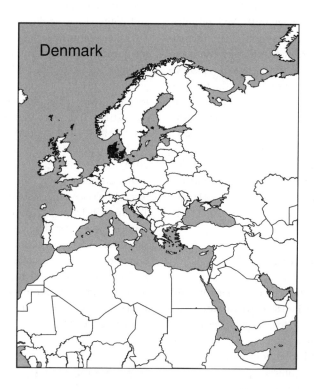

7.1 The beginnings

Danish forensic science probably evolved much in the same fashion as in the rest of Europe. That is, a gradual transition from pre-Medieval and Medieval notions of evidence as being signs from God, for example, that an innocent man could bear red hot iron without getting burns, to the more rational, scientific ideas in the 16th century Reformation period, reflecting a closer study of causality of events and the study of evidence. Probably one of the first cases in Danish jurisprudence, where

forensic evidence is registered, concerned a fatal shooting in Copenhagen in 1727. The round was recovered from the chest of the deceased and analyzed, although somewhat inconclusively. The presumed weapon was found in the saddle on the horse belonging to the suspect. Combined with the testimony of various witnesses, this evidence was presented in court. The Police Chief noted in his account that in this case he had used "much diligence and Science" (Hoeck, 1951a).

Medical science had been brought to bear on criminal court cases almost 100 years earlier. The first attempts

---

The Global Practice of Forensic Science, First Edition. Edited by Douglas H. Ubelaker.

at forensic medical science, in the terms of deliberating over medical evidence for a court of law, date back to the 16th century, when the King at times requested the assistance of the professors of the medical faculty of the University of Copenhagen. One such case concerned a woman suspected of having killed her newborn child (Tryde, 1939). The professors Ole Worm[1] and Thomas Bartholin[2] ascertained that milk could be produced not only when a woman was lactating an infant or when she was pregnant or had just given birth. Milk production could in fact, although uncommonly, be initiated without the woman being pregnant, and had also been described to have happened in men. Thus, the professors could not with certainty conclude that the woman had recently been pregnant even though milk had been seen to be produced by her breasts. The woman in question was acquitted; milk production from her breasts was not strong enough evidence for her having recently given birth, and hence that she must have killed her infant (though at the time not an uncommon practice for women getting pregnant out of wedlock) (Tryde, 1939).

7.2 Forensic technical science

Modern Danish forensic technical investigations are said to have been implemented in 1869, when "the best" policemen could be assigned to special investigative duties (Hoeck, 1951a). Up to then, investigation and the practice of securing technical, forensic evidence was very much up to the local police officers, possessing often rather varying degrees of competence. This is probably also why the Police Chief in the above-mentioned case from Copenhagen specifically stated that he had used "much diligence and Science": this was otherwise rare. The need for better investigative techniques and securing evidence and interpretation clearly became an issue, leading to the police specifically assigning these tasks to the best and brightest policemen.

Among the many forensic technical problems was not least the question of identity. At a time when identity documents were virtually unknown, securing the proper identity of criminals was of paramount importance. A criminal could simply claim different names and it

might be impossible to properly establish whether the person had been apprehended or sentenced before. Therefore, a bureau for identification was established by the police in 1900, also marking the first true forensic technical unit under the police (Brockmann, 2009; Duedahl et al., 2013). The bureau used the methods of Bertillion, including, since 1904, fingerprints. While laborious, the Bertillion method did provide a first attempt at securing proper identification of suspects and criminals. A verdict in the Danish High Court in 1915 concerning fingerprints confirmed their value, and this meant that fingerprint analyses became routine in Denmark (Brockmann, 2009). The full Bertillion system gradually became obsolete, so that only facial photographs were taken along with fingerprints (Duedahl et al., 2013). Today, the Danish Police uses an automated system, AFIS, and approximately 335,000 individuals are now registered in the database (The Danish Police, 2014).

Identification aside, the first real police technical forensic service was established in 1922 as "The Police Technical Laboratory" (Hoeck, 1951b). This technical service came over time to consist of several subdivisions, for example, ballistics, photography, documents and trace evidence. A major reform of the Danish Police in 2007 has centralized these functions on a national level, so that these are now handled by the "National Police Forensic Technical Center" (Brockmann, 2009; Danish Police, 2014).

7.3 The Danish judicial system, the police and forensic science

The main act regulating Danish criminal law, including laws about the police, criminal prosecution and the courts, is the Danish Administration of Justice Act (Retsinformation, 2014). This act was passed and implemented in 1919, setting up a comprehensive, modern, judicial system. Some years before, in 1911, a national police force had been established (although it was first in 1938 that the Danish police force, then consisting of State police and county police, was truly centralized into one common police force) (Hoeck, 1951b). Thus, the police in Denmark is now one national force, employed

---

[1] Ole Worm (1588–1655) described the small intercalated bones in the calvarium, hence the name Wormian bones.
[2] Thomas Bartholin (1616–1680) published one of the first descriptions of the human lymphatic system.

directly by the state. A major reform of the Danish police was initiated in 2007. It meant that 54 police districts were transformed into 12 districts and a National Police (Danish: "Rigspolitiet"). The Minister of Justice, who is the chief police authority, exercises his powers through the National Commissioner and the Commissioners of the police districts (The Justice Department, 2014). The National Police includes areas known as operative departments engaged in investigation into IT crime, road traffic tasks, the surveillance of environments involving drugs, bikers, gangs and prostitution, international cooperation with the police in other countries, as well as forensic technical investigations. It is also from the National Police that individual police districts can request assistance for various investigations and special duties. There are approximately 11,000 police officers in Denmark (Justice Department, 2014).

According to the Administration of Justice Act, it is the duty of the police to investigate crimes. Gathered evidence and the results of the investigative efforts are presented to the attorneys of the Prosecution Service. This service comprises the Director of Public Prosecutions, the regional public prosecutors, the chief constables and the Commissioner of the Copenhagen Police. The Minister for Justice is also the chief authority of the Prosecution Service. The attorneys work closely together with the investigative police officers. It is the Prosecution Service attorneys who will have to assess whether a case is likely to stand up in court. If so, the attorneys will appear before a judge in an attempt to have the perpetrator convicted in a District Court. The Director of Public Prosecutions heads the Prosecution Service, and when a case is to be conducted before the High Court, which is the tier above the District Court, the regional public prosecutors will conduct the case. It is the Director of Public Prosecutions who conducts proceedings in criminal cases before the Supreme Court, which is the highest tier of the Danish legal system (Justice Department, 2014).

It may be noted that Danish courts have no formalized requirements for expert witnesses or forensic technical evidence (like, for example, the "Daubert rules" known from the USA; James and Nordby, 2003). It is in principle solely for the Judge to evaluate whether forensic technical evidence and expert witnesses are admissible. The results of the various forensic technical and medical analyses, as well as expert statements, may play a part in court procedures, and the forensic specialists may be called to testify in court proceedings.

7.4 Forensic medicine

While forensic medicine had been introduced in a few professorial lectures at the University of Copenhagen in the 17th century, the first real, systematic teaching of the specialty began in 1819, at which time Forensic Medicine also became a specialty included in the exams for the medical degree (Gormsen, 1979). However, forensic medicine was not a wholly independent specialty; this first happened in 1905 (Gormsen, 1979). In 1935 the Department of Forensic Medicine was organized into three sections: forensic pathology, forensic serology (now forensic genetics) and forensic chemistry.

The forensic medical department at Aarhus University was founded in 1959 and the forensic medical institute at Odense University, now the University of Southern Denmark, in 1971 (Aarhus University, 2014; University of Southern Denmark, 2014). However, regional offices for forensic autopsies had been in place in Aarhus and Odense since 1916 and 1937, respectively.

It is perhaps noteworthy that the three Danish forensic medical institutes belong to universities. They are not part of the Danish health care system, nor the police or the judiciary. This autonomy means that cases brought to the institutes, concerning, for example, medical malpractice at a hospital, fatalities in connection with police work or deaths in prisons or other state institutions, may be handled independently and be unbiased. The forensic medical institutes also handle forensic medical investigations at the request of the Danish National Board of Industrial Injuries, the Military Prosecution Service and insurance companies.

7.5 Forensic pathology

Forensic pathology finally became a fully recognized, independent medical specialty in 2008. Until that time most forensic pathologists were specialists in pathology. All medicolegal autopsies in Denmark are performed at the three university departments. According to Danish law, a medicolegal autopsy must be performed if a punishable act has been carried out or is suspected, if the cause of death is not established and the death holds aspects of interest to the police, if the manner of death is unknown, or if an autopsy is considered necessary to prevent suspicion from arising at a later point in time. Furthermore, the Ministry of Justice has decided that an autopsy shall be performed when a death is related to drug abuse (Retsinformation, 2014). A medicolegal autopsy is preceded by a medicolegal external examination performed by a forensic pathologist or a health medical officer in collaboration with the police (Retsinformation, 2014).

The forensic pathological sections perform approximately 1500 autopsies per year; this number has, though, been decreasing over the last decade. The distribution (2007) of the manner of death determined by the autopsies is 35–38% natural, 37–41% accidental, 6–9% suicides, 3–5% homicides and 12–15% unknown (Tangmose Larsen and Lynnerup, 2011).

All three sections of forensic pathology have a CT scanner. This makes it possible to perform a CT scan of the whole body before each autopsy. It has been an important supplement to the autopsies and an improvement in the documentation of several conditions, for example, fractures, pathologies and traumatic lesions, foreign bodies and free air in the body. The technique is valuable for producing three-dimensional reconstructions of the body with specific lesions.

7.6 Clinical forensic medicine

The forensic pathologists at the three university institutes also carry out clinical medical examinations. Unlike autopsies, the number of these examinations has been rising, and they are now more numerous than forensic autopsies. The clinical forensic medical examinations are made at the request of the police and comprise perpetrators and suspects as well as victims, focusing on the documentation of lesions. The examinations may also include securing biological trace evidence. Examinations of victims of severe violence, including gunshot and stab wounds, may take place at the hospital trauma care unit, where such victims may have been brought in. Thus, the forensic medical examiner works alongside the doctors treating the victim, and may thus document lesions and wounds at or even before surgical revision. In such cases the forensic medical examiner also considers whether the victim's life was in danger.

Rape victims constitute the largest group of victims being examined clinically. These examinations take place at special centres for rape victims, and are made

in close cooperation with specially trained nurses and medical specialists in gynecology, who are also responsible for the subsequent treatment of the rape victims. Likewise, child victims of physical and sexual abuse are examined at hospital child care units or at special centres for child victims. The examinations are made in close cooperation with pediatricians and pediatric nurses.

Torture victims may also be examined at the forensic medical institutes. Such examinations may be made at the behest of the Danish immigration authorities in cases of asylum applications, where the result of such examinations may play a part in the full assessment of an application.

7.7 Forensic genetics

Serological analyses using the ABO blood typing system of Landsteiner were introduced at the department in Copenhagen in1926 (Gormsen, 1979). A section for forensic serology was set up in 1935. Obviously, this section has seen a huge expansion with the advent of the modern forensic DNA methods in the late 20th century. A unit for forensic anthropology was started in 1958 at the Department in Copenhagen for determining paternity, combining tissue typing, serological analyses and morphological examinations (e.g., head shape, facial features, etc.). The modern DNA techniques have since completely replaced these analyses.

Today, the section of Forensic Genetics at the University of Copenhagen, which is also the only forensic genetic laboratory in Denmark, analyzes material to types of cases: criminal cases and paternity cases. In criminal cases such as burglary, rape or murder, DNA profile analyses from biological material such as blood, saliva, tissue or semen from a crime scene are compared with the DNA profile analyses found in a suspect or a person in the DNA register (University of Copenhagen, 2014).

In paternity cases the DNA profiles from one or more males are compared to the child's DNA profiles. The mother's DNA is usually also investigated as this strengthens the overall results. Similar studies may be made in immigration cases (in these cases it is examined whether the alleged relationship between an immigrant and a person seeking permanent residence in Denmark may be present) (University of Copenhagen, 2014).

7.8 Forensic toxicology

Forensic chemistry and toxicology became part of the remit of the Forensic Medical department in Copenhagen in 1972; until then, these analyses had been performed by the Institute of Pharmacology (Gormsen, 1979). Analyses for alcohol, not least in connection with traffic offenses, have though been made at the Forensic Medical Department since 1922.

Today, forensic chemical (toxicological) analyses are performed at the departments of Forensic Medicine in Copenhagen, Aarhus and Odense. The analyses concern forensic toxicological analyses in connection with autopsies and of living persons in connection with driving under the influence of drugs and narcotics as well as criminal offences. This also includes blood alcohol measurements. The toxicological investigations include screening, identification and quantification of alcohol, drugs, narcotics and technical poisonings. Furthermore, effects/seizures received from the police and the juridical system are investigated for narcotics, drugs and anabolic steroids (University of Copenhagen, 2014; Aarhus University, 2014; University of Southern Denmark, 2014).

7.9 Forensic odontology

Forensic odontology emerged in Denmark as a specialty at the Copenhagen School of Dentistry in 1964 (Severin, 2005). Preceding this, forensic odontological examinations had been performed sporadically, mostly in connection with identification, following Nordic awareness of how odontological identification had been performed in Paris, France, after the fire at the Bazar de la Charité in 1897 (Keiser-Nielsen, 1992). The impetus for organizing the specialty, and ultimately including it as a proper specialty at the School of Dentistry, was no doubt also influenced by an airplane accident in 1947, where 22 people were killed at the Copenhagen Airport, the Swedish Crown Prince being one of the victims (Severin, 2005).

The Copenhagen School of Dentistry is now incorporated in the Faculty of Health Sciences, University of Copenhagen, and in 1993 the section for forensic odontology was transferred to the Department of Forensic Medicine, Section of Forensic Pathology. The remit for the section comprises odontological identification of the deceased and age determination of the living, the latter especially determining the age of asylum seekers, that is, whether an age above or below 18 years may be determined as well as bite mark analyses (Severin, 2005). At the University of Copenhagen, Department of Forensic Medicine, Section of Forensic Pathology, there is a forensic odontologist employed on a permanent basis. Furthermore, there are forensic odontologists associated with the three forensic institutes in Aarhus, Odense and Copenhagen comprising 10–15 active forensic odontologists nationwide (Danish Society for Forensic Science, 2014). These forensic odontologists work as consultants employed on a freelance basis, and may be called upon by the Disaster Victim Identification (DVI) team under the National Police (see below). In addition to the forensic odontologists there are 60–70 dentists (members of the Danish Society for Forensic Odontology, DROF) with sufficient forensic dental skills to be able to assist in forensic dental work (Danish Society for Forensic Science, 2014).

7.10 Forensic anthropology

Forensic anthropology, in the terms of specifically analyzing human skeletal remains, is practiced at all three university institutes. The Unit of Forensic Anthropology at the Department of Forensic Medicine at the University of Copenhagen further performs analyses of surveillance pictures and videos. These analyses may comprise comparison of facial images, gait analyses and photogrammetry. A typical case would be a bank robbery, where the perpetrator has been caught on camera. If the police find a suspect, any likeness between a suspect and the perpetrator can be evaluated (University of Copenhagen, 2014).

The Unit of Forensic Anthropology in Copenhagen also curates a major collection of human skeletal findings from Danish archaeological excavations. The collection includes more than 30,000 items from Danish pre-historical and historical periods ranging from the Mesolithic age (10,000 to 6,000 BCE) to the 17th century. It also holds material from Greenland, the Faroe Islands, Egypt and other cultural areas (University of Copenhagen, 2014). The University of Southern Denmark also curates a major skeletal collection, mostly from the Danish medieval period (Anthropological Database Odense University, 2014). The size of the collections and the extensive archaeological documentation of the materials make them unique in a national and international research perspective.

7.11 Disaster Victim Identification (DVI) team

The National Police has a DVI team consisting of police officers and technicians, forensic pathologists and anthropologists from the Danish universities. The Danish DVI team was activated in connection with the tsunami disaster in South-East Asia in 2004. This was a major task for the team (Schou *et al.*, 2012).

7.12 National forensic societies

The Danish Society for Forensic Odontology has already been mentioned. There is also a Danish Society for Forensic Science, which regularly meets for the exchange of forensic scientific knowledge. The Society also organizes courses, not least with a view for other medical specialties as well as nonmedical participants, for example, police and attorneys (Danish Society for Forensic Medicine, 2014). A key role for the Society is to oversee and regulate the specialty education for forensic pathologists. This is done in close cooperation with the Danish Health and Medicines Authority and the three university institutes.

The Society also participates in a Scandinavian joint effort in publishing the *Scandinavian Journal of Forensic Science*. The journal papers are freely accessible online, and a hard copy journal is published twice yearly (*Scandinavian Journal of Forensic Science*, 2014).

References

Aarhus University (2014) AU.dk, viewed on 10 February 2014, http://forens.au.dk/en/.

Anthropological Database Odense University (2014) adbou.dk, viewed on 10 February 2014, http://www.adbou.dk/.

Brockmann, O. (2009) *Fældende beviser. En kriminaltekniker fortæller*, Gyldendal, Copenhagen, Denmark.

Danish Police (2014) The Danish Police, viewed 10 February 2014, https://www.politi.dk/en/servicemenu/home/.

Danish Society for Forensic Medicine (2014) viewed 10 February 2014, http://www.forensic.dk/?pageid=0801.

Duedahl, P., Wodskou Christensen, P., Bergendorff Høstbo, G. (2013)*Forbrydelsens ansigt*, Gads Forlag, Copenhagen, Denmark.

Gormsen, H. (1979) Retsmedicin, in *Københavns Universitet 1479–1979, Det Lægevidenskabelige Fakultet, bind VII*, Eds. J. Melchior, E. Andreasen, K. Brøchner-Mortensen, A. Gjedde, V. Møller-Christensen, D. Trolle, University of Copenhagen, Copenhagen, Denmark, pp. 479–488.

Hoeck, E. (1951a) Den politimæssige bekæmpelse af forbrydelser i Danmark med træk af krminalpolitiets historie, 1. Del, in *Kampen mod Forbrydelsen, bind I*, Emil Wienes Forlag, Copenhagen, Denmark.

Hoeck, E. (1951b) Den politimæssige bekæmpelse af forbrydelser i Danmark med træk af krminalpolitiets historie, 2. Del, in *Kampen mod Forbrydelsen, bind II*, Emil Wienes Forlag, Copenhagen, Denmark.

James, S.H., Nordby, J.J. (Eds.) (2003) *Forensic Science*, CRC Press, New York.

Justice Department (2014) Justitsministeret.dk, viewed on 10 February 2014, http://www.justitsministeriet.dk/generelt/english.

Keiser-Nielsen, S. (1992) *Teeth that Told*, Odense University Press, Odense, Denmark.

Retsinformation.dk, (2014) *Retsplejeloven*, viewed 10 February 2014, https://www.retsinformation.dk/Forms/R0710.aspx?id=157953.

Scandinavian Journal of Forensic Science (2014) De Gruyter Publishing, viewed on 10 February 2014, http://www.degruyter.com/view/j/sjfs.2013.19.issue-1/issue-files/sjfs.2013.19.issue-1.xml.

Schou, M.P., Knudsen, P.J.T. (2012) The Danish Disaster Victim Identification effort in the Thai Tsunami – organisation and results, *Forensic Sci. Med. Pathol.* 8, 125–130.

Severin, I.P. (2005) *Tandlægeskolen I København 1888–2000 – Liv og Historie*, Munksgaards Forlag, Copenhagen, Denmark.

Tangmose Larsen, S., Lynnerup, N. (2011) Medico-legal autopsies in Denmark, *Danish Medical Bulletin* 58(3): A4247.

Tryde, G. (1939) *Retsmedicinske Erklæringer afgivet af Københavns Universitets medicinske Fakultet i Aarene 1630–1662*, Nyt Nordisk Forlag-Arnold Busck, Copenhagen, Denmark.

University of Copenhagen (2014) KU.dk, viewed 10 February 2014.

University of Southern Denmark (2014) SDU.dk, viewed 10 February 2014, http://www.sdu.dk/en/om_sdu/institutter_centre/ri_retsmedicinsk_institut.

CHAPTER 8

The practice of forensic science in Egypt: a story of pioneering

Dina A. Shokry

Faculty of Medicine, Cairo University, Cairo, Egypt

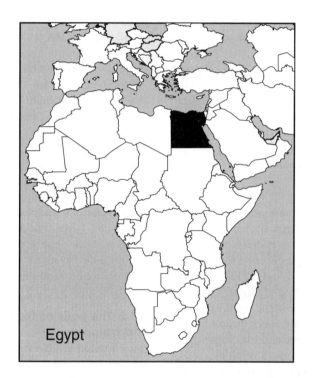

Egypt

The practice of forensic sciences in Egypt is the responsibility of three governmental bodies: the Egyptian Medicolegal Authority (*Ministry of Justice*), the Departments of Forensic Medicine and Toxicology (*Egyptian universities – Ministry of High Education*) and the General Administration for Criminal Evidence Investigations (*Ministry of Interior*) (Figure 8.1).

Throughout this chapter we are going to explore the different aspects of forensic science practice via throwing light on the practice in each of these justice bodies.

8.1 Departments of Forensic Medicine and Toxicology and Egyptian universities – Ministry of High Education

8.1.1 Historical background

The origin of forensic medicine is hidden in the mists of antiquity, dating from the beginnings of family and tribal life. Recorded human history goes back for 6000 years. The ancient Egyptians were the first to apply forensic practice – as it is known now – to call experts

The Global Practice of Forensic Science, First Edition. Edited by Douglas H. Ubelaker.
© 2015 John Wiley & Sons, Ltd. Published 2015 by John Wiley & Sons, Ltd.

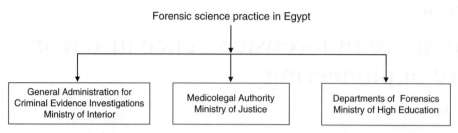

Figure 8.1 Forensic science practice in Egypt.

to question them and to do autopsies on corpses. The history of autopsy is intimately related to medicine and anatomy. According to the Egyptian historian Manetho, the king-physician Athotis (BC 4000) wrote books on medicine, the first of which contained some anatomic descriptions (King and Meehan, 1973).

The Egyptian Imhotep (BC 2667–2648) was probably the first real medicolegal expert. He combined in his person the offices of Chief Justice and of physician to Pharaoh Zoser, much like some of the English coroners with dual qualifications in law and medicine (Deadman, 1965).

In ancient Egypt, the acts of the medical man were circumscribed by law. Stab wounds were differentiated in the 17th century BC. The Egyptians had a thorough knowledge of poisons. There is evidence that priests made determinations regarding the cause of death and whether it was natural or not (Oliver, 1932).

In modern times, a committee of foreign doctors in 1820 was invited to initiate teaching medicine at the School of Medicine in Abu Zaabl, which included teaching forensic medicine in its curricula. By the time of Khedive Ismail Dr. Ibrahim Hassan was advised to travel to Germany to be trained in forensic medicine at the University of Berlin after returning from his medical studies in France in 1862.

In 1870, Dr. Ibrahim Hassan started teaching forensic medicine as a separate subject at the school of medicine. His followers were Professor Dr. Colin and Professor Dr. Hamilton. In 1928, The School of Medicine became the Faculty of Medicine and Professor Dr. Sidney Smith was the first Chairman of the Department of Forensic Medicine that served both academic and field work. The establishment of the Museum of Forensic Medicine at Cairo University was done by that time, which is so far one of the greatest museums of forensic medicine in the world, having more than a thousand life specimens with different injuries and causes of death. Professor Dr. Glaister followed him until 1932, the date when

separation between the academic and field forensic practice took place. Then, Professor Dr. Mohamed Omara came to the position to be the first Egyptian to chair the department of forensic medicine at Cairo University (Ramzy, 1992).

Nowadays, there are 17 public schools of medicine (Kasr El-Aini, Alexandria, Ain Shams, Al-Azhar University – for males and females, Al-Fayum, Al-Minya, Assiut, Banha, Bani Suwayf, Sohag, Mansoura, Minufiya, South Valley, Suez Canal, Tanta and Zagazig Universities) and two private schools of medicine (Misr University of Sciences and Technology (MUST) and 6th of October University), each with a department of forensic medicine and toxicology (Supreme Council of Universities–Egypt, www.scu.eun.eg/).

The academic departments of Forensic Medicine and Science at the Egyptian Universities encompass two disciplines, forensic medicine and toxicology.

8.1.2 The policies for recruitment and training

Demonstrators in different departments in Egyptian universities are recruited from the medical graduates who apply for the job and following the best ranking among applicants. Through Master (MSc) and Medical Doctorate (MD) postgraduate studies, the candidate should fulfill training requirements stated in the postgraduate university curriculum (clinical forensic medicine, forensic pathology and forensic sciences).

8.1.3 Manpower

There are hundreds of staff members in these departments; full professors, assistant professors, lecturers, assistant lecturers and demonstrators.

After the doctorate degree the assistant lecturer becomes a lecturer. To be promoted to the next Chair, the staff member should pass the supreme forensic council discussion for the researches and scientific activities proposed by him. The candidate cannot be proposed to the next Chair before a lapsed period of five years.

8.1.4 Responsibilities

1. *Teaching.* Staff members in the departments of forensic medicine and toxicology in Egyptian universities are responsible for the academic teaching of undergraduate and postgraduate students. Forensic sciences and toxicology are core curriculum subjects in the Egyptian medical education for 4th year undergraduate medical students (clinical phase) who should pass written, practical and oral exams. The syllabus includes topics in forensic medicine, forensic and clinical toxicology and medical ethics and laws. Postgraduate degrees of forensic medicine and toxicology (Diploma, Master and Doctorate degrees) are also granted by various universities.
2. *Research.* Research projects are in accordance with the strategic plan for each university. Personal academic research initiatives are also part of university academic activities.
3. *Training workshops, seminars and conferences* are also among university activities.
4. *Consultation in forensic cases* after a court mandate to write down medicolegal reports. These reports should be approved by three or five professors according to the court mandate. Egyptian universities receive about 2000–3000 cases annually.
5. *Consultation on personal basis* for the cases that asked for medicolegal reports in different forensic issues.
6. *Laboratory analyses.* Chemical and analytical analyses are made for samples from individuals and agencies for screening of drugs of abuse and different toxicological screening. DNA typing in paternity testing is also accomplished in some forensic departments.
7. *Clinical toxicology practice in poisoning control centers.* The majority of forensic departments at Egyptian universities have a clinical toxicology unit that deals with cases of acute poisoning.

8.2 The Egyptian Medicolegal Authority – Ministry of Justice

The Egyptian Medicolegal Authority has a pivotal role that contributes significantly to the achievement of justice and unraveling of the mysteries of many crimes.

8.2.1 Historical background

This dates back to the date of initiation of the Ministry of Justice. In the early days, the authority was run by a physician who was appointed as a part time worker in forensic cases by the Ministry of Health. Starting from 1890, the forensic practice was the responsibility of physicians commissioned from the Ministry of Health and by that time the emergence of forensic interest had been launched.

On the first of June 1890, Dr. Hassan Pasha Refky was commissioned from the Ministry of Health to the Ministry of Justice (or Alhakania by this time) to be the first forensic expert in the history of the Medicolegal authority. His office was in the Court of Appeals building and only serious cases were referred to him.

In September 1897, Dr. Nolon was appointed as the first forensic physician. His office was in the Ministry of Justice but he was transferred to the public prosecutor building in January 1902.

In April 1906, Dr. Thomas Hamilton was appointed as the assistant of Dr. Nolon, who transferred later in April 1909 to the Ministry of the Interior. Dr. Mahmoud Maher was appointed as the assistant of Dr. Thomas Hamilton in July 1909.

Dr. Sidney Smith was upgraded to be the Chief Medical Examiner in January 1928 and Dr. Mahmoud Maher became the senior forensic physician. On November 24, 1928, His Excellency Ahmed Pasha khashba, Minister of Justice, issued the first Bylaws of the Medicolegal authority in Egypt (Ramzy, 1992).

Now there are a large number of forensic science experts working in branches covering most of the Egyptian governorates (Figure 8.2).

8.2.2 Forensic field work

This deals with both autopsy and clinical forensic practice. The departments cover 19 governorates out of 28 all over the country. The head office and central mortuary are in Cairo – the capital city – at the Zenhom area. There are forensic medicine areas in most provinces (Cairo, Alexandria, Beheira, Menoufia Qaliubiya, Zagazig, Ismailia, Beni Suef, Fayoum, Qena, Aswan and Sohag–Port Said–Kafr El Sheikh–Mansoura) and the provinces that do not have a legitimate medical area are covered by the closest region (as in the case of Damietta covered by Mansoura).

The photography and photocopy unit covers photographing of living cases and corpses as well.

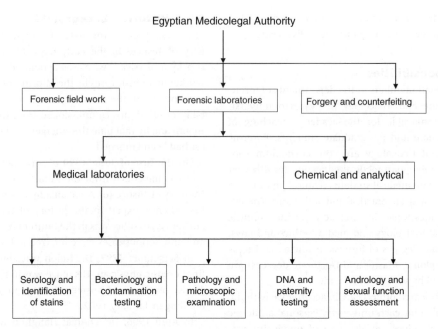

Figure 8.2 Departments and administrative units.

Photocopying of the documents and reports are also part of its work.

In the forensic imaging unit X-rays were used for cases of injuries including firearm injuries. A comparison microscope for examination of the weapons is also part of the department.

8.2.2.1 Manpower

The total number of forensic experts are 160. The number of working forensic experts covering the whole provinces of Egypt are 90 physicians and specialists, 15 of whom work in the head office in Cairo. There are 70 experts working in different Arab countries.

8.2.2.2 Responsibilities

Their responsibilities are to issue medicolegal reports for the referred cases from prosecutors and courts.

Living cases include different types of injuries with an estimation of disabilities, suspected criminal abortion, suspected rape and sexual offences, attempted homicide and suicide, malpractice and medical responsibility, suspected impotence and sexual dysfunction, and workplace accidents and an estimation of disabilities.

External examination and autopsy for suspected cases of homicide or suicide are among the forensic expert's workload.

Crime scene investigation is done in a very limited number of cases in which examination of the scene by the forensic expert is necessary for the report. This cannot be offered in every case as there is a limited number of forensic physicians.

8.2.2.3 Workload and number of cases

During 2013 the number of autopsied cases in Cairo were 3141, while the clinical cases accounted for 5252.

8.2.2.4 Recruitment and training

The new forensic physicians are recruited after been selected via a newspaper announcement and passing the interview. The training program takes place for six months before each trainee can begin his/her professional career.

8.2.2.5 Consultants and consultancy

Consultants from different medical specialties (surgery, orthopedics, radiology, psychiatry, urology, neurosurgery, anesthesia, cardiology and cardiac surgery) give their scientific opinion to the forensic expert if needed, especially in malpractice cases. The consultant's opinion is then included in the final medicolegal reports.

8.2.3 Forensic laboratories

Forensic laboratories are part of the forensic practice. The Medicolegal Authority includes two main laboratories:

1. Medical laboratories. These specialized laboratories are only located at the headquarters in Cairo. They are further subdivided into five specialized laboratories:

   • Serology laboratory, which is responsible for grouping of biological fluid samples (blood, semen and saliva) taken from cases or extracted from the scene of the crime. The manpower of the Laboratory is 35 physicians and the total cases received during 2012 were 1941.

   • DNA laboratory, which deals with cases of paternity testing and personal identification via examination and analyses of blood, blood stains, semen, nails and bones. There are 11 specialized physicians working in this laboratory, who aremedical graduates who receive hands-on training and specialty degrees; 2774 cases were displayed during 2012. Samples from unidentified dead bodies have been examined and the results were stored for future matching.

   • Forensic pathology laboratory, where the tissue samples from the autopsied bodies have been processed and examined. Classic H&E staining and examination via an electric microscope are the routine approach for these cases, where 13 medical pathology specialists are the manpower of the unit and have accomplished 729 cases during the year 2012.

   • Andrology laboratory, which is a specialized laboratory that deals with cases of suspected impotence and sexual dysfunction. They are concerned with routine laboratory testing (blood sugar, CBC, liver and kidney function tests, etc.), semen analysis and tests to assess sexual functions. There are five physicians, who received and accomplished 372 cases during the year 2012. As for the assessment of sexual function, cases of suspected impotence are referred to an andrology consultant.

   • Bacteriology laboratory. The responsibility of this laboratory is to analyze samples taken from cases and utensils in suspected cases of bacteriological contamination. The laboratory received 24 cases during the year 2012.

2. Chemical and analytical laboratory. The administrative structure of the Egyptian Medicolegal Authority includes six chemical and analytical laboratories covering all provinces in Egypt (Alexandria, Ismailia, Assuit, Mansoura, Algharbia and Banisuef governorates), with the central laboratory in Cairo.The number of experts is 86, who graduated from schools of sciences and pharmacy. Chemical analyses of biological samples for screening of different poisons and drugs of abuse are the main duty of this laboratory. The total number of cases displayed from January through December 2012 were 7297.Analyses are done using chemical and instrumental techniques.

8.2.4 Counterfeiting and forgery department

8.2.4.1 Terms of reference

This department specializes in forgery scans of all types of currencies, official and customary documents that are needed for justice. These cases should be referred from the prosecutors or the court.

8.2.4.2 Types of referred cases

1. Criminal cases: those cases concerning the rights of the state.
2. Civil cases: those mainly based on the presence of a prosecutor of civil rights.

8.2.4.3 Tasks

1. Comparing handwritings.
2. Examination and comparison of signatures.
3. Checking the fingerprints of government and personal seals.
4. Examinations of documents for total or partial forgery.
5. Examination of all types of local currencies and the global ones (whether coins, paper or plastic and electronic cards).
6. Checking all types of passports and visas, and travel permits local and global.
7. Checking weapons and car chassis.
8. Identification of cases of writing under different pathological situations and under the influence of coercion, alcohol or drugs, etc.
9. Dating of the document writing.

10. Restoration and reappearance of writings that have been erased automatically or chemically.
11. Examination of electrostatic copying machines (regular and colored).
12. Examination of computers and their accessories, like scanners and printers, searching for physical evidence – if any.
13. Examination of printing machines, both traditional and updated ones, searching for physical evidence – if any.
14. Examination of documents for sorting their chronological order and to identify the relation between the core of the document and signatures.
15. Linking the output of the printing devices and the questioned documents.
16. Examination of suicide letters and writings in terminal diseases and imminent deaths.
17. Revisualization of the scripts written with volatile and vanishing inks.

8.2.4.4 Sections

1. The central administration: located at the Medicolegal building, which investigates cases referred from Cairo governorate.
2. Public administration: located at the Ministry of Justice building and investigates the cases referred from the provinces of Giza, Fayoum and Beni Suef.
3. Department of Alexandria.
4. Department of Tanta.
5. Department of Assiut.
6. Department of Qena.
7. Department Kaliobeya.
8. Department of Ismailia.
9. Department of Port Said.
10. Department of Mansoura.

8.2.5 Manpower and number of forgery and counterfeiting experts

The total number of experts working in the department of counterfeiting and forgery is 262. The majority of them are graduates from schools of the sciences and pharmacy. Some of the qualified experts share in the training courses for bank workers and prosecutors.

The total number of cases displayed during the year 2012 was 29,931.

8.3 General administration for criminal evidence investigations – the Ministry of the Interior

The department of personal identification in the Ministry of the Interior was established in 1898, and since then there has been an increasing contribution of police in the justice achievement.

The general administration for criminal evidence investigations – theMinistry of the Interior (Figure 8.3) – has two main agencies.

8.3.1 Fingerprints agency

This agency was established in 1957 for registration of fingerprints of the Egyptian population and later on computers replaced the manual registration. It is now fully digitalized and the database includes almost all Egyptians.

8.3.2 Criminal laboratories agency

This agency includes the following administrative departments:

1. The Crime Scene Investigation Department is responsible for the documentation and photography of the scene. The crime scene investigators have the responsibility of protecting crime scenes, preserving the physical evidence and collecting and submitting the evidence for scientific examination. The evidence includes fingerprints, suspected stains, fibers, hairs, clothes, weapons, etc.
2. The Counterfeiting and Forgery Department has the role of investigating the suspected documents and currency. The unit of voice print analyses and acoustic analyses, which involves tape filtering and enhancement, tape authentication, gunshot acoustics, reconstruction of conversations and the analysis of any other questioned acoustic event, is also a part of this department.
3. The Crime Scene Photography Department is responsible for taking photos and making video tapes from the crime scene. The photos and videos are used to produce an accurate reproduction of crime or accident scenes to be used in court and/or an investigation. It is part of the process of evidence collection. It provides investigators with photos of victims, places and items involved in the crime. The duties of

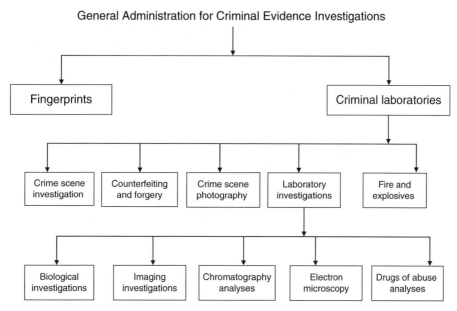

Figure 8.3 The general administration for criminal evidence investigations.

this department extend to cover face recognition and matching via manual sketching or digital reproductions together with facial reconstruction and personal identification.

4. The Fire and Explosive Investigation Department has the major role of sponsoring and fostering the collection and analysis of fire and explosion debris.
5. The Laboratory Investigations Department is further subdivided into five units:
   a. The biological investigations unit, whose duties include analysis of the biological samples of blood, saliva and semen tissues and matching these with the suspects or the putative and biological fathers in cases of paternity testing.
   b. The imaging investigations unit.
   c. The chromatography unit.
   d. The electron microscopy unit.
   e. The drugs of abuse analyses unit.

Most of the human power working in these laboratories and departments are officers with a science background and qualifications.

The administrative structure of the General Administration for Criminal Evidence investigations is divided into a central administration covering Cairo, Giza and Qualyobia governorates and five local administrations in the West Delta Region, Suez Canal and Sinai Region in Ismailia city, Middle Delta Region in Tanta city, northern upper Egypt in Assiut city and southern upper Egypt in Qena city.

It is not possible to miss the overlap between duties of the forensic laboratories affiliated to the Ministry of Justice and those of the Ministry of the Interior. The prosecutors or the court are the ones who mandate the work for any of them.

8.4 Funding policy

All the bodies included in the justice system were mostly funded by the Government of Egypt through a balance of payments method. The Medicolegal Authority is funded by the Ministry of Justice, medical schools by the Ministry of High Education and crime scene investigation laboratories by the Ministry of the Interior.

8.5 Political influences

Egypt offered humanity the oldest political system in the world. On the banks of the River Nile the first unified central government in history was established, so politics is always a crucial part of people's lives.

All workers in the field of forensic science in Egypt believe that independency is the cornerstone in the achievement of justice.

Political turbulence adds a burden to the forensic practice workload due to the increasing number of cases that necessitate the development of a concrete strategic plan for management crises.

8.6 Future steps for development of the forensic science sector

The regulatory status of forensic science practice in the Arab Republic of Egypt differed over time. It was run by the Head of the Department of Forensic Medicine – Cairo University, who is also the chief medical examiner, that is, he chaired both the academic and field work of forensics. This administrative system was applied until the year 1932 when the administrative separation between academic and field work took place. Bernard Knight described the separation of those who practice forensic pathology from those who profess to teach it in universities as a serious defect (Knight, 1996).

The core recommendation for development is to establish an integrated cooperation between scientific and academic work, which is the primary objective of the departments of forensic medicine in different Egyptian universities and the fieldwork that is the responsibility of the Egyptian Medicolegal Authority. This kind of cooperation may be accomplished in many ways. The forensic staff members of different universities should take part in the clinical forensic practice by being responsible for the documentation and medicolegal handling of trauma victims referred to different university hospitals to compensate for the limited number of forensic examiners in the Ministry of justice. The forensic staff will cover clinical work 24/7 (24 hours a day for 7 days a week), which will offer better preservation of biological evidence, especially in cases of sexual assaults, where victims often present to medicolegal authority some days after the assault due to its limited working hours.

The other way of integration is to develop unified training programs for the forensic sciences practitioners from universities and the Ministry of Justice. These training programs will be structured by the supreme forensic council of both parties.

Other points of concern in the process of development in the field of forensic practice in Egypt are:

- The development of training programs, logistics and equipment, especially in the light of rapid and successive progress in forensic sciences, is considered as a basic need for upgrading the Egyptian forensic science practice.
- Introduction of different forensic subspecialties, i.e. forensic anthropology, archeology, dentistry, imaging, psychiatry, etc. This step will allow specialized forensic examiners to be part of the justice system in Egypt and will offer better management of forensic cases.
- Implementation and restructuring of the crises management strategies is mandatory to cope with crises and disasters. This should be accomplished via a distinctive body dedicated to this purpose.
- To ensure the continued outstanding performance we must develop strategies for auditing and internal control to seek for international accreditation of forensic laboratories and forensic practice.

Egyptian civilization was the first great civilization on this planet and the first forensic practice evolved in its land. Egyptian forensic science practitioners have great potential to proceed in the process of development for better enforcement of justice and regaining the leadership.

I leave you with the wise words of Aristotle (Greek philosopher BC 384–322):

> We are what we repeatedly do, therefore excellence is not an act, but a habit (Durant, 1926).

Acknowledgements

The author is deeply indebted to Dr. Hisham A. Farag, the Director of Zenhom Mortuary, for the information he gave to me about the administrative structure and flow of cases to the Egyptian Medicolegal Authority, Ministry of Justice, Egypt. The sources of the administrative structure and statistics of the received cases were the paper archiving systems in each organization.

References

Deadman, J.W. (1965) Forensic medicine: an aid to criminal investigation. *Can. Med. Assoc. J. 27*; 92(13): 666–670.

Durant, W. (1926) *The Story of Philosophy. The Lives and Opinions of the World's Greatest Philosophers*, Simon and Schuster, New York, pp. 76.

Gradwohl, R.B.H. (1954) The history and development, in *Legal Medicine*, Ed. R.B.H. Gradwohl, St. Louis, USA, pp. 3.

Imhotep sculpture: the Egyptian Museum, Berlin in Encyclopedia *Britannica*. http://www.britannica.com/EBchecked/topic/283435/Imhotep.

King, L.S. and Meehan, L.C. (1973) A history of autopsy, a review. *Am. J. Pathol.* 73: 514–544.

Knight, B. (1996) Forensic autopsy, in *Forensic Pathology*, Ed. B. Knight, Hodder Arnold Publishers, London, pp. 2.

Oliver, J.R. (1932) Legal medicine in Europe and America. *A.B.A.J.* 18: 405–411.

Ramzy, A.M. (1992) The history of forensic medicine, in *Forensic Medicine Between Prosecution and Defense*, Eds. A.M. Ramzy *et al.*, Lawyer's Library Publisher, Cairo, Egypt, pp. 58–61.

Supreme Council of Universities – Egypt (http://www.scu.eun.eg).

CHAPTER 9

The practice of forensic science in Estonia

Marika Väli[1,2], Üllar Lanno[2] & Ivar Prits[2]

[1] Department of Pathological Anatomy and Forensic Medicine of the University of Tartu, Estonia
[2] Estonian Forensic Science Institute, Tallinn, Estonia

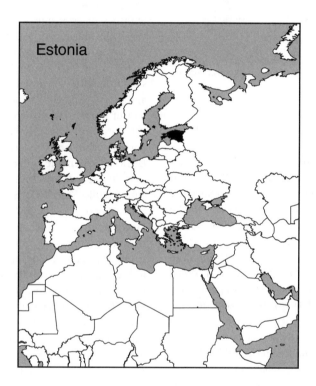

9.1 Introduction

The Estonian Forensic Science Institute (EFSI) is a State Agency established on 1 January 2008 and governed by the Ministry of Justice (Figure 9.1).

The principal objectives of the Institute are the provision of forensic science expertise in criminal cases according to the competence, the development of the fields of forensic science, the forensic training of police agencies and consultation on matters related to the duties of the Institute, and the administration of national databases and registers. The Institute comprised at that time its Forensic Science Departments, the DNA Department, the Document Department, the IT Department, the Chemistry Department, the Fingerprint Department, the Crime Scene Department, the Traffic Department, the Technical Department, the Forensic Science Division of the Security Police, the Forensic Psychiatry Division, the Economy Division, the Administration Division, the Quality Division and the Personnel Division. The Institute is not continuing the activities of the Crime Scene Department and the Forensic Science

The Global Practice of Forensic Science, First Edition. Edited by Douglas H. Ubelaker.
© 2015 John Wiley & Sons, Ltd. Published 2015 by John Wiley & Sons, Ltd.

Figure 9.1 Map of Estonia. *Source:* Estonian Forensic Science Institute archives.

Division of the Security Police as both were transferred to the initial bodies.

The Quality Management System was based on two internationally recognized standards: EVS-EN ISO/IEC 17025:2006, General requirements for the competence of testing and calibration laboratories (ISO/IEC 17025:2005) and EVS-EN ISO 9001:2008, Standard for Quality Management Systems (ISO 9001:2008). Also, the Quality Management System was expanded with the third standard, EVS-EN ISO/IEC 17020:2006, General criteria for the operation of various types of bodies performing inspection (ISO/IEC 17020:1998). In its activities, the Institute follows the principles of the European Network of Forensic Science Institutes (ENFSI): to be impartial, to operate on a high professional and technical level, to be cost-effective, to guarantee the reliability of its expertise results and to be acknowledged at the national and international levels in its activities. The EFSI has been an ENFSI member since 1998.

9.2 History

The first mentioned activity in Estonia was the Cabinet of Forensic Science (CFS) (Figure 9.2) at the Court Prosecutor's Office, established on 5 August 1921. The founder of the CFS, chemist Professor Karl Schneider, was invited from Riga, Latvia.

The Cabinet reorganization started in 1938. The Forensic Science Institute (FSI), as the first forensic service institution, officially started its activities after the release of the *Declaration of the Code of Courts* on 6 April 1938. The FSI was mainly serving at that time the Prosecutor's preparations for court proceedings. Professor Feliks Wittlich was nominated to the position of Director.

The activities of the FSI were randomly stopped during World War II.

Starting in 1944, the Soviet Union annexed the Baltic States as the Estonian, Latvian and Lithuanian SSRs. The judiciary was not independent from other branches of government. The Supreme Court supervised the lower courts (People's Court) and applied the law as established by the Constitution or as interpreted by the Supreme Soviet. The Constitutional Oversight Committee reviewed the constitutionality of laws and acts. The Soviet Union used the inquisitorial system of Roman law, where the judge, procurator and defence attorney work together to establish the truth. Forensic examinations were carried out throughout the USSR in systematic order where the "Militia" (Russian "Police") Crime Investigation Laboratory, Prosecutor's Office Technical Examination Laboratory and University of Tartu Legal Medical Unit operated simultaneously side-by-side. At the end of 1944, the position of the chief expert of legal medicine was created. In the 1950s and 1960s, implementation of legal medical examinations was complicated and to support the demand autopsies were performed by the doctors of other specialities, which resulted in a number of exhumations. In the Soviet era the continuous training of Estonian forensic pathologists took place in Russia (mostly in Leningrad, the present name of which is St. Petersburg). Forensic psychiatry examinations were carried out in hospital psychiatry clinics by regular doctors.

Estonia regained its independence from the USSR on 20 August 1991. After this, Estonia needed to deal with the consequences of almost 50 years of Soviet totalitarian rule, while taking measures for the rapid and efficient integration into the European economic area. Estonian reforms were aimed at lustration, the economy, and the law enforcement and judicial systems.

In 1993 the first reform in the Forensic field started when the Police Crime Investigation Laboratory and Prosecutor's Office Technical Examination Laboratory were merged into a united structural unit in the National Police Board. The name of this new organization was the

Figure 9.2 Cabinet of Forensic Science, 1921. *Source:* Estonian Forensic Science Institute archives.

Forensic Service Centre. At the same time, in 1993, the institution in charge of forensic medical expert analyses was renamed the Estonian Bureau of Forensic Medicine (EBFM). Furthermore, in 2002, the EBFM was removed from the jurisdiction of the Ministry of Social Affairs and was moved under the jurisdiction of the Ministry of Justice.

The second major merging reform of the two main agencies – the Estonian Bureau of Forensic Medicine under the Ministry of Justice and the Forensic Service Centre under the government of the Ministry of the Interior – started in spring 2006. Introduction of the new initiative was made at a regular ministers' meeting in March.

In June 2006, the Ministers of Justice and Interior agreed to merge the agencies into one governmental authority under the area of government of the Ministry of Justice. In October 2006, the merging of the Estonian Bureau of Forensic Medicine and the Forensic Service

Centre was approved at the sitting of the Government of the Republic.

In February 2007, a decision was made to merge the agencies on 1 January 2008 (both to minimize the personnel risks arising from prolonging the merging and to start with the levelling of the forensic examination system). In June 2007 the amended *Forensic Examination Act* was adopted in the Estonian Parliament, or *Riigikogu*. In the same period the Government decided that the activities of the Forensic Service Centre would be terminated and its tasks, rights, obligations, public property and records management would be transferred to the Estonian Bureau of Forensic Medicine from 1 January 2008. In August 2007, a decision was made at the sitting of the Government of the Republic to establish a liquidation committee for the Forensic Service Centre and ministers were assigned the task of organizing the amendment of legislation in view of the merging. In December 2007, the amendment of the legislation

Figure 9.3 EFSI Headquarters Tervise 30 TALLINN. *Source:* Estonian Forensic Science Institute archives.

necessary for the merging was decided at the sitting of the Government of the Republic and in 14 December 2007, the Minister of Justice signed the statutes of the merged agency.

The re-established Estonian Forensic Science Institute started its activities on 1 January 2008 with a united, 185 strong staff (Figure 9.3).

9.3 Types of cases

Every year about 1800 forensic psychiatric, 2500 forensic medical, 4600 forensic criminalistic and 6400 forensic toxicological examinations are performed in the EFSI (Figure 9.4).

9.4 Structure

The Estonian Forensic Science Institute is administered by the Ministry of Justice, Criminal Policy Department. The Institute is governed by a five-member Supervisory Board that directs its operations on the basis of the views submitted to it by agencies on matters of forensic science. The Board is led by the Deputy Secretary General of the Ministry of the Interior and consists of the Deputy Secretary General of the Ministry of Justice, Prosecutor General of the State Prosecutor's Office and a Judge from the Criminal Chamber of the Supreme Court. Council meetings are 4 times per year.

The Institute is guided in its operations by its statutes and other legal acts that apply at the national level.

The structural units of the Institute are its departments and divisions. Divisions may form parts of departments. The Institute comprises its Forensic Science Departments, the DNA Department, the Document Department, the IT Department, the Chemistry Department, the Fingerprint Department, the Vehicle and Road Accident Investigation Department, the Technical Department, the four Forensic Medical Departments, the Forensic Psychiatry Division, the Economy Division, the Administration Division, the Quality Division and the Division of Human Resources and Development and Management Board (Figure 9.5).

Regional forensic science departments are located in four regions; northern, southern, western and eastern.

The main functions of structural units in their working areas are set out in the Statutes of the Institute. More detailed tasks for each unit are set out in the statutes of individual units, as approved by the director. The structure of the Institute is enacted in accordance with Annex 1 to the regulation of the Minister of Justice produced on the basis of § 43 (5) of the *Government of the Republic Act* and § 301 (1) and (2) of the *Forensic Examination Act*.

The EFSI today has 176 employees including 87 forensic examiners. The staff of the Institute consists of forensic criminalistics examiners, forensic pathologists, forensic psychiatrists, forensic psychologists and specialists. The EFSI's scope is currently over 40 different examination areas. The final updated list of EFSI examinations and tests is published in the *Forensic Examination Act*, along with relevant price categories.

In accordance with the statutes, the Institute has in its structure a Research and Development Committee (RDC). The RDC consists of employees and specialists who meet four times a year and advise the management on the directions the Institute should be taking in terms of new methods and technology to adopt. The active chairman of the RDC is the Deputy Director of Development and the vice chairman is the Quality Manager. Both are selected by RDC members. The committee makes decisions by voting. There are 20 councillors participating in the committee, including the representative from the Ministry of Justice.

The EFSI's task is to administer the nationally approved List of Officially Certified Experts, which includes 60 experts in 12 areas of science. The purpose of the list is to provide courts with a qualified selection of experts who can be appointed in order to expand the scope of

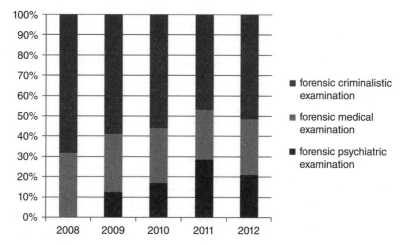

Figure 9.4 Forensic examinations in 2008–2012. *Source:* Estonian Forensic Science Institute archives.

the Institute's activities. The list is officially located on the Institute's website.

9.5 Estonian Forensic Science Institute Departments

The DNA Department conducts DNA analysis and testing. The object of testing is human DNA. Analyses with the objective of comparing the DNA profile obtained from the scene of an event or accident with the DNA profile of a person provide the biggest work volume. The DNA Department also conducts relationship analyses with the objective of identifying a person or determining filiation. DNA analyses for establishing paternal filiation may also be ordered from the DNA Department by private persons outside criminal or civil proceedings. The DNA Department of the EFSI is an authorized processor of the National DNA Database. The Database contains over ten thousand profiles obtained from scenes of events or accidents that have not yet been related to a person and 34,000 DNA profiles of persons.

In the Document Department, data media of paper or plastic, such as identity documents, vehicle documents, cash, contracts, wills, invoices, applications, diplomas, certificates, etc., are analysed and technical comparative analyses are conducted with regard thereto.

Handwriting analysis is a classical forensic science analysis field with the main goal of determining the writer. The long-term work experience of the experts is

essential as merely a magnifying glass and a microscope are used as the main technical means for the comparative analysis of handwriting features. Document analysis examines printed products (passports, drivers' licences, cash, contracts, etc.) in order to provide an opinion concerning the authenticity of such documents or their manner of production.

It is possible to implement both microscopic and spectral methods upon the conduct of document analyses and document materials can be analysed in cooperation with the Chemistry Department (see below). Identifying euro banknote forgeries, collecting the technical data related thereto and exchanging information with other competent authorities are among the tasks of document experts. The objective of accounting analysis is to help the body conducting proceedings resolve complex economic criminal offences. Depending on the criminal offence, the organization of the accounting and reporting of the accounting entity, falsification of accounting data or presentation of incorrect data, causing material damage and the extent thereof, accuracy of audit conclusions and other circumstances that are essential as evidence is analysed. In 2009, a new video spectral comparator (Foster + Freeman VSC6000) was acquired. In 2010, the equipment was modernized with a stereomicroscope (Leica Stereo ZOOM Fluorescence Microscope) (Figure 9.6).

The IT Department conducts keyword, correspondence, document and file searches as requested by the body conducting proceedings from computers serving

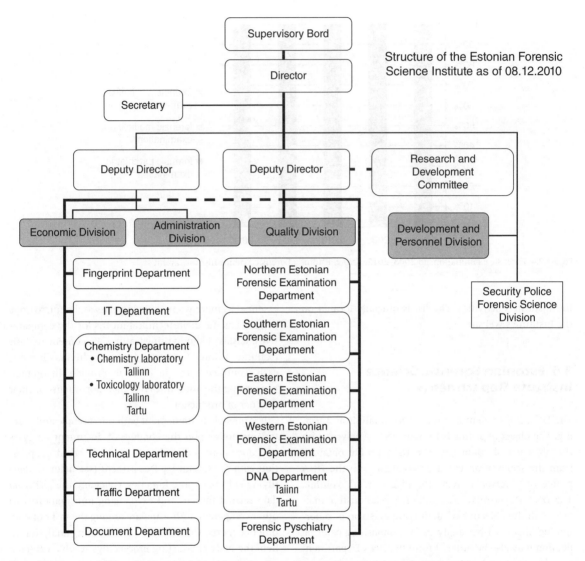

Figure 9.5 Structure of Estonian Forensic Science Institute. *Source:* Estonian Forensic Science Institute archives.

as the objects of the analysis and the data media related thereto (hard disk drives, CDs/DVDs, floppy disks, memory sticks and memory cards).

It is also possible to analyse other digital or electronic devices that may contain data that are essential for proceedings. The most commonly analysed data media are hard disk drives from PCs and laptops, but also from various special purpose devices (computers) such as video security recording devices, DVD recorders with hard disk drives, video game consoles, etc. The Department is always prepared to assist the body conducting

proceedings by conducting image analysis in issues related to video recordings or digital images (converting video recordings in various formats, processing and quality improvement, resolving issues related to playing video recordings, frame extraction, responding to questions related to digital images, image and video file search from data media and devices in relation to the proceedings).

Voice analysis includes analysing the authenticity of recordings, improving the quality of recordings, that is removing background noise, telephone interference,

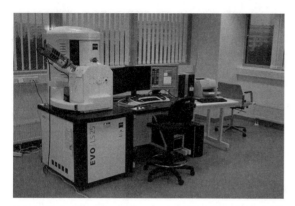

Figure 9.6 Scanning electron microscope. *Source:* Estonian Forensic Science Institute archives.

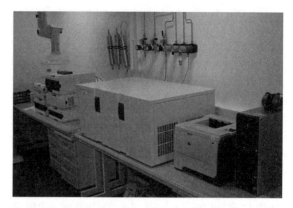

Figure 9.8 Liquid chromatographmass spectrometer Agilent 6410. *Source:* Estonian Forensic Science Institute archives.

radio interference, slow-playing music, street noise, etc., in order for the speech on the recording to be as user-friendly and comprehensible as possible. It also deals with transcription, that is writing down the text of the recording and identifying the speaker (Figure 9.7).

The Chemistry Department conducts expert assessments and analyses pertaining to narcotic substances, toxicology and residues of coats of paint, fibres, explosives, metals and gunshot. The regional Chemistry Department is located in Tartu, where toxicology expert assessments and analyses are conducted. The majority of the work volume comprises toxicology and narcotic substance expert assessments and analyses and most of the methods used for determining narcotic substances and toxicology are accredited. Gunshot residue and

Figure 9.7 Voice analyses. *Source:* Estonian Forensic Science Institute archives.

element analysis electron microscopic methods are also accredited.

The thoroughly amended legislation concerning the identification of intoxication entered into force on 1 July 2009, centralizing all analyses pertaining to the identification of intoxication in the country in the Chemistry Department of the EFSI.

In 2010, the Chemistry Department acquired two chromatographs, the ion chromatograph Dionex ICS-1600 and the liquid chromatograph/mass spectrometer Agilent 6410 (Figure 9.8).

The Department has a gas chromatograph/mass spectrometer Agilent 7890/5975 for conducting narcotic substance and toxicology analyses, a gas chromatograph/mass spectrometer Agilent 7890/5975 with a pyrolysis device for conducting combustible liquid and coat of paint analyses and a gas chromatograph Agilent 7890 for determining the percentage of narcotic substances.

Forensic Medical Departments are located in four regions in Estonia: in Tallinn for Northern Estonia, in Tartu for Southern Estonia, in Pärnu for Western Estonia and in Kohtla-Järve for Eastern Estonia.

All Departments conduct forensic medical examinations on living persons and dead bodies, including forensic radiology and medical criminology expert assessments and analyses in Tallinn and medical toxicology expert assessments and analyses in Tartu. Forensic medical examinations are conducted on living persons in order to assess health damage (injuries), verify offences against a person's state of health or sexual self-determination or resolve any other medical issues that law enforcement authorities encounter. Forensic medical examinations are conducted on dead bodies when the elements or a suspicion of a criminal offence become apparent; a forensic autopsy of a dead body is prescribed if the impact of a factor arising from the external environment is involved (e.g. hanging, drowning, traffic accidents, etc.).

Medical toxicology analyses are conducted in order to assess the impact of toxic substances on the basis of examination rulings of pre-trial investigation authorities or courts. Medical criminology expert assessments are prescribed in order to verify the cause or mechanism of death on the basis of a skeleton or a part of skeleton.

As of 2010, it is also possible to order analyses that are not related to proceedings from the Forensic Medical Departments in order to assess injuries.

As of October 2010, a three-dinemsional technology for digital autopsies and digital examinations of injured persons was implemented. A CT scanner (Siemens Somatom Emotion 6) (Figure 9.9) and an MRI scanner (Siemens 1.5T Magnetom Avanto) were installed in the new rooms in Tallinn.

As of 2009, the Institute organizes forensic psychiatry, psychology and sexology expert assessments in the Forensic Psychiatry and Psychology Department. The expert assessments cannot be conducted by means of a privately ordered paid service; they are instead prescribed by a body conducting proceedings on the basis of legislation and within the framework of a certain court case or proceedings. On average, 1500–1600 expert assessments are conducted per year, of which the

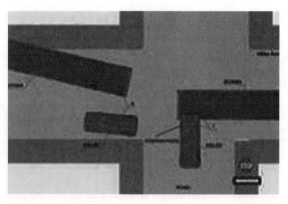

Figure 9.10 PC-CRASH software. *Source:* Estonian Forensic Science Institute archives.

majority comprise expert assessments prescribed in the course of guardianship proceedings in relation to restriction on active legal capacity or assignment of involuntary care. Another big part of expert assessments comprise assessments in criminal cases during which the condition of the suspect or victim at the time of committing the offence is determined. Expert assessments are also prescribed in disputes related to wills, determining a parent's right of custody, etc.

The Vehicle and Road Accident Investigation Department conducts technical traffic analyses, technical examination of vehicles and traffic traceology examinations.

The field of technical traffic analyses includes issues related to the reconstruction of traffic accidents and any issues requiring a calculated analysis of the estimated movement processes of vehicles. Among other methods, the analysis also uses the traffic accident reconstruction program PC-CRASH, which is commonly used all over Europe (Figure 9.10).

The objective of a technical examination of vehicles is to inspect the working capacity of systems that ensure the traffic safety of vehicles and identify any breakdowns and damage in order to determine what aspects could have affected the movement or controllability of the vehicle regardless of the intention of the driver. The objective of technical examination of vehicles is not to inspect the technical condition of the vehicle in compliance with the Regulation "Requirements for the Technical Condition of Motor Vehicles and Trailers" but instead to analyse the technical condition of the vehicle in relation to a specific assessment task and/or traffic situation (traffic accident).

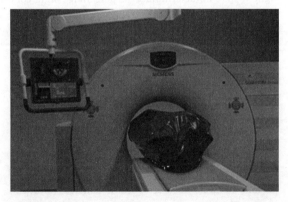

Figure 9.9 CT scanner (Siemens Somatom Emotion 6). *Source:* Estonian Forensic Science Institute archives.

The field of traffic traceology examinations includes issues that are related to the identification of vehicles and identification and examination of traces left by vehicles or left on vehicles.

The fields of activity of the Fingerprint Department are detecting and photographing fingerprints, identifying persons on the basis of fingerprints, mutual linkage of various scenes of events and maintaining the National Fingerprint Database.

Various physical, physical/chemical and chemical methods are used in the course of collecting friction ridge impressions. The holistic approach and the internationally recognized ACE-V principle, consisting of qualitative/quantitative trace analysis, comparative analysis, assessment and verification of the analysis, serve as the basis for the identification process.

The Fingerprint Department maintains the National Fingerprint Database. Fingerprint cards from over 145,000 persons are preserved in the database both on paper and electronically. Approximately 3800 expert assessments and analyses are conducted in the Fingerprint Department every year (Figure 9.11).

The Technical Department conducts marks examination, explosive device and explosion examination and fire and firearms examination.

The objective of *marks examination* is to identify an object that has left a mark on the basis of the characteristics of the marks left on the scene of an event. The objects of marks examination are marks left by an object used for breaking in; marks left by footwear, footprints and tyres; locks; parts separated from an object; plastic bags; die markers; seals; damage to clothing and other marks (e.g. traces of blood, marks left by ears, gloves, etc.).

Explosive device and explosion examination is divided into two main groups depending on whether the objects need to be identified or the explosion has already occurred and the event and the exploded object need to be reconstructed. Both industrially manufactured and homemade objects are analysed. Upon identifying the objects presented for examination, the main objective is to identify their structure, properties and explosive content and to verify the type and mark of objects, possible function in the explosive device and their usability. In the case of post-explosion examination, the additional objectives are to determine the centre of the explosion, identify the connections between the objects found from the scene of the event and the explosion, identify the possible structure and explosive mechanism of the explosive device and reconstruct the event.

The objective of *fire examination* is to identify the technical cause of the fire and collect data concerning the progress of the fire (location of the source of the fire, number of sources of the fire, routes by which the fire has spread, creation of the combustion process and temporal characteristics of its progress, and circumstances favourable for the spread of fire).

Firearms examination is conducted for firearms, gas weapons and pneumatic weapons, cartridges and the traces left by the latter, with the objective of identifying whether the presented objects belong among weapons, identifying the type, system, model and modification of the weapon, method of manufacture and usability of the weapon, identifying the weapon on the basis of the shot bullets, shells and other cartridge components in exceptional cases, identifying the direction and distance of the shot on the basis of the traces left on various objects and other circumstances related to shooting (Figure 9.12).

9.6 National Fingerprint Database and National DNA Database

The National Fingerprint Database and National DNA Database were established and the statutes thereof were approved by a regulation of the Government of the Republic. The chief processor of the National DNA and Fingerprint Databases is the Ministry of Justice and the authorized processor thereof is a state forensic institution – the EFSI.

Figure 9.11 Identification of 10 print cards. *Source:* Estonian Forensic Science Institute archives.

Figure 9.12 Automated Ballistic Identification System. *Source:* Estonian Forensic Science Institute archives.

9.7 NAC and CNAC service to the Estonian Central Bank

As of 1 January 2011 the euro, the single currency of the European Union, is the official currency of Estonia. In order to detect and update the European Central Bank database of counterfeit euro banknotes and coins the EFSI is acting under the supervision of the National Central Bank as the national NAC and CNAC.

9.8 Laboratory accreditation/quality control

In order to achieve its goals, the Institute has implemented a quality management system, which is based on three internationally recognized standards:

EVS-EN ISO/IEC 17025, General Requirements for the Competence of Testing and Calibration Laboratories

EVS-EN ISO/IEC 17020, Conformity Assessment. Requirements for the operation of various types of bodies performing inspection

EVS-EN ISO 9001, Quality Management Systems, Requirements.

The Institute was accredited by the Estonian Accreditation Centre in 2003. The accreditation scope of ISO 17025 (accreditation certificate no. L127) covers the Institute's activities in the fields of toxicology, determination of narcotic drugs and psychotropic substances, gunshot residues and electron microscopy, DNA analyses, mass measurement, investigation of questioned counterfeit euro banknotes, also development and identification of fingerprints and information technology.

The accreditation scope of ISO 17020 (accreditation certificate no. I072) covers activities in the fields of forensic medical examinations of living persons and dead bodies.

The Institute is certified by the Bureau Veritas Eesti OÜ since 2009 (initial certificate no. EST90645A, now EST62212A). Certification gives the confirmation of an independent third party that forensic examinations and analysis and activities related to them comply with the requirements of the internationally recognized management standard ISO 9001.

In addition to their everyday work, the staff of the Institute develop and implement innovative ideas, methods and technologies of expertise.

9.9 Competence assurance

By the *Forensic Examination Act*, the person may be employed as a forensic expert in the EFSI if the person: has active legal capacity; is proficient in Estonian to the extent established by law or on the basis of an Act; has acquired higher education required in his or her field of expertise in an institution of higher education of the Republic of Estonia or if the person's education corresponds to the said level and has been employed in his or her field of expertise in a forensic or research institution or in another position for at least two years immediately prior to commencing employment as a forensic expert. All restrictions are mentioned in the same Act. Upon entry into a contract of employment, a forensic expert shall take the following oath before the employer:

I (name), swear to perform the duties of a forensic expert with honesty and to provide expert opinions impartially, according to my specific knowledge and conscience. I am aware that knowing provision of a false expert opinion is punishable pursuant to the provisions of § 321 of the Criminal Code.

A forensic expert shall sign the oath and indicate the date of taking the oath. The signed text of the oath shall be annexed to the copy of the employment contract kept by the employer.

The competence of forensic medical experts is regulated by the occupational qualification standards approved by the Law and Public Defence Professional Council on 11 December 2006. Qualification standards of levels III, IV and V have been established for forensic experts.

The competence of forensic science (criminalistics) experts is regulated by the occupational qualification standards (Expert IV and V) approved by the Law and Public Defence Professional Council on 12 May 2009.

To ensure the competitive and highly qualified technicians and scientists in fields of the Institute's scope, the EFSI is following the ENFSI (European Network of Forensic Science Institutes) Education and Training standing committee best practice guidance documents: ISO 17025 and ISO 9001 standard documents; the in-service training curriculum of the Faculty of Medicine of the University of Tartu; and the EFSI long-term training programme and annual training activities plan.

The Institute is confirming its professional quality by participating regularly in cooperation exercises and International proficiency tests.

Officially certified experts are entered in the list by scientific field. Entry of officially certified experts in the list is regulated by the *Forensic Examination Act*. By this Act the applicant shall be entered in the list, if the person:

1. has worked for at least three years immediately before application for entry in the list, in the scientific field in which he or she applies for official certification and which provides the qualifications in compliance with the nationally recognized requirements for conducting examinations;
2. has the opportunity to use the technical resources necessary for expert research;
3. has a permanent income.

The EFSI acts as the national training facility for all its partners in the Law Enforcement Community.

9.10 Funding

Conduct of examinations in a forensic institution is financed from funds allocated from the state budget. The EFSI Annual Budget is allocated in the budget of the Ministry of Justice. The fiscal period is reported from 1 January until 31 December.

By the *Forensic Examination Act* the EFSI can accept external income from the sales of forensic services, which cannot exceed 20% of the volume in the specific field. This includes private persons' orders of analyses

of parental testing, toxicology, graphology, electron microscopy measurement and forensic medial inspections that do not conflict with open cases.

Customers shall pay a charge for the conduct of studies to a forensic institution according to the price list of examinations. In the absence of a price corresponding to the type of study for a charge, the price for the closest type of examination shall be used as the basis upon agreeing on the charge.

9.11 Research

In accordance with the statutes of the Institute a research and development committee has been formed, comprised of employees and specialists, which meets four times a year and advises the management on the directions the Institute should take in terms of new methods and technologies to adopt.

Three persons with a PhD degree work in the Estonian Forensic Science Institute: one in the field of forensic science and two in the field of DNA. Three forensic experts are also enrolled in PhD studies in forensic medicine in the University of Tartu and their research topics are as follows:

- Alcohol-related molecular and pathomorphological damage
- Forensic medical differentiation of injuries caused by different pistols
- Clinical findings and significant biochemical tests of acute ethyl alcohol intoxication in different age groups of children
- The possibilities of using biochemical and virological investigations in postmortem diagnostics.

The experts in the Chemistry Department of the Estonian Forensic Science Institute are elaborating a methodology for determining hypoxanthine within the framework of their research with the objective of using the methodology for determining the time of death.

During the past few years, two doctoral theses have been defended at the University of Tartu's Institute of Pathological Anatomy and Forensic Medicine and three doctoral theses are in progress. Every year two or three international articles are published.

Since 6 April 2011 the Institute has celebrated its anniversary with the traditional Forensics Day Scientific Conference. Moreover, every calendar year a special award is given to the most outstanding scientist or scientific research.

The Institute has published Estonian language scientific books and training materials: Kohtuarstiteadus (Legal Medical Science, 2006), Kohtuhambaarstiteadus (Forensic Odontology Science, 2009) and Kriminalistikaekspertiisid (Forensic Scientific Examinations, 2013). In 2011 the history book of the EFSI 1918–2011 was issued.

As the Institute is the only forensic institution to conduct forensic examination in Estonia, international contacts are required to ensure a high scientific level (participating in the meetings, seminars and conferences of the ENFSI workgroups, exchange of experience with other forensic institutions, etc.). Close international cooperation is conducted with Latvia, Lithuania, Finland, Sweden, the Netherlands, Denmark, Germany, Switzerland, Poland, Russia and numerous other foreign countries.

The employees of the Estonian Forensic Science Institute participate in various projects financed by the ENFSI: Quality Manager in the "European Mentorship for Forensic Accreditation 2" (EMFA 2) and "Establishment of New Process for the Conduct of Proficiency Tests (PT) and Collaborative Exercises"; Head of the IT Department in the projects "Cyber Attack Against Critical IT Systems of the Police, Their Protection and Proceedings for Cyber Attacks" and "Fight and Investigation of Cyber Attacks Against Critical Governmental Infrastructures"; and experts of the DNA and Fingerprint Departments participated in the project "Impact of Dactyloscopic Investigation Methods on DNA Analysis".

9.12 Future trends

The Institute will follow the strategies of European main networks – ENFSI and ECLM. Future trends are directed by "Council conclusions on the vision for European Forensic Science 2020 including the creation of a European Forensic Science Area and the development of forensic science infrastructure in Europe", released on 13 November 2011.

The objectives of the Conclusions are the achievement of a Pan-European accreditation of forensic science institutes and laboratories; establishment of minimum competence criteria for forensic science personnel; establishment of common best practice manuals and their application in the daily work of forensic laboratories and institutes; mandatory participation in proficiency tests/collaborative exercises; application and implementation of minimum quality standards for scene-of-crime investigations by forensic science personnel; Pan-European legal harmonization of forensic activities with a view to avoid duplication of effort, reduce technical and qualitative differences and reduce the time taken to process crimes with a cross-border component; creation of optimal possibilities for exchange of data and joint updating and usage of the databases of the Member States; use of the advances in forensic science in the fight against terrorism, organized crime and other criminal activities; increasing forensic knowledge through appropriate training and education for the law enforcement and justice community; promotion of research and development projects in order to support the sustainable development of the forensic science infrastructure.

CHAPTER 10

History and current status of forensic science and medicine in Finland

Erkki Sippola[1] & Pekka Saukko[2]

[1] Forensic Laboratory, National Bureau of Investigation, Vantaa, Finland
[2] Department of Forensic Medicine, Institute of Biomedicine, University of Turku, Turku, Finland

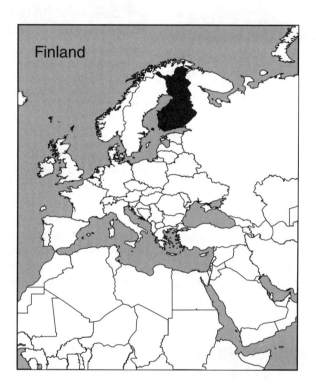

10.1 Forensic science

10.1.1 History of forensic science

Forensic science started in Finland in 1908 with the establishment of the so-called Anthropometric Office belonging to the Helsinki police department. The office never carried out anthropometric examinations, but it was responsible for fingerprint examinations. In the beginning only one forensic expert was employed to the

laboratory (Figure 10.1). His only actual tool was a light microscope. In 1914 the personnel was increased to three persons.

The Anthropometric Office was later named the Office of Distinguishing Marks and in 1926 as the Crime Investigation Centre. In the 1920s several homicides were solved thanks to the fingerprint and firearms examinations. The caseload gradually increased while more police officers were trained to carry out crime scene

The Global Practice of Forensic Science, First Edition. Edited by Douglas H. Ubelaker.
© 2015 John Wiley & Sons, Ltd. Published 2015 by John Wiley & Sons, Ltd.

Figure 10.1 Harald Rosenberg was the first photographer of the police. He studied crime scene photography in Sweden and Russia. He was a recognized professional despite the rather simple tools he had in his use. *Source:* Reproduced with permission of the National Bureau of Investigation, Finland.

Figure 10.3 Due to the outburst of the Winter War in 1939 the Crime Investigation Centre was transferred to Ostrobothnia where it functioned in a school building in the village of Koivulahti. *Source:* Reproduced with permission of the National Bureau of Investigation, Finland.

investigations. The total case number in 1926 was only 56, but after five years it was already over 500. In that time the Centre's forensic disciplines included fingerprints, marks, handwriting and firearms examinations (Figure 10.2).

Quite soon it became obvious that a chemistry laboratory was also needed and it was established in 1930. The newly hired forensic chemist carried out chemical analyses of toxins, blood and accelerants. In 1931 the Crime Investigation Centre moved to new facilities and

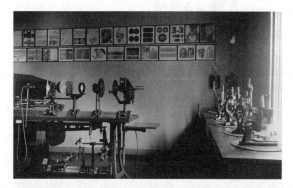

Figure 10.2 The main instrument in the figure is a microphotograph, which was purchased in 1929. During the same time period also various microscopes were obtained. *Source:* Reproduced with permission of the National Bureau of Investigation, Finland.

its organization was divided into the Optical Department and Chemistry Department. In the 1930s staff still only numbered four persons. In 1937 the status of the Crime Investigation Centre was confirmed in the new law. The staff already included 18 persons and the annual case number had increased to 800. The fingerprint collection included nearly 100,000 convicted persons' fingerprints.

The Second World War decreased caseload, but also personnel, as six staff members were sent to the Front. Unfortunately two of them were killed in 1942. To avoid bombings, the Centre was transferred further north to Ostrobothnia and functioned in a school building in the village of Koivulahti (Figure 10.3). The laboratory was temporary placed in classrooms.

After the war, the caseload started to grow again thanks to increased criminality, but also to the activity of the police. In 1955 a new agency, the National Bureau of Investigation (NBI), was established. The Crime Investigation Centre became a part of the NBI and was then renamed the Forensic Laboratory.

In the 1960s the methods and utilization of forensic science started to grow again (Figure 10.4). Gas chromatography enabled measurements of drastically increased accuracy and crime scene photography reached a new level after the introduction of 35 mm film cameras. Also, color photography was introduced in the 1960s. The popularity of illicit drugs abuse increased the caseload rapidly.

Figure 10.4 The second crime scene investigation vehicle of the Finnish police. All the equipment was normally packed in the car. The picture has been taken in Helsinki in 1964. *Source: Reproduced with permission of the National Bureau of Investigation, Finland.*

Expansion of the Forensic Laboratory caused problems regarding the facilities. These became too small and inappropriate for the rapidly developing methodology. Finally, in 1976 the laboratory moved to new facilities. In 1978 the first scanning electron microscope was purchased followed by the first FTIR microscope in 1985. International collaboration started to grow in the 1980s, especially with other Scandinavian countries but also with Germany and the USA.

In 1994 the NBI got a completely new building and the laboratory was for the first time in facilities entirely designed according to modern forensic standards. One of the main areas of development in the 1990s was the introduction of an accredited quality system. The first accreditation against EN45000 standard was received in 1996, later being switched to the ISO 17025 standard. Also the caseload increased considerably; in 1991 the Forensic Laboratory received 8500 requests and in 1999 there were 14,000. Growth of the DNA examination was primarily responsible for these figures. The number of staff members had increased to 90 persons.

The new millennium brought massive development of the IT infrastructure through the introduction of the laboratory information management system (LIMS). The new system was first used in drugs and DNA areas only. Ten years later the system was revised, covering the whole laboratory. Unlike in most other countries, in Finland the LIMS is directly interfaced with the police

case registration system and enables to both upload and download data between the systems. Also other major data systems were introduced or revised during that time (Kaartinen, 2008).

In the 2010s the NBI Forensic Laboratory employs 125 persons and examines 30,000 cases annually. The laboratory is an active member of the European Network of Forensic Science Institutes (ENFSI). The laboratory provides services to the Police and also to the Customs, Frontier Guard, Immigration service, Defense Forces and some other Finnish authorities.

Unlike in many other European countries, the Finnish Forensic Laboratory is part of the Police, not under the Ministry of Justice. Experience of over 100 years has proven that also the Finnish system works very well and there are no signs that the impartiality or neutrality has been jeopardized.

10.1.2 Types of forensic cases

In Finland the NBI Forensic Laboratory is solely responsible for a wide range of forensic examinations. However, the toxicological analyses of samples from drunken driving and traffic offence cases are carried out by the National Institute of Health and Welfare (THL) on a subcontracting basis, whereas all postmortem toxicology from forensic autopsies are investigated at the Forensic Toxicology Division of the Department of Forensic Medicine of the Hjelt-Institute, University of Helsinki. Moreover, the Customs Laboratory is responsible for the examinations of illicit drugs and medicines, which are seized by Customs.

The NBI Forensic Laboratory is responsible for over 20 forensic disciplines. The Chemistry group has expertise to examine illicit drugs (including drugs profiling), designer drugs, doping agents, poisons, arson materials, environmental pollutants and explosives.

The Comparisons Group has expertise to examine firearms and ammunition, gunshot residues, elemental composition of various microscopic samples, fibers and hair, glass and paint, marks, bloodstain patterns, electric fires and various types of vehicle-related issues.

The DNA Group is responsible for various DNA-related examinations.

The Document and Digital Technology Group is responsible for the documents area, handwriting area, banknote and coin authenticity examinations, information and telecommunication area (computers, mobile phones, GPS systems, cameras and various types of digital storage devices) and digital imaging area.

The Fingerprint Group is responsible for fingerprint examinations and for forensic anthropology (Figure 10.5).

Additionally, the Forensic Laboratory has specialized units for the Customer Service, CSI Support Services and In-House Support Services. The Customer Service is responsible for all logistics regarding samples and cases, but it also includes a Coordination Centre, which helps the customer in high profile cases to prioritize samples and examinations. The CSI Support Service is responsible for the quality audits of the CSI units and also help the CSI units to draw up SOPs. Forensic training of the Police personnel is also under their responsibility. The In-House Support Services is responsible for the

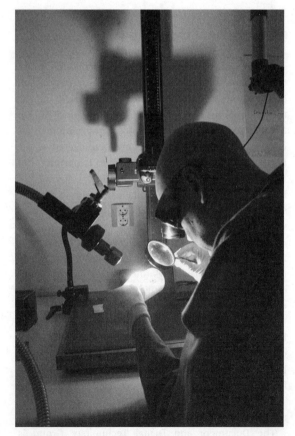

Figure 10.5 Practically all modern forensic technology is nowadays widely exploited by the Forensic Laboratory. Various different light sources are commonly used in fingerprint development. *Source:* Reproduced with permission of the National Bureau of Investigation, Finland.

Laboratory's quality system, procurements, ICT systems and communication services.

The NBI Forensic Laboratory manages the national DNA and fingerprint databases. Other databases under the Laboratory include voice, footwear impressions, firearms and ammunitions as well as drug profiling databases (see Table 10.1). The Laboratory is also responsible for the European exchange of DNA and fingerprint data within the concept defined in the Prüm Treaty (National Bureau of Investigation (NBI), 2012).

10.1.3 Structure and funding of forensic science

The NBI Forensic Laboratory is part of the Police organization, and thus it has a very good relationship with the local police units – especially the CSI units. The CSI units are responsible for all demanding crime scene investigations. In volume crime cases the crime scene investigation is typically carried out by the first responders, that is, the ordinary police patrols. In Finland all police units use the same case management system, which provides equal tools for documentation and chain of custody.

The reports (statements) made by the Forensic Laboratory are very seldom challenged in the courts. The forensic experts need to give a testimony in only about 50 cases per year.

The Forensic Laboratory acquires some laboratory examinations from forensic laboratories in the neighboring countries or from trusted laboratories in Finland. Subcontracting is used to avoid situations where rarely needed services need to be maintained, thus sacrificing overall efficiency of the Forensic Laboratory. The

Table 10.1 The NBI Forensic Laboratory caseload in 2012

Drunken driving	11,500
DNA	7,000
Drugs	3,800
Fingerprints	2,200
Documents and banknotes	2,000
Arson	500
Marks	500
Firearms	300
Other	2,200
Total	30,000
Additionally:	
DNA and fingerprint reference samples	30,000

most common outsourced service is blood analyses of the drinking and driving cases.

The NBI Forensic Laboratory is funded by the Police within the state budget. Thus the services provided by the laboratory are free of charge for the customers. Over recent years there has been a tremendous pressure to reduce personnel. The Forensic Laboratory has carried its share of this burden, which has caused occasional backlogs.

In the 2010s the annual funding has been from 12 to 13 m€, including all expenses (National Bureau of Investigation (NBI), 2013a).

10.1.4 Recruitment and competence of forensic experts

Recruitment of forensic experts is based on open announcements on the public domain of the State of Finland. Every citizen has an equal opportunity to apply for any vacancy. In practice the announcements are formulated to specify what kind of education and experience are expected. Qualifications most typically sought are chemists, engineers and technicians.

In Finland there are no universities or schools giving forensic education (except forensic medicine) and thus every new employee needs to be further trained at the Forensic Laboratory. A tailored orientation plan is formulated for each and every new employee. The orientation program includes elements of legislation, pre-trial investigations, examination methods and a quality system. The new employee needs to pass a proficiency test prior to starting to work as an expert.

Only Finnish citizens can be nominated to permanent positions. A security clearance of the Finnish Security Intelligence Service is required for all nominations – also for temporary personnel and students (National Bureau of Investigation (NBI), 2013a).

10.1.5 Quality system in the NBI Forensic Laboratory

The NBI Forensic Laboratory was first accredited against the EN45000 standard in 1996 and later against the ISO 17025 standard. Currently all routine methods belong to the scope of accreditation. The Forensic Laboratory has been very active in recommending to the national accreditation body the best European forensic experts to carry out the technical assessment. This has proven to be a great asset as it has improved quality to a great extent.

In Finland there is not a system that would require the forensic experts to be formally registered. The certification given by the Forensic Laboratory is sufficient to demonstrate required competence.

The Forensic Laboratory is currently working on a development project with the aim to get the SCI units also under the ISO accreditation (National Bureau of Investigation (NBI), 2013a).

10.1.6 Technology used in the NBI Forensic Laboratory

The NBI Forensic Laboratory is using modern technology in all disciplines. Laboratory instrument line-up is mainly less than seven years old. When new instrumentation is purchased, the main selection criteria are high reliability, stability and performance. Very often the cutting-edge technology is avoided due to its questionable suitability for high volume routine work.

A lot of resources have been used to develop laboratory automation and data systems. A laboratory information management system (LIMS) covers the entire laboratory. Similarly a document management system is used for the management of all formal documents. The system also enables electronic archiving. Laboratory automation is mainly applied in the DNA laboratory, but plans to exploit this technology also in the drugs area are in place (National Bureau of Investigation (NBI), 2013a).

10.1.7 Research and development in forensic science

The NBI Forensic Laboratory has a project management system, which is steered by the R&D director. All project ideas are evaluated against existing strategies and accepted projects are managed in the project portfolio.

The Forensic Laboratory mainly focuses on development. Basic research is very seldom carried out. Most of the development projects during the past ten years have aimed at developing new methods, computer systems, working processes or services.

During the past decade the Forensic Laboratory has coordinated or participated with many European funded projects, where the workload has been shared between several European forensic laboratories. Also US and Australian based laboratories have participated with these project consortia (National Bureau of Investigation (NBI), 2013a).

10.1.8 Future directions of forensic science

In 2013 the Forensic Laboratory defined the strategic goals for the next two to three years (National Bureau of Investigation (NBI), 2013b):

1. Interactive cooperation
   - The Laboratory further develops its services together with the personnel and clients.
   - The Laboratory obeys the principle of early caring to all staff members and develops the interaction skills of the entire personnel.
   - The Laboratory ensures that the personnel has sufficient competence to provide and develop services.
   - The Laboratory develops management and leadership skills by utilizing an extensive training program.
   - The Laboratory develops project implementation skills by training project managers and steering group members.
   - The Laboratory informs and communicates actively, appropriately and in a well-justified manner; the Laboratory develops interactive communication such as to support implementation of strategies and well-being of the personnel.
   - The Laboratory is managed such that it constructs trust within the entire personnel.

2. Watertight life cycle of forensic investigations
   - The Laboratory helps the Police to develop data systems such that they provide platforms for seamless documentation and chain of custody and that they support the Laboratory's services.
   - The Laboratory develops the competence of the police officers to enable reliable sampling, sample preparation and laboratory examinations.
   - The Laboratory helps the Police to develop the quality systems of the CSI units such that they can reach ISO accreditation.
   - The Laboratory will ensure that all registers under its responsibility meet the requirements of current legislation.
   - The Laboratory will carry out necessary actions to ensure that the competence of all subcontractors can be demonstrated.

3. Uniform, modern and organized forensic investigations
   - The Laboratory will set requirements for the participation with ENFSI activities such that they support the development of forensic science in Finland to meet the highest European standards.
   - The Laboratory will define the minimum standards to all CSI units covering human resources, competence, facilities, consumables and equipment.
   - The Laboratory will promote policies that the quality systems of the SCI units and the Laboratory will be merged in the future.

4. Service-based funding
   - The Laboratory will help the National Police Board to define the minimum objectives for all CSI units regarding crime scene investigations; the Laboratory will make service level agreements with the Police Board to ensure that the service capacity of the Laboratory is compatible with the customer needs.
   - The Laboratory will exploit all relevant sources of external funding for R&D projects.
   - The Laboratory will increase cooperation with other public laboratories in Finland to achieve cost savings and to avoid duplication of work.
   - The laboratory will draw up an HR strategy to help future recruitments and to help allocation of human resources.

10.2 Forensic medicine

10.2.1 History of forensic medicine

The legislation regulating the medical profession and medicolegal activities in Finland has its origin in the period of time when Finland was a part of the Swedish Kingdom (c. 1150–1809). A uniform Swedish rule was extended to Finland in the 17th century and accordingly the Swedish legal system was adopted in Finland.

In the 18th century several regulations concerning medicolegal death investigations were introduced. In 1726 the King gave permission to perform autopsies to determine the causes of maternal deaths during labor.

A comprehensive Swedish Code was enacted in 1734. According to this Code of 1734: "when it is unclear whether a person has died due to a disease or involuntary manslaughter, a Judge or King's governor shall let the body be examined before burial" (author's translation) (Sveriges Rikes Lag, 1734, Chapter XXVIII, §6).

In 1744 the King's Instructions obliged Provincial Medical Officers to advise and provide expertise to courts in medicolegal matters. It also regulated the payment and remuneration for various services rendered, including examination of a dead body and an autopsy performed in the presence of the Provincial Medical Officer by a Barber-Surgeon, suggesting that autopsies were occasionally performed.

When Sweden lost the war against Russia, Finland became for a century a Grand Duchy of Russia (1809–1917) but was allowed to retain its own legislation, religion and the old Swedish system of law and government. In 1811 the Finnish Collegium Medicum was established in Turku and in 1832 the instructions for Provincial Medical Officers concerning their duties in general as well as the medicolegal ones were updated. In 1841 the first detailed instructions were given to regulate the legal framework and the performance of medicolegal autopsy as well as sampling for toxicology in the case of a suspected intoxication. In 1878 Collegium Medicum was unified with two other government offices, forming the National Board of Health.

In 1991 the traditional National Board of Health was merged with the National Board of Social Affairs into one authority, which again in 1992 was replaced by the National Authority for Medicolegal Affairs (Saukko, 2008).

10.2.2 Present organization of forensic medicine

Since 2010, the competent authority in charge of forensic medicine in Finland is the National Institute for Health and Welfare (THL), which was formed in January 2009 with the merger of the National Public Health Institute (KTL) and the National Research and Development Centre for Welfare and Health (STAKES). In the Service System Department of the Division of Health and Social Services of the THL, there is a Forensic Medicine Unit, which employs full-time medicolegal officers (forensic pathologists) who are associated with the University Departments of Forensic Medicine in the five cities with a medical school. They deal mainly with medicolegal autopsies, guidance and supervision of health care professionals with regard to the cause of death investigation, and to some extent with other administrative matters such as scrutinizing all death certificates from their respective region before they are sent further to Statistics Finland (Central Statistical Office of Finland).

10.2.3 Specialization in forensic medicine (forensic pathology)

The first Chair of Pathological Anatomy and State Medicine was established at the University of Helsinki in 1857, followed by an Extraordinary Chair of Forensic Medicine in 1902, which in 1946 was changed into a Chair of Forensic Medicine. An Associate Professorship of Forensic Toxicology was established in 1948 and changed into a Full Chair in 1998.

A further three Chairs of Forensic Medicine were established at other universities: the University of Turku (1963), the University of Oulu (1966) and the University of Tampere (1989).

The medical specialty dealing with forensic pathology is called "Forensic Medicine," and has existed in Finland as a separate medical specialty since 1955. In 1986 training of medical specialists became a responsibility of the medical faculties of the universities and a postgraduate university degree. Since 1999 the specialist curriculum in Forensic Medicine takes a minimum of 5 years after graduation from medical school (which takes 6 years), comprising at least 3.5 year's specific training at a department of forensic medicine (performing during this training as a rule 175 forensic autopsies/year), at least 6 months training in a Department of Clinical Pathology, 9 months of general practice and the rest of service in other fields of medicine, finishing with a written National Examination, usually in the final year of specialization (Saukko, 2008).

There are altogether five universities with a medical faculty (Helsinki, Turku, Tampere, Kuopio and Oulu) and four Chairs of Forensic Medicine. For historical reasons the Professor at Tampere University has the obligation to teach the undergraduates also at Kuopio University. All university units of Forensic Medicine participate in medicolegal autopsy work. This activity is based on separate service contracts between the THL and the university in question. The university employs the necessary personnel, such as secretaries, autopsy technicians, etc., to provide the services and the facility, the cost of which is remunerated to the university from the THL budget. The Ministry of Social Affairs and Health has the main supervisory role and budgetary responsibility for medicolegal autopsy work.

10.2.4 Cause of death investigation

According to the decree about the criteria of death a person is dead when all the brain functions have irretrievably ceased (Decree about the criteria of death, 2004). A death must be immediately reported to the attending physician or a physician of the local municipality or police (Act on the inquest into the cause of death, 1973;

Decree on the inquest into the cause of death, 1973; Circular of the National Board of Health,1983).

As a rule only a physician can establish the fact of death and before a death certificate can be issued, the body must be examined, death officially established and the cause(s) of death must be determined. Depending on the circumstances of death there are two alternatives for determining the cause of death: medical or medicolegal, of which the latter has always priority. The police shall make an investigation when it is not known that death has been caused by a disease or when the deceased during his last illness has not been treated by a physician or death has been caused by crime, accident, suicide, poisoning, occupational disease, investigative or therapeutic procedure or there is reason to suspect that death may have resulted from such a cause or when death has been otherwise sudden and unexpected. Also deaths under special circumstances, such as death during military service, in custody, being arrested, in captivity or involuntary psychiatric hospitalization, or if the identity of the deceased is unknown, are always subjected to a medicolegal investigation. In medicolegal cases the police investigation is not a criminal inquiry, but if indicated it can turn into one. As a rule there is a full medicolegal autopsy performed by a forensic pathologist of the THL or one of the University Departments.

Roughly two-thirds (72% in 2011) of all death certificates are based on clinical investigation. A medicolegal autopsy will be ordered by the police in the majority of nonnatural cases of death and quite a few sudden unexpected deaths assumed to be natural, resulting in altogether 10,042 medicolegal autopsies, that is, 19% of all deaths in 2012.

The hospital autopsy rate has been decreasing since 1979 (23%), being about 7% of all deaths in 2011. All death certificates are scrutinized by the Medico Legal Officers of the THL, or in some major cities also by other officials of the Municipal Department of Health. This gives an additional possibility for quality assurance of the certification of deaths before they are sent further to Statistics Finland.

10.2.5 Postmortem forensic toxicology

All postmortem toxicology samples from forensic autopsies in Finland are investigated at the Forensic Toxicology Division of the Department of Forensic Medicine of the Hjelt-Institute, University of Helsinki. In 2011, the Laboratory investigated 6661 cases of postmortem

toxicology. The number of samples related to clinical forensic toxicology, clinical pharmacology or drugs of abuse testing was nearly three thousand. The focus of the investigation is on broad-scale screening analyses for alcohol and volatile substances, drugs of abuse, prescription medicines, date-rape drugs, LP gases, carbon monoxide, cyanide and some pesticides. Since 1997, the Laboratory has acted in the capacity of Testing Laboratory T 115, accredited by the Finnish Centre for Metrology and Accreditation (FINAS).

10.2.6 Forensic biology

The Laboratory of Forensic Biology of the Department of Forensic Medicine University of Helsinki offers services in human identification by DNA testing. DNA testing is mostly requested in cases of unidentified corpses by the forensic pathologist or police, and in cases of refugee family reunion or paternity testing by child welfare officers, courts of justice or individuals on a private basis. In addition, the laboratory serves other laboratories in cases of suspected sample mix-up. Scientific research projects include utilization of DNA methods in human identification, pharmacogenetics, history of Finno-Ugric language-speaking populations and genetics of sudden death.

10.2.7 Forensic odontology

Forensic Odontology/DVI Unit of the Department of Forensic Medicine University of Helsinki employs one full-time forensic odontologist and performs at the request of authorities identification and age assessment based on tooth findings and X-ray of bone structures as well as bite mark analyses. Other University Departments engage odontologists qualified in forensic odontology case-specifically.

10.2.8 Forensic psychiatry

Forensic psychiatry is a separate medical specialty in Finland with Chairs at the Universities of Helsinki and Kuopio.

The THL coordinates all forensic psychiatric examinations required to assess the criminal responsibility of homicide or other criminal perpetrators ordered by courts. It takes place in special hospitals where forensic psychiatrists conduct an extensive, hospital-based psychiatric study of the offender lasting a maximum of two months.

10.2.9 Clinical forensic medicine

Clinical forensic medical cases are usually handled by general practitioners or hospital doctors with the exception of the Helsinki University Department of Forensic Medicine. This department is the only forensic one in the country providing forensic physician services 24 hours a day, investigating cases involving driving under the influence, drugs of abuse, assaults, sexual crimes, crime scenes and also sampling for paternity testing and for refugee family reunion. Other forensic departments are involved in clinical forensic medicine only to such a degree it is needed for postgraduate training of forensic specialists.

10.2.10 Research in forensic medicine

All academic Departments of Forensic Medicine are actively involved in scientific research in their respective areas of interest. The key areas of research at the Department of Forensic Medicine in Helsinki include causes and mechanisms of death as well as understanding post-mortem developments with a focus on unnatural deaths. The Department also studies the recognition, effects and use of various intoxicants. Forensic research contributes to legal protection both on a societal and individual level and is closely connected to public health.

10.2.11 The past, present state and future challenges in forensic medicine

For decades the Finnish medicolegal system suffered from a lack of leadership and coordination by various Ministries, neglecting their respective sectors in developing and supporting these activities. The Ministry of Education did not provide enough resources to increase the number of training posts at the University Departments, which caused a bottleneck in specialty training, leading to a shortage of forensic pathologists, and at the same time with growing autopsy rates, to increasing workload among those already in the profession. The Ministry of Internal Affairs, in charge of the Police and the Provincial Governments, the latter of which were then the only authority offering permanent full-time posts for forensic pathologists (in addition to University Chairs), refused to establish new posts for forensic pathologists. This again made it more difficult to recruit new trainees. The Ministry of Social Affairs and Health, who in the course of time had established a number of Committees, a Working Party (1991) and a One-Man Committee (1997) to solve the problems in Forensic Medicine, never took action to put any of the recommendations of the experts into practice, losing valuable time to reform the system (Saukko, 1998).

With the THL as the new responsible authority for forensic medicine the medicolegal system in the country is now under a uniform organization and professional leadership. The greatest challenges are now the shortage of forensic pathologists both in the service system as well as of those interested in an academic career to hold future Chairs. The THL employs altogether 13 specialists of which 11 work full-time. A further six specialists are employed by the University Departments including four professors. With regard to the relatively high medicolegal autopsy rate, the workload of individual forensic pathologists at the THL varied in 2012 from a minimum of 169 autopsies/year (of a part-time pathologist) up to a maximum of 630 autopsies/year. This situation has driven the service system close to breaking point and forced the new authority to take active measures in recruiting more trainees and simultaneously trying to reduce the workload by scrutinizing the indications for autopsy in individual cases more thoroughly in order to avoid unnecessary medicolegal autopsies. Only time will tell whether the reform of the system and these measures were taken in time.

References

Act on the inquest into the cause of death (No. 459/1973).

Circular of the National Board of Health on the inquest into the cause of death (1.4.1983/1789).

Decree about the criteria of death (No. 27/2004).

Decree on the inquest into the cause of death (No. 948/1973).

Kaartinen, K. (Ed.) (2008) *Hundred Years of Forensic Investigation – A Photographic Journey*, Otava Book Printing Ltd, Keuruu

National Bureau of Investigation (NBI) (2012) Annual report.

National Bureau of Investigation (NBI) (2013a) Internal presentation.

National Bureau of Investigation (NBI) (2013b) Strategic goals of NBI Forensic Laboratory, Internal report, Vantaa.

Saukko, P. (1998) Report on the Evaluation of the Finnish Medico-Legal System, Ministry for Social Affairs and Health, Helsinki. ISBN 952-00-0464-5.

Saukko, P. (2008) Forensic medicine in Finland, in *Forensic Medicine in Europe* (1st ed.), Eds. B. Madea and P. Saukko, Schmidt-Römhild, Lübeck, Germany.

Sveriges Rikets Lag (1734) Chapter XXVIII, §6.

CHAPTER 11
Forensic medicine in France

Bertrand Ludes

Institut Medico-légal de Paris, Paris, France

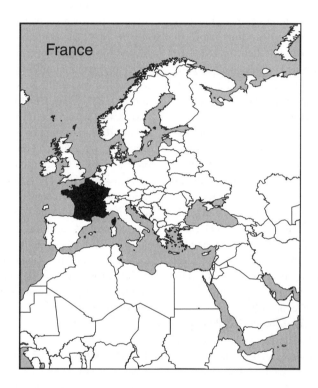

11.1 The history of forensic medicine

This subject was for the time described in the book entitled *Forensic Medicine in Europe* (Ludes, 2008). After giving a taste of the historical background of this field in France, the author will give the new organization of forensic medicine according to French governmental decisions.

Modern forensic medicine was born after the French Revolution (1789) with the creation of three new Faculties of Medicine in Paris, Strasbourg and Montpellier.

In 1794, medical studies were reorganized and professorships of forensic medicine in the new Faculties were established. In 1798, Francois Emmanuel Fodere (1764–1835) was the first to publish a treaty that establishes the distinction between civil, criminal forensic medicine,

The Global Practice of Forensic Science, First Edition. Edited by Douglas H. Ubelaker.
© 2015 John Wiley & Sons, Ltd. Published 2015 by John Wiley & Sons, Ltd.

administrative forensic medicine as well as health and medicine policing (Sournia, 1989).

Under the French Directoire, Nicolas Pierre Gilbert (1751–1814) considered forensic medicine as "one of the noblest professions". He reformed the teaching of the forensic medicine field, so that "wisely motivated reports" may be used in Court. He proposed also to instruct health professionals in this discipline in medical schools near the Courts of Appeal.

During this period, clinical forensic medicine was introduced in the curriculum, and the importance of forensic medicine was highlighted when, in 1814, Le Roux des Tilliets, Dean of the medical school of the Paris Faculty of Medicine proposed the creation of professorships in clinical forensic medicine. However, until then teaching remained mostly theoretical.

In 1813, Fodere, who held the Chair of Forensic Medicine and Public Health in Strasbourg, published a treaty, entitled "Treaty of forensic medicine, public health or health policing". He gave the following definition of forensic medicine in 1818: "By forensic medicine one means the application of physical, natural and medical knowledge to the legislation of the people, the administering of justice, local government, the maintenance of public health" (Chaumont, 1997a, p. 247). He also wrote: "How wrong are those who think that forensic medicine deals only with the right way to write a judicial report!" (Chaumont, 1997a, p. 247).

Victor Balthazard had a more restrictive definition of forensic medicine than Fodere in his "Summary of forensic medicine" (1906) when he stated that "Forensic medicine is the application of medical knowledge to civil and criminal cases that could only be solved using its tools" (Chaumont, 1997a, p. 248).

New horizons were opened for this field by the development of pathological anatomy and toxicology as developed by Matteo-Jose Bonaventure Orfila (1787–1835), and widespread use of microscopical investigations. One must also note the rise of forensic psychiatry with Jean-Dominique Esquirol (1772–1840) (Chaumont, 1997b).

At that time, the major work of forensic medicine specialists was limited to autopsies in morgues where bodies were displayed to be claimed by the public. Ambroise Tardieu heralded social forensic medicine with his 1860 work on child abuse (Tardieu, 1860, pp. 361–398).

The teaching of forensic medicine as proposed by Dean Le Roux des Tilliets remained at the theoretical level

despite the introduction of clinical forensic medicine as a discipline. Around 1877, Dean Alfred Vulpian (1826–1887) organized practical teachings in morgues, conducted by Paul Brouardel (1837–1906). Brouardel held the chair of forensic medicine in Paris between 1879 and 1906 and became Dean of the Faculty of Medicine. In Lyon, forensic medicine was developed by Alexandre Lacassagne (1843–1924), who held the Chair of forensic medicine in the Faculty of Medicine in Lyon for over 30 years, between 1880 and 1913. This position was created in 1870. Lacassagne's work focused on the medical and social aspects of criminality. The Faculty of Lyon developed criminal anthropology and created the first technical and scientific police laboratory by Dr. Edmond Locard (1877–1966). The Institute of Forensic Medicine was located within the University of Lyon.

The creation of the first forensic medicine institute in Lyon took place in 1853 on a barge of the Rhone River, on the opposite side of the Hotel Dieu hospital.

A few words about Professor Louis Roche: he was born in St-Etienne on 10 September 1916. He was appointed as university professor specialist of forensic medicine and deontology, and director of the Forensic Institute in 1955. The publishing house he founded, Alexandre Lacassagne Editions, has published 200 original works to date including forensic medicine and medical economy books. He remained exceptionally active until his retirement in 1985.

11.1.1 Examples of historical backgrounds

A particular situation worth noting is forensic medicine at Strasbourg and how the discipline could be maintained after two world wars. The curriculum of the college of medicine of Strasbourg has included a course in forensic medicine since its creation in 1795. This course began on 20 April 1795 and was given by military surgeon Joseph Noel (1753–1808), the future director of the college. The Chair of forensic medicine was created in 1796 and Noel was appointed professor of forensic medicine and in time director of the college.

The transformation of the college into the Faculty of Medicine took place on 17 March 1808, and confirmed the position of forensic medicine in higher education. The directive of 7 February 1809 organized 12 Chairs, including the Chair of forensic medicine. Jean-Louis Michel Tinchant (1741–1835), also a military surgeon, succeeded Noel in 1809. He taught forensic medicine until his death, on January 23rd, 1813 (Chaumont, 1997a).

Francois-Emmanuel Fodere (1764–1835) joined the Faculty of Medicine in 1814, and remained in Strasbourg until his death in 1835. Fodere gave a definition of forensic medicine as "the art of applying the knowledge and principles of different branches of medicine in the interpretation of law items" (Chaumont, 1997a, p. 248).

Gabriel Tourdes was the head of the department of forensic medicine in 1840. He was the real founder of a practical approach to teaching this discipline.

In those times, the teaching of forensic medicine took an important part in medical studies in Strasbourg, as evidenced by the fact that out of 2064 questions in the final examination, 306 pertained to forensic medicine. Tourdes died on 26 January 1900 in Strasbourg. His long career is one of the most remarkable in the history of forensic medicine (Chaumont, 1997a).

The French victory in 1918 marked a resurrection for forensic medicine, and Chavigny (1869-1949) who was appointed in 1919, brought forensic medicine in Strasbourg to the forefront. Pr. Chavigny came from the Val de Grâce hospital in Paris where he had been teaching forensic medicine since 1907. He studied under Lacassagne in Lyon, himself a student of Pr. Gabriel Tourdes during the Second Empire. In Strasbourg, Chavigny created a teaching structure, laboratory, equipment, library and collection from scratch. He was succeeded in the chair of forensic and social medicine by Professor Camille Simonin (1891-1961), who had been his student since 1930.

In 1932, this Chair was renamed the Chair of forensic and social medicine. Camille Simonin continued to develop forensic medicine in Strasbourg, followed by Professor Chaumont in 1961.

During World War II, the Institute of Forensic Medicine was located in the so-called historical part of the medical school of Strasbourg, built by the Germans during the period 1870–1890. It had not been destroyed by the occupation forces and C. Simonin found after 1945 an institute that could be satisfactory run (Chaumont, 1997a).

11.1.2 The new organization of the discipline in France

The founding of the Higher Council of Forensic Medicine on 30 December 1994 (décret 94-1210 du 30/12/1994)

has led to a more structured framework for the activities of forensic medicine in the past 18 years.

Major concerns were raised by numerous colleagues involved in the field of legal medicine and forensic sciences about the former organization (Gosset, 2007; Demichel, 2004; Hecketsweiller, 2006; Penneau, 2003, 2006; Proust, 2007) who highlight the weakness of the low rate of forensic autopsies against the necessity of enhancing the university education in forensic sciences.

The Higher Council of Forensic Medicine inspired the following directives:

27 May 1997 (DGS/DH No. 97-380). Creation of regional centres for the treatment of victims of sexual abuse. These centres provide not only medical treatment for victims but also legal and psychological supports.

13 July 2000 (DGS/DH No. 2000-399). Extension of these centres for the support for child abuse.

22 October 2001 (DHOS/E1/2001/503). Directive on the emergency admission in hospitals for victims of violence and persons in psychological distress. This Directive covers victims of violence and other distressing events.

27 February 1998 (DH/AF1/98/No 137). Creation of emergency medicolegal centers. This follows the creation under an interdepartmental project of the Departments of Health and Justice of 26 forensic medicine units in regional university hospitals. These units associate thanatological as well as clinical practices, carried out 24 hours a day by university clinicians, hospital consultants and private consultants. The location of these structures within teaching hospitals guarantees a high technical and scientific level.

The Higher Council of Forensic Medicine published on 1 February 1995 a report on the different services provided by thanatological structures within university hospitals as well as in others teaching hospitals. A national report on this matter was given to the French Prime Minister by O. Jarde, deputy of the region Somme, on January 2006 (Jarde, 2006; Rapport IGAS).

From an educational perspective, the Higher Council proposed the creation of university degrees in forensic medicine and health law.

These structures led to:

- the creation of clinical research positions in forensic medicine,

- the creation of clinical research departments in hospitals and universities,
- the creation of forensic medicine units in hospitals located near courthouses,
- new diplomas in forensic medicine (DESC and Capacity, see below),
- the teaching of forensic medicine during the first years of medical studies,
- the development of new fields in biological research (toxicology, genetic fingerprinting, etc.).

The major modifications of the practice of Legal Medicine in France were induced by the "Circulaire du 27 décembre 2010 relative à la mise en oeuvre de la réforme de la médecine légale, NOR: JUSD1033099C (circul CRIM-2010-27/E6)."

This reform on a national level came into effect on 15 January 2011, and included funding by global budgets instead of fee-for-service paid by the Criminal Justice Department. This new organization is supposed to clarify the medicolegal activity on the national level and allows an easier identification of the forensic medical units. After two years of application of those rules (organization and funding), we can highlight the better consideration of our discipline in the hospital organization and the recruitment of numerous medical doctors in clinical units (Chariot, 2012).

The framework of the different departments of clinical and thanatological forensic activities is shown in Figure 11.1 and Table 11.1.

11.1.3 Activities of the forensic medicine departments

Clinical forensic medicine includes either the examination of living victims (child abuse, battered women, assaults, rape cases) or the examination of people in custody. One of the French characteristics is the determination of a given period called "incapacité total de travail (ITT)" (occupation incapacity), which represents the loss of autonomy of the victim, and its length is of legal importance. An ITT of less than eight days is a minor contravention of the law; a criminal offense occurs when the ITT is more than eight days.

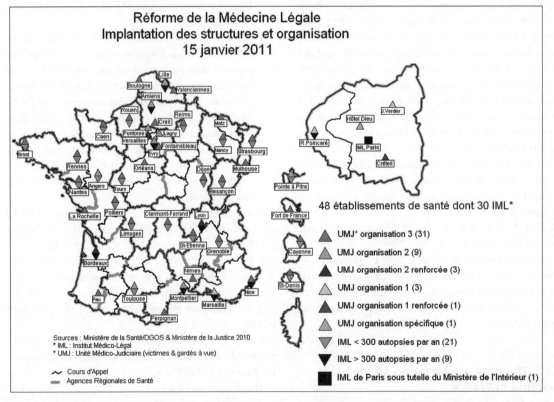

Figure 11.1 The framework of the different departments of forensic activities. *Source:* http://eclm.org/docs/France/Forensic_Medicine_in_France.pdf

Table 11.1 Names and addresses of hospitals having a medicolegal unit

Name of the hospital having a medicolegal unit	Addresses	Région
Centre Hospitalier Régional d'Orléans	1 rue Porte Madeleine - BP 2439 - 45032 Orléans	Centre
Centre Hospitalier Régional Universitaire de Tours	2 boulevard Tonnellé - 37044 Tours	Centre
Centre Hospitalier Sud Francilien	59 boulevard Henri Dunant - 91106 Corbeil-Essonnes	Ile-de-France
Centre Hospitalier de Lagny Marne-la-Vallée	31 avenue du Général Leclerc - 77405 Lagny sur Marne	Ile-de-France
Centre Hospitalier Intercommunal de Créteil	40 avenue de Verdun - 94010 Créteil	Ile-de-France
Centre Hospitalier de Versailles	177 rue de Versailles - 78157 Le Chesnay	Ile-de-France
Centre Hospitalier René Dubos	6 avenue de l'Ile-de-France - BP 90079 - 95303 Pontoise	Ile-de-France
Centre Hospitalier de Fontainebleau	55 boulevard Joffre - 77305 Fontainebleau	Ile-de-France
Centre Hospitalier Universitaire de Dijon	1 boulevard Jeanne d'Arc - BP 77908 - 21079 Dijon	Bourgogne
Centre Hospitalier de Mulhouse	87 avenue d'Altkirch - 68051 Mulhouse	Alsace
Centre Hospitalier de La Rochelle-Ré-Aunis	Rue du Docteur Schweitzer - 17019 La Rochelle	Poitou-Charentes
Centre Hospitalier Félix Guyon	Bellepierre - 97405 Saint-Denis	La Réunion
Centre Hospitalier A. Rosemon	Rue des Flamboyants - 97306 Cayenne	Guyane
Centre Hospitalier de Perpignan	20 avenue du Languedoc - BP 49954 - 66046 Perpignan Cedex	Languedoc-Roussillon
Centre Hospitalier de Valenciennes	114 avenue Desandrouin - BP 479 - 59322 Valenciennes	Nord-Pas-de-Calais
Centre Hospitalier de Boulogne-sur-Mer	Rue Jacques Monod - BP 69 - 62321 Boulogne-sur-Mer	Nord-Pas-de-Calais
Centre Hospitalier de Creil Laënnec	Boulevard Laënnec - BP 72 - 60109 Creil	Picardie
Centre Hospitalier de Pau	4 boulevard Hauterive - 64046 Pau Cedex	Aquitaine
Centre Hospitalier Régional Universitaire de Lille	2 avenue Oscar Lambret - 59037 Lille	Nord-Pas-de-Calais
Centre Hospitalier Universitaire de Besançon	2 place Saint-Jacques - 25030 Besançon	Franche-Comté
Assistance Publique - Hôpitaux de Marseille	80 rue Brochier - 13005 Marseille	Provence-Alpes-Côte d'Azur
Centre Hospitalier Universitaire de Toulouse	2 rue de la Viguerie - 31059 Toulouse	Midi-Pyrénées
Centre Hospitalier Universitaire de Caen	Avenue de la Côte de Nacre - 14033 Caen	Basse-Normandie
Centre Hospitalier Universitaire de Rennes	2 rue Henri le Guilloux - 35033 Rennes	Bretagne
Centre Hospitalier Universitaire de Limoges	2 avenue Martin Luther King - 87042 Limoges	Limousin
Centre Hospitalier Universitaire de Nancy	29 avenue Lattre de Tassigny - 54035 Nancy	Lorraine
Centre Hospitalier Universitaire de Nantes	5 allée de l'Ile Gloriette - 44093 Nantes	Pays de la Loire
Centre Hospitalier Universitaire d'Amiens	Place Victor Pauchet - 80054 Amiens	Picardie
Centre Hospitalier Universitaire de Reims	45 rue Cognacq-Jay - 51092 Reims	Champagne-Ardenne
Centre Hospitalier Universitaire d'Angers	4 rue Larrey - 49933 Angers	Pays de la Loire
Centre Hospitalier Régional Universitaire de Brest Carhaix	2 avenue Foch - 29609 Brest Cedex	Bretagne
Centre Hospitalier Universitaire de Rouen	1 rue de Germont - 76031 Rouen	Haute-Normandie
Centre Hospitalier Universitaire de Poitiers	2 rue de la Milétrie - BP 577 - 86021 Poitiers	Poitou-Charentes
Centre Hospitalier Universitaire de Grenoble	Boulevard de la Chantourne - BP 217 - 38700 Grenoble	Rhône-Alpes
Centre Hospitalier Universitaire de Saint-Etienne	1 chemin de la Marandière - 42055 Saint-Etienne	Rhône-Alpes
Centre Hospitalier Universitaire de Pointe-à-Pitre Abymes	BP 465 - 97159 Pointe-à-Pitre	Guadeloupe
Centre Hospitalier Universitaire de Fort-de-France	BP 632 - Route de Châteauboeuf - 97261 Fort-de-France	Martinique
Centre Hospitalier Universitaire de Nice	4 avenue Reine Victoria - BP 1179 - 06003 Nice	Provence-Alpes-Côte d'Azur
Centre Hospitalier Universitaire de Nîmes	Place du Professeur Robert Debré - 30029 Nîmes	Languedoc-Roussillon

(Conituied)

Table 11.1 *Continued*

Name of the hospital having a medicolegal unit	Addresses	Région
Centre Hospitalier Universitaire - Hôpitaux de Bordeaux	12 rue Dubernat - 33404 Talence	Aquitaine
Centre Hospitalier Universitaire de Montpellier	191 avenue Doyen Gaston Giraud - 34295 Montpellier	Languedoc-Roussillon
Centre Hospitalier Régional de Metz -Thionville	28 rue XXème Corps Américain - BP 90770 - 57019 Metz	Lorraine
Centre Hospitalier Universitaire de Clermont-Ferrand	58 rue Montalembert - 63003 Clermont-Ferrand Cedex 1	Auvergne
Centre Hospitalier Universitaire de Strasbourg	1 place de l'Hôpital - BP 426 - 67091 Strasbourg	Alsace
Hospices Civils de Lyon	3 quai des Célestins - BP 2251 - 69229 Lyon Cedex 02	Rhône-Alpes
Assistance Publique - Hôpitaux de Paris : Groupe Hospitalier Hôtel-Dieu	1 place du Parvis de Notre-Dame - 75181 Paris	Ile-de-France
Assistance Publique - Hôpitaux de Paris : Groupe Hospitalier Raymond Poincaré-Berck	104 boulevard Raymond Poincaré - 92380 Garches	Ile-de-France
Assistance Publique - Hôpitaux de Paris : Hôpital Jean Verdier	Avenue du 14 Juillet - 93143 Bondy	Ile-de-France

In the university hospitals, forensic doctors are on duty around the clock year round to perform the clinical examinations and, if possible, the external examination on the crime scene when called by the police forces (Martrille and Baccino, 2005).

Thanatological activities include body examination at the scene and medicolegal autopsies ordered by legal authorities. Most of the units develop radiographic post-mortem imagery.

These structures have their own laboratories or often collaborate with laboratories within the same university hospital structure for toxicological analyses and in some cases for genetic or dental identification.

It must be emphasized that all the forensic activities are performed under the control of the prosecutors and judges from the scene of crime throughout the investigations until the end of the trial. For example, the order to perform an autopsy is left in the hands of the magistrates on a case-by-case basis and there is no statue-defined policy despite the European protocol published in 1999. At the year 2012, about 8500 autopsies were performed in the forensic field and 570,000 deaths were registered in France.

11.2 Scientific and research bodies

The scientific body in the field of legal medicine is the French Society of Legal Medicine (Société Française de Médecine Légale). It is a nationwide forensic society of about 400 members having educational and scientifical goals. A special section is dedicated to young scientists called "club junior" open to assistants and people involved in the hospital internship. The Society gives also, every two years, a prize for scientific projects of great interest called "Prix Louis Roche."

Most of the French professors and heads of departments are associated or running research units of the two major research organizations in France, named the National Institute of Medical Research (INSERM) or the National Centre of Scientific Research (CNRS).

11.3 Teaching

In French medical schools, 20 to 40 hours of lectures are dedicated to forensic medicine to enable students to provide appropriate medical certificates for living victims and death certificates. These lectures also give some basic principles on medical law, that is, medical liability and medical confidentiality. It must be emphasized that during the first year of medical school, a few hours are spent on bioethics. Lectures concerning other aspects of legal medicine and health law are also given within modules in humanities, social sciences, clinical practice and gynaecology as well as modules relating to abuse and sexual violence.

Following the two-year specialization internship, medical students can then study for the DESC (Diplôme d'Etudes Specialisées Complémentaires) in Forensic Medicine and Medical Expertise. This includes students who have completed specialization internships in occupational medicine, public health, psychiatry, pathological anatomy, internal medicine, surgery, as well as specialization in general practice.

Legislation passed on 10 January 2000 under the influence of the Higher Council of Forensic Medicine introduced a new diploma called "Capacity in Medicolegal Practice." The Capacity should compensate the lack of places in the DESC programmes, and is open to family practitioners or specialists who would not qualify for a DESC. This teaching also takes two years, and students must conduct over 100 autopsies supervised by an experienced professional before they can practice forensic medicine autonomously (Martrille and Baccino, 2005).

Postgraduate lectures are also often given to train future experts in the evaluation of bodily damage for the civil courts or insurance companies in order to explain how to take care of a victim from the medical, psychological and judicial points of view. Other lectures are given in the field of social security medicine and in the law school about the medical aspects.

Forensic medicine is also part of the curriculum of a number of university diplomas. The University Diploma in bodily impairment is delivered following university studies that do not encompass the whole range of forensic medicine activities but deal with compensation for physical injuries. Finally, a number of Masters and University Diplomas nationwide include different aspects of forensic medicine.

It must be noted that forensic medicine is a medical activity that is not recognized as a medical speciality, but as a competence, by the French Medical Association Ordre National des Médecins.

Students engaged in professional courses can get Masters lessons in different scientific fields. Masters take two years and are organized by medical schools or other schools such as law and life sciences. Among these are Masters in anthropology, forensic biology, toxicology, medical law, ethics and different domains of biology.

A list of experts is established by each Court of Appeal, under the Forensic Medicine chapter. About 530 doctors having a diploma delivered in forensic medicine are registered. Magistrates do not always have a precise knowledge of the diplomas delivered and the corresponding level of formation. Magistrates are not limited to experts registered under these chapters, but experts who are not registered have to swear an oath in court proceedings, and magistrates can be required to motivate their decision to choose an expert outside the register.

Within continuous education, one can note a course given nationally by the Society of Forensic Medicine, which includes teachings on the crime scene, the medical file and child abuse. Local and regional courses by the Mediterranean Society of Forensic Medicine and the Belgian-Italian-French-Swiss Association of Forensic Medicine yearly are organized by Professor Daniel Malicier of Lyon and the annual symposium on forensic anthropology held in Nice is organized by Professor Gérald Quatrehomme. Numerous other regional courses are also organized by hospital and university centres. It should be mentioned that workshops are organized by Professor Cristina Cattaneo and Professor Eric Baccino on clinical subjects under the umbrella of the International Academy of Legal Medicine. Online e-learning is also being developed, especially on the site of the Faculty of Medicine of Grenoble.

Continuous education courses tend also to be undertaken by people in the police force, lawyers and forensic medicine practitioners.

11.4 Forensic organization in criminalistics in France

11.4.1 The Institute of Criminal Research of the National Gendarmerie (IRCGN) (www.gendarmerie.interieur.gouv.fr)

Located in Rosny-sous-Bois (93) near Paris, the judicial division of the National Gendarmerie is based on the capacity of the IRCGN and on the Department of Legal Documentation and Research. It employs 500 military and civilian personnel as well as forensic pathologists, odontologists and pharmacists. This organization may give some help to French investigators and judges for technical, scientific investigations at a high level.

The Department of Legal Documentation and Research has been established for the treatment of information to judicial finality. Its main mission is to maintain national databases, to make cross-check information and to duplicate and strengthen the fight against cybercrime. Forensic sciences are essential to resolve cases and allow gathering evidence and reconciliations of facts and knowledge about criminality.

The Institute of Criminal Research of the National Gendarmerie is accredited by the French accreditation body (COFRAC) and groups on one site all activities related to forensic sciences. It has a laboratory and a tactical and operational component available 24 hours a day, allowing specialists to be quickly sent on to complex crime scenes or major disasters with specific and adapted material resources. This component includes two operating units:

The Gendarmerie Disaster Victim Identification Unit (UGIVC). During a major disaster, this DVI unit composed of multidisciplinary trained teams is in charge of the different steps of the identification procedure based on the recovery of bodies, the ante- and postmortem information collection and the crosscheck of these data.

The National Criminal Investigation Unit is a special unit of scientists of the Institute of Criminal Research of the National Gendarmerie, able to carry out in specific circumstances all or part of the investigations and coordination of forensic operations. Specialists from different departments (fingerprints, biology, biochemistry, microtraces, etc.) carry out the analyses with the multidisciplinary competences to perform the sampling in different areas of the forensic field and may perform the analyses of the samples on-site or in the laboratory.

11.4.2 The National Police Institute of Forensic Science (www.inps.interieur. gouv.fr)

This institute, created in 2001, is a public institution placed under the authority of the French Minister of the Interior (Home Office). It has the quality of national expert approved by the Supreme French Court and is accredited for the analyses performed in casework. Its mission is to conduct examinations and scientific and technical analyses ordered by the judges and police investigators in a criminal context. The Institute is constituted by six police laboratories, namely the forensic laboratories of Lille, Lyon, Marseille, Paris and Toulouse and the toxicology laboratory of the Prefecture of Police of Paris. These laboratories have a national competence and the central support body is located in Lyon. Approximately 700 employees work at the Institute who are mostly scientists. The activity of this Institute covers the entire field of forensics, going from the exploitation of

genetic samples to traces of papillary fingerprints, document analysis, ballistics and analysis of ballistic injuries, expertise on digital technologies, analysis of drugs, toxicology as well as physical chemistry analyses on various media (fire residues, soil, paints, inks, fibers and gunshot residue).

Forensic specialized analyses are performed either by national or university laboratories as well as private ones. This is particularly the case for toxicological and forensic DNA analyses. Another example is the entomology samples examination to determine the postmortem delay. These are processed essentially in two centers, the Medico-Legal Institute in Lille and at the IRCGN; the diatom test, which was reintroduced in France by the university laboratory of the Medico-Legal Institute of Strasbourg in 1992 today has an experience of over 1500 cases.

Diatoms are unicellular algae belonging to the class of Bacillariophycae, which includes more than 15,000 species living in fresh water. These algae can be considered as particles present in submerged water that are inhaled during drowning. Once in the bloodstream they reach the closed organs. Under strict extraction and identification conditions, these particles can be considered as good markers of drowning.

Due to this hard siliceous skeleton, diatoms can be recovered from putrefied or burnt tissues by either enzymatic or acid digestion (Ludes *et al.*, 1994). The identification of these algae is based on the structure of their valves, which show different symmetry, thus allowing the distinction of two main groups, namely the centric diatoms and the elongated or pennate diatoms.

Analysis will be considered as positive when at least 20 diatoms are identified per 100 µl of a pellet sediment extracted from a 2 g lung sample and the identification of more than five complete diatoms (with exclusion of fragments) per 100 µl of a pellet sediment extracted from 2 g tissue samples from, for example, the brain, kidney, liver and bone marrow. Bone marrow is described as a sanctuary organ and if diatoms reach this tissue, the diagnostic of drowning could be assessed.

This test cannot be proposed to assess the diagnostic of drowning in a bathtub or in water containing very few algae, for example, in ice water.

The site of drowning may be determined by comparison between the water microflora with the diatoms found in the lungs.

11.5 Conclusion

The organization of the Legal Medicine in France was reinforced by a new regulation, which has been applied since January 2011 and enhances the strength of this field in France. All the examinations, autopsies and additional analyses are only performed on prosecutor or judge orders. The *Journal of Legal Medicine* is the official voice of the "Société Française de Médecine Légale," which is the scientific body of French legal medicine. Important support is given to the research teams to be internationally recognized.

References

Chariot, P. (2012) Organisation nationale de la médecine légale en France. *La Rev. Prat.* 62: 796–798.

Chaumont, A. (1997a) L'âge d'or de la médecine légale – Histoire de la médecine à Strasbourg – Edition, *La Nuée Bleue*, pp. 246–249.

Chaumont, A. (1997b) La brillante reviviscence de la médecine légale – Histoire de la Médecine Légale Edition, *La Nuée Bleue*, pp. 510–513.

Demichel, F. (2004) Les contradictions actuelles du Droit et de la Santé. *Revue Générale du Droit Médical* 13: 169–181.

Gosset, D. (2007) Les structures hospitalières et hospitalo-universitaires de médecine légale: quel avenir en 2007? *Gestion Hospitalière* 2007: 676–679.

Hecketsweiller, Ph. (2006) Trajectoire de la médecine légale. *Gestion Hospitalière* 2006: 657–664.

Jarde, O. (2006) Rapport au Premier Ministre sur la Médecine Légale, 2003, rapport IGAS/IGS – Mission interministérielle en vue d'une réforme de la médecine légale, Janvier.

Ludes, B. (2008) Forensic medicine in France, in *Forensic Medicine in Europe*, Eds B. Madea and P. Saukko, Schmidt-Römhild, Lübeck, Germany, pp. 113–141.

Ludes, B., Quantin, S., Coste, M., Mangin, P. (1994) Application of a simple enzymatic digestion method for diatom detection in the diagnosis of drowning in putrefied corpses by diatom analysis. *Int. J. Med.* 107: 37–41.

Martrille, L., Baccino, E. (2005) Professional bodies, France – forensic medical and scientific training, in *Encyclopedia of Forensic and Legal Medicine*, Eds J. Payne-James, R.W. Byard, T.S. Corey, C. Henderson, Elsevier Ltd, pp. 495–499.

Penneau, M. (2003) Plaidoyer pour une médecine légale moderne. *Gaz. Pal.* 4–6, Mai.

Penneau, M. (2006) La médecine légale, discipline hospitalière. *Gestion Hospitalière* 2006: 665–669.

Proust, B. (2007) La réforme de la médecine légale sur le pas de tir. Plaidoyer pour un passage à l'acte politique en 2007. *Gestion Hospitalière* 2007: 670–675.

Sournia, J.-Ch. (1989) *La Médecine Révolutionnaire (1789–1799)*, Payot ed., p. 198. Rapport IGAS: http://lesrapports.lado cumentationfrancaise.fr.

Tardieu, A. (1860) Etude médico-légale sur les sévices et mauvais traitements exercés sur des enfants. *Annales Hygiène Publique et Médecine Légale*, 1860: 361–398. www.gendarmerie.interieur.gouv.fr.www.inps.interieur.gouv.fr.

CHAPTER 12
Forensic medicine in Germany

W. Eisenmenger & O. Peschel

Institute of Forensic Medicine, Ludwig Maximilians University, Munich, Germany

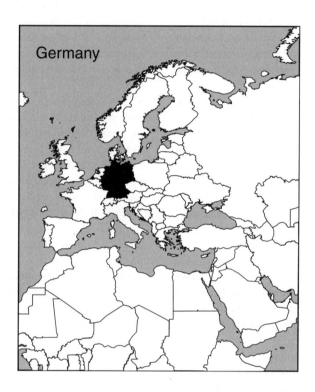

The origins of forensic medicine in Germany date back some 500 years and are rooted in the codification of the criminal law that was in force at the time and that was, in essence, municipal law. It was largely due to the pressure exerted by the Imperial Chamber Court, founded in 1495, that Johann von Schwarzenberg drew up the so-called *Constitutio Bambergensis* in 1507. This formed the basis for the *peinliche Halsgerichtsordnung* of Emperor Charles V, a legal code involving corporal punishment for the judgement of capital crimes, better known as the *Constitutio Criminalis Carolina*. It was passed into law for the whole of the German Reich in the Reichstag of 1532. This legal code stipulated that experienced specialist doctors had to be consulted in cases involving murder, manslaughter, grievous bodily harm resulting in death, infanticide, suspicion of medical malpractice, and autopsies of people who had died a violent death. The same was true for cases of abortion or sterilization, as well as for establishing the degree of criminal liability in cases involving juveniles and the mentally ill. This marked the starting point of forensics as a specialist field in the German-speaking regions of Europe.

In the period that followed, programmes of training in forensic medicine evolved at universities, which

The Global Practice of Forensic Science, First Edition. Edited by Douglas H. Ubelaker.

were the educational establishments where doctors were given their scientific training. Although forensic medicine was not yet a separate discipline in its own right, a number of lectures dealing with forensic-medical issues were held. The first books to address this subject matter were published in the 16th and 17th centuries; because they were published in Latin, they quickly spread across the whole continent of Europe. The most renowned were the works of Ambroise Paré from France and Fortunato Fedele and Paolo Zacchia from Italy.

In the second half of the 17th century and especially in the 18th century, professors at German-speaking universities also published works relevant to the discipline. These included Welsch, Amann and Bohn in Leipzig, Alberti in Halle, Löw in Prague, Teichmeyer in Jena, Albrecht v. Haller in Göttingen and Büttner and Metzger in Königsberg, to name but a few.

Of particular significance was the contribution made by Johann Peter Frank in Vienna. He saw the fields of forensic medicine and public healthcare, particularly in association with hygiene, as being the communal responsibility of an absolutist state, thereby creating the concept of *Staatsarzneikunde*, or the study of public health and hygiene.

Combining two medical fields in this way transpired to be an impediment to the scholarly development of both subdisciplines in the longer term, because an ever-increasing degree of specialization meant that the knowledge and practical expertise acquired could no longer be managed as a single, common task. Indeed, the two fields were still not ultimately separated until the second half of the 19th century.

The development of forensic medicine into a university discipline in its own right was a slow process. Although lectures did take place in forensic medicine at individual universities, they were being held by professors who were specialists in other fields such as surgery, physiology or anatomy. In 1804, Emperor Francis II created the first specific Chair of legal medicine and medical police by decree in Vienna. The *Ordinarius* Professor, Ferdinand Bernhard Vietz, carried out autopsies in the presence of students; initially, they took place in the Vienna General Hospital, the *Allgemeines Krankenhaus*. His successor, Joseph Bernt, was subsequently given his own small institute in 1818 with storage rooms for corpses and a lecture theatre where he could carry out autopsies.

In accordance with the standardized nature of *Staats-arzneikunde* in the various countries of the Habsburg Empire, the next professorial Chair to be created was in 1807 in Prague. The Kingdom of Prussia also viewed the establishment of a public health sector as progressive and in accordance with the Enlightenment, creating so-called *Physicat* positions. It was the task of those entrusted with these jobs to cater to the medical needs of the population, a remit that included issues of a forensic nature. It was in this spirit that an *Extraordinariat für Staats- und Gerichtliche Arzneikunde* – an associate professorship of public health and legal medicine – was created at the Friedrich-Wilhelms-University in Berlin in 1820. Further professorships in legal medicine followed in 1855 in Bern/Switzerland, 1863 in Graz, 1867 in Kiel, 1869 in Innsbruck, and in a total of 15 universities by the turn of the century. A further six universities created professorships in the years before the Great War. Nevertheless, it was not until 1980 that all German-speaking universities could boast a Chair in the field. The last new professorship to be created was in 1980 at the University of Ulm, which was founded in 1967.

Forensic medicine as a university discipline in its own right came under serious threat in 1966 when the German Council of Science and Humanities – the *Wissenschaftsrat* – recommended, in its new regulations on the licensing of doctors, that forensic medicine should no longer be taught as a specialism, but that forensic issues should be integrated into lectures dealing with clinical matters. It was only thanks to the enormous effort invested by the German Association of Forensic Medicine, the West German Medical Faculty Association, the Ministries of Education in the *Länder* and the Federal Ministry of Youth, Family and Health that the implementation of these plans could be prevented.

Although forensic medicine had been written into the regulations on the licensing of doctors as a university course of study in 1970, and although the German Medical Assembly had decided in 1976 to include its own specialist doctor of forensic medicine in its regulations governing advanced specialist training, the German Council of Science and Humanities tried once again, in 1976, to abolish forensic medicine as a discipline in its own right. It suggested that it be classified as a subdiscipline in the field of pathomorphology. This plan was also thwarted by the President of the German Association of Forensic Medicine.

In the 1990s and into the 2000s, financial considerations led many universities to consider whether it still made sense for the smaller medical fields to continue being represented by full professors, or *Ordinariate*. This concerned fields such as the history of medicine, social medicine, dentistry and also forensic medicine. In 1999, the institute at the University of Marburg closed, with its teaching and other services being taken over by the University of Giessen. In 2003, the Institute of Forensic Medicine at Aachen University transferred its duties to the Institute of Legal Medicine in Cologne. In Berlin at around the same time, the institutes at the Humboldt University and the Free University were merged, although the State Institute of Legal and Social Medicine Berlin, which was administered by the healthcare authorities, had already had its staff merged with the institute at the Free University and the two institutes had already been run on the basis of a single common staff. At a later date, a merger took place between the institutes at the Medical University Lübeck and at Kiel University. This was also the case with the institutes at Magdeburg University and the University of Halle. Several institutes were no longer run by full professors, but as a subsection in the department of pathology, as was the case at Göttingen.

In addition to the university institutes, there have been and still are other institutes that are assigned to the public health authorities in large towns or the *Länder*. For example, there is one such institute in each of the following cities: Bremen, Dortmund, Berlin (which shares a common staff with the Institute of Forensic Medicine at the Humboldt University) and Potsdam. The German military – the *Bundeswehr* – also maintains its own institute at the Airforce (Luftwaffe) Institute of Aviation Medicine, which deals primarily with the forensic examination of aeroplane and helicopter crashes.

Recently, certain individual specialists in forensic medicine have opened their own private practices. They tend to restrict themselves to minor forensic procedures, such as alcohol assessment or autopsies.

The most common areas of activity in the field of forensic medicine are the following: autopsies, clinical forensics including the examination of living people, in particular of the victims of sex offences, sexual abuse and child abuse; toxicology relating to controlled substances, medication and serious cases of poisoning of all kinds; the analysis of DNA in the context of criminal evidence and in establishing parentage; the process of identification in cases of unknown deceased persons and large-scale disasters; determining the age of individuals in asylum cases and establishing their degree of accountability in cases requiring the application of juvenile law; biomechanics, traffic medicine and accident reconstruction, and a number of specialist areas such as forensic insectology (entomology) or paleopathology. Since the 1930s, alcohol research has occupied a position of importance in forensic medicine, both in respect to detecting levels of blood alcohol as well as establishing the effect of alcohol on a person's fitness to drive and their criminal liability. In contrast to the law in other countries, German criminal law permits a blood sample to be taken in the process of securing evidence. This is why extensive research has been undertaken into the metabolism of ethanol in the human body and also the setting of so-called limits to prohibit drivers of motor vehicles or cyclists from taking part in road traffic on the basis of their blood alcohol levels. In 2003, the breath test was deemed admissible in assessing a person's relative fitness to drive.

German law requires a proof of abstinence from anyone who has repeatedly committed alcohol-related traffic offences, who has exceeded certain blood alcohol concentrations or who has been found to have traces of controlled substances in their blood whilst taking part in road traffic. Because of this, forensic medicine also includes research into and the provision of services associated with examining markers of alcoholism or providing evidence of drug consumption by conducting a longitudinal analysis of a suspect's hair.

The field of biomechanics, in both its research and provision of services, has given rise to considerable discussion. The effects of physical parameters on the human body, especially the effects of forces including acceleration, often constitute part of a judicial report. Investigations of this nature require natural scientists, for instance physicists, engineers and computer scientists, to collaborate with medical doctors. Only very few institutes of forensic medicine can afford such a complex staff structure, meaning that there are only two university institutes in Germany that currently maintain a department of biomechanics.

One area that has seen rapid development in forensic medicine is the use of medical imaging techniques. The first research findings in this field were yielded by

Professors Dirnhofer and Thali at the University of Bern. Since then, a large number of German institutes have acquired their own machines and are now in a position to routinely carry out X-ray examinations, CT scanning and, in individual cases, NMR. Recently, studies have been conducted using targeted biopsy techniques and the creation of a postmortem circulation using a heart–lung machine. The value of such studies for the field of forensic medicine is currently under discussion.

A further procedure that might be integrated into the canon of forensic methods is the study of stable isotopes for use in clarifying the regional background of unknown persons.

Clinical forensic medicine has grown particularly rapidly in recent years, with new departments in this field being established in Hamburg, Mainz and Munich, for example. Here, the focus is on assessing domestic violence, child abuse and sex offences. In cases involving the latter, procedures are limited to the use of specula. In cases where it becomes necessary to assess injuries deep in the vagina, then a gynaecological examination is required.

Forensic psychiatry has completely separated itself from forensic medicine. Until the 1970s, permanent positions for psychiatrists still existed at individual institutes of forensic medicine. However, the viewpoint prevailed that psychiatric exploration would be best undertaken by admitting the subject to a clinic as an inpatient: because the institutes of forensic medicine do not allow periods of residency, this field of study became completely integrated into clinical psychiatry.

In Germany, procedures for processing fingerprints and examining the authenticity of documentation lie outside the scope of forensic medicine. This is also the case with the examination of fibres, traces of paint and ballistics. These types of examination have long been the responsibility of the State Criminal Police Offices – the *Landeskriminalämter* – or police laboratories. Because these police bodies also carry out other types of scientific examination, there is a certain degree of competition between themselves and the institutes of forensic medicine, particularly in the fields of toxicology and DNA analysis, and to some degree in anthropology and biomechanics. German judges are free to choose their expert witnesses, whereas the public prosecutor's office and the police themselves tend to turn to police institutions when they need to call on expert opinion. The central argument underlying this was always that

the services required could be provided less expensively by the police, because the university institutes did not primarily exist to provide such services and they received payment for them. In contrast, the State Criminal Police Offices only received payment for their services through a system of internal accounting with the contracting authority. Over the last few years, many services at the university institutes have been reclassified to include them in their main duties, and the staffing costs at the State Offices of Criminal Investigations proved to be extremely expensive, so that the arguments cited above have lost much of their former significance. The vast majority of the contract work undertaken by the institutes of forensic medicine comes from the state investigating authorities, that is from the police, the public prosecutor's office or from the courts. Contracts issued by private individuals or by insurance companies are far less numerous and are often limited to specific problem areas. The biomechanic assessment of whiplash injuries, in particular as a consequence of road traffic accidents, is included in this category.

The vast majority of the institutes of forensic medicine are indeed financed by the income they receive for compiling reports for the police and the public prosecutor's office. Since these reports are now paid for as part of the main duties of the institutes, the income they generate, which flows to the universities as the parent institutions, can be used in no small measure to finance their staffing costs. Payment for the services provided by the institutes of forensic medicine occurs under a specific law that governs the compensation of witnesses, including expert witnesses (JVEG). Private institutions and individual specialists in forensic medicine operating their own private practices are also subject to this law, although the cost of certain services, for instance autopsies, is not covered in its entirety by the compensation payments. A university-based institute of forensic medicine that possesses a molecular genetic and a toxicological section is in a position to offer and charge for these rather more lucrative services, whereas those operating in private practice might find this structure problematic.

As a consequence of the legal requirement to put all contracts out to public tender, competitive pressure has increased, as has the downward pressure on pricing. As a result, some institutes are no longer able to provide those services, which are manpower-intensive and require considerable material input, because they are insufficiently remunerated within the parameters of the law.

Currently, most of the German institutes are accredited according to certain norms (DIB-ISO), either as a whole institute or by section, so that procedural codes and examination procedures have been largely standardized across the country and are therefore comparable with one another. In addition, round robin tests (e.g. DNA, alcohol) exist for specialist laboratories as a form of quality control. They are repeated regularly and passing them is a precondition for submitting bids in public tenders.

Forensic odontology is largely conducted at university institutes of forensic medicine in collaboration with interested odontologists. Working together with the Federal Criminal Police Office – the *Bundeskriminalamt* – it is repeatedly called upon by the so-called identification commission (German DVI-Team = IDKO) to identify the victims of air crashes. At its core, the team is made up of officers from the *Bundeskriminalamt* who are then supplemented on a case-by-case basis by specialists from the institutes of forensic medicine.

Besides being involved in several domestic catastrophes involving German victims, most of which were road traffic accidents and air crashes, German forensic specialists were also active internationally in 1991 following the crash of an Austrian passenger aircraft near Bangkok; under the auspices of the International Criminal Tribunal for Yugoslavia's mission to exhume the victims of the Bosnian conflict in 1998, as well as in 1999 in Kosovo; following the fire on the mountain railway in 2001 in Kaprun, Austria, which claimed the lives of 156 people; and in 2004/05 in Thailand and Sri Lanka in the aftermath of the tsunami.

The causes of death covered by autopsies cover a broad spectrum. Among these there are typically cases of homicide including murder and manslaughter, but also cases of negligent homicide arising from road traffic and occupational accidents. Added to this are household accidents, sport-related accidents, suicides and cases where the cause of death by natural causes is unclear. In recent years, the number of autopsies conducted as a result of medical malpractice has risen sharply. The statistics for the number of autopsies carried out show significant regional variation. Whilst the very high proportion of autopsies being carried out in Munich, at 10% of deceased persons, is unusual, many rural areas have extremely few autopsies, with statistics in some cases showing numbers below 0.5% of all deceased persons. This appears to be particularly the case when it

is necessary to cover large distances to reach the nearest university institute of forensic medicine. Such situations arise partially due to the legal requirements to which postmortem examinations and certification of death are subject. In Germany, each individual *Land* determines its own legal framework, meaning that there is no standard for the country as a whole. A postmortem examination and certification of death can only be carried out by licensed doctors, although irrespective of their specialization; most often it is the practically active, established doctors and general practitioners who are called upon to conduct postmortem examinations. If these doctors do not certify a natural cause of death, or certify the cause of death as unknown (and here too there are no national, standardised legal definitions), the police must be informed. The police then initiate an investigation and submit it to the public prosecutor's office, which decides whether an autopsy is required by making an application to the district court – the *Amtsgericht*. Classical pathology has seen doctors applying for autopsies with the consent of the next of kin (albeit with very low and continually declining numbers of autopsies being conducted), but this has never played much of a role in forensic medicine in Germany. According to a Multicenter study carried out in 1997, some 1200–1400 homicides a year are not identified as such (as against approximately 700–900 homicides a year according to police crime statistics) as a result of these regulations and because general practitioners are not well versed in forensic matters and the interpretation of evidence, and also because of the investigating authorities' cost-saving interest in having people's deaths certified as being the result of natural causes (which means that the police are not required to conduct an investigation).

Irrespective of police crime statistics, which are based purely on issues of policing, no other statistics exist covering the number of autopsies being carried out in Germany either nationwide or in the individual *Länder*. Neither is there any unified law or legal framework covering autopsies.

If earlier and/or regional studies are used as a point of orientation, and if the steadily sinking number of autopsies over many years is taken into account, then the number of forensic autopsies being carried out across the country nowadays might be estimated at below 1–1.5%.

The assessment of cases involving accusations of medical malpractice poses a particularly complex challenge. Many questions can only be answered by consulting a specialist from the relevant clinical field. Heart and vascular surgery or neurosurgical operations can serve as an example here: it is usually the case that an institute of forensic medicine becomes involved when there has been a fatality and an autopsy is required in the early stages of an investigation. Experience has shown that it makes good sense to tackle cases of this kind in a team of colleagues and, where necessary, to involve the relevant specialists even as early as the autopsy stage. Cases like these have become more frequent in recent years due to a rise in complaints by next of kin.

After having submitted his written investigation report, a forensic pathologist will also usually be summoned to the main trial as an expert witness and consulted in court. This means he will deliver an oral report based on the information that has emerged from the main trial and the examination of the witnesses. The code of criminal procedure contains a principle of orality, meaning that during the main trial the only information that can be used in reaching a verdict is that which has been debated orally during the trial, including the questioning of the expert witness. The expert witness is summoned in the vast majority of cases by the court and is independent and impartial, meaning he or she is under no obligation to either the public prosecutor's office or the defence. The expert witness is remunerated by the court and not by either of the parties, and whilst this is certainly legally possible, it is fairly uncommon.

In Germany, forensic medicine is an established course of study in the regulations on the licensing of doctors. Every medical student must therefore complete a course of study in this subject and have their knowledge tested in an examination. Teaching methods differ from university to university, but in the main they are a combination of lectures and practical classes. Additionally, it falls under the remit of forensic medicine to teach the medical students the legal and ethical essentials of being a doctor. Accordingly, some colleagues' work addresses questions of medical law and forensic medicine plays a role in the ethics commissions of many universities.

In order to qualify for a course of advanced training to become a specialist in forensic medicine, candidates must first have been in full-time employment in the field for at least 3.5 years and at least half a year each in the fields of pathology and psychiatry (minimum 5 years all together). In this time, a catalogue enumerating a specifically defined quantity of occupations and tasks must have been completed; the following list of procedures serves as an example (numbers differ between the *Länder* – the numbers cited here are for Bavaria): description and evaluation of postmortem examinations (400); findings reports and evaluations from crime scenes and places where evidence has been discovered (25); forensic autopsies and reports on the correlation between morphological findings and the sequence of events (300); histological examinations (2000); evaluation of pictorial evidence and storage of evidence (10); oral and written reports for the law courts (200); forensic-osteological and/or odontological expert reports (25).

In addition, expertise in the following areas is integral to the training of specialists in forensic medicine: assessing and diagnosing poisoning; the essentials of forensic molecular genetics related to paternity and identification; knowledge of forensic anthropology and odontology; questions of traffic and insurance medicine, together with the forensic application of imaging procedures.

The course of study takes place in the institutes according to individual curricula and not in externally held courses, although in exceptional cases optional specialist courses (e.g. bloodstain pattern analysis) are offered. The course of training to become a specialist in forensic medicine ends with an oral exam held by the State Chamber of Physicians. The field of forensic medicine is currently experiencing a heightened level of public awareness due to forensics in general and the field of forensic medicine as a whole being a central theme in many crime films and thrillers. This has resulted in increased interest in the field on the part of medical graduates, enabling institutes of forensic medicine to select their academic assistants from a larger field of applicants. In contrast, however, many institutes are struggling to find specialists with professional experience.

Experience suggests that predicting the future is no easy matter. Clearly, the question of whether forensic medicine can sustain its long-standing and extensive links to universities as a course of study in its own right will prove decisive for the field in Germany and the whole of the German-speaking world. Partly out of financial considerations, the future of forensic medicine at some universities is open to discussion. But one thing is certain: if the field of forensic medicine survives only as the provider of services for the police and the public prosecutor's office, then research in the field will grind to a standstill, leading to a serious loss of academic potential in this field, which is of such crucial importance both to the medical profession and society as a whole.

CHAPTER 13

Forensic science in Hong Kong

Sheilah Hamilton[1] & Philip Beh[2]

[1] Forensic Focus, Hong Kong
[2] Department of Pathology, The University of Hong Kong, Hong Kong

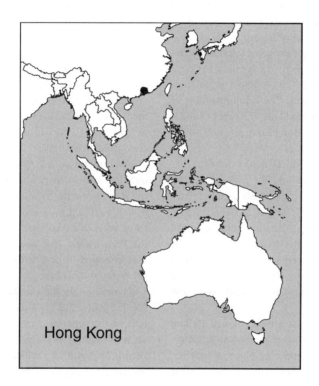

Hong Kong

13.1 Background

Forensic science in Hong Kong has a long and colourful history, although the term "chemicolegal" – not "forensic science" – was used for many years, and the number of professionals employed in its practice remained very low until the early 1970s (Clarke, 2004). However, since the late 1870s, one constant is the fact that the operation of forensic science in Hong Kong has been a predominantly "Government" matter. There were, and still are, few private forensic consultancies or forensic professionals in Hong Kong, and those in the latter category are often former or retired professional staff of the Hong Kong Government Laboratory (HKGL).

In 1842 the island of Hong Kong was ceded to the British by the terms of the Treaty of Nanking, although settlement had begun the previous year. Thus was born the Colony of Hong Kong. Lord Palmerston, British

The Global Practice of Forensic Science, First Edition. Edited by Douglas H. Ubelaker.
© 2015 John Wiley & Sons, Ltd. Published 2015 by John Wiley & Sons, Ltd.

Foreign Secretary, famously referred to it as "a barren rock with hardly a house upon it". This so-called "barren rock" covered a mere 80 km². Some two decades later, the size of the territory increased due to the acquisition of the Kowloon peninsula (opposite the northern shore of Hong Kong Island), and the quaintly named "Government Gardens and Tree Planting Department" set about beautifying the previously stark hillsides that had irked Lord Palmerston 30 years before. Still later in 1898, the lease of the New Territories and several islands resulted in the formation of a much larger area comprising 1104 km².

Since July 1997 Hong Kong has been a Special Administrative Region (SAR) of the People's Republic of China and, at the time of writing (2013) has a population of approximately 7.15 million. The administration of Macau, the former Portuguese colony and other Chinese SAR, is separate from that of Hong Kong and will not be mentioned further.

Although this is not a political book, the fact that Hong Kong was a British colony for more than 150 years should not be ignored, particularly as this relates to the different "Hong Kong Government Departments" that were formed as part of its development, operated within the overall administrative framework and, much to historians' delight, produced some detailed Annual Reports. Without intending to, these reports illustrate how forensic science developed in the early days and operates in the 21st century.

An interesting feature about British colonial staffing is that some expatriate personnel employed in different administrations moved from one place to another. This may be considered in the Hong Kong context in relation to acquiring new forensic expertise. As late as 1960, Ron Edgley, an experienced forensic scientist, transferred from Tanganyika (later Tanzania) to the Hong Kong Government Laboratory (HKGL), where he worked until his retirement in 1984 (Clarke, 2004). As forensic science became more internationally accepted during the 1970s, staff of the newly formed (1969) Forensic Science Division of the HKGL developed close ties with the UK Home Office and Metropolitan Police Laboratories, both of which seemed to regard their Hong Kong cousin, geographically at least, as a rather distant UK forensic laboratory. Home Office Central Research Establishment (HOCRE) reports were sent regularly to staff of the Forensic Division of the HKGL throughout the 1970s, as were quality

photographic collections of glass headlights (Hamilton, 2013).

13.2 Early history

One of the first examples of forensic analysis being required in Hong Kong occurred in 1857 when an attempt was made to poison the European community by lacing its bread supply with a large amount of arsenic. However, because the criminals had been heavy-handed, the poison was noticed before the bread was eaten. Even so, analysis of the tainted bread was necessary. The tests did not take place in Hong Kong but in the War Department in England, suggesting that either no analyst with appropriate knowledge, equipment and experience was available in Hong Kong, or at least none who wished to become involved in such chemicolegal matters.

It was not till some 20 years later, in 1879, that the first qualified "Apothecary and Analyst" was recruited into the Hong Kong Government. This was Hugh McCallum, a well-qualified Scot who had previously worked for three years as a dispenser in the Royal Naval Hospital in the West Indies. The "analyst" part of McCallum's title was intended to deal with any forensic or chemicolegal work, and his first two Annual Reports for 1880 and 1881 mention the fact that he analysed material from suspected poisoning cases during both years. McCallum's immediate superior was the Colonial Surgeon, head of what would become known as the Medical and Health Department (M&HD). Over time the names of the parent department, subdepartment and the officer-in-charge altered, but one thing remained unchanged: with few exceptions that will be mentioned later, traditional forensic scientific work was performed in the HKGL which, until 1978, was part of the Medical and Health Department of the Hong Kong Government but then became an independent Government agency composed of two divisions, a "Forensic Science Division" and an "Analytical and Advisory Services Division".

When McCallum was transferred in 1883 to the newly formed Sanitary Board, a "replacement Apothecary and Analyst" was recruited from England. Although William Crowe was only 21 at the time of his appointment in 1883 and had no prior overseas experience, he was remarkably farsighted during his early years, particularly when it came to "forensic thinking", as can be seen from his views of the value of what might now be termed "alternative" or "negative" evidence – see Box 13.1 (Crow, 1885).

Box 13.1 (Crow, 1885)

The murder at Kowloon, on April 16th, furnished material for investigation. A garment was sent by the Police with a request that the stains thereon might be examined in order to determine whether or not they were due to human blood. Although very like, the stains were not due to blood but to some oxides of iron. The man under arrest was an engineer and had possibly been using, when at work, some paint made of iron pigments known in commerce as "Indian and Venetian red".

Leaving the term "human" out of the question, for it is impossible to distinguish, with certainty, the blood of a human from that of other mammals, the Inspector took a proper course in having the coat examined. *In chemico-legal cases negative evidence is equally as valuable as that of a positive nature* (Emphasis added).

13.3 Early changes and challenges

In 1903 the pharmacy aspect of the "Apothecary and Analyst" responsibilities was removed from the title, and future chemists were known, at least initially, as either "Government Analysts" or "Assistant Analysts". More importantly, the change meant that these analysts were no longer dispensers. A decade later another major change occurred when the management of the laboratory was removed from the Government Civil Hospital and transferred to the parent department (MH&D).

There were many recurring problems during the early years of analytical work in Hong Kong, not least because Hong Kong was an unhealthy place to live. These challenges included but were not limited to:

i.   chronic illness of personnel coupled with associated sick leave;
ii. lengthy periods of overseas home leave (obviously by ship) as part of officers' conditions of service;
iii. inadequate premises for the laboratory and
iv. insufficient laboratory equipment and chemicals.

Even when the number of personnel appeared to increase on paper, this was often not reflected in the actual staff available because of continuing unfilled vacancies.

Despite these many challenges, the number, variety and complexity of criminal cases handled by Government Laboratory personnel increased over the years to include:

- Toxicology (many poisonings of different types – both accidental and intentional)
- Narcotics, initially mostly opium and heroin
- Counterfeit coins, including manufacturing equipment
- Counterfeit banknotes and metal plates
- Forged cheques
- Detection of removed cancellation marks on stamps
- Detection of delay mechanisms at fire scenes
- Detection of fire accelerants
- Identification of blood on weapons and clothing
- Detection of semen
- Fibre identification
- Oil identification on cloth
- Detection of gunshot residues
- Detection of pepper residues in nail parings
- Examination of bomb residues.

Over time the number of operational staff in the Government Laboratory rose slowly. By December 1941, when Hong Kong fell to the Japanese, the total establishment had grown to eight officers including the Government Chemist, two assistant Government Chemists and five Assistant Chemists, including some local Chinese (Clarke, 2004).

Unsurprisingly, due to lack of staff, equipment and chemicals after 1945, it took some time and a lot of commitment before Hong Kong resumed anything like normality and the Government Laboratory was able to function as before.

13.4 Court attendance

Chemists from the HKGL were required to give oral testimony in Court on many occasions, something that was particularly time-consuming as new Courts opened in Kowloon. Because the Cross Harbour Tunnel linking Kowloon to Hong Kong Island (where the Government Laboratory was located) did not become operational until August 1972, all previous journeys to Kowloon had to be made by ferry. Relevant Annual Reports show that in 1930, laboratory staff presented expert evidence on 50 occasions, and this number had risen to more than 120 by 1962. Just over a decade later, court attendances had declined slightly to 97 during 1975 and 103 for 1976 (Hamilton, 2013).

13.5 Attendance at scenes

Information about early crime scenes attended by laboratory staff is limited but there is no doubt that during the troubled year of 1937 the Government Chemist, Victor Branson, personally investigated one suspicious fire and a destructive explosion, the former on the Kowloon Canton Railway and the latter on a launch in Hong Kong harbour. Both incidents resulted in many deaths but Branson found no evidence of deliberate acts.

A decade later, Richard Terry, a recently recruited Assistant Government Chemist, meticulously investigated the scene of the disastrous fire at the Wing On Godown premises in the western part of Hong Kong Island that claimed the lives of some 200 people. Interestingly, from a "scene" view point, Terry and the investigating Police officer also visited Macau to examine a further 80 drums of washed nitrocellulose to determine whether this was identical to the material that Terry had determined was the cause of the fire. It is reasonable to surmise that other, less publicized, scenes would have been attended even if they were not documented in the Annual Reports.

As the years passed and the population rose, the need for chemists to attend crime scenes also increased. One reason was the growth in population (see Box 13.2) whilst another was the rise in serious crimes in the years following the 1967 riots (Jones and Vagg, 2007). Yet another was a Police General Order (PGO) by the Royal Hong Kong Police (RHKP) requiring a chemist from the HKGL (and, by implication, after 1969 from its newly formed Forensic Science Division) to attend all suspicious deaths and assist police officers in the investigation and collection of potentially useful physical evidence.

Jones and Vagg (2009) suggested that, "The 1970s" was a pivotal decade both for the criminal justice system and for the governance of Hong Kong generally. It might be claimed that it was also a pivotal decade for the progress of forensic science in Hong Kong. Not only had violent crime escalated as a whole, this increase included more homicides, many of which occurred outside normal working hours. Moreover, a large number of these attacks were in remote parts of Kowloon and the New Territories (NT) where larger settlement blocks

had been built to cater for the increasing population. During the years 1969 to 1972, three HKGL staff, namely Ab Nutten, Ron Edgley and Sheilah Hamilton shared this extra work (see Figure 13.1).

The opening of the Cross Harbour Tunnel in 1972 was a welcome development since it enabled speedier access to homicide and other crime scenes in far-flung parts of the territory without having to rely on vehicular ferries. However, despite being able to reach scenes more quickly, this remained work performed outside regular "office" hours and in addition to normal laboratory work. In 1972 the first of several new Scientific Evidence Officer (SEO) posts was created, and this extra pair of hands helped reduce the workload. Since the scheme's inception, all SEOs have been Cantonese speakers with many years of previous experience in the HKGL. During 1975 and 1976, chemists and the recently appointed SEO attended respectively 219 and 253 crime scenes of various types within and outside normal working hours (Hamilton, 2013).

The most recent statistics given in the 2012 Annual Report of the HKGL show that, during this year, HKGL staff attended 447 crime scenes including 287 general crime scenes, 6 scenes with bloodstain pattern analysis, 26 fire scenes, 116 traffic accidents or vehicle related scenes and 12 drug-related scenes. However, it should be stressed that by 2012 the number of professional staff in the Forensic Division of the HKGL was many times that of the mid-1970s.

13.6 "New" dangerous drugs legislation and consequences

1968 saw the introduction of new legislation that had major consequences on the workings of the Forensic Science Division. Thereafter anyone arrested with (i) more than 0.5 g of heroin or (ii) five packets containing any amount of heroin could be charged with "Trafficking in a Dangerous Drug" rather than mere possession. At this time heroin was classified in the Ordinance under the catch-all term "salts of esters of morphine". One result of this legislation was the need for a dedicated Narcotics Section comprising one chemist and five laboratory assistants. Each morning at 9 a.m. (public holidays excepted), police constables delivered sealed packets of suspected narcotics and returned the next day at 10 a.m. to collect the analysed, sealed drugs and the signed Government Chemist's certificate. If the seizure

Box 13.2 Hong Kong's population after World War II

Year	Population	Year	Population	Year	Population
1945	500,000 (est.)	1965	3.598 million	1985	5.456 million
1950	2.360 million (est.)	1970	3.959 million	1990	5.705 million
1955	2.500 million (est.)	1975	4.462 million	1995	6.156 million
1960	3.075 million	1980	5.063 million	2000	6.665 million

(and police officer!) came from the NT, a special arrangement existed whereby he came back to the laboratory at noon the same day to collect the drugs and certificate. This 25-hour (or 3-hour) service only applied to small routine seizures of suspected narcotic substances, not large quantities of drugs like opium or paraphernalia seized from heroin manufacturing cases. Seizures of raw opium as large as 1–2 tons were not uncommon.

In the 1970s most of these routine seizures consisted of:

- Raw opium
- Prepared opium
- Morphine and morphine hydrochloride
- Heroin
- Heroin pills
- Barbitone.

13.7 Training of forensic scientists

Soon after the Forensic Science Division became operational in 1969, a new method of training forensic chemists was introduced. Experienced laboratory assistants from the HKGL could apply for scholarships to

Figure 13.1 Sheilah Hamilton, Ronald Belcher, Ron Edgeley and Albert "Ab" Nutten

study at a UK university for a BSc (Hons) degree in Chemistry followed by an MSc degree in Forensic Science at the University of Strathclyde in Glasgow, Scotland. On successful completion of both degrees, these new graduates were promoted to the grade of "Chemist" within the Forensic Science Division as posts became available. Naturally, he had to sign a contract agreeing to work in the Government Laboratory for a specified number of years. All candidates of this scheme were male. With the exception of women medical doctors, no female graduates within the Hong Kong Government were paid the same as their male counterpartos until 1975.

13.8 Training in fire investigation

In later years, forensic chemists with prior experience in fire investigation attended successive annual "Fire Science and Fire Investigation" courses at the University of Edinburgh, Scotland, followed by an examination equivalent to the Institution of Fire Engineers pass in the same subject.

13.9 Training in blood grouping and blood typing

When the HKGL separated from its long-time parent in 1978, the Forensic Science Division took over the typing of liquid blood from individuals and bloodstains on articles from crime scenes. Although analysts/chemists in the Government Laboratory had examined bloodstains for many decades before World War II, even as far back as 1884 (Crow, 1885) this changed when a separate (Police) Forensic Laboratory was established in 1949 under the direction of Dr Pang Teng-cheung, who was also appointed Hong Kong's first Police Surgeon on his return from studying in the United Kingdom (Pang, 1959). For most of the next 30 years, ABO grouping techniques were applied to blood and/or semen stained items by staff of Dr Pang's unit, not personnel from the HKGL (see separate section).

However, by the 1970s, the importance of forensic blood *typing* had been accepted by the international forensic community. A person involved in a crime needed only to possess one rare blood type and the evidential value of the results could be significant. Thus, in the run-up to the separation of the HKGL from the MH&D, it was agreed – at the highest level – that blood typing in Hong Kong should be transferred to what had become the Forensic Science Division of the HKGL. Its introduction was challenging for several reasons. Firstly, the number of systems introduced (ABO, PGM, EAP, Hp, EsD and Rhesus) was ambitious.

Equally important, the frequency of alleles in a Hong Kong Chinese population was unknown and had to be determined before the new system could be applied to casework samples. The Hong Kong Red Cross was most helpful. In return, many forensic lab staff became new blood donors! Relevant assistance was needed! Not long after this new work began, a secondment was arranged whereby a forensic scientist from the Metropolitan Police Forensic Science Laboratory (MPFSL), with considerable experience in serology and blood typing, was attached to the Hong Kong laboratory for a year. Additionally, as new graduates were recruited into the Forensic Science Division, some were specifically required to have appropriate experience in this new field.

Not long afterwards, what had become informally known as the 'Blood Grouping' section acquired another task when the examination of saliva and stains containing seminal material was inherited from the Forensic Pathology Unit, by this time under the leadership of Dr Frederick Y.K. Ong. Fortunately this was yet another area where the expertise of the seconded UK forensic expert proved to be invaluable.

13.10 Training in blood spatter interpretation

Following the good relations established with MPFSL forensic scientists during the late 1970s and early 1980s, experts from the UK Forensic Science Service (Clarke, 2004) later gave a week long practical "blood spatter interpretation" course for scene-going staff in the Forensic Science Division of the HKGL. By 1998, when the course was held, the name of the Metropolitan Police Laboratory had changed to become part of the Forensic Science Service or FSS. From the 2012 Annual Report of the HKGL, it can be seen that similar training courses continue to be held for officers attending scenes where blood has been spilt.

13.11 Introduction of DNA in Hong Kong

Although considerable success had been achieved with ABO grouping and blood typing results, by the late 1980s it was necessary to consider introducing DNA into local casework. This was done gradually and not until considerable work had been carried out by HKGL forensic scientists to determine the DNA frequencies of Hong Kong Chinese.

13.12 Hong Kong DNA database

This DNA database was introduced in June 2000 after the controversial passage of the necessary legislation. By this, "provisions were made for the setting up and maintaining by the Government Laboratory, on behalf of the Commissioner of Police, of a database storing DNA information of persons convicted of a serious arrestable offence".

By the end of 2012, as reported in the Annual Report of the Government Laboratory the total number in this DNA database had grown to 42,465.

13.13 The Vietnam War and its impact on Hong Kong forensic caseload

1. During the 1960s and early 1970s, many service personnel fighting in the Vietnam War came to Hong Kong as part of a "Rest and Recuperation" programme, more commonly known simply as "R & R". The presence of so many young combat troops letting off steam in the bars of Wanchai and Kowloon brought an unexpected and tragic problem. Some of these men, mostly Americans, apparently thought they were buying LSD from illegal sources in Hong Kong whilst, in fact, they were being sold capsules of Seconal (Secobarbital). When taken with large quantities of alcohol, the results were not merely additive but synergistic, and fatalities were not uncommon. Toxicological examinations of the blood and organs removed at autopsy confirmed their presence, and the Government Chemist's staff repeatedly advised the American authorities to warn their servicemen that in Hong Kong LSD did *not* come in bright red gelatine capsules.

2. Two other unusual forensic cases resulted from the aftermath of the Vietnam War. One involved the Panamanian freighter, *SKYLUCK* (see Figures 13.2 and 13.3), containing 2651 Vietnamese "boat people". In June 1979, after a standoff of almost five months, the vessel was beached off the island of Lamma (opposite Hong Kong). The authorities believed that the *SKYLUCK* was identical to a similar freighter that went by the name *KYLU*, and had been spotted off the coast of Vietnam. Chemists from the Forensic Science Division examined samples of paint that had been sampled from sets of the seven letters comprising the longer name. Cross-sections of this paint showed that the outer "S—-CK" contained several alternating layers of white and black paint whilst the central "KYLU" contained fewer. The explanation was obvious – that the outer three letters had been painted with black or white paint to change the name of the ship and the suspicions were justified.

3. Earlier the same year, forensic staff of the Hong Kong Laboratory examined 3000 taels (1 tael = 37.4 g) of suspected gold found hidden in a disused oil tank of the *HUEY FONG* (see Figures 13.4 and 13.5), another Panamanian freighter that had been stopped by officers of the Marine Police branch of the RHKP as it approached Hong Kong with 3300 refugees (2400 ethnic Chinese and 400 Vietnamese). The hidden gold leaflets were a small part of the total payment for the boat people's voyage from Vietnam to Hong Kong (although the first port of call was meant to be Kaohsiung in Taiwan).

Forensic staff cleaned the leaflets of the thick sticky oil embedded in surface crevices, weighed each leaflet individually and confirmed that every one contained 100% gold and was not base metal coated with gold. The estimated value of the gold leaflets was HK$6.5m (Ward, 1999).

13.14 Interaction between forensic scientists and HK Government Departments

Since its early days more than a century ago, successive staff of what became known as the HKGL examined and analysed materials supplied by other Hong Kong Government Departments, as well as items

Figure 13.2 *SKYLUCK.*

submitted by the general public and semi-official organizations (Clarke, 2004). Despite requests for assistance, in recent years chemists in the Forensic Science Division have been unable to undertake any "non-Government" work due to the high caseload and the priority that is given to "Government" samples.

Although the Hong Kong Police is probably the Government Department most readily associated with the Forensic Science Division, others include the following:

- Customs and Excise Department (formerly – Preventive Service)
- Fire Services Department (FSD)
- Immigration Department
- Independent Commission against Corruption (ICAC)
- Correctional Services Department
- Department of Justice (formerly – Legal Department)
- Medical Department (formerly – Medical and Health Department).

As far back as the mid-1970s, personnel in the Forensic Science Division gave frequent lectures to operational staff of the various departments involved in law enforcement matters and as well as members of the Judiciary.

The HKGL operates a 24-hour service offering advice to Law Enforcement officers (see above list).

Whenever a Police (or other) officer from one the Disciplined Services wishes to discuss a crime scene or arrange for it to be attended by a forensically trained officer, (i) a request is made to the Forensic Science Division of the HKGL, (ii) the nature of the request is considered by a qualified officer and (iii) if deemed appropriate, an SEO (or chemist) will attend the scene to undertake its examination and arrange for the collection of potential evidence. If attendance by a professional from another discipline is also required, the SEO (or chemist) will often suggest this to the officer making the original request. Potentially relevant items from scenes will be identified for collection by the SEO and, where appropriate (e.g. debris from deceased persons), personally collected by the SEO and handed to the "Exhibits Officer" who will be responsible for subsequent delivery of the items to the Forensic Science Division.

Figure 13.3 *SKYLUCK.*

Finally, a designated Police (or other) officer will transport items from scenes or individuals to the HKGL together with a request form containing information about the items submitted, examinations requested, details of who delivered the items and the date of submission. Since more than 200 forensic personnel work in the Government Laboratory, it is not surprising that expertise is available in most of the usual subfields, including:

1. DNA of blood, body fluids, hair and body parts;
2. Species identification of the above;
3. Analysis of narcotics, pharmaceuticals and poisons;
4. Toxicological analysis (including urinalysis, drink driving service, drug driving service and hair drug testing service;
5. Trace evidence of various kinds (including fibres, glass, paint, rubber, plastic, pepper);
6. Identification and comparison of marks of different types (including shoeprints, tyre tracks, prints made by clothing and surfaces cut by sharp edges);

7. Document examination including handwriting comparison in different scripts;
8. Examination/analysis of debris and other items from fires and explosions;
9. Various others.

13.15 Forensic subfields undertaken by the (Royal) Hong Kong Police

The Ordinance establishing and regulating the *Hong Kong Police* was passed in 1844, and this name was retained until 1969 when it became the *Royal Hong Kong Police* in recognition of the work done by police officers during the 1967 riots. When the territory returned to China in July 1997, the title reverted to the *Hong Kong Police*.

13.15.1 Fingerprints

As early as 1904, fingerprints were used to identify Hong Kong's criminals. All prisoners were fingerprinted before

Figure 13.4 *HUEY FONG.*

Figure 13.5 *HUEY FONG.*

their release from jail and everyone arrested for a criminal offence was also fingerprinted. As the scheme developed, it was found that many alleged "newcomers" to the system already had prior convictions (Criswell and Watson, 1982). Interest in fingerprinting grew within the Hong Kong Police and Mr Ng Bing-wu, a clerk working in CID, produced *The Art of Fingerprints* in 1919, the first book of its kind written in Chinese (Sinclair, 1983). Since the Identification Bureau's birth over a century ago, the examination and comparison of fingerprints has remained exclusively a Police duty although, in the 1970s, documents thought to contain latent fingerprints were submitted to the Government Laboratory where chemists of the Forensic Science Division treated the paper with Ninhydrin before returning the items to the Police. As detection techniques became more advanced and "chemical" in nature, the Advanced Technical Unit (ATU) was formed within the main Identification Bureau in 1986 and staffed by Police officers who were also qualified chemists.

13.15.2 Bullets and guns

Compared to many countries in the region, Hong Kong is fortunate in having relatively few firearms used during the commission of crimes. When guns are involved, most examinations to associate the individual weapons with bullets and cartridge cases are performed by officers of the Ballistics unit of the Hong Kong Police. However, if a gun has been handled but not fired during an incident, then the *Ferrozine* (*Ferrotrace*) test may be applied, assuming that the suspect is apprehended soon after the event. In past years, the *Ferrozine* method was used by chemists in the Forensic Science Division as well as Ballistics officers in the (R)HKP.

13.15.3 Gunshot residues (GSRs)

The examination of debris from a variety of surfaces, including flesh and clothing, for the presence of gunshot residues GSRs) is something that can be done by a scientist with experience in using a scanning electron microscope (SEM) or Police officers with similar practical knowledge. In the past the Ballistics section of the (R)HKP employed an officer with this ability. However, the use of SEM to detect GSRs appears to have fallen out of favour with the departure of this officer.

13.15.4 Forensic computing

As computers and similar smaller devices found at crime scenes or otherwise involved in criminal activities became more prevalent and important, a dedicated unit within the Hong Kong Police was tasked with their investigation. This technical capability has grown considerably with several other disciplined forces, such as the Immigration, Customs & Excise and Independent Commission Against Corruption (ICAC) Departments, developing their own forensic computing units.

13.16 Political aspect of DNA typing by scientists of the HKGL

The following quotation from the 2012 Annual Report of the HKGL is included since it describes an unusual use of DNA testing that is not related to crime but is pivotal in allowing legal immigration of Chinese persons from the PRC into the HKSAR:

> In close liaison and co-ordination with the Forensic Science Centre of Guangdong Provincial Security Department, GL accomplished 2,093 cases in connection with the Certificate of Entitlement (CoE) applications that are controlled under the Immigration (Amendment) Ordinance 2001. … The GL also assisted Immigration Department in other Right of Abode applications by providing genetic testing to verify claimed kinship relation. 74 non-CoE cases have been completed in 2012.

However, similar DNA parentage testing by the HKGL is not available to the members of the general public and must be done through a private laboratory.

13.17 Recruitment of forensic scientists in the HKGL

Like other appointments in the HKSAR Civil Service, when new entry-grade posts arise in the Forensic Division of the HKGL, advertisements are placed in local newspapers. However, it is likely that "cold" requests are often received. As well as having the necessary qualifications (usually a Masters and/or PhD degree in one or more relevant subjects), and preferably previous forensic or related experience, the applicant must speak Cantonese and be able to read and write Chinese. Additionally, they must pass the Hong Kong Government Civil Service examination, proving their knowledge of the HKSAR "Basic Law". For these last reasons, it is difficult for a non-Chinese person to be successful in their application.

13.18 Non-Government or privately employed forensic scientists in Hong Kong

From the foregoing, it can be seen that most forensic scientists in Hong Kong have worked in the HKGL at one time or another. In June 2013, the department employed 484 people in seven sites, the main laboratory at Homantin, Kowloon, custom-built in 1992, and six satellite laboratories in different parts of the territory.

Whilst the precise breakdown of staff employed in the two divisions is not stated in the report, approximately the same number of personnel used to work in both the "Forensic Science" and the "Advisory and Analytical Services" divisions, whilst the administration of the Department was dealt with by far fewer nonscientific staff.

For obvious reasons, the Forensic Science Division of the HKGL is not actively involved in matters relating to the "defence side" of criminal cases, nor is it permitted to act in a professional capacity in civil disputes.

This does not mean that no forensic science expertise is available in Hong Kong for defendants in criminal trials or parties involved in civil disputes, but it certainly means that there are far fewer experienced forensic professionals available.

Some retired or former HKGL forensic scientists, particularly those with expertise in handwriting and signature comparison, have set up their practices after long and successful careers in the HKGL. Most of these former civil servants work alone or in small consultancies, and their existence is usually made known by word-of-mouth, the placement of advertisements in legal publications or by personal websites. Others may give lectures about their forensic specialty to organizations such as the Hong Kong Law Society or the Hong Kong Bar Association. Many consultants starting up in private practice inform both the Legal Aid Department and other legal personnel about their new venture.

Additionally, a few international firms dealing with the investigation of fires, explosions and related issues have branch offices based in Hong Kong.

However, to date there is no register of private forensic experts based in Hong Kong. Those who are members of the Academy of Experts (TAE) may list their experience and qualifications in TAE publications, but the effectiveness of this depends on the "searcher" knowing about the list. Others who are professional Members or Fellows of the American Academy of Forensic Sciences (AAFS) may have their contact details included in the annual Membership Directory but, since these are distributed to AAFS members (not outside bodies), it is doubtful how useful they are in reaching a Hong Kong audience.

Some of the local Hong Kong universities employ professionals who also undertake forensic consultancy work – if it is within their areas of expertise. However, knowing who these people are often depends on word-of-mouth.

Amongst its members, the Hong Kong Medico-Legal Society contains a wealth of unofficial information about forensic experts who have presented lectures on various topics. However, as useful as this may be on occasion, it is nevertheless anecdotal.

At least one locally based company claims to be able to provide the names of contacts in many different forensic subfields.

13.19 Forensic pathology

It is highly likely that forensic medicine was introduced to Hong Kong with the establishment of the College of Medicine in 1877 as it had essentially adopted a curriculum used in Scotland. Nonetheless, very little is known about how forensic medicine was practised in the early years of Hong Kong other than that there was a succession of academic appointments at the University of Hong Kong of individuals who held positions in Medical Jurisprudence.

It is also clear that autopsies were performed with increasing regularity after 1850. Interests and numbers increased with the introduction of the Coroner's Ordinance (1889) in Hong Kong following the passage of the Coroner's Act (1887) in the United Kingdom. The plague epidemic of 1894 opened the eyes of the local Chinese population to the advantage of an autopsy in accurately determining the cause of death. The Hong Kong authorities had decreed that the belongings of all plague victims were to be incinerated. Relatives of victims whose deaths were proven by autopsy not to be due to plague were therefore spared such destruction of property.

Much later, in the late 1940s, Dr T.C. Pang was the first local doctor employed to work full-time as a police surgeon. On his return to Hong Kong after studying in the United Kingdom, he gradually built up a unit of doctors, police officers and technical staff to provide coverage for scene of deaths, clinical forensic examination, forensic autopsies and blood grouping. However, with the later development of serology and the forensic sciences, the forensic pathology services essentially focused on their core competencies in clinical forensic medicine and forensic pathology. Until the turn of the new millennium, many young local doctors were sent to the United Kingdom for relevant training under world-renowned forensic pathologists.

In later years the influx of refugees fleeing China during the formative years of the People's Republic of China exerted a huge strain on the autopsy services because of the large number of unfortunates drowning in their attempt to swim to Hong Kong.

Currently the Forensic Pathology Service has approximately 16 full-time forensic doctors and operates out of three public mortuaries in different parts of the territory. Each year the Service deals with nearly 10,000 cases and performs close to 4000 autopsies. Forensic pathologists require a total of six years postgraduate training and all forensic pathologists first need to have qualified as medical doctors before they can enter training in forensic pathology.

13.20 Forensic odontology

At the time of writing there is no unit or department in forensic odontology and such services are provided by a few dedicated individuals in private dental practice. One of these pioneers, Dr Carl Leung, obtained his forensic training in Australia and often assists in cases where forensic odontology is required.

13.21 Forensic anthropology

There are no trained forensic anthropologists based in Hong Kong and, when this skill is required, investigations of human skeletal remains are undertaken by forensic pathologists, who are mainly self-taught in this discipline.

13.22 Academic forensic expertise

There is a glaring absence of academic forensic practitioners in Hong Kong. The forensic disciplines do not appear to be well recognized or represented. There is only one full-time associate professor in forensic pathology at the University of Hong Kong. There are several individuals who are computer scientists and engineers and these provide specialist consultation services to the community on an ad hoc basis.

Abbreviations

AAFS	American Academy of Forensic Sciences
ATU	Advanced Technical Unit
CoE	Certificate of Entitlement
DD	Dangerous Drugs
FSD	Fire Services Department
GSR	Gunshot residues
HKP	Hong Kong Police
HKSAR	Hong Kong Special Administrative Region
ICAC	Independent Commission Against Corruption
MHD	Medical and Health Department
MPFSL	Metropolitan Police Forensic Science Laboratory
NT	New Territories
PGO	Police General Order
RHKP	Royal Hong Kong Police
SAR	Special Administrative Region
SEM	Scanning electron microscope
SEO	Scientific Evidence Officer
TAE	The Academy of Experts

References

Annual Report of the Government Laboratory, 2012, p. 30

Clarke, D.J. (2004) *Hong Kong – Under the Microscope*, Government Laboratory, Hong Kong

Crisswell, C., Watson, M. (1982) *The Royal Hong Kong Police (1841–1945)*, MacMillan, Hong Kong, p. 98.

Crow, W.E. (1885) In Ayers, P. (Ed.) *Annual Report of the Hong Kong Government Analyst and Apothecary*.

Hamilton, S.E. (2013) Personal communication.

Jones, C., Vagg, J. (2007) *Criminal Justice in Hong Kong*, Routledge, London, p. 358.

Pang, T.C. (1959) *A Study in Medical Jurisprudence in Hong Kong (1950–57)*, University of Hong Kong.

Report of the Commission of Enquiry into the Wing On Fire on 22 September 1948, p. 42.

Sinclair, K. (1983) *Asia's Finest*, Unicorn Press, Hong Kong, p. 209.

Ward, I. (1999) *Mariners: The Hong Kong Police 1948–1997*, IEW Publications, United Kingdom, pp. 156–160.

CHAPTER 14

The practice of forensic science in Hungary

Eva Keller[1], Peter Sótonyi[2] & Agnes Dósa[1]

[1] Department of Forensic and Insurance Medicine, Semmelweis University, Budapest, Hungary
[2] National Institute of Forensic Medicine, Budapest, Hungary

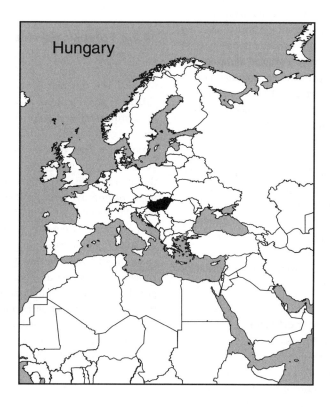

14.1 Current and historical accounts of forensic science in Hungary

14.1.1 History within the country

Teaching of forensic sciences has a long tradition in Hungary, dating back to the end of the 18th century. It was in 1793 that the first faculty of Forensic Medicine was established in Budapest (medicina forensis), and

forensic medicine has been a compulsory part of undergraduate training ever since.

There are five types of forensic science institutions: the National Institute of Forensic Medicine, departments of forensic medicine of the medical universities, the Network of Forensic Science Institutes (NFSI), the criminal forensic medical service of the police (including HIFS) and finally the Board of Forensic Medicine Experts of

The Global Practice of Forensic Science, First Edition. Edited by Douglas H. Ubelaker.
© 2015 John Wiley & Sons, Ltd. Published 2015 by John Wiley & Sons, Ltd.

the Health Scientific Council. The history of these institutions is described in details below.

14.2 Types of cases

14.2.1 Postmortem examinations

While there has been a substantial decrease in clinical autopsy rates in Hungary over the past 20 years, forensic autopsy rates have been relatively steady: 6500 forensic autopsies are carried out yearly by the four university departments and the ten institutes of the Department of Forensic Science and Research. Forensic autopsies are performed in accordance with the "Recommendations No. R(99)3 of the EU Committee of Ministers to Member States on the Harmonization of Medico-Legal Autopsy Rules" (http://www.coe.int/t/dg3/healthbioethic/texts and documents/RecR(99)3.pdf).

Forensic autopsies are carried out in all cases of unnatural death, based upon the decision of the prosecution or police. If crime is suspected, special forensic autopsy is performed by two forensic medical experts.

Forensic autopsies are performed within a centralized system: only university institutes and the institutes of the Network of Forensic Science Institutes have competence to perform forensic autopsies. This centralized system was created in 2008.

14.2.2 Clinical forensic medicine

The importance of clinical forensic medicine has been growing over the past two decades. Clinical forensic medicine includes traditional areas, such as assessment, documentation and evaluation of injuries, in criminal cases and in civil courts and insurance procedures alike (traffic and insurance medicine). Besides these traditional areas, new territories have emerged recently. For example, a major area of clinical forensic medical activity is now the assessment of health impairment (in cases where certain health impairment is a prerequisite of various social security benefits). In Hungary the decisions brought within the social security system are subject to court review, and in the court proceedings forensic experts give an expert opinion regarding the degree of health impairment. Another important territory is medical malpractice (both criminal and civil); with the growing number of medical malpractice court cases the need for forensic evaluation has increased substantially. These

cases cannot be decided by the court without forensic expert opinion; usually this is prepared by a specialist in forensic medicine and a specialist in the relevant clinical discipline. The latter does not have to be a registered forensic expert: in most clinical disciplines the relatively low number of cases does not encourage clinicians to go through the registration process and to take all the duties associated with being a forensic expert (training, exams and fees).

14.2.3 Forensic psychiatry

The need for expert opinions in forensic psychiatry has been growing over the past two decades, for various reasons. The increase in the number of forensic psychiatry expert opinions was partly due to the reform of guardianship legislation introduced in 2001. Since then, if guardianship is ordered, it has to be reviewed periodically. The review period should not exceed 5 years. The only exception is if the court declares that the mental state of the patient is final and there is no hope for improvement. In these rare cases there is not periodic review. Before the guardianship law reforms no periodical review was performed. The other factor leading to the increased numbers of forensic psychiatry examinations was the new legislation on drug crimes. However, the structure does not necessarily reflect its growing importance; there is no independent chair of forensic psychiatry at either medical university. Forensic psychiatrists are trained at the forensic institutes of the four medical universities. Many forensic psychiatry experts are not affiliated with institutions, but work as independent forensic experts.

14.2.4 Forensic toxicology

Forensic toxicology laboratories are either part of university institutes, or of HIFS and NFSI. On the one hand they investigate postmortem toxicology samples, but they also perform blood alcohol determinations and toxicological investigations on blood samples. This is mainly needed for cases where driving under influence is an issue to be decided, and in cases related to illegal drug possession and consumption. In addition, university toxicology labs are also performing clinical toxicology investigations for the university hospitals or other contracted hospitals. The toxicology labs are accredited according to ISO standards.

14.2.5 Forensic genetics, DNA investigation

Most forensic DNA case work (criminal cases) is done by HIFS. It was in 1992 when the first DNA expert opinion was issued by their DNA Department in a murder case. Since then the lab keeps up with modern developments in DNA technologies and it has a highly qualified personnel (30 staff members).

The Department takes part annually in five proficiency tests organized by two companies (GEDNAP and CTS). The laboratory has validated the internationally accepted methods for the local Hungarian population and laboratory circumstances. These results are also utilized by several other DNA laboratories in Hungary. The application of these methods and the long term experience enabled the expert group to take the challenges of various criminal and genetic issues in accordance with internationally compatible standards

The main activity of the Department is the DNA expert reporting for the Police, for the Prosecutor's Department and for the court. The reliability of expert reports is supported by permanent national and international training, by introduction of new methods of international compatibility and by strict documentation. In special cases the experts of the Department take part in crime scene investigations as well. To support this activity the Department has been participating in proficiency tests of bloodstain pattern analysis since 2003.

The Department maintains and manages the national criminal DNA profile database. The database is set up on CODIS software, which is fully compatible with the international data exchange system of the Prüm Treaty.

NIFS also has a well-equipped DNA lab active in civil court cases (paternity testing).

14.2.6 Forensic materials testing

The HIFS has the only department providing services in the field of forensic materials testing. The Department has a highly qualified staff (chemist, geologist and physicist) to investigate a wide range of trace evidences, both organic and inorganic material residues, excluding those of human origin. Furthermore, physicist experts answer the questions in connection to theoretical problems such as case reconstruction (way of a human body falling). Chemist experts additionally take part in building up national databases and spectrum libraries of dyes, fibers, paints, etc.

14.3 Structure

There are five types of forensic science institutions: the National Institute of Forensic Medicine, departments of forensic medicine of the four medical universities, the Network of Forensic Science Institutes (NFSI) (in Hungarian: ISZKI), the criminal forensic medical service of the police (including HIFS) and finally the Board of Forensic Medicine Experts of the Health Scientific Council. Besides these institutions private forensic experts do a significant part of routine case work.

14.3.1 National Institute of Forensic Medicine

The National Institute of Forensic Medicine was established in 1975 by the Minister of Health in agreement with the Ministers of Internal Affairs and National Defense and the public prosecutor. The Institute is a publicly financed institution, with its headquarters at the Department of Forensic and Insurance Medicine of the Semmelweis University. Its most important task is to elaborate professional guidelines of forensic medicine. The Institute has issued a total of 21 guidelines, takes part in research and has been playing an important role in the modernization of undergraduate and postgraduate training. The Institute collects and publishes data on forensic medical activities. The Director of the Institute is appointed by the Minister responsible for health care. The first director was Endre Somogyi who was followed by Péter Sótonyi, the holder of the current Chair of the Institute.

14.3.2 Police forensic Medical Service and HIFS

The history of the criminal forensic medical service dates back to the 19th century. Act No. XIV of 1876 created the post of the "police medical officer" and determined its tasks: among others, performing forensic autopsies in forensic cases and evaluating offences leading to death and suicides.

From 1922 forensic autopsies were assigned to the physicians of the public health service and this situation did not change until the end of World War II. After 1945 the reorganization of the police forensic medical service began. It was established at county level, and from 1963 most forensic autopsies were performed by the experts of the police forensic Medical Service. The numbers were impressive: the Service performed around 2000 inquests, 7000–8000 autopsies and 30,000–35,000 clinical forensic examinations per year. As of 1 July 1990 the Service functioned within the Health Department of the National Police.

This situation changed substantially in 2007, when Act XLVII came into force. This Act modified Criminal Procedure and stated that forensic experts employed by the police are not allowed to perform forensic autopsies. This change of criminal procedure had far reaching consequences: the competence of forensic medical experts employed by the police was restricted to crime scene investigations. Therefore the number of forensic medical experts employed by the police decreased dramatically. The current forensic medical expert staff was integrated into the Hungarian Institute for Forensic Sciences (HIFS) (in Hungarian: BSZKI), which was established in 1990, and is part of the Hungarian National Police. Its legal predecessor from 1906 was the Criminal Technical and Registry Subdivision, later from 1961 the Criminal Technical Institute.

The HIFS currently has 269 staff members: physicians, engineers, biologists, chemists, physicists, technicians specialized in various fields of criminal sciences and assistants. The equipment of the department is outstanding, even by international standards. It is equipped with instruments for scanning electron microscopy and microspectrophotometry and modern techniques are also available for personal identification, technical separation, as well as automated DNA-typing methods. Significant scientific results have been obtained in the following fields: blood group and DNA characterization, research on writing and ballistics, criminalistics utilization of X-ray studies. Both in respect to practical activities and scientific research, emphases are laid on the physical–chemical examination of microsized material residues, as well as on the qualitative and quantitative determination of drugs. In 1989, the Registry Department of the Dactyloscopy Unit, which has an automated fingerprint identification system, was integrated into HIFS; this provides for the dactyloscopic database and registry system of Hungary.

HIFS takes part continuously in the international quality control system, with excellent qualifications. It has been a member of the European Network of Forensic Science since 2000, working actively together with the DNA, dactyloscope, drug accreditation work groups and also carrying out activities in the field of classic criminology. Within the frame of international collaboration, it works together with Interpol and Europol on standardization of fingerprint and DNA databases. The scientific achievements of the department are significant, both regarding publications and participation at international congresses. The Department is state financed. Throughout its existence, outstanding scientists of the department have been Dr. Imre Kertész, Dr. Vilmos Földes and Dr. Zsófia Santura and recently Dr. Gabor Nagy.

Within the armed forces, the Hungarian Army has its own department of judicial medical experts, functioning within the Central Army Hospital as the Department of Military Judicial Medical Experts (founded in 1949). The department collaborates with the pathology department of the hospital. It carries out high standard judicial medical expert duties occurring within the armed forces. It is maintained from the budget of the Ministry of National Defense. The leaders of the department have always been forensic medicine experts with pathology qualifications (Dr. Viktor Fáber, Dr. György Dallos and currently Dr. Miklós Molnár).

14.3.3 Network of Forensic Science Institutes (NFSI)

The first unit of NFSI was founded in 1964 by the Ministry of Justice, and gradually new units were added (see Table 14.1). At present it includes 12 institutes, which are the following:

- NFSI Institute of Auditing, Taxation and Technical Experts of Budapest, established in 1965
- NFSI Institute of Forensic Medicine of Budapest, established in 1964
- NFSI National Institute of Toxicology, established in 1872
- NFSI Institute of Debrecen, established in 1976
- NFSI Institute of Gyor, established in 1977
- NFSI Institute of Kaposvar, established in 1992
- NFSI Institute of Kecskemet, established in1985
- NFSI Institute of Miskolc, established in 1972
- NFSI Institute of Szeged, established in1981
- NFSI Institute of Szolnok, established in 1980
- NFSI Institute of Szombathely, established in 2000
- NFSI Institute of Veszprem, established in 1977.

These Institutes have a highly qualified team of forensic experts and they perform routine casework in forensic medicine, psychiatry, psychology, human biology,

Table 14.1 Institutes of the NFSI showing the number of opinions

Institutes	No. of court ordered expert opinions	No. of police ordered expert opinions	No. of expert opinions ordered by other authorities	No. of expert opinions based on contract	Sum
NFSI Institute of Auditing, Taxation and Technical Experts of Budapest	248	30	7	2	287
NFSI Institute of Forensic Medicine of Budapest	4 407	668	197	150	5 422
Szekszard Group of NFSI Institute of Forensic Medicine of Budapest	213	458	8	3	682
NFSI National Institute of Toxicology	28	8 124	200	0	8 352
NFSI Institute of Debrecen	101	43	44	5	193
NFSI Institute of Gyor	1 638	4 417	75	42	6 172
NFSI Institute of Kecskemet	720	1 506	38	73	2 337
NFSI Institute of Miskolc	3 066	2 601	34	47	5 748
Eger Medical Expert Group of NFSI Institute of Miskolc	410	539	16	5	970
NFSI Institute of Kaposvar	899	770	14	56	1 739
NFSI Institute of Szeged	125	85	40	29	279
NFSI Institute of Szolnok	1 092	5 084	68	13	6 257
Bekescsaba Medical Expert Group of NFSI Institute of Szolnok	21	199	10	0	230
NFSI Institute of Veszprem	881	2 212	18	70	3 181
Szekesfehervar Medical Expert Group of NFSI Institute of Veszprem	385	586	5	3	979
NFSI Institute of Szombathely	657	807	39	22	1 525
Zalaegerszeg Medical Expert Group of NFSI Institute of Szombathely	40	684	1	0	725
ÖSSZESEN	14 931	28 813	814	520	45 078

DNA, personal identification (anthropology) and toxicology, auditing and taxation, and provide technical expertise for the prosecution, court, police and other authorities. In 2012 the Institutes gave 45,000 opinions (including 2725 forensic autopsies).

The NFSI has 268 staff members, including 101 forensic experts and 11 forensic expert trainees.

The NFSI also functions as a major center for applied forensic research, carrying out national and international research projects.

14.3.4 Institutes of Forensic Medicine of the Universities

There are four medical universities throughout the country, each of which has an independent Institute of Forensic Medicine.

14.3.4.1 Department of Forensic and Insurance Medicine, Semmelweis University, Budapest

The legal predecessor of the Faculty of Medicine of Semmelweis University was the Medical Faculty of Nagyszombat, established in 1770. At the beginning it only had five departments. The independent department of forensic medicine was founded in 1793.

József Jakab Plenk was the first tutor of obstetrics and surgery at the Nagyszombat Medical Faculty. He published two books on forensic medicine: *Elementa Medicinae et Chirurgiae Forensis* in 1871 (Plenk, 1871) and *Toxicologia seu Doctrina de Venernis et Antidotis* on forensic medical toxicology in 1875 in Vienna (Plenk, 1875). His books were used in teaching at various European universities. A new course called state medicine (forensic medicine and medical public administration) was introduced in 1793. Ferencz Schraud (1793–1802) and later Ferencz Bene Sen (1802–1816) were the first lecturers.

Ferencz Schraud published three books on forensic medicine: Aphorismi de Politia Medica (Schraud, 1795), De Forensibus Judicum et Medicorum Relationibus. In Vicem Introductionis ad Medicinam Forensem Disserit (Schraud, 1797) and Elementa Medicinae Forensis (Schraud, 1802).

However, the very first work on forensic medicine written by János Jakab Neuhold (1700–1738) under the title *Introduction ad Jurisprudenciam* has never been published. Neuhold was the chief medical officer of Komárom County and a member of the German Academy of Natural Sciences.

The Department was led by Sándor K. Ajtai between 1822 and 1915. He had worked previously in Vienna with Rokitansky and then became the lead of the Pathology Department in the Szent Rókus Hospital. Between 1874 and 1882, he was the director of the Department of Forensic Medicine in Cluj.

Later Sándor K. Ajtai became the first director of the Department of Forensic Medicine of the Medical Faculty in the Royal Hungarian University of Sciences, which was opened in Budapest on 1 January 1890. He established the units for forensic psychiatry and chemistry within the department in 1872 and 1892, respectively. His name is also associated with the planning in 1902, and then the introduction, of the forensic medicine examination system in 1904.

Balázs Kenyeres chaired the department between 1915 and 1935. He started his career as a pathologist under the supervision of Ajtai. In 1895 he was appointed as the head of the forensic department in Cluj, and later in Budapest, in 1915. He was a dedicated scholar and professor, six of his students later qualifying as university lecturers. He was member of the Hungarian Academy of Sciences. He played a decisive role in the expansion of the material proof branch of science. His contributions are of considerable value even internationally. He founded the scientific journals entitled *Archiv für Kriminologie* and *Kriminalistische Monatsheft*, and also the "Gesellschaft für Kriminologie" Society. His book *Sachliche Bewewise bei der Klärung von Todesfällen* was published in 1935 (Kenyeres, 1935). He also published a textbook entitled *Forensic Medicine* in three volumes, the first in 1909 (Kenyeres 1909). He became an honorary member of the Imperial Academy of Halle in 1930.

Ferenc Orsós followed Balázs Kenyeres as the head of the department between 1935 and 1944. Previously, between 1918 and 1935, he was the director of the Department of Pathology and Forensic Medicine at the University of Debrecen. He pioneered research on vital reactions and connective tissue metachromasia. He was also the chief specialist of personal identification in Katyni, Poland. In 1944, he settled in Halle.

He was pronounced a war criminal by the people's court in 1946 and was therefore deprived of all his positions, including his academic membership. Despite pressure from the Soviet Union, the Americans did not hand him over to the Hungarian authorities. In 1946, he received an invitation to become tutor of artistic anatomy in the University of Mainz. He died in Mainz in 1962 and was buried in the university graveyard.

During the period of 1946–1955 Gyula Incze led the Forensic Department. He was extensively involved in studies on the pathology of electrical injuries and the biological effects of electricity. His study conducted on diatomes, which can be used in the verification of water drowning, gained him recognition all over Europe (Incze, 1942).

During the street battles in 1956, the department located on Üllői Street sustained serious damages. In 1956–1957 the assigned director of the department was Dr. László Haranghy, who also acted as the head of the 2nd Department of Pathology in the Semmelweis Medical University. Laszlo Haranghy had training and practical knowledge of forensic medicine.

From 1958 until 1969 Dr. Sándor Ökrös became the director of the department, invited from Debrecen. He was a student of Ferenc Orsós, receiving significant pathology training, and was an illustrious representative of forensic pathology. He spent a long period of time in Vienna in the Institute of Haberda, becoming friends for life with Breitenecker. His scientific activities were prominent and memorably his research on the papillary pattern was published as a book (Incze, 1965).

In the years between 1969 and 1992 Dr. Endre Somogyi became the director of the Department. He was an extremely dynamic personality with wide international relations. He showed particular interest towards the introduction of new morphological research techniques. He made significant contributions to our knowledge of the pathomechanism of fine structural tissue damage developing on the effect of electricity. He received recognition on several accounts both nationally and internationally. He achieved 241 publications and 20 books and book-chapters define his scientific work. His textbook *Forensic Medicine* had six editions (Somogyi, 1968). He also edited a book entitled "Sudden Cardiac Death" with Péter Sótonyi, which was published in 1984 (Somogyi and Sótonyi, 1994).

Péter Sótonyi was the head of the department from 1992 until 2003. His basic pathology training determined his professional profile. He established new laboratories (DNA, scanning electron microscopy and immunohistochemistry) in the department. From his scientific work, it is important to mention his studies on the cytochemistry analysis of the localization of heart glycosides and the cell model of isolated cardiac muscle. Several universities awarded him as a doctor honoris causa and honorary senator. He conducted a Ph.D. school program in Semmelweis University. Four editions of his textbook *Forensic Medicine* were published and are still used in teaching (Sótonyi, 2011). His book on the history of forensic medicine in Hungary was published in 2009 (Sótonyi, 2009). He became a member of the Hungarian Academy of Sciences. He is currently the director of the National Institute of Forensic Medicine.

Since 2003, the director has been Éva Keller. She introduced insurance medicine into the repertoire of the department.

14.3.4.2 Department of Forensic Medicine, University of Debrecen

University education in Debrecen dates back 400 years. The University of Debrecen incorporating a medical faculty was opened in 1918. Originally pathology and forensic medicine departments operated as one unit; then in 1946 it was divided into two independent departments. Ferenc Orsós led both departments between 1919 and 1935. He started his career at the Department of Pathology at Budapest University. His excellent pathology background enabled him to direct pathology-based forensic medicine. His conclusions regarding vital reactions are still cited in current literature (Orsós, 1935). Upon invitation from the Budapest Medical Faculty, in 1935 he became the head of the Department of Forensic Medicine in Budapest. Between 1936 and 1944 László Jankovich was director of the Department of Forensic Medicine functioning within the organizational unit of the Pathology Department. His scientific activities focused on the morphology of changes occurring in alkali poisoning.

Between 1945 and 1957 Sándor Ökrös was the assigned and then the appointed director of the independent Department of Forensic Medicine. He was one of the most successful members of the Orsós school. His research included studies on skull trauma-related liquor circulation problems, the role of Paccini granules and the traumatic changes of the pituitary and the pituitary stem. He carried out noteworthy studies on the traumatic alterations of muscle tissue with polarization optical analysis, and also on the changes of the protein components actin and myosin. He started research on dactyloscopy in Debrecen. He became the head of the department in 1958, upon invitation.

His student, János Nagy, became director of the Department from 1957 until 1961 by assignment and then from 1961 until 1980 by appointment. His scientific research involved the alcohol breakdown and detection, elaborated the error potentials of the Harger technique and modelled a semi-quantitative method for the determination of alcohol and ether. His name is associated with the Nagy–Zsigmond probe. Between 1980 and 2000 László Buris headed the department. He established widespread international connections with the United States and Israel. He also established an Eastern–Central European toxicological reference center in the department. He was also a member of several international societies and a subcommittee member of the European Council.

The next head of the department was Mihály Varga from 2000 until 2006. He was a specialist with extensive knowledge of pathology. Previously he worked as a lead of the pathology unit in a large district hospital. He was involved in the research work on alcoholic liver damage as a team member and later as the lead. Unfortunately, he died suddenly at an early age.

The present director of the department by assignment is László Herczeg.

14.3.4.3 Department of Forensic Medicine, University of Pécs

The medical faculty was established in 1918 in the Hungarian Royal Elisabeth University of Sciences in Bratislava. King Karoly IV conferred the title of full professorship on Béla Entz and appointed him as a director of the Departments of Pathology and Forensic Medicine. The medical faculty moved to Budapest after Trianon and from 1923 it finally settled down in Pécs.

The first complete academic year of the medical faculty in Pécs was during 1924–1925. Béla Entz directed the two departments until 1948 when the departments were separated.

Béla Entz was an outstanding student of Antal Genersich, and he was also a highly qualified pathologist and paleopathologist. He was a member of the Hungarian Academy of Sciences. He was awarded the state fellowships to the Universities of Dresden and Munich, conducting scientific research work.

From 1934 Konrád Beöthy became the lead of the Department of Forensic Medicine.

Konrád Beöthy was also the director of the Department of Forensic Medicine from 1948 until 1958. Between 1927 and 1929 he worked in Vienna in the department of Haberda, and then together with Entz. He progressed as a recognized university tutor in 1931 and became a private tutor in 1932. Between 1945 and 1948 he was the professor of forensic medicine in Cluj and Marosvásárhely. Upon invitation, from 1 September 1948 he became director of the independent forensic department in Pécs. His scientific contributions included the pathogenesis of silicosis and the rehabilitation of the injured.

From 1958 Lóránt Tamáska became head of the department until he left for Germany in 1961. He worked as a medical expert in Augsburg, Cologne, Aachen, Lübeck and Düsseldorf. During the years 1961 and 1962 Gyula Farkas was the assigned lead of the department.

The next director was Robert Budvári from 1962 until 1976. His scientific interest was blood alcohol research and serology. He was the director of the National Institute of Medical Experts between 1976 and 1978. During the years 1976 and 1977 Péter Guth chaired the department.

From 1977 László Harsányi was the director until his death in 1992. His research focused on forensic osteology, the comparative analysis of skeletal findings as well as medical expert identification. Together with Vilmos Földes he published a book entitled *Medical Expert Identification* (Harsányi and Földes, 1968). He played a significant role in the identification of the victims of reprisals following the 1956 events (e.g. Imre Nagy and Pál Maléter). He was superseded by Árpád Németh in 1992. His research focused on respiratory distress syndrome and hyalin membrane disease. He died at an early age in 1993.

Then István Bajnoczky was appointed as the head of the department in 1994. He followed the impeccable work on "personal identification school of Pécs" founded by Harsányi. He was involved in the modernization and improvement of the video-superimposition technique. Regarding medical expert identification, he developed the scientific methods of personal identification.

14.3.4.4 Department of Forensic Medicine, University of Szeged

Following World War I, the József Ferenc University of Sciences moved from Cluj to Szeged in 1921.

Between 1921 and 1925 Károly Demeter led the department. Then after Kenyeres moved to Budapest, he became the director of the Department of Forensic Medicine in Cluj. His research on radiography and histology awarded him international recognition. His research on shot wounds is also important from a criminalist perspective.

From 1925 until 1934 László Jankovich was the head of the department. His comparative pathological and forensic pathological studies on poisoning related to central nervous system changes were prominent.

Between 1934 and 1945 the well-known pathologist, József Baló, the founder of the elastase enzyme, directed the Department of Pathology and Forensic Medicine. From his forensic pathology research, the mechanism of fat embolism and the effect of ammonia poisoning on blood haematogenesis were recognized. In 1945 József Baló became the head of the Department of Forensic Medicine in Budapest and later undertook the responsibilities of the leadership of the First Institute of Pathology and Experimental Cancer Research.

Between 1946 and 1973 Gyula I. Fazekas was the lead of the independent forensic medicine department. His scientific studies incorporating endocrinology, free total-histamine content of embryonic bones and injuries are well recognized. In accolade of his scientific research, he was elected a member of numerous international scientific societies and academies. He also contributed in publishing a book entitled *Forensic Fetal Osteology* co-written with his colleague Ferenc Kósa in 1978 (Fazekas and Kósa, 1978).

From 1973 until 1993 Vilmos Földes directed the department. His scientific research work mainly focused on criminology. He also published a book entitled *Medical Expert Identification* with László Harsányi (Harsányi & and Földes, 1968).

From 1994, Tibor Varga, former director of the forensic medicine department in Budapest, became the lead of the department by invitation. He established the foundations of modern analytical laboratories focusing on toxicology and DNA analysis. His main scientific interest involved the vital reactions of heart muscle injury, the clinical and comparative morphological characteristics of alcohol and drug abuse, and the problems of road traffic incidents-related medical science. He was also president of the Board of Forensic Medicine Experts of the Health Scientific Council and edited a book entitled *Health Insurance* in 2004 (Varga, 2004).

14.3.5 Board of Forensic Medicine Experts of the Health Scientific Council

The history of the Board of Forensic Medicine Experts dates back to the times of the Habsburg Monarchy. Medical experts were regularly heard in court as early as the 16th century, mainly in cases of homicide, suicide, infanticide, poisoning and sexual assaults. If the court heard more than one medical expert and their opinions diverged it was extremely difficult for the court to decide. Therefore the *Constitution Criminalis Theresiana*, which entered into force in 1768, created a special procedure to help the courts solve the cases where the opinions of the medical experts differed substantially: in these cases the courts had the option to order the universities to review these cases and to give a so-called priority opinion, which decided the controversial medical issues. Later the structure changed and an independent Board was created for this task, the members of the Board being the most experienced forensic medical experts appointed by the Minister of Justice. Originally the opinions of the Board were only signed by the president and the Board was not obliged to testify in court. This situation changed in 2005; the opinions of the Board are delivered by committees consisting of 3–5 members, each of them sign the opinion and if needed the members of the committee testify in court. The Board delivers approximately 400 expert opinions per year.

At present, Eva Keller is the president of the Board. Her predecessors were: Tibor Varga (2001–2011), György Berentey (1989–2000), Imre Zoltán (1957–1989) and Frigyes Doleschall (1954–1956).

14.3.6 Private forensic medical experts

Forensic medical experts used to work within a very centralized structure: they were all affiliated with one of the above-mentioned institutions. This structure started to change in the 1990s when substantial changes in legislation made it possible to work as an independent forensic medical expert. Many experts left the police and the university institutes and started to work as independent forensic experts. Police and courts are in most cases free to choose among the registered forensic experts, and private forensic experts step by step took over a substantial part of forensic casework, mainly in the field of clinical forensic medicine. There are some exceptions, however; for example, autopsies are still done within the institutions – private experts are excluded. Just like any other forensic medical expert, private forensic medical experts have to take part in continuing medical education (CME); they also have to attend the legal courses organized by the Ministry of Justice.

14.4 Integration of forensic science

Some forensic medicine experts work within the criminal division of the Hungarian police. Their duties consist of crime scene investigation, case analysis and legal presentation, apart from postmortem examinations in particular during recent years. There is also a significant involvement in clinical forensic science and in drink-and-drive cases. They have also an active role in the university education, such as teaching and training forensic doctors.

There is a continuing teaching and education program in conjunction with judges, prosecutors and police officers. Semmelweis University is the center of scientific meetings and continuing medical education in forensic medicine.

14.5 Training

14.5.1 Undergraduate training

Forensic medicine is a compulsory requirement of undergraduate training for fifth year medical students. The curriculum is standardized in the four universities (Budapest, Szeged, Pécs and Debrecen), consisting of two academic semesters. Teaching is delivered through lectures, seminars and visits to the autopsy rooms.

The first semester focuses on health law, the course covering areas such as medical malpractice, liability of health care providers, consent to treatment, patient's rights and social services. The second semester focuses on traditional areas of forensic medicine: thanatology, forensic traumatology (mechanical injuries, electrocution, transportation injuries), sudden and unexpected death, toxicology, traffic medicine, DNA, forensic histology, forensic anthropology and clinical forensic medicine, etc. In this semester students visit the autopsy room and participate actively in seminars and lectures.

Forensic odontology is a compulsory requirement of undergraduate training for fourth year dental medicine students, and is for a period of one semester.

All institutes also feature lecturing at the faculty of law.

14.5.2 Postgraduate training

Specialization in forensic medicine takes 60 months. The first 12 months are similar to the final year residency program. The following 12 months are spent in the anatomical pathology department, followed by 3 months in an internal medicine department, 3 months in a traumatology department and 3 months in a psychiatry department. One month should be spent in an institute for disability evaluation. The remaining time is used for forensic autopsies and clinical forensic medicine.

The requirement at the end of the curriculum is to have performed at least 300 autopsies with histology and to have given expert opinion in at least 200 different clinical forensic cases.

The board exam consists of two parts, a practical and an oral exam.

Specialization in forensic psychiatry takes 36 months for certified psychiatrists who have at least three years of experience. The training consists of mandatory courses and practical training.

There is a relatively new specialization called insurance medicine. Training is provided by the forensic medicine departments of the universities. Physicians specialized in all clinical disciplines can fulfill the course requirements and sit for the board exams, which consist of an oral and a practical exam. The training period is 24 months.

Like every physician, specialists in legal medicine are required to maintain their knowledge through continuing education. Compulsory courses organized or accredited by the universities have to be fulfilled (attendance and exam) and scientific achievements and publications are awarded extra credits. Compliance with continuing education requirements is rigorously controlled – incompliance results in losing the right to exercise the profession.

14.6 Funding

Funding of forensic services is diverse and controversial. University forensic departments are under the surveillance of the Ministry of Education which only finances their undergraduate and postgraduate training activities. It is very controversial in that the universities train forensic professionals basically for the legal system and law enforcement. The Ministries of Justice and Interior Affairs still do not finance the training at all and this is very disadvantageous for the university institutes.

The other source of income for the universities is the fees for autopsies, clinical forensic examinations and toxicology tests they do for the court, prosecution and police, and the fees for clinical autopsies. The fees in most cases (especially in cases of clinical forensic medicine examinations) do not cover the cost; this is mainly due to the fact that a special law regulates the fees for expert evidence nationwide.

The National Institute of Forensic Science is financed by the Ministry of Human Resources. The NFSI is financed by the Ministry of Justice.

14.7 Political influences

There is no political influence in forensic practice and the forensic experts are independent; they cannot be instructed by anyone regarding their expert opinion. Before implementing legislation having influence on forensic medicine, the Division of Forensic Medicine of the National Medical College has to be consulted and thus it indirectly influences the content of new legislation.

14.8 Certification

All forensic experts have to become certified and registered. The process of certification and registration is done by the Ministry of Justice; the registry of forensic experts is available online. The registration is open for specialists in forensic medicine, forensic psychiatry and insurance medicine, and also for specialists in clinical disciplines. They all have to be members of the Chamber of Forensic Experts, attend a mandatory legal course organized by the Ministry of Justice, take the mandatory legal exam and repeat it periodically. For those who specialize in a clinical discipline (e.g. surgery, traumatology, internal medicine), the registration is very similar, but they also have to attend a special course organized by the Chamber of Forensic Experts. Once registered, the experts can give expert opinions within their competence for court, police and prosecution. However, there are some cases in which it is mandatory for forensic experts in clinical disciplines to collaborate with experts of forensic medicine and give a joint opinion (injuries, medical malpractice, etc.).

14.9 Laboratory accreditation

All DNA and toxicology laboratories of university forensic departments and NFIS take part in national and international accreditation procedures, and gain a license from GEDNAP, which is successfully renewed every year. The laboratories are accredited according to the ISO 17025 standard.

14.10 Technology

The academic and forensic network has made major advances in development, using funds granted by ministries. Universities also have found resources to develop the laboratories. The NFSI and HIFS have performed significant improvements to the DNA and toxicology laboratories. The postmortem rooms of Semmelweis University have been refurbished and toxicology and histology laboratories have been modernized recently at different universities.

14.11 Disaster preparedness

Currently, there is no DVI team in the country, but the first steps to set up a DVI team have been taken by the police. According to preliminary plans, a new DVI team will be established in 2014 under the surveillance of the HIFS.

14.12 Legal issues

Forensic medicine is strictly regulated by law. The Acts on Criminal, Civil and Administrative Procedure all have regulations regarding forensic medical opinion and forensic experts, and the Act 47 of 2005 regulates the rights and duties of forensic experts.

The forensic medical experts are supervised by the Ministry of Justice (in professional matters in conjunction with the relevant ministry, which is in the case of physicians the Ministry of Health).

Membership of the Chamber of Forensic Experts is compulsory for all medical experts. The Chamber was founded in 1996. The Chamber adopted a Code of Ethics and has the right to conduct a disciplinary procedure if the forensic expert is accused of unethical behavior, where the most serious punishment is exclusion from the Chamber (which means that the forensic expert has to be deleted from the central registry and therefore loses his right to act as a forensic expert).

14.13 Research

The various institutions of forensic medicine all take part in various research activities, in national or international cooperation. Among others, research conducted on drug-related death, addiction, neurobiology of drug abuse, heroin-related pathologic changes of the brain, and drink and driving deserve special mention. The NFSI took part in an international DNA population study recently.

14.14 Future direction

Forensic medicine faces many challenges nowadays. The age distribution among forensic pathologists and forensic psychiatrists is a big problem in Hungary; it has become absolutely necessary to recruit young colleagues into these professions. However, it would only be possible if our profession was attractive for them – this would take many steps. First of all the authorities will have to take responsibility for finding financial means so that appropriate persons can be recruited into this field. We are hoping for the recognition of Legal and Forensic Medicine as a European specialty.

It is important to improve research activities in the future and is essential first of all for university institutes to carry out high quality research and strengthen their positions within the academic world.

Acknowledgments

The authors thank Dr. Gabor Nagy, Dr. Sandor Kosztya, Dr. Antal Kricskovics and Dr. David Petretei for data provided for the Police Forensic Medical Service and HIFS section and Dr. Eva Susa for her assistance with the Network of Forensic Science Institutes (NFSI) section.

References

Fazekas, I. G., Kósa, F. (1978) *Forensic Fetal Osteology*, Akadémiai Kiadó, Budapest, Hungary.

Harsányi, L., Földes, V. (1968) *Orvosszakértői Személyazonosítás*, BM Tanulmányi és Kiképzési Csoportfőnökség, Budapest, Hungary.

Incze, G. (1942) Fremdkörper in Blutkreislauf Ertrunkener. *Zentralbl. Allg. Pathol. Anat. 79.*

Incze, G. (1965) *The Heredity of Papillary Pattern*, Akadémiai Kiadó, Budapest, Hungary.

Kenyeres, B. (1909) *Törvényszéki Orvostan I–III*, Magyar Orvosi Könyvkiadó Társulat, Budapest, Hungary.

Kenyeres, B. (1935) *Sachliche Bewewise bei der Klärung von Todesfällen*, Walter de Gruyter, Berlin-Leipzig, Germany.

Orsós, F. (1935 Die vitalen Reaktionen und ihr Gerichtsmedizinische Bedeutung. *Beitr. Path. Anat.* 95.

Plenk, J. J. (1871) *Elementa Medicinae et Chirurgiae Forensis*, Vienna, Austria.

Plenk, J. J. (1875) *Toxicologia seu Doctrina de Venernis et Antidotis*, Vienna, Austria.

Schraud, F. (1795) *Aphorismi de Politia Medica*, Pest, Hungary.

Schraud, F. (1797) *De Forensibus Judicum et Medicorum Relationibus. In Vicem Introductionis ad Medicinam Forensem Disserit*, Pest, Hungary.

Schraud, F. (1802) *Elementa Medicinae Forensic*, Pest, Hungary.

Somogyi, E. (1968) *Az igazságügyi orvostan alapjai*, Medicina, Budapest, Hungary.

Somogyi, E., Sótonyi, P. (Eds.) (1994) *Sudden Cardiac Death*, Semmelweis Kiadó, Budapest, Hungary.

Sótonyi, P. (Ed.) (2009) *A Magyar Törvényszéki-Igazságügyi Orvostan Története*, Medicina, Budapest, Hungary.

Sótonyi, P. (2011) *Igazságügyi Orvostan* (4th ed,), Semmelweis Kiadó, Budapest, Hungary.

Varga, T. (Ed.) (2004) *Egészségbiztosítás*, Szeged, Hungary.

CHAPTER 15
Forensic science in India

P.K. Chattopadhyay

Amity Institute of Forensic Science, Noida, India

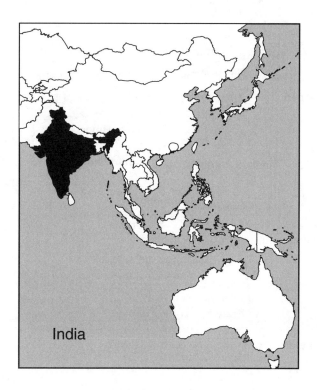

India

15.1 Introduction

Forensic Science, the application of scientific methods and techniques for the purposes of justice, is quite ancient in India. There are several instances where fingerprint patterns, such as Chakra (circular meaning the whorl), Sankh (Conch meaning the Loops) or reference to poisons/poisoning, their signs and symptoms, etc., have been mentioned in the ancient texts and literature. As a matter of fact, fingerprints have been in use as signatures on land deeds, etc., and continue to be used even today by people all over the country (Figure 15.1). However, laboratories for the analysis and identification of poisons in cases of poisoning were established in the form of the Chemical Examiner's Laboratory starting from Madras (1849) followed by Calcutta (1853), Agra (1864) and Bombay (1870); Forensic Science Laboratories, as we know them today, came much later with the establishment of the West Bengal State Forensic Science Laboratory in Calcutta in 1952. Ayenger (1961), Bami (1982), Chatterjee (1961), Nanda and Tewari (2000), Tewari and Ravikumar (1999) and Tewari (1999) have

The Global Practice of Forensic Science, First Edition. Edited by Douglas H. Ubelaker.

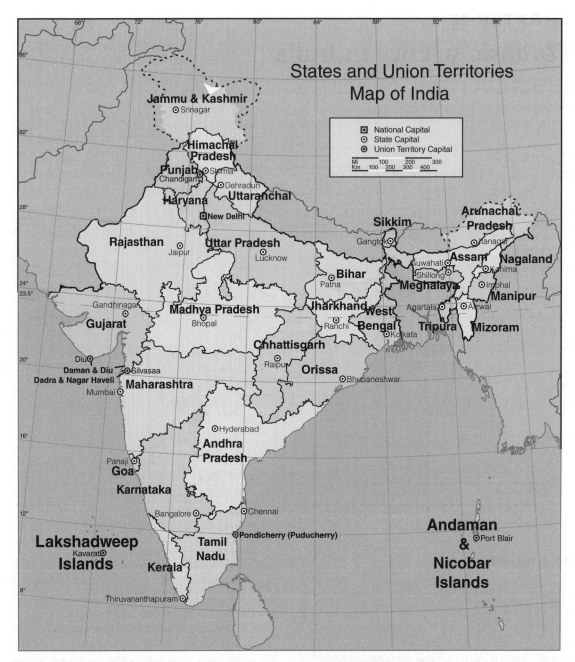

Figure 15.1 Map of India showing the various states. *Source:* Aotearoa at pl.wikipedia [GFDL (http://www.gnu.org/copyleft/fdl.html) or CC-BY-SA-3.0 (http://creativecommons.org/licenses/by-sa/3.0/)], via Wikimedia Commons from Wikimedia Commons.

Table 15.1 Chronological establishment of forensic science laboratories

Name of the State	Location of the Laboratory	Year of establishment
Andhra Pradesh	Hyderabad	1974
Assam	Guwahati	1963
Bihar	Patna	1960
Chattisgarh	Raipur	2002
Delhi	Rohini	1994
Gujrat	Gandhinagar	1974
Haryana	Madhuban, Karnal	1970
Himachal Pradesh	Junga	1971
Jammu and Kashmir	Jammu, Srinagar	1963
Karnataka	Bangalore	1968
Kerala	Trivandrum	1961
Madhya Pradesh	Sagar	1964
Maharashtra	Bombay	1967
Manipur	Pangei near Imphal	1989
Meghalaya	Shillong	1987
Mizoram	Aizwal	1998
Nagaland	Dimapur	1982
Orissa	Bhubaneswar	1969
Punjab	Chandigarh	1976
Rajasthan	Jaipur	1959
Tripura	Agartala	–
UP	Lucknow	1964
Uttarakhand	Dehradun	2006
Central Forensic Science Laboratories	Calcutta	1957
	Delhi (CBI)	1968
	Chandigarh	1978
	Hyderabad	1966
	Guwahati	2013
	Pune	2013
	Bhopal	2013

written on the development of forensic science in India. The chronological order of the establishment of various state and central forensic science laboratories is given below and in Table 15.1:

The Anthropometric Bureau was established in Calcutta in 1892 for maintaining records of criminals according to Bertillon's System.

The Finger Print Bureau, the first of its kind in the world was set up in June 1897 at Calcutta.

The Government Examiner of Questioned Documents was set up at Shimla in 1906.

Serologist to the Government of India for examination of blood, semen, etc., was established in Calcutta in 1910.

The Ballistics Laboratory was established under the police in Calcutta in 1930.

The organizational structure of the Laboratories by and large is similar and is given in Figure 15.2.

The number of divisions (subjects covered) varies from one laboratory to another; the divisions that are mostly there are:

- Ballistics and Explosives Division
- Biology Division/DNA Profiling Unit
- Chemistry Division
- Computer Forensic Division
- Toxicology
- Criminalistics/Instrumental Analysis
- Fingerprint/Footprint Division

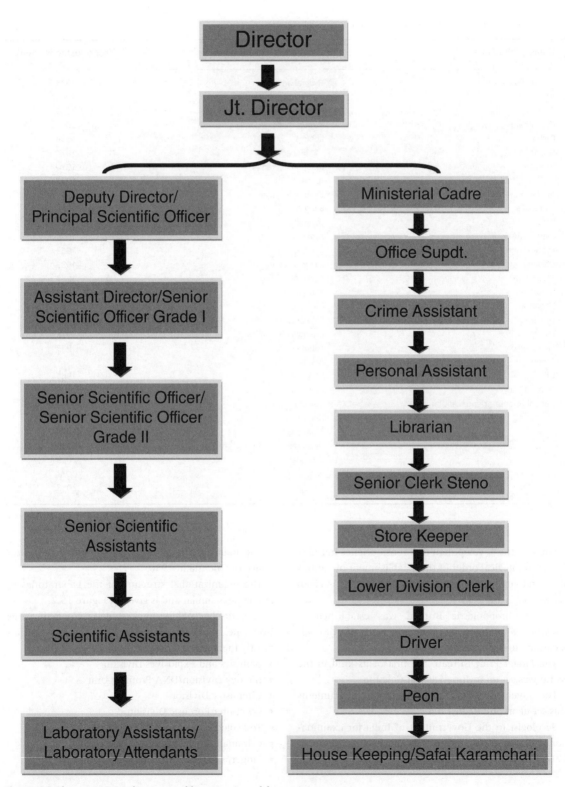

Figure 15.2 The organizational structure of forensic science laboratories.

- Forensic Psychology Division/Lie Detection
- Document Division
- Physics Division
- Photo/Scientific Aid Division
- Serology Division.

15.2 Biology division

Identification of blood, semen and other body fluids, vomit, foecal matter, tissues, hairs and fibres, wood, leaf, skeletal remains, etc.

15.3 Serology division

Determination of species origin and ABO groups from blood and other body fluid stains.

15.4 Physics division

Examination of paint, glass, metals including metal coins, comparison of tool or cut marks, deciphering erased/altered numbers on automobiles, seals, etc.

15.5 Ballistics and explosives division

Examination of firearms, bullets, cartridges, gunshot residues, traces of explosive materials collected from crime scene or suspected examination of defused/exploded devices to determine their operation and origin.

15.6 Documents division

Comparison and identification of hand writings, erasers, obliteration, addition, alteration, detection of forgeries, typewriting/printed matter, inks, paper, charred documents, etc.; secret/disguised writing, relative aging of documents, etc.

15.7 DNA unit/division

Extraction and profiling for STR types, mt-DNA, etc., from blood and body fluids, tissues, bone, etc., for identification.

15.8 Chemistry division

Analysis of petrol/petroleum products and other inflammable materials in case of arson, qualitative analysis of narcotic and psychotropic substances, alcohol, etc.

15.9 Toxicology division

Extraction and identification of poisons from viscera, etc.

15.10 Fingerprint/footprint division

Developing, lifting, comparison and identification of fingerprints and footprints/footwear impressions, preparation of cast, etc.

15.11 Forensic psychology/lie detection division

Verification of statements of suspects, witness and complaints with the help of polygraph, scientific interrogation of suspects, etc.

15.12 Photography division

Photography/videography of scene of crime and crime-related exhibits/objects, to decipher indented writing marks, micro- and macrophotography of documents, etc., preparation of posters, charts, etc.

15.13 Computer forensic

All computer-related cases including hacking, source of message, etc.

15.14 Discussion

The administrative control of the Laboratories also varies from state to state as also for the Central Forensic Science Laboratories. While the Central Forensic Science Laboratory in Delhi is under the control of the Central Bureau of Investigation, the other Central Forensic Science Laboratories located in Calcutta, Chandigarh, Delhi, Hyderabad, Pune, Bhopal and Guwahati are under the control of the Directorate of Forensic Science located in Delhi. While most of the State Laboratories are under the administrative control of the Police, the others are controlled by the Department of Home directly.

The Departments of Forensic Medicine that are under the administrative control of the Ministry of Health and Family Welfare are primarily concerned with the conduct of autopsy examinations to determine the cause of death, examine the victim or the assailants (clinical forensic medicine), type and cause of an injury, etc., and teaching of courses to undergraduates and postgraduates. Research is of secondary importance and is mostly case based.

Although most of the Laboratories are equipped with the latest sophisticated instruments, lack of adequate qualified manpower, coupled with a resource crunch, has hampered their progress. The National Human Rights Commission under the Chairmanship of Mr Justice M.N. Venkatchalia in its annual report of 1998–1999 observed that ".... Criminal cases delayed for a variety of reasons, are also often further delayed because matters remain pending in Forensic Science laboratories. This has added yet another impediment to the dispensation of Justice. Realising the critical importance of improving the functioning of the Forensic Science Laboratories, as this is essential to the proper administration of the criminal justice system, the commission felt it was necessary to look into the problems bedeviling these laboratories with a view to evolving guidelines for their better working...." Although a Core Group was constituted for the purpose to suggest measures for improving laboratories the position has not changed much. Nevertheless, within the limitations commendable work has been done in solving many of the cases that are referred to the laboratories from time to time. Further, most of the state laboratories have a number of Regional Forensic Science Laboratories with the districts being covered by Mobile Forensic Science Laboratories, which are especially useful for crime scene visits including collection, packing and onward transmission of the exhibits to the nearest Regional Forensic Science Laboratory or the main laboratory where required facilities for analyzing the particular type of exhibits are available.

Funding of the Central Forensic Science Laboratories is from the central government while the State Forensic Science Laboratories are funded by the respective state governments. It must be added that all the Laboratories are supported by a central grant under the Modernisation Scheme for equipments, etc.

The tremendous advances made in science and technology and their application in forensic problems require that all aspirants who want to make a career in forensic science must be trained and oriented in various aspects of forensic science, including instrumental analysis. In order to fulfill this objective, courses at the undergraduate and postgraduate level were started in the universities, with Dr H.S. Gaur University at Sagar, Madhya Pradesh starting courses on criminology and forensic science in 1961 followed by Delhi University, which started a one year postgraduate course in forensic science in 1968. Subsequently several universities in India including the Punjabi University, Patiala (numbering about 25), are now offering courses in forensic science. However, the universities suffer from a serious resource crunch and the nonavailability of qualified and committed teachers to train the students. The problem is further aggravated by the lack of uniformity in the teaching curriculum. In terms of research activities in the laboratories the less said the better. While acute shortage of manpower, the work load, etc., are advanced as causes for the lack of research activities these are lame excuses. The main reason is the lack of aptitude for research, as has been highlighted in the Report by a Committee formed by the Government of India on Perspective Planning in Forensic Science. This, however, is not the case in the universities where serious researches on basic problems related to Forensic Science are being carried out despite the lack of facilities since regular publications in peer reviewed journals are a must for career advancements and promotions in the universities. Some of the important publications on different aspects of forensic science ranging from identification of hand and finger from single fingerprints to STR types are mentioned in various papers (Chattopadhyay, 1972, 1982, 1990; Mukherjee and Chattopadhyay, 1976; Chattopadhyay and Sharma, 1989; Gonmori et al., 1994; Sharma and Chattopadhyay, 1994; Kaur et al., 1997; Chattopahyay et al., 2000; Singh et al., 2005; Yuasa et al., 2006; Chattopadhyay and Chattopadhyay, 2006; Chattopadhyay and Bhatia, 2008).

References

Ayengar, N.K. (1961) Growth and development of forensic science in India. *Indian Police Journal* (Special Centenary Issue) : 145–151.

Bami, H.L. (1982) Forensic science in India. *Journal of Indian Academy of Forensic Science, Calcutta* 21: 71–76.

Chatterjee, S.K. (1961) History of fingerprinting in India. *Indian Police Journal* (Special Centenary Issue): 152–157.

Chattopadhyay, P.K. (1972) A new method for classifying Palmprint. *Journal of Indian Academy of Forensic Science, Calcutta* 11: 12–17.

Chattopadhyay, P.K. (1982) Teaching of Forensic Science. *Journal of Indian Academy of Forensic Science, Calcutta* 21: 60–64.

Chattopadhyay, P.K. (1990) ABO blood groups from hairs, in *Proceedings of the International Symposium on Advances in Legal Medicine*, Kanazawa, Japan, pp.111–114.

Chattopadhyay, P.K., Bhatia, S. (2008) Morphological examination of the ear: a study of an Indian population, paper presented at the *Seventh International Symposium on Legal Medicine*, Osaka, Japan, April 2009, pp. 192–193.

Chattopadhyay, Prasun, Kr., Chattopadhyay, P.K. (2006) Identification of individuals from teeth. *Indian Journal of Physical Anthropology and Human Genetics* 25 (2): 221–226. Published in 2007.

Chattopadhyay, P.K., Sharma A.K. (1989) Teeth as aid to personal identification: a study for species origin and ABO blood groups. *Journal of Indian Academy of Forensic Science, Calcutta* 28: 25–30.

Chattopahyay, P.K., Cleef, S., Duelmer, M., Henke, L., Henke, J. (2000) Human autosomal short tendem repeats types in Jatt Sikhs from North India. *Forensic Science International, Elsevier, Ireland* 113: 29–32.

Gonmori, K., Yoshioka, N., Chattopadhyay, P.K. (1994) Identification of human semen stains by thin layer chromatoghaphy. *Acta Crim. Japon., Japan* 60: 149–154.

Kaur, H., Chattopadhyay, P.K., Mishra, G.J. (1997) Chlorinated insecticides in human blood and milk. *Journal of Forensic Medicine and Toxicology, New Delhi* 14: 13.

Mukherjee, J.B., Chattopadhyay, P.K. (1976) Blood groups from teeth. *Medicine Science and Law, London* 16: 232–234.

Nanda, B.B., Tewari, R.K. (2000) Development of Forensic Science Services at the State level. *Indian Police Journal* 66: 109–119.

Sharma, A.K., Chattopadhyay, P.K. (1994) Blood groups and enzyme types from teeth. *Journal of the Forensic Science Society UK.*

Singh, I., Chattopadhyay, P.K., Garg, R.K. (2005) Determination of the hand from single digit fingerprint: a study of whorls. *Forensic Science International* 152: 205–208.

Tewari, R.K. (1999) Application of forensic science in criminal justice administration in the developing countries. *Indian Police Journal* 66: 78–83.

Tewari, R.K., Ravikumar, K.V. (1999) *Journal of Indian Academy of Forensic Science* 38: 17–32.

Yuasa, I., Umetsu, K., Harihara, S., Kido, A., Miyoshi, A., Saitou, N., Dashnyam, B., Jib, F., Lucotte, G., Chattopadhaya, P.K., Henke, L., Henke, J. (2006) Distribution of F37 allele of SLC45A2 (MATP) gene and founder haplotype analysis. *Annals of Human Genetics, London* 69: 1–10.

CHAPTER 16
Forensic sciences in Italy

Cristina Cattaneo[1], Antonio Grande[2] & Luigi Ripani[3]

[1] Sezione di Medicina Legale, LABANOF (Laboratorio di Antropologia e Odontologia Forense), Dipartimento di Scienze Biomediche per la Salute, Università degli Studi di Milano, Milan, Italy
[2] Servizio di Polizia Scientifica, Polizia di Stato, Rome, Italy
[3] RaCis, Servizio Investigazioni Scientifiche Arma dei Carabinieri, Rome, Italy

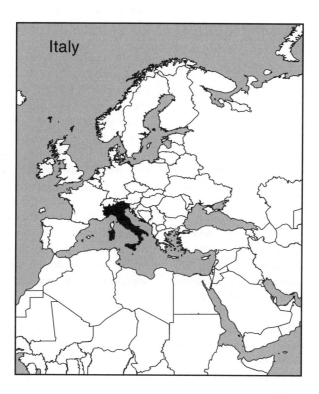

16.1 Introduction

It is extremely difficult to clearly delineate how forensic sciences are structured and organized in Italy. Italy is a country that is renowned for being disorganized but certainly full of resources, though the ways such resources can be applied may be complicated. In a country where in 2010, for example, the number of total crimes recorded by all police forces amounted to

2,621,019, cases of voluntary homicides amounted to 567 and robberies to 47,996 (Clarke, 2013), forensic science has an obvious role and is of paramount importance. Qualified personnel exist across the country, but at times efficiency is not maximized because of lack of communication and inadequate awareness of judges concerning the multifaceted nature of a forensic investigation. Forensic activity can be performed by different agencies – the Polizia Scientifica (the forensic

The Global Practice of Forensic Science, First Edition. Edited by Douglas H. Ubelaker.
© 2015 John Wiley & Sons, Ltd. Published 2015 by John Wiley & Sons, Ltd.

team of police forces, which is represented both within the Polizia di Stato (Ministry of Internal Affairs) and the Carabinieri (Ministry of Defense)), universities and even private institutions or individuals. Training of single experts can be at various levels; more traditional disciplines, such as DNA analysis and pathology, provide greater guarantees as concerns the quality of the investigation as opposed to relatively newer fields (botany and anthropology, for example) for which there is still little regulation and training.

In order to be able to fully understand the ins and outs of forensic sciences in Italy it is necessary first of all to concisely explain the judicial system and how and when it uses forensic sciences and scientists.

16.2 How forensic sciences enter the judicial scenario

In Italy the judicial initiative is taken by the prosecutor ("Pubblico Ministero", public minister or PM). Criminal investigation actually begins with a *"notizia di reato"*, literally "information on a crime", i.e. the presence of sufficient data to officially open a case or to verify if a crime has been committed and if it can be attributed to a specific subject. This activity is performed by the PM and the judicial police (JP) which usually work by proxy. The term JP refers to officials and agents coming from police corps (in Italy, for example, the Polizia di Stato and Carabinieri) but also from other public administrations, recruited specifically by the PM for criminal investigations. The *notizia di reato* can come from several sources: judicial police, police corps, privates, doctors, etc. If a private citizen witnesses a crime he or she is under no obligation to report it to the PM. However, some professions such as that of teachers and physicians are in fact under the obligation to notify the PM if they have encountered a situation that may represent a serious crime. In these diverse manners a *"notizia di reato"* is created. Once the PM receives such a report he must immediately, with no delay, transcribe it to a specific registry at the Procura della Repubblica (i.e. the Public Prosecutor's Office) of the Tribunale Ordinario (Ordinary Court) (article 335, Codice Procedura Penale, i.e. Criminal Procedure Code). From this moment onwards the PM is the *dominus* of the enquiry and will commission all necessary investigations (Gentilomo, Travaini and D'Auria, 2009).

The forensic scientist may come into action during these very preliminary steps, that is during the acquisition of the *notizia di reato*, but in a more marginal manner. An example could be a death scene investigation. The analysis of something as preliminary as a death scene is included within the activities described by article 354 of the Codice di Procedura Penale which "urges verification of environments, things and persons..." and states what the judicial police must do concerning documentation and preservation of the environment and evidence when further delay would be critical since it could lead to modifications. This article declares that *"the officials and agents of the judicial police take care that traces and things referring to the crime are preserved and that the condition of the scene does not change before the prosecutor is involved and appointed. If there is the risk that the things, traces and places previously indicated can change or be modified and the prosecutor cannot immediately intervene or has not taken lead of the investigation yet, the judicial police perform all the necessary evaluations and surveys ...."*

In these scenarios the Polizia Scientifica intervenes together with its forensic experts as auxiliaries of the JP. However, other forensic scientists from other institutions (universities for example) can be called. This is frequently the case for the forensic pathologist since the Polizia Scientifica does not have forensic pathologists within their teams (with the exception of the Polizia Scientifica of the Polizia di Stato in Rome). This forensic scientist is usually involved in the investigation of the crime scene, together with police officers and personnel of the police scientific divisions. The forensic pathologist in such cases is usually considered an auxiliary of the judicial police (article 348 of the Codice di Procedura Penale), who aids police personnel in the "evaluation and survey" of places and things where they require "specific technical competence". In detail, article 348 states that *"after communication of the potential crime, the judicial police...collect any evidence useful for the reconstruction of the event and the identification of the culprit, they search for evidence related to the crime and guarantee preservation of the scene...after the prosecutor is contacted, the judicial police...follow the orders of the prosecutor and may proceed on their own all the investigations needed to ascertain the crime..... When the judicial police have to perform activities which require specific technical competence, they can call adequate personnel, who cannot refuse"*.

Legislation of the crime scene investigation does not request that the defence be informed, since in this early phase the prosecutor and the judicial police are not yet "a part" of the judicial activities.

In conclusion, the first moment where forensic sciences come into a criminal case scenario is in a very preliminary phase with less guarantees for other parties; in this instance the PM who can definitely count on the availability of forensic experts within the teams of the Polizia Scientifica may not be able to take advantage of the presence of other types of experts who are not within these teams (e.g. pathologists, odontologists, entomologists) because they are not part of the police forces and thus may not be involved or called at all in this delicate phase. This is a (perhaps inevitable) flaw in the system. It may happen that a pathologist will not even be called to a crime scene, or that appropriate entomological evidence will not be collected. Finally, regardless of who is called and present at the scene, these scientists are usually nominated as auxiliaries and not consultants, for the above-mentioned procedural purposes, with therefore much less responsibility.

An interesting and frequent example of the lack of appropriate personnel at the crime scene is in cases of buried bodies or human remains. Most forensic investigators are aware of the fact that archaeology is the only discipline that can guide an appropriate excavation and retrieval of the body, without creating postmortem lesions. Nonetheless police forces do not have archaeological personnel and frequently such remains are poorly excavated with bulldozers, picks and shovels, creating complete dispersal and loss of crucial information concerning the manner of deposition, trauma, identification, time since death. More and more proper acculturation of magistrates and especially of police forces is reducing this kind of gross error and forensic archaeologists are becoming involved.

Going back to the magistrate's action, one must stress that activity of the PM has as its scope that of verifying whether the elements coming from the investigation, collected directly or through the activity of the judicial police, are appropriate for sustaining the accusations and therefore transforming the person on whom he or she is making enquiries into the accused (or defendant). The PM, however, must also collect evidence in favour of the investigated party since art. 97 of our constitution requires PMs to work impartially. At this moment of the judicial activity the PM may need an expertise, which is technically called "consulenza tecnica" (CT). Here is where forensic scientists, again, may

come in, this time with a more specific and perhaps responsible role – when they are appointed as the consultant. The CT is described by articles 359 and 360 of the Codice di Procedura Penale (which they must be aware of because of the consequences described below). If what needs to be performed (e.g. a DNA analysis) is considered to be repeatable (i.e. there is enough material to perform the expertise more than once), the PM does not need to inform the other parties involved, namely the defense and the injured party. If, on the contrary, the analyses concern persons, things or places that will change following these tests, the PM has to inform the defendant and the injured party of such tests and these parties can, and usually, appoint their own consultants, who can be present at all technical activities the PM's consultant will perform (during which they can also make suggestions and requests).

The role of the consultant is described by article 359 of the Codice di Procedura Penale, which states that "*the prosecutor, when he asks for descriptive and photographic evaluations and surveys or other technical operations which require specific competence, can call consultants which cannot refuse. The consultant is allowed to attend to every act of the investigation*". The consultant therefore can be anyone the PM decides is adequate for the task. He or she can come from a university, represent a private institution or belong to Polizia di Stato and Carabinieri, especially for what concerns genetics, criminalistics and analysis of digital images. After his or her investigations, if the PM thinks the information and data point towards a criminal responsibility, he will ask for a "rinvio a Giudizio", in other words he will ask for there to be a trial. In this case there will usually be a preliminary hearing in front of the Giudice per l'Indagine Preliminare (GIP) or preliminary investigation judge. This judge, if not satisfied with the expertise requested by the PM, can ask for further tests. This is another scenario in which forensic scientists can be requested to be consultants, for all parties – only that the forensic scientist for the GIP will be called perito (expert) and not consultant (consulente) anymore. The GIP can then establish whether to send the defendant to trial or to acquit him or her. If he decides the defendant goes to trial, then the defendant can decide in which way to go to trial: by a *patteggiamento*, where there is an agreement between prosecution and defendant on the sentence (maximum 5 years) or by a *rito abbreviato*, which is a request for an immediate sentence, without going through a real trial and hearings and therefore without the acquisition of evidence – in this case the eventual sentence will be reduced by a third.

If a trial occurs, this is where all evidence will be taken on by all parties in front of a court, that is a judge (a third, impartial party). The Court can be Monocratic (one judge), Collegial (three judges) or d'Assise (a Crown or Supreme Court with two judges and six layman judges), depending mainly on the type and modality of the crime. All consultants from all parties (i.e. forensic scientists) involved in the previous phases of the case will/can be heard in court and questioned by the prosecution, the damaged party, the defense and the court. The judge can then request further evidence and appoint his own expert (perito). If so the other parties will/can appoint more experts.

The appointment of a perito is stated by article 221 of the Codice di Procedura Penale, which establishes that *"the judge can call his expert by choice on specific boards or among persons with a particular competence in that specific discipline....The judge can call more persons if the investigations and evaluations are of special complexity or they require different areas of competence in different disciplines"*. This is valid also for the scientific departments of police forces (Polizia and Carabinieri) who are involved in investigations especially for what concerns genetics, criminalistics and analysis of digital images. The trial will then end in an acquittal or in a guilt sentence. As one can see, therefore, if we use genetics as an example, a single case can involve as many as nine DNA experts (one (at least) for each party, namely the PM, the defense and the damaged party in the preliminary phases, if necessary again before the GIP, and finally during the trial).

Final judgment in the first degree can be contested. Both the defense and the prosecution can appeal; an Appeal trial has a further, although exceptional, possibility of appointing new forensic experts. After an Appeal there can be a Cassation trial, with a similar procedure to the Appeal but the object is limited to the logical criteria of the written motivations and in checking for formal or procedural errors.

Through all these steps, the consultant or the expert can be virtually anyone, at times regardless of qualifications and experience. Here lies a common but important problem. As one can see from the criminal codes, the forensic expert is usually called upon by the prosecutor or the judge who base their choice on their personal opinion in the end: in other words, a board or list of experts in the forensic field does not exist, or rather it

exists in all courts but is of no practical relevance and significance. One has also to consider that certification in Italy is not mandatory at the moment for most forensic expertises and has and is being acquired within a limited number of fields (such as genetics and toxicology). In court rarely do questions such as qualification come up – this, however, is bound to change in the near future. At the moment, this may lead to the choice of personnel without specific knowledge or experience in the forensic field.

16.3 Evaluation of goodness of evidence

For what concerns the criteria and rules by which the validity of evidence is evaluated, Italian academia has a long and philosophical history. The most relevant rule concerns the "contrafactual judgment" ("giudizio controfattuale"), which provides an indication for the reconstruction of causal links: the contrafactual judgement is defined by article 40 of the Italian Codice Penale (Criminal Code), according to which *"nobody can be punished for a crime if the damaging or dangerous event upon which the existence of the crime depends is not a consequence of his action or omission. Not preventing an event which one is obliged to prevent is the same as producing it"*. This means that in judicial cases the point of view of the judge consists of mentally eliminating the possible causes in order to verify if the event would actually have occurred.

For what concerns the admissibility of scientific results in the trial, for the Italian judicial system the judge himself states the admission of the evidence based on his conviction. From this point of view, in Italy the judge is considered "expert of experts" (peritus peritorum) as he decides on admissibility of the results provided by the experts, and whether they provide scientific information. This may lead, although rarely, to decisions that are discordant from the results provided by the expert witness, if other sources of evidence provide a different opinion or the conclusions given by the consultant do not convince the judge.

There is in Italy a long history of medicolegal "criteriologia" (the discipline dealing with criteria by which to justify causal links), which is unfortunately more popular in the medicolegal environment than among other forensic scientists. It started with the evaluation of the causal link by Cazzaniga (1938) who identified specific criteria by which to establish if an event can be considered as the cause of another one, namely criteria based on topography, chronology and whether the entity of the event was important enough. More modern theoretical models have been proposed, such as those referring to statistical laws of modern jurisprudence. In other words, the expert should always seek laws that will prove, for example, that a certain conduct will always lead to that specific event according to statistical probability. Concerning statistics, Italian jurisprudence intervened in 2002 with the so-called "sentenza Franzese" (Cassazione Penale, SS UU sentenza 11.09.02 n° 30328) concerning a case of medical malpractice. It established how statistical laws are not *per se* prohibited but that they should have a controllable degree of certainty and be checked for repeatability through empirical testing. Also they must resist epistemological trials of falsification. This has actually led to a relatively new article of our Codice di Procedura Penale, article 533, which establishes that the defendant cannot be condemned unless there is evidence beyond reasonable doubt. These applications of logic and epistemology in fact represent an innovative approach, which was already somewhat anticipated with the Daubert and Kumho rulings (Grivas and Komar, 2008). All this may truly resemble philosophy more than forensic sciences; however, the rules of logic, which are equally well expressed in a more practical and less redundant manner in the Daubert and Kumho rulings, are of paramount importance. All forensic scientists should work by these criteria. They are traditionally, or should be, part of the forensic culture of the forensic scientist but are beginning to be seriously considered only now within other forensic disciplines that are encompassing this way of thinking in presenting evidence.

A last interesting comment, in this statistical perspective, should be made concerning the excessive and quasi-paradoxical use of quantifying error. Geneticists especially have virtually spoiled judges by always providing them with an apparently precise quantification of the error of their methods, which can automatically be translated into a quantification of the risk a judge is taking. This has led in our country to excessive and impossible demands for quantification for all disciplines. It may happen that a judge will ask an odontologist, who has just identified a victim by several reliable dental traits, what the chances are of another person sharing the exact same dental asset. Though statistics and methodology

have an important role in presenting evidence, forensic scientists in Italy are aware of the fact that not all can be quantifiable and that other ways of sustaining evidence can be sought (Grivas and Komar, 2008).

16.4 Who are the forensic scientists?

Forensic science expertise may be delegated generally to one of four entities: Polizia, Carabinieri, universities and privates. The different professional figures will be treated in detail in the following sections.

16.4.1 Polizia Scientifica of the Polizia di Stato (Ministry of Internal Affairs)
16.4.1.1 Background and history
The scientific section of the Police was born in 1902 when in Rome the first course of forensic sciences for the Police was held by Professor Salvatore Ottolenghi. On October 25th 1903, the Minister Zanardelli (State Secretary for Interior Affairs), established the first course in forensic sciences for the Scientifica. The course was finally made official by the King's Decree of December 7th 1919.

The Scientific Section of the Police (Polizia Scientifica) is included within the Anti-Crime Central Direction of the Police, and is structured as follows:

i. First Division comprises:

1st Section of judicial authority and personnel
2nd Section for coordination and management of resources
3rd Section for International relations, projects, training and teaching
4th Section for computerized analysis and support

ii. Second Division comprises:

1st Section of preventive identification
2nd Section of judicial identity
3rd Section of graphic analyses
4th Section AFIS (Automated Fingerprint Identification System)
5th Section for the analysis of latent fingerprints

iii. Third Division comprises:

1st Section Unit for the Analysis of Violent Crime (UACV) and operational technical support
2nd Section for forensic genetics

3rd Section for legal medicine, psychology applied to criminalistics

iv. Fourth Division comprises:

1st Section of analyses of drugs

2nd Section for analyses of explosives, inflammable substances, soil

3rd Section for questioned documents, inks, paints,
inorganic analyses and fibers

4th Section for electronics

5th Section for ballistic and gunshot residues

On the entire national territory the Polizia Scientifica is organized into six inter-regional centres (Torino,
Milano, Padova, Roma, Napoli, Bari) and eight regional
centres (Genova, Bologna, Firenze, Ancona, Cagliari,
Reggio Calabria, Palermo, Catania), which depend
directly on the General Service of the Polizia Scientifica,
and 89 provincial centres (c/o Questure), 198 places
for photoidentification and documentation (c/o Com-
missariati di P.S.) and 18 photoidentification places (c/o
Uffici Polizia di Frontiera).

16.4.1.2 Types of cases and case load

The Polizia Scientifica operates at a central level in
the organization of training, coordinating and leading
technical scientific investigations for all activities of the
Police on the national territory of the judicial author-
ity and of other investigation forces. In the Servizio di
Polizia Scientifica there are, among others, AFIS and
IBIS databases, as well as specialized groups and units
for DVI (Disaster Victim Identification), Experts in Trace
Research (ERT), the group for fingerprint identification
(GID), Unit for the Analysis of Violent Crime (UACV)
and Unit for Cold Cases (UDI), in cooperation with the
Central Operational Service. At the Servizio di Polizia
Scientifica and at the interregional centres of Naples
and the regional centre of Palermo there are genetic
laboratories for identification by comparison of DNA
profiles.

The Scientific Section of Police performs tests in the
fields of:

- -Fingerprint recording
- -Investigation of the crime scene
- -Fingerprint comparison
- -Sketching for identikits
- -Genetic analyses
- -Enhancement of latent fingerprints

- -Graphic analyses
- -Ballistic analyses
- -Analysis of abraded serial numbers in cars and
  weapons
- -Questioned documents
- -Qualitative and quantitative analysis of drugs
- -Video-photographic documentation of the investiga-
  tive services and of public order.

The Scientific Service of the Police every year perform 15,000 investigations of crime scenes (both for suspicious deaths and robberies) and several thousands of
interventions for public order (sports and public meetings, etc.); new cases entered in the AFIS system are
over 13.5 million. The genetic laboratories every year
perform thousands of analyses. Recently the Polizia Scientifica has operated within the DVI mission (with the
DVI-Polizia which counts over 100 components) in the
naval disaster of *Costa Concordia* and in the naval disaster
of *Lampedusa* (more than 400 corpses).

16.4.1.3 Recruitment and training

Recruitment occurs by selection of personnel already in
service at the Police, who wish to attend training courses
organized by the Polizia Scientifica. Recruitment of high
ranking personnel of the Police and of physicians and
scientific technical staff on the other hand occurs directly
through advertisement of the post, selection by CV and
interview.

Training of personnel of the Polizia Scientifica *involves* an initial course in photo-identification (*fotoseg-
nalatore*) and fingerprinting, after which they can
perform institutional tasks linked to the investigation of
the crime scene, with fingerprinting and video-photo-
documentation (e.g. events involving public order).
Every year refresher courses and updates are given.
Further courses and updates are offered to specialized
groups and units and to lab personnel.

16.4.1.4 Funding and certification

Funding is provided according to availability of the Ministry of Internal Affairs and eventually from EU funds.
The Polizia Scientifica is UNI EN ISO 9001 certified, and
the laboratory of forensic genetics, drugs and gunshot
residues is ISO/IEC 117025 accredited.

16.4.2 The Raggruppamento Carabinieri Investigazioni Scientifiche (RaCIS), of the Carabinieri Corps (Ministry of Defence)

The RaCIS, **the** forensic science Institute of the Carabinieri Corps, is the structure in charge of the technical-scientific investigations of the Arma dei Carabinieri for the judicial authority as well as for the police forces. The RaCIS, located in Rome, is the headquarters of a complex structure articulated in several departments: four "Reparti Investigazioni Scientifiche (RIS)", scientific investigation departments located in Rome, Parma, Messina and Cagliari with operational competence over the main criminalistics fields (fingerprints, forensic biology, forensic chemistry, etc.) and other departments, all located in Rome, which are the "Reparto Tecnologie Informatiche" dealing with all the ICT investigations, the "Reparto Dattiloscopia Preventiva" dealing with the preventive fingerprint database and the "Reparto Analisi Criminologiche" involved in criminological analyses. The RaCIS also has further units operating on the Italian territory within the Operational Sections of the Provincial Headquarters, functionally linked with their respective RIS units, named "Sezioni Investigazioni Scientifiche" (SIS). The personnel employed in the SIS is specifically skilled in evidence collection at the crime scene and drug analyses.

16.4.2.1 The history of the RaCIS

On December 15th 1955, at the School for Officers in Rome, the "Gabinetto Centrale di Documentazione e di Investigazioni Tecnico-Scientifiche" was created, and on December 1st 1965 it took the name of "Centro Carabinieri Investigazioni Scientifiche" (CCIS). Subsequently, with the increasing role of technical-scientific analysis in the Italian legislation, both structure and operational activities of the CIS were further revised and implemented with the institution of the peripheral departments located in Parma, Messina and Cagliariup until 1999 when the CIS took on its present name (RaCIS) and organization with the four Reparti Investigazioni Scientifiche (RIS) of Roma, Parma, Messina and Cagliari. The RaCIS was also implemented by the creation of the Reparto Analisi Criminologiche since 2004, of the Reparto Dattiloscopia Preventiva since September 1st 2005 and of the Reparto Tecnologie Informatiche since November 1st 2006.

16.4.2.2 RaCIS international affiliations, cooperations and relationships

The RaCIS in the international scenario is, as a founding member, a part of ENFSI (European Network of the Institutes of Forensic Sciences), an organization that includes 63 institutes of forensic sciences from 34 European Countries. RaCIS participates, with its expert personnel, in different fields of forensic sciences, in the activities organized by Interpol (OICP) (such as the "AFIS Expert Group", "International DNA Users' Conference for Investigative Officers", "International Forensic Science Symposium", "Disaster Victim Identification" and "International Firearm Forensics Symposium") and Europol (e.g. participation to EEODN – Europol EOD Network for neutralization of explosives).

16.4.2.3 Organization and activities of RaCIS

RaCIS, by its forensic departments, cover the main fields of criminalistics and criminology. The operational activity of each department is reported below:

The four **Reparti Investigazioni Scientifiche** (RIS) of Roma, Parma, Messina and Cagliari perform technical investigations in the different fields of criminalistics when requested by the Carabinieri Commands spread over the Italian territory and/or judicial authorities or other police forces according to the following criteria:

The RIS department in Parma performs technical analyses for Northern Italy.

The RIS department in Rome performs technical analyses in Central and Southern Italy (but for the regions of Calabria, Sicily and Sardinia).

The RIS department in Messina performs technical analyses for Calabria and Sicily.

The RIS department in Cagliari performs technical analyses in Sardinia.

When the crimes are complex, RIS ensure through adequate personnel from the Operational Intervention Section (SIO) the necessary analyses and technical investigations on the scene of crime for integrating and supporting the activities performed by the SIS/Section of Technical Analyses.

RIS are articulated in different sections for each field of criminalistics: "Ballistics", "Biology", "Chemistry, Explosives and Inflammable

Substances", "Fingerprints", "Voice Analysis", "Digital and Image Sciences" and "Graphics".

In the above-mentioned forensic areas, the RaCIS case load is quite relevant, especially considering the capillary distribution of the Carabinieri Command on the territory with a mean number of caseworks exceeding 20,000 per year.

Reparto Tecnologie Informatiche. This operates on the entire Italian territory and performs technical investigations in the field of *Digital Forensics* and on technological devices, providing management and development for the scientific databases of RaCIS. It includes three units: a telematics section, an electronic section and a database section.

Reparto Dattiloscopia Preventiva. This operates on the entire Italian territory, performing activities of preventive fingerprint identification, verifying the identity of persons who undergo photo identification by personnel of the Carabinieri, feeding and searching the Central Identity AFIS Database (for fingerprints) and the APIS (for palm prints).

Reparto Analisi Criminologiche. This operates on the entire territory and employs the Section of Investigative Psychology and Analysis to provide support in cases of violent and particularly cruel crimes, by identifying the psychological profile and behaviour of the criminal and the connection with other crimes. In addition, through the Persecutory Acts Unit, created in 2009 by the Department for the Equality of Rights of the President of the Council of Ministers and the General Command of the Carabinieri, the unit analyses and monitors violent persecutory acts characterized by sexual or detrimental actions against vulnerable victims who are not otherwise protected.

16.4.2.4 Recruitment and training, certification

Technical personnel in Ra.CIS are exclusively recruited within the military of the Carabinieri and can have the following roles:

The role of Officers. These are specialized personnel who act as the Head of a Laboratory appointed as Commander and/or is responsible for a Technical Section. Such personnel belong to the technical-logistic role in scientific investigations and are specialists in physics (with a degree in physics,

engineering, mathematics), in chemistry (with a degree in chemistry, industrial chemistry, pharmaceutical technologies), in biology (with a degree in biological sciences, biotechnologies, medicine) and in computer technologies (with a degree in computer, computer engineering, electronic engineering, telecommunications engineering, managing engineering). Recruitment occurs after passing an examination organized by the Ministry of Defense where candidates present their CV and are then evaluated through a test on the scientific and technical notions of the area they are applying for (e.g. chemistry, biology, physics, etc.).

Those who pass the test are admitted to the Training Course at the School of the Carabinieri, which lasts about 9 months, where they study jurisprudence, military and technical subjects with lectures and laboratory exercises on the techniques and analytical procedures of the various Ra.CIS sections. At the end of the course, the RTL officers are assigned to the Sections where they are employed according to operational and personnel needs and they then acquire the title of Director of the laboratory after two years of employment.

Roles of Warrant Officers and Brigadiers. These are personnel specialized as Laboratory Analysts, employed in the RIS laboratories with evaluation tasks. Such military personnel come from other departments of the Carabinieri and are assigned to Ra.CIS after a selection based on: academic CV (at least a three-year undergraduate degree in a scientific subject), and after passing an oral and written examination on scientific culture related to the subjects he or she will be destined to; they then follow a specialized course for analysts of 4 months divided into two phases – a first theoretical phase lasting one month on criminalistics (biology, forensic chemistry, forensic computing, ballistics, fingerprinting, voice analysis, graphics, digital and image analysis, technical drawings and sketches, anthroposomatic examinations, criminal procedure and legislation), followed by an intensive course in the English language, which lasts 4 weeks; a second practical phase, which lasts 2 months, where the trainee follows and assists in the specific laboratory activity to which he or she will be destined. In this phase the personnel is specifically trained through the midterm examination and final examination.

Role of Corporals. These personnel specialize as a "laboratory assistant", employed in RIS laboratories with technical duties. This role requires a high school diploma in scientific subjects and passing an examination both written and oral on general scientific knowledge. They must then follow a Specialization course for lab assistants, which lasts about 5 months, divided into two phases: an initial theoretical phase lasting one month for improving their knowledge in specific scientific fields; a second practical phase, which lasts 2 months, where the personnel help the laboratories in performing technical analyses.

The training of personnel employed in the Territorial Commands, who go to the crime scene and perform sampling, is brought forth by the Superior Institute for Investigative Techniques of the Carabinieri (ISTI) in Velletri, where there is specialized teaching personnel from RaCis. ISTI is certified UNI EN ISO 9001:2008 for teaching activities and development of guidelines in the specific areas.

16.4.2.5 Certification of laboratories and accreditation of evidence

RIS laboratories in the sections of Drugs, Explosives and Inflammable Substances, Biology and Fingerprints and Preventive Fingerprinting adopt a quality management system, which is UNI EN ISO 9001:2008 certified. The extension of such ISO certification to the other sections (Ballistics, Voice Analysis, Graphics) is in progress.

With reference to biology, RIS in Rome and Parma obtained UNI CEI EN ISO/IEC 17025:2005 accreditation for procedures that entail all kinds of traces and forensic samples. The extension of such ISO certification to the other sections of RIS in Messina and Cagliari, and to the Section of Fingerprint Analysis, is in progress, according to the 2009/905/GAI Decision of the Council of Europe.

16.4.2.6 Disaster Victims Identification (DVI)

Within RaCIS the Unit of the Carabinieri for the Identification of Victims of Great Disasters was created. This unit aims at providing a relevant contribution for the identification of victims of mass disasters and the scientific support it is capable of; it is called to the scene of the disaster by the General Command of the Carabinieri, according to technical guidelines for the postmortem and antemortem activities adopted by Interpol. In several minor and major DVI cases RaCIS was called

to operate. Among them the DVI team of the Carabinieri was employed for the identification of the victims: after the terrorist attack of Nassirya (Iraq, 2013), the South-East Asian tsunami (Thailand, 2004), the air accident in Kabul (Afghanistan, 2005), the terrorist attack in Sharm ElSheikh (Egitto, 2005) and the earthquake at L'Aquila and surrounding area (Italy, 2009).

16.4.3 University centres, hospitals and private institutions

Once one exits the realm of the Carabinieri and the Polizia, where the laboratories and the forensic experts are somewhat institutionalized, and therefore subject to internal training and control, the forensic expert can be anyone. This does not mean necessarily that quality decreases, but it does imply that there is less control and guarantee of at least some internal training or regulation.

The first question that comes to mind is: If the Carabinieri and Police have forensic science sections, why is there a need for other forensic scientists? The answer is multifaceted. First of all, as one can see from the previous section, Police and Carabinieri do not cover all specialities. For example, there are no forensic pathologists in the police force, apart from the exception of the Polizia Scientifica in Rome, which has recently reinstated three forensic pathologists within its ranks. Similarly there are no forensic odontologists, anthropologists, archaeologists, entomologists or natural scientists: this means that such experts have to be recruited by the PM or the judge from "outside", mainly from universities, which are usually a local reference point for PMs and judges. For example, judges from Rome will usually call experts from the Roman Universities unless expertise that is not within reach is needed. However, it is not uncommon for them to refer to hospitals (especially for pathology and toxicology) or to private institutions or citizens. Courts may also call upon non-Police and non-Carabinieri experts because of personal reasons or because they think more objectivity will be guaranteed. For example, although the police forces have DNA labs sometimes courts and judges will appoint a university laboratory. Furthermore, universities and private institutions are recruited also by the defense and the injured party, where the Police and Carabinieri usually cannot be involved. So experts in fields that are both not dealt with and dealt with by the Polizia Scientifica are numerous and much called for.

The Codice di Procedura Penale states that the consultant or expert will be appointed by the judge. This virtually means that the judge is free to make any choice, and this has made the fortune of many self-made forensic experts and the misfortune of many trials. Apart from the actual autopsy, which by law has to be performed by a physician (if the cause of death must be diagnosed and registered in the National Health Registry), all assessments can be done by laymen, regardless of qualifications. The Italian juridical system does not yet require *strictu sensu* certification or accreditation of labs and experts, even in the most commonly certified fields, such as toxicology and DNA analysis. DNA laboratories will in the future have to be certified if they are to enter DNA profiles into the national DNA database – but as this does not yet exist, certification is not an issue. In Italy in fact there still is at the moment no official DNA database; it has, however, been approved and will be administrated by the Polizia Penitenziaria (Penitentiary Police) and hopefully will be functioning in a few years. Then DNA profiles from noncertified laboratories will not be allowed to enter the system, so it will become convenient to accredit or certify one's own laboratory. An inability to enter the profile into the national database will in fact certainly be a drawback for potential experts. Many toxicological laboratories are also striving for certification. Here, too, the reason is not directly or necessarily related to court work or forensics but to the fact that Regional and National Health regulations require that laboratories which provide toxicological information on issues such as drunk driving or capacity to work require certification (but not courts).

Registers for consultants and experts exist in all courts, but are scarcely considered even by judges themselves as they are a mere list of names of those who wish to be appointed as experts, with no kind of filter or control. No accreditation for any discipline is requested and not always during a trial will a consultant or expert be asked what his or her detailed qualifications are. Fortunately some parties, such as the defense, usually catch on to the crucial issue of qualification and sometimes will ask the expert to list degrees and experience in court.

Forensic pathology, through the skin of its teeth, is somewhat more quality-guaranteed than other disciplines. However, anthropologists, botanists and geneticists may have multivariate qualifications. This means that on the one hand there are many very qualified and competent geneticists (biologists or doctors who have specialized with several postgraduate courses and much experience) in forensic genetic analysis, but there are also armies of nonqualified individuals playing CSI. One of the authors has seen a parapsychologist and a researcher in paranormal activities appointed for positive identification from videosurveillance systems. Training for most disciplines is not homogeneous nor is it regulated; for some disciplines it is not there at all. If one were asked to envisage the perfect scenario, as seen for the police forces, the formation of experts should certainly involve a basic degree in the area of interest (biology, anthropology, entomology or natural sciences), some teaching in forensics, specifically regarding legal issues, and then a period of working as an apprentice. This, however, does not or cannot always occur.

Such a scenario is backed up by the extremely confused, equally multifaceted and sometimes embarrassing plethora of postgraduate courses in forensic topics. The university scenario is virtually bogged with hundreds of "Corsi di Perfezionamento" (postgraduate short courses) and first and second level Masters in all types of forensic sciences. Some courses are led by competent and prepared teaching staff, others are not. Therefore judges and PMs who clearly have no way of discerning useful from damaging experts will chose according to faith in Institutions (Police, Carabinieri, Universities), the forensic grapevine, or even more subjective parameters. What sometimes, unfortunately not always, makes up and compensates for this haphazard system where forensic sciences end up in court in the hands of whomever, is the hearing, with a severe cross-examination, where the multitude of consultants hired by the defense and the damaged parties sometimes act as a quality control. One example of how this can change the face of trials was a famous court case in the north of Italy, concerning the area of sexual child abuse. Two children seen by the same expert physicians with no training in paediatrics or forensics who acted as consultants for the PM were diagnosed as having been victims of child sexual abuse, the first because of anal lesions, the second because of hymenal scars. These physicians had been working for several years as renowned experts in the field of child abuse and were constantly appointed by courts across the north of Italy. In these two specific cases the defense provided a very qualified expertise, which convinced the judge to appoint new experts. The judge's experts showed that in the first case the child had, and subsequently died of, an anal tumor; in the other case the hymenal anomaly, which had been seen to consist of a septate hymen – that is a hymen with a septum running across it, a frequent anomaly found in little girls – had no scars. After a series of trials of this type the physicians were signalled to the Consiglio Superiore della Magistratura, but no further action was taken that is known of. Similar and more subtle scenarios can be seen in the fields of juvenile pornography, identification of the living and at more subtle levels even DNA analysis.

In the absence of certification and accreditation (which may not always be a guarantee of quality but at least proves some effort to filter incompetence and haphazard administration of science) PMs and Judges have very few tools by which to select a good expert. This is also due to the fact that they receive very little scientific education in their study curriculum, and therefore are not aware of which disciplines they need in different cases and what dangers they may encounter.

In such an uncontrollable forensic scenario outside the neat ranks of the Police and Carabinieri it is impossible to give statistics on case load, budgets, education. What can be done is to focus on universities, which are perhaps the main container of most non-Police and non-Carabineri expert work: for these also there is no national account of workloads and budgets or protocols, but at least a general idea can be given of how they function. No information whatsoever can be obtained on privates.

The other premise that should be made before entering the next section is that if the Police and Carabinieri are almost automatically involved in DNA and toxicological analysis, fingerprinting (exclusively theirs), criminalistics (fiber analysis, etc.), behavioural sciences and computer sciences are usually their domain – also because of their history. The other disciplines, particularly those practiced in universities, rotate around forensic pathology and therefore in their development are strictly related to it.

The present scenario does not guarantee that forensic sciences will be practiced by qualified forensic experts. Italy is a country where there is plenty of forensic science malpractice. However, on the other hand, there are plenty of qualified forensic scientists with credentials, a large workload of experience, who have even exported Italian forensic sciences in European courts. One advantage of case work performed in universities is that it

can take advantage of facilities, personnel and a *modus operandi* typical of research facilities.

The next sections will therefore focus on the specific forensic disciplines found within universities.

As mentioned previously, hundreds of short (usually 50 hour) postgraduate courses exist across the country in various forensic topics, targeted for various types of undergraduate degrees and disciplines, but have no academically qualifying status. Several Master courses in Forensic Sciences in general exist, for example at the Universities of Parma, Roma, Pavia and Palermo, and these usually are intended for other scientific (and sometimes nonscientific) degrees. Access to such courses is on the basis of CV and an interview.

PhDs in any forensic discipline have been severely reduced: very few PhD programs bear the name "legal medicine" or "forensic sciences" or "criminalistics" (for example at the Universities of Verona, Rome and Macerata); many times forensic academics have to insert their PhD students into nonforensic programs. Very few national textbooks exist that encompass forensic sciences *per se* (Picozzi and Intini, 2009; Loré, 2012): most forensic sciences, if at all, are dealt with in subsections of books in forensic medicine.

16.4.3.1 Forensic pathology

Forensic pathology is a forensic science. In Italian university forensic scenarios it is the discipline around which all other forensic sciences developed. The history of forensic sciences in Italy therefore lies mainly in the trail of that of forensic pathology.

It is in fact within the Roman period, characterized by the codification of laws and the practice of court challenges or cross examinations, that main medicolegal issues started appearing concerning violent deaths, poisoning (Lex Cornelia de sicariis et veneficis, III sec. A.C.), rape and compensation (Lex Aquilia de damno, 81 A.C). During early Mediaeval times, political and territorial fragmentation made it difficult to pin down any form of medicolegal activity, although it is known that in certain Italian cities physicians with a role similar to that of forensic pathologists would by law examine bodies of the dead in order to verify if any fowl play had occurred. Later on, in the 13th century the first rules for expert witnessing in court proceedings appear, particularly in the ecclesiastic world, as one can see from the *Decretali* of the popes Innocenzo III (1209), Onorio III (1220) and Gregorio IX (1234). Medicolegal testimony became more and more important in the first communal statutes of the 13th and 14th centuries, which envisage that the surgeon was to be called in all cases of personal lesions, violent deaths and rape. After having performed all his examinations, surgeons would dictate a report to the barrister (notaio), subsequently discussed in court during cross examination. Along with communal legislation, there was another growing institution that helped to stabilize and strengthen the role of the surgeons in court: this consisted of the Church's canonical law. In the realm of Christian philosophy, an in-depth examination of acts committed but even more an analysis of intentions behind one's actions (i.e. the subjective element of a crime) started gaining importance.

With the development of the importance of the expert witness in court (and in particular the doctor or surgeon as such) the first written documents of the discipline that tried to give it a structure can be seen. In this sense the main ones are A. Parè (1575) and F. Fedele (1602), who developed the issue of expert testimony in court, and Giovanni Filippo Ingrassia di Recalmuto, whose *Opus Methodus dandi Testificationes (On How to Testify)* constitutes the first "book" of legal medicine in Italy. However, only with Paolo Zacchia, in 1612, was the first encyclopedic text on legal medicine written, *Quaestiones Medicolegales*, which, for almost two centuries, was considered the classical text of the discipline across all Europe. The final step forward towards modern legal medicine and sciences in general was taken in the 18th century, when Illuminism introduced the adoption of a scientific method of inductive reasoning within this discipline, up to then characterized by the study of single cases. In this manner the discipline reached its modern form, more or less as we know it today.

University Institutes usually have a Department or Section of Legal Medicine, around which the academic nucleus of all other forensic sciences (from genetics to criminology) has been built. This is usually the place where judicial autopsies are performed (autopsies in Italy are performed under two main umbrellas – the judicial one and the sanitary "health service" one when no crime is suspected). All services usually have access to histopathology facilities and radiology (either of their own or of an adjacent hospital), genetics and toxicology. As previously mentioned, sometimes hospital departments have a similar development, especially in cities where universities are not present. Pathologists, as well as laboratory specialists already employed for clinical

purposes, will perform some forensic casework. In both cases the budget comes from the Ministry of Education or from the National Health Service as concerns equipment and personnel, but usually not for forensic purposes. Courts will pay the single person appointed as the expert separately along with the laboratory expenses that the university or hospital department has anticipated.

Another type of medicolegal activity always related to forensic pathology is that on the living (clinical forensic medicine): this is the case of child sexual abuse, child maltreatment, torture assessment and interpersonal violence in general.

In Italy the actual specialization a physician undergoes is in "legal medicine", in the pure Mediterranean tradition, which comprises forensic pathology but which encompasses much more (perhaps too much in this day and age). There are in fact many medicolegal activities less or not strictly related to forensic sciences. Particular kinds of medicolegal activity are performed in previdential institutes, concerning invalidity and incapacity, as well as evaluation of the capacity to drive vehicles; capacity to drive boats; exemption from using safety belts; exemption from the military service; fitness for work; suitability for handicap parking; assessment of bodily damage, particularly in the insurance scenario, is a large source of work, as is assessment of civil invalidity. A relevant portion of this part of the medicolegal profession is perpetrated in private medical cabinets, where, usually on a part time basis, the pathologist examines persons and expresses evaluations mainly on bodily damage both for judicial and extrajudicial purposes. A great amount of this activity is on behalf of insurance companies, with respect to policies against accidents or civil responsibility.

From now on, however, this section will focus only on the realms of legal medicine that involve forensic sciences, that is forensic pathology and, to a certain extent, clinical forensic medicine.

Forensic pathology usually enters the judicial scenario at the scene of a crime, for an autopsy and for the examination of living victims of violence (sexual assault, child abuse, torture, lesions in general). This usually occurs at universities and, to a lesser extent, in hospitals.

As previously mentioned, forensic pathologists are not part of the state police forces (apart from three in Rome belonging to the Polizia Scientifica of the Polizia di Stato). Therefore at the scene of death they do not automatically go on site with the Polizia Scientifica, which is activated by the PM or by the JP. It is only subsequently decided by the PM or JP if the forensic pathologist is to be called. A recent survey in the north of Italy has shown that even in suspicious deaths pathologists are called on site only in 60% of cases. This means that whereas fingerprint and DNA sampling on site is guaranteed by the Polizia Scientifica, body temperature or collection of larvae is not.

It is then completely up to the PM to request an autopsy. If he or she does not believe the body to be the object of a crime, then the body will be handed over to the national health authority which will request a nonjudicial autopsy only in the case where the general practitioner will not certify cause of death and simply because Italian Police Mortuary Regulation states that in order to bury someone a cause of death has to be diagnosed. Again reasons for requesting an autopsy may differ between PMs and Courts. In Milano, for example, all victims of traffic accidents are subjected to a judicial autopsy, but not in Rome. Many PMs in fact are under the impression that if the cause of death is evident (e.g. severe head damage) it is not necessary to perform an autopsy, only to regret this when after burial parties request information on the manner of death, whether there was abuse of substances, etc., or when witnesses change their testimony. If the autopsy is requested usually in suspicious deaths it should be performed by a forensic pathologist. Unfortunately sometimes the PM will appoint an anatomical pathologist (because, for example, in remote areas of Italy it is easier to find a general pathologist in hospitals than to look for a forensic pathologist) who has a different training. In cases of evident voluntary homicide, the autopsy is usually performed by two pathologists, according to European Union recommendations. Then the pathologist may ask to be associated with other specialists (e.g. entomologists, toxicologists) or ask to hire an auxiliary in such disciplines where he may have little or no competence. Such "associated" expertises, when conceded, allow for a thorough and complete approach to questions such as identity, postmortem interval and cause and manner of death. It is usually the forensic pathologist who will involve other specialists, from the DNA expert to the entomologist. Even when the forensic issue does not concern a dead body, frequently PMs or judges will use medicolegal institutes at least to enquire about the proper type of expertise.

In cases concerning the living (e.g. child abuse) the victim may be taken to pre-existing structures (such as rape centres), which are usually within hospitals or universities, and clinicians and pathologists here may act as auxiliaries of the JP or they can be directly appointed by the PM, which usually, in every city, has identified his or her expert pathologists within a university structure or hospital (or other). Large cities and centres usually have agreements with the courts and set rotas for all medicolegal and forensic activities.

The pathologist, just like other forensic experts, will work along with the consultants nominated by other parties and conclude the work within a deadline, which has been set by the PM or the judge. He or she will then present a report and an invoice within the following 100 days. When working for the defense or the injured party, the invoice does not need to follow any rules or does not need to be motivated. When working for the PM or judge, the invoice has to be motivated and formulated according to set regulations, depending on the hours or number of samples examined. All expenses are anticipated by the consultant or expert in most cases. Courts usually pay no earlier than 6 months after having received the report, but usually much later. All this leads to much bureaucracy and to large waiting lists for the cheaper labs, which frequently leads to delays and/or to the use of less qualified laboratories. The PM or judge can also decide whether to pay the entire sum on the invoice or reduce it. The general budget that courts have for forensic expertise is unclear. It may happen that they may not be able to pay for an entire year due to lack of funding from the Ministry of Justice and are therefore very careful in spending. This has led to a decrease in the number of autopsies performed and forensic science assessments in general that are being requested, unless it is the Polizia Scientifica performing it, in which case it has its own funding up to a certain extent. In some cases, however, personnel from the Polizia Scientifica can be appointed as the consultant or expert in the same manner as others external to the police forces and be paid similarly.

A forensic pathologist in Italy becomes so by gaining a Specialization in Legal Medicine, which now lasts 5 years (soon to be changed to 4), after having earned a degree in Medicine. There is a test for candidates who wish to enter. The winners are granted a monthly wage equivalent to a hospital assistant's for the following 5 years. Contrary to other European countries, training is quite long, but there is no obligation to first specialize in pathology and/or jurisprudence. These subjects are included in the 5 year curriculum. In agreement with European Union indications, the specialization of legal medicine includes pathology, forensic pathology, clinical forensic medicine, civil and criminal law, civil aspects of legal medicine, forensic sciences and ethics. Practical training on autopsy and casework in general is favored in larger centres such as Milano, Rome, Padova, Naples and Palermo, where between 500 and 800 autopsies per year are performed in each centre.

Politics has severely affected the budgets of Universities and the National Health System. On the one hand criteria for university appointments have changed, in part for the better, in favor of university personnel with adequate teaching and research curricula. Nonetheless the bad economy and the plight in which Italy now finds itself has drastically reduced the number of academics performing forensic medicine in universities (some universities have seen a decrease of 10 milion euros this year in their budgets from the Ministry of Education). The same can be said for the National Health System. Furthermore, many academic posts in legal medicine are for nonpathologists. Nonetheless, the increasing awareness concerning child abuse, interpersonal violence and the problem of political refugees requesting asylum and thus evaluation for signs of ill treatment has opened clinical forensic activity to such areas, possibly creating the perspective for new jobs in the future. Italy, however, is still far from the interesting French *reforme* in legal medicine and from the French system in general, where frequently emergency wards have among their staff clinical forensic physicians or pathologists.

About 20 years ago a national poll on the orientation of medicolegal research among the younger generations was performed. Fiori (1969) underlined the intense development of the professional activity and indicated the areas of research in the following manner: studies in doctrine and medicolegal methodology; forensic pathology, particularly as regards casuistic approaches; studies on the living; postmortem interval; identification of human remains; medicolegal psychiatry and criminology; and laboratory techniques in haematology applied to legal medicine, medicolegal analytical toxicology and experimental forensic pathology. More recently Canepa (1995) performed a study on the most significant contributions in research. It has been observed that research in forensic pathology coming from Italy has definitely increased (Viel *et al.*, 2011) and scientific publications

in both national and international journals by Italian authors have definitely increased in the past 10 years, although many, especially from the older generation, limit their academic publishing to legal and civil issues.

SIMLA (Società Italiana di Medicina Legale e delle Assicurazioni) is the main scientific society that brings together all aspects of legal medicine, including related forensic sciences and nonforensic aspects of legal medicine such as insurance issues. Within this group are various subgroups. In this instance there is the Gruppo Italiano di Patologi Forensi (GIPF), born in 1998, which organizes conferences, workshops and scientific events in forensic pathology. Textbooks in this field are certainly numerous: each school or university has produced its own textbook, such as Milano or Rome (Giusti, 1998; Cazzaniga *et al.*, 2006).

The main medicolegal academic centres are in the following cities: Ancona, Bari, Brescia, Bologna, Cagliari, Camerino, Catania, Catanzaro, Ferrara, Foggia, Firenze, Genova, l'Aquila, Macerata, Messina, Milano, Milano Bicocca, Modena, Napoli (two), Novara, Padova, Palermo, Parma, Pavia, Perugia, Pisa, Roma (three), Sassari, Siena, Terni, Torino, Trieste, Udine, Varese and Verona.

National journals include *Rivista Italiana di Medicina Legale* (soon to be indexed), *Minerva Medico-legale*, *Archivio di Medicina Legale*, *Jura Medica*, *Zacchia*, *Quaderni Camerti* and *Medicina e Diritto*. These journals also encompass other forensic sciences; however, no Italian journals dedicated only to Forensic Sciences exist.

Academically, Legal Medicine and related Forensic Sciences go under the heading MED 43 (all university disciplines have a numerical code). MED 43 thus includes forensic pathology, genetics, toxicology, criminology and most forensic sciences and houses professors of different origins, that is with Degrees in Medicine, Biology, Chemistry, Jurisprudence and Psychology. Currently there are 48 full professors, 64 associate professors and 118 teaching assistants or lecturers.

Postgraduate qualifications (apart from the Specialization in Legal Medicine) in areas of Legal Medicine (apart from a Masters in Legal Medicine offered in Messina and in Forensic Nursing also in Messina) usually consist of a PhD.

16.4.3.2 Forensic anthropology

Forensic anthropology is becoming more and more popular, thanks not only to scientists conveying the role of this discipline in helping justice with complex cases but also to the only too well known CSI effect of many television series, where experts in anthropology can be seen on crime scenes, around autopsy tables, next to boiling units, measuring bones, looking down a microscope or reconstructing faces.

Forensic anthropology is indeed crucial for recovering skeletal or quasi skeletal remains, for their identification, for determining postmortem interval, as well as for proper trauma analysis; in some countries it is even beginning to be functional for the identification of living individuals by physiognomic traits. This is beginning to become clear to many in the field of forensics and to pathologists. It is a discipline which, however, sits delicately in between forensic pathology and physical anthropology, since it by definition deals with human osteology (more typical of the purely anthropological scenario) but is related to diagnostic procedures, which only a physician or pathologist can perform. This has frequently created some discussion as to who or what a forensic anthropologist is or should be, especially in this day and age of accreditation and general awareness of the implications of court work. In Italy, as in many countries, a strong divide or lack of communication still exists between the two categories.

Lectures concerning anthropological issues (biological profile, taphonomy (the study of post-mortem alterations), estimation of PMI, assessment of trauma, etc.) are usually included in the course of legal medicine for medical students and in the courses of anthropology and archaeology for the arts and natural sciences. As a consequence of this fragmentary scenario, a unique professional figure who can be named "forensic anthropologist" does not exist, and is therefore replaced by "experts" with various professional backgrounds ranging from forensic pathology to natural sciences, who can be called by judicial authorities.

Again, courses and good training are difficult to come by. There is a Master's course in Physical Anthropology, Palaeopathology and Forensic Anthropology run jointly by the University of Bologna, Pisa and Milano – here, however, the forensic component is limited to two months. Few national books exist on the topic (Introna and Dell'Erba, 2000; Marella, 2003; Cattaneo and Grandi, 2004); a fairly intense research activity is now visible through the numbers of publications from Italy on the subject, which has increased, particularly at the international level, in the past few years.

There are only two known anthropological skeletal collections in Italy useful for training, particularly in forensic anthropology. One is in the Sardinian (Sassari) collection in Bologna and consists of about 800 known individuals belonging to the 19th century. Age and sex are known. The other is a joint collection between the University and the City of Milano, consisting of 2000 known individuals who died in the late 20th century, of which 150 are infants, with known age, sex, stature, cause of death, many of which have autopsy reports and clinical records.

A similar situation can be described for forensic odontology. The discipline is performed outside the police forces by odontologists who have gained experience in the forensic field. In addition, in Italy forensic odontologists are usually involved in civil issues concerning the quantification of bodily damage for compensation, similarly to legal doctors. There is a Master's course in Forensic Odontology in Florence, which, however, has as its larger focus noncriminalistic aspects.

Again, few national books exist specifically dedicated to the topic (Cameriere, 2003). International publications and research activity is far less at the moment compared to anthropology.

A scientific group within the Italian Society SIMLA was founded in 1996 called GIAOF – Gruppo Italiano di Antropologia e Odontologia Forense – which has remained silent for the past few years, but lately had begun focusing mainly on bodily damage and dental issues.

16.4.3.3 Genetics and toxicology

Genetic and toxicological tests account for a relevant part of forensic analyses on biological samples from the investigation of crime scenes and autopsies. In Italy these services can be provided both by university structures and the scientific sections of the police forces. In universities the laboratories of genetics and toxicology usually are led respectively by physicians with a specialization in genetics, biotechnicians, biologists, in the first case, and physicians with a specialization in toxicology and chemists (usually with a specialization in pharmaceutical technologies), in the second case. As mentioned previously, no accreditation or certification at the moment is required for specific court work.

Education is variable. At the moment for genetics, a dedicated Master course is run by the University of Tor Vergata in Rome and for forensic toxicology in Catania and Bologna.

There are quite a few national textbooks for toxicology (Gagliano Candela, 2001; Zacà and Pellegrino, 2006;

Fucci and De Giovanni, 2007; Froldi, 2011), but less so for genetics (Tagliabracci, 2010; Giardina, Spinella and Novelli, 2011; Marelli and Boeri, 2012), with publications in both national and international literature having significantly increased in the past 10 years.

There is one main association for forensic genetics, GEFI, Genetisti Forensi Italiani, which was formed in 1966, and GTF, Gruppo Tossicologi Forensic Italiani, for toxicologists, founded in 1974. They are both subsections of SIMLA – Società Italiana di Medicina Legale e delle Assicurazioni – and have national meetings every year.

16.4.3.4 Natural sciences (entomology, botany, geopedology)

The collaboration between some institutes of legal medicine with departments in other faculties, such as natural sciences, has led to the awareness that entomology, botany and geology in particular can be extremely useful, and these have since been slowly developed. This closeness has also led to botanists and geologists working closely with pathologists and, therefore, regardless of the lack of specific courses and long term dedicated forensic training, learning to apply their disciplines to the forensic scenario.

Entomology is the best known so far and most developed. There are many university short courses in entomology across the country as well as several Masters not in Forensic Entomology specifically but in Forensic Sciences, which deal with the topic. In 2007 the Gruppo Italiano di Entomologia Forense (GIEF) was created by university based forensic pathologists and entomologists in order to harmonize the discipline and promote it. They are at the moment very active and have one yearly scientific meeting. Very few handbooks on forensic entomology exist in the national scenario (Introna and Campobasso, 1998; Magni, Massimelli and Messina, 2008). Publication of articles occurs both at the national and international level, although they are not as extensive as those on genetics and toxicology.

Expertise in botany and geology at the moment is usually performed outside the Police forces and within universities. Articles from Italy on this topic are few and far between, both in national and international journals.

16.4.3.5 Psychiatry and behavioral sciences

As previously mentioned, it is the Police forces that have true Behavioural Sciences Units, for criminal profiling for example. Forensic psychiatry, on the other hand, has its experts usually within medicolegal departments. Usually those who work in this area are psychiatrists who have in some way trained in the area of forensics.

Psychiatric assessment is usually requested by judicial authorities in order to ascertain imputability and reliability of the culprit. There is, however, an absolute lack of certification and the discipline can entail many different types of experts, ranging from psychiatrists to psychologists or even jurists with some knowledge in psychology. This too is a very debated issue, similarly to forensic anthropology, where many think that psychopathological assessments in the end should be performed only by physicians. Criminology is a discipline frequently related to forensic psychiatry and psychology, albeit with different connotations; it is slightly more popular and has led to the appearance of many criminologists whose qualifications are actually unclear in public arenas. This is somewhat reflected through the CSI effect visible in the myriad of talk shows with "criminologists" appearing from all sorts of backgrounds and disciplines.

There are innumerable associations registered under the headings of forensic psychiatry, psychology and criminology, the most ancient and accredited one being the SIC – Società Italiana di Criminologia – formed in 1957. Several national textbooks also exist (Fornari, 2008; Ferracuti and Lagetti, 2010). Forensic psychiatrists, psychologists and criminologists have a fairly large national editorial activity and publish in the above mentioned local journals, which encompass all forensic sciences within legal medicine. This activity is, however, at the moment not yet reflected in the international scenario, where there are very few Italian articles on these subjects.

16.4.3.6 Questioned documents, engineering and computing, fingerprints, criminalistics

Fingerprint analysis is almost entirely delegated to the Polizia Scientifica, for several reasons. Police forces are the only ones administrating what is called "fotosegnalamento", that is identification of culprits via photography, description and fingerprinting, and inserting such data within the AFIS (Automated Fingerprint Identification System). They are also the only ones working using the AFIS and then actually performing positive identification by fingerprints. It is extremely rare that external experts will take on this kind of expertise, also because in Italy training of any sort or quality is absent outside the forces. Pathologists or anthropologists may be involved only in the very preliminary steps of treating mummified, decomposed or burnt finger tips and enhancing the prints. Therefore scientific groups or activities or even textbooks for that matter are not very common and nor are publications both in the national and international scenario.

Analysis of questioned documents, computer sciences and traditional criminalistics is a very similar scenario. Occasionally chemists or graphologists from universities or even privates will act as experts on the odd fragment of glass, paint, fiber, gunshot residue or paper. For computer sciences Politechnics and Engineering faculties are slowly becoming involved. However, most of this kind of work at the moment remains with the police force. Within criminalistics some exceptions, which have been mentioned above, such as geology and botany, are beginning to emerge.

16.5 Conclusions

The condition of forensic sciences in general in Italy is multifaceted, with many assets and several defects. Some of the latter, in order to be ameliorated, still need academic and political changes as well as a more thorough education of investigating authorities. Others, however, seem to be finding some solution, particularly those stemming from the lack of collaboration between Universities, Police and Ministerial Agencies. Recent DVI and RISC (Ricerca Persone Scomparse, see below) activities seem to be an example of a better scenario.

In the previous sections concerning the police forces the Interpol Disaster Victim Identification layout was described, which envisages both the Police and the Carabinieri. However, as has been previously mentioned, neither of these forces has forensic odontologists, anthropologists or, for that matter, many forensic pathologists. In many southern European countries the DVI teams will recruit nonmilitary or nonpolice personnel from universities for example. This so far has not been possible in Italy, with some negative consequences. Nonetheless the Ministry of Internal Affairs is seeking to create a protocol by which, if a disaster occurs, the Police and Carabinieri DVI team is always called in, but if it does not have enough or the necessary personnel, then it will call upon the nearest qualified university to assist. This may take some time to occur, however, because in case of a disaster related to a crime the PM's office will automatically be involved. The PM may not

necessarily delegate the DVI team. He or she can, but has the option of appointing any expert. The Linate aircraft disaster is an excellent example. When an MD80 crashed into a small Cessna aircraft at the Linate airport in Milan on October 8th 2001, causing 118 victims, the PM did not call in the DVI team, although this was requested by foreign authorities, and "preferred" to appoint her own experts, namely two pathologists, two toxicologists, an odontologist, a geneticist, who in turn selected several auxiliaries. This may happen in many cases when the judicial authority is not acquainted with protocols concerning other institutions.

Finally, an event that is shedding some positive light on collaboration among forensic experts belonging to different agencies is, hopefully, the creation of the RISC (RIcerca Scomparsi) system and database for missing persons and unidentified bodies. The problem of unidentified bodies on our national territory (national and migrants) (Cattaneo *et al.*, 2009) has finally been realized in Italy on behalf of authorities who have begun searching for a solution. A special office of the Ministry of Internal Affairs with a Commissioner for Missing Persons has been created. Along with the institution of this office a database is being set up, destined to collect information on missing persons and on unidentified bodies in order to find possible matches. This will and is already leading towards a collaboration between the Polizia, the Carabinieri, the Prefettura (another office within the Ministry of Internal Affairs) and University and National Health Pathologists in order to collect appropriate post-mortem data.

The multifaceted world of forensic sciences and the will to create a more compact and uniform discipline in Italy is in fact represented by the diverse origins of the authors of this chapter.

References

Cameriere, R. (2003) *Identificazione in Odontologia Forense*, Ed. Minerva Medica, Turin, Italy.

Canepa, G. (1995) *Nuovi Orizzonti della Ricerca in Medicina Legale*, Giuffrè, Milan, Italy.

Cattaneo, C., Grandi, M. (2004) *Antropologia e Odontologia Forense: Guida allo Studio dei Resti Umani – Testo Atlante*, Monduzzi Ed., Bologna, Italy.

Cattaneo, C., Porta, D., De Angelis, D., Poppa, P., Gibelli, D., Grandi, M. (2009) Unidentified bodies and human remains: an Italian glimpse through a European problem. *Forensic Science International* 195 (1–3): 167.e1-e6.

Cazzaniga, A., Cattabeni, C.M., Luvoni, R., Zoja, R. (2006) *Compendio di Medicina Legale e delle Assicurazioni* (12th ed.), UTET Giuridica, Milan, Italy.

Clarke, S. (2013) Trends in crime and criminal justice, 2010 – *Eurostat, Statistics in Focus*, 18/2013.

Ferracuti, S., Lagazzi, M. (2010) *Psichiatria Forense Applicata*, Centro Scientifico Editore, Rome, Italy.

Fornari, U. (2008) *Psichiatria Forense*, UTET Giuridica, Turin, Italy.

Fiori, A. (1969) *L'orientation de la Recherche Médico-légale Scientifique Moderne dans le Pensée des Jeunes*, VII rapporta u XXXII Congrès International de Médecine Légale et de Médecine Sociale de langue francaise, Genes, 7–11 May 1969.

Froldi, R. (2011) *Lezioni di Tossicologia Forense*, Giappichelli G. Ed., Turin, Italy.

Fucci, N., De Giovanni, N. (2007) *Il Laboratorio di Tossicologia Forense*, Selecta Medica, Pavia, Italy.

Gagliano Candela, R. (2001) *Tossicologia Forense*, Giuffrè, Milan, Italy.

Gentilomo, A., Travaini G., D'Auria, L. (2009) *Medico e Giustizia*, Raffaello Cortina Ed., Milan, Italy.

Giardina, E., Spinella, A., Novelli, G. (2011) Past, present and future of forensic DNA typing. *Nanomedicine (Lond)* 6 (2): 257–270.

Giusti, G. (1998) *Trattato di Medicina Legale e Scienze Affini*, CEDAM Ed., Padua, Italy.

Grivas, C.R., Komar, D.A. (2008) Kumho, Daubert and the nature of scientific inquiry: implications for forensic anthropology. *Journal of Forensic Science* 53 (4):771–776.

Introna, F., Dell'Erba, A. (2000) *Determinazione dell'età da Resti Scheletrici*, Essebiemme Ed., Bari, Italy.

Introna, F., Campobasso, C.P. (1998) *Entomologia Forense – Il Ruolo dei Ditteri nelle Indagini Medico Legali*, Essebiemme Ed., Bari, Italy.

Lorè, C. (2012) *Scienze Medico-legali Sociali e Forensi*, Giuffrè Ed., Milan, Italy.

Magni, P., Massimelli, M., Messina, R. (2008) *Entomologia Forense. Gli Insetti nelle Indagini Giudiziarie e Medico-legali*, Minerva Medica, Milan, Italy.

Marella, G.L. (2003) *Elementi di Antropologia Forense – Dalle Indagini di Sopralluogo Agli Accertamenti di Laboratorio*, CEDAM, Padua, Italy.

Marelli, L., Boem, F. (2012) *Elementi per una Genetica Forense*, Mondadori Bruno Ed., Turin, Italy.

Picozzi, M., Intini, A. (2009) *Scienze Forensi – Teoria e Prassi dell'Investigazione Scientifica*, UTET Giuridica, Milan, Italy.

Tagliabracci, A. (2010) *Introduzione alla genetica forense: indagini di identificazione personale e di paternità*. Milan: Springer

Viel, G., Boscolo-Berto, R., Cecchi, R., Bajanowski, T., Vieira, N.D., Ferrara,S.D. (2011) Bio-medicolegal scientific research in Europe. A country-based analysis. *International Journal of Legal Medicine* 2011 September; 125(5): 717–725.

Zacà, V., Pellegrino, S. (2006) *Manuale di Tossicologia Forense*, Giappichelli G. Ed., Turin, Italy.

Websites

SIMLA (Società Italiana di Medicina Legale e delle Assicurazioni). Available from: www.simlaweb.com

LABANOF (Laboratorio di Antropologia e Odontologia Forense). Available from: www.labanof.unimi.it

Legislation

Codice Penale Italiano
   Codice di Procedura Penale Italiano
   Cassazione Penale, SS UU sentenza 11.09.02 n° 30328

CHAPTER 17

History and current status of forensic science in Japan

Hitoshi Maeda[1], Takaki Ishikawa[1,2] & Toshikazu Kondo[3]

[1] Osaka City University Medical School, Osaka, Japan
[2] Faculty of Medicine, Tottori University, Yonago, Japan
[3] Wakayama Medical University, Wakayama, Japan

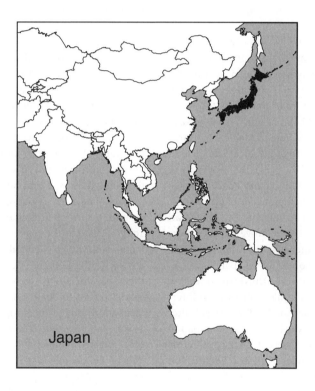

Japan

17.1 History

17.1.1 Forensic/medicolegal autopsy in death investigation

The history of forensic science represents the development of a civilized society. During the *Edo* period (the 17th–19th centuries) under the rule of the *Tokugawa* shogunate, the final part of the *samurai* family feudal age in Japan, involving national isolation, a legal system was established covering the whole country; military officers (*Bugyo*) controlled administrative, criminal justice and court systems. Early in the 18th century, three classical Chinese publications on death investigation, *Sen-en-roku* (Xi-Yuan-Lu, 1247), *Hei-en-roku* (Ping-Yuan-Lu, n.d.) and *Mu-en-roku* (Wu-Yuan-Lu, 1308), were brought to Japan. *Mu-en-roku* was

The Global Practice of Forensic Science, First Edition. Edited by Douglas H. Ubelaker.
© 2015 John Wiley & Sons, Ltd. Published 2015 by John Wiley & Sons, Ltd.

translated into Japanese, entitled *Mu-en-ruku-jutsu* (1736); the title implied "Instruction for preventing a false accusation" (Tsunenari and Suyama, 1986; Misawa and Honda, 1996). In this period, however, European culture was gradually introduced through trade with the Netherlands, an exception to the country's isolation. In the city of Nagasaki, which had the only Japanese port open to foreigners, Dr. Pompe van Meerdervoort from the Netherlands gave lectures on forensic medicine at his private school in 1862.

After the *Meiji* Restoration in 1868, Western civilization including its legal systems and science was introduced rapidly, involving the major influence of Germany (Prussia) on the modernization of Japanese law and medicine (Oda, 2009). The Ministry of Justice and the Tokyo Court of Law were founded in 1871. Initially, forensic autopsy was performed at/near the site where the body was found, but a dissection room was later installed at the Administration of Justice. A German anatomist, Dr. Wilhelm Doenitz, gave lectures on forensic medicine at the School of Medical Jurisprudence (the forerunner of the Tokyo Medical School, later reorganized as the Faculty of Medicine, the University of Tokyo) affiliated to Tokyo Metropolitan Police Hospital in 1875, followed by a German professor of physiology, Dr. Ernst Tiegel, and a German surgeon, Dr. Julius Carl Scriba, at the University of Tokyo; however, they were not specialists of forensic medicine/legal medicine. Dr. Kuniyoshi Katayama, a pioneer of legal medicine in Japan, was a medical student at the University of Tokyo, and assisted Professor Tiegel in his lectures as an interpreter. Dr. Katayama studied under Prof. Tiegel after his graduation (1879) and was officially sent abroad to Germany and Austria (Prussia) to study forensic medicine and psychiatry under Professor Eduard von Hoffmann at the University of Vienna (1884–1888). After his return from abroad, Dr. Katayama was appointed as the first Japanese professor of forensic medicine at the Imperial University of Tokyo (1888), and forensic autopsies started at the university (1897). Thereafter, departments of forensic medicine chaired by Japanese professors were established at five universities in Kyoto, Kyushu, Tohoku, Osaka and Hokkaido (1899–1923), and the number of medical schools/colleges with forensic medicine departments had increased to 46 by 1950. After the Second World War, the medical education system was reorganized, and medical schools/colleges were newly founded according to the policy of one medical school/college in each prefecture to improve healthcare services (1970–1974); thus, in Japan there are now 80 medical schools/universities (as of January 2014), at which practical activities in forensic/legal medicine vary greatly (see below for details). During these periods, forensic autopsies were also performed by police surgeons outside of medical schools. There are eight university institutions for forensic odontology at present.

Under the new constitution (1946) introduced after the Second World War, the Code of Criminal Procedure was revised to incorporate rules for the rights of suspects and defendants (Oda, 2009); however, investigation of unnatural death is under the control of police officers termed "coroners" without a medical license, who categorize criminal and noncriminal cases, and decide which cases should include autopsy for criminal investigation (see below for details). This system implies that the police force is fully responsible for criminal investigation, but obstructs investigation of the cause of death by autopsy in so-called "noncriminal" cases, involving possible infringements of the rights of the deceased in the context of civil and administrative affairs as well as even neglected criminal cases. Against this background, a medical examiner system was organized in Tokyo (1946) at the request of the American Occupational Authorities (General Headquarters, GHQ), the advisor to the Supreme Commander of Allied Powers; the initial aim was to investigate the cause of death with special regard to death related to mal-/undernutrition (starvation) under the occupation (Misawa and Honda, 1996; Shoji, 1996). Thereafter, medical examiner's offices were founded in seven major cities, namely, Tokyo, Yokohama, Nagoya, Kyoto, Osaka, Kobe and Fukuoka, under the provision of the law for examination of deaths from unknown causes (1947). The primary task of the Japanese medical examiner system, now based on the Postmortem Examination and Corpse Preservation Act (1949), is to investigate the cause of "noncriminal" unnatural death by external examination and autopsy when necessary; thus, it is quite different from the systems in other countries (Misawa and Honda, 1996; Shoji, 1996; Tsunenari and Suyama, 1986). However, the medical examiner system now remains active only within the limited areas of Tokyo, Osaka and Kobe.

17.1.2 Police forensic science

Forensic science of police in Japan started at the Tokyo Metropolitan Police, with the installation of a hygiene science laboratory for toxicological analysis (1904) and official introduction of fingerprinting for identification (1909) (Nagano and Miyake, 1996). Thereafter, criminal identification sections were launched for police science (1920). Following revision of the Code of Criminal Procedure (1947) under the new constitution (1946) introduced after the Second World War, incorporating rules on the rights of suspects and defendants, scientific evidence became essential for accusation and in trials. In 1948, the Scientific Crime Detection Laboratory was established in the Criminal Identification Department of the National Rural Police Headquarters (forerunner of the National Police Agency). In 1959, the laboratory was reorganized as the National Research Institute of Police Science, in which a training institute of forensic science was established in 1983. This institute supervises forensic science laboratories and criminal identification sections of prefectural police headquarters.

17.1.3 Research and academic bodies

Experimental forensic science was introduced from Germany and Austria (Prussia) by pioneers of forensic/legal medicine at the University of Tokyo at the beginning of the 20th century (Misawa and Honda, 1996). Early fundamental research mainly included that on serology by Professor Sadanori Mita, followed by Professor Tanemoto Furuhata, who extended the research to blood typing, fingerprinting, genetics, histology and toxicology.

The first meeting of the Medico-legal Society of Japan (the forerunner of the Japanese Society of Legal Medicine) was held by Professor Katayama as the president in Tokyo in 1914. The Japanese Association of Criminology was also founded in the same year. Other branch academic bodies include the Japanese Association of Forensic Pathology (since 1993) and the Japanese Association of Forensic Toxicology (since 1982) affiliated with the International Association of Forensic Toxicology (TIAFT), as well as the Japanese Association of Forensic Science and Technology (since 1995), mainly organized by police forensic scientists. The Japanese Society of Legal Medicine has connections with the International Academy of Legal Medicine (IALM), the International Association of Forensic Sciences (IAFS) and the Indo-Pacific Association of Law, Medicine and Science (INPALMS), and founded the International Symposium Advances in Legal Medicine (ISALM) in 1990 in cooperation with the German Society of Legal Medicine.

17.2 Practice

17.2.1 Routine casework
17.2.1.1 Postmortem examination

All unnatural deaths are investigated by police officers, accompanied by medical professionals (physicians or surgeons), while medical professionals (clinicians) are obligated to provide notification on identified unnatural death (including stillbirth at four gestational months or over) to the district police authorities under the provision of the Medical Practitioners' Act; however, there is no legal definition of unnatural death. For a provision to promote legislation for establishing the system of organ transplantation from brain-dead donors (1997), the Japanese Society of Legal Medicine published the *Guidelines for Notification of Unnatural Death* (1994), which state that unnatural deaths include any deaths other than those due to clinically established natural disease: (a) external causes of death (violent deaths, independent of the history of clinical care), including accidents, suicides, homicides and unknown causes; (b) deaths from complications or sequelae of bodily injury; (c) deaths alleged to be included in (a) and (b); (d) unexpected deaths related to medical care or alleged to be included in this category; and (e) deaths from unknown causes.

Police death investigation includes criminal and administrative inspections. Criminal inspection concerns criminal or alleged criminal deaths, usually attended by judicial police officials supervised by public prosecutors, accompanied by medical professionals. The bodies undergo legally ordered autopsy, usually at a university forensic/legal medicine institute on the decision of police "coroners" and with permission of the judge at the district court under the provisions of the Code of Criminal Procedure (without consent of the family members or relatives). For categorization of unnatural deaths into criminal and noncriminal cases in police investigations, a recent trend is the supplemental application of postmortem imaging using computed tomography (CT) to detect violent deaths; however, traffic fatalities are usually not autopsied when there are no particular legal issues, for example, involving cases of hit-and-run, multiple vehicle accident and undetermined cause of death. Another issue is the investigation of unnatural death related to medical practice; clinicians often oppose police intervention in such clinical cases. However, police intervention usually occurs in response to public or a family member's interest in cases of alleged medical negligence involving a disrupted patient–physician relationship; this is an ethical rather than a legal issue.

Administrative inspection is concerned with deaths where police officers did not find possible evidence of a crime (noncriminal deaths). In such cases, the bodies are examined in the medical examiner's system in the central urban areas of Tokyo, Osaka and Kobe, including autopsy on the decision of the medical examiner; the consent of the family members or relatives is not essential for this. In other regions, however, the bodies are usually cremated without autopsy, except in several special cases with legal or social issues in which autopsy is undertaken with the consent of the family members or other relatives. Occasionally, however, forensic autopsy is legally ordered, following the suggestion of medical examiners or other medical professionals in the police investigation, or notification under the provision of the Postmortem Examination and Corpse Preservation Act, which includes the responsibility of an anatomist/pathologist who has found death in a crime-related unnatural state (i.e., violent death) during autopsy to notify the chief of the district police station of it.

17.2.1.2 Forensic/medicolegal autopsy

Under the aforementioned Japanese legal provisions for postmortem examination of unnatural death, forensic/medicolegal autopsy is categorized into: (a) legally ordered autopsy in cases of criminality and alleged criminality cases under the provisions of the Code of Criminal Procedure and (b) administrative autopsy in cases where the police investigation did not detect evidence suggesting the involvement of crime. Administrative autopsy comprises autopsy in the medical examiner system provided by the Postmortem Examination and Corpse Preservation Act (see above), as well as autopsy under the provisions of the Quarantine Act and the Food

Hygiene Act. An additional forensic autopsy system for police investigation started in April 2013, provided by a new law, the Cause-of-Death Investigation and Identification Act (2012), which was established to improve postmortem investigation in regions without a medical examiner system.

Legally ordered autopsies for crime investigation are usually entrusted to professors of forensic pathology at university institutes. Related forensic activity includes radiology, anthropology and odontology for identification; however, dental identification is partly performed by clinical dentists affiliated with police criminal identification sections. The annual number of legally ordered autopsy cases at individual university institutes is not large, widely ranging from around 10 to 400 in recent years, depending on the location and situation. Major causes of nonaccidental homicidal death (around 600–1000/year/population of 127–128 million, according to criminal statistics during the last 10 years) are sharp instrument injury, strangulation and blunt injury. Gunshot injury is infrequent, mostly involved with crime organizations, and also including suicides. Other cases include falls, fire fatalities, drowning, asphyxiation, traffic fatalities, labor accidents and drug abuse, as well as atypical suicides. Methamphetamine is a major drug of fatal abuse, followed by tranquilizers, while narcotics and other illicit drugs are infrequently involved.

Administrative autopsy is performed at the medical examiner's offices, as well as university institutes when requested or in regions without a medical examiner system. Medical examiner's offices investigate: (a) apparently noncriminal traumatic deaths; (b) natural deaths without clinical care or clinical diagnosis of the cause of death, including cases of cardiopulmonary arrest on arrival (CPAOA), infections or food poisoning, onsets of disease in unusual circumstances and unexplainable deaths; (c) unexpected deaths under medical care (alleged malpractice not included in routines); (d) unknown cause of death; (e) deaths of pregnant women at four gestational months or later; and (f) some alleged criminal cases (Shoji, 1996). The annual case numbers during the last 20 years (1992–2011) at individual medical examiner's offices have been increasing, mainly due to unnatural deaths of elderly people: 8507 to 13,997 in Tokyo (approximately 9.0 million inhabitants), 2697 to 4825 in Osaka (approximately 2.6 million inhabitants) and 922 to 1626 in Kobe (approximately

1.5 million inhabitants). Major causes of death are natural deaths (around 70%), mainly including ischemic heart disease (around 40%) followed by cerebrovascular disease (around 10%), accidental falls, drowning, asphyxiation and traffic fatalities (not included in routines in Osaka and Kobe), as well as suicidal hanging, falls from a height and drowning. However, the autopsy rates at medical examiner's offices are low and gradually declining from 32.8% (1992) to 18.4% (2011) in Tokyo and from 37.5% (1992) to 26.7% (2011) in Osaka, while a high autopsy rate (around 65%) is maintained in Kobe. The rate of forensic autopsy cases in all unnatural deaths has been around 9–11% during the last 10 years (see below for details).

Forensic autopsy provided by the aforementioned new law is performed at university institutes. There are no differences in the autopsy procedure and laboratory investigation among these types of autopsy at university institutes.

17.2.1.3 Police forensic science
Forensic science institutions of individual prefectural police headquarters, consisting of forensic science laboratories and criminal identification sections, are responsible for routine criminal investigation, including crime and accident scene investigation, and examination of biological and other trace evidence as well as firearms and explosives, drug and chemical analysis, document examination and psychological tests. Prefectural police science laboratories investigate hundreds of thousands of specimens in total per year, mainly including bloodstains, body fluids, drugs and chemicals of abuse, as well as handwritings, printed material, chemical substances, gunpowder, vehicles, banknotes, coins and postage stamps (Nagano and Miyake, 1996). The National Research Institute of Police Science described above supervises prefectural police institutions and also undertakes special casework.

DNA analysis for identification in criminal cases is almost exclusively performed at police laboratories, except for specific markers, and a database system has been created; this is one of the major tasks in police science, involving an increasing number of cases. Investigation of drugs and poisons is another major point since the large scale of attacks using arsenic in Wakayama (1998) and domestic terrorist attacks

perpetrated by a religious sect (Aum Shinri-kyo) using nerve gases including sarin and VX (chemical weapon) in Matsumoto, Osaka and Tokyo (1994–1995), as well as the spread of the abuse of illicit drugs despite strict control. Computer-aided investigation systems, including mugshot retrieval using surveillance cameras on the street and in public facilities, have been established for criminal investigation and traffic control.

17.2.1.4 Additional casework
Examination of biological evidence
University institutes of forensic/legal medicine also contribute to biological, anthropological, dental and radiology identification of skeletal remains and biological materials as well as toxicological analysis in criminal cases at the request of the police under the provision of the Code of Criminal Procedures. DNA analysis in criminal cases is not major routine work at university institutes. Veterinary and entomological examination may be undertaken by specialists in respective disciplines. Civil cases are very rare but possible when officially requested by the attorney at law, or other legal or administrative officers; paternity testing is also not included in major casework.

Examination of documents
In both criminal and civil cases, clinical and postmortem documents are investigated by experts at university institutes of forensic/legal medicine, requested by the judge, public prosecutor, police and attorney at law, for assessment or reassessment of legal issues including the causal mechanism and severity of injury, cause and process of death, contributory disorders including alcohol or drug influence and pre-existing disease, and possible survivability, as well as physical disability or mental disorder in survivors. Clinicians also contribute to such medical assessment upon request. Experts in other disciplines may participate in forensic examination of documents upon request, for example, regarding engineering issues in traffic accidents and pharmacology issues in drug misuse/abuse.

Examination of living persons
The contribution of university institutes of forensic/legal medicine to the examination of victims and assailants as part of clinical forensic medicine is infrequent in Japan;

the police usually request help from the clinicians in charge of victims or assailants in need of medical care for the assessment of bodily injury or mental disorder following crimes or accidents. However, in cases without clinical care or positive cooperation of the clinician, or insufficient clinical interpretation, experts in forensic/legal medicine are requested to examine victims or assailants with permission from a judge at a district court under the provision of the Code of Criminal Procedure, for example, for assessment of bodily injury, injection mark or mental disorder with regard to the consequence of a violent crime, a traffic accident, physical abuse or neglect, and drug abuse. In civil cases, a similar medical examination is performed at the request of the court or attorney at law.

17.2.2 Court-supporting activities
17.2.2.1 Treatment of offenders and criminals
The roles of forensic/legal medicine in criminal proceedings include physical and mental medical examinations of suspects and defendants for evaluation of their capacity to be subjected to criminal investigation or stand trial. Psychiatric examination is provided for assessment of mental disorders related to "insanity" (criminal responsibility and diminished responsibility) as well as possible medical care, treatment and rehabilitation, and also for risk management to prevent further offenses in relation to prosecution and judicial judgment under the legal provisions (Nakatani *et al.*, 2010). Psychiatric and psychological assessments also contribute to the management of family or domestic abuse cases. These functions are usually fulfilled by clinicians in respective specialties.

In juvenile cases, family court probation officers investigate cases involving domestic personal status and relations as well as juvenile delinquency, and coordinate human relationships. They are specialists in behavioral science, including psychology, sociology, pedagogy and social work, and are engaged in the scientific function of family courts.

17.2.2.2 Support of crime victims
Under the provision of the Basic Act on Crime Victims (2004) and the Act on Support for Crime Victims (1980), crime victim support services are available from support officers and hotlines throughout the relevant period. Victims and their family are provided with mental, legal and financial support when necessary (details

are available from: http://www.moj.go.jp/ENGLISH/CRAB/crab-02.html).

17.3 Organization and institutions

17.3.1 General aspects
Institutions for forensic science in Japan include: (a) police science institutes focusing on criminal investigation, (b) university institutes of forensic/legal medicine, odontology, pharmacology, psychiatry and criminology, as well as fields related to casework that can contribute scientific expertise in both criminal and civil cases on the basis of research work in their own specific disciplines and (c) medical examiner's offices for postmortem examination primarily in non-criminal cases. These institutions are independently organized, with some cooperation in their casework and research work (Figure 17.1).

17.3.2 University institutions for forensic/legal medicine
There are 80 university medical schools, comprising 43 national, 8 prefectural and 29 private schools; each has a forensic/medico-legal institute, except for a private school (Figure 17.1). Each institute is small in size, generally with three or four regular posts including one or a few forensic pathologists, supported by part-time staff for education, research and office work. The number of forensic autopsies is in the range of around 10–400 at each institute, as described above. Facilities and equipment vary depending on the financial and staffing conditions and the policy of individual institutes regarding research and routine forensic casework, which is largely related to the amount of routine casework. There is no standardization or guidelines in connection with forensic practice, except for autopsy facilities; however, most institutes have facilities for histology, toxicology and storage, as well as partly for chemistry, biochemistry, molecular biology and ultrasonography and radiology, including computed tomography (CT) for postmortem imaging, in relation to their routines. In general, most institutes have insufficient facilities for toxicology, while several institutes are almost specialized in toxicology. Eight institutes for forensic odontology are located in the east of Japan.

The major task of these university institutes of forensic/legal medicine is education of medical students;

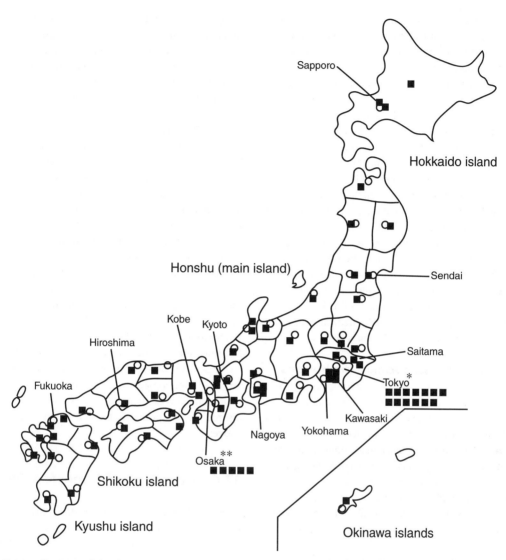

Figure 17.1 Localization and distribution of 79 university institutes of forensic/legal medicine (■) and 3 medical examiner's offices (★), as well as the National Research Institutes of Police Science (●) and 47 prefectural police institutes of forensic science (○) in Japan. *The Tokyo metropolitan area and **Osaka Prefecture have 13 and 5 university institutes of forensic/legal medicine, respectively. Cities of more than one million people are indicated.

forensic/legal medicine is a compulsory subject for graduation. Research work is also obligatory for academic qualifications of the education staff and institutes. In addition, the staff have routine forensic casework at the request of the police, public prosecutor or court in the district (see above for details). There is mutual consultation or cooperation in casework among university institutes, but these institutes are as a rule independent of police institutions of forensic science.

17.3.3 Medical examiner system

Prefectural governments are authorized to establish a medical examiner system for investigating the cause of death, including autopsy, under the provision of the Postmortem Examination and Corpse Preservation Act. The medical examiner's offices, which were established in seven major cities after the Second World War, are maintained in Tokyo, Osaka and Kobe at present; these offices belong to the section of medical affairs in each prefecture, but cover only the central urban areas (Figure 17.1). The other four offices described above were discontinued, predominantly due to financial crises of the prefectures.

The Medical Examiner's Office of Tokyo Metropolitan Government is the largest one, mainly covering the central urban area of the 23 wards (Shoji, 1996). This office has facilities for autopsy as well as histology, toxicology, storage, education and administration, staffed by 63 medical examiners (12 regular members and 51 part-timers, as of January 2014), assisted by technicians and office workers. Postmortem examination is performed at the scene, hospital or police station, accompanied by an authorized police officer, and the bodies are brought to the office when autopsy is needed for determining the cause of death. In Osaka and Kobe, the Medical Examiner's Offices also investigate the cause of death in urban areas. These offices are smaller in terms of the facilities, equipment and staffing than those in Tokyo, having only one or no post for a regular medical examiner, being mostly or fully supported by part-timers.

17.3.4 Police forensic science institutions

Each prefectural forensic science laboratory of police, belonging to respective prefectural headquarters, has specific sections for routine activities in the identification of biological and other trace evidence, and for chemistry, toxicology, physics, mechanics, engineering and psychology, and is equipped with a DNA typing facility and advanced instruments for chemical, toxicological and micro- and ultramicroscopic analyses, as well as for other sections. The approximate number of scientific experts ranges from 10 to 70 (Nagano and Miyake, 1996).

The National Research Institute of Police Science acting as the central police science laboratory consists of a general affairs department, two forensic science departments, comprising a wide range of research sections including biology, chemistry, document examination, psychology, physics, acoustics, fire investigation, explosion investigation and engineering/mechanics, as well as a crime and delinquency prevention department, comprising juvenile guidance, social environment and crime prevention sections, a traffic department, comprising traffic control, traffic safety and driver–vehicle system sections, an identification center and a training institute of forensic science. The Institute has updated facilities and equipment for research and technical development,

with about one hundred scientific staff members. The functions include research as well as special casework, training, international exchange and advisory function, supervising routine criminal investigations at forensic science laboratories and criminal identification sections of 47 prefectural police headquarters.

17.3.5 Others

Police surgeons and dentists are organized in their individual prefectures, affiliated with the police headquarters, for assisting police inspection and dental identification, respectively. Police surgeons also have roles in the healthcare of suspects under detention in police stations. In special regions, a postmortem examination including autopsy is performed at private institutions; however, the actual situations are obscure.

There are institutes for pharmacological or chemical jurisprudence in several pharmaceutical departments of universities. These institutes are involved in analyses of illicit drugs and natural biological toxins including tetrodotoxin and aconitine. There are several private institutes for forensic science services in criminal and civil cases. A substantial number of specialists in psychiatry and criminology at university institutes contribute to criminal investigations, and assessment of mental disorders of criminals and crime victims as described above.

17.4 Integration of forensic evidence

A criminal investigation under the provisions of the Code of Criminal Procedure includes scene investigation and evidence collection by the police, followed by forensic examination at police laboratories, as well as examination by experts, including a legally ordered autopsy and related forensic investigation at university institutes or other institutions including medical hospitals and clinics. These activities provide a range of evidence for accusation of a suspect(s) by the public prosecutor in charge or to be presented in court. Thereby, the public prosecutor is responsible for the decision on accusation of the suspect, integrating criminal evidence in cooperation with police officials; however, the decision of prosecutors not to prosecute is later reviewed by the Committee for the Inquest of Prosecution, established in conjunction with branch courts (Oda, 2009).

Forensic experts contribute to the integration of forensic evidence when requested officially under the provisions of law and also privately at the request of the police or prosecutor. This includes reassessment by another expert (second opinion); such expert opinions may also be requested from the defense counsel in the court process. In court, the judges primarily inquire into the documents presented by the public prosecutor, and thereafter summon experts to supplement individual evidence when needed, but not always.

17.5 Professional recruitment

17.5.1 University institutions for forensic/legal medicine

The standard staff at university institutes of forensic/legal medicine generally include forensic pathologists, toxicologists and scientists specializing in chemistry, biochemistry and molecular biology. However, the staffing varies depending on the situation and policies of individual institutes, mainly regarding the priority of forensic casework or research work, owing to the limited number of regular staff members as well as varied amount of routine casework. Japanese university institutes of forensic/legal medicine are primarily responsible for the educational course of basic medicine and are not suited to casework. The educational staff members need academic degrees (Master's or doctorate) with substantial publications, and thus are recruited from among the postgraduates. Medical doctors are also recruited from among research scientists in other medical disciplines and clinicians; however, there are an insufficient number of members with a medical license. To resolve this difficulty, several universities have set up a predoctoral course for medical students to encourage recruitment. No specific academic degree or professional career history is essential for technical staff. There are insufficient posts related to office work.

17.5.2 Medical examiner system

Medical examiners are appointed from among forensic pathologists, clinical pathologists and anatomists with a medical license, as well as clinicians; most of them are part-timers. Specific academic degrees are not required. Other staff members include technicians for autopsy, histology, chemistry and toxicology, as in university forensic/medicolegal institutes described above, as well as office workers and other technical officials. There is a history of professional personnel exchanges between medical examiner's offices and university institutes.

17.5.3 Police forensic science institutions

Forensic scientists at local police institutions are prefectural employees, recruited as technical expert officials. This post is one of the most attractive jobs for highly motivated young scientists in Japan. Their academic degrees are mostly Bachelor's, with some of Master's and doctorate level (Nagano and Miyake, 1996). The National Research Institute of Police Science, as the central police science laboratory, also recruits scientists with high academic grades, for whom there are exchanges with university institutes of forensic/legal medicine and other related disciplines.

17.6 Professional training

17.6.1 University institutions for forensic/legal medicine

Each institute is responsible for professional training including forensic pathology, toxicology and genetics, as well as other related specialties, under the guidelines of the Japanese Society of Legal Medicine, including those for the board certifications of medical specialists in legal medicine and postmortem examination. There is no legal or government administrative control except for the approval of medical licenses and qualifications for autopsy in forensic/legal medicine, or clinical pathology or anatomy.

Professional training includes forensic case studies in routine and research work, for academic degrees and the board-certified specialists of legal medicine. Domestic and international exchanges are encouraged in training courses, including participation in regional, domestic and international academic meetings, cooperation with other institutes and study abroad, as well as the acceptance of foreign students and young scientists; foreign scientists stimulate the globalized training of Japanese members.

17.6.2 Medical examiner system

The training program depends on the situation of individual offices; however, candidates are usually supervised by senior medical examiners before employment.

17.6.3 Police forensic science institutions

In-house training courses have been established at the National Research Institute of Police Science (Nagano and Miyake, 1996). Recruited staff members finish the junior course in the training institutes of forensic science before official investigation in casework. Some members study at university institutes of relevant disciplines for further professional training and academic qualifications.

17.7 Funding

17.7.1 University institutions for forensic/legal medicine

University institutions for forensic/legal medicine share the budgets of their respective universities founded by the central or prefectural government, or private educational foundations. The facilities, equipment and staffing, as well as running costs for education and research, are financed by individual founders. However, provisions and running costs of equipment, staffing and costs for routine casework depend on payments from clients, which are almost exclusively the police; this in particular obstructs standardization of routine laboratory work in forensic/medicolegal autopsy. For larger research projects, each scientist applies for grants from the central government and other sources.

The level of payment from the police for legally ordered forensic autopsy had been very low for a long time, only providing a fee for "dissection" without any expenses for laboratory investigation including histology and toxicology. In 2006, the payment system was revised to include the necessary expenses, supported by civil movements that emerged following several cases of negligence in crime investigation by the police.

17.7.2 Medical examiner system

The medical examiner's offices are established and financed by the respective prefectural governments (Shoji, 1996). The budget is large in Tokyo, but markedly smaller in Osaka, and very low in Kobe; the latter two have difficulty in maintaining the quality of routine work. In Kobe, however, a high autopsy rate (around 65%) is maintained by the endeavors of staff members.

17.7.3 Police forensic science institutions

Staff members of prefectural forensic science laboratories are employed by individual prefectural governments. Running costs are supplied by the central government. The National Research Institute of Police Science is affiliated with the National Police Agency, and is fully funded by the central government (Nagano and Miyake, 1996).

17.7.4 Other institutions

The financial situation of other university institutes involved in forensic science is similar to that of institutes of forensic/legal medicine. The major interest of laboratory staff is academic research work for application to casework. Besides the fundamental funding from the university, each scientist applies for grants from the central government and other sources for specific research projects.

17.8 Political influences

17.8.1 University institutions for forensic/legal medicine

There is no positive political influence on the activity of university institutes of forensic/legal medicine. However, since the allotted task of these university institutes is the education of medical students and research work as described above, the capacity for routine casework is insufficient, substantially obstructing the social contribution; this is a negative influence of politics. There are no effective measures to resolve this problem at present.

17.8.2 Medical examiner system

This system is financially controlled by the respective prefectural government; thus, several offices were closed as described above. In recent years, medical affairs officers of central and local governments have had insufficient interest in investigating the causes of unnatural death. This is also a negative influence of politics.

17.8.3 Police forensic science institutions

From the political perspective of maintaining and improving social security by preventing crimes and arresting criminals, the budgets of the police are maintained, with special consideration for DNA analysis and database management. On the basis of the separation of the three state powers of legislation, administration and judiciary, there is as a rule no political influence on or interference with forensic activity.

17.9 Certification

17.9.1 Forensic/medicolegal autopsy
In general, professors and associate professors of anatomy, pathology and legal medicine at medical schools as well as medical examiners are authorized to undertake autopsy as provided by the respective articles of the Postmortem Examination and Corpse Preservation Act. The Minister of Health, Labor and Welfare certifies other individuals with a medical license and regular staff members in the above-mentioned educational specialties by determination of the pre-scribed experience of autopsy, under the provision of the same law. Independent of these qualifica-tions, a public prosecutor or another agency (assis-tant officer or judicial police official) is allowed to request an expert of forensic/legal medicine to perform legally ordered forensic autopsy with permission from a judge under the provisions of the Code of Criminal Procedure.

As a general rule, a medical license is needed for forensic expertise involving postmortem examination with/without autopsy and issuing the death certifi-cate. Other qualifications are not essential legally. How-ever, the Japanese Society of Legal Medicine and the Ministry of Health, Labor and Welfare (to be taken over by the Japan Medical Association) certify the qualifica-tions of board-certified specialists of legal medicine and provide official approval for postmortem examinations without autopsy, respectively. Police officials involved in the inspection of bodies have no medical or co-medical license.

17.9.2 Other
17.9.2.1 Forensic sciences
For investigations involving forensic toxicology, DNA analysis and odontology, there is no domestic certifica-tion system at present, only guidelines. In-house qual-ifications have been established for DNA analysis by forensic scientists at police science institutes (Nagano and Miyake, 1996).

17.10 Laboratory accreditation/ quality control

This is an important issue that has developed; at present, no systematic accreditation or quality control is orga-nized for university institutes and medical examiner's offices in Japan. The present situation of university insti-tutes is far from providing board accreditation or qual-ity control because of the small amount of casework in several institutes and the small budget for the pro-vision of adequate facilities and equipment with rel-evant staffing of technicians, under the political and financial conditions described above. In this situation, however, guidelines for forensic autopsy were issued by the Japanese Society of Legal Medicine, involving the autopsy procedures, sample collection and storage, laboratory investigation, reporting and documentation; thus, quality control is a matter of individual institutes, including traceable listing for sample storage, automa-tized analyses, double checks of laboratory findings and systematic data documentation. Re-examination or reassessment is required in cases of dispute. Police insti-tutes are under the control of the National Research Institute of Police Science with in-house accreditation and quality control.

17.11 Technology

17.11.1 General aspects
Key technology issues in forensic practice vary substan-tially, depending on the roles of individual institutions in legal systems (see above for details), although with some overlaps. University institutes of forensic/legal medicine mainly perform legally ordered autopsies for crime investigation and administrative autopsy when requested or in regions without a medical examiner sys-tem. Medical examiner's offices mainly investigate the cause of noncriminal unnatural death, which includes unexpected onsets of disease and environmental haz-ards, as well as alleged violent death that needs fur-ther police investigation (screening of criminal death). Police institutes are specialized in criminal investiga-tion to provide evidence for arresting and accusing the suspects, as well as presenting the evidence in court.

17.11.2 University institutions for forensic/ legal medicine

Key technology issues are mainly concerned with establishing evidence of trauma and disease as well as the cause and process of death in alleged criminal cases by forensic autopsy combined with radiology, and with laboratory investigation, including histology, toxicology, biochemistry and biology, followed by comprehensive data analysis. From the traditional background of experimental forensic medicine, biochemical and molecular biological techniques are used in combination with immunohistochemistry to detect local and systemic functional alterations after insults, and for interpreting and visualizing the death process. In addition, postmortem imaging is used not only for detecting pathologies but also for analyzing terminal cardiopulmonary dysfunction. Limited numbers of autopsy cases at individual institutes allow precise investigation in each case, including comprehensive histological and toxicological screenings when adequately prepared (Maeda, 2012).

Some university institutes have special technology, for example, including that for advanced DNA analysis and toxicological analysis of specific chemicals such as natural biological toxins (e.g. tetrodotoxin and aconitine), which contributes to identification and death investigation in unusual autopsy cases, respectively. This unique technology is also applicable in the examination of other biological materials.

17.11.3 Medical examiner system

Since the primary task of medical examiners is to determine the cause of noncriminal death and screen criminal cases, no specific technology other than pathology and toxicology is needed in the routines. Major environmental hazards are extreme temperatures and air pollution; the latter includes asthma as a pollution-related illness and several specific malignancies related to labor environment. Chemical analysis is needed for the detection of pollutants, including asbestos and other carcinogenic substances.

17.11.4 Police science institutions

Police institutes have a diverse range of advanced technology for criminal investigation. Recent forensic issues include the conflicts between criminal investigation and an infringement of personal privacy in DNA analysis with the establishment of databases, and in computer-aided investigation systems using surveillance cameras on the street and in public facilities (Nagano and Miyake, 1996). The accuracy and reliability of DNA analysis are argued about in complicated cases. Detection and profiling of illicit drugs including designer drugs is a global issue in relation to smuggling. In traffic accidents, the reliability of documents and data analysis, as well as computerized simulation, is often discussed.

17.11.5 Others

In criminal proceedings, psychiatric examination is needed for the assessment of mental disorders related to "insanity" (criminal irresponsibility and diminished responsibility), as well as possible medical care, treatment and rehabilitation. This is a major issue in criminology; however, inconsistent results lead to complications. In addition, comprehensive support of crime victims is now essential in criminal investigations.

17.12 Disaster preparedness

During the last 50 years, Japan has experienced various mass disasters involving over one hundred deaths, including coal mine explosions in 1963 (458 fatalities) and 1965 (237 fatalities); airplane accidents in 1971 (162 fatalities), 1985 (520 fatalities) and 1994 (264 fatalities); railway accidents in 1963 (161 fatalities) and 2005 (107 fatal fatalities); an earthquake accompanied by conflagration involving Kobe and the surrounding city areas in 1995 (the Hanshin–Awaji Great Earthquake, with 6434 deaths and 3 missing) and earthquakes involving a tsunami in Hokkaido in 1993 (226 deaths and missing) and Tohoku in 2011 (the Higashi–Nippon Great Earthquake, with 18,131 deaths and 2829 missing). Other disasters included house fires, typhoons, localized downpours and volcanic eruptions. However, there was insufficient systematic provision until the Hanshin–Awaji Great Earthquake (1995); temporary postmortem examination teams were organized by those working in forensic/legal medicine, and by police surgeons and dentists, voluntarily gathering mainly from the neighboring regions. University institutes or medical examiners in the local area handled smaller disasters. The Hanshin–Awaji Great Earthquake (1995) caused damage over an extensive area including Kobe, being beyond the control of the medical examiner's office and two university institutes. Thereafter, the Japanese Society of Legal

Medicine established the postmortem examination supporting system (1997) in cooperation with the administrative authorities concerned and related organizations to prepare for large-scale disasters. Its first operation was on the occasion of the Higashi–Nippon Great Earthquake involving a tsunami (2011), which destroyed many cities and towns, associated with around 20,000 deaths and missing people. Official operation in foreign countries depends on requests by the Ministry of Foreign Affairs.

17.13 Legal issues

Current criminal proceedings are based on the adversarial system (Oda, 2009). Forensic specialists are summoned to appear in court at the request of a public prosecutor or defense counsel. The expert involved in criminal investigation under provisions of the Code of Criminal Procedure is termed as an "expert witness", who cannot be substituted; the situation in court is similar to that for other witnesses. The expert who has examined the evidence by the order from a court under the provisions of the law is termed an "expert", as a specialist who can be substituted. Because of the difficult access of courts to forensic specialists for expertise in cases involving disputes over the presented evidence, the Japanese Society of Legal Medicine provided a list of specialists at the request of the Supreme Court. Other scientific experts in science and engineering, as well as clinical physicians and healthcare professionals, participate in court processes depending on the case. The experts and their expertise should be "natural" and "neutral", excluding any preconception, prediction or conflict of interest. Public prosecutors and defense counsels may present expert opinions prepared at their own discretion in court; however, there are poorer opportunities for reassessment or re-examination for defendants because of the difficulty in both access and cost due to the lack of an official support system.

Public prosecutors prefer visual presentations in court. This trend has been accelerated, and also requested by defense counsels, since the introduction of the *Saiban-in* (lay/citizen judge) System for trials of certain serious cases, including homicide, in district courts (2009), as part of the Justice System Reform since 1999 (Oda, 2009; details are available from: http://www.moj.go.jp/ENGLISH/index.html). Since the presentation of photographs of the scene of the crime and victim to the Saiban-in is often limited or rejected in court, forensic specialists are requested to prepare illustrations or modified photographs, which involves extra work; however, the application of postmortem imaging using CT or magnetic resonance imaging (MRI) greatly contributed to this process.

17.14 Research

17.14.1 General aspects

University institutes of forensic/legal medicine and related disciplines, medical examiner's offices and police institutes are major institutions involved in forensic science, which have specific functions for research activity to develop and improve casework and social services. Research activity is closely related to the tasks of individual institutions in medical and forensic education, professional training, casework and other social services.

17.14.2 University institutions for forensic/legal medicine

The major trend in research at university institutes is fundamental and experimental approaches to develop and improve the technology in death investigation, as well as single or serial case studies. Systematic mass data analyses are performed as part of the activity of the Japanese Society of Legal Medicine since individual university institutes have an insufficient amount of routine casework under the legal, political and institutional background. The updated objectives include visualization of the evidence for interpreting pathologies of trauma and diseases with regard to the cause and process of death by means of immunohistochemistry, biochemistry and molecular biology, and postmortem imaging using CT or MRI; the trend is gradually shifting to autopsy data collection. Several institutes have specialized in research activities on genetics, including DNA analysis, or toxicological analysis. In forensic psychology and criminology, recent research has developed focusing on the strategies for crime investigation and prevention as well as the management of criminals and the support of crime victims. Forensic pathologists can also contribute to investigation of the psychological reactions of crime victims and bereaved family members (Ogata, Nishi and Maeda, 2009; Ogata *et al.*, 2011).

Research using human materials is performed following the ethics guidelines of individual institutes and academic bodies under the provisions of official guidelines of the Ministry of Education, Culture, Sports, Science and Technology, and the Ministry of Health, Labor and Welfare, in accordance with international standards. For animal experimentation, there are institutional and national guidelines. International exchanges with European countries have been encouraged historically, especially with Germany, as well as with the United States and Australia.

17.14.3 Medical examiner's offices

The research at medical examiner's offices is mainly postmortem data analysis. The data include statistics of sudden natural deaths, suicides, deaths of the elderly, deaths due to extreme environmental temperatures in summer and winter, as well as traffic and labor accidents. Because of the Japanese bathing style, differentiation between drowning and natural death is of special interest in elderly deaths in a bath, which often involves issues related to casualty insurance. These data contribute to administrative management of respective fatalities. There is also the possibility of cooperative research with university institutes in specific study projects.

17.14.4 Police science institutions

Research at police institutions for forensic science is focused on technology for criminal investigation. The National Research Institute of Police Science as the central police science laboratory in Japan has broad research activities, including DNA analysis, anthropology, chemistry/toxicology, document examination, psychology/sociology, physics, acoustics, fire investigation, explosion investigation and mechanics/engineering (Nagano and Miyake, 1996). Prefectural police science institutes are encouraged to participate in research work for the development and improvement of criminal investigation procedures in connection with the central laboratory and also related university institutes.

17.14.5 Academic bodies

Academic bodies of professionals involved in forensic or legal routine casework include societies/associations of a multidisciplinary nature for legal medicine, criminology and compensation science, as well as those for specific fields of forensic pathology, toxicology and police science (see also History). The Japanese Society of Legal

Medicine and the Japanese Association of Forensic Toxicology publish the official international journals *Legal Medicine* and *Forensic Toxicology*, respectively. Other academic bodies also issue Japanese publications.

17.15 Past and current issues

17.15.1 Postmortem examination and forensic/medicolegal autopsy

Major issues derived from the historical background in Japan described above include: (a) physical examination of human bodies by nonmedical police officials on their own, or even accompanied by physicians/surgeons, (b) categorization of criminal and noncriminal deaths by police officials, lacking insight into possible legal and social issues involved in healthcare and welfare, as well as civil affairs, and (c) systems and institutions unsuitable for unnatural death investigation and insufficient funding for maintaining routine activity of forensic/legal medicine, despite a large budget for the police. Police officials lose interest in investigating the cause of death of the deceased when they find no apparent traces of crimes, without understanding or neglecting the social significance of investigating the cause of noncriminal but unnatural deaths. Japanese clinicians also have insufficient understanding of the social and legal significance of establishing the cause of death. In addition, the officials of medical affairs administrations have insufficient understanding of the significance of investigating the cause of unnatural deaths and closed some medical examiner's offices, while there are many social and medical issues related to suicides and social deprivation involving solitary deaths of the elderly as well as the poor and needy.

In the districts with the medical examiner's system, police mishandling may be resolved by forensic medical checks including autopsy; however, another problem exists in the decreasing tendency to perform autopsies. Until quite recently, there was also a serious problem involved in forensic autopsy without systematic laboratory investigation by private police surgeons outside medical schools in some regions, which in part remains unresolved. In April 2013, a new forensic autopsy system for police investigation started as a measure for the regions without the medical examiner system, provided by the Cause-of-Death Investigation and Identification Act (2012); however, a relevant autopsy system has not been established and cases where this has been practically applied have been very few. Criminal evidence is lost without an adequate forensic/medicolegal autopsy system for cases categorized into "noncriminal" death by the police. Even in university institutes, facilities and equipment are insufficient, especially for toxicology, owing to inadequate organization and insufficient funding.

Against the above-mentioned political background, there were, although sporadically, overlooked homicide cases in police investigations; the mass media reported at least 13 homicide cases during a period of 20 years (1987–2007) in which victims had been cremated without forensic autopsy: presumed causes of death included asphyxiation (strangulation and smothering), drowning, intoxication, venous air injection and even head injury and stabbing. There were also cases of lost evidence due to incomplete or unfulfilled forensic autopsy, or serious misinterpretation even in cases of forensic autopsy. The total number of annual deaths during the last 10 years (2003–2012) in Japan increased from approximately 1,015,000 to 1,256,000/population of 127–128 million, which included around 13–14% of unnatural deaths with a gradually increasing tendency in the number (approximately 134,000–174,000), while homicidal deaths were gradually decreasing; however, only approximately 12,000–19,000 unnatural deaths (9–11%) underwent forensic autopsy, including legally ordered and administrative cases (excluding traffic fatalities). The total forensic autopsy rate differed greatly between the regions with and without the medical examiner system (around 1.5–30%), as well as among the regions without the medical examiner system (around 1.5–11.5%); the rate of legally ordered forensic autopsy also varied among prefectures (1.2–9.8%). Furthermore, the autopsy rate substantially varied among medical examiner's offices (around 20–65%), depending on the situation and/or policies of individual offices or medical examiners. These factors imply that Japanese people are suffering substantial inequality and unfairness regarding unnatural death investigation, which is closely related to fundamental human rights as well as social security and welfare.

17.15.2 Police forensic science

Before 2000, there were serious experiences of doubtful blood and DNA typing in the identification of suspects in homicide cases, in which the accused or convicts were proved to be not guilty by counter-expertise at the request of the defense counsel.

Thereafter, training and quality control of DNA typing were tightened, along with improving technology. Further issues included the accuracy of toxicological analysis; counter-expertise is often difficult in other organizations since police institutions are equipped with the most advanced facilities, and most pieces of evidence are used up, leaving insufficient amounts for re-examination. In a similar manner, the adequacy of traffic accident analysis is often discussed, but reassessment is difficult for the defense counsel. These issues remain unresolved. In addition, recent issues include the conflict with people's privacy in updated computer-aided identification systems using surveillance cameras.

17.16 Future directions

17.16.1 Postmortem examination and forensic/medicolegal autopsy

On the basis of the past and current issues mentioned above, the most important and urgent points for reform in postmortem examination of unnatural deaths in Japan are: (a) establishing a system to ensure medical examination of the bodies by board-certified experts of forensic/legal medicine on their own, which is the responsibility of the government, to provide optimum medical information for police criminal investigation, as well as adequate suggestions for further investigation from a medicolegal viewpoint in possibly noncriminal cases; (b) establishment of an effective system and institutions optimized for unnatural death investigation with sufficient funding for maintaining routine activity of forensic/legal medicine in both criminal and noncriminal cases in individual districts; and also (c) education and training of police officials as well as medical students and clinicians for comprehension of the social significance of investigating the cause of noncriminal but unnatural deaths. Forensic autopsy routines with sophisticated laboratory investigation are also important for professional training and quality control as well as reassessment in cases of dispute (Maeda, 2012). The sophistication of laboratory investigation, in terms of updating technology and databases on the basis of research work involving postmortem human data analyses, is important to meet social and legal requirements, with relevance to the advances in medical science (Maeda, Ishikawa and Michiue, 2011, 2014; Maeda *et al.*, 2010). Under such conditions, individual institutes and professionals can be prepared for systematic accreditation and quality control, as well as for contributions to national and international operations in mass disasters. With respect to these issues, the Japanese Society of Legal Medicine officially proposed establishing a medical center for death investigation, including the foundation of a toxicological analysis center and network in 2009. A discussion on reorganization of the postmortem investigation system is ongoing under administrative coordination, although a lot of difficulties remain.

In addition, cooperation with related medical specialties including emergency medicine and psychiatry, as well as social organizations and activities including healthcare and mental care, is needed for supporting crime victims and bereaved families as well as management of criminals and crime prevention. Such cooperation also contributes to the development of respective specialties and organizations through feedback from forensic case studies.

17.16.2 Police forensic science

Since police forensic science institutions have the dual tasks of identifying suspects and excluding innocent people, excluding political and social influences, independent and autonomous internal accreditation and quality control are essential in relation to the updated scientific standards in respective disciplines; however, outside inspection will be needed to establish public understanding. In routines, systematic and strictly controlled storage of pieces of evidence is needed as a provision for re-examination. It is also essential to respect people's privacy in personal data storage and retrieval in criminal investigations.

References

Maeda, H. (2012) Histology in forensic practice. *Forensic Science Medicine and Pathology* 8: 62–63.

Maeda, H., Ishikawa, T., Michiue, T. (2011) Forensic biochemistry for functional investigation of death: concept and practical application. *Legal Medicine (Tokyo)* 13: 55–67.

Maeda, H., Ishikawa, T., Michiue, T. (2014) Forensic molecular pathology: its impacts on routine work, education and training. *Legal Medicine (Tokyo)* 16: 61–69.

Maeda, H., Zhu, B.-L., Ishikawa, T., Michiue, T. (2010) Forensic molecular pathology of violent deaths. *Forensic Science International* 203: 83–92.

Misawa, S., Honda, K. (1996) History of the medico-legal system in Japan. *Forensic Science International* 80: 3–10.

Nagano, T., Miyake, B. (1996) The present situation of forensic sciences of police in Japan and the National Research Institute of Police Science. *Forensic Science International* 80: 11–22.

Nakatani, Y., Kojimoto, M., Matsubara, S., Takayanagi, I. (2010) New legislation for offenders with mental disorders in Japan. *International Journal of Law Psychiatry* 33: 7–12.

Oda, H. (2009) *Japanese Law* (3rd ed.), Oxford University Press, Oxford, pp. 426–442.

Ogata, K., Nishi, Y., Maeda, H. (2009) Psychological effects on the surviving family members seeing the deceased person after forensic autopsy. *Psychological Trauma* 1: 146–152.

Ogata, K., Ishikawa, T., Michiue, T., Nishi, Y., Maeda, H. (2011) Posttraumatic symptoms in Japanese bereaved family members with special regard to suicide and homicide cases. *Death Studies* 35: 525–535.

Shoji, M. (1996) History and present status of the Tokyo Metropolitan Medical Examiner System. *Forensic Science International* 80: 23–31.

Tsunenari, S., Suyama, H. (1986) Forensic medicine in Japan. *American Journal of Forensic Medicine and Pathology* 7: 219–223.

CHAPTER 18
Forensic science in Korea

Heesun Chung[1], Soong Deok Lee[2] & Sikeun Lim[3]

[1] Graduate School of Analytical Science and Technology, Chungnam National University, Daejeon, South Korea
[2] Department of Legal Medicine, Seoul National University College of Medicine, Seoul, South Korea
[3] Division of Forensic DNA Analysis, National Forensic Service, Wonju, South Korea

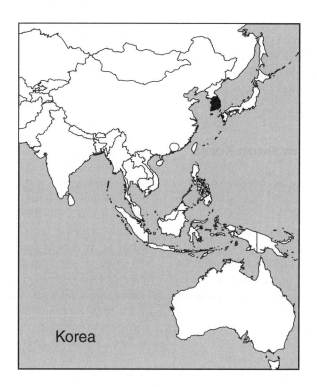

Korea

18.1 Overview, history of forensic science in Korea

Recently, it seems fairly difficult to classify or define forensic science as its field has been expanding. Forensic engineering can be an example. No one would deny its forensic relevance and it may be increasing, but its possibility to be incorporated into traditional areas of Forensic Science, or the point of its division, is hard to declare.

The situation is no different in South Korea; even at this moment, the area of Forensic Science is expanding.

In the aspect of postmortem examination, Forensic Science has a long history in Korea. Since the Goryeo dynasty (918–1392), publications on forensic medicine imported from China were already used in the forensic field. In 1438, under King Sejong in the Joseon Dynasty, *Shinjumuwonrok* (the meaning of this book title is the "annotation of Muwonrok with Korean") was

The Global Practice of Forensic Science, First Edition. Edited by Douglas H. Ubelaker.
© 2015 John Wiley & Sons, Ltd. Published 2015 by John Wiley & Sons, Ltd.

published (see Jong-Min Chae, 2007, *A Textbook of Legal Medicine*, JeongmoonGaak). It was written by annotating the Chinese book *Muwonrok* (the meaning of this book title is the "elimination of resentment"). This publication was widely used to practically include forensic medicine analysis in trials. Also, officials were sent to the scene for first-hand autopsies. Modern forensic science started to be established after the Republic of Korea's independence from Japan. In 1948, 3 years after independence, three major areas, forensic medicine, forensic chemistry and physics, and fingerprints were systematically set up to help the police scientific investigations. With democratization, the necessity of scientific investigation and the appropriateness of legal judgments based on scientific evidence have been emphasized in Korean society; the need for forensic science in Korea is expanding rapidly.

18.2 Judicial system in South Korea

In common with other countries, forensic science in South Korea is closely related to the judicial system. In South Korea, all authority and responsibility in investigation eventually belongs to the prosecutor. However, police officers carry out most of the investigation because the prosecutor cannot perform all the investigative works by themselves. Of course, in certain parts of cases, the prosecutor directly proceeds to investigation. Every prosecution is done by the prosecutor. The court does not become involved in the investigation and judge the prosecuted case.

Meanwhile, there is a special judicial police in South Korea. Judicial systems in military or maritime police (Korea Coast Guard, KCG) can be an example. In this Korean judicial system, forensic science has developed with related organizations like the police, the prosecutor's office, military or maritime police, and even reflects significant aspects of their characteristics.

18.3 Forensic science related organizations in South Korea

Most forensic science institutes in South Korea are closely related to the judicial system, like the prosecutor's office, the police or the special judicial police, which is run for police works in specific fields such as

the railroads, environment, food and corrections service related areas.

18.3.1 National Forensic Service (NFS), formerly the National Institute of Scientific Investigation (NISI)

The NFS started as a department within the police and was in charge of works related to forensic medicine, forensic chemistry and fingerprints in 1948. It separated from the police and became an independent institute in 1955. Since then, it has supported the police's first investigation by identifying most of the forensic evidence collected at crime scenes. Also, it has played a major role in developing forensic science techniques. The NFS has rapidly expanded since the 1970s with Korean economic development. In 1986, it moved into the newly built building with further increased duties. Starting from 1993, the NFS opened branch offices in regions outside Seoul, currently maintaining four branch offices. In the fall of 2013, another branch office is planned to open with the relocation of the main office. At present, the NFS is focusing its capability on ensuring substantiality to become a world-class forensic institute. In 2010, NFS's status was promoted administratively, reforming from the National Institute of Scientific Investigation (NISI) to its current name. Being independent from the police, it now belongs to the Ministry of Security and Public Administration (MoSPA), managing scientific examinations, research and development, and education in broad areas including forensic medicine, forensic chemistry or toxicology, digital forensics including video analysis, forensic engineering including a car accident analysis unit and several other forensic specialties. At present (July 2013), 328 employees are working for the NFS and 247 employees are managing analysis.

18.3.2 Forensic science and the Prosecutor's Office, National Digital Forensic Center (NDFC)

Scientific investigation in the prosecutor's office started from the introduction of lie detectors in 1979. Then until 1991, related works like authenticating documents, analyzing images, forensic genetics and forensic toxicology were introduced one by one. Systems got into shape as professionals were hired and research labs were set up in 1992. Since then, continuous hiring of professionals and expansion of facilities were carried out. In October 2008, the Digital Forensic Center (DFC) in the Supreme

Prosecutor's Office opened and later changed its name to the NDFC.

In particular, the digital forensic area should be mentioned. The NDFC supports the prosecutor's investigation over various areas, including special investigation, like restoring and analyzing databases, cell phone analysis, e-mail and finance account analysis, and code-breaking by using rapidly developing IT. Digital Forensic teams are in operation in seven district public prosecutors' offices, including Seoul and Busan. They are developing education systems to train digital specialists and supply them with necessary talent. Now 120 forensic specialists are working in the NDFC.

18.3.3 Forensic science in the military, Ministry of National Defense affiliated Institute of Scientific Investigation (ISI)

This Institute started as a research department of the Military Police inside the military establishment in 1953. Afterwards, there were several expansions and unit re-titles and in 1987 it became a forensic science organization under the Ministry of National Defense (MND). The missions undertaken include technological support to scientific investigation, forensic tests for evidence, research and managing equipment. The Institute is active in the fields of forensic medicine, forensic chemistry, documents analysis, teams on explosives and fires, and lie detectors. Particularly in the forensic genetics section, they are identifying corpses from the Korean War by DNA analysis.

18.3.4 Korea Coast Guard Research Institute

This initiative refers to the Korea Coast Guard (KCG) affiliated research institute. In 2007, the KCG Research and Development (R&D) Center was established and was promoted to the KCG Research Institute in 2010. Its goals include research and development for KCG support and improvement of the ocean environment. Its main tasks are building the support systems for maritime crime and scientific investigation, developing equipment, enhancing identification and analysis capability of contaminants, systematic confrontation strategy for contaminants through marine exhaustion, supervising ocean dumping wastes, investigating pollution level of exhausted waters, etc.

In addition to the Forensic Science research and investigation institutes described above, the Supreme Prosecutors Office and Police have administrative systems for managing forensic science related matters. However, a detailed explanation will not be presented in this document. Also, there are education and research institutes run by universities and other small, separate initiatives that will not be summarized here.

18.4 Current affairs of forensic science – outcomes and challenges

18.4.1 Scale of current affairs

The National Forensic Service (NFS) and the Supreme Prosecutors Office affiliated National Digital Forensic Center (NDFC) are the two main institutes that are in the front line of forensic science current affairs in South Korea. During 2012, the NFS and NDFC carried out 298,729 and 87,943 examinations, respectively. In the case of the NFS, its number of examination cases is continuously increasing; 256,386 in 2008, 278,040 in 2009, 276,614 in 2010 and 297,357 in 2011 (Figure 18.1). To look closely into the number of investigation cases in 2012, there were 5150 cases of autopsy, 104,164 of forensic DNA analysis, 61,132 of drug and toxicology, 17,371 of forensic engineering, 14,183 of questioned documents and image analysis, 536 of crime psychology and 35,878 of alcohol and trace evidence. Especially, starting from July 26, 2010, the NFS DNA Identification Center and the Supreme Prosecutor's Office affiliated NDFC's DNA Investigation Office are building a national forensic database for criminal evidence, confined suspects and prisoners convicted for certain designated crimes. Until September 30, 2012, the site database included 36,010 cases, confined suspect database 23,755 cases and prisoner database 45,789 cases.

18.4.2 Outcomes of forensic science examination

Among many cases in which forensic science played a big role in their solution, there is a case called "*Seorae* Village Infanticide Case." In 2006, two corpses of infants were found in a freezer of a Frenchman's house located in Seorae Village, Seoul. The infants were killed after born living, were not identical twins, and had valid parent–child relationships with the French house owner "C" who notified the police. The Frenchman "C" went to

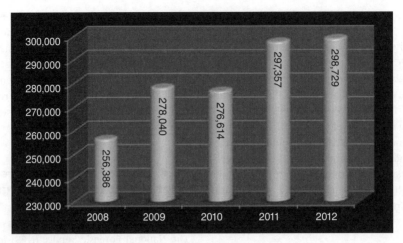

Figure 18.1 The number of examination cases in the NFS during recent five years.

France with his wife "B" for the summer vacation. The Frenchman C was proved to be the father of the two infants after DNA typing. So the police thought that the killer of the two infants must be a woman who knows the Frenchman C and might be their mother. An investigation was launched to find the criminal who killed the infants, presumed to be their mother because the infants were autopsied and it was determined they were killed after being born living. The police searched for the mother of the two infants. From the household items such as a toothbrush and comb that were collected from C's house, the NFS found a woman's DNA that showed a parent–child relationship with the deceased infants. This woman's DNA also had a parent–child relationship with the two sons (in addition to the deceased infants) of B and C, and consequently the police could throw suspicion on B. However, B and C denied the charge, disregarding the level (or standard) of Korean forensic DNA technology. In order to prove that B was the mother of the dead infants, B's specimen was necessary but she refused to hand in the specimen. The Korean police found out that B's uterus tissues were kept in a neighboring hospital. With this tissue, they carried out DNA testing and it was identical to the one found in C's house, also having a valid parent–child relationship with the two dead infants. The test results and specimen were sent to a French DNA identification laboratory. There, the same results were presented. In the end, B was sentenced for killing two infants after they were born. By this incident, countries in the world including France appreciated Korea's forensic DNA technology.

18.4.3 Challenges of South Korean forensic science analyses

There is the "Murder Case of Dentist Mother and her Daughter," which is also referred to as South Korea's OJ Simpson case. It went through 8 years of court debate but resulted in a pronouncement of innocence. In 1995, a fire broke out in an apartment located in Seoul. After the fire, a female dentist and her daughter were found dead in the bathtub inside the apartment. The prosecutor targeted her husband "L" as the culprit. However, the presumed time of their death and the time of the outbreak of the fire, which were considered most important in this case, were indefinite and the accused was declared innocent. Circumstantial evidence led the prosecutor to have a firm belief that the husband was the culprit but they lacked tangible evidences. After this case broke, the importance of organized collection of evidence and scientific analysis at the scene was magnified in South Korea.

Overall, forensic science in South Korea has substantially expanded with the rapid progress of the society. However, additional efforts are still necessary. Therefore, continuous R&D, social systems with high completeness, exchanges and harmony between the forensic society and judicial systems are considered to be important.

18.5 Research and development (R&D)

R&D was gradually handled on a small scale by individual forensic science institutes. It is not long since systematic forensic science research started. In the middle of year 2000, the South Korean government started to support R&D. Recently, they are planning a new R&D system as a consensus that investment in forensic science is critical to forming a social safety net and to protect human rights. The budget of South Korea's national R&D investment in 2013 was about 16 trillion, ranking 6th worldwide and ranking 2nd in terms of taking 4% of South Korean Gross Domestic Product (GDP). However, R&D in the forensic science field still remains relatively low in rank. Isolating the validity of the result, sharing the research results or industrializing and linking to human resource development is still lacking. The NFS, the largest forensic science institute in South Korea, itself had 3.7 billion for its R&D budget in 2013. Except government institutes, the R&D level in universities, contributed research institutes and corporations still have a low level of research but they are expected to gradually improve in the future.

The main academic journals where one can publish the research results in South Korea include *The Korean Society of Forensic Science Journal* (http://www.ksfs.org), *The Korean Society for Legal Medicine Journal* (http://www.legalmedicine.or.kr), *The Korean Academy of Scientific Criminal Investigation* (http://kasci.or.kr) and *The Korean Society of Analytical Sciences* (http://www.koanal.or.kr).

Recently, South Korea's forensic science increased its global presence by the NFS hosting the 43rd international meeting of The International Association of Forensic Toxicologists (TIAFT) in 2005 and the 3rd meeting of the Asian Forensic Science Network (AFSN) in 2011. Also in 2014, South Korea is preparing the 20th international meeting of the International Association of Forensic Science (IAFS) as the presidential nation. Efforts to attract the 27th meeting of the International Society of Forensic Genetics (ISFG) in 2017 were also approved during the last ISFG meeting.

18.6 Education and forensic personnel

In the forensic medicine field, MDs have continuously expressed concern about raising their succeeding generation. From the 1970s some medical colleges have established departments of Forensic Medicine, and now about a quarter of medical colleges are operating this department. From this education network, newly trained medical examiners or researchers in forensics are supplied. Compared to the above, there has been no established training school that is focused only on forensics. There are no official training schools offering an undergraduate course such as basic classes of forensic science including chemistry, physics and biology.

With the effect of mass media like CSI, many young students have become interested in forensics and attempt to search for forensic training. As a result some universities have launched graduate forensic training courses, such as Kyungpook National University, Chungnam National University and Soon Chun Hyang University. The police have made special rules that allow those forensic specialists to be recruited as easily as their CSI members. In this manner, many different efforts are being implemented for training the succeeding forensic generation. For the ultimate users of forensics like the police, prosecutors or lawyers, various lectures are given now based within their own training courses, like law school or training courses for policeman.

18.6.1 Graduate School of Scientific Investigation, Kyungpook National University

This was established in 2003 and was organized on a five semester basis. Three specialties are provided including forensic nursing, scientific investigation and legal medicine and the quota is 30 for each. The major topics include the following: criminal identification, forensic medicine, IT-based techniques, psychology, anthropology, etc. They also stress the safety and prevention of the public from industrial accidents.

18.6.2 Graduate School of Peace and Security, Chungnam National University

This was first established in 2002 for peace and security purposes. In 2004 the department of scientific investigation was added to the previous department of peace and security and the department of military science and military art. In 2013, they started to set up an integrative system providing school–industry–military cooperation.

18.6.3 Graduate School of Forensic Science, Soon Chun Hyang University

This was established in 2011. They also opened a private forensic lab and are trying to take part in crime scene evidence examinations, which had mainly been handled through the official institute. At present (2013), 72 students are studying in the department of forensic science and the department of crime investigation.

18.7 Communication with judicial system and standardization of related works

18.7.1 Legislation

The ultimate application of forensic science is for the law, so forensic science cannot be divided from the judicial system of a country. The judicial system reflects its own peculiarity depending on each different country, so forensic science is closely related with how the law regulates forensics. In South Korea there is no law that directly rules forensics and the will of the lawyers seems to be not very strong to prepare this. In contrast, forensic scientists have wanted to prepare common law for the forensic field and the process is still ongoing.

The effect of legislation on forensics has become evident with the criminal DNA database construction. Like NDNAD in England or CODIS in the US, South Korea has also tried to establish a nationwide criminal DNA database for over 10 years and at last it became possible from 2010. Whatever the purpose, the DNA related database needs specific law, so the so-called Criminal DNA Database Act was made and passed by the National Assembly. After this process the forensic genetics society in South Korea has jumped up to a more advanced stage with reinforced personnel and a well-established standard that must be followed. The legislation process has not only made the process possible but has also made it open for all citizens, thus potentially indicating its clearness and providing a bastion for citizens and criminals. In South Korea there is another legislation that is related to personal ID, the Act for Protection and Support of Missing Children. It was established in 2005, and revised in 2013. It is focused on the ID for missing children under 18 or dementia patients, with a database of them or their relatives.

18.7.2 Communication with lawyers or judicial system

Considering the purpose or application of forensic science, the lawyers or related personnel also have to know about forensic science or know what is going on in forensic societies, but the situation is rather different in South Korea. They usually pay little of their concern to forensics and the communication between the forensic and lawyer societies seems not to be very active. In some real caseworks, some argue that the fact was misunderstood or misapplied. Among this kind of dispute, there are many misunderstandings between both disciplines, from both lawyers and forensic scientists. This must be considered for the widening and strengthening of forensics in South Korea.

18.7.3 Standardization and quality assurance (QA)

This initiative is operated mainly by the KOLAS (Korea Laboratory Accreditation Scheme); it is based on ISO 17025 and also gives accreditation for forensic laboratories. The NFS was first accredited on drug and DNA aspects, and the topics have been subsequently widened. It also was designated as the SRM (Standard reference material) producing institute in 2010. Thereafter the NDFC in the Supreme Prosecutor's Office was accredited, and many forensic labs have participated in the process by several different tests.

18.8 Shortage and the future

As with South Korea in general, the Korean Forensic Society has made great advancement in a short period. For further advancement and to reach a mature and refined status, much additional work is required. For this the effort of the whole forensic community is most important, but this is not all. Social support must also be added to this. Especially the following seems to be important: (1) strengthening of education for the whole field of forensics and the research and development for this is needed; (2) continuous communication between the forensic and the judicial communities needs to be strengthened; and (3) an adequate legislation process needs to be established to address the needs of the forensic community.

Besides government driven institutes, forensic activity in the general academic field and private arenas are also important. They must be in harmony and the government must be aware of this and supportive. For the future, we feel it is rather promising considering the increasing awareness of both government and public for the importance of forensics in national security and social safety.

CHAPTER 19
Forensic medicine in Libya

Fawzi Benomran

Department of Forensic Medicine, Dubai Police General Headquarters, Dubai, United Arab Emirates

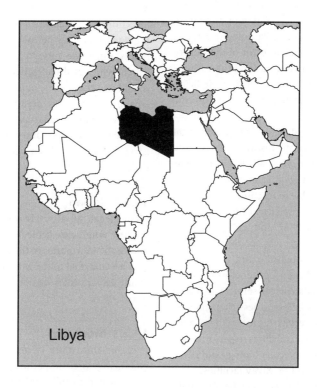

Libya

19.1 An overview and a historical background

The contemporary Libya was under Ottoman rule from 1551 until the Italian invasion in 1911. During the Second World War it was a setting of hard fought battles between the Axis and Allied Forces until the defeat of the Italians and the Germans in 1943 when it became under British administration. Libya gained its independence in 1951 where it became a Kingdom until 1969 when an army lieutenant, Gaddafi, led a military coup and overthrew the king. The lieutenant made himself

a colonel, and ruled the country for 42 years. On 17 February 2011, Gaddafi's armed forces killed scores of peaceful demonstrators in Benghazi, an act that started a revolution and armed conflict that ended with the killing of Gaddafi and defeat of his forces with the help of NATO forces. During the dictator regime of Gaddafi, the country had been in chaos that destroyed everything that was achieved during the previous reign of the king.

Although medicolegal services had existed since the early 1960s, it had been a modest section of a centralized governmental expert witness services located in the

The Global Practice of Forensic Science, First Edition. Edited by Douglas H. Ubelaker.
© 2015 John Wiley & Sons, Ltd. Published 2015 by John Wiley & Sons, Ltd.

capital, Tripoli, with a branch in Benghazi, and attached to the Ministry of Justice. It had not gained much attention from the Gaddafi regime, and consequently it continued to be a less than satisfactory establishment. It depended entirely on expatriate doctors from neighboring Egypt working on a contract basis. In the 1960s, there had been very few Libyan doctors, and none in the field of forensic medicine.

In December of 1983 the author, a native of Libya, finished his training in Glasgow, Scotland, and came back to become the first Libyan Forensic Pathologist. He was based in Benghazi and was made director of the Centre of Expert Witness Services, as well as the senior forensic pathologist. He also joined the Faculty of Medicine and was made the head of the Department of Forensic Medicine and Toxicology.

The author tried hard to develop the medicolegal services and establish a separate Institute of Forensic Medicine in Benghazi, but to no avail. His vision was to establish an Institute with good resources and properly qualified personnel capable of teaching medical students and performing service practice at the same time. He gave up trying in August 1997, and left for the UAE to join Dubai Police, where he was made Director of the Department of Forensic Medicine and managed to develop the department and train local doctors to partly replace expatriates. The medicolegal services in Libya continue to be the same as before, a less than modest section of an expert witness service centre, with no laboratory facilities. There are no possibilities to perform toxicological investigations, no molecular biology and DNA, no histopathology facilities and no X-ray facilities.

The concept of the separation between the university department teaching forensic medicine to medical students and the department performing real forensic services, and the combination of medicolegal services with the rest of expert witness fields in a body attached to the Ministry of Justice has been adopted from Egypt, and likewise, this system was adopted by many other Arab countries.

19.2 Forensic medicine in the Arab countries

What is known as the Arab World or Arab countries are a number of independent states, totaling 22, that speak the Arabic language with diverse local dialects. The total population amounts to over 370 million. Although largely of the Muslim faith, there are many Christian Arabs, Jew Arabs and a small proportion who adopt different faiths. There are subtle but important differences in the criminal law between Arab states that use the practice of forensic medicine and forensic sciences.

19.2.1 The United Arab Emirates
Medicolegal services started in 1982 in Dubai, where a section was established within Dubai Police General Headquarters, and became a Department in 2004. In nearly the same time, a crime laboratory was established, which is also attached to the police and currently considered the most sophisticated in the region. In Abu Dhabi, however, the setup has been a little different, with two separate departments of forensic medicine, one attached to the police and another attached to the Ministry of Justice, with one crime laboratory attached to the police.

19.2.2 Sudan
Medicolegal services are offered by the Ministry of Health, where medicolegal autopsies are carried out within the mortuaries of the hospitals. Forensic pathologists are attached to the Ministry of Health, but they use Crime Laboratories of the Police Department for their tests.

19.2.3 Morocco
It seems that there is no separate professional body embracing forensic pathologists. Forensic pathologists are attached to the Ministry of Health and practice in hospital mortuaries. Some do practice in the university teaching hospitals, and those would probably be staff members of the medical faculty. Other aspects of forensic sciences would be handled by the police laboratories.

19.2.4 Algeria
In a way this is similar to Morocco, in which all forensic pathologists are basically university staff who are dispatched to perform medicolegal work all over the country. They use hospital facilities, which are either attached to the Ministry of Health or teaching hospitals attached to the different faculties of medicine. As far as forensic science is concerned, it is performed by police laboratories, including samples referred by the forensic pathologists.

19.2.5 Tunisia

Practicing forensic pathologists are either attached to the Ministry of Health or the different universities. By and large, autopsies are carried out within hospital mortuaries. Forensic science, on the other hand, is provided by the Police Department.

19.2.6 Bahrain

A forensic pathologist would belong to one of three governmental bodies, the ministry of interior, the military judiciary or the public prosecution. Whatever their affiliations, they use the facilities at the hospitals of the Ministry of Health. All of the practicing forensic pathologists are expatriates.

19.2.7 Kuwait

There is a Department of Forensic Medicine, which is attached to the police which is part of the Ministry of the Interior. They have their own mortuary and autopsy facilities. Forensic science is attached to the police. Again, medicolegal services do not collaborate with the staff of the Faculty of Medicine at the university.

19.2.8 Saudi Arabia

Forensic Medicine Services are provided through departments attached to the Ministry of Health. Forensic Science is provided by a department of the Police Services. Although all Medical Schools teach forensic medicine to the medical students, they do not take an active part in actual medicolegal work.

19.2.9 Jordan

There has been a sort of collaboration between the department of forensic medicine and toxicology of the Faculty of Medicine and the medicolegal services that belong to the Ministry of Health. Forensic Medicine of the Ministry of Health is located within hospital facilities. Some of its staff would contribute in teaching in exchange of reciprocal treatment, where university staff are allowed to do some work within the medicolegal service.

19.2.10 Lebanon

The forensic pathologists are attached to a separate body called the Medico-legal Service, which belongs to the Ministry of Justice. The laboratory, which carries out other aspects of Forensic Science is attached to the police.

19.2.11 Syria

The service is provided by the Ministry of Justice through its personnel, and the logistics are provided by the Ministry of Health. Apparently there is not a proper crime laboratory to back up the forensic pathologists.

19.2.12 Yemen

A Department of Forensic Medicine exists in the Capital, with some branches. It is attached to the Director of Public Prosecution, with a few offices within its building, but no separate mortuary or laboratory. The forensic pathologists rely on a very primitive mortuary located within the hospital, which in turn belongs to the Ministry of Health.

19.2.13 Iraq

The forensic pathologists and the medicolegal services are run by the Ministry of Health. A laboratory is attached to the department in Baghdad, where it includes toxicology, histopathology and X-ray facilities. The university staff members in forensic departments adhere to "teach only policy".

19.2.14 Qatar

The Ministry of the Interior provides medicolegal services through its Police Departments. The crime laboratory, which belongs to the police, performs forensic science and toxicological tests. Forensic medicine is not taught in the only School of Medicine in Doha. The work is carried out, however, within the hospital mortuary.

19.2.15 Oman

Forensic medicine and forensic science services are provided through departments attached to the Police organization.

CHAPTER 20

The practice of forensic science in Mexico

Mario Alva-Rodríguez[1] & Rolando Neri-Vela[2]

[1]National Autonomous University of Mexico, Anahuac University, La Salle University and the Military Medical School, Mexico City, Mexico
[2]Department for the History and Philosophy of Medicine of the Faculty of Medicine at the National Autonomous University of Mexico, Mexico

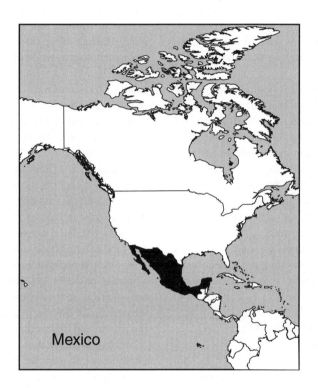

Mexico

20.1 Introduction

Mexico is organized under a federal system. The forensic services and laboratories work, with some exceptions, under the dependency of the National Attorney General's Office in federal cases and under the dependency of the Attorney General's Office of the corresponding State and the Federal District in local cases. The Attorney General Offices, as a part of the Government, cover the annual budget of the forensic services, according to the needs and the available resources. In general, the experts, professional, technical or empirical, have adequate preparation to fill their functions.

There are many institutions that offer careers and courses related to the various forensic specialties: the National Institute of Penal Sciences, the various local institutes of professional formation, many universities and private ones. The forensic services recruit their personnel from these graduates through a curriculum evaluation and, generally, an entrance examination.

The Global Practice of Forensic Science, First Edition. Edited by Douglas H. Ubelaker.
© 2015 John Wiley & Sons, Ltd. Published 2015 by John Wiley & Sons, Ltd.

The forensic services are far from the political shifts because they are always working with technical and urgent cases.

It is convenient to say that the forensic services in Mexico have different dimensions and capacities: there are some of a high level situated in the capital cities, from the Republic or the States, with higher economical resources; then come intermediate cities and lastly are the smallest ones in a third economical level. The first level services have sufficient personnel and equipment in all or in the majority of the forensic specialties. They organize conjoint sessions, evaluate and certify periodically the experts and the laboratories as well.

In the second and third level services a wide variety of conditions exist and they work hard according to their capabilities. However, when they reach their limits, there is always the option to ask for help from the upper steps. It is important to know that thanks to the good results that the forensic services have produced in favor of justice, the judicial and the administrative authorities are supporting the budget increases, the purchase of modern equipment and the construction of new laboratories, within the existing resources.

In the field of research, there are some interesting advances. The goal is there, but not the sufficient financial means to materialize it now. That is our challenge.

20.2 The practice of forensic medicine in Mexico

Forensic medicine is one of the medical disciplines that appeared in Mexico as a scientific branch of human endeavor. Regulations that applied to legal medical cases already existed in pre-Hispanic Mexico in the 15th century, as reported in the chronicles that came from the New World. People were condemned to death for statutory rape, stoned for adultery, skinned when they abused a woman, drowned for incest with their mother or father, and hung for homicide for abortion by poisoning, facilitation abortion or raping their mother. They were condemned to slavery for homicide with pardon, for lesions, for poisoning a slave or getting a slave pregnant if she died during childbirth, or for copulating with a slave who was a minor or who belonged to someone else. To repair the damage caused by homicide, if the widow gave her pardon, the aggressor was sold as a slave and the money was given to her (Lima, 1986, pp. 7–29).

The first autopsy that was performed in Mexico City was in 1576, during colonial times. Its objective was to clarify the etiology of *matlazáhualt*, an epidemic that hit Mexico City and its surroundings.

In John Tate Lanning's opinion (1997), if one was an official or salaried surgeon one had the responsibility of healing broken skulls, and would be obligated to tend to the sick on weekends or vacations, often without help, even if this meant that he would have to walk hesitantly and half asleep through the streets to minister to a bloodied beggar, while his colleagues lay sprawled in their beds. When a wealthy person called, they would wake with an inhalation of snuff, tend to the scene and charge a good fee.

The same author added that medicine in the Spanish territories (or New Spain) was frequently a matter for the police. Not only was it a matter of calling a medic, if the call came in the middle of the night it usually fell on the police to solve the problem. Fights were common, and the quarrelsome, who were tended to by doctors without licenses at the Hospital Real de Naturales in Mexico City, were such a problem that in 1763 the administrator, overriding the Real Protomedicato, solicited permission of the viceroy to prohibit the admission of said bullies. The wounded, who frequently arrived drunk, may have caused the fight, and it was not uncommon for a doctor or surgeon to show up, examine the patient and inform the authorities.

Lanning added that in this grey zone between the purely medical and the purely judicial, there never existed total security as to who was in charge of the admission to the hospital. In 1815 authorities were still so unorganized that it became necessary for a scribe to gather all the previous regulations available to solve the case and determine the correct procedures.

Based on this list, when a patient was admitted to hospital his name had to be registered in the books along with that of the person who accompanied him and the jurisdiction to which he belonged. Afterwards the doctor had instructions to examine the patient and he then left his certified report with the intern to be handed in to the corresponding authorities.

This practice required that the surgeon who performed the examination was required to say whether the wound was recent or had been inflicted a few days before; a precaution that could lead to the conclusion that the patient was trying to hide a crime. To prevent alterations or fraud these data were registered in another certification book. Therefore, if the case arose, the corresponding certification on the gravity of the wound or the state of the injured was made, in order to expedite the process. It is a given that when the wounded died, the surgeon would have to certify this as soon as possible and the scribes, who expected this contingency, would have to be at the hospital (daily if necessary) to pick up the certificate so that the case would not be delayed. In individual cases, the hospital sent to the appropriate courts and judges a list of the wounded, those who died and those who recuperated, and a statement of whether or not the certificates had been collected (Lanning, 1997, pp. 308–309).

Even when the Real Protomedicato was in place, in 1830 Doctor Manuel de Jesús Fables compiled existing laws and provisions related to medical practice and published them as news of the law and police orders that govern the art of healing (Alva-Rodríguez, 2010, pp. 3–14).

In Mexico, once higher education was restored, the Faculty of Medicine of the Real y Pontificia Universidad de Mexico was replaced by the Establecimiento de Ciencias Médicas. Its founders, while organizing the campus, created the corresponding team of professors of Legal Medicine, which was made up of the doctors Agustín Arellano, Dávila and Tender. Arellano was the first appointee on 27 November 1833, and was sworn into office on the 2 December of that same year.

Agustín Arellano was part of the Commission of Public Hygiene and Medical Police of the Establecimiento de Ciencias Médicas, along with doctors Pedro Del Villar and Salvador Rendón. He was also part of the History of Medicine Commission with doctors Olvera and Ignacio Erazo.

Agustín Arellano was born in Mexico City, and as a student of the old university, he took his exam on 20 March 1819, and lectured on the lessons of Luis José Montaña, on the Aphorisms of Hippocrates, on the beginnings of medicine and the first and second volumes of physiological investigations of Francisco Xavier Bichat. On 21 April he received his degree of bachelor in medicine from doctors Fables, Flores, Contreras, Liceaga and Vara. Two years later he sat for his professional examination before the Protomedicado and in 1831 he graduated as a surgeon.

The Legal Medicine course was abolished in 1834, to appear again in 1839, under the charge of the then director of the Institution Casimiro Liceaga, leaving Arellano as a second, who then replaced Liceaga temporarily in 1841. The subject was then taught by Casimiro Liceaga, José Ignacio Durán, Rafael Lucio, Manuel Robredo and José María Espejo.

In 1849 the subject was then taught by José Ignacio Durán, who was succeeded by Luis Hidalgo y Carpio, who is known as the pioneer of Mexican legal medicine. The lawyer Rafael Roa-Bárcena wrote in 1860 the first edition of a book that combines Penal Law, Criminal Procedure and Legal Medicine, under the title *Manual Razonado de Práctica Criminal y Médico-Legal Forense Mexicana*. The second edition was edited and printed in 1869 by Eugenio Maillefert (Roa-Bácena, 1869). The author explains that his objective in writing this book was to make available to students of law and medicine a text in which knowledge of criminal proceedings are tied to Legal Medicine.

There was no other Mexican author covering such topics, which forced one to consult foreign authors, mainly Spaniards, in the criminal part and French or Spanish authors in the medical legal part, with the grave consequences of facing significant discrepancies in the laws of said countries as opposed to those of Mexico.

Roa-Bárcena has the double merit of being the first person to publish a book that ties Mexican criminal law to legal medicine, and of doing so in strict compliance with the laws valid in 1860. The work consists of 529 pages and is divided into four books or parts. The first mentions laws in force for criminal matters and the organization and allocations of tribunals. The second describes the classification of crimes in general and the corresponding judgment and procedures, as well as the forensic participation that the case warrants. The third refers to the crimes (prosecuted when sued) examining in general and in particular each of the procedures in question, both forensic matters and its laws and practice. In the fourth book he talks about extraordinary means, especially pardons and asylum.

To give an idea of the wide coverage of the text, we list some of the most prominent issues: the definition and classification of crimes, the procedures in public criminal trials, verbal and written criminal trials, preliminary statements, witnesses, crime investigation, indictments and freedom, bail, evidence, arguments, judgments, penalties, appeals, and the execution of judgment. In relation to forensic matters, he speaks of injuries or bodily lesions, their classification and characteristics, homicides, autopsies, burial and exhumation, suffocation, poisoning, abortion, infanticide, rape, statutory rape, incest, insanity, and expert statements or certifications. In the final part of the book, Don Rafael includes a brief alphabetical glossary of surgical, medical and pharmaceutical terms for law students.

Luis Hidalgo y Carpio was born in Puebla on 18 May 1818. He belonged to a family of limited financial resources. He was a scholar at the theological seminary of Puebla, where he studied mathematics and physics in 1835. He gained the reputation of being diligent and intellectual, and on the 25 September 1843 he obtained a medical degree from the *Escuela Nacional de Medicina*, having already published 12 papers in the *Gaceta Médica de México*.

As professor of the *Escuela Nacional de Medicina* he studied the endemic diseases of Mexico. He demonstrated through his clinical histories and pathological pieces that typhus and typhoid fever are different diseases. As a chemist and technician, he made studies on the histological and chemical constitution of blood; he performed toxicological analysis on blood and published a general and practical method for the study of poisonous substances in blood. He also dedicated time and effort to the study and use of the microscope and spectroscope.

According to Francisco Flores, Hidalgo y Carpio, had many original ideas on different medical subjects. He made comparative studies on the blood of Europeans and Mexicans; he undertook research on the role of chloral on the blood. He made various experiments on blood clotting in wounds and formed original theories on the legal definition of suicide. He gave a description of a type of suffocation, which was not yet known. He also gave certain precautions that could be taken to avoid burying people alive and was well versed in toxicology studies, where he found a general method of analyzing poisonous substances (Flores y Troncoso, 1982, pp. 741–742).

During these years Hidalgo y Carpio contributed to the creation of the new pharmacopoeia. As a hygienist he worked with the board of sanitation and health to create the bases for a cemetery. He granted a prize for the discovery of the cowpox virus and together with doctor José María Reyes, proposed the establishment of a civil registry and a register for mortality statistics.

As a surgeon he made his debut in the *Cuerpo Médico Militar de Instrucción*, by attending to the sick and wounded in the war of 1847. While established in the field hospital of *San Hipólito*, he went on to lend his services, in the absence of Pedro Vander Linden, as head of the Army Medical Corps. He later went to the *San Pablo* field hospital, first as a doctor and then as director, a position which he held until 1874.

At the *San Pablo* hospital alongside doctors Miguel Jiménez and José Vilagrán, he conducted a magnificent study on thoracic effusion, advocating expectorants in the beginning and toracentesis afterwards as the best treatment. As a bold surgeon, he pioneered the search for biliary fluids by puncturing through the intercostal spaces and the liver itself. He gave great insights into the severity of the dislocation of the glenohumeral joint and made detailed studies of injuries to the head of the humerus and on purulent infections.

As a result of his inquiries and observations, he wrote *Medicina Legal Mexicana*, in which he revealed data on the careful study of the signs of death, while believing that the tales of people being buried alive were exaggerated or apocryphal. He investigated suicides and the maximum length of gestation. He proved, experimentally, that blood clotting was not an infallible sign of injury while being alive. He also demonstrated that the mummification of the umbilical cord in newborns is not a vital phenomenon, but is subject to physical and chemical laws. He described a new type of suffocation caused by the breathing in of dust-laden atmospheres and he showed that many of the people who drown actually die because of food residues that return from the stomach to block the airways.

Hidalgo y Carpio wrote the book *Introducción al estudio de la Medicina Legal Mexicana* (Hidalgo y Carpio, 1869), published by Imprenta de Ignacio Escalante.

Introducción al estudio de la Medicina Legal Mexicana is divided into two parts, medical jurisprudence and medical law. Medical jurisprudence consists of eight chapters, where topics such as forensic medical education, medical police, medical practice, medical confidentiality, the physician's responsibility in general, medical proficient and forensic medical practice and the physician's fee are seen. The second section is medical law and is divided into twenty chapters, including incontinent crimes, notes on marriage, divorce, criminal and medical abortion, birth and viability of the newborn, infanticide, murder, poisoning, suicide and burials and exhumations of corpses.

Hidalgo y Carpio allotted a large section of his book to mental illness: to the treatment of mental alienation and its laws, responsibilities and diagnosis. He also spoke on the importance of the identification of people and diseases that exempt young people from military service (Zacarías-Prieto, 2010, pp. 25–28).

In the words of José Torres-Torija, two chapters caught his attention, the forensic classification of injuries, which were ruled by *Auto de Heridores* in 1765, which established the division of wounds as minor or serious injuries and whether they were caused by accident. The sanction that should be received was confusing, since on occasion the civil and criminal sanctions did not correspond to the severity of the damage caused. It called for doctors from the beginning to determine the cause of injury. The second was the conditions doctors practice under, particularly in relation to the authorities.

Torres-Torija continues by saying:

Because I believe it is of interest and because of the differences in the law between Spaniards and natives, I cannot resist the temptation to transcribe it partially. It reads: "Those who produced minor injuries, after paying the diet, the cure and the costs, would suffer the penalty of exactly fifty lashes… in the beginning, and more lashes depending on the time it took for health to be restored, if they were dark skinned, and if they were Spaniards they would have to pay $25.00 fine and spend two months in prison; and if they were poor, the punishment was four months in prison the first time and double for the second time; if the injury was serious but by accident, the first (i.e. the dark skinned), after fifty public lashes were sentenced to work in a closed office for a year, and the Spaniards wound be sentenced to two years in prison on the first occasion and double on the second; if the wound was serious and not caused by accident… the first were condemned to one hundred lashes as a form of justice and would be sentenced to two years of work in a closed office, to earn to pay for themselves, the diet, the cure and the costs, and Spaniards, would be obligated to pay these same penalties and would be sentenced to four years in prison…. All of which were established as punishment for a single wound; if there were two or more injuries the Real Sala had the right to increasing the lashings, labor or imprisonment, depending on the qualities and circumstances of the case, even if health was already restored" (Torres-Torija,1934, pp. 234–235).

Hidalgo y Carpio accepted the classification system of injuries as minor or serious, the latter being by accident or not, but he clarified what was confusing and of dubious appreciation. He insisted on separating the damages caused to the injured from that caused to the interests, and he advocated that physicians should not

be required to grant a definitive classification from the beginning.

His influence in the Mexican forensic area was of such importance that in 1868, while he was part of the committee that was in charge of writing the draft of the Penal Code, he managed to share his ideas. The Penal Code was enacted by President Benito Juárez-García in 1871.

Due to his moral and political convictions he was forced to leave his professorship, and went on to write the aforementioned *Introducción al estudio de la Medicina Legal Mexicana*, and later, in collaboration with doctor Gustavo Ruiz Sandoval, the *Compendio de Medicina Legal arreglado a la legislación del Distrito Federal*, which was published in 1877 (Hidalgo y Carpio and Ruiz-Sandoval, 1877, 2 Vols.). The latter was used as a textbook at the *Escuela Nacional de Medicina* for a few years (Archivo Histórico de la Facultad de Medicina, 1851–1883: libro 26).

In his work on criminal responsibility, being a philosophical partisan of free will, he advocated for the personal study of criminals, admitting that the criminals were such because of physical or mental conditions or abnormalities, thereby suggesting suspended sentences. Don Manuel Hidalgo y Carpio died on 12 May 1879.

During 1870 there was an opening for the then vacant position of associate professor, which was covered by Agustín Andrade, who had studied at the Colegio de San Gregorio and then gone to Paris to take the corresponding courses in medicine to receive his professional degree in 1859. Among his most interesting works are: *De los signos Profesionales Desde el Punto de Vista de Identificación de las Personas; De la Estatura en la Identificación; El Himen en México; Contribución a la Estadística del Suicidio en la República Mexicana; Estudio Comparativo entre la Estrangulación y la Suspensión; and A qué edad Empieza la Nubilidad y Cuándo Desaparece en la Mujer Mexicana.* Other works by Agustín Andrade are *Los Médicos y la Administración de la Justicia,* as well as another publication related to the morals of the indigenous race, considered by him as an important means of identification of race.

Another relevant forensic observation made in Mexico at that time was that physiological birth had some difficulties in Mexico, and Andrade assumed that the configuration of the pelvis, and consequently the birth channel of Mexican women, presented certain particularities. Francisco de Asís Flores y Troncoso's thesis states that the pubis of Mexican women is higher than in women from other races, also its downwards and backward inclination is notable, which shortens the distance between its edge and the lower limb as well as from the coccyx. In that same work, Francisco Flores comments on the introduction of life insurance in Mexico (Flores y Troncoso, 1982, pp. 744–745).

Another topic studied by Mexican medicine in the 19th century was the tears in the hymen caused by rape and statutory rape. They came up with a theory about how it resisted external violence, calculating formulas of the mechanical force expended to overcome the resistance of each form, applying the theory about its resistance to forensic issues, drawing special attention about the changes in the hymen's shape with age and the convenience of taking this into account while collecting observations.

On infanticide, Flores recounts his partner Miguel Barragán's experiences, who wrote his inaugural thesis on the national practice of medical legist Ignacio Maldonado y Moron, who brought to light the fact that the umbilical cord constituted the most important proof of fetal life, indicating that there are three parts that must be the medical forensic expert's objective for examination: the external apparatus, the intermediate zone and the internal umbilical apparatus. Maldonado carried out his observations of the intermediate zone, taking into account that for the umbilical cord to fall off it had to be preceded by the phlegmastic work of the surrounding tissues, which would be evident on the exterior, recognized by swelling, inflammation and redness, which he deduced by making two cuts on the newborn's cadaver, one on the umbilical region and the other on another body region. If the umbilical incision shows exudate and blood extravasation into the tissues, it would be probable that the fetus had lived. By contrast, the outside incision does not show those alterations.

In this same thesis, other signs found in internal organs are mentioned. With the bases on how the auditory system developed in the fetus and the mechanisms of how breathing is established in children during the first hours of life, Maldonado looked for and found air in the tympanic cavity of children who had breathed. Then he established his procedure, "dosimasia auricular". He began by beheading the fetus or by separating both temporal bones from the skull; then he made sure to expunge the gases or bubbles that might be present. Once he was sure they no longer had any air in them,

he submerged them in a vessel filled with water and proceeded to perforate the tympanic membrane with a needle; once the perforating instrument had been removed, if an air bubble was visible and came out of the hole, it was proof that the child had breathed, and therefore had been born alive. The author explained that the result was constant in children who had breathed and negative in the opposite case. This observation was most valuable when the death had been recent (Flores y Troncoso, 1982, pp. 746–747).

The 19th century in Mexico is rich in forensic publications; a monograph written by Andrade is *Aplicaciones del Microscopio en Medicina Legal* (Flores y Troncoso, 1982, pp. 746–747). Among the theses written in this century at the *Escuela Nacional de Medicina de la ciudad de México* are: José Ramos, *Bajo el Punto de Vista de la Identificación de las Personas* (from the point of view of the identification of people), 1880; Agustín Andrade, *De Algunas Aplicaciones del Microscopio en las Pesquisas Médico-legales* (some applications of the microscope to forensic inquiries), 1870; T.G. Cadena, *Juicio Crítico de la Interdicción por Demencia Seguida ante el Juzgado Tercero de esta Capital, por el Ministerio Público, contra el Sr. Lic. D. Felipe Raigosa* (critical judgment of the ban for dementia followed before the third court of this capital city, by the public prosecutor's office against Mr. D. Felipe Raigosa), 1873; Jesús García Fuentes, *Signos para Distinguir las Lesiones hechas Durante la Vida, de las que son Hechas Después de la Muerte* (signs for distinguishing injuries caused in life from those caused after death), 1878; Antonio A. Tapia, *Reflexiones sobre Algunos Artículos del Título II del Código Penal* (reflections on some articles of the II title of the Penal Code), 1877; Alfonso Ruiz-Erdozaín, *La Responsabilidad Médica ante el Código Penal del Distrito Federal y Territorio de Baja California* (medical responsibilities before the Penal Code of the Federal District and the territory of Baja California), 1887; Nicolás Ramírez de Arellano, *Profanación de Cadáveres Humanos* (desecration of human corpses), 1877; Joaquín Rivero y Heras, *Breve Estudio sobre Clasificación Médico-legal de las Lesiones* (a brief study of the forensic classification of injuries), 1880; Eduardo Corral, *Algunas Consideraciones Médico-legales sobre la Responsabilidad Criminal de los Epilépticos* (some medical considerations on the criminal responsibility of patients with epilepsy), 1882; José Hernández-Ortega, *Algunas Consideraciones sobre los Certificados de Defunción* (some considerations on death certificates), 1882; José

Antonio de Echávarri y Fernández, *Breves Apuntamientos para Coadyuvar al Estudio de la Visión Distinta en sus Relaciones con la Medicina Legal* (brief notes to facilitate the study of the view capacity in its relations with the Legal Medicine), 1883; Nicolás Mendiola, *Consideraciones Sobre la Actual Organización de las Secciones Médicas en las Inspecciones de Policía* (considerations on the current organization of the medical sections in police inspections), 1885; Luis G. Ezeta, *Policía Sanitaria. Conducción de Cadáveres* (sanitary police, management of corpses), 1887; Manuel Ortega-Reyes, *La Medicina Legal y el Médico Legista* (legal medicine and the forensic medic), 1893; Alberto López-Hermosa, *Juicio Crítico Sobre los Artículos 599 y 570 del Código Penal Vigente* (censorious judgment on articles 599 and 570 of the Penal Code), 1897.

Additionally, in magazines and newspapers such as *Gaceta Médica de México, La Independencia Médica, La Escuela de Medicina, Anales de la Asociacion Larrey*, among others, that appeared in Mexico City, we can see the interest that existed on forensic topics.

Andrade's successor as Legal Medicine Professor was Nicolás Ramírez-Arellano, who gave that cathedra up to 1915. His associate professor was Alfonso Ruiz-Erdozaín. Ramírez-Arellano was named Director of the Servicio Médico Legal in 1915. Juan Peón-Del Valle completed an interim period in 1907, who as well as being a doctor was a great novelist; he died prematurely.

In 1880 the Police Medical Services were created to take in the wounded from each of the eight districts that existed in Mexico at that time; the physicians from each district were allied with the prison doctors and with those from *San Pablo* Hospital (which later came to be named the *Hospital Juárez*). In the courts the Body of Medical legalist experts and the Forensic Council were created; they were intended to be auxiliaries in the administration of justice.

A Forensic Service was created in the District and each of the Federal Territories as a result of the Judicial Organization Law issued in 1903 by the government. It stated in the 114th article that the Forensic Service was to be made up by the police station doctors, the physicians at hospitals, the prison doctors and the medical legalists. In the 119th article it stated that there would be four forensic experts, two chemists, a practitioner, a filing clerk and two porters in Mexico City. There would also be a forensic expert for each of the judicial districts of *Tacubaya, Tlalpan* and *Xochimilco*. It also stipulated that

to perform the duties of a forensic expert, being moral and notoriously honest was required, as well as being a professor with an official degree in surgery, medicine and obstetrics, also being over thirty years old and having, at least, five years of professional experience. This law also assigned a daily wage of four pesos, ninety-four cents for each forensic expert.

By 1909 the Central Relief Station was founded in Mexico City, whose function from the beginning was primarily to tend to the uninsured population (poor people) who had been victims of assault, fights or accidents on the streets. These "blood facts", as these misfortunes were named, exemplify the close relationship between medical services and the police and, therefore, with legal medicine.

To work at these new services, named Police Medical Services, assigned to each of the eight existing districts in the city, the physicians had to have a degree and be residents of the district they would work at, which is why for some years physicians had police officer designation and their boss was the police general inspector. These medical services were identified, during their first years of existence, as Green Cross, since that was the name of the street where the Central Relief Station was located.

In 1911, President Francisco I. Madero appointed Dr. Xavier Ibarra as head of the Services, who then changed the name Central Relief Station to Green Cross; he intended to distinguish it from the White Cross, which was founded that same year and whose mission was to provide first aid and transport the wounded during the revolutionary struggle/Mexican revolution (Castañeda-Jaimes and Herrera-Franyutti. 2009, pp. 52–55).

With the enactment of the Federal District and Federal Territories Penal Code, the Supreme Council of Defense and Social Security was created. As of then the Forensic Service no longer depends on the Supreme Court/Superior Tribune of Justice.

In 1931, the police doctors no longer relied on the police office and were ascribed to the General Direction for Social Action of The Federal District Department.

Well into the 20th century, on the 28 January 1935, the Common Courts of the Federal District and the Federal Territories Law was issued; the 219th article stated that the Forensic Service for the administration of justice in Mexico City would be run by the delegation, hospital, prison physicians and the medical legist expert. This law established that the position of the medical legist expert would be obtained by opposition before a jury. The applicant would have to take a practical examination and would have to present a theoretical subject on forensic medicine, as well as being over 30 years old and having at least five years of professional experience.

The Federal District Forensic Service was located in the offices attached to the Penal Courts that were next to the Federal District's Penitentiary where the experts solved the classification of injuries, determination of age, sexual assaults, psychiatry, etc. The Toxicology Laboratory was also in this building. The practice of autopsies was carried out at the *Hospital Juárez*, both by experts from the Forensic Service and by the hospital's doctors.

Regarding the Forensic Medicine Cathedra, named by the Technical Council of the Faculty of Medicine of the National Autonomous University of Mexico in 1958, when the student role increased, the number of professors increased as well. Once it was evident that most of the new teachers were improvising, the first Training Course in Forensic Medicine was organized, in 1964, led by Alfonso Quiroz-Cuarón, with a duration of 10 months. That was backed by the Division of Higher Education of the same Faculty of Medicine, the Attorney General of the Federal District and the Forensic Service of the Federal District.

Professors such as Samuel García, Enrique C. Aragón, Francisco Castillo-Nájera, Luis Gutiérrez and José Torres-Torija have been heads of the Forensic Medicine class, and Francisco Osorio, Xavier López-Portillo, José Alfaro, Aurelio Becerril, Alfonso Millán, among others, have been associate professors, during the 20th century (Torres-Torija, 1939, pp. 223–242).

Francisco Flores y Troncoso, in his book *Historia de la Medicina de México*, recorded names of the authors of the textbooks used at the National Medical School. These authors are Joseph Michel Briand, Louis Bayard, Peyró y Rodrigo, Pedro Mata-Fontanet, Johann Ludwig Casper, Briand y Chaudé and Hidalgo y Carpio y Paulier y Hetet (Flores y Troncoso, 1982, 744–745). In the early 20th century some of these authors continued their work, following *Medicina Legal* by V. Balthazard and Ch. Vibert (Torres-Torija, 1934, pp. 1–15). *Toxicología Médica* written by Mateo Orfila was used at the National Medical School during the mid-19th century (Fernández del Castillo and Castañeda Velasko, 1986).

The Hospital Rubén Leñero was founded in 1943 and has been a prominent center of forensic activities in Mexico City. It was named after Dr. Rubén Leñero who died heroically after being infected by a patient who suffered from typhus.

In 1958 the Medical Faculty of the National University updated the subject's program, and by agreement of the Technical Council (as mentioned above) Legal Medicine was given the designation of Forensic Medicine.

The Rubén Leñero Hospital had a Public Prosecutor's office to facilitate the intervention of medical experts, and since 1960, it was authorized to conduct autopsies, similar to the hospital that depended on the General Direction of Medical Services of the Federal District, Emergency Hospitals Xoco and Balbuena, which received authorization in 1962.

The construction of the Forensic Service building in Mexico City was ordered in 1960 by the Federal District Department, under the direction of the architect Leónides Guadarrama.

In Mexico there are high quality forensic services, such is the case of Guadalajara, Jalisco, which since 1998 has the Jalisciense Forensic Sciences Institute. There are others in Monterrey, Toluca, Culiacán, Veracruz, etc.

In 1971 campaigns for the professional improvement of the medical experts were organized at the port of Veracruz; during that same year the Colegio de Médicos Forenses del Estado y de la República Mexicana (School of State and Country Forensic Physicians) was founded. Also in Veracruz, the Forensic Institute of the Veracruz University was founded, in 1974,

At the Medical Service of the Federal District Department a Course for Specialization and Masters in Legal Medicine was organized, in 1974. It was taught by the Legal Medicine Association, with recognition from the National Autonomous University of Mexico (UNAM), which is the institution that since 1986 has recognized and endorsed this specialty as a formal postgraduate course with a two year residency.

In that same year, 1974, public statements made the authorities understand the need to modify the specialty in this area of medicine. It was then decided that forensic medics were improvised, and that specialists in psychiatry, toxicology and other branches of medicine were indispensable; this was instigated by Miguel Gilbón-Maitreit, who had started at the Federal District Forensic Service in 1936 and had retired in 1974, after 38 years of service.

By 1980 the Forensic Medicine Masters program began at the Military School for Health Graduates, founded and coordinated by Mario Alva-Rodríguez.

The Specialty in Forensic Medicine began in 1984, and was held at the Federal District's Forensic Service, with the academic support of the Graduates Section of the Superior School of Medicine of the National Polytechnic Institute, also under Mario Alva-Rodríguez. In the same way courses on forensic odontology, forensic anthropology and embalming techniques were conducted for the first time.

The 1st World Congress of Forensic Medicine was held in Mexico, at the city of Queretaro, in 1994, with lecturers from Europe, Asia, Latin America and the USA. as well as from Mexico.

Forensic Medicine, in Mexico, has reached such a level of excellence that on 25 January 2013, the Honorary University Council of The National Autonomous University of Mexico approved the study plan for the bachelor degree in Forensic Science. The medical faculty of this University has initiated formal courses in this branch of knowledge.

20.2.1 Current practice and new developments of death investigations in Mexico

Mexico is a Federal Republic with 31 States and one Federal District. The States are partitioned in a variable number of "Municipios" (regions), each with its own government, importance and size. The Federal District, also known as Mexico City, is the country's capital (8.8 million inhabitants). Each State and the Federal District have their own laws and legal dispositions, but all are very similar with some specific differences; nevertheless they operate autonomously and all of them follow the medical examiner system.

The medical examiners, called "peritos" or experts in forensic or legal medicine, work in official facilities known as Forensic Medical Services (SEMEFO). In the States they are, in general, under the jurisdiction of the corresponding State Attorney General's Office, but in the Federal District they are under the Superior Tribunal of Justice of the same city. In both locations the medical examiners conduct autopsies and practice clinical forensic medicine.

20.2.2 Autopsy conduction

The autopsies are authorized by the District or State Attorney and are mandatory. The most frequent cases are: transit accidents, homicides, suicides, sudden and unexpected deaths, deaths without medical attendance or charged as a result of malpractice; and exhumations with or without a previous autopsy.

Occasionally, in cases of inpatient death in private hospitals, the families may request an autopsy from the Attorney General's Office, which is then performed by the SEMEFO.

20.2.3 Crime scene investigation

When a death is reported to the "Ministerio Publico" (Prosecutor's Office), there is an initial forensic scene investigation by a team made up of the prosecutor as the head, some police investigators who interrogate witnesses, explore the site and arrest suspicious persons, and criminalistic experts such as a forensic photographer, a field criminalist, a fingerprint specialist, a chemist, a ballistics expert and so forth, depending on the case. A forensic physician in attendance confirms the death, detects external injuries and diagnoses the probable time of death.

From the obtained data the prosecutor may decide to order a forensic autopsy. At this point the body is transferred to the morgue. The body usually undergoes necropsy within a couple of hours of arrival.

20.2.4 Autopsy procedure

The law requires that two forensic physicians sign off on each autopsy report, so often one of them performs the procedure while the other takes notes. They are assisted by an autopsy technician and a forensic photographer. Whenever they consider it necessary, they ask the pathologist to be in attendance or any other of the forensic specialist on staff to discuss a point, give a suggestion or take a sample to the lab.

All autopsies include a complete external and internal examination. The description of the injuries is detailed and made to assess the type of agent involved. It is also intended to estimate the time of death. In certain cases, X-rays are obtained, either before or during the course of the dissection.

Following external examination and photography, the intracranial anatomy and pathology are studied. After dissection of the central nervous system and removal of the dura mater for viewing of the intracranial skeleton, the thorax and abdomen are approached via a midline incision. The oropharyngeal structures and neck organs are examined in situ, then excised together with the thoracoabdominal viscera. During dissection, photographs are taken of significant findings. Histological specimens, toxicological and DNA samples are also collected. Autopsy reports specifying the mechanism of injuries, mechanism of death and possible cause of death are dictated immediately following the necropsy, and are usually signed within hours.

Death certificates in Mexico contain all the demographic information usually present on death certificates in many countries, because they are in accordance within the guidelines of the World Health Organization. There is a separate death certificate in cases of fetal demise, which includes data on maternal health and gestational course.

The question arises as to how histological and toxicological results are included in the death certification, when those studies may take two or three weeks to be completed. This problem is solved by the convention of using "visceral congestion" as a cause of death in cases where it is not readily apparent by results of a gross autopsy examination. When toxicology and histology results become available, the cause of death may then be amended by "amplification of the report", so that this will read: "visceral congestion due to acute heroin intoxication" or "visceral congestion due to lobar pneumonia".

This convention substitutes for the diagnosis of "undetermined", which is very rarely used. The manner of death (homicide, suicide, accident or none of the above) is also noted on the death certificate, as is the "opinion" of the forensic physician, but final certification of the manner of death is made by the Attorney General's Office.

The whole process works quickly, so that the family of the deceased can usually receive the remains within one day of the death. The driving force behind this rapid turnaround time is the National Commission for Human Rights acting on the behalf of the families of decedents.

20.2.5 Clinical forensic medicine

The medical examiners evaluate injuries, illnesses and disabilities of individuals where the apparent cause is not of a natural origin. In addition to their clinical examination, they can order any kind of lab tests and radiological studies needed. They provide impartial documentation and testimony on the nature, extent and sequel of physical and mental injuries to living persons.

The clinical forensic examinations include, for the most part, the following cases: wounds and their sequels,

sexual assaults, women coming from recent abortion, injuries indicative of familial violence or torture, symptoms of poisoning or drug abuse, mental evaluation of crime victims and the victimizers. Some medical examiner's offices have psychiatrists and psychologists on the staff to determine the mental competency of accused perpetrators and for the psychological autopsies of decedents.

Sometimes the clinical case is so complex that it surpasses the competency of the medical examiner. In such cases, the medical examiner asks the General Attorney's Office to designate a suitable specialist who can be found at a hospital, an institute or university.

20.2.6 Work setting

Generally the medical examiners work in shifts; these could be of four, six or eight hours a day, depending on the organization of the different forensic services (SEMEFO). At any given time, even beyond work hours, they respond to emergency calls, for example, in cases of multiple victims from a catastrophe.

The forensic services work every day of the week, throughout the year. In many cases they conduct autopsies during the night, especially if there is any legal or investigative urgency.

Of course there are many differences between the SEMEFOs throughout the Republic. At the first level are the ones pertaining to the Federal District and to the capital cities of the most important states. These have a sufficient number of medical examiners, the majority of them accredited with a specialty in forensic medicine. They also rely on forensic anthropology and forensic odontology specialists.

They are lodged in appropriate buildings, some being fairly new, with photography, criminalistics and toxicology, DNA and pathology laboratories. The toxicology laboratory performs screen testing by immunoassay and then does quantification tests by gas chromatography–mass spectrometry and mass spectrometry–mass spectrometry. Toxicological results are usually available within two to three weeks. The DNA laboratory uses a polymerase chain reaction for amplification of samples and then automated sequencing for quantification of the 13 CODIS loci for identification and amelogenin alleles for sex determinations. They also count on forensic anthropology and forensic odontology specialists.

It is important to explain that medical examiners, with exceptions, are not specialists in pathology. So when they perform the autopsy, they send the selected organs and tissues to the pathology lab, where a certified pathologist on staff, processes the specimens and reports the findings.

At a second level there are the SEMEFOs with a nucleus of medical examiners and some of the afore-mentioned laboratories and collaborators. When they need some tests outside their capabilities, they ask for support from the adequate institution at the State or even from the Federal District.

Finally, at a third level, there are the small units with few medical examiners, sometimes only one or two, an autopsy technician and, maybe, a photographer and a field criminalist. These units may request help from the upper levels, which may send personnel or ask for the transfer of the body. Fortunately, because they are in small communities, criminal cases do not often happen.

20.2.7 Role in court
In Mexico an arrested individual is presumed innocent, with the burden of evidence being on the State to prove culpability. The prosecution and defense present their cases before a judge who must then weigh the evidence and give a verdict.

Until now the Mexican judicial system tries an individual with a judge only, but that is changing progressively, because of the new laws that will be implemented throughout the Republic in the course of seven years, having an adversary system and a jury system.

The medical examiner in his or her role as official expert can be summoned by the judge to clarify doubts or to discuss face to face with the opposing expert. This is done under the system of full disclosure and therefore all the files are available to both parties. The medical examiner is called by the judge, but he is independent and he has the right to sustain his technical conclusions.

20.2.8 Training and certification
Since the 1980s, to qualify as a legal medicine specialist it is mandatory to have, at the very least, two years of graduate training. For that purpose, there are several postgraduate courses promoted by universities and schools of medicine that count on the full support of the SEMEFOS of the Federal District and of the most important States. These courses are formal, with a competent faculty, a complete program, practical activities and periodical evaluations.

There is a so-called Mexican Board of Legal and Forensic Medicine that certifies the newly graduated from the above-mentioned courses. This certification is valid for five years, after which another examination is required for recertification.

20.2.9 Education
Education is very active at all the national SEMEFOs. They receive medical and law students at both pre- and postgraduate levels, criminalists, police investigators, odontology and anthropology professionals and students from other disciplines. The students have access to laboratories, mortuaries and other installations and, on certain occasions, they participate with the professors as assistants. The idea is to give a predominately practical education.

As sources of learning, students use modern textbooks, journals and the Internet. The books on forensic medicine are not only from Mexican authors but also from South American, American and European authors.

20.2.10 Working relations with other personnel
The Medical Examiner's Office personnel have constant and close contact with the field criminalists, law enforcement personnel, as well as with those corresponding to the forensic sciences laboratories and public hospitals. In general this relationship is productive and cordial.

20.2.11 Final considerations
After a long period of empirical practice, Mexico now relies on modern forensic medicine. The medical examiners are required to have graduated from a formal and recognized specialty course.

The Medical Examiner's Offices are, for the majority, lodged in adequate, sometimes even new, buildings. The laboratories have better equipment and well-trained personnel.

Currently forensic medicine activities are receiving an increased recognition from the legal authorities, from the medicine and law professionals and from the public in general.

Medical examiners in Mexico are working closely with forensic scientists and are asking for even better installations and lab equipment to enable them to keep pace with scientific advances and to produce better results in the field of justice, as requested by society at large.

20.3 The practice of criminalistics in Mexico

Throughout the 16th, 17th and 18th centuries, the forensic investigation of crimes fell to civil authorities or judges, who with the help of police and, if warranted, doctors, received evidence or went to the place where the crimes were committed. With the global rise in science in the 19th century, professionals in physics, chemistry, biology and pharmacology contributed their valuable knowledge.

In the second half of the last century to these were added the forensic arsenal: fingerprinting, the various methods of identification of people (as influenced by Alphonse Bertillon's studies), as well as ballistics and toxicology. It has been in the early 21st century, however, that laboratories have been instigated and official services, usually assigned to the prosecutor's offices of the States and the Federal District, have been given greater formality and several of the different branches of Criminalistics have developed.

In 1904 Carlos Roumagnac, police investigator and journalist, received a report on the fundamentals of anthropology based on studies made at Belem prison, and in 1907 he founded the Servicio de Identificación de la Inspección General de Policía de la Ciudad de México and published *Elementos de la Policía Científica* (Franco-Ambriz, 1999, pp. 14–20).

In 1914 the fingerprint specialist, Luis Lugo-Fernández, founded in the city of Merida, in the State of Yucatan, the Bureau of Identification, which was named Departamento de Identificación Dactiloscópica and later called Departamento de Registro de Identificación de Delincuentes; much later it was named by Ernesto Abreu-Gómez the Bureau of Identification and Forensic Services or Dirección de Identificación y Servicios Periciales (Franco-Ambriz, 1999, p. 15).

In 1920, in Mexico City, Professor Benjamin A. Martinez created the Office of Identification and Forensic Laboratory of the Police Headquarters. He wrote the first known manual on Police and Judicial Scientific work: *Dactiloscopía, Mis Lecciones y una Guía del Operador Dactiloscópico* (Franco-Ambriz, 1999, p. 20).

In 1935 a Scientific Police College was established and in 1938 José Gómez-Robleda, as Director of Expert Services, added Criminology to the Attorney General of the Federal District and Federal Territories, as Escuela Policial de Investigación Científica. In the Directorate of Forensic Services of the Federal District several specialties were integrated into Criminalistics: questioned documents, ballistics, valuation, transit, fires and explosions, and the Crime Laboratory and judicial identification were consolidated.

In 1938, in the city of Toluca, Estado de Mexico, José Rodríguez-Sandoval founded the Bureau of Identification and Criminal Police Headquarters, which in 1954 became a Crime Laboratory.

In 1955, in the State of Jalisco, the Laboratorio de Investigación was created. In addition to fingerprint profiling, ballistics, questioned documents and the investigation of fires were added and in 1977 the Directorate of Forensic Services was founded.

In 1959, José Amezcua-Manjarrez founded the Forensic Laboratory of the State of Chiapas. In 1960, he founded the Laboratory in Michoacan and in 1968 in the State of Durango (Franco-Ambriz, 1999, p. 18).

In 1961 the Technical Forensic Training Institute under the directorship of Dr. Salvador Iturbide-Alvírez was created.

In 1971, Dr. Rafael Moreno-Gonzalez as Director of Forensic Services of the Attorney General's Office of the Federal District and Federal Territories upgraded the facilities and equipment, and implemented new techniques. He counted on the help of Dr. Raúl Jimenez-Navarro (Jiménez-Navarro, 1980, pp. 15–17) as head of the Department of Scientific Research, the chemist Martha Franco-Ambriz (who later wrote the book *Hematología Forense*) (Franco-Ambriz, 1984, p. 14), the dactiloscopyst Arminda Reyes-Martínez (Reyes-Martínez, 1977, pp. 1–16) and the photographer Julio Tiburcio-Cruz, as well as other collaborators.

In 1977, Dr. Rafael Moreno-González published the book *Manual de Introducción a la Criminalistica* (Moreno-González, 1977, p. 15), which was followed by many more texts on various themes of the forensic sciences. He also participated as a distinguished Criminalist and Professor in numerous courses, lectures and meetings.

In 1976, the National Institute of Penal Sciences was inaugurated, and with great breadth of vision has held numerous training events for forensic science personnel. Many prosecutors' offices of the various States (which depend on their respective Forensic Services) have created their own professional training institutes, and are a constant source of generations of new experts in all branches of forensic science.

In 1981, in the State of Puebla, la Dirección General de Servicios Periciales was born.

On 19 September 1985, the country suffered a devastating earthquake that affected a large number of buildings. The facilities of the Forensic Services of the Federal District were destroyed along with lab computers. This resulted in an urgent need for new equipment which meant (on top of everything else) getting data up to date. The following were acquired, among others: spectrophotometers, ultraviolet and infrared light, an atomic absorption spectrophotometer, a gas chromatograph, equipment for automatic processing of photography and an immunoassay kit with a scanning electron microscope X-ray analyzer.

Later an Automatic Fingerprint Identification System (AFIS) was implemented and by 1994 the Laboratory of Forensic Genetics was launched. It is worth noting that in Mexico, criminalistics has been exercised in a unitary manner, in which there is close collaboration between experts working in different specialties.

In the major cities these specialties are mostly covered by technicians or specialized professionals, but as we move to smaller towns, expert services or criminalists have to cover several branches given that the forensic personnel is not available. In these cases support from professional laboratories is requested to resolve specific issues.

The following is a breakdown of the different branches of criminalistics.

20.3.1 Fingerprinting

The country's forensic laboratories historically had for the vast majority a fingerprinting unit to which other specialties were gradually added. Fingerprint experts became competent after a long period of apprenticeship with the leading experts who were self-taught and had forged the way. Little by little guidelines appeared and in 1977 the book *Dactiloscopía y otras Técnicas de Identificación* by the leading fingerprint expert Arminda Reyes-Martínez (Reyes-Martínez, 1977) could be counted on.

The road of fingerprinting has been a long one; from finding, cataloguing and the painstaking sorting by the expert, who was confronted with tokens or cards from large files, to the present automation of the process (AFIS), which offers speed and multiple chances of a successful identification. In Mexico, there are now many laboratories that have this resource. Experts in this field are taught in various official institutions and by learned

individuals. To become an expert they must sit for an examination of selection and then are given refresher courses. If necessary, these experts are called upon to go before the judge to testify and to clear up doubts on their opinions.

20.3.2 Questioned documents

Questioned documents have long remained in the realm of the empirical, as it was not until the 1970s that it underwent serious systematization. María de la Paz Vega-Corona is considered one of the pioneers in the field, as a trainer as much as an expert. Josefina Mendoza-Vargas and Elsa Fernández-Brondo developed a guide for the recommended analysis methodology and for drawing conclusions. This guide was used for a long time in the courses offered by the Technical Training Institute of Criminology Office of the Federal District (Franco-Ambriz, 1999, pp. 19–20). Later, these courses were provided at official and private institutions, most notably the *Instituto Nacional de Ciencias Penales* and the *Institutos de Formación Pericial de las Procuradurías and Universities* throughout the country.

The recruiting experts are subjected to an entrance exam and are offered periodical refresher courses. They also may be asked to appear before the courts to defend their opinions.

20.3.3 Ballistics

The study of firearms and projectile weapons has evolved from the 18th century, in which the same basic visual inspection was made, through the use of simple microscopes, to increasingly sophisticated comparisons, to the latest computerized technology (IBIS).

As in the above-mentioned disciplines, to be employed in the Forensic Services one is required to have taken accredited courses at recognized institutions (that typically add military retirees, from the service of war materials), which in any event are continuously updated activities. It goes without saying that they are expected to come before the judges, if needed.

20.3.4 Traffic accidents

In this section accidents in land, air and water vehicles are studied. The experts are professionals in mechanical engineering related to the type of vehicle. They also receive courses and training for research on the methodology of accidents; from where they occur, to the reconstruction of the scene, to careful surveys determining if the accident originated due to mechanical failure or if there was a human error involved.

In this specialty, the usual work of field experts is to collect evidence such as skid marks, paint chips of the vehicles, fragments thereof, etc., to be sent to an appropriate laboratory. It is also the routine activity of the forensic photographer. If multiple deaths are recorded, medical experts intervene.

20.3.5 Field criminalistics

Specialized experts in the methodology are required to go to the place where a crime took place. Usually several of them go as a team to the crime scene; it consists of a forensic, chemical and ballistics expert, a photographer, a fingerprinting expert, a forensics expert, etc., depending on the crime involved in each case. They collect all kinds of evidence, pack it and label it, and initiate a chain of custody that is destined for the laboratory that such materials require. This is a truly multidisciplinary work, in which the experts are constantly updating their knowledge.

20.3.6 Forensic chemistry

The laboratories are well equipped in the State capitals and in Mexico City. The provision in smaller and less important cities is less varied and in some cases only has equipment for basic tests. When the need is beyond the scope of these places, they ask for help from senior levels within the expert system.

An equivalent phenomenon occurs in regard to specialized technical personnel who, in most cases, have a previous career in the field of chemistry. At the start of their careers they are trained in the preparation of reports for the judicial authorities, as well as the behavior to be observed when they are required to go to the scene of the crime.

20.3.7 Toxicology

As part of chemical laboratories or specialized laboratories working on the identification and quantification of drugs, drug abuse, pesticides and poisons in general, they count on equipment that can detect these substances, even in minimal concentrations.

Before advances in technology, in the early laboratories, color development reactions, thin layer chromatography and crystallography were used, which at the time, and with the dedication of the experts, yielded useful results. In 1980, Dr. Raul Jiménez Navarro published

the text entitled *Materia de Toxicología Forense* that contributed to the improvement of this important branch (Jiménez-Navarro, 1980, pp. 15–17). Today's experts are skilled professionals with a high level of competence.

Of course, not all geographic locations have the expensive sophisticated equipment necessary. Here again, there are varying degrees of competence and there may be cases where they solicit aid from other institutions.

20.3.8 Fires, explosions and building collapses

These areas have qualified professionals, who are able to make good field studies, draw correct conclusions regarding the causes, sequence the events and results of such disasters, and finally write technical reports that are useful to the judicial authorities in front of whom they may be called to testify. These experts often participate in meetings and refresher courses in their field of work.

20.3.9 Disaster preparedness

In Mexico the government has implemented a National Center for Disasters Prevention, which intends to apply the technologies for the prevention and mitigation of natural and man-made disasters. Many official institutions participate to this purpose, particularly the Army with its Plan DN-III-E in protection of the civil population. Of course the Forensic Services collaborate in those actions whenever they are requested.

20.3.10 Forensic genetics

In Mexico, the application of genetics to forensic investigation is very recent, dating from the late 20th century, and due to the high cost, is limited to senior institutions that are located in Mexico City and in some State capitals. However, the profitability of DNA technology is well known and it is relied upon with increasing frequency, which means the number of laboratories that can have such a valuable resource will, in the near future, increase in the country.

In functioning genetic laboratories specialized personnel perform their duties with efficiency and reliability. To date the most frequent use of genetics is for the identification of live and dead persons and establishing paternity.

20.3.11 Specialties of limited development

In Mexico there are some specialties that are under-represented in institutional laboratories, namely, entomology, psychiatry and digital sciences and multimedia in a forensics application. Except for a small number of expert services (particularly located in the city of Mexico), laboratories do not count on specialized personnel in these disciplines. When studies are needed, they collaborate with other agencies or hire qualified people from the private sector.

20.3.12 Final considerations

Forensic science in today's Mexico gets the attention it demands. It is important that laboratories develop in varying degrees, according to their geographic location, ranging from laboratories in Mexico City to the State capitals to the minor towns of these States. However, there is ongoing concern that the staff recruited only has a minimum of training needed for the tasks they are expected to perform and, once hired, that they cannot count on regular activities that lead to constant improvement.

20.4 Practice of physical anthropology in Mexico

The remotest antecedent in this field is the Department of Anthropology of the Penitentiary in the Puebla State, Mexico. It was founded on 2 April 1891 by Dr. Francisco Martinez-Baca and Dr. Manuel Vergara. They made meticulous measurements, statistics, photos, etc., and published the results in 1892 (Rodríguez-Manzanera, 2013, pp. 404–405).

By the mid-20th century few marginally scientific articles relating to Physical Anthropology and Criminology were published: *Breves notas Acerca de la Colección de Cráneos de Delincuentes del Museo Nacional* by Javier Romero-Molina (Romero-Molina, 1939, pp. 167–176), *La Criminología y una Técnica de Craneologia Constitucionalista* by Anselmo Flores (1945), *Ensayo de Antropología Criminal el Reclusorio de Perote, Veracruz* by Felipe Montemayor-García (Montemayor-García, 1995, pp. 35–58) and *Craneología y Criminología* by Anselmo Marino-Flores (Marino-Flores, 1964, pp. 123–146).

One work published in 1973 with the title *Método de Superposición Radiológica Craneal con Fines de Investigación Identificativa* by Luis Vargas-Guadarrama and

Mario Alva-Rodríguez (Vargas-Guadarrama and Alva-Rodríguez, 1973, pp. 353–358) and another, *Aspectos Anatómicos del Método de Superposición Fotográfica Cara-cráneo con Fines Identificativos* by Mario Alva-Rodríguez (Alva-Rodríguez, 1974, pp. 5–12) could be the obvious way of connecting the two disciplines: Criminalistics and Physical Anthropology (Romano-Pacheco, 2003, 185–186).

In 1975, the Laboratorio de Investigación Criminal de los Servicios Periciales de la Procuraduría de Justicia del Distrito Federal received human remains that were in an advanced state of putrefaction, partially skeletonized, among which a human head was found. The Director of Forensic Services, Dr. Rafael Moreno-González, at the suggestion of Dr. Felipe Pardinas, Anthropologist and Philosopher, invited the Master Physical Anthropologist, Arturo Romano-Pacheco, to undertake the study of the remains (Romano-Pacheco, 2003, p. 188). From this case, Professor Romano was called upon to act as an expert witness, whenever any corpses, skeletons or parts thereof came to the institution that had not been identified previously and those for which the cause of death was not known.

This prompted interest from other Forensic Services that were interested in having this specialty and this gave rise to numerous courses in Mexico City and in several States, some of which were with the valuable participation of experienced Physical Anthropologists Douglas H. Ubelaker, Ted A. Rathbun and John W. Verano. Later (in 1997), the National Institute of Forensic Science, under the guidance of Physical Anthropologist Dennis C. Dirkmaat, held a course on techniques for locating and the recovery of cadaveric remains of clandestine burials.

To date there are now many laboratories that have at least one physical anthropologist, or, lacking one, hire a specialist to solve specific cases or ask the support of institutions of such specialty. Experts in forensic physical anthropology have the corresponding title and have completed one of the many courses at various public universities, prominent among which are those offered by the Institute of Anthropological Research of the National Autonomous University of Mexico.

In 1993 an agreement was signed between the Attorney General of the Federal District and the National Autonomous University of Mexico to study the physical characteristics of the face of the Mexican. Anthropologists traveled all over the country to take pictures of the face and profile of many people from diverse communities, including indigenous groups, mestizos and creoles. In a brief interview an information card stating age, sex and place of birth of the person and his ancestors was filled. Color photographs, accurately obtained, were subjected to sharpness and digitized studies. Phenotypic variables of facial features, with metric, morphological and pigment data were recorded. Metric data and angles to 145 variables for each subject were obtained, which was useful for computerized facial reconstruction as well as to predict the changes of aging individuals. Thus a catalog of Mexican faces was obtained in a single computer image, which reflects the face of a single subject. It is an example of our heritage and a way of locating people. From then on, this study was to be known as "the face of the Mexican".

20.5 The practice of forensic dentistry in Mexico

After the recognition of the usefulness of dentistry in criminal investigation in the second half of the 20th century, Forensic Services began incorporating dental professionals. In 1987, the first course in Forensic Dentistry was held at the Servicio Médico Forense del Tribunal Superior de Justicia del Distrito Federal under the guidance of the prestigious forensic odontologist Dr. Thomas C. Krauss. Following this course, similar ones appeared in the same city and in various States (particularly in Querétaro). In the year 1990 and supported by the Autonomous University of Querétaro, the first formal postgraduate course in the specialty in forensic odontology was held, with a curriculum that lasted for two years.

Today, many Forensic Services have on their staff dentists who are dedicated to the specialty, practicing routine dental examination and applying the results for identification purposes. The boom this specialty received expanded the scope of the clinical observation of bites in cadavers and living persons, which has already led to locating the aggressor in many cases and making the information available to the authorities.

Dental schools around the country introduced forensic dentistry into their curricula, and institutions and private organizations have offered training and upgrading courses in the art. It has been shown that in cases of accidents or natural disasters, as well as clandestine burials, the participation of expert forensic dentists is already required.

20.6 The practice of criminology in Mexico

In Mexico we often turn to the science of criminology as an important auxiliary for the administration of justice. There are multiple definitions of this science, but in this paper we present a relatively simple definition, which has the advantage of demonstrating the lines of work of an expert criminologist: criminology is the science that is responsible for (a) the study of crime as a human and social behavior, (b) the investigation of the causes of crime, (c) crime prevention and (d) the treatment of offenders (López-Vergara, 2000, pp. 17–20).

From these four components we can deduct which objectives will be of use to the criminologist, so that he may assist in solving the problem. For example, an objective is that the offender should be studied comprehensively (as a whole, since this is the only way to individualize sentences and accurately point out the necessary treatments).

Dr. Francisco Martinez-Baca and Dr. Manuel Vergara were the first to make criminological studies of criminal and military men in Puebla, Mexico, and published their findings in 1899 (Rodríguez-Manzanera, 2013, p. 405).

In 1929, Dr. José Gómez-Robleda, when he was Director of the Medical Section and the Laboratory of the Supreme Council of Defense and Social Prevention, integrated criminological medical records (Villarreal-Rubalcava, 1987, p. 175). Dr. Alfonso Quiroz-Cuarón was the first graduate of Criminology, at the National Autonomous University of Mexico, in 1939 (Rodríguez-Manzanera, 2005, p. 144). Both professionals worked together on a series of crimes with great social impact and their conclusions led, decisively, to the discovery and the punishment of the corresponding perpetrator. They were persistent promoters of the discipline and spread it through conferences, courses and publications.

Professors Raúl Carrancá-Trujillo (Carrancá-Trujillo, 1955) and Hector Solís-Quiroga (Solís-Quiroga, 1962) published, respectively, books about Criminal Sociology, which have had an important impact in the field of criminology.

The first edition of *Criminología* by Dr. Luis Rodríguez-Manzanera, who has had a distinguished career as a Professor and Investigator, was published in 1979 (Rodríguez-Manzanera, 1979).

In 1971 Professor Javier Piña y Palacios took over the Technical Institute of the Federal District Justice Attorney and three years later he was able to set the postgraduate criminology specialty in motion, which was upgraded to a Master's program in 1978 (Villarreal-Rubalcava, 1987, pp. 177–178).

In 1976 the National Institute of Penal Sciences was officially established, which in the short term and to date has been providing the Master's program of this discipline, as well as in other areas of criminal sciences (Villarreal-Rubalcava, 1987, p. 178).

Moreover, the Autonomous University of Nuevo León instituted a degree in criminology in 1974, which has been an example for the implementation of this career at other institutions of higher education across the country (Fernández-Sánchez, 2005, pp. 52–54).

As seen, throughout the 20th century and the beginning of the current century, criminology has received great interest in Mexico. It should also be mentioned that its scope has widened, as in the case of professional care to victims of crimes and to those imprisoned in correctional facilities.

References

Alva-Rodríguez, M. (1974) Aspectos anatómicos del método de superposición fotográfica cara-cráneo con fines identificativos. *Criminalia* año XL, nos. 5–12: 459–462, Mayo–Diciembre, México.

Alva-Rodríguez, M. (2010) *Compendio de Medicina Forense* (4ª Edición), Méndez Editores, México.

Archivo Histórico de la Facultad de Medicina, Universidad Nacional Autónoma de México. Fondo Escuela de Medicina y Alumnos 1851–1883, Sección libros, Libro 26, Libro de Juntas de Profesores, México.

Carrancá-Trujillo, R. (1955) *Principios de Sociología Criminal y Derecho Penal*, Ediciones Imprenta Universitaria, México.

Castañeda-Jaimes, A., Herrera-Franyutti, A. (2009) Cien años de la Secretaría de Salud del Distrito Federal. Bayer Health Care, Bayer Schering Pharma, México, pp. 52–55.

Fernández del Castillo, F., Castañeda Velasco, H. (1986) Del Palacio de la Inquisición al Palacio de Medicina, Universidad Nacional Autónoma de México, México.

Fernández-Sánchez, N. (2005) El Criminólogo en México. *Iter Criminis*, Núm.1, Tercera época, Agosto–Septiembre, México.

Flores y Troncoso, F. (1982) *Historia de la Medicina en México*,

tomo III, Edición Facsimilar, Instituto Mexicano del Seguro Social, México.

Franco-Ambriz, M. (1984) *Hematología Forense*, Editorial Porrúa, S.A. México.

Franco-Ambriz, M. (1999) *Apuntes de Historia de la Criminalística en México*, Editorial Porrúa S.A., México.

Hidalgo y Carpio, L. (1869) *Introducción al Estudio de la Medicina Legal Mexicana*, Imprenta de Ignacio Escalante, México, 239 pp.

Hidalgo y Carpio, L., Ruiz-Sandoval, G. (1877) *Compendio de Medicina Legal Arreglado a la legislación del Distrito Federal*, 2 Vols, *Imprenta de Ignacio Escalante*, México.

Jiménez-Navarro, R. (1980) *Materia de Toxicología Forense*, Editorial Porrúa S.A., México.

Lanning, J.T. (1997) El Real Protomedicato. La Reglamentación de la Profesión Médica en el Imperio Español, Facultad de Medicina, Instituto de Investigaciones Jurídicas, Universidad Nacional Autónoma de México, México.

Lima, M. (1986) Control social en México-Tenochtitlan. *Criminalia*, año LII, nos. 1–12, Enero–Diciembre, México.

López-Vergara, J. (2000) *Criminología, Introducción al Estudio de la Conducta Antisocial*, Textos Iteso, México.

Marino-Flores, A. (1964) *Craneología y Criminología. Anales*, t.16, INAH, México.

Montemayor-García, F. (1995) *Ensayo de Antropología Criminal en el Reclusorio de Perote, Veracruz. Anales*, t.6, INAH, México, pp. 35–58.

Moreno-González, L.R. (1977) *Manual de Introducción a la Criminalística*, Editorial Porrúa S.A., México.

Quiroz-Cuarón, A. (1980) *Medicina Forense*, 2ª.Ed., Editorial Porrúa S.A., México.

Reyes-Martínez, A. (1977) *Dactiloscopía y otras Técnicas de Identificación*, Editorial Porrúa S.A., México.

Roa-Bárcena, R. (1869) Manual Razonado de Práctica Criminal y Médico-Legal Forense Mexicana, Segunda edición, Ed. Eugenio Maillefert, México.

Rodríguez-Manzanera, L. (1979) *Criminología*, Editorial Porrúa S.A., México.

Rodríguez-Manzanera, L. (2013) *Criminología*, 27ª ed., Editorial Porrúa S.A., México.

Rodríguez-Manzanera, L. (2005) Alfonso Quiroz Cuarón. *Iter Criminis*, Núm.1, Tercera época, Agosto–Septiembre, México.

Romano-Pacheco, A. (2003) Algunos datos para la historia de la Antropología Física Forense en México y su estado actual. Antropología Física, Disciplina Plural, Instituto Nacional de Antropología e Historia, México, pp.185–198.

Romero-Molina, J. (1939) Breves notas acerca de la colección de cráneos de delincuentes del Museo Nacional. Revista Mexicana de Estudios Antropológicos, Num.3, México, pp. 167–176.

Solís Quiroga, H. (1962) Introducción a la Sociología Criminal. Universidad Nacional Autónoma de México, México.

Torres-Torija, J. (1934) Fundación e historia de la cátedra de Medicina Legal en el Instituto de Ciencias Médicas. Revista de Cirugía Hospital Juárez, año V, núm. 9, Septiembre, Suplemento de la Revista de Cirugía, México.

Torres-Torija, J. (1939) Elogio del Dr. Don Agustín Arellano, primer catedrático de Medicina Legal. In: *El Establecimiento de Ciencias Médicas y sus Primeros Catedráticos*, D.A.P.P., México.

Vargas-Guadarrama, L.A., Alva-Rodríguez, M. (1973) Método de superposición radiológica craneal con fines de investigación identificativa. *Criminalia*, año XXXIX, nos. 9–10, Septiembre–Octubre, 353–358, México.

Villarreal-Rubalcava, H. (1987) La Criminalística en México y sus aportaciones a la investigación judicial. *Criminalia*, año LIII, nos. 1–12, Enero–Diciembre, México, pp. 173–181.

Zacarías-Prieto, M.J. (2010) Luis Hidalgo y Carpio a 140 años de su Introducción a la medicina legal mexicana. LABORATacta, Vol. 22, núm. 1, México.

CHAPTER 21
The Netherlands

Arian van Asten, Wim Neuteboom, Sijtze Wiersma & Zeno Geradts

Netherlands Forensic Institute Ministry of Justice, Den Haag, The Netherlands

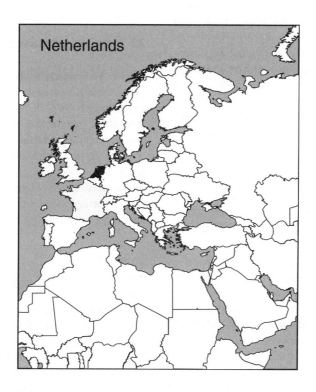

21.1 History

It is generally agreed that modern forensic science started in the beginning of the 20th century with the work of Edmond Locard, Alphonse Bertillon, etc. In those days, the daily practice of forensic science was organized quite differently from how it is today. The work was done by individual scientists without the support of or embedding in a forensic science institute. In those days the forensic scientists were pioneers.

The history of forensic science in The Netherlands is similar to those in most other European countries.

Before World War II, a limited number of Dutch scientists was active (mostly part-time and not as a day job) in what is now called the forensic domain. A well-known name is Co van Ledden Hulsebosch, a pharmacist in Amsterdam, who did his first case in 1902 without any experience after a desperate request from a prosecutor. He wrote his memoirs on 40 years of forensic practice in 1945. This amusing book (Hulsebosch, 1945) without any scientific pretensions has become a classic in The Netherlands. Emile van Waegeningh (1870 – 1944) (Van der Pol and van Boxtel, 2010) was a multitalented man (pharmacist, military, inventor, business man) who

The Global Practice of Forensic Science, First Edition. Edited by Douglas H. Ubelaker.
© 2015 John Wiley & Sons, Ltd. Published 2015 by John Wiley & Sons, Ltd.

contributed substantially to the developments of scientific photography. Police and Judiciary consulted him frequently for these skills with sometimes striking results. Finally, the University of Leiden must be mentioned. Its Faculty of Toxicology (Professor Van Itallie) had a very good reputation regarding forensic toxicology, although it was not its core activity.

A few weeks after the end of World War II in The Netherlands (5 May 1945), a national forensic laboratory (in Dutch: Gerechtelijk Laboratorium[1]) was established as part of the Ministry of Justice. At that time the Ministry of Justice was preferred over the Ministry of Home Affairs (supervising the police forces already). It was presumed that these separate responsibilities would guarantee a more independent position for the newborn institute. The first director was Wibo Froentjes, who held this position till 1974. In 1949 another forensic institute was established in the same building: the Laboratory of Forensic Pathology[2]. Jan Zeldenrust was the director and worked till he was over 80 years of age. Both men are recognized as the founding fathers of forensic science in The Netherlands. In 1999 the two institutes merged and the new name became the NFI (NFI, 2013). It can be called remarkable that their separate status had lasted over 50 years.

From the very start, the NFI was welcomed enthusiastically by prosecutors and judges, as well as defense lawyers. It was emphasized as an important improvement that a forensic institute was in place within the criminal justice system. Its independent and neutral position – truth finding was and is the driving force – was seldom questioned.

During the past decades the NFI has developed steadily in terms of scope of expertise fields, number of employees (from 15 in 1950 to 650 in 2014), adequate premises and budget.

The NFI has been the only forensic institute in The Netherlands for a long time, except for some specialized disciplines. It was not a monopoly position laid down in the Dutch law, but no initiatives were taken by anybody else to establish another forensic institute. This situation changed at the beginning of the 21st century when other, smaller forensic institutes were established.

Finally, the stimulating role of the NFI in the early 1990s as a founding member of the European Network of Forensic Science Institutes (ENFSI, 2013) must be remembered. The aim of the NFI to create a European platform for forensic scientists as well as directors of forensic institutes has been fully met.

21.2 Types of Cases

In the Netherlands several forensic laboratories are active. The government laboratory is the NFI where approximately 90% of the forensic cases are handled. Due to this circumstance, the following overview gives a representative reflection of the Dutch situation. In recent years private labs have entered the forensic market. In several fields of expertise the police will also do investigations, such as fingerprints and digital evidence. For civil cases a wider range of private services for insurance companies exists.

21.2.1 NFI
The NFI covers a wide range of expertise, ranging from chemical identification to medical forensic investigation and from digital to human biological traces. However, Psychiatry and Odontology are not included in these. The NFI is composed of several departments for forensic analysis. Since the organization has a different structure in terms of defining and naming the expertise field compared to the AAFS sections, the links to the different sections are shown in this paragraph.

Within Digital Technology and Biometrics the digital section has expanded very rapidly in the last few decades and contains the following fields of expertise: digital technology ranging from investigations or computers, interception, data analysis, mobile (smart) phones, GPS systems, silicon chip forensics and intelligent data analysis (AAFS: Digital and Multimedia Sciences).

---

[1]The name Gerechtelijk Laboratorium has been changed a number of times, the latest being the Nederlands Forensisch Instituut (NFI) in 1999. For reasons of convenience, the name NFI is always used in this chapter, even if the actual name of the institute was different at the particular time.

[2]This institute has also changed its name a few times before it became part of the NFI.

The biometric part consists of a document and investigation printer, machine and hand writing (AAFS: Questions Documents), finger marks (Criminalistics), speaker audio analysis (AAFS: Digital and Multimedia Sciences), image analysis and biometrics (AAFS: Digital and Multimedia Sciences) and traffic accidents (AAFS: Engineering).

The Department of Forensic Chemical Investigation is composed of a variation of expert fields: chemical identification research (AAFS: Criminalistics) ranging from fire investigation, tear gas and pepper spray investigation, comparison of fuels and oil products and other chemical identification investigation, explosions and explosives (AAFS: Criminalistics), a toxicology laboratory where the analyses for the toxicology department are conducted (AAFS: Toxicology), narcotics (AAFS: Toxicology/Criminalistics), systematic drug analysis, drug comparison and investigation of drug manufacturing plants.

The Front Office has a central Front Desk for the administration of cases that enter and exit the institute, where a separate team gives forensic advice. The Mobile Forensic Team works on the crime scene on request from the prosecutor or police. Furthermore, forensic archeology (anthropology), environmental waste and risks of fire, technical and material research (Engineering Sciences) are located in this department.

The Human Biological Traces Department (AAFS: Criminalistics) has the expert groups on biological traces, DNA research, examining blood trail pattern research and relationship testing.

The Department of Medical Forensic Investigation has the product groups of forensic anthropology (AAFS: Anthropology), forensic pathology (AAFS : Pathology and Biology), forensic medicine (AAFS: Pathology and Biology), forensic toxicology (AAFS: Toxicology) and a photo service.

The Department of Micro Traces (AAFS: Criminalistics) analyses glass and tape, gunshot residue, paint, fibers and textiles, nonhuman biological traces, striation and impression marks and weapons and ammunition.

The Dutch DNA database is a separate organizational unit within the NFI. This unit also manages the DNA databases of the Netherlands Antilles and Aruba and the DNA database for missing persons. The unit performs comparisons within the cross border exchange of information within the European Union under the mandate of the EU Prüm Treaty.

The number of cases are published in the annual report 2012 of the NFI (rounded up to 100):

Digital Technology and Biometrics	1200
Forensic Chemistry Research	8000
Front Office	300
Human Biological Traces	1600
Forensic Medical Examination	2900
Micro Traces	1300

21.2.2 Odontology

In The Netherlands regional odontologists are united in the National Consultation Forensic Odontology (Lofo). Forensic odontologists also form part of the Disaster Identification Team (LTFO, 2013).

21.2.3 Forensic psychiatry

The Netherlands Institute of Forensic Psychiatry and Psychology (NIFP) (NIFP, 2013) is the center of expertise for forensic psychiatry and psychology. It is a national service of the Ministry of Justice and Security, incorporated in the National Agency of Correctional Institutions. The NIFP provides independent psychiatric and psychological expertise (diagnosis, care and advice) to judicial and social chain partners. In this way it contributes to the due course of justice, effective implementation of custodial psychiatric care and treatment, and a safer society.

The Pieter Baan Centre (PBC) is the forensic psychiatric observation clinic of the Ministry of Security and Justice. The clinic is unique due to the fact that it offers multidisciplinary clinical examination, under strict security, with regard to:
– The suspect's person
– The degree of legal accountability of the suspect, at the time of the crimes of which he or she is suspected
– The chance of reoffending.
An examination at the Pieter Baan Centre can lead to a recommendation to the judiciary on possible treatment.

Approximately 250 suspects are examined at the Pieter Baan Centre each year. The magistrate or the judge at the hearing orders the suspect to be placed at the Pieter Baan Centre, after which the suspect is admitted for seven weeks for observation and examination. The Pieter Baan Centre can also be involved for (six-year) extension recommendations of persons held under hospital order, or for recommendations with regard to placement in a long-stay department.

21.3 Structure

As already stated in Section 21.1, History, the NFI has been the only major forensic science provider in The Netherlands for many decades since the late 1940s. Apart from the NFI, a limited number of others – individuals as well as institutes – were involved in forensic science. A number of categories can be distinguished.

There have always been a number of private handwriting experts. The main reason was that there was a need for these experts in cases under civil law. The NFI was very reluctant to do casework under civil law, because it had the opinion that its focus should be on cases under criminal law. Thus a forensic market in this field arose. Moreover, starting a career as a private handwriting expert did not require the purchase of expensive instruments. However, the number of private handwriting experts has never been more than seven individuals. Nowadays, the number is even decreasing because in the digital era handwriting is of less importance.

For practical and economic reasons the NFI cannot cover all forensic disciplines. This applies especially for disciplines that are requested with a (very) low frequency. In these situations, the NFI takes the role of a broker and liaises with universities or other specialized, technological centers. In the course of many years this has resulted in a network of specialists who can be consulted if needed. It is obvious that the NFI scope of forensic disciplines is dynamic; that is, if the frequency of "rarely requested" disciplines increases, the adoption of such a discipline by the NFI is considered. Following this approach, forensic archaeology and forensic knotting have recently been added to the scope of the NFI.

In Dutch drunk driving legislation, the suspect has traditionally the right for a second (contra) analysis of the blood sample by another institute. The suspect can make a choice out of four selected hospital laboratories spread over the country. A similar provision was created in 1994 for DNA analysis. The Department for Human Genetics of the Leiden University (FLDO) (FLDO, 2013) is legally assigned to perform the contra-analysis on the request of the suspect. These two kinds of analyses (alcohol and DNA) are the only ones for which the suspect has – under strict rules – the legal right to have a contra-analysis performed in another forensic institute, checking the reported results of the NFI. Within the Dutch jurisdiction, there is not a universal right to have a contra analysis. If a suspect has serious doubts on the correctness of the report by the NFI or another forensic institute, the judge can decide to repeat the forensic examinations elsewhere.

The identification of fingerprints belongs to the domain of the Dutch National Police. A specialized department is responsible for the central, digital database (AFIS). In 10 regional police stations, spread over the country, data input facilities are in place; the database can be consulted on-line at about 150 police stations and prisons. Currently, the database includes 30,000 million fingerprints and 3 million hand palm prints, which requires a computer capacity of 30 terabytes. The number of unknown perpetrators in the database is 115,000; the number of the fingerprints of known individuals is over 900,000. On the average 250 identifications per day are done by the National Police.

The privatizing of the forensic institutes in England and Wales in the first decade of the 21st century had an influence on the debate in The Netherlands as well. Voices were heard to follow this approach, that is, to transfer the forensic institutes to the private sector. Others were of the opinion that a forensic institute is a fundamental part of the national criminal justice system and should thus be positioned under the full responsibility of the government. Besides these views, it was also stated that a monopoly position (whether in the private or in the public sector) is for reasons of principle not appropriate. Although unintended, the NFI had de facto achieved a monopoly position. From a legal point of view, there have never been any objections for having more than one forensic institute in The Netherlands. The police, prosecutors and lawyers are free to involve other forensic institutes or experts. It is up to the judge to admit their conclusions in the court room.

An important reason that other forensic institutes were not established is due to the funding system. The NFI is financed by the Ministry and does not charge its customers (police and prosecution for over 90%). Potential, new forensic institutes lack the funding by the Ministry and have to charge their customers. It is obvious that this situation gives the NFI a great advantage. In spite of the above-mentioned barrier, a number of new forensic institutes on a commercial basis have entered the field in the past 10 years. These are the main ones:

- Verilabs (Verilabs, 2013) – established in 2002 – cooperates closely with a series of partner institutes, e.g. Baseclear and LGC Forensics in the UK. It has a focus on pathology and toxicology. Furthermore, Verilabs has the ambition to operate also in other countries.
- Independent Forensic Services (IFS) (IFS, 2013) was founded in 2003 with expertise in the fields of forensic medical issues and bloodstain pattern analysis. In 2011 a second laboratory was built in the USA. IFS performed investigations and appeared in court in some famous cases in various countries.
- The Maastricht Forensic Institute (TMFI) (TMFI, 2013) was established in 2008 by the Maastricht University and DSM Resolve with financial support from the European Commission and the Province of Limburg (region in the south of The Netherlands). It aims for a broad range of forensic disciplines.
- The Centre for Forensic Pathology (CFP) (CFP, 2013) has its focus on pathology, but cooperates with other institutes, resulting in a broader, medical-oriented scope.
- Fox-IT (Fox-IT, 2013) was established by two former employees of the NFI in 1999 and has a forensics division that is specialized in digital investigation and also has divisions on crypto and cybercrime.

Given the current financing system of the forensic institutes in The Netherlands, the sustainability of these new institutes will become clear in the future.

21.4 Integration of forensic sciences

Investigations at the crime scene are primarily the responsibility of the police. The first responders decide on the need for involvement of special crime scene investigation (CSI) teams. Formally the public prosecutor is the head of the investigation, but in practice this role is only actually played in serious crime cases.

The Dutch National Police is structured into 10 regional units, geographically spread over the country. Each regional unit has a forensic department equipped for crime scene investigations. Besides collecting evidence at the crime scene, the CSI teams have facilities to perform some types of forensic examinations, like tool marks, foot, ear or tire prints and drugs screening. Apart from these examinations, usually the CSI teams

submit evidence to the forensic laboratory for regular or additional examinations.

In order to control the caseload of the laboratory, each year an agreement on the maximal number of exhibits to be submitted is made between the police and the NFI. A set of criteria for various types of crimes were formulated on this maximal number. Another element of the agreement is a maximal turnaround time guaranteed by the NFI. This way of working has the advantage that the turnaround times of cases in the laboratory are reasonable and predictable.

On the request of the police, the forensic laboratories are prepared to advise and assist the CSI units in complex and/or specialized cases. The NFI has created a mobile forensic team, focused on capital crimes. The number of attendances of the mobile forensic team is 70–100 a year. The members in this team work in close cooperation with the NFI experts in the laboratory.

Incidentally, the NFI organizes a so-called forensic intake. This is only done for very complex cases and happens about 20 times a year. Prior to the start of the laboratory investigations, a strategy for the investigation is discussed with all partners: police officers, prosecutor and forensic experts. This has proven to be very useful for these types of cases.

Integration of reports (from various expertise fields and from police, forensic institutes and others) is a goal, but in daily practice it is seldom realized. Serious attempts are going on to structure this process, but have showed to be an intractable problem.

21.5 Recruitment

Forensic scientists are hired by vacancies that are published on the public website of the forensic science provider. It has a wide variety of fields that are hired, ranging from pathologists, physicists to biologists or computer scientists. The announcement includes – among other things – the job requirements in terms of education and experience, and the requirement for reporting officers to have a good general knowledge of the Dutch language. Furthermore, a certificate of good conduct is necessary (Justis, 2013) and for several positions a security clearance of the General Intelligence and Security Service (AIVD) is necessary (AIVD, 2013).

21.6 Training

In the early 1990s, the NFI – the dominating forensic institute in The Netherlands – started an internal education and training program for its employees. The underlying notion was that an academic degree in, for example, chemistry or physics followed by an undefined introduction on the job by a senior colleague was too little. The program is meant for incoming as well as experienced employees and is rounded off with an examination. A successful exam gives the employee the authority to sign a forensic report and to be called as an expert witness in court. This status as a reporting expert is limited to a period of 4 years and can be prolonged after having passed another examination. It must be emphasized that this approach is not laid down in any formal law or requirement – it was started by the NFI on its own initiative during the establishment of its quality management system. It can be qualified as an internal certification.

What are the features of the NFI education and training program? Firstly, it was recognized that – on top of a set of general principles — forensic science includes a broad scope of many (sub-) disciplines. It is obvious that the competences for experts on handwriting, DNA, ballistics, etc., are quite different. This recognition has led to different programs for each and every forensic discipline; the NFI has defined about 35 forensic disciplines. The actual program is divided into two major parts: a general part (identical for all disciplines) and a specific part (different for the particular disciplines). The basis of the program is the question: "What are the needed knowledge, skills and attitude to perform adequately as a forensic expert in discipline X?" Elements of the general part are Dutch law, forensic reporting, statistics and practices in a moot court. The specific part focuses on experience with the techniques and methodologies within the particular discipline. During the exam for the specific part, the candidate expert is interviewed by a panel of experts about a series of draft reports written by the candidate expert. Furthermore, participation in scientific meetings and publishing in scientific journals are taken into account. Finally, it must be demonstrated that an expert has executed a minimal number of cases annually to get a prolongation of his or her expert status. Usually the panel consists of internal as well as external experts in order to enhance its independence.

In The Netherlands several Universities provide forensic education:

- A Master in Forensic Science is available from the University of Amsterdam, which is the only MFS program in The Netherlands. Within the University of Amsterdam there is also a track on Forensics within the MSc System and Network Engineering.

The full time Bachelor programs within The Netherlands on Forensic Science are from:

- The University of Applied Sciences in Amsterdam.
- The University of Applied Sciences Saxion.
- The Universities of Applied Science Zuyd and Leiden provide a Bachelor program on Forensic ICT.

Within the University of Applied Sciences in Amsterdam a minor on Forensic ICT is provided within the Bachelor program Informatics.

21.7 Funding

Within The Netherlands a large part of the forensic investigations in criminal investigations is funded by the Ministry of Security and Justice. For the NFI a budget of 67 million euro is foreseen in 2014 with 4 million euro additional income, such as EU funding, additional casework, training and R&D paid by other agencies. In Forensic Psychiatry 683 million euro will be spent in 2014 for various institutes.

Since 2007 police, public prosecution and the NFI set up a "service level agreement (SLA)" where the amount of casework, research and development (R&D) and education research capacity of the NFI was fixed. Specifically herein are the agreements related to the influx, production and delivery of products and services of the NFI. If the number of cases exceeds the SLA, additional casework can be bought by extra funds from the customers.

Other forensic providers within The Netherlands get paid on a case by case basis.

21.8 Political Influences

Within The Netherlands, the influence of political climate and shifts of political orientations do not influence the forensic science reporting. With austerity measures from the government and reduction of funds, the number of cases that can be handled within the SLA and the amount spent on Research and Development will become lower.

21.9 Quality assurance

As a logical consequence of the introduction of quality management systems (usually based on ISO 17025) in the 1990s and 2000s in a lot of European forensic laboratories, the attention for the competences of forensic scientists increased. It was recognized that the competence of forensic scientists is a keystone in the quality of the work performed by the forensic laboratories.

In later years, the competences of court experts became the subject of Dutch legislation, not only for experts in the natural sciences but also for experts in, for example, forensic psychiatry. The Netherlands Register of Court Experts (NRGD, 2013) was created in response to the new Experts in Criminal Cases Act. This Act was unanimously adopted in 2009 by the Upper House of the Dutch parliament and took effect on 1 January 2010. The NRGD has been realized under the auspices of the Ministry of Security and Justice. This took place by means of a number of expert meetings and with a broad working group, including the Public Prosecution Service, the Council for the Judiciary, the Dutch Bar Association, the National Police, the NFI and The Netherlands Institute for Forensic Psychiatry and Psychology.

The NRGD is the first register for court experts with a legal basis, independent position and structural financing. To date the appointment of experts is possible for the following disciplines: DNA analysis and interpretation (source level), handwriting, weapon and ammunition, forensic psychiatry and psychology, toxicology and drugs.

During 2013, 470 experts were registered in the Netherlands Register of Court Experts divided over the following distinguished disciplines:

Discipline	Number of registered experts
DNA analysis and interpretation	20
Handwriting	3
Weapon and ammunition	6
Forensic psychiatry and psychology	431
Toxicology	7
Drugs – analysis and interpretation	3

The aim of the new Experts in Criminal Cases Act is dual. On the one hand it is intended to strengthen the position of the defense counsel. The Act explicitly grants a suspect the right to request an additional investigation or counter inquiry. On the other hand, the Act signifies a tightening up of the quality, reliability and competence of court experts. In the near future, the Public Prosecutor will – in principle – only appoint experts from the Register.

21.10 Laboratory accreditation and quality control

Dutch law does not require forensic laboratories to be accredited. Exceptions are made for DNA and some environmental analyses. However, the current situation shows that all forensic laboratories in The Netherlands are accredited. The accreditations are based on ISO 17025 (ISO, 2005) in conjunction with the ILAC Guideline 19 (ILAC, 2002). The NFI already achieved its accreditation in 1994 being the second forensic institute in Europe – the first one was the Forensic Science Service (FSS) in the UK. The Raad voor de Accreditatie/Dutch Accreditation Council (RVA) (RVA, 2013) is signatory to the International Laboratory Accreditation Cooperation (ILAC, 2013) and the World Association of Conformity Assessment Accreditation Bodies (IAF, 2013). Due to the existence of the ILAC Mutual Recognition Arrangement, the accreditations of the Dutch forensic laboratories are recognized in over 60 countries worldwide. Furthermore, the RVA is a member of the European cooperation for Accreditation (EA, 2013), the association of national accreditation bodies in Europe. The EA cooperates with the European Network of Forensic Science Institutes (ENFSI, 2013), resulting in joint documents,[3] which are relevant for the European forensic community.

Current developments within the forensic quality assurance domain in The Netherlands are:
- Increasing the segment of laboratory analyses
- Including nonstandard analyses
- Including opinions and interpretations (at source level)
- Introducing of flexible scopes

[3] Example: Guidance for the Implementation of ISO/IEC 17020 in the Field of Crime Scene Investigation, ref. EA-5/03 (December 2008).

- Introducing of ISO 17020 to crime scene activities and some particular fields (e.g. archaeology)
- Introducing of ISO 15189 to pathology and toxicology.

Since the late 1980s the NFI and the Dutch police cooperate in formulating so-called forensic technical norms. The aim of these joint norms is to harmonize the work processes from the crime scene to the submission of evidence to the forensic laboratory. Currently, about 75 norms are in place, indicating issues like collecting, transport, storage and labeling of evidence. Additionally, special investigations kits (DNA, hair, gunshot residues, textile, fire accelerators, etc.) were developed. It is obvious that for both parties this way of cooperation is very beneficiary in terms of quality and efficiency.

21.11 Technology

In this section the main areas of R&D covered by the NFI are described, although this does not cover the whole forensic arena in The Netherlands. Due to the NFI's dominating position, it reflects the situation within The Netherlands adequately.

In forensic investigation and innovation the availability of state-of-the-art technology plays a key role. The NFI maintains a substantial investment budget to ensure that the latest analytical, medical, physical and IT equipment can be used to study forensic evidence and conduct forensic investigations. In recent years the NFI invested in the following state-of-the-art equipment:

- Dual beam SEM (scanning electron microscope) with a focused ion beam mainly for gun shot residue and forensic digital technology application including physical hardware decryption
- High resolution orbit trap LC-MS (liquid chromatography–mass spectrometry) system for highly selective and sensitive compound identification and quantification in complex matrices
- Gas chromatography coupled to an isotope ratio mass spectrometer for pure compound isotope ratio measurements
- Fully automated and custom made system for DNA extraction, quantification, multiplication and extract storage
- Comprehensive GCxGC-TOF MS (comprehensive two-dimensional gas chromatography with a time-of-flight mass spectrometer) system for full two-dimensional separation of complex samples of forensic interest for chemical profiling and target compound analysis
- Infinite focus microscope for the three-dimensional investigation and quantitative characterization of tool and firearm marks laser ablation ICP-MS (inductively coupled plasma mass spectrometry) system for quantitative analysis of trace elements in microtraces such as glass fragments, paint chips, human hair, ink lines and fibers.

In the case of highly specialized and expensive equipment that is not used frequently or for which the investment is not economically viable the NFI seeks strategic partnerships with institutes, companies and universities to ensure access to the equipment and required expertise. Forensic radiology is, for instance, often applied in forensic autopsies but medical imaging on human remains is not performed at the NFI but in two Dutch hospitals with which the NFI has made special arrangements.

Forensic technology is not always available as commercial equipment or accessible through partnerships. In dedicated innovation programs the NFI has recently developed in-house forensic technology. Through the new NFI products, business line in-house technology is sold to international customers. For several products patent applications have been filed and a professional tool or product has been developed. These products and tools are offered "not for profit" but to cover development costs and to ensure sufficient funds for R&D at the NFI in future.

Examples of such tools and products developments include a special Faraday cage to shield smartphones and mobile phones (without shutting them down) that have been secured as evidence. Additionally, the NFI has developed a state-of-the-art Memory Toolkit that allows the read-out of recorded digital data on mobile phones for a large range of makes and models. The institute also offers various tailor-made forensic software packages such as Bonaparte for familial DNA searching for rapid and accurate human identification in Disaster Victim Identification (DVI) situations. Another example is a PRNU (photo response nonuniformity) compare, a software package allowing digital pictures to be compared and linked to cameras on the basis of camera sensor pixel artefacts. The XIRAF/Hansken system of the NFI offers a complete digital forensic platform where digital evidence can be uploaded. The large and often heterogeneous data are indexed and mapped by the system, allowing case officers to search the evidence in an efficient and effective manner.

Finally, great potential exists for ICT applications in the criminal justice system. In The Netherlands, as in many other countries, criminal investigations are still recorded and documented in paper-based dossiers. It is anticipated that great improvements in terms of speed, efficiency and quality can be achieved in the entire criminal justice chain if all documents, reports and dossiers were to be made up digitally. At the NFI a comprehensive program is currently in progress to change from a paper-based archive to a digital archive including an LIMS for processing laboratory data and a system for fully digital forensic case files. This would allow customers to receive NFI information almost in real time and to monitor the progress of ongoing forensic investigations. A fully digital forensic archive would also facilitate intelligent data analysis and knowledge management of the data that are created on a daily basis from the casework at the NFI.

21.12 Disaster preparedness

Since 2005 the NFI has invested in knowledge, expertise and capacity with regard to forensic investigation under disaster conditions, that is, in the aftermath of serious industry incidents or terrorist attacks. Under the umbrella of an institute-wide CBRN program (C = chemical agents, including warfare agents, B = biological agents and RN = radioactive and nuclear agents), forensic expertise has been developed to provide a fast and effective forensic response after a major incident in The Netherlands or abroad.

This capability has been embedded in the standing forensic organization of the NFI and this new expertise has been added to existing forensic expertise areas:

- Forensic expertise of C agents is provided by the forensic toxicology and forensic engineering specialists.
- Forensic expertise of B agents is provided by the non-human biological traces specialists.
- Forensic investigation of RN agents is provided by the forensic explosives and forensic engineering specialists.
- Disaster Victim Identification capability is provided by the human biological traces (familial searching experts) and forensic anthropological specialists.

- Medical diagnosis of CBRN victims is provided by the forensic physicians.

Additionally, a CBRN R&D and innovation program has been established focusing on traditional forensic investigations (digital evidence, finger marks and other human biological traces) under CBRN conditions and on CBRN forensics, that is, the forensic identification, classification and individualization of C, B and RN agents.

The NFI currently has the following capabilities to perform forensic investigations after a national or international disaster:

- Forensic support at the scene of crime or scene of incident by C, B, RN, digital, explosive, medical and trace experts capable of performing an investigation with protective gear including gastight suits. This includes full logistic support with several specialized vehicles.
- Forensic investigation of evidence secured after a CBRN incident or terrorist attack (direct investigation at partner laboratories equipped to handle C, B or RN agents or investigation at the NFI after decontamination).
- A portfolio of new forensic methods to investigate C and B agents as such and in toxicological samples.
- Rapid and accurate identification of deceased victims in the case of mass fatalities through familial DNA searching using a special software package (i.e., Bonaparte, developed with Radboud University in Nijmegen) and forensic anthropological sampling and study (the methodology was used for the identification of the 103 victims in the airplane crash of Afriqiyah Airways Flight 771 on 12 May 2010 in Tripoli).

The development of the forensic CBRN expertise at the NFI has been financed by the Dutch government but recently the NFI has been successful in raising international funds for its CBRN program. The NFI currently participates in several CBRN related projects funded by the European Union under the Framework 7 Program FP7 (CORDIS, 2013). The recently submitted FP7 GIFT proposal involves a consortium of 21 partners from nine countries. This CBRN project is the first granted EU effort to be fully coordinated by the NFI and will start early 2014.

21.13 Legal issues

In 2010 a reform took place to the law on experts and expert evidence in criminal procedures. The establishment of a national public register of experts became law in Dutch legislation and can be found in a new Title in the Code of Criminal Procedure (CCP, 2013). The judge, the public prosecutor and the defense counsel have the opportunity to appoint experts who meet generally approved standards. Not only the special knowledge but also the expert's ability to work in a forensic context is important.

Rules can also be found in the Register of Experts in the Criminal Cases Decree (Besluit Register Deskundige in Strafzaken, 2009). An independent Board of Registered Experts (College Gerechtelijk Deskundigen) have the task to set standards to registered experts and decide on applications to be registered (Besluit Register in Strafzaken, 2009). An application for registration will only be considered if the application relates to a field of expertise, which can be reviewed and substantiated on the basis of established norms. If so, the Board will set specific standards in a specific field of expertise (e.g., DNA), based on an advice of representative international experts in this specific field of expertise. Not only is special knowledgerequired but also familiarity with the role and position of the expert in the criminal procedure (Besluit Register in Strafzaken, 2009).

The expert must fulfill his assignment independently, impartially, with due care and attention, professionally and with integrity. These requirements are elaborated in the Code of Conduct, established by the Board of Registered Experts.

The appointment of experts is bound by new rules. The public prosecutor and the assistant public prosecutor (police) may only appoint an expert who is listed in the Register of Experts. Appointment by the police is restricted to experts in a technical field, except the appointment of DNA experts for research only on traces.

In practice the police do not appoint an expert because the Board of Procurators General did not decide which fields of expertise are labeled as technical. Not all research in preliminary investigations has to be executed by forensic experts. Forensic standard investigation in the context of a criminal investigation is often done by the police.

The CCP contains several articles that give the investigating judge the right to appoint experts on his or her own initiative or on the request of the defense counsel or the public prosecutor. He or she can also appoint experts to check the report of a previous expert or an expert who observes or reviews an investigation carried out by a previous expert. The CCP contains some specific articles covering the appointment of a counter-expert in DNA research.

Only the (investigating) judge may appoint an expert who is not listed in the register of experts. Testing this expert by the requirements of Article 12 of the Decree is a necessary condition. If an expert is appointed by the investigating judge he or she will inform the public prosecutor and defendant of this decision. This information can temporarily be withheld in the interest of the criminal investigation. It is now a legal possibility for an expert to contact the investigating judge to get clarity about the content and the reach of his or her appointment.

The law on experts has also strengthened the position of the defendant. It grants a suspect the right to be informed by the prosecutor of the appointment of an expert, although this information can temporarily be withheld in the interest of the criminal investigation.

The defendant may also request the public prosecutor as well as the (investigating) judge for an additional investigation or counter inquiry (Art. 150 a.b, 2012). If the prosecutor rejects a defendant's request, it may be in writing and should be well substantiated, but the investigating judge is authorized to overrule this refusal. Furthermore, the defendant can also decide to approach an expert, but has to pay the expert's costs. The CCP contains a provision which gives the defendant the right to request the clerk to advance money for expenses and to request the court to refund the amounts expended for the expert.

In addition to that the law on experts requires that the expert provides an opinion "that his knowledge teaches him". The expert has to provide an explanation as to how he arrived at his conclusion in his report. Furthermore, he has to mention which method of research he applied, why he considers this method reliable and to what extend he is competent in his application of the method. The expert declares that he drafted his report truly, complete and to his best opinion.

During the pre-trial investigation the defendant has access to the content of written documents, for example, expert's reports, except if the interest of the criminal investigation requires that this information should temporarily be withheld from the defendant.

An expert may report verbally at the court session or in writing. Both are types of evidence. The oral opinions of experts, written down by a police officer in an official police report, may also be used as evidence.

A formal requirement that the Court of Cassation applies strictly is that experts – if heard by the court – must take the oath. The Court of Cassation considers the oath as a guarantee of the validity and reliability of the testimony

In Dutch law there is an absence of admissibility rules. The rules take the form of decision and argumentation rules. The court does not have to restrict itself to the evidential material presented by the public prosecutor and/or the defense. In the end it is up to the trial court to decide whether (forensic evidence) is reliable and can be used as evidence.

The court has the right to engage the help of a counter-expert, whether on the court's initiative or that of the defendant or public prosecutor (Art. 315,328 CCP). The Dutch Court of Cassation has decided that defendants have a right to counter-expertise. They must make an explicit, motivated and timely request in order to be allowed to retest (forensic) evidence.

Dutch courts are bound by the requirements of the European Convention on Human Rights and particularly the requirements set forth in Article 6 of that treaty (the right to a fair trial). In some cases the European Court has decided that the court must ensure that the expert is neutral and that there are circumstances under which the use of court experts may breach the right to a fair trial, for example, that the court does not treat the experts on behalf of the defendant in the same way as it treats the experts against the defendant. Furthermore, courts must afford defendants the opportunity to contest and refute the expert evidence against them at trial.

21.14 Research

The NFI has three primary tasks:
1. Conduct forensic investigations in casework
2. Develop and innovate forensic methods and tools
3. Center of knowledge and expertise on forensic science.

To ensure a state-of-the-art portfolio of forensic investigative methods the NFI maintains a substantial R&D program. Research findings and innovations form the basis for new forensic investigation methods that are added to NFI's product portfolio after successful validation.

Recently introduced novel, state-of-the-art forensic methods, tools and products from NFI's innovation program include:
- RNA analysis to determine the origin of human biological traces
- Bullet cytology based on RNA typing
- High speed products: DNA profiling within 6 hours
- Three-dimensional tool mark investigation with infinite focus microscopy
- Investigation and comparison of partial and distorted finger marks
- Web based service center for digital evidence investigation
- Advanced chemical profiling of illicit drugs and explosives
- Characterization and comparison of nonhuman biological traces
- Forensic statistics product portfolio
- Microanalysis invasive traumas
- Interdisciplinary investigations.

The NFI operates from a strong customer focus and hence innovations aim at maximizing the forensic information value added whilst minimizing the delivery time and cost of the investigation. Starting from 2014 the NFI will focus its innovation efforts even further by establishing seven innovation programs.

21.14.1 Real time, on-site chemical identification
Developing robust methods that allow chemical analysis and identification directly at the crime scene without the need for experts.

21.14.2 Forensic recognition and individualization
State-of-the-art analyses of forensic biometric, biological and chemical crime scene traces in order to provide investigative leads on suspects in the absence of reference material.

21.14.3 Digital Forensic Service Center
Creating a digital platform that will allow police investigators to effectively search large amounts of "heterogeneous" digital evidence. The platform also includes a toolbox with intelligent data analysis methods to assist and direct the data search.

21.14.4 From source to activity

Fundamental scientific studies and the use of statistical methods for combining evidence to allow evidence evaluation at the activity level.

21.14.5 Advancing forensic medicine

Using modern technology and medical imaging for minimal invasive autopsies and introducing interdisciplinary forensic approaches to enable the manner of death instead of the cause of death investigations.

21.14.6 CSI innovations

Introducing state-of-the-art technology and tools allowing crime scene officers to record, detect, select and analyze crime relevant traces and to record and document the crime scene investigation.

21.14.7 CBRN forensics

Developing an extensive toolbox for forensic investigation of incidents, crimes and terrorist attacks involving chemical, biological and/or radioactive nuclear agents.

21.14.8 Benefits of the programs

Each program will consist of a set of interdisciplinary projects to ensure relevant innovations in each area to meet the customer needs and advance forensic science. For projects to be successful it is important that customer participation is ensured, relevant academic expertise is available and the innovation capability of high tech companies is included. As forensic science is an applied science, emerging technology in other domains can provide substantial forensic potential. This is why the NFI maintains a broad international innovation network of companies, knowledge institutes and companies. Various special forensic chairs (biological traces, statistics, analytical chemistry, criminalistics and speech comparison and analysis) have been created at three Dutch universities to ensure a sound academic connection and to create opportunities for collaboration and funded forensic research. The NFI participates in several forensic projects and consortia that are funded nationally and internationally.

21.15 Future directions

In 2013 the CEO of the NFI published a vision white paper titled "Trends, Challenges and Strategy in the Forensic Science Sector", which can be downloaded in English and Spanish from the website of the NFI (NFI, 2013). This document reflects a vision of the NFI on the rapid changes in the forensic sector in recent years and years to come. These changes are linked to the increasing importance and impact of forensic science in the criminal justice system and thus not only lead to challenges but also to great opportunities in the forensic sector.

The NFI has recognized four important trends both on a national and international level that will shape the future of forensic science:

1. Growth. The NFI has seen spectacular growth since its start in 1945. The case load handled by the NFI in 2012 was roughly six times higher than the number of requests processed in 2000. In the meantime the workforce of the institute nearly tripled from 200 to 600 coworkers. This growth has been typical for the forensic sector and has been fueled by the introduction of new forensic technology, allowing a more detailed analysis of even smaller forensic traces. Typical examples of new forensic capability include DNA profiling of human biological traces and the extraction and investigation of digital forensic evidence. Interestingly, the largest departments of the NFI dealing with these types of evidence did not exist at the institute 20 years ago. Additionally, with the ongoing technological developments in forensic science the demand for forensic investigations is also increasing. In the criminal justice system new methods that can solve crime quickly gain popularity and lead to an increasing number of requests. This can be considered as a very natural phenomenon, successful innovations leading to new and relevant forensic possibilities will grow the forensic market.

2. Customer focus. The forensic institutes are changing from internal, expertise-oriented and skill-based organizations into professional, technology driven institutes with a strong customer focus. As customers inside and outside the criminal justice system are relying increasingly on forensic information they become more demanding in terms of the quality, robustness, versatility, speed and cost of the provided forensic services. As a result the NFI has instigated a strong sense of customer focus in its organization. In a special effort, including the introduction of a lean six sigma process optimization, in a period of five years the substantial case load was

diminished and average delivery times were reduced by more than 90% to an overall average delivery time of less than 14 days at the end of 2012. An important instrument in the fight against the backlog was the introduction of a Service Level Agreement with key national customers. By balancing supply and demand for over 30 forensic expertise areas an increasing workload is prevented and a fast delivery of results is guaranteed.

3. Defragmentation. Forensic science is intrinsically a fragmented domain. It is fragmented in the sense that a large number of individual forensic expertise areas are recognized, covering a wide range of scientific fields. Forensic experts usually only work within a single expertise area and do so in a relatively independent, solitary manner. Furthermore, each country usually handles and maintains its own forensic investigations. This is caused by the fact that criminal laws have a strong domestic character. Penal laws and proceedings tend to differ from country to country and consequently on a global scale there is a large number of relatively small forensic institutions. From an efficiency and quality perspective this is a far from ideal situation and from a purely forensic viewpoint there are no limitations to a more global and interdisciplinary approach. As the forensic community develops into a high-tech, customer focused sector, the NFI anticipates that custom-made interdisciplinary investigations will evolve and that institutes with sufficient critical mass for constant innovation and improvement in given forensic expertise areas will provide forensic services on a global scale.

4. Forensic awareness. With an increasing role of forensic science in the criminal justice system and with new technology leading to complex forensic investigations there is an increasing demand for forensic training and education. Customers of forensic services will require an increased knowledge and awareness to use the forensic information that has been generated upon their request effectively and efficiently. For this reason the NFI created the NFI Academy in 2010. The NFI Academy maintains and develops a professional portfolio of forensic training and courses for the customers of NFI products, services and investigations. This portfolio includes basic awareness courses, e-courses on criminalistics principles, hands-on workshops, table-top exercises and expert training up till the complete forensic

conferences. Course attendants represent the entire criminal justice system (police, public prosecutors, lawyers and judges) but forensic courses are also provided for a broader customer base including, for instance, military personnel and first responders.

21.15.1 Forecast
21.15.1.1 The Netherlands
Within the Netherlands it is expected that complicated forensic investigations using a Bayesian approach will be commonly used in the criminal justice system. Also the results of examinations should be available faster by using new technologies and first results should be available within 48 hours after a crime has happened. It is foreseen that the number of forensic scientists within The Netherlands remains stable, but shifts between expert fields can occur.

21.15.1.2 European Union
Also within Europe it is expected that fields that require high costs and are not often used will be concentrated in certain locations. Furthermore, the vision for European Forensic Science 2020 (European Commission, 2012) will provide more standardization within forensic science in Europe, so cross-border examinations can be easily used in other member states:

> In order to foster cooperation between police and judicial authorities across the European Union with a view to creating a European Forensic Science Area by 2020, Member States and the Commission will work together to make progress in the following areas, aiming to ensure the even-handed, consistent and efficient administration of justice and the security of citizens:

- accreditation of forensic science institutes and laboratories;
- respect for minimum competence criteria for forensic science personnel;
- establishment of common best practice manuals and their application in daily work of forensic laboratories and institutes;
- conduct of proficiency tests/collaborative exercises in forensic science activities at international level;
- application of minimum quality standards for scene-of-crime investigations and evidence management from crime scene to court room;
- recognition of equivalence of law enforcement forensic activities with a view to avoiding duplication of

effort through cancellation of evidence owing to technical and qualitative differences, and achieving significant reductions in the time taken to process crimes with a cross-border component;

- identification of optimal and shared ways to create, update and use forensic databases;
- use of advances in forensic science in the fight against terrorism, organized crime and other criminal activities;
- forensic awareness, in particular through appropriate education and training of the law enforcement and justice community; research and development projects to promote further development of the forensic science infrastructure.

References

AIVD (2013) *Veiligheidsonderzoek.* [Online] Available at: https://www.aivd.nl/onderwerpen-0/item-2800/forms-security/ [Accessed 8 8 2013].

Art. 150 a.b (2012) Book I CCP.

Besluit Register Deskundige in Strafzaken (2009) Stb. 330.

Besluit Register in Strafzaken (2009) Stb. 330.

CCP (2013) *IIIC Book I.* Staatsdrukkerij, Den Haag.

CCP (n.d.) CCP. In: *Title IIIC.* s.l.:Rijksoverheid, p. Book I.

CFP (2013) *CFP.* [Online] Available at: www.forensischpatholoog.nl [Accessed 8 8 2013].

EA (2013) *European Co-operation for Accreditation.* [Online] Available at: www.european-accreditation.org [Accessed 8 8 2013].

ENFSI (2013) *ENFSI.* [Online] Available at: http://www.enfsi.eu [Accessed 8 8 2013 and 13 8 2013].

European Commission (2012) *Vision for European Forensic Science 2020.* [Online] Available at: http://www.consilium.europa.eu/uedocs/cms_data/docs/pressdata/en/jha/126875.pdf [Accessed 8 8 2013].

FLDO (2013) *FLDO.* [Online] Available at: www.fldo.nl [Accessed 8 8 2013].

Fox-IT (2013) *Fox-IT.* [Online] Available at: www.foxit.nl [Accessed 8 8 2013].

Hulsebosch, C. v. L. (1945) *Veertig jaar Speurderswerk*, Kemink en Zonen, Utrecht.

IAF (2013) *IAF.* [Online] Available at: www.iaf.nu [Accessed 8 8 2013].

IFS (2013) *IFS.* [Online] Available at: www.forensic-services.nl [Accessed 8 8 2013].

ILAC (2002) *ILAC Guideline*, ILAC, Silverwater, Australia.

ILAC (2013) *ILAC.* [Online] Available at: www.ilac.org [Accessed 8 8 2013].

ISO (2005) ISO 17025, s.l.: s.n.

Justis (2013) *Justis.* [Online] Available at: http://www.justis.nl/Producten/verklaringomtrentgedrag/information-in-english/ [Accessed 8 8 2013].

LTFO (2013) *Over LTFO.* [Online] Available at: http://www.ltfo.nl/index.php?option=com_content&view=article&id=16:slachtofferidentificatie&catid=7:over-ltfo&Itemid=135 [Accessed 13 08 2013].

NFI (2013) *Netherlands Forensic Institute.* [Online] Available at: http://forensicinstitute.nl [Accessed 19 08 2013].

NIFP (2013) *NIFP.* [Online] Available at: https://www.nifpnet.nl/default.aspx?tabid=164 [Accessed 8 8 2013].

NRGD (2013) *NRGD.* [Online] Available at: http://english.nrgd.nl [Accessed 8 8 2013].

RVA (2013) *RVA.* [Online] Available at: www.rva.nl [Accessed 8 8 2013].

TMFI (2013) *TMFI.* [Online] Available at: www.tmfi.nl [Accessed 8 8 2013].

Van der Pol, P., van Boxtel, H. (2010) *Kapitein van Waegeningh.* Breda's Museum, Breda.

Verilabs (2013) *Verilabs.* [Online] Available at: www.verilabs.nl [Accessed 8 8 2013].

CHAPTER 22

History and current status of forensic science in Singapore

George Paul & Paul Chui

Forensic Medicine Division, Health Sciences Authority, Singapore

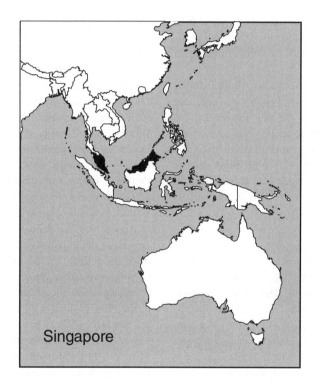

Singapore

22.1 History within the country

The Republic of Singapore is a sovereign city-state and an island country at the southern tip of the Malay Peninsula in Southeast Asia. Its geographic location is 137 kilometres (85 miles) to the north (or 1 degree north) of the equator. Made up of the lozenge-shaped main island (widely known as *Singapore Island* but also as Pulau Ujong (its native Malay name) and over 60 much smaller islets, it is separated from Peninsular Malaysia by

the Straits of Johor to its north and from Indonesia's Riau Islands by the Singapore Strait to its south. The country is highly urbanized, with very little primary rainforest remaining. Its territory has consistently expanded through land reclamation.

The earliest recorded settlement on the island dates back to the 2nd century AD. Modern Singapore was founded in 1819 by Sir Stamford Raffles as a trading post of the East India Company with the permission of the Johor Sultanate (the ruler or Sultan of Johor,

The Global Practice of Forensic Science, First Edition. Edited by Douglas H. Ubelaker.
© 2015 John Wiley & Sons, Ltd. Published 2015 by John Wiley & Sons, Ltd.

one of the southern states of Royal Malaysia). At that time the settlement was largely Chinese in population, with a tiny but important European minority. The British obtained sovereignty over the island in 1824 and Singapore became one of the British Straits Settlements in 1826 (*Singapore Free Press*, 3 January 1861). It became the penal settlements for Indian civilian and military prisoners (Anderson, 2007), earning them the title of the "Botany Bays" of India (Nicholas and Shergold, 1988), with minor uprisings by convicts in Penang and Singapore in 1852 and 1853 (Turnbull, 1970). From 1867 it became a Crown colony, directly answerable to the Colonial Office in London instead of the Indian government in Calcutta, India, with a colonial constitution also granted.

After the Japanese overran British Malaya during World War II, Singapore was invaded in February 1942 shortly afterward. After the war, the colony was dissolved in 1946, with Singapore becoming a separate crown colony – ultimately getting freedom from the British in 1963, to initially unite with other former British territories to form Malaysia, from which it separated two years later. Since then it has had its independent constitution. Singapore is a parliamentary republic with a Westminster system of unicameral parliamentary government representing constituencies. Its constitution establishes representative democracy as its political system (US Central Intelligence Agency, 2014). Executive power rests with the Cabinet of Singapore, led by the Prime Minister and the President (http://en.wikipedia.org/wiki/Politics_of_Singapore). The president is head of state and is elected through popular vote and has some veto powers for a few key decisions but otherwise occupies a ceremonial post (http://www.istana.gov.sg/content/istana/thepresident.html).

Singapore practices the common law legal system, where the decisions of higher courts constitute a binding precedent upon courts of equal or lower status within their jurisdiction, as opposed to the civil law legal system in continental Europe. Some of the laws reflect the influence of its former colonial association with England and English laws applicable to and prevalent in Singapore before 1867, as well as Indian Laws and Imperial Laws, and Strait Settlement Acts and laws after this period (Chan, 1995). In addition, certain Indian Laws such as the Penal Code and Evidence Act, of Indian origin (Chang and Lin, 1995), were adopted when Singapore was a crown colony. Criminal law, company law and family law are completely statutory in nature.

The legal system of Singapore is based on English common law, albeit with substantial local differences. The decisions of higher courts constitute binding precedent upon courts of equal or lower status within their jurisdiction, as opposed to the civil law legal system in continental Europe. Major areas of law – particularly administrative law, contract law, equity and trust law, property law and tort law – are largely judge-made, though certain aspects have been modified by statutes.

However, the criminal law of Singapore is largely statutory in nature. Trial by jury was entirely abolished in 1969 leaving judicial assessment performed wholly by judgeship, and the Criminal Procedure Code was amended in 1992 to allow for trials of capital offences to be heard before a single judge (*Milestones in Singapore's Legal History*, http://app.sup remecourt.gov.sg/default.aspx?pgID=39, retrieved: 22 February 2014). Singapore has penalties that include judicial corporal punishment in the form of caning for rape, rioting, vandalism and some immigration offences (World Corporal Punishment Research, 2012; Kuntz, 1994). Previously the final court of appeal was the Privy Council in London, but in 1994, after a permanent Court of Appeal was established in Singapore, the process of appeals in death penalty cases to the Privy Council was done away with by the Constitution of the Republic of Singapore (Amendment) Act 1994 (No. 5 of 1993), repealing article 100 of the Constitution, with reference to the Privy Council of appeals from the Supreme Court (of Singapore). There is a mandatory death penalty for murder, and for certain drug-trafficking and firearms offences (US Department of State, 2013), though, with increasing public and legislative discussions on the need to be humane, certain situations among these cases have of late been attracting life imprisonment instead of the death penalty. The Court of Appeal is Singapore's final court of appeal after the right of appeal to the Judicial Committee of the Privy Council in London was abolished in April 1994. The President of Singapore has the power to grant pardons on the advice of the cabinet (Attorney-General of Singapore, 2013).

In the late 18th and early 19th centuries, all toxicological and other forensic analyses were conducted by the Analyst, Government of Singapore. The Analyst was also responsible for all kinds of medical and other scientific investigations, including microbiological and parasitological investigations, and thus was an integral part of the health care system and was integral to the early Singapore Medical School for teaching and training in these subjects.

Inquiries into deaths were reportable to the Coroner (State Coroner) under the tenets of the Criminal Procedure Code. After the enactment of the Coroner's Act 2010, those relevant sections were deleted from the Criminal Procedure Code, with the Coroner's Act governing procedures and penalties related to reportable coroner's cases and inquiries into those deaths.

22.2 Types of cases

As Singapore is a city-state, the nature of forensic cases bear a similarity to that in other major cities in the world, except for a low crime rate, attributed largely to effective policing, strict drug laws, strict firearms control and the imposition of capital punishment for serious offences such as murder and drug trafficking. Caning or corporal punishment may be imposed over and above incarceration. The drug control measures are calculated to deter both trafficking into the local scene and cross-border activities through Singapore, as well as to reduce addict recidivism. Although a large majority of Singapore males form the conscript army and are well versed with the use of military weapons, the strict control of access to firearms by the civilian population has meant that firearm related incidents and deaths have been few and far between.

22.3 Structure

The first documented involvement of scientists in criminal cases is through the Annual Reports of Straits Settlements, in 1885, when the Government Analyst. Dr Bott, reported toxicological, food and drug, points of dangerous petroleum and blood tests. In 1907 the Singapore laboratory was serving the whole of Malaya and Singapore, but 2 years later, a branch was opened in Penang and in 1946 in Kuala Lumpur. In 1939 the title was changed to Chief Chemist and the department was the Department of Chemistry, a legacy still continuing in Malaysia. In 1947 the three departments in Penang, Kuala Lumpur and Singapore were headquartered in Singapore. The early interests of the department were mainly related to commercial issues and commercial crimes – testing opium, liquors and drugs, as well as petroleum, denaturation of alcohol, explosives and ship

inspection – much less in criminal cases. A 1946 report talks of the change from caustic soda for suicide shifting to the use of barbiturates, as well as an accidental admixture of barium salts in baker's flour. Methanol deaths were also reported (DSS Annual Report '89, 1989, pp. 1–37).

In 1955 an Inspectorate of Dangerous Materials was established under the Department of Chemistry. After Independence in 1957, all three departments became independent of each other, with each having its own regional chemist. The first non-British Director of the Singapore Department of Chemistry was appointed in 1959. By this time, reports such as that of 1958 mentioned blood stained exhibits from frequent gang clashes.

Before World War II and immediately after, medicolegal autopsies were conducted mainly by surgeons, in fact any government doctor of authority, with annual reports mentioning names of surgeons and their findings in autopsy cases.

Anatomical pathologists started conducting autopsies in the late 1960s with a full time forensic pathologist finally taking over medicolegal autopsies.

In 1976, the Department of Chemistry was renamed the Department of Scientific Services, directly under the Ministry of Health. Gradually various testing units came up under it, viz. the Radiation Protection Inspectorate (1972), Microbiology Laboratory (1973), Chemical Engineering Section (1974), Narcotics Unit (1976), Urine Testing Unit (1977), Regulatory Drugs Unit (1980), Carcinogenic Laboratory (1988), Advanced Instrumentation Laboratory (1988), Computer Centre (1988) and Cigarette Testing Laboratory (1988). By this time there were three divisions within the Department of Scientific Services: Forensic Science, which had the Forensic, Narcotic, Toxicology and Document Examination laboratories under it; the Health Science Division, which had Food, Pharmaceutical, Industrial Health, Environmental Cigarette Testing laboratories and R&D Coordination and Planning under it; and lastly the Resource and Radiation Division, which had Radiation Protection, Advanced Instrumentation, Customs Laboratories and Material Management and Computer Centres under it. Soon emergency toxicology, including clinical toxicology analysis, was set up within the Toxicology Laboratory for analytical services to hospitals in suspected overdose and poisoning cases.

Subsequently, the Department of Scientific Services (DSS) was formed, comprising the Health Science

Division, Forensic Science Division and Resource and Radiation Division, while the Department of Forensic Medicine (DFM) comprised both the Forensic Pathology Division and the Clinical Forensic Medicine Division.

With the devolution of hospitals into autonomous operational entities and the subsequent formation of vertically integrated healthcare clusters (from primary healthcare to tertiary care) in the 1990s, the Ministry of Health moved, with Parliamentary approval under the Health Sciences Authority Act, to form the Health Sciences Authority in 2001.

The Health Sciences Authority brought together the Forensic and Scientific Services (previously under ISFM), the Bloodbanking Services and the National Drug Regulatory Services. Over a period of organizational reorganization, three major operational groups were formed:

a. The Applied Sciences Group, which comprises the Analytical Science (Chemical Metrology, Food Safety and Pharmaceutical Divisions), Forensic Medicine and Forensic Science (Biology, Forensic Science, Illicit Drugs and Analytical Toxicology Divisions), the Quality Department along with the Group Director's Office.

b. The Blood Services Group secures the nation's blood supply and comprises the following branches: Blood Resources, Blood Supply, Patient Services and Clinical Services.

c. The Health Products Regulation Group comprises the Pre-marketing Division (Western Medicine, Medical Devices, Complementary Health Products and Cosmetic Products branches), Post-marketing Division (Vigilance, Compliance Enforcement and Medical advertisement branches), the Audit and Licensing branch and the Group Director's Offices.

A brief description is now given of the various divisions and their nature of work.

The Forensic Medicine Division (FMD) provides forensic medical consultancy services in the examination of Coroner's cases. Its forensic consultancy services (including autopsy work) have also been provided to clients from neighbouring regional countries. The pathologists also attend crime scenes, in order to support scene investigation by the Singapore Police Force (SPF) in homicides and suspicious deaths. They work closely with the Criminal Investigation Department (CID). The division is constantly reviewing its work processes and upgrading its technical capabilities (including the implementation of postmortem CT since 2010). In addition,

FMD offers clinical forensic medical consultations by transferring and applying its professional expertise gained in understanding trauma and injury in the dead, to the living cases on subjects of violence resulting from child abuse, sexual offences and spousal abuse. As part of a one-stop service to the next-of-kin, it acts as an agent of the Registry of Births and Deaths, providing the death certification services for Coroner's cases.

In the SARS outbreak in 2003, the FMD provided its autopsy services in support of Singapore's effort to understand the pathophysiology of SARS, and made significant improvements in biosafety practices in the handling of suspected highly infectious cases. This culminated in a patented novel invention, a mobile containerized BSL4 autopsy suite. Forensic Odontologist services are provided through a former Singapore Armed Forces ex-colonel Forensic Odontologist, who is currently in private practise but still responds to forensic odontology calls. A few more army odontologists are training overseas to be forensic odontologists. A full-time Forensic Anthropologist is not available, as there are not enough skeletal remain cases to justify hiring one. Overseas Forensic Anthropologist consultants have been appointed, along with similar experts in radiology, anatomical pathology, etc. Similarly, the various other divisions have their overseas consultants appointed on a nominal retainer arrangement, to be activated for consultation, as and when important cases crop up for their independent opinions.

The Forensic Science Division offers forensic examination for physical evidence: viz. fire, firearms and explosions, chemical analysis and trace evidence, marks, impressions, etc. The Division also carries out scene analysis and reconstruction. Its Documents Lab is one of the few worldwide that is qualified to examine both English and Chinese handwriting and signatures, tampered and counterfeit documents, differentiation of inks, etc. For arson and fire scenes, the preliminary scene investigation is carried out by the Singapore Civil Defence Force (SCDF). In shipboard incidents, the primary investigator is the Port of Singapore Authority, while that of worksite incidents is the Ministry of Manpower. Evidence that is recovered is then submitted to the HSA for testing by the Forensic Science Division.

The Illicit Drugs Division offers analytical services and consultancy to law enforcement agencies in the examination of drug seizures and detection of controlled drugs, as listed in the Misuse of Drugs Act (Cap. 185). The Division also provides test services to support the routine urine testing of drug suspects and parolees as part of the drug control program.

The Analytical Toxicology Division offers analytical services on drugs of abuse testing in urine and clinical and forensic toxicological testing in biological fluids, and supports the Forensic Medicine Division in their routine autopsy cases by screening their biological fluids and tissues for drugs and poisons, etc.

The Biology Division provides human identification and forensic biological services. The DNA Profiling Laboratory at the Health Sciences Authority was established in 1990. The Laboratory is the only DNA laboratory in Singapore to be accredited by the American Society of Crime Laboratory Directors/Laboratory Accreditation Board (ASCLD/LAB). The Laboratory also adheres to the DNA Advisory Board (DAB) Quality Assurance Standards for Forensic DNA Testing Laboratories. The Division collaborates with the Singapore Police Force in establishing and operating a DNA database for convicted offenders in Singapore.

The Pharmaceutical Division of the Health Sciences Authority provides analytical services for the quality and safety of drugs (Western medicines, traditional medicines, health supplements), cosmetics and cigarette testing. Testing services are offered to hospitals, clinics, traders and the Health Products Regulation Group, the HSA. HSA's Cigarette Testing Laboratory analyses tar, nicotine and carbon monoxide in mainstream smoke constituents and tobacco products.

The Food Safety Laboratory specialises in testing of processed foods, in support of the Agri-Food Veterinary Authority of Singapore (AVA) for contaminants that occur naturally (e.g. Mycotoxin), contaminants from the environment (e.g. organic/inorganic pollutants), contaminants migration from food contact materials (e.g. Bisphenol A), as well as contaminants from food processing (e.g. 3-MCP).

Digital and multimedia investigations are not covered by the HSA but by specialized officers of the CID, who have had training in these aspects. The CID also has its own cyber crime division, which investigates and testifies in court relating to evidence discovered and proving of cyber crimes.

22.4 Integration of forensic science

While crime scenes are handled by the scene of crime officers from the Police, forensic scientists and pathologists may be called to attend to the scene, as the case dictates. At the scene, professional advice is sought and given as to how the crime scene may be preserved, documented and evidence recovered optimally. Training and education outreach to law enforcement enable the value of forensic testing services to be more appreciated. Regular interagency operational meetings translate to closer working ties and closure of feedback loops for process improvements. In addition, a high level cross-agency taskforce has been formed to oversee the development of forensic science and better process integration between the Investigator and the Scientist.

Within the HSA, cross-entity interactions are formalized into standard operating procedures so that evidence may be examined by different laboratories efficiently and effectively, without the need for resubmission or inconvenience to the Investigator.

Reports are submitted to the law enforcement agencies and then forwarded to the Public Prosecutor. Forensic autopsy reports are sent to the Police Investigator as well as the Coroner, and may be accepted as prima facie evidence in court if not challenged by the defence, without the need for court attendance by the expert. In the decision to prefer charges against the accused, the Public Prosecutor may discuss the case with the Scientist or Pathologist in order to understand the findings better. Access to the scientist for interviews by the Defence is upon request and concurrence of the Public Prosecutor.

Legal presentation in court is in response to summons to the officers of the HSA to give evidence and be cross-examined. Evidence is individual and specific to his/her specialty so that no charge of collusion can be brought on the expert. Although forensic experts are called by the Prosecution, forensic experts present their cases objectively, without fear or favour.

22.5 Recruitment

Recruitment for scientists and staff is carried out both locally and overseas. Local recruitment is done via local media. Incumbent staff may apply for vacant positions. For overseas recruitment, external agencies are used to head-hunt persons with particular skillsets and experience. Advertisements in professional journals may be used to publicize the vacancies. A formal job application and interview process is in place to assess suitability of candidates. Applications are evaluated on the basis of merit, aptitude and suitability. Scientists are generally brought in at graduate level Second Class Honours or higher scores. Laboratory officers are either graduates or diploma holders from local polytechnics.

A young doctor who wishes to specialize in forensic pathology has first to opt for a 6 month posting with the Forensic Medicine Division in order for his/her suitability to be assessed. An annual traineeship selection exercise is held nationally for medical graduates to apply for specialization, and this applies to forensic pathology as well. The applicant has to undergo a formal interview with a panel under the Joint Committee for Specialist Training (JSCT) of the Specialist Accreditation Board (SAB) for evaluation before training can commence.

22.6 Training and certification

The HSA has put in place various in-house training programs to ensure that their staff are properly trained to perform their roles.

Forensic scientists at the HSA are individually certified by his/her peer group in the lab duties that he/she perform, per accreditation requirements, eg. ASCLD-LAB, SINGLAS (Singapore's equivalent of ISO certification), before they are allowed to sign out cases independently. In addition, HSA also has technical training attachment/exchange programs with some overseas institutions of repute in the same disciplines.

Medical Officers who are accepted for specialization in forensic pathology will train in both forensic pathology as well as spend time with anatomical pathology departments, over a period of seamless training that lasts for 5 to 6 years. To become qualified practising specialists, they will have to either pass the Royal College of Pathologists (UK) examinations or the Royal College of Pathologists Australasia examinations for them to be recognized by the Specialist Accreditation Board and placed on the roll of specialists in Pathology. The training period also includes an overseas attachment to a forensic pathology department so that the individual gains greater exposure in various types of cases. Only those Pathologists working as Forensic Pathologists with the HSA can be notified in the national government Gazette as being Forensic Pathologists (under the Coroner's Act 2010), thus enabling them to independently undertake forensic autopsies at the HSA.

While some of the US specialty boards in Forensic Pathology may be recognized, the need to clear basic residency fellowship followed by Anatomical Pathology and then Forensic Pathology makes the US route too lengthy for Singapore's training considerations.

Postspecialization, there is a mandatory Continuing Medical Education (CME) program that requires all medical practitioners to fulfil a minimum of CME points every two years before they can continue to practice.

For all scientific and medical staff, in-house courtroom training is also conducted, with mock-trials involving public prosecutors and district judges participating and presiding, shadowing one of the senior scientists/consultants to court, etc., as well as attending difficult or complicated scene or case analysis. During the course of their dealing with in-house live cases under supervision, they also learn the legal framework of their work, as well as come to know many of the persons involved in these cases, from investigators, including police and CID, the coroners, Forensic Pathologists (if they are from a scientific background), etc.

The HSA has further put in place in-house training programmes to ensure that its staff remain updated and competent. A minimum target of 40 training hours a year per employee is set as the performance appraisal target to be achieved. Attendance at conferences for presentation and publications for peer-reviewed journals are encouraged. A modest amount is also made available for research projects.

The HSA also has its own funded scholarships and training programs for deserving candidates, to be trained locally or even overseas, for development of various subdisciplines or expertise, subject to bond for continuance of service after successful completion of their training and qualification by serving the HSA. Such opportunities are offered right up to doctorate levels (PhD) in their specialty.

22.7 Funding

Operational Funding of the HSA is through a combination of fee recovery from users of its services, as well as government subvention. The formula for subvention is negotiated with its parent Ministry periodically. Depending on the nature of the projects, capital or investment funding for strategic development may be injected into the HSA from the parent Ministry of Health from time to time.

Forensic laboratories, in following the prescribed practices and services model of the Singapore government, have to negotiate service level agreements (SLA) with their key clients (e.g. the Singapore Police Force, Central Narcotics Bureau). Some analytical laboratories have to compete in tendering processes for work with other government agencies. Certain scientific laboratories that service internal clients (other departments in the HSA) adopt cross-charging models to promote financial accountability and efficient usage (e.g. the Toxicology Laboratory charges the Forensic Medicine Division for the latter's use of its toxicology services).

The Forensic Medicine Division is expected to achieve full-cost recovery for its operations. It has a standard fee schedule for all the cases it does – with a lower fee for externals only (signed outs) and a larger single fee for full autopsies (which would include all necessary ancillary investigations relevant to the case). Revenue collected is expected to cover all nature of expenses from expenditure on manpower to equipment acquisition, rental and expenditure on testing services requested (e.g. toxicology, microbiology and testing for channelopathies – the latter by looking for gene markers associated with conduction defects, etc.).

The funding model has enabled ongoing improvement in terms of technology and capabilities as the expectations on funding by the FMD continue to increase over the years.

Funding has no bearing on the outcome of cases. Funding is forecasted annually through a series of senior management discussions and iterations before the Board approves the finalized budget. Fee increases are notified in advance to clients. Billing is carried out in accordance with a schedule of fees approved by the Board. Billing takes place after the cases are reported, regardless of the outcome in court proceedings.

22.8 Governance

The HSA is governed by a Board of Directors whose members are professionals from both the public and private sectors and are appointed by the Ministry of Health. The Chairman of the Board is appointed by and reports directly to the Minister of Health. The Board oversees the Chief Executive Officer, who sees to the day to day running of the organization. Professionals of the specialty oversee the scientific operations and have freedom

within the framework to report on their cases independently without influence from higher management.

22.9 Political influences

Singapore is conscious and proud of its international reputation of honest dealings and fairness. Behind the cases, there is a constant drive to achieve efficiency and optimization while performing at the highest level. The speed at which things turn around may seem to the "outsider" to be unrealistically fast or "acquiescent" to external influence. However, if the truth be told, forensic practitioners have full scientific independence in how their cases are managed and they defend the integrity and independence of their work rigorously.

The Courts and Attorney-General's office demands no less objectivity from the reports that are produced by the scientists and pathologists of the HSA and expect them to stand up to international scrutiny when the situation occurs. Often, when contested, the expectations are that the work complies with international standards and can withstand external audit.

From time to time, interagency interaction between the HSA and stakeholder agencies takes place, to identify future directions for the development of forensic pathology and forensic sciences in order to meet future challenges.

22.10 Laboratory accreditation/ quality control

The forensic analytical and toxicology labs. The forensic laboratories achieved accreditation by the American Society of Crime Laboratory Directors/ Laboratory Accreditation Board (ASCLD/LAB) under the ASCLD/LAB Legacy Program in June 1996. In June 2012, the forensic laboratories successfully transferred to the ASCLD/LAB International Testing Program. The ASCLD/LAB International Testing Program incorporates ISO/IEC 17025:2005 requirements in addition to the ASCLD/LAB supplemental requirements specific to forensic science testing laboratories. The Scientific Analytical laboratories are accredited under SINGLAS.

Forensic medicine. The former Centre for Forensic Medicine (2005) and subsequently the Forensic Medicine Division (2011) have been accredited by the National Association of Medical Examiners (NAME), and is currently the only Centre outside North America that is fully accredited by NAME.

22.11 Technology

The HSA strives to obtain the latest analytical and scientific equipment and validated techniques to implement in its labs. It collaborates with academia, such as the National University of Singapore, in various joint projects and research activities. It continues to monitor the forensic scene abroad and adopt relevant and appropriate technologies and best practice to keep up with "cutting-edge" international standards.

Scientists and forensic pathologists plug into various international and overseas professional networks to keep abreast of developments and contribute to the international dialogue. There is a conscious effort to plough back surpluses from operating activities to invest in technology and strategic development in a consistent manner over the decades.

22.12 Disaster preparedness

The HSA works jointly with the Singapore Police Force and Singapore Civil Defence Force (Fire and Rescue) as a key player in the management of mass casualty scenarios. To maintain operational readiness, staff participate in various interagency exercises.

The HSA has also developed a response plan to dealing with suspected highly infectious diseases with a mobile containerized BSL4 autopsy facility. The program involves regular practices and biennial mobilization to maintain staff operational competency and team coordination effectiveness.

The HSA has also build up its preparedness by participating in regional mass disasters, such as the Asian Tsunami in 2004 and the 2011 Christchurch, New Zealand, earthquake, in the Disaster Victim Identification morgue as well as assistance in DNA profiling of some of the victims in order to confirm identity.

22.13 Legal issues

Singapore has an adversarial legal system, inherited from the British as it was a former colony of the British Empire. Since independence, the Singapore legal system has moved gradually away from the UK system.

Evidence for criminal trials are introduced and led by the Public Prosecutor, which is then challenged by the Defence. Scientific reports are provided to the Defence before the trial for their preparation if these reports are to be introduced. Recent changes to the law have made the process of discovery more transparent and accessible to the defence. If there is material evidence that is in the defence's favour, these also should be made known to them. The defence may call their own experts but, in practice, such challenges are infrequent.

The Judiciary is keenly aware of the role of science in trials and has been proactive in engaging the scientific community in gaining awareness and basic understanding of the science behind the work that goes into the reports. In the course of proceedings, judges often engage in querying the scientists and pathologists, in seeking clarification on scientific matters. Digital technology has found its way into court processes, including the recording, documentation and display of evidence, exchange of court documents, court presentations, etc. Teleconferencing technologies with overseas experts who cannot be physically present have been adopted.

Court trials are generally open to the public. However, the media and public are not allowed to record the events by photography or videography, and there are no televised courtroom proceedings.

Coroner's cases are heard by the State Coroner in the State Courts. The State Coroner is appointed by the President of Singapore and is a legally trained judge. The roles and responsibilities of various players in the Coroner's death investigation process are spelt out in the Coroners Act 2010. The rules of evidence in a Coroner's Inquiry are much more relaxed than in criminal trials. Hearsay evidence is admissible. The next of kin is given the privilege to ask question of witnesses, with or without counsel. Following the new Act, the Coroner no longer makes a determination of manner but records the findings regarding the circumstances of the death and may make recommendations as he/she deems fit, that will help to prevent a recurrence of the tragedy. The Public Prosecutor may also direct the Coroner to reopen an inquiry or redirect examinations if required in the public interest. Where an individual is charged with an offence related to the person's death, the Coroner's Inquiry is held in abeyance until the prosecution for the offence(s) have been completed and the Inquiry is summarily closed.

Section 16 of the Health Sciences Authority Act indemnifies any employee of the HSA from prosecution for acts done in good faith, while section 17 declares all employees to be public servants. Thus there is no risk of outright litigation on the reports of employees of the HSA. However, like colleagues in other specialties of medicine, the HSA takes out medical indemnity insurance for its Forensic Pathologists.

22.14 Research

Current research in Forensic Science is directed towards newer methods of detection, increased sensitivity of detection and newer methodologies of drugs and substances of abuse, adulteration, etc. While some of this is within the HSA, most of this research is multi- institutional and spans many of the universities' departments and laboratories. Some overseas collaboration through MOUs and focus-group research is also taking place. The HSA has also spearheaded rapid processing kits for the investigating officers and is collaborating with the technical universities to develop nanotechnology based rapid identification kits for various forensic screening purposes.

22.15 Future directions

Being an open society, Singapore is highly porous to external influences, both sociocultural and economic. As such, there is a strong need to remain vigilant in anticipating the evolving scene in criminal and illegal activities. It is recognized by the judiciary, legal system and law enforcement that science plays an important role in the detection and solving of crime. The challenge is to try to stay ahead of the curve by being plugged into developments abroad and developing the tools before the wave hits. One anticipates there will be an ongoing investment in resources to keep up with the changing

technology. However, as resources are not unlimited and with pressure to shorten turnaround times, there will inevitably be a move towards automation and adoption of kit-technologies that will inevitably displace some of the current jobs.

Finding enough people and the right people will be a significant challenge, as the population ages and births continue to decline. This together with constraints on headcount growth as the country grows at a slower pace will require innovative solutions, and further drive automation and adoption of kit-technologies. Public pressure that believes in the use of CT scans that will obviate the need for autopsies will persist.

So far, the HSA has been the national lab for all the services it offers. However, from time to time, some independent overseas private analysis groups have appeared on Singapore's horizon, offering some competing and limited services. Defence experts may become a more frequent occurrence in the longer term.

References

Anderson, C. (2007) The Indian Uprising of 1857 – 8: Prisons, Prisoners, and Rebellion, Anthem Press, p. 14.

Attorney-General of Singapore (2013). Part V (The Government). In: *Constitution of the Republic of Singapore*. Archived and retrieved from the original on 18 December 2013.

Chan, H.M. (1995) *The Legal System of Singapore*.

Chang, W. (1995) Historical overview. In: *Legal Systems in ASEAN – Singapore* Chapter 1, http://www.aseanlaw association.org/papers/sing_chp1.pdf.

Kuntz, T. (1994) Ideas & Trends; Beyond Singapore: Corporal Punishment, A to Z, *The New York Times*, 26 June 1994.

Nicholas, S., Shergold, P.R. (1988) Transportation as global nigration In: S. Nicholas (ed.) *Convict Workers: Reinterpreting Australia's Past*, Ed. S. Nicholas, Cambridge University Press, Cambridge, p. 29.

Turnbull, C.M. (1970) Convicts in the Straits Settlements 1826–1867. *Journal of the Malaysian Branch of the Royal Asiatic Society* 43 (1): 91.

US Central Intelligence Agency (2014) *World Factbook – Singapore*. Retrieved: 22 February 2014.

US Department of State (2013) *Singapore Country Specific Information*, 5 September 2013.

World Corporal Punishment Research (2012) *Judicial Caning in Singapore, Malaysia and Brunei*. Retrieved: 22 February 2014.

CHAPTER 23

The history and current status of forensic science in South Africa

Herman Bernitz[1], Michael Kenyhercz[2], Burgert Kloppers[3], Ericka Nöelle L'Abbé[4], Gérard Nicholas Labuschagne[5], Antonel Olckers[6], Jolandie Myburgh[7], Gert Saayman[8], Maryna Steyn[9] & Kyra Stull[9]

[1] Department of Oral Pathology and Oral Biology, School of Dentistry, University of Pretoria, Pretoria, South Africa

[2] Department of Anthropology, University of Alaska, Fairbanks, USA

[3] Ballistics Section, Forensic Science Laboratory, South African Police Service, Pretoria, South Africa

[4] Department of Anatomy, Faculty of Health Sciences, University of Pretoria, Pretoria, South Africa

[5] Investigative Psychology Section, South African Police Services, Pretoria, South Africa

[6] DNAbiotec (Pty) Ltd; Department of Immunology and Department of Forensic Medicine, Extraordinary Professor, University of Pretoria, Pretoria, South Africa

[7] Forensic Anthropology Research Centre, Department of Anatomy, Faculty of Health Sciences, University of Pretoria, Pretoria, South Africa

[8] Department of Forensic Medicine, Faculty of Health Sciences, University of Pretoria, Pretoria, South Africa

[9] Forensic Anthropology Research Centre, Department of Anatomy, Faculty of Health Sciences, University of Pretoria, Pretoria, South Africa

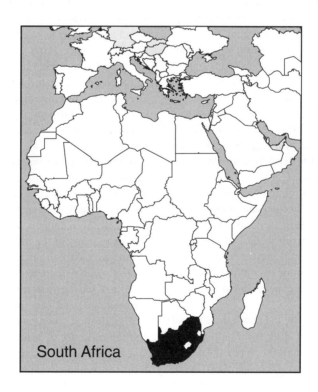

South Africa

The Global Practice of Forensic Science, First Edition. Edited by Douglas H. Ubelaker.

© 2015 John Wiley & Sons, Ltd. Published 2015 by John Wiley & Sons, Ltd.

23.1 History of forensic sciences in South Africa

23.1.1 Introduction

Each discipline of forensic science has its own history, its own pioneers, its inception problems and its historical achievements. Together these forensic science disciplines have all had to deal with a past that was dominated by a segregated community with both Eurocentric and African traditions. This has influenced, and still affects, the day to day activities of all forensic scientists functioning within the country. The impact of apartheid, divided families, bantu education and racial domination as institutionalized in the past South African judicial system, must take some blame for the extremely high levels of crime that prevail in our current society (Centre for the Study of Violence and Reconciliation, 2009). The new democratic South Africa has seen little progress towards the elimination of extreme poverty, with resulting populations of rich and poor living side by side, creating a natural osmotic climate for criminality. The influx of illegal foreign nationals has also been blamed for the high levels of crime (Humanitarian News and Analysis, 2013), a claim that has been questioned. The crime levels as indicated in the 2012/2013 official SAPS crime statistics are: 16,259 murders, 66,387 sexual offences and 105,888 robberies with aggravated circumstances (South African Police Services Crime Statistics, 2013). The quality and validity of these official statistics has often been called into question, primarily due to relatively poor raw data collection and interpretation of findings. Understaffed forensic services with budget restraints together with overworked police officers, who have to investigate, analyse and present to the courts evidence related to the multitude of criminal acts, contribute to the current problems experienced in the forensic community.

South Africa was colonized by the Dutch in 1652 and the English in 1795, with the result that South African law is based primarily on Roman Dutch principles with a strong English law influence. Post-apartheid South Africa has seen the abolition of many discriminatory laws coupled with pioneering decisions in the area of the death penalty, visiting rights, free access to medical services and the acknowledgement of language diversities. The right to a fair trial in South Africa is now entrenched in Section 35(3), which assures the right to be tried in a language that the accused person understands (Du Preez, 2013). The present "South African law" is composed of at least five layers, namely: Roman Dutch law as common law, Roman Dutch law as civil law, Tribal law, Islamic law and English law (Beat, 2002). An area of concern is the fact that the prosecution and the investigative arms of the state are housed under the same umbrella, causing distrust in several sections of the community. The legal system with its continually changing legislature has a direct impact on the forensic science community, as was seen when the so-called "DNA bill", the Criminal Law (Forensic Procedure) Amendment Bill B09-2013, was introduced into parliament on 8 May 2013. Chapter 8 of the "National Health Act" includes several aspects of international law pertaining to issues such as the use of stem cells and aspects related to the use of human tissue in research. While the promulgation of Chapter 8 and regulations thereto might be a welcome step towards partial relief from the regulatory vacuum, several important gaps still exist and several newly introduced inaccuracies have added further complexity to the situation (Pepper, 2002).

The end of apartheid in 1994 saw drastic changes in all spheres of society including forensic science services. The dramatic increase in acceptance of all social races into tertiary institutions of learning has seen a more representative profile in all scientific spheres of our forensic services.

Health care practitioners including forensic pathologists, forensic odontologists and medically qualified forensic anthropologists are highly regulated by the statuary Health Professions Council of South Africa (HPCSA). Accreditation and professional audit with respect to many of the other disciplines in the domain of forensic sciences is not at the same level of regulatory control. The remaining forensic sciences have been neglected, having no statutory governing body. This has led to unsatisfactory and insufficient national standards and guidelines, questions concerning quality control and the existence of facilities running without accreditation, certification or a general code of ethics (Olckers, Blumenthal and Greyling, 2013). Notwithstanding the above, South Africa has a large fraternity of highly qualified and extremely competent forensic scientists. This chapter only addresses a select group of forensic disciplines, but it must be stated that forensic services are available by experts in a wide range of fields, including forensic entomology, forensic engineering, criminology, questioned documents, computer forensics, forensic nursing and fingerprint identification.

23.2 Medicine and pathology in South Africa

23.2.1 Historic overview

For the past approximately 100 years, professional forensic medical services in South Africa were primarily rendered by medical practitioners who held official appointment as District Surgeons (DSs). Forensic medical services include clinical forensic medical services (referring to the evaluation of living patients with respect to rape and sexual assault, interpersonal violence, elder and child abuse, driving under the influence, etc.) and morbid forensic pathology (medicolegal/autopsy investigation of sudden, unexplained and/or unnatural deaths).

District Surgeons were generally medical practitioners in private practice but who held part-time official appointments to render services on behalf of the National or Provincial Departments of Health, incorporating three broad categories: routine medical services to indigent population groups and the elderly, duties of an official nature (vaccination services, issuing of travel certificates, pre-employment examination for civil servants, etc.) and forensic medical services (both clinical forensic and morbid pathology services). Such appointments were made in virtually every magisterial district (approximately equivalent to counties in the United Kingdom, and of which there are more than 350 across the nine provinces of South Africa). In many districts, only one DS held appointment, although larger or more populous districts may have had more than one DS. One distinct advantage of this system was that, over time, these designated medical practitioners developed substantial experience and expertise in forensic medicine, not only in diagnostic skills but also in medicolegal report writing, courtroom skills, etc. DSs were responsible for evaluating virtually every incident and/or case involving interpersonal violence that was reported to the police and thus became highly experienced medicolegal practitioners in most cases.

After the first democratic elections in 1994, the official designation and post of District Surgeon was abolished, and all cases that had previously been attended to by the DS would attend local clinics and hospitals, where the resident medical officer (casualty officer) would render the requisite forensic medical (diagnostic and therapeutic) service. Due to the relatively junior profile of medical practitioners at such centres, their unwillingness to become involved in matters that could result in court proceedings and the relative lack of interest displayed by most of these clinicians, etc., there has been a dramatic decline in clinical expertise and experience of medical practitioners who now must testify in courts of law.

Historically, District Surgeons also rendered morbid pathology services, including medicolegal investigation of death in cases of sudden, unexplained and/or unnatural death. In most magisterial districts, both clinical forensic medical services and morbid pathology services were rendered by the same medical practitioner. Such a DS would therefore conduct medicolegal autopsies on a regular basis, prepare his/her report and subsequently testify in a court of law. In some larger towns and cities, District Surgeons may have been appointed to render exclusively clinical or morbid pathology services. In larger metropolitan centres, specialist forensic medical practitioners (forensic pathologists), were appointed to render medicolegal investigation of death services.

Although professional forensic pathology services were rendered by medical practitioners, the physical infrastructure (medicolegal mortuaries) and administrative and functional organization, as well as overall logistic and budgetary responsibility, were the responsibility of the SAPS, who provided the human resources, vehicles, equipment and other facilities required for a comprehensive death investigation service. Thus, police officers were responsible for collecting bodies from crime/death scenes, overall functioning of medicolegal mortuaries, providing autopsy assistants for pathologists, interacting with the public and funeral undertakers, etc. Medical practitioners were, however, in the service of the national or provincial Departments of Health and were not on the payroll of the South African Police Service.

In the 1990s, negotiations began for medicolegal mortuaries and the entire forensic pathology service to be transferred from the budgetary, administrative and operational control of the South African Police Service to the Provincial Departments of Health. This was effected in 2006, with all medicolegal mortuaries becoming the responsibility of Provincial Directorates or Divisions of Forensic Pathology Service, across all nine provinces in South Africa. The involvement of the SAPS is now limited to securing crime/death scenes and the requisite police/criminal investigation including most aspects of identification and collection of physical evidence, but excluding the responsibilities for the collection, handling and examination of bodies and related evidentiary material at scenes and medicolegal mortuaries. The Provincial Departments of Health now also employ Forensic Pathology Officers (FPOs), who are responsible for collecting bodies from death scenes, admission of such bodies at medicolegal mortuaries, assisting pathologists during medicolegal autopsies, victim identification procedures and other administrative requirements.

23.2.2 Legislative framework

The legislative framework within which the medicolegal investigation of death service is conducted in South Africa is provided for primarily within the following statutory framework:

- The Inquests Act (Act 58 of 1959) prescribes that all non-natural deaths have to be reported to the police, who must then investigate the circumstances of death and make the body available to a medical practitioner, who shall examine the body for purposes of establishing the cause of death with greater certainty.
- The Registration of Births and Deaths Act (Act 18 of 1969), which prescribes that medical practitioners must issue Notification of Death forms (specifying the primary medical cause and/or mode of death) in all cases where death has been due to natural causes. Where the practitioner is of the opinion that death was not entirely due to natural causes, the matter must be referred to the SAPS and the Forensic Pathology Service for further investigation.
- The National Health Act (Act 61 of 2003). Chapter 8 of this act provides for the use of human tissues for purposes of research, teaching and training, transplantation and therapeutic applications. In addition, the performance of postmortem examinations of a nonforensic nature is provided for. The Act provides for the Regulations Regarding the Rendering of Forensic Pathology Services in South Africa, which further define the scope of death investigation responsibilities and provides the mandate for Forensic Pathology Service divisions of the Provincial Departments of Health to perform medicolegal autopsies and render related services in cases of unnatural death. Unnatural deaths are by law defined to include all deaths that were brought about by the effects of physical and/or

chemical forces or agents, all sudden, unexpected or unexplained deaths and all deaths that may have been due to intrinsically natural causes or conditions but where (in the opinion of a medical practitioner) negligence may be implicated as well as all deaths that take place during a surgical/anesthetic procedure or where medical treatment may have resulted in complications that may have contributed to the demise of the patient.

- The Health Professions Act (Act 56 of 1974). Recent amendments to the Health Professions Act prescribe that medicolegal investigation including autopsy must be undertaken in all cases where death may have taken place during a surgical/anaesthetic procedure or had resulted from a complication related to any form of medical treatment (diagnostic, therapeutic or palliative).
- The Criminal Procedure Act (Act 51 of 1077) makes provision for the acquisition of specimens and scientific investigations related to bodily tissues and/or samples for purposes of establishing facts and/or conditions that may be relevant at future criminal proceedings.

23.2.3 Academic teachings and training in forensic medicine in South Africa

There are presently eight tertiary academic institutions that have Faculties of Health Sciences producing medical practitioners in South Africa. In total, approximately 1200 medical practitioners graduate from these medical schools annually. There are currently approximately 28,000 active medical practitioners in South Africa servicing a population of 52 million. No one is allowed to practice medicine in South Africa without official registration with the Medical and Dental Professions Board of the Health Professions Council of South Africa (HPCSA). Medical practitioners may hold registration as general medical practitioners or as specialists in defined clinical or pathology disciplines recognized by the HPCSA.

All medical schools teach basic principles of forensic medicine at the undergraduate level, including medical law and jurisprudence, basic thanatology, basic postmortem techniques, principles and procedures of medicolegal investigation of death, legal and ethical perspectives of certification and notification of death, as well as aspects of clinical forensic medicine. There is wide divergence amongst medical schools as to the scope and detail of such undergraduate courses, varying from a few hours of total tuition time to a cumulative total of almost 100 hours of theoretical and practical tuition at some institutions. At most medical schools it is mandatory for senior medical students to attend a number of medicolegal autopsy sessions at designated medicolegal mortuaries.

Nearly all medical schools offer postgraduate residency training in forensic pathology, leading to recognized academic degrees registerable with the HPCSA, thus allowing successful candidates to register and practice as specialist forensic pathologists. Such training generally comprises four to five years of residency training, including formal assessments in a variety of pathology disciplines, predominantly comprising anatomic and forensic pathology modules. Proof of research capacity and output is now also a prerequisite for successful completion of residency training. Until recently, most medical schools offered the postgraduate degree of Master of Medicine (MMed) in forensic pathology, but currently final examinations are conducted under the auspices of the Colleges of Medicine of South Africa, with the degree of Fellowship of the College of Forensic Pathologists (FCForPath[SA]) being conferred on successful candidates.

Faculties of health sciences generally have between four and ten accredited residency training posts, with a combined annual national output of only four or five qualified specialist forensic pathologists in South Africa. Despite the great need for increased numbers of specialist forensic pathologists in this country, the total number of active registered specialist forensic pathologists here remains steady at between 35 and 45 pathologists.

General medical practitioners may also undergo further discipline specific and vocational training without formally embarking on residency training programs, after which they may sit for the Diploma in Forensic Medicine or Pathology with the Colleges of Medicine of South Africa. However, the diploma does not allow for the registration of a specialist degree or designation as specialist pathologist with the HPCSA.

23.2.4 Forensic pathology services: demographic and related service perspectives

South Africa has a total population of approximately 52 million people. Mortality statistics are regularly provided by Statistics South Africa, the official national agency responsible for supplying population figures. Although

official figures would suggest lower numbers, it is likely that at least 70,000 non-natural deaths take place annually in South Africa, if regard is had for the full spectrum of cases included in the definition of "non-natural death". The reliability and accuracy of crime statistics and homicide/murder figures (as released by official agencies, including the SAPS) are a topic of intense debate, not least because the government has placed a moratorium on the release of such data. Up to 25,000 homicidal deaths, 15,000 road traffic accident fatalities and almost 10,000 suicidal deaths form part of the overall annual mortality figure in South Africa.

South Africa is geographically divided into nine provinces, of which Gauteng Province (population of approximately 12 million people) and KwaZulu-Natal (approximately 10 million people) constitute by far the most populous regions. Both Pretoria, the political capital, and Johannesburg, the economic hub of South Africa, are situated in Gauteng Province. Recent reports suggest that the metropolitan area where citizens are at highest risk of violent or non-natural death is Cape Town.

Every Provincial Department of Health now has a Forensic Pathology Service Directorate or Division, responsible for providing the physical infrastructure and human resources in order to render a medicolegal investigation of death service. In the larger cities and towns, one or more forensic pathologists may be attached to larger medicolegal mortuaries, but the bulk of medicolegal autopsies are still being conducted by nonspecialist medical officers and trainee pathologists (residents). It is rare for forensic pathologists to practice in rural communities and/or smaller towns. On average, forensic medical practitioners conduct between 400 and 600 medicolegal autopsies per annum, although significantly larger numbers of cases may be attended to in some regions.

23.2.5 Support services

A full spectrum of specialist support services across virtually all forensic science disciplines is available to forensic medical practitioners at medicolegal mortuaries across South Africa. Due to relatively poor functional organization and logistic deficiencies, access and use of these services is often limited. Routine access to histology and toxicology services generally exists, but other specialized scientific services (including anthropology and odontology services, forensic genetics/molecular biology and entomology services) are less readily available. These services are generally provided either from within the auspices of the SAPS Forensic Science Laboratories or from within academic/scientific departments at universities or other tertiary education colleges or scientific institutions.

23.2.6 Defined problem areas

South Africa has a generally well-developed legal framework and service platform for the rendering of a medicolegal investigation of death service, with a systematized and routine delivery of service in all geographic areas. The quality of diagnostic service and efficiency of processing of cases remains questionable in many areas, especially outside of larger cities and facilities. The following specific problems exist:

- Inadequate professional manpower, with far too few formally trained forensic pathologists and very few appropriately trained forensic pathology officers who are responsible for attending scenes, gathering appropriate information and assisting pathologists at autopsy.
- Suboptimal mortuary facilities and poor autopsy and related investigative equipment, including inadequacies in modern diagnostic and service aids such as photographic equipment, diagnostic radiologic support, etc. Despite a substantial recent increase in funding for forensic pathology services countrywide, much still remains to be done on this front in order for an appropriate service to be rendered in South Africa.
- Poorly developed and nonstandardized operational protocols pertaining to death investigation, with a general lack of interinstitutional and interagency memoranda of understanding, SOPs, service level agreements, etc.
- The lack of an efficient, reliable forensic toxicology service.
- Poor mortuary information management systems and inadequate use of statistics to procure appropriate funding and to empower managers to improve service delivery.
- Lack of accreditation processes and inadequate measures to ensure professional and institutional audit and quality control, undermine ongoing efforts at improving diagnostic accuracy and compiling reliable and authoritative medicolegal reports for use in adversarial legal proceedings.

23.3 Forensic odontology in South Africa

23.3.1 History of forensic odontology in South Africa

The first notable reports regarding forensic dentistry in South Africa appear in the book *Forensic Odontology, Its Scope and History* (Hill *et al.*, 1984). The first forensic dental position was established in 1966 when Professor C.W. van Wyk was appointed as Honorary Consultant Forensic Odontologist to the South African Police Services. In 1977 the South African Society for Forensic Odonto-Stomatology (SASFOS) was formed with close links to the International Organisation of Forensic Odonto-Stomatology (IOFOS). South Africa can be very proud of the fact that the first dedicated forensic dental journal was established by Professor H.A. Shapiro in 1983. The journal, known as the *International Journal of Forensic Odonto-Stomatology* was first published in 1983 with Shapiro as its editor. Since then forensic dentistry has flourished, with most dental schools having forensic dentists on their staff. In several mass disasters on the continent of Africa, forensic dentists have played a role in the identification of victims: Windhoek air disaster, 1968 (Professor C.W.van Wyk), terrorist bombing in Pretoria, 1983 (Professor A.J. Ligthelm), Helderberg air disaster, 1987 (Professor A.J. Ligthelm), Kenya air disaster, Douala, Cameroun, 2007 (Professor H. Bernitz) and Maputo ammunition explosion (Professor H. Bernitz). Professor H. Bernitz was the first South African to be elected as International President of IOFOS, a position he held from 2005 to 2011. During his term the paper based journal (*JOFOS*) was changed to an open access web-based journal.

23.3.2 Types of cases in forensic odontology at the University of Pretoria

Forensic dental cases are received from the Department of Forensic Medicine, Department of Forensic Anthropology, Victim Identification Centre of SAPS, Silverton Forensic Laboratory and the Forensic Mortuary in Pretoria. The services rendered include:

- Corpse identification
- Age, race and gender determination of skeletal remains
- Age determination of crime suspects and refugees
- Bite mark analyses

- Mass disaster management
- Odonto-stomatological investigations of child abuse cases
- Forensic jurisprudence

23.3.3 Recruitment and training in forensic odontology

Academic courses related to forensic dentistry are offered at several universities in South Africa. These courses are offered at the level of diploma, honours, masters and doctoral. The courses are advertised on the respective university web pages and the local dental journals. South Africa is one of the few countries in which only university trained postgraduates work as forensic dentists.

23.3.4 Disaster victim identification (forensic odontology/forensic pathology)

South Africa was one of the first countries to have a National Disaster Management Act, Act 57 of 2002 (Government Gazette, 2003). This Act has been recognized internationally as a model for disaster risk management as it gives effect to the concept of disaster management through legislation.

The Disaster Management Act also makes provision for emergency preparedness, rapid and effective disaster response and recovery, and the participation of volunteers. A disaster is defined as a progressive or sudden, widespread or localized, natural or human-caused occurrence that causes or threatens to cause: death, injury or disease; damage to property, infrastructure or the environment; or disruption of the life of a community. South Africa has a formal DVI team comprised of police officials under the direct supervision of a senior police official. All medical and dental services are ad hoc and the number of protagonists is determined by the size and nature of the disaster. These are primarily university staff, but, when needed, suitably qualified private forensically trained dental practitioners can be included.

23.3.5 Research in forensic dentistry

Current research in forensic dentistry has focused mainly on bite mark analysis techniques, frequency of features within demarcated/representative population samples and age estimation in different racial groups within the country. These aspects of research are being addressed in research projects that form part of academic

degrees as at various institutions in South Africa. South Africa has a proud record of publications in the field of forensic dentistry. The publications include research into: age estimation, mass disaster management, materials used in forensic dentistry, dental concordance and bite mark analysis. Currently the Universities of Pretoria and of the Western Cape are leaders in forensic odontological research.

The estimation of age in younger individuals between the ages of ten and eighteen has always been problematic when handing down sentences to suspects with little or no documentation. Many data are available to estimate the ages of young individuals in England, Canada and Belgium, but little or no data are available in South Africa for black populations. Research into the estimation of black South African children is ongoing.

The role of dental cementum in age estimation is also being investigated. This research project will investigate the possibility of determining life events, which manifest as changes in the mineralization of this fascinating structure, which is laid down in yearly annulations similar to the growth rings seen in trees.

Collaborative projects with researchers from the Department of Mathematics and the Department of Statistics using probabilities in analysing bite marks for presentation in court cases is currently underway. The research is applying Bayesian statistics to the prevalence of selected dental features observed in the Gauteng population in an effort to determine the probability of guilt in bite mark related cases.

A research project is also being undertaken that forms part of an MSc in which the student aims to collect and analyse a representative sample of five commonly used dental features in the province of Gauteng. This ambitious project aims to include 4300 bite mark registrations obtained within the province and will analyse the prevalence of five selected dental features in the anterior dentition.

A research projects using CBCT scans for identification purposes is also being investigated.

23.4 Forensic anthropology in South Africa

23.4.1 History of physical anthropology

The development of a discipline is dependent on prominent researchers in the field as well as the social, political and environmental circumstances of a country. In the early 20th century, R.A. Dart, T.J. Dreyer, M.R. Drennan and R. Broom, who were originally trained as a medical doctor, a zoologist, an anatomist and a paleontologist, respectively, introduced and gave rise to the discipline of physical anthropology in South Africa (Morris, 2012). Research focused on the origin of South African populations, the typology of modern and historic groups and human evolution (Morris, 2012). The most outstanding example of South African scholarship was Raymond A. Dart's discovery of *Australopithecus africanus*, or the Taung child, in 1924 (Dubow, 1995).

In the middle of the 20th century, research in physical anthropology began to diverge from the typological approach towards a more modern description of human variation in South Africans. A turning point in physical anthropological research was De Villiers' (1968) study on the crania of modern black South Africans, which laid the foundation for later development of population specific formulae among South African groups and the application of these methods to unknown remains (L'Abbé and Steyn, 2012).

Devoid of theoretical influence from either social or cultural anthropology, South African physical anthropology was taught and researched exclusively in medical schools and not the humanities, which makes physical anthropology in South Africa distinct from the North American emergence of the discipline. Thus, physical anthropologists in South Africa are not always exposed to anthropological theory but in contrast receive a much stronger education founded in the anatomical and medical sciences.

23.4.2 Recruitment/training/certification

The impact of forensic anthropology on the large number of missing people and unidentified corpses in South Africa is only as valuable as the efforts placed into the investigation of these cases. As such, a skeletonized case found in the veldt logically receives less attention from overburdened investigating officers than a recent homicide.

Within the last 10 years, various academic institutions have opened research facilities to cope with unidentified skeletal remains. The Forensic Anthropology Research Centre was established in the Department of Anatomy at the University of Pretoria in 2008. Similar groups have also been formed at the University of Cape Town in the

Western Cape in 2010 and the University of Witwatersrand in Johannesburg in 2013.

Anatomy departments at the University of Pretoria, University of Witwatersrand, University of Cape Town and Stellenbosch University offer postgraduate degrees from BSc Honours to PhD in physical anthropology and the University of Cape Town also offers an MSc in Biomedical Forensic Science. At the various institutions, students are often recruited from the Basic Medical Sciences programmes with their only experience in anthropology being a course in human evolution and often in physical, or forensic, anthropology. No clear guidelines are available as to who can call him/herself a forensic anthropologist; neither are there specific requirements with regard to minimum qualifications for this type of expertise. Without minimum qualifications or standards in training or expertise, the proficiency level of each anthropologist varies and thus the aptitude to conduct forensic anthropological analyses is a paramount problem in South Africa.

23.4.3 Types of cases in the Department of Anatomy, University of Pretoria

Since 1993, the Department of Anatomy at the University of Pretoria has received requests to conduct anthropological analyses from either the SAPS or local forensic pathologists (L'Abbé and Steyn, 2012). Between January 2002 and September 2012, a total of 555 cases were analysed at the Forensic Anthropology Research Centre. Most of the bodies were collected from the veldt (26%) in various stages of decomposition; the most common was skeletonized (50%), followed by partially skeletonized (31%), advanced decomposition (15%) and fresh (2%). Due to increased economic growth in the country, several skeletons were also inadvertently removed from historical cemeteries and early and late Iron Age period archaeological sites.

On average, males were estimated to comprise 52% of the cases, with a distinctly larger incidence of estimated black (76%) than white South African ancestry (5%); these numbers are reflective of the demographics of the country. In about 11% of cases the sex could not be established, as the remains were either incomplete or very young. The majority of cases involved adult remains (86%), while only 5% were estimated to be between 11 and 18 years old at death and 4.5% were 10 years and younger. Traumatic bone injuries primarily included antemortem trauma, focused mainly on the skull and thorax. Perimortem bone trauma ranged from – in order of frequency – blunt, ballistic to sharp injuries. Approximately 9% of the bodies were found burned, which included two cases of necklacing, post-mortem burning in the veldt and garbage dumping sites, and two house fires.

23.4.4 Research

Current anthropological research in South Africa is strongly focused on exploring human variation within the population and subsequent comparison with other populations, with emphasis on countries that con-tributed to the genetic composition of modern South Africans. Evaluation of human variation is directly asso-ciated with forensic applicability. The consistent deriva-tions of population specific techniques in all realms of the biological profile strive to make forensic anthropol-ogy in South Africa comparable to other countries.

Many studies on modern human variation in South Africa focus on the cranium. Historically, cranial research was limited to univariate measures, such as cranial indices, but this approach has not adequately captured human variation within the country. Using multivariate statistics on the cranium, Steyn and Iscan (1997) distinguished black and white South Africans with classification accuracies between 75% and 94%, with the mid-face shown to be more discriminatory than the vault dimensions. Nasal breadth and height, particularly, yielded consistently higher classification accuracies than other mid-face dimensions. The pattern re-emphasized that mid-facial features have the most discriminatory ability in ancestry estimation (Hefner, 2009; L'Abbé et al., 2011; McDowell, L' Abbé and Kenyhercz, 2012). Expanding on the mid-face analyses, McDowell, L'Abbé and Kenyhercz (2012) achieved sim-ilar classification accuracies for the size and shape of the mid-face dimensions for white and black South Africans.

A custom database has been created for use with the software program FORDISC3.0 (FD3) and has offered a means to apply multivariate statistical analyses to cran-iometric data to explore population variation and thus ancestry estimation in South Africa. A large, modern South African sample comprises the custom database that includes the three largest population groups in South Africa, namely black ($n = 158$), white ($n = 114$) and coloured ($n = 247$). Utilizing craniometric measures in a three-way DFA (black, white, coloured with sexes pooled) has resulted in classification accuracies as high as 82% (L'Abbé et al., 2013). The use of the entire crania instead of solely the mid-facial region has improved classification accuracies. Interestingly, when population and sex are incorporated into the analyses, different misclassification patterns by population are obvious. Whereas white and black males and females misclassify into the opposite sex but same ancestry, coloured males and females misclassify into the same sex but different ancestry.

Using the entire cranium and geometric morphomet-rics rather than linear measures, L'Abbé et al. (2013) compared cranial shape among three modern South Africans and achieved an increase in classification accu-racy to 90%. In their analyses, they found two major separations: between whites and the remaining groups, and between blacks and coloureds. The first separation between whites and the non-white groups is due in large part to the relatively higher and more anteriorly placed euryon, overall reduction of the facial skeleton and comparably taller crania of white South Africans. The second separation between black and coloured South Africans involves cranial breadth, as blacks demonstrated a much more infero-anteriorly placed euryon in comparison to coloureds. The large within-group variation is expected for South African coloureds, who represent one of the most unique populations in the world, exhibiting more inter- and intracontinental contributions than any other population.

The ability to estimate ancestry using postcranial measurements is currently being assessed. Historically, postcraniometric variables were never explored even though South African populations demonstrate dispar-ities in final attainment of stature (Steyn and Smith, 2007). Population differences in stature are even appar-ent in South African subadults between the ages of 6 and 10 years (Anholts, 2013).

Several postgraduate students explored research topics in estimating the postmortem interval and decomposition rates with body size in northern South Africa (Myburgh, L'Abbé and Steyn, 2013). Keough et al. (2012) assessed burn patterns on fleshed, wet and dry remains and then quantitatively recorded burn pat-terns on pig carcasses ranging from fresh to skeletonized and provided information on burn patterns associated with wet and dry bone as a means for discussing the possible timing of the burn event on a body recovered from the veldt.

23.4.5 Future directions

South Africa has become a centre for research, primarily due to the overhauling of forensic standards to meet the requirements/standards presented in other countries. In addition to developing population-specific standards for the diverse population, new methodologies, such as geometric morphometrics, and new analytical techniques, such as flexible discriminant function analysis and multivariate adaptive regression splines, are being utilized to demonstrate not only their applicability in South Africa but also in forensic anthropology at large. For the future, in order to improve the value of research methodology for South African populations, South African students need additionally to be exposed to anthropological theory as well as the basic medical sciences, as the value of an applied method in forensic casework is only as strong as the reliability and validity of the research used to create it.

With large skeletal collections and strong collaborative research ties with leading experts throughout Europe and North America, South Africa has the potential to become a leader in the study of human variation and forensic anthropological techniques applicable to the country, specifically, and sub-Saharan Africa, in general. Some constraints include the overwhelmingly high rates of crime, the general unimportance of skeletal remains in death investigations and the relative isolation of the country from the general academic community (L'Abbé and Steyn, 2012).

23.5 DNA evidence in South Africa

23.5.1 Introduction

The largest forensic DNA laboratory in South Africa is the South African Police Service (SAPS) Forensic Science Laboratory (FSL). The main DNA analysis laboratories are situated in Pretoria, Gauteng and Cape Town, Western Cape. These are currently the only laboratories that perform DNA analysis within the FSL network. Two other DNA laboratories are located in Port Elizabeth and Durban, but perform only DNA evidence recovery.

Private laboratories are prohibited by law from analyzing DNA profiles for criminal cases. There are, however, several private pathology firms that perform DNA typing used in civil cases, mainly paternities. Several efforts in the past to convince the FSL to outsource DNA typing for criminal cases have been unsuccessful. However,

the call for higher quality in forensic services is increasing and even the option of a public–private partnership to improve forensic services in South Africa is being discussed (Barnard, 2014).

23.5.2 Cases using DNA evidence

DNA evidence has been used in South African courts since the late 1990s, with State v. Parker (2000) being one of the first cases where short tandem repeat (STR) technology was used. Since then the technology has been implemented widely and in 2013 there were 314,613 cases processed in the DNA analysis unit of the FSL (Smith, 2014). Of all cases received annually, approximately 70% are sexual assaults (Lucassen, as cited by Omar, 2008) with the rest being other violent crimes including murder and other assaults. Of all the cases received per year 60% will not be typed for DNA profiles, due to no DNA being detected in the preliminary testing phase on the evidence submitted and only approximately 10% of all samples will yield sufficient DNA for DNA typing (Omar, 2008).

23.5.3 Integration of forensic science

The process from collection at the crime scene is outlined in Table 23.1 for a case involving DNA evidence.

The chain of custody is critical not only outside of the laboratory, from collection at the crime scene until it reaches the laboratory, but also inside the laboratory. A so-called paper trail is in place inside the laboratory that documents each step and test that is performed on the sample. This trail is auditable from raw data that can be recovered by the defence. Inside the laboratory all actions that are taken with regard to the samples are taken according to the quality manual's prescriptions, which are documented in standard operating procedures (SOPs) up to the level of generating the final report, Section 212(4)(a) affidavit. This provides a thoroughly documented record of the entire analysis workflow. During interpretation one of the key outcomes is the final statement. In the forensic DNA laboratory only one of three statements should be made to convey the valid interpreted result (Essential DNA Evidence Short Course, 2013):

(a) Inclusion
(b) Exclusion
(c) Inconclusive

The distinction between the different categories is important as it is part of the interpretation of DNA results

Table 23.1 Outline of the process followed with DNA evidence (adapted with permission from Meintjes-van der Walt, 2010)

	Crime scene	• Identification • Collection • Packaging • Storage	
South African Police Service	Investigating officer opens docket	• Case Administration System number assigned to the case • Chain of custody • Samples from victim/accused • Transfer to laboratories • Storage • Charge and suspect arrested, reference blood sample obtained	
SAPS Criminal Record and Forensic Science Service (CRFSS)	Forensic Science Laboratory (FSL) Biology Section	• Chain of custody • Samples received at FSL • Presumptive testing • DNA extraction • Quantification • PCR • Electrophoresis • Electropherogram • DNA profile generated • Evaluation of profile quality • Profile submitted to database • Comparison with other profiles on database • Interpretation within case context • Match declared if applicable • Laboratory report: Section 212(4)(a) Affidavit	National Forensic DNA Database (NFDD) • Sample collection • DNA profile comparison • Arrestees • Convicted offenders • Cold hits
National Prosecuting Authority	Prosecutors	• Indictment • Pre-trial proceedings • Discovery	
Court System	Criminal courts	• Evidence at trial • DNA expert testimony • DNA match • Significance of match • Adjudication • Sentencing • Post sentencing • Database entry of samples: convicted offenders	
Department of Correctional Services	Correctional services	• Convicted offender DNA collection • Appeals • Parole	

The DNA case process flows from the crime scene where evidence is collected via the FSL to the courts and ultimately to correctional services. The interface between the DNA database and other elements in the process are indicated by dotted lines.

that is open to bias and misinterpretation. It requires skill and objective evaluation of the data. It is thus imperative that training is appropriate and sufficiently in depth to provide a solid foundation for these skills to be honed over time.

23.5.4 Education and training

In the past when potential DNA analysts entered the FSL for employment they were trained in-house according to an unaccredited syllabus. In 2007 the first formal forensic science qualification, the National Certificate in

Forensic Science, was developed and registered on the National Qualifications Framework of South Africa. It is currently used as an entry level qualification for personnel at the FSL.

Prospective employees of the FSL are now required to hold an appropriate degree in science depending on the section of the FSL into which they will be deployed (SAPS, 2014). In the biology unit where DNA analysis is performed, it is imperative that a thorough scientific background is present since the analyst should not only be able to perform satisfactorily in that unit but also explain their results in court. The FSL uses a system of induction and in-house training, followed by competency testing and operational mentorship prior to the analyst being able to work independently (Omar, 2008).

In the past 3 years several academic institutions in South Africa have initiated forensic science programs to meet the growing demand in the market. These programs are determined by the institutions themselves and nationwide uniformity in these programs is not a key priority at present. It is envisaged that there will be national guidelines in the future stating a minimum criteria to which programs must adhere to in order for graduates to be able to register at the regulating body SACNASP (the South African Council for Natural Scientific Professions).

It is encouraging that Legal Aid South Africa, which employs by far the largest number of legal professionals in South Africa, if not Africa, is empowering their legal professionals with training on DNA evidence. Legal Aid SA is an independent body that provides legal assistance to those who cannot afford it. Legal Aid SA is dedicated to training their legal practitioners in the skills they require, in order for them to have the technical competencies to deal with, for example, DNA expert evidence (Hundermark, 2014).

23.5.5 Funding

The budget for public funded forensic science services originates from the government and is revised annually. This is allocated to the different departments at the national level including the Department of Police. In this department, the FSL resorts under the Criminal Record and Forensic Science Service division. Accountability for this division resorts under the Divisional Commissioner: Criminal Record and Forensic Science Services (SAPS, 2014).

In the case of a large project such as the fully robotized Genetic Sample Processing System (GSPS) external funding from, for example, the European Union was obtained. These large scale infrastructure projects generally are of national importance in terms of crime prevention and management.

23.5.6 Regulation of the forensic science profession

The SACNASP is the body mandated by law to regulate the field of natural science professions, including forensic science. In Schedule 1 to the Natural Scientific Professions Act, Act 27 of 2003, Forensic Science is listed as a field of practice regulated by this Act. The Forensic Science category was recently removed and the field is currently unregulated in South Africa.

There are current efforts underway to form a Forensic Science Academy in South Africa during the coming year (Olckers, Blumenthal and Greyling, 2013). After organizing the profession, the Academy will be able to petition the SACNASP to reopen the category of forensic science for regulation of the forensic science profession. The SACNASP has to date worked diligently with the tasked professionals in the field to get forensic science regulated again at the earliest date possible.

It is envisaged that the formation of a Forensic Science Academy in South Africa will ultimately bring about a system of continued professional development that will allow forensic scientists to stay up to date, which will be a requirement of their registration with the SACNASP. The Academy should also host events to foster healthy scientific discussion about DNA evidence between peers and the exchange of values and ideas to ensure that forensic science is practiced with integrity.

23.5.7 Quality assurance and laboratory accreditation

The accreditation of laboratories according to the standards of the International Organization for Standardization (ISO) is performed by the South African National Accreditation System (SANAS) in South Africa (Act 16 of 2006). The SANAS has been a signatory to the International Laboratory Accreditation Co-operation (ILAC) agreement since 2000, which facilitates the acceptance of accredited laboratory results across national borders (ILAC, 2014). The SANAS is organized in several fields, one of which is forensic science. The Specialist Technical Committee (STC) of forensic science within the

SANAS sets the guidelines for accreditation in forensic science laboratories at the national level. This STC is comprised of several key stakeholders in the forensic science national landscape. SANAS accreditation implies that minimum quality standards are in operation in the laboratory and that on the day of inspection the laboratory was declared competent to perform the specified tests.

South Africa has a widely publicized high crime rate. It flows logically that the major State forensic laboratory in the country would have a high case load, which is indeed the case for the FSL. This laboratory, which has the highest case throughput in the world in terms of forensic samples processed per annum, is not accredited by the SANAS. There are currently two forensic laboratories in South Africa that are accredited and neither is connected to the FSL. The Forensic Chemical Laboratory of the Department of Health in Cape Town was accredited in 2010 (SANAS, 2014) in the field of chemistry and performs toxicological analyses. The University of Pretoria Forensic Toxicology Laboratory was accredited in 2012 (SANAS, 2014). The only two forensic science laboratories accredited in South Africa are thus both in the field of chemistry, specifically toxicology. Each cycle of accreditation is for a period of five years after which it can be renewed.

The issue of accreditation is thus urgent but fortunately has been noted by the Portfolio Committee of Government. "The lack of accreditation of Forensic Science Laboratories (FSL), even though not legally required, is a problem as some cases have been dismissed by the courts due to the lack of accreditation" (Report of the Portfolio Committee, 2012). Monitoring of this aspect by the Portfolio Committee on Police will hopefully assist in getting the accreditation of the Forensic Science Laboratory realized in the near future.

23.5.8 Testimony in DNA evidence

There is no national review system in place for testimonies delivered by the State laboratories' analysts. If this were the case, it would be unlikely for science mistakes and/or unethical testimony by the same analyst (State v. Rapagadie, 2010; State v. Mlanga, 2012; Bokolo v. State, 2013) not to have been detected and rectified. A system of monitoring and evaluation is a powerful tool for any forensic laboratory to identify areas where the

training of their analysts requires attention at both the technical and ethical levels. Regulation of the forensic science profession is thus imperative to elevate the quality of testimony by scientists in court in South Africa.

23.5.9 Technology of DNA typing

South Africa started to use STR technology in the late 1990s with the first cases going to trial after 2000. State v. Parker (2002) was one of the first STR based DNA cases, although it was used prematurely by the State laboratory before it was validated for use in casework. Initially kits with nine STR markers were the international norm (see Table 23.2), but this was found to be inadequate and 15-STR kits were developed, validated for use and implemented in most forensic laboratories. The current norm at the international level is to use 23 or more STR markers per DNA profile. In South Africa the FSL will finalize "full implementation" of 15-STR kits in 2014 (Smith, 2014). Other methods, for example X and Y haplotypes and mitochondrial analyses, are not routinely used in the FSL.

In terms of throughput, the FSL was, in 2007, with the commissioning of the fully automated robotics Genetic Sample Professing System (GSPS), the first laboratory in the world to have such a processing platform operational (Omar, 2008). The GSPS was single-handedly responsible for eliminating the backlog in DNA cases that hampered the efficient delivery of justice for many years. Early in 2013 the GSPS was switched off, first due to disposable shortages (Barnard, 2013), and subsequently it was permanently switched off and is being disassembled. Semi-automated processes are being instituted in its place (Smith, 2014). This defies logic at both the technology and justice levels, as South Africa has not only forfeited its leading role in automated DNA profiling but is again facing substantial DNA backlogs that are not conducive to the timely delivery of justice.

23.5.10 Legal aspects affecting DNA evidence

Forensic evidence is science based and an objective scientific evaluation of the data presented in court is essential. Unfortunately in court there is an emphasis on convictions by the National Prosecuting Authority (NPA) since this metric is primarily used to evaluate their performance (Redpath, 2012).

Table 23.2 DNA profiling kits launched by one commercial company for use in forensic DNA analyses (Life Technologies, 2014)

Kit name	No. of STR loci in kit	Launched
GlobalFiler™ PCR Amplification Kit	23	2012
AmpFLSTR® Identifiler® plus PCR Amplification Kit	15	2010
AmpFLSTR® Identifiler® PCR Amplification Kit	15	2001
AmpFLSTR® Profiler Plus® PCR Amplification Kit	9	1997

Independent experts in DNA evidence are more often than not regulated by the Health Professions Council of South Africa (HPCSA) since they all also perform work outside forensic science, which is mandatory (Health Professions Act, 1974). The HPCSA has a strict code of conduct and emphasis is placed on eradicating unethical practice. Although this does not guarantee the ethical practice of independent experts, there are severe consequences for them should they testify unethically in a court of law. This is not the case for the FSL expert witnesses, as they are exempt from the HPCSA Act.

The Criminal Procedure Act (CPA), Act 51 of 1977, together with the South African Law of Evidence (Zeffertt, Paizes and Skeen, 2003), is the legislation that governs how scientific evidence is introduced and handled in a court of law in South Africa. The South African Law of Evidence contains a mere nine lines on how to deal with DNA evidence and it pre-dates the advent of STR technology. The CPA also requires updating to keep track with the developing field of DNA evidence. To this end the new Criminal Law (Forensic Procedures) Amendment Bill was passed by the National Assembly in Parliament. This Bill will provide legislation, for example, for the National Forensic DNA Database and database hits, to facilitate the management of crime. Until the promulgation of this Amendment Bill, a legal vacuum existed for the use of DNA databases hits in court.

23.5.11 Future direction

Interpretation. Although new technology will always be adopted if it is fit for the purpose of forensics, focus has now globally shifted to the interpretation of the data generated (Butler, 2014).

Ethical practice of science. This is a clear goal towards which the proposed South African Forensic

Science Academy must strive. The regulation of the forensic science profession by SACNASP, with its formalized code of conduct and mandatory consequences for unethical conduct, will go far to rid the field of the scourge of unethical testimony that is often observed today.

Accreditation. As is the case with private pathology laboratories today, it should be a requirement for forensic laboratories in South Africa to be accredited.

Science discussion in forensics. There is a need to elevate the discussion about forensic science to the academic level between State and private experts. It is also necessary to foster discussion between the scientific and legal professions. The situation in South Africa is not dissimilar to that of the rest of the world: science professionals do not receive training in the law and legal professionals receive no training in science. Yet these professionals today both operate in an area where their fields of expertise overlap. It will be optimal if forums are created where these professionals can discuss how science can serve justice at the national level, without the pressure of a pending court case. This will be a positive step towards serving the people of the Republic with the justice they deserve.

23.6 Forensic toxicology in South Africa

It is unfortunate that forensic toxicology has not developed in pace with many of the other forensic science disciplines in South Africa. Although substantial analytical capacity exists in many academic and service laboratories, there are notable deficiencies in the domain of forensic toxicology, specifically as it applies to post-mortem diagnostic requirements, but also in routine drug and alcohol screening and analyses for DUIs (Driving Under the Influence), etc. Perhaps the major reason for this has been the striking absence of an appropriate academic platform for forensic toxicology as a discipline in tertiary teaching and training institutions.

There are three state-run forensic chemistry laboratories (Cape Town, Johannesburg and Pretoria), which provide analytical services to all nine provinces in respect of postmortem samples (blood, urine, vitreous humour, stomach content, etc.). However, minimal capacity exists in terms of analytical services with respect to enzymes/bioassays, nail and hair analysis, integrated advisory and/or diagnostic support service by experienced toxicologists, etc.

A large number of medicolegal postmortems are conducted annually in South Africa by nonspecialist medical practitioners (i.e. who are not forensic pathologists) and, accordingly, greater reliance is placed on support diagnostic services (histology, toxicology, etc.). This places an even greater burden on strained diagnostic resources and capacity, in a country that has one of the highest levels of interpersonal violence as well as driving under the influence violations (as reflected in the exceptionally high numbers of road traffic fatalities).

The large routine service workload, coupled with the physical separation of diagnostic laboratory facilities from medicolegal mortuaries (sometimes over great geographical distances), has resulted in the development of a huge operational backlog of case analyses, which is undoubtedly hampering and frustrating the administration of justice. In many long overdue cases, the validity of test results will inevitably be questioned in courts of law.

There has been a very rapid increase in the use of illicit drugs in South Africa over the past two decades, whilst South Africa has also become a crossroad for shipments of drugs being moved on intercontinental routes. The need for improved diagnostic capacity in respect of illicit drugs is great, not only in the medicolegal (postmortem) context but also with respect to the investigation of numerous clandestine and illicit laboratories that are being discovered and drug shipments that are being intercepted. Most of these activities are attended to by the Toxicology Section of the South African Police Service Forensic Science Laboratories, which is not affiliated to the National Department of Health Laboratories. This separation of major toxicological diagnostic services (South African Police Services and National Department of Health), also results in a lack of uniformity in diagnostic approach and service rendering.

Recently, substantial initiatives have been taken by the government to improve diagnostic capacity by implementing further tertiary training programs, improving human resource allocations and procuring new and sophisticated diagnostic equipment. Nonetheless, forensic toxicology service delivery in South Africa remains an area in urgent need of reformation and expansion.

23.7 Offender profiling in South Africa

23.7.1 History of offender profiling in South Africa

Offender profiling as an investigative tool has been used by the SAPS since 1994. Retired FBI Profiler, Robert Ressler, who visited South Africa in 1994 to assist with South Africa's most prolific serial murderer, Moses Sithole, later returned to train members of the SAPS in serial murder investigation. Ressler was one of the original FBI offender profiler pioneers and claims to have coined the term "serial murder".

The Investigative Psychology Unit (IPU) was first created in 1997 to assist in the investigation of psychologically motivated crimes and later expanded to a Section (a larger organizational structure) in 2011. At the time of its creation the main focus was on serial murder investigations due to a sharp increase in the detection of these types of cases between 1994 and 1997. The focus expanded over the years to include a wide variety of psychologically motivated crimes. These types of crimes typically have no external (usually financial) motive. They include but are not limited to serial murder, serial rape, sexual murders, muti- (ritual) murders, child sexual offenders, intimate partner murders, child abductions and kidnappings, mass murder, spree murder, cold cases and equivocal death scenarios, to name a few.

In its early days the Unit was staffed only by members with a psychology background, later augmented by a detective. Since then detectives have been a permanent part of the Unit; currently the majority of staff are officers with a detective background.

The Unit was originally stationed within the Detective Service Head Office in Pretoria. The SAPS is a national police service with a mandate for all policing in South Africa, with the result that the IPU would assist throughout the whole of South Africa. In 2009 the Unit was relocated to the Forensic Services Division where it remains today.

Between 2012 and 2013 the Section underwent a rapid expansion in terms of staff. At the beginning of 2012 the Section consisted of two support staff and five sworn police officers, all of whom were based at the National Head Office of the SAPS. By the end of 2013 the National IPS consisted of four members who were licensed psychologists, six detectives, two researchers, and two support staff, with plans to employ more detectives and psychologists. By mid-2013 the IPS had opened satellite units in each of the nine provinces, each staffed by a single detective. Plans are to expand these provincial units with between 10 and 15 members. Currently with its overall complement of 21 members providing services related to offender profiling and the investigation of psychologically motivated crimes, this makes the IPS one of the largest such units in the world.

Along with the rapid expansion of staff came an increase in training for the existing and newly appointed members. After 2012 training was provided to the members by International Criminal Investigative Analysis Fellowship accredited profilers from the Royal Canadian Mounted Police, Ontario Provincial Police in Canada and the Los Angeles Sheriff's Department. Further training focused on threat assessment and management, medicolegal death investigation, forensic pathology, psychopathy assessment and diagnosis, sexual offences investigation, serial arson investigation, anatomy of sharp force injuries, homicide and death investigation, Schedules for Clinical Assessment in Neuropsychiatry training, bloodstain pattern analysis and geographic profiling. Essentially the training program for the IPS members follows that of the curriculum of the understudy program of the International Criminal Investigative Analysis Fellowship.

23.7.2 Mandate of the section

While initially the IPS focused on serial murder investigations this has expanded over the years. Currently the mandate is to assist in the identification and investigation of psychologically motivated crimes, by means of investigative support, training and research.

Roles of the Section:
- Investigative support
- Training
- Research

23.7.3 Investigative support

Assistance is provided upon request to any investigator in the SAPS. The Section acts in an advisory capacity (like consultants) in the investigation of psychologically motivated crimes by providing services of a criminal investigative analysis nature such as: offender profiling, investigative guidance, risk assessments, interviewing of witnesses and suspects, crime scene analysis, case linkage analysis and courtroom testimony. The Section's experience with such cases is offered to the investigator who most likely has never dealt with a case of a similar nature.

Some of the members have worked on over 100 murder series since joining the Section, thus making the members some of the most experienced investigators of serial crimes in the world.

The Section has also assisted foreign law-enforcement agencies such as the Finnish National Bureau of Investigation, New Scotland Yard, Netherlands National Police, Central Bureau of Investigation – India, Royal Swazi Police and the Namibian Police, to name but a few.

23.7.4 Training

The Section provides training to investigating officers in the identification and investigation of psychologically motivated crimes. Training is given to various members of the SAPS, for example detectives and crime scene investigators. Ad hoc training is given upon request to prosecutors and other interested parties such as forensic pathologists, psychologists and parole board members of the Department of Correctional Services. Not only does this aid in the identification and successful investigation and prosecution of such crimes but it also educates investigators as to how and when behavioural analysts can be of assistance. The Section provides training to SAPS members by means of:
- Crime scene investigators' refresher course
- Serious and Violent Crime Course
- Family Violence, Child Protection and Sexual Offences Course
- Organized Crime Course

- Training tours through provinces upon request of a particular province
- Psychologically Motivated Crimes (PMC) Course

The PMC course is presented once a year to 30 members of the Detective Service and Forensic Services. The aim of the course is to train investigators to be able to identify and investigate these types of crimes. The course has a high academic standard and members are evaluated by means of daily tests, practical exercises and assignments.

The Section has also trained members of foreign law enforcement agencies such as the Belgian Police, Scotland Yard, Botswana Police, France Police, Namibia Police, the Australian Federal Police and the Royal Swazi Police.

The Section also provides practical training placements to students from overseas universities such as the Centre for Investigative Psychology at the University of Liverpool, UK, and the California School for Forensic Studies at Alliant International University, USA.

23.7.5 Research

Research into understanding psychologically motivated crimes aids in the investigative support and training provided. A local understanding of how crimes present themselves is imperative as foreign research has proved to be of limited use. This has resulted in the SAPS being one of the few law enforcement agencies that has a thorough database of its solved and unsolved serial murders. Suspects' details are meticulously recorded for research purposes and offender profiling purposes.

In 2013 for the first time, a full-time research capacity was approved within the Section.

23.8 Forensic ballistics in South Africa

23.8.1 History

The Ballistics Section of the Forensic Science Laboratory had its origins in the South African Defence Force. During the 1930s Major M.S. Barraclough, Inspector of Armaments for the Union Defence Force, performed certain firearms examinations for the Police. He was assisted later by Colonel G.C. Britz, a photographer attached to the South African Police Criminal Bureau.

The ballistics examinations were transferred to the South African Police during the 1940s and Colonel Britz

became the Commander of the Ballistics Section. The Ballistics Section was established as part of the Criminal Bureau and functioned as part of the Criminal Bureau until the Forensic Science Laboratory was established.

With the establishment of the Forensic Science Laboratory, all Forensic Science related examinations were incorporated into the Laboratory. The Ballistics Section became part of the Forensic Science Laboratory during 1986. The Laboratory was established in Silverton Pretoria and provided forensic services nationally.

The Ballistics Section performed firearms and toolmark examinations and included crime scene reconstructions. During the late 1980s stock theft and poaching case examinations were added to the examinations performed.

Due to the vast distances travelled for crime scene examinations, the Ballistics Section established Regional offices in Natal, the Eastern Cape and the Western Cape during the 1990s. These Regional offices developed into fully fledged Regional Forensic Science Laboratories.

The development of automated examination technology improved during the 1990s and the Integrated Ballistics Identification System (IBIS) was implemented at the Ballistics Section during 1997 to assist with the automated comparison of bullets and cartridge cases in a database.

The Mechanical and Metallurgical Engineering Section was incorporated into the Ballistics Section to perform vehicle accident reconstructions and metallurgical failure examinations.

The Ballistics Section diversified to include the following examination services:
- Firearms and toolmark examinations
- Shooting incident examinations and reconstructions
- Mechanical and Metallurgical Failure Analysis
- Vehicle Accident Reconstructions
- Stock Theft and Poaching Analysis

In 2013, approximately 38,000 ballistic cases were analysed by the Ballistics Section of the Forensic Science Laboratory.

References

Accreditation for Conformity Assessment, Calibration and Good Laboratory Practice Act, Act 16 of 2006 (South Africa).

Anholts, A. (2013) *Secular trends in the height and weight of South African children aged 6 to 10 years*, BSc Honours, Department of Anatomy, University of Pretoria.

Barnard, D.K. (2013) *SAPS bungle essential tenders*, Politicsweb, accessed: 7 January 2014, http://www.politicsweb.co.za/politicsweb/view/politicsweb/en/page71654?oid=363317&sn=Detail.

Barnard, D.K. (2014) *South Africa: 52 748 Forensic samples backlog is hampering fight against crime*, All Africa, Cape Town, South Africa, accessed: 14 January 2014, http://allafrica.com/stories/201401120251.html.

Beat, L. (2002) *History of South African law*, accessed: 4 October 2013, http://www.lenel.ch/docs/history-of-sa-law-en.pdf.

Bokolo v. State (2013) Supreme Court of Appeal of South Africa, Judgment, pp. 10.

Butler, J.M. (2014) *Advanced Topics in Forensic DNA Typing: Interpretation*, Elsevier Academic Press, San Diego, CA, USA.

Centre for the Study of Violence and Reconciliation (CSVR) (2009) *Why does South Africa have such high rates of violent crime?*, accessed: 4 October 2013, http://www.csvr.org.za/docs/study/7.unique_about_sa.pdf.

De Villiers, H. (1968) *The Skull of the South African Negro*, Johannesburg: Witwatersrand University Press.

Du Preez, J. (2013) *Language rights in South African courts*, accessed: 5 October 2013, http://www.politicsweb.co.za/politicsweb/view/page71654?oid=353910&sn=Detail&pid=71616.

Dubow, S. (1995) *Scientific Racism in Modern South Africa*, Cambridge University Press, Cambridge, pp. 117, 283.

Essential DNA Evidence Short Course (2013) DNAbiotec (Pty) Ltd, Pretoria, South Africa, pp. 46, 47.

Government Gazette (2003) Disaster Management Act, 2002, accessed: 14 December 2013, http://www.info.gov.za/view/downloadFileAction.

Health Professions Act, Act 56 of 1974 (South Africa).

Hefner, J.T. (2009) Cranial nonmetric variation and estimating ancestry. *Journal of Forensic Sciences* 54: 985–995.

Hill, I.R., Keiser Nielsen, S., Vermylen, Y., Free, E., De Valk, E. and Tormans, E. (1984) *Forensic Odontology, Its Scope and History*, The Old Swan Bicester, pp. 193–201.

Humanitarian News and Analysis (2013) *South Africa: Police blame "illegal immigrants" for crime*, accessed: 15 December 2013, http://irinnews.org/report/88303/south-africa-police-blame-illegal-immigrants-for-crime.

Hundermark, P. (2014) Chief Legal Executive of Legal Aid South Africa. Personal communication on 10 January 2014.

International Laboratory Accreditation Co-operation (ILAC) (2014) Rhodes, NSW, Australia, accessed: 12 January 2014, https://www.ilac.org/ilacarrangement.html.

Keough, N., Colman, K., L'Abbé, E.N., Symes, S.A., Cabo, L. (2012) Distinguishing features of thermal destruction on fleshed, wet and dry remains. In: *Proceedings of the 64th Annual Meeting of the American Academy of Forensic Sciences*, Vol.18, 386 pp.

L'Abbé, E.N., Steyn, M. (2012) Forensic anthropology in South Africa. In: *A Companion to Forensic Anthropology*, Ed. D,C. Dirkmaat, Wiley-Blackwell, London, pp. 626–638.

L'Abbé, E.N., Van Rooyen, C., Nawrocki, S.P., Becker, P.J. (2011) An evaluation of non-metric cranial traits used to estimate ancestry in a South African sample. *Forensic Science International* 209: 195.

L'Abbé, E.N., Kenyhercz, M., Stull, K.E., Ousley, S.D. (2013) Craniometric assessment of modern 20th century black, white and "coloured" South Africans. In: *Proceedings of the Annual Meeting of the American Academy of Forensic Sciences*, Vol. 19, 444 pp.

Life Technologies (2014) Life Technologies, Carlsbad, CA, USA, accessed: 9 January 2014, www.lifetechnologies.com.

McDowell, J.L., L'Abbé, E.N., Kenyhercz, M.W. (2012) Nasal aperture shape evaluation between black and white South Africans. *Forensic Science International* 222: 397.

Meintjes-van der Walt, L. (2010) *DNA in the Courtroom: Principals and Practice*, Juta & Co. Ltd, Cape Town, South Africa.

Morris, A.G. (2012) Biological anthropology at the Southern Tip of Africa: Carrying European baggage in an African context. *Current Anthropology* 53: S152–S160.

Myburgh, J., L'Abbé, E.N., Steyn, M. (2013) Estimating the post-mortem interval using accumulated degree-days in a South African setting. *Forensic Science International* 229: 165e.1–e.6.

Olckers, A., Blumenthal, R., Greyling, A. (2013) Forensic science in South Africa: status of the profession. *Forensic Science International: Genetic Supplement Series* 4: e146–147.

Omar, B. (2008) Are we taking physical evidence seriously? The SAPS criminal record and forensic science service. *SA Crime Quarterly* 23: 29–36.

Pepper, M.S. (2002) Partial relief from the regulatory vacuum involving human tissue through enactment of Chapter 8 of the National Health Act and regulations thereto. *South African Medical Journal* 102: 736–737.

Redpath, J. (2012) Failing to prosecute?: assessing the state of the National Prosecuting Authority in South Africa. *Institute for Security Studies Monograph* 186: 26–27.

Report of the Portfolio Committee on Police (2012) Report on the Detective Dialogue held on 5 September 2012, South Africa, accessed: 5 January 2014, http://www.pmg.org.za/files/doc/2012/comreports/121024pcpolicereport.htm.

SANAS (2014) South African National Accreditation System, Pretoria, accessed: 10 January 2014, http://home.sanas.co.za/?page_id=38.

SAPS (2014) South African Police Service, accessed: 11 January 2014, http://www.saps.gov.za/_dynamicModules/internetSite/faqBuild.asp?myURL=273.

Smith, J. (2014) Brigadier and Section Head: Forensic Database Management, Quality Management, Division: Forensic Services, SAPS, Personal communication on 6 January 2014.

South African Police Services (2013) Crime statistics, accessed: 5 October 2013, http://www.saps.gov.za/statistics/crimestats/2013/crime_stats.htm.

State v. Mlanga (2012) Regional Court held in Port Elizabeth, Testimony transcript, p. 279 lines 3–4, p. 289, lines 11–12 and 24–26, p. 294, lines 10–13, p. 284, pp. 289–294.

State v. Parker (2000) High Court of the Cape of Good Hope (subsequently renamed High Court of the Western Cape) in Cape Town, on Appeal (Full Bench).

State v. Rapagadie (2010) Regional Court held in Parow, Cape Town, Testimony transcript, p. 24, line 24, p. 25, lines 12–14, p. 68, line 16.

Steyn, M., İşcan, M.Y. (1997) Sex determination from the femur and tibia in South African whites. *Forensic Science International* 90: 111–119.

Steyn, M., Smith, J. (2007) Interpretation of ante-mortem stature estimates in South Africans. *Forensic Science International* 171: 97–102.

Zeffertt, D.T., Paizes, A.P., Skeen, A.St.Q. (Eds) (2003) *The South African Law of Evidence*, LexisNexis Butterworths, pp. 713–714.

CHAPTER 24
Forensic science practice in Spain

Angel Carracedo & Luis Concheiro

Institute of Forensic Science, University of Santiago de Compostela, Spain

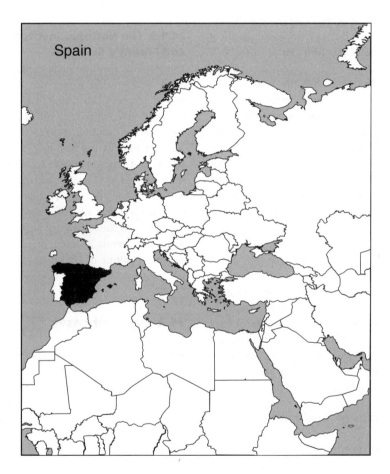

24.1 History

Although the first references to legal medical issues in Spain appear in *Fuero Juzgo* (642–653), and the *Fuero Real* (1255) and *Código de las Siete Partidas* (1265) and deal with numerous forensic references, the influence of the *Constitutio Criminalis Carolina* (1532) was essential for the

development of the legislation of medicolegal issues in Spain, as in many other continental European countries, and can be considered the beginning of the official intervention of doctors in judicial cases.

In the 16th and 17th centuries the influence of French and Italian legal medicine was notable in Spain and especially the work of Paolo Zachia, Fortunato Fidelis

---

The Global Practice of Forensic Science, First Edition. Edited by Douglas H. Ubelaker.
© 2015 John Wiley & Sons, Ltd. Published 2015 by John Wiley & Sons, Ltd.

and Ambrosio Paré. Among the Spanish authors Juan Fragoso and his work *Cirugia Universal* (1601) – whose second volume is dedicated to forensic science – is remarkable. Later, Mateo Orfila (1787–1853), a scientist of Spanish origin but teaching in Paris, marked the beginning in Spain, as in the rest of Europe, of forensic toxicology and the start of a stage of strong French influence in Spanish legal medicine. Pedro Mata y Fontanet (1811–1877), politician, writer and first professor of forensic medicine at the Complutense University of Madrid (1843), was the most important figure of Spanish legal medicine in the 19th century. His book *Tratado teórico-práctico de Medicina Legal y Toxicología* was the reference text in Spain well into the 20th century. However, of most importance was his influence on the structure of forensic science because he was the architect of the creation of the figure of *médicos forenses*, public servants of the Ministry of Justice, assigned to the courts, including those in rural areas, with the main function of assisting judges in any type of medicolegal issues (including – but no exclusively – forensic pathology). This original model favored at that time was that the judges were assessed with the same expert quality throughout the country and not just in large cities.

The problem is that this model remained unchanged until recently with a deep separation of academic legal medicine and forensic practice despite the enormous effort of some people who wanted to join both and to adopt the structure of the European institutes of legal medicine. Among those people should be mentioned Professor Lecha-Marzo (1888–1919), an extraordinary figure who tried to modernize Spanish legal medicine, in efforts surely curtailed by his early death.

24.1.1 The institutes of legal medicine

Spanish institutes of legal medicine were finally created in 1985 (Law 6/1985) and *medicos forenses* were integrated in this structure, but not the Academia, and this division persists today. The possibility of collaboration in teaching remains open through the "Teaching and Research Committees" (institute regulations) and in some cases the collaboration of the Universities with Institutes of legal medicine is remarkable.

From 1998 the following institutes were created (by date of approval):

1998 Valencia, Basque Country
2000 Navarra
2001 Catalonia
2002 Murcia, Aragon, Andalucia, Rioja, Asturias, Castilla-Leon, Castilla-La Mancha, Canary Islands
2003 Extremadura, Cantabria, Balearic Islands
2005 Galicia
2006 Madrid

The organization of the institutes is different from one to another but in general they have services of forensic pathology and clinical forensic medicine and have different seats distributed in the areas they serve.

24.1.2 The National Institute of Toxicology and Forensic Sciences

The National Institute of Toxicology and Forensic Sciences was created under the denomination of the Forensic Science Laboratory in 1886 as an official institution to give support to the work of *médicos forenses* with seats in Madrid, Barcelona and Seville. Later it was renamed as the National Institute of Toxicology (1935) and was responsible for all toxicological analyses requested by the *médicos forenses*. Finally a new seat was created in the Canary Islands and its work was extended to histopathology, biology, biochemistry and in general all the laboratory analyses needed in forensic cases. Recently its name was changed again to "The National Institute of Toxicology and Forensic Sciences" (INTCF). It belongs to the Ministry of Justice.

24.2 Types of cases

Forensic expertise can be requested directly by the judge alone or by the judge after a proposal from the prosecution or defense. There is also the possibility of private expertise when the prosecution or defense directly requests a forensic investigation at their own expense, in support of a hypothesis.

Crime investigation is conducted by examining magistrates (*jueces de instrucción*) who cannot be involved in the trial and therefore in the verdict. Investigation at the scene of the crime is performed by police officers and all forensic pathology issues by the *medicos forenses*.

According to Spanish criminal law, it is mandatory to perform autopsies in all cases of violent and suspicious death, including unexpected death.

There are few institutes of legal medicine with facilities for histopathological analysis, so this type of test is usually sent together with a toxicological analysis to the INTCF or to university institutes in some cases.

This is also the system for other complementary analyses in the field of biology, biochemistry or molecular pathology.

Ballistic, fingerprinting and criminalistics are mainly performed in labs of the *Cuerpos y Fuerzas de Seguridad del Estado* (National Police, Guardia Civil and Polices of the autonomous regions) (Ministry of Interior).

DNA typing for criminal cases is performed in the labs of INTCF, Police, Guardia Civil, Police forces of the autonomous regions and Institutes of Legal Medicine. Private DNA labs mainly carry out DNA testing for paternity cases.

Forensic anthropology, odontology and entomology are carried out in some of the official institutions but the services of some reference labs and experts in universities are often requested.

Clinical forensic medicine is usually performed by *médicos forenses* but specialists in other disciplines are increasingly requested. This is especially true for forensic psychiatry, where psychiatrists are often required. Injury assessment is usually performed by *médicos forenses* but there is a lot of private activity in this area.

24.2.1 Legal medicine in hospitals

In some hospitals in Spain, specialists in legal medicine are starting to be hired and legal medicine units implemented to assess medicolegal problems that arise in the clinical activity of the hospitals as well as to implement procedures and protocols to reduce a number of legal problems, especially those related to medical liability, which have continued to increase.

It is difficult to estimate the number of cases due to the lack of registries and official statistics. Information is only publically available from some institutions but not from most of them.

24.3 Structure

As stated by Luna and Pérez-Cárceles (2008), the organization of legal medicine in Spain is the result of an organizational model designed at the end of the 19th century, and the tensions created by intentions to adapt the model to modern day scientific reality and expertise.

From a practical point of view forensic science in Spain is currently structured around institutes of legal medicine. The work at institutes is carried out by *médicos forenses*, members of the *Cuerpo Nacional de Médicos forenses* (National Forensic Medical Corps), which, along with other institutions detailed below, form the organization of legal and forensic medicine in Spain.

The Forensic Medical Corps depends on the Ministry of Justice of Spain or the Ministry of Justice of the autonomous regions with competence in this matter.

Other institutions include:

– National Institute of Toxicology and Forensic Sciences (INTCF). The Institute of Toxicology depends on the Ministry of Justice for technical support of judges and *médicos forenses*. The main activities at the INTCF are forensic toxicology, forensic genetics (analysis of any type of biological material at the scene of the crime) and histopathology. It also provides advice and information to the public on issues related to poison prevention and consequences. They have facilities in Madrid, Barcelona, Seville and Canary Islands.

– University Institutes and Departments of Legal Medicine. These institutes provide teaching and educational resources and carry out official and private casework, mainly for toxicological analysis, forensic genetics (DNA typing), clinical forensic medicine and also when some specific expertise is required (i.e. anthropology, odontology, entomology, biochemistry).

There are university chairs of legal medicine and toxicology in most of the faculties of medicine across the country, university departments often associated with clinical pathology and two university institutes of forensic science: Seville and Santiago de Compostela. The latter is an institute created by an agreement of the autonomous government of Galicia with the University of Santiago de Compostela.

At the present time five Spanish universities are accredited for teaching the specialty of legal and forensic medicine: Barcelona, Granada, Madrid, Murcia and Seville.

– Medical Colleges and Royal Academies of Legal Medicine are also occasionally requested to provide expertise by judges.

24.4 Integration of forensic science

In general there is a lack of integration of forensic science reports. Crime scene experts, case analysis and complementary analysis are all independently reported by different experts. Although *médicos forenses* can assist the judge about doubts or questions regarding the different reports, experts involved in the case are called to give evidence at the courtroom since the reports only have validity after being confirmed at the hearing.

24.5 Education, recruitment and training

Legal and forensic medicine is mandatory subject matter in a medical career so it is offered in all faculties of medicine across the country. Forensic odontology is also part of the curriculum of Spanish faculties of dentistry. In addition, legal medicine is offered in many universities to students in law as an optional matter.

Some universities also offer master degrees in forensic medicine and different forensic disciplines such as forensic psychiatry, injury assessment, forensic anthropology, forensic genetics, forensic odontology, forensic toxicology, among others.

To become a *médico forense* it is necessary to have a degree in medicine and to pass an examination in a number of topics (*oposición*). They then become public servants of the Ministry of Justice. Once selected they have to acquire practical experience for a few months and after this period are considered official experts with full capacity to perform any type of forensic science report.

Médicos forenses are then ascribed to the different sections of an institute (pathology, clinical forensic medicine) according to the needs but without any specific formal training in the respective area. However, training courses are offered on a regular basis.

A similar system is used for other public institutions such as the INTCF. Applications for positions at the INTCF require a Bachelor of Science title in a biomedical discipline, and to pass the examination on a program with forensic science topics adapted to the type of work to be carried out at the institute. They then become public servants of the Ministry of Justice and are ascribed to one of the seats of the INTCF. Courses for updating knowledge are offered on a regular basis. The university does not have any role in the selection and education of the experts.

Legal Medicine was one of the first medical specialties in Spain (Health law of 20 November 1855) and is included in the list of specialties still recognized in Spain today.

Access to the specialty is through the MIR (postgraduate resident interns). The title of specialist in forensic and legal medicine, issued by the Ministry of Education, is provided after three years of training (two years rotating in different hospital areas such as pathology, psychiatry and traumatology and the last year spent at an institute of legal medicine.

The possession of the title of specialist in legal medicine is not a requirement for the examination to apply for the position of *medico forense* and therefore the practical usefulness of the title is limited. Due to this fact and despite the efforts of some relevant forensic scientists (from both the Ministry of Justice and academia) to integrate both systems and to have a similar system to other medical specialists, the Ministry of Health has recently proposed the exclusion of legal or forensic medicine from the list of medical specialists awarded in Spain, pending a final decision.

24.6 Funding

Funding for public institutions is obtained through the national government. The budget for the institutes of legal medicine, INTCF or police departments, is established on an annual basis in the Spanish national budget or the budget of the autonomous communities in some cases. University institutes usually have agreements with the Ministries of Justice of the corresponding autonomous communities.

24.7 Political influences

There is no political influence in the practice of forensic science, with the institutes of legal medicine, the INTCF and the other institutions involved in casework absolutely independent.

24.8 Certification

There is no certification program in Spain. After the examination for public servants is passed and the mandatory period of formation finished, public servants officially enter in the correspondent corp (Corps of Medicos Forenses, Corp of specialist at the INTCF, Police and so on). From that moment no additional evaluations or certifications of further qualifications are required in most cases, although forensic practitioners commonly attend courses organized by the different institutions.

24.9 Laboratory accreditation/ quality control

Only in forensic DNA typing is accreditation officially required. In this particular case ISO 17025 guidelines are mandatory and a few labs (including police labs, justice labs, National Institute of Toxicology and the University Institute of Forensic Science in Santiago). Since accreditation is not required for paternity testing, most of the private labs are not accredited (only four are accredited so far).

24.10 Technology

Infrastructures have clearly improved after the implementation of institutes of legal medicine. INTCF and police departments have improved facilities in general terms and there are no major limitations in technology affecting the practice of forensic science. However, there are differences in resources among different institutions.

24.11 Disaster preparedness

Medicolegal intervention and disaster victim identification has been regulated by Royal Decree 32/2009, where the role of the *médicos forenses* and the scientific police has been clearly established. Disaster preparedness and the role of different experts are clearly regulated in law. The protocol has been successfully applied in a number of disasters, particularly in the Santiago de Compostela derailment that occurred on 24 July 2013.

24.12 Legal issues

Single reports only have validity after being confirmed in the hearing. Experts are requested to give testimony in most of the trials where they have submitted reports. Expert testimony is always the last part of the trial.

Due to the duration of the trial (difficult to predict in some cases) and the lack of adequate planning, hearings are very time consuming for forensic experts. However, since teleconferences have been allowed and facilities implemented in many courtrooms, the situation has improved.

24.13 Research

Research is mainly performed in academic institutions and around 80% of the scientific production is carried out in university departments or university institutes of legal medicine. Three universities, Santiago de Compostela, Granada and Murcia, account for more than 60% of the scientific production in legal medicine in Spain. Since academic institutions are mainly involved in forensic genetics and toxicology, these are the most active areas, especially research linked to DNA typing.

Most of the scientific papers are published in international English language journals but there are a variety of journals in the Spanish language, including *Revista Española de Medicina Legal, Cuadernos de Medicina Forense, Ciencia Forense* and different local journals linked to the institutes of legal medicine.

The scientific level of some institutions is excellent. As an example the Institute of Forensic Science at the University of Santiago de Compostela was reported by Thompson and Reuters (http://archive.sciencewatch. com/ana/fea/11julaugFea/) to be the first at an international level in number of publications, number of citations and H index.

24.14 Future directions and challenges

24.14.1 Medical specialty

The fact that legal medicine is following a different scheme than the other medical specialties (through schools of medicine and not through hospital structures) and the fact that the title of specialist is not required to obtain a position as *médico forense* is a major challenge. The latter is a major limitation for the adequate training of *médicos forenses* since presently there is no real specialization, even in major areas such as forensic pathology or forensic psychiatry. The idea still remains that forensic doctors should carry out autopsies but in most cases they do not carry out microscopic histopathological studies, which are not performed in the institutes of legal medicine but at the INTCF, with the limitations that this implies.

There is a climate in favor of the integration of legal medicine in the MIR system (the Spanish educational system for medical specialties) and to make mandatory the title of specialist to apply for the position of *médico forense*, but since this has not been achieved so far the Ministry of Health has recently proposed the elimination of the specialty of legal and forensic science.

24.14.2 Integration academy/justice institutions

The fact that teaching of legal medicine is carried out by university professors that in general have little contact with practical forensic casework is a serious drawback for good quality teaching. At the same time, forensic practitioners are not benefiting from an adequate level of teaching and specialization and are not integrated in research projects.

The advantages of the integration of academia and forensic practitioners is so clear and it has been claimed for so many years for relevant personalities in the field that there is not any logical explanation why this has not been achieved so far.

24.14.3 System of public servants and public servants corps

Selection of personnel using the traditional Spanish system (a theoretical examination) for public servants is controversial. Once the candidate has been appointed to the corresponding corps (*médicos forenses* or personnel at the INTCF) promotions and executive positions are not based solely on merit and they are not open to people not already public servants of that particular corp.

24.14.4 Funding for research

Funding for research in forensic science has also been a considerable limitation. While the health system has its own funding scheme (National Institute of Health, Carlos III), forensic science is not included in this, since it is considered a responsibility of the Ministry of Justice, which does not have funding for research. Forensic researchers have therefore to apply for funding to general research funding programs, competing with basic research of higher impact, so the chances to obtain the approval for research programs is increasingly difficult.

Simultaneously, the possibilities of funding at the European level have decreased during the last two funding periods of the Directorate of Research of the EU (Framework Program 7 and Horizon 2020). Forensic Medicine is neither in the Health Program nor in the Security Program so the possibilities for funding are also limited.

24.14.5 Organization

The organization of forensic science is too complex with overlaps of activity in different institutions and should be simplified for better efficiency. This is becoming more complicated by the fact that many responsibilities in organization have been transferred to the autonomous communities while some others remain under the control of central government.

References and further reviews

Castellano, M. (2012) *La construcción de la Medicina Legal y Forense en España: Después de ciento Setenta Años, una tarea Inacabada. Discurso de Ingreso*, Real Academia de Medicina. Instituto de España. Madrid.

Concheiro, L. (2006) *La Medicina Legal en la Distoria. Discurso de Ingreso*, Real Academia de Medicina y Cirugía de Galicia, La Coruña.

Luna, A., Pérez-Cárceles, M.D. (2008) Forensic Medicine in Spain. In: *Forensic Medicine in Europe*, Eds. B. Madea and P. Saukko, Verlaf Schmidt-Römhild, Lübeck.

Sánchez, J.A. (2010) Organización de la medicina legal y forense en España. *Jano* 12: 77–80.

Villanueva, E., Gisbert Calabuig, J.A. (2004) *Medicina Legal y Toxicologia*, Ed. Masson, Barcelona–Madrid.

CHAPTER 25

Legal medicine and forensic science in Switzerland

Patrice Mangin[1] & Pierre Margot[2]

[1] The University Center of Legal Medicine, Lausanne-Geneva, Switzerland
[2] School of Criminal Justice, University of Lausanne, Switzerland

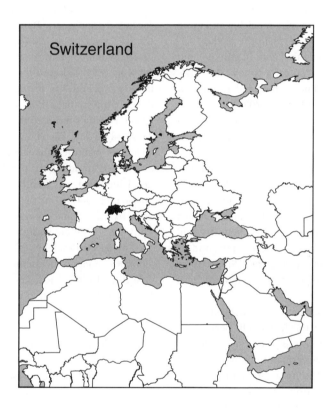

Switzerland has seen a strong and early academic development of both forensic medicine and forensic science that is unheard of elsewhere. This has helped in creating a strong culture and research within a continental legal environment. This dual development is described thereafter.

25.1 Legal medicine

25.1.1 History (Mallach, 1996; Mund and Bär, 2004; Mangin and Barras, 2008)

The roots of legal medicine in Switzerland are to be found in the Middle Ages, its customary laws

The Global Practice of Forensic Science, First Edition. Edited by Douglas H. Ubelaker.
© 2015 John Wiley & Sons, Ltd. Published 2015 by John Wiley & Sons, Ltd.

and its specific social and sanitary organizations. Surgeons, matrons, physicians and apothecaries all acted as early forensic experts in numerous cases of suspected infanticides, sorcery, bawdry, poisoning or any other bodily harm. At the end of the Middle Ages, every important city had its own official physician who would often let the activity of a medical expert earn its spurs as a valuable service to the community and justice. Such was the case for Felix Platter (1536–1614), a physician from Basel who is generally considered as the founding father of legal medicine in Switzerland (Figure 25.1). In the Modern Times, several other Swiss leading medical experts took an interest in legal medicine and more generally in the ties that exist between the medical sciences and different legal activities, both in criminal and civil law. Even though it is too early to talk about the emergence of a new discipline in those times, different authors, including Albert de Haller (1708–1777), were already publishing a variety of case collections and treatises explaining the art of writing medicolegal reports and other dissertations.

The field of legal medicine, such as it is understood today, emerged at the end of the Enlightenment period. The sanitary and academic organization of the modern state, the advent of anatomoclinical localization methods, the discoveries in chemistry and the invention of many laboratory techniques and of their biological applications during the 19th century all contributed to the emergence of the new medical specialty.

In fact, the birth of the science of legal medicine coincided with the creation of the first public services of forensic medicine and forensic psychiatry. Because of Swiss federalism, these services had to be organized at the level of the different cantons. At the same time and in practice, the strictly forensic tasks overlapped with the activities carried out by sanitary police and public hygiene authorities.

The changes also impacted the academic world: legal medicine began to be taught at the law faculties of the different Swiss universities. Soon thereafter, however, all scientific and teaching activities pertaining to legal medicine were gradually transferred to the five newly created or reorganized faculties of medicine, and in some cases even to independent urban institutions (in Locarno, St-Gallen or Chur).

Several legal medicine university chairs and teaching programs were thus created within the various faculties of medicine: in Bern (Professor Carl Friedrich Emmert in 1855, followed by Professor Max Howald in 1903), in Geneva (Professor Hippolyte-Jean Gosse in 1876, followed by Professor Louis Mégevand in 1902 and Professor François Naville in 1925), in Basel in 1882 (Professor Ernest von Sury in 1890, followed by Professor Adolf Streckeisen in 1895 and Professor Salomon Schönberg in 1924), in Lausanne in 1890 (Professor Jacques Larguier des Bancels, followed by Professor Georges Spengler in 1904 and Professor Paul Reinbold in 1922) and in Zürich (Professor Hans Konrad von Wyss in 1895, followed by Professor Heinrich Zangger in 1912 and Professor Fritz Schwarz in 1941).

The professionalization and institutionalization of legal medicine continued throughout the 20th century. At the same time, the volume and the types of activities of all the institutes increased significantly, causing an acute need for additional physical space at all locations. Legal medicine was clearly outgrowing its traditional boundaries, defined in the 19th century by pathology and toxicology and sometime later also by genetics. Thus, the different institutes introduced a number of new specialties: physical anthropology, antidoping laboratory analysis, penitentiary medicine, forensic psychiatry and traffic medicine. A milestone was reached in 1980 with the creation of the Swiss Society of Legal Medicine.

25.1.2 Organization

There are currently five institutes of legal medicine in Switzerland, located respectively in Basel, Bern, Lausanne-Geneva[1], St-Gallen and Zürich. They are all administered by different cantonal authorities, such as the cantonal government itself, the Department of Health and Social Affairs, the Department of Justice and Police or the Department of Education. Some cantons that do not have an institute of legal medicine (Grisons, Neuchâtel, Ticino, Zug) offer their judicial authorities a cantonal medical examiner that can conduct the necessary forensic investigations.

---

[1]Both institutes of Lausanne and Geneva merged into a single one under the name "University Center of Legal Medicine Lausanne-Geneva".

Figure 25.1 Felix Platter (1536–1614).

25.1.2.1 The institutes of legal medicine

University status

The institutes of legal medicine of Basel, Bern, Lausanne-Geneva and Zürich operate under university status. The director of each institute is a medical doctor who must be an ordinary professor at the faculty of medicine of the university to which the institute is affiliated. He or she is also in charge of teaching legal medicine at both undergraduate and postgraduate levels.

The institute of legal medicine of St-Gallen has a hospital status. Nevertheless, it is headed by a medical doctor who is a member of the Faculty of Medicine of the University of Basel. The Institute's Director is responsible for undergraduate teaching of legal medicine at the University and is also in charge of postgraduate training at the Institute.

Structure

The institutes, which are structured identically, always include a forensic medicine unit, a unit of traffic medicine, a laboratory of toxicology and forensic chemistry and a laboratory of forensic genetics.

The forensic medicine units are headed by a medical examiner. These units are active in three different domains: forensic pathology (on-site investigations, autopsies, external examinations, identifications), clinical forensic medicine (examination of victims of physical and sexual assault, abuse, age determinations, etc.) and forensic expert evaluations (medical malpractice).

The units of traffic medicine are in charge of assessing the driving capacities of individuals suffering from alcohol-related or drug-related problems, specific diseases or age-related psychomotor impairment. These units are headed by a medical doctor specialized either in internal medicine or in forensic medicine.

The toxicology and forensic chemistry units are usually headed by a forensic chemist. The tasks carried out include the determination of blood–alcohol levels, toxicological analyses of samples collected during autopsies or clinical examinations and analyses of samples in cases of suspected driving under the influence of illegal drugs or medication. The quality of the latter analyses, as well as that of blood–alcohol level determinations, is rigorously controlled by the federal government, which delivers accreditation based on mandatory external quality control procedures. In addition, the laboratories are accredited according to the ISO 17025 standard.

The forensic genetics laboratories, headed by a forensic geneticist, are responsible for analyzing biological traces, carrying out paternity tests and determining genetic profiles that are then added to the national registry at the Federal Police Office for Police in Bern. These activities are rigorously controlled by the federal authorities and require ISO 17025 accreditation.

In addition to these common services, certain institutes also include some specific units and laboratories like a forensic psychiatry unit (Basel, Bern, Lausanne-Geneva), a forensic imaging unit (Zürich, Bern, Lausanne-Geneva), a forensic physics and ballistics center (Bern), a violence medicine unit and a laboratory for doping analysis (Lausanne-Geneva).

Funding

The different activities of the five Institutes are financed in part by the fees charged for the forensic services rendered and in part by funds provided by the relevant cantonal authorities.

Staff

The institutes' staff is composed entirely of employees. A number of professions are represented: physicians, biologists, chemists, psychologists, laboratory technicians and assistants, secretaries and administrators. In the case of university-affiliated institutes, the supervisory staff, the physicians, the chemists and the biologists usually hold a university degree.

25.1.2.2 Legal medicine outside of the institutes

In the cantons of Grisons, Neuchâtel, Ticino and Zug the medical examiners have a different status:

- In Neuchâtel, he or she is considered as a liberal professional.
- In the other three cantons, they work as employees of the cantonal administration.

All the medical examiners in these cantons hold forensic medicine specialty diplomas. As a rule, they have undergone training in one of the institutes of legal medicine in Switzerland and with which they collaborate on a regular basis, in particular with regards to the laboratory analyses that need to be conducted.

25.1.3 Forensic evaluations

In Switzerland, different organizations may ask an institute of legal medicine or an extra-institute forensic science expert to carry out a forensic evaluation. In most cases, these evaluations are ordered by judicial and police authorities. Occasionally, federal authorities may also be involved. In addition, cantonal administrations may also request an evaluation of one's driving capacities. Finally, forensic evaluations may also be carried out on the request of private individuals or nongovernmental organizations such as the IRCC, the WHO, the World Antidoping Agency or international sports federations.

The Swiss institutes of legal medicine do not conduct evaluations of bodily damage due to accidents or to any other cause when such assessments are requested by insurance companies. Instead, this particular task is carried out by other expert physicians (internists, rheumatologists, orthopedists, etc.).

Requests for forensic evaluations are usually addressed to the director of the institute. Once the evaluation is completed, the institution issues a bill for the services rendered. The situation is different for extra-institute experts, who either bill their services directly or receive salaries as state employees.

Judicial evaluations are principally aimed at determining the cause of death of a victim, the possible involvement of a third party in a death and the nature of such involvement, as well as the date and time of death. In this respect the units of forensic medicine of each institute in charge of these evaluations are provided with all the equipment needed in terms of autopsy facilities, imaging techniques and laboratory of histopathology. The identification of victims and the characterization of traumatic injuries inflicted during any type of assault, including sexual assault, are also common requests.

Forensic investigations often require complementary forensic toxicological analyses, such as the determination of blood–alcohol levels at the time of the event of interest, regular monitoring in substance abusers and tests certifying the absence of alcohol consumption using the appropriate biological markers.

In more general terms and whenever possible, the institutes of legal medicine always readily assist the judicial authorities by offering their expert medical opinion so that justice may prevail. The issues at stake may concern medical liability, drunk driving and even forensic psychiatry when the institutes have the appropriate expert staff.

Finally, the institutes of legal medicine also play an important role in providing expert advice in medical law and ethics when such advice is requested by hospitals or private practitioners.

25.1.4 Disaster response

According to the recommendations of Interpol, Switzerland created a Disaster Victim Identification (DVI) team in 2002. The team consists of some members of the federal police, forensic pathologists and technicians from the different university institutes, forensically trained odontologists and members of the different cantonal police forces. The legal basis of the DVI team is an intercantonal agreement in which all members agree to send trained professionals to the canton in need, in some cases at the request of the federal police or the federal department of foreign affairs. The DVI team is meant to support and reinforce the canton in need, mainly by conducting the postmortem operations. The canton that requests this aid grants a fixed financial compensation on a per man and day basis. All members of the Swiss DVI team (www.dvi.ch) follow at least three training modules of one day each, which are provided by experienced DVI members. The Swiss DVI team has now 270 members and has been engaged several times, for example, in Thailand after the 2004 Tsunami, in the St Gothard tunnel fire and the crash of a Belgian bus.

25.1.5 Training
25.1.5.1 Undergraduate training

Forensic medicine is part of the mandatory courses taken by every medical student in Switzerland and is one of the subjects of the Federal Medical Diploma examination. Although the medical diploma is indeed federal, undergraduate education is organized independently by each faculty of medicine. Forensic medicine is thus taught in different ways in different universities. In some cases, the subject is addressed exclusively in ex cathedra lectures. In other cases, a more interactive format is offered: workshops designed for groups of 8 to 10 students. Each faculty is also at liberty to decide which specific topics should be included in the course and which specific format, practical or theoretical, is used during the final examination. At the same time, a certain level of homogeneity is guaranteed thanks to a common, nationwide list of learning objectives in forensic medicine.

As a rule, the teaching of forensic medicine in every faculty covers classical issues such as forensic pathology, clinical forensic medicine, forensic toxicology, forensic genetics, traffic medicine and medical law, and ethics.

Finally, it should be noted that in some cases, the academic members of the institute of forensic medicine also participate in the teaching offered to law students.

25.1.5.2 Postgraduate training

A specialist diploma in forensic medicine may be obtained after receiving a Federal Diploma in Medicine and attending a five year program, which must include at least three years of training in an institute of legal medicine, between six months and one year spent in a department of clinical pathology and one year training in a defined clinical setting. A scientific activity within a forensic institute or a PhD program can be counted for up to six months. The training can be partly accomplished in an accredited foreign institution for up to one year.

The postgraduate training required to obtain a given specialty Diploma is defined by the Swiss Medical Association (FMH), a privately held nonprofit institution where every recognized medical specialty is represented by two members nominated by peers. In the case of legal medicine, the requirements for obtaining a specialty Diploma are relatively complex. The successful candidate must be familiar with a number of different forensic methodologies as specified by the Swiss Society of Legal Medicine. In practice, each candidate is required to carry out a specific number of forensic investigations including examination of bodies, external examinations and autopsies. The candidate must also be knowledgeable about forensic toxicology, in particular with regards to the interpretation of analytical results. He or she must be familiar with forensic genetics, including paternity testing, analysis of trace material and interpretation of results. There are also other requirements such as demonstrated active participation in psychiatric evaluations, the ability to conduct driving capacity assessments, evaluations of traumatic lesions in an assault victim, determination of blood–alcohol levels, age determination, evaluation of a potential medical error and others.

The successful candidate is also expected to be knowledgeable about medical law and ethics and to participate in different scientific meetings in legal medicine.

When all of these conditions are met, the director of the institute where the candidate has been trained issues a certificate testifying that all the prerequisites for a specialist Diploma have been met. The candidate must then pass a full-day examination. The morning session includes an autopsy in the presence of two experts,

followed by a written autopsy report and its conclusions. In the afternoon, the candidate is first asked to conduct an evaluation of traumatic lesions, either by examining a live victim or analyzing previously collected data. A second evaluation follows. It may focus on another set of traumatic lesions or address a different topic, such as forensic toxicology, forensic genetics or traffic medicine. The examination also includes a series of general questions about legal medicine pertaining to medical law, determination of blood–alcohol levels, paternity searches, driving ability, etc. Once the examination has been passed, the candidate submits all work certificates and case numbers to the FMH, who then decides if all conditions are met.

25.1.5.3 Continuing education

Every specialist in legal medicine is required to maintain his or her knowledge through continuing education. Continuing education activities usually consist in attending congresses, seminars and other scientific meetings. Compliance with continuing education requirements is rigorously controlled on behalf of the FMH by the Society of Legal Medicine. Thus, every specialist must earn a certain number of continuing education credits every year.

25.1.6 Research

Research activities in legal medicine are carried out for the most part within the university institutes. Indeed, only these institutions can provide the technical framework, all the competent staff and the critical mass of investigations necessary to conduct quality research. Research is funded by national or international granting agencies, such as the Swiss National Fund for Scientific Research, different Federal Departments (Health, Justice, Transportation, Sports) and a number of private foundations. Institutional grants are allocated to specific projects on a competitive basis and using independent evaluators.

The institutes of legal medicine participate in a number of collaborative research projects. At a national level, the institutes collaborate among themselves and also with the Lausanne School of Criminal Sciences, currently headed by Professor Pierre Margot. International collaborations involve a number of different institutions and laboratories abroad. In practice, medical and nonmedical scientists employed by the Swiss institutes have many opportunities to undergo additional training abroad. Funding is provided either by research grants or within the context of sabbatical stays granted by the home institution.

Current research projects in Switzerland cover many different areas of legal medicine. In some cases, individual institutes have focused on specific research subjects leading to international recognition in very precise domains such as forensic imaging, imaging mass spectrometry or transcriptome investigations.

The Swiss Society of Legal Medicine was founded on 13 December 1980 by the Directors of the Institutes of Legal Medicine. Its first president and founding father was Professor Hubert Patscheider, the Director of the Institute of Legal Medicine of St-Gallen. According to the Society's articles of association, its members may include both legal medical doctors and other professionals involved in forensic activities, such as chemists, biologists and psychologists.

The Society meets twice a year. The winter meeting always takes place in Bern and has a fairly standard agenda. Firstly, reports are made by the different commissions and experts that represent the Society vis-à-vis other learned societies or international organizations. Secondly, a number of administrative issues are addressed, such as changes in the articles of association, admission of new members and approvals of the treasurer's financial statement and of the President's activity report. The summer meeting is organized by a different institute every year and is more scientific in nature. Thus, the members can usually attend at least one presentation made by a Swiss or foreign invited speaker on a topic of interest to forensic scientists.

The Swiss Society of Legal Medicine is also active through its specialty commissions, which represent different domains of legal medicine (forensic medicine, forensic chemistry and toxicology, forensic genetics, traffic medicine). The specialty commissions play two important roles. The first role consists in ensuring good practices in the specialty. This may be accomplished by coordinating different activities through institutional directives and by conferring specialty titles on the basis of ad hoc directives. The second role is to represent the specialty vis-à-vis the Swiss political authorities. Indeed, the political authorities often require expert opinions that the specialty commissions are capable of providing. One example is the revision of the law that sets the maximum allowable alcohol levels when driving a vehicle.

Another example is the introduction of tests aimed at identifying drivers that use illegal drugs or dangerous medical substances. Some of the issues are extremely complex: directives aimed at properly defining death in the context of organ transplantation, construction of human tissue banks, ethical issues surrounding end-of-life treatments, and many others.

Our description of the Swiss Society of Legal Medicine would not be complete if we did not mention its central role in the training of forensic specialists. Not only is the Society responsible for defining the conditions necessary to obtain the specialty Diploma but it is also instrumental in ensuring lasting professional excellence through mandatory continuing education. Indeed, every physician with an FMH specialization in legal medicine must be able to demonstrate that he or she is maintaining and updating his or her knowledge by engaging in continuing education activities. Oral presentations or written publications in relevant domains as well as active collaboration with the official organizations in a given specialty constitute additional requirements. The overall control of continuing education is indeed possible and enforceable because the minimum number of credits that a physician must earn each year is determined for each given specialty.

25.1.7 The five Swiss Institutes of Legal Medicine

BASEL:

Institut für Rechtsmedizin der Universität
Pestalozzistrasse 22, Postfach, CH-4004 Basel
Telephone: +41 61 267 38 73
Telefax: +41 61 267 39 07
E-mail: irm.basel@bs.ch
Director and Head Physician: Prof. Volker Dittmann, MD

BERN:

Institut für Rechtsmedizin der Universität
Bühlstrasse 20, CH-3012 Bern
Telephone: +41 31 631 84 11
Telefax: +41 31 631 38 33
E-mail: contact@irm.unibe.ch
Director and Head Physician: Prof. Christian Jackowski, MD

LAUSANNE-GENEVA:

University Center of Legal Medicine
Rue du Bugnon 21, CH-1011 Lausanne

Telephone: +41 21 314 70 70

Telefax: +41 21 314 70 90

E-mail: curml.central@chuv.ch

Rue Michel-Servet 1 - CH-1211 Genève 4

Telephone: +41 22 379 56 16

Telefax: +41 22 789 24 17

E-mail: claudine.kuffer@hcuge.ch

Director and Head Physician: Prof. Patrice Mangin, MD, PhD

St-GALLEN:

Institut für Rechtsmedizin am Kantonsspital

Rorschacherstrasse 93, CH-9007 St-Gallen

Telephone: +41 71 494 21 52

Telefax: +41 21 494 28 75

E-mail: irmsg@kssg.ch

Director and Head Physician: Prof. Roland Hausmann, MD

ZÜRICH:

Institut für Rechtsmedizin der Universität Zürich

Winterthurstrasse 190/52, CH-8057 Zürich

Telephone: +41 44 635 56 11

Telefax: +41 44 635 68 51

E-mail: contact@irm.uzh.ch

Director and Head Physician: Prof. Michael Thali, MD

25.2 Forensic science

25.2.1 History

The industrial revolution and the humanization of the law, forbidding torture as a means of proof in the late 18th and early 19th century in most of Europe, led courts to rely occasionally on expert's advice to decide on issues in criminal proceedings. The use of chemistry, biology, physics and technologies such as photography is documented in many cases in the 19th century but there is no professional or academic discipline developing expert's services except in medicine. Reforms in police organization, the disappearance of marking criminals with hot wires, the lack of systematic classification of condemned criminals combined to highlight the need of the development of a scientific and administrative profession within law enforcement. The development of criminal anthropometry, scene of crime documentation and forensic photography by Bertillon in Paris were the seeds of identification bureaus around Europe, created to help identify habitual criminals (recidivists) at the end of the 19th century. Switzerland was the first country outside France to introduce Bertillon's identification system after a chief of police meeting in Bern in 1890. The first identification bureau was opened in Geneva in 1891. Switzerland was also strongly influenced by Hans Gross who published in Vienna (Austria) his famous handbook presenting "Kriminalistik" as the fundamental method for criminal investigation in 1893 (led by the investigative magistrates of the continental European legal systems) (Gross, 1893). It relied heavily on physical evidence for both tactical as well as evidential purposes.

A young German researcher (Figure 25.2), established in Switzerland, became convinced that forensic photography, criminalistics or police science were to become a science and a profession in the 20th century: Archibald Rodolphe Reiss (1875–1929). His passion for scientific photography and his contact with Bertillon and Gross were the seeds of a course in forensic photography and police science already given for students at the University of Lausanne in 1902, developments published in an unsurpassed book in forensic photography (Reiss, 1903). In parallel, Reiss described and developed a full range of scientific expertise for courts and fought for the development of the discipline in academia (Collectif, 2009). His international reputation convinced the University to create a new institute, accepted by authorities in 1906 and officially opened in 1909: the Institute of Police Science. This was the first full university programme in forensic science worldwide. Soon, major contacts and initiatives saw intensive collaborations and meetings of scientists in Europe, one of whom was marked by intensive collaboration: Edmond Locard from Lyon, who created the first forensic science laboratory in 1910. Scientists strongly opposed social science theories on criminals, such as those by Lombroso, and focused on a cynegetic culture of trace evidence. Lausanne made Reiss an honorary citizen.

A major book combining scientific knowledge with the knowledge of criminal activities showed the potential of combining forensic science and criminology in understanding and solving crimes (Reiss, 1911). This was to be the first volume of a four volume contribution, but the First World War put an end to the academic career of Reiss. Hired to witness atrocities in the Balkans, he denounced and documented the use of forbidden ammunitions (explosive projectiles), mass executions, bombing of hospitals (probably the

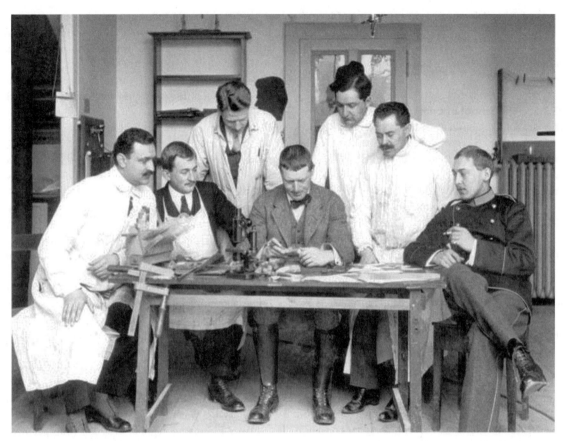

Figure 25.2 Rodolphe Archibald Reiss (1875–1929) as a young professor (center with the bow tie) teaching toolmark identification in 1913. From left to right: Mr Costescu (Romania), Mr Burnier (collaborator), Reiss, Grigoriu (Romania), Vamesch (Romania) and Bischoff (student, future professor of forensic science).

first documentation using photography from a plane was used by Reiss at the time) and soon took sides for Serbia, to become a war hero. After the War, Reiss came briefly back to Lausanne, saw that his students had pursued the development of the Institute and went back to Belgrade to become consultant for King Pierre of the Serbs, Croats and Slovenes.

Jean Burnier, first graduate, and Bischoff, third graduate, combined their efforts during and after the War and Bischoff (1892–1969) became the second professor of forensic science at the University of Lausanne officially in 1923 after the withdrawal of Reiss. He was followed in 1963 by Professor Jacques Mathyer (1921–2010) and in 1986 by Professor Pierre Margot (1950–). In 1954, the Institute of Police Science created the first academic programme in criminology in Switzerland and changed its name to become the Institute of Police Science and Criminology (IPSC), under the impulsion of Bischoff, Locard and the then professor of forensic medicine M.A. Thélin. A first doctoral programme was also initiated.

The continuous increase in student population as well as the development of interdisciplinarity saw the development and offer of full academic forensic science specializations.

Since 2003, the disciplines of criminal law and criminal procedure joined the school, to become the School of Criminal Justice, its current name, in 2013.

25.2.2 Organization

There are currently two large institutes of forensic science in Switzerland in Lausanne and Zürich administered by cantonal authorities. They cover most specialized forensic science cases. Further, 25 small cantonal crime laboratories are extensions of identification bureaus within state (cantons) police forces and process most routine forensic science cases (fingerprints, various marks, documents, scene of crime, etc.).

25.2.2.1 The School of Criminal Justice – Lausanne

The School of Criminal Justice (Ecole des sciences criminelles – ESC; www.unil.ch/esc) operates under a university status. The Director of the School is a full professor at the Faculty of Law, Criminal Justice and Public Administration of the University of Lausanne to which the School is affiliated. The School has a vice-dean of the Faculty and participates in the overall administration of the Faculty. It provides full undergraduate and postgraduate studies in Forensic Science and Criminology.

Currently the School offers a full-time BSc in forensic science (180 ECTSs (European Credit Transfer Units)) in 3 years, completed by 3 to 4 semesters (full-time equivalent) Master programme either in:

- Science (MSc in forensic science, with emphasis on "identification – physical evidence", or "chemical criminalistics", or "identification – digital evidence). A new MSc in traceology and crime analysis was created in 2013, which combines three semesters in forensic science and one semester in criminology in collaboration with the University of Montreal, Canada (who is offering a master in criminology with three semesters in criminology and one semester in forensic science, in Lausanne)
- Law (MLaw in criminology and security or MLaw for magistrates in criminal proceedings)
- Law, interdisciplinary (MLaw criminality and security in communication technologies) that extends over two faculties (Business and Law) and the School of Criminal Justice.

The School offers two successful PhD programmes, one in Forensic Science (64 candidates in 2014) and one in Criminology (currently 21 candidates) (Margot and Al, 2009).

Continuing education is offered in the form of day conferences, week's workshops as well as a wide range of web-based distance learning certificates (CAS – certificate of advanced studies with university credits), interpretation and evaluative opinions, DNA interpretation, Bayesian networks and crime statistics.

The School has 11 full-time equivalent professors and includes about 100 collaborators (researchers, tutors) with full laboratory facilities and in 2013–2014 over 550 students.

Besides teaching and research, the school provides experts services for courts (in fingerprints, toolmarks and firearms, fire investigation, illicit drugs, documents, handwriting expertise, microtraces, forensic imaging, forensic intelligence and crime analysis), for administrations (policing, criminological expertise – crime prevention, statistics, penology) as well as private and civil cases.

The funding is provided by the state of Vaud (with a Federal contribution) or for casework by fees charged, and research mandates by National or International research funds (Swiss National Research Foundation, European Funds, NIJ, etc.).

Graduates from the School become scientists within crime laboratories, criminals investigative services, three are currently state police chiefs, border control agencies, drug control agencies or work in private companies (insurances – crime-related insurance frauds; fighting against counterfeit products) for the forensic scientists or in administration (crime statistics, preventive programmes, prison and rehabilitation centers) for the criminologists or court officers and magistrates.

It was a founding member of ENFSI (European Network of Forensic Science Institutes) in 1994.

25.2.2.2 The Forensic Science Institute – Zürich

The City of Zürich created a Forensic Science Laboratory within the City Police Deparment in 1952 under the Direction of Dr Frei-Sulzer. It developed full laboratory services as well as a Federal Research Center in the field of explosives investigation and public security (under the acronym WFD – Wissenschaftlicher Forschungsdienst). It covers all specialities of a full forensic science laboratory with civil (scientists) and police trained personnel except in matters of documents, handwriting, and fingerprints. In parallel, the state Police (Canton of Zürich) developed an extensive identification bureau that covered specialties not covered by the City Laboratory, with some overlap. Both were also founding members of ENFSI.

In 2010, State and City authorities decided to combine both laboratories to develop synergies within what is now known as the Forensic Science Institute of Zürich (http://www.stadt-zuerich.ch/pd/de/index/stadtpolizei_zuerich/WD_WFD.html). It is one of the large European laboratories with over 60 scientists and police personnel. Its current legal status is under discussion. It provides full forensic science services for the Canton (state) of Zürich and for most German speaking Cantons in a fee for service arrangement.

25.2.3 Research

Research activities are mostly conducted within university institutes, with the exception of the WFD in Zürich, but many projects are conducted in collaboration with the Forensic Medicine Institutes and the various administrations (magistrates, crime laboratories, state of Federal authorities) as well as with international working groups (such as ENFSI–WG) and laboratories.

Switzerland has also created specialist working groups to share experience and developments within the country and the Lausanne and Zürich Institutes are heavily involved in these gremiums. Both Institutes participate in the Swiss Society of Legal Medicine.

The Lausanne Institute has also created prototypes and protocols that are tested within operational facilities such as a full interstate coordination of forensic intelligence and is also participating in the harmonization procedures of crime laboratories.

For many years Lausanne has provided active research in collaboration with international partners in drugs, fingerprint, fire investigation, interpretation of evidence and has published extensively the outcome of these research projects (over 200 publications within the last ten years in forensic science alone and over 100 publications in criminology), to be found on the School website.

Finally, a research collaboration developing investigating means for industries such as the Swiss watchmaking or pharmaceutical industries in fighting against counterfeiting has been on-going for many years.

25.2.4 The two Swiss Forensic Science Institutes

LAUSANNE:
Ecole des sciences criminelles
Faculté de droit, des sciences criminelles et d'administration publique Batochime, Quartier Sorge
CH-1015 Lausanne
Telephone: +41 21 692 4600
Telefax: +41 21 692 4605

E-mail: info.esc@unil.ch
Director and Vice-Dean: Prof. Pierre Margot, BSc, MSc, PhD, Dr hc, Douglas Lucas Medal

ZURICH:
Forensisches Institut Zürich
Zeughausstrasse 11
CH-8004 Zürich
Telephone: +41 44 295 4111
Telefax: +41 44 295 4099
E-mail: info@for-zh.ch

25.2.5 Conference and meeting organizations

All institutes take an active role in communicating with judicial, political and economic partners in Switzerland.

The Zürich Medico-legal Institute (IRM) and the then City of Zürich Forensic Science Institute (WD) combined to organize a successful International Association of Forensic Science Meeting in 1975.

The School of Criminal Justice has been at the origin and first European Academy of Forensic Science Meeting in 1997 as part of ENFSI activities.

Both Lausanne/Geneva University Institute of Forensic Medicine (CURML) and the School of Forensic Science have held combined international meetings and organized joint regular information days for magistrates and police.

References

Collectif (2009) *Le Théâtre du Crime*, Presses Polytechniques et Universitaires rRomandes, Lausanne.
Gross, H. (1893) *Handbuch für Untersuchungsrichter als System der Kriminalistik*, Leuschnen und Lubensky, Graz.
Mallach, H.J. (1996) *Geschichte der Gerichtlichen Medizin im Deutschsprachigen Raum*, Schmidt-Römhild Verlag, Lübeck.
Mangin, P., Barras, V. (2008) Legal Medicine in Switzerland. In: *Forensic Medicine in Europe*, Eds. B. Madea and P. Saukko, Schmidt-Römhild Verlag, Lübeck.
Margot, P., Al., E. (2009) Sciences forensiques: dossier spécial. *Revue Internationale de Criminologie et de Police Technique et Scientifique* 62: 1–128.
Mund, M., Bär, W. (2004) Legal Medicine in Switzerland. *Forensic Science International* 144: 151–155.
Reiss, A.R. (1903) *La Photographie Judiciaire*, Mendel, Paris.
Reiss, R.A. (1911) *Manuel de Police Scientifique (Technique)*. Vols et Homicides, Payot Alcan, Lausanne.

CHAPTER 26

Forensic medicine and sciences in Turkey

Mete Korkut Gulmen[1] & Cengiz Haluk İnce[2]

[1] Department of Forensic Medicine, School of Medicine, Cukurova University, Adana, Turkey
[2] Department of Forensic Medicine, School of Medicine, Istanbul University, Istanbul, Turkey

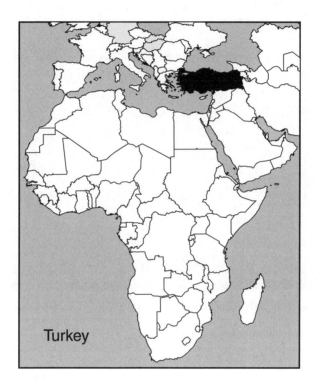

Turkey

26.1 History

The first official records of autopsy and forensic curiosity date from early 1768 during the Ottoman Empire period as one of the Turkish forensic sciences early steps.

In 1839 The Military Medical School was established in Istanbul under the influence of France and Germany, as was also forensic sciences in the medical school.

In 1841 Professor Dr. Claude Bernard of the Vienna University School of Medicine came to Istanbul University as a guest lecturer and started to practice forensic medicine and also systematic autopsies for medicolegal interests (Gok, 1995).

The first civil medical school and the first medicolegal society developed in 1846 and 1856, respectively. The first independent Morgue Department and Police Courthouse was established in 1908, which was followed by an Independent Forensic Medicine and Sciences Institute in 1913 (Figures 26.1 and 26.2). The Institute was part of the Ministry of Interior between the years 1923 and 1926, which became a part of the Ministry of Justice and had also been accepted as an independent

The Global Practice of Forensic Science, First Edition. Edited by Douglas H. Ubelaker.
© 2015 John Wiley & Sons, Ltd. Published 2015 by John Wiley & Sons, Ltd.

Figure 26.1 The forensic medicine law original handwriting in the year 1913. *Source:* From Haluk Ince, 'Forensic medicine and sciences in Turkey', in "Health in Istanbul from Past to Present Congress", 3–6 of November 2010, published as "Council of Forensic Medicine in The Light of Historical Documents' (Belgeler ile Adli Tıp Kurumu).

educational organization for forensic purposes (Gok and Ozen, 1982; Gok, 1995).

During the Second World War period medical education and expertise had been changed and improved with the University Reform. The Institute established inside the university as a separate organization as a part of the Ministry of Justice, although most of the professionals were also academicians of the university and were in collaboration with the academy. In 1953 the organization was extended and widened with new legislation. In the meantime a new Department of Physics developed. This department was a special section that was responsible for the laboratory investigations of ballistics, forensic documents and stylistic evidence. The others sections were well-defined Pathology, Toxicology, Chemistry and Biology departments (Gok and Ozen, 1982; Gok, 1995).

The French–German Medical and Scientific School started to be a part of the Ottoman Empire, which was at the end of the 18th century and at the beginning of the 19th century. It was displaced by the USA School after the Second World War. The structure of the US system became the model of today's Forensic Medicine and Sciences in most parts of the world and helped Turkey to bring about progress in forensic medicine. However, the Forensic Sciences and Medicine system completely altered after the coup in 1980. The legislation article number 2659 was accepted on 20 April 1982 and became valid on 1 May 1982 and the Forensic Medicine Council of Turkey was established in Istanbul (İnce, 2013; Forensic Medicine Council Law, 1982, 2003).

The Forensic Medicine Council works under the authority of the Ministry of Justice and the President and the Vice-presidents, and the board members are directly

Figure 26.2 Professor Dr. Semsi Gok, the founder and the first president of the Turkish Forensic Medicine Council: medical doctor and forensic pathologist. *Source:* From Haluk Ince, 'Forensic medicine and sciences in Turkey', in "Health in Istanbul from Past to Present Congress", 3–6 of November 2010, published as 'Council of Forensic Medicine in The Light of Historical Documents' (Belgeler ile Adli Tıp Kurumu).

appointed by the Minister himself. The Council has a President and a General Assembly. The general assembly consists of expert section presidents and/or representatives, a general secretary and the president. Each section has its own expertise units in accordance with the division, such as a physics section and ballistics (Salacin *et al.*, 1994; Gulmen *et al.*,1995).

Criminal Police Laboratories or Criminalistics first started in 1910 with fingerprint analyses in the Police Departments, headed by a Hungarian immigrant Yusuf Cemil Bey, when it was first getting to be known and extending worldwide. Yusuf Cemil Bey had a great influence on the Turkish Police systems. He first taught the fundamental technique for fingerprint analyses to the Turkish Police departments and then it became a part of the police education until the reforms of the new Turkish Republic. It became an official lecture in the Police Institutes and a small Criminal Laboratory had been developed as a scientific branch of the Police Academy or, as it had previously been named, the Police Institute in 1938. During the first years almost every student in the Academy had the knowledge of analyzing fingerprints, but the increase in the number of students in the Academy led to a change for more talented selected students. During the Second World War an expert from Switzerland became the founder of the modern Criminal Laboratories and gave great effort in educating Turkish experts. The criminal investigation of the assassination attempt of the German Ambassador, Mr. Von Papen, turned out to be a great chance to put criminalistics and ballistics to the foreground. The forensics succeeded to read the engraved serial numbers of a handgun and it was the turning point for the evaluation of forensic science in Turkey. This extraordinary incident led the laboratory to become an expert in the forensic field. With continuing successes, the authorities decided to develop a small model of the FBI laboratories and much technologic equipment for the forensic laboratory had been supplied to the Istanbul division. On the other hand, many of the talented forensics in the police departments were sent to the United States to obtain better practice and certification. The success stories of this department caused a serious work load in those years and the laboratories became insufficient again, so in 1967 the laboratories became a separate unit of the police departments for the first time in Istanbul. The terror actions and crime levels all around the country created the need to develop another Police Forensic Department in Izmir and other cities in Turkey continuously from 1967 till now. The Criminal Laboratories and Forensic Units remained inside the Police Academy in Ankara until 2004. The Criminal section became a separate division and was named the Criminal Police Head Quarters nationwide (Cakici, 2006).

The ordinary cases vary in all sections of the spectrum, as in most of the countries. The firearm use also had been increased after acceptance of firearm use legislation in late 1980s. Our data are very similar to those of most of the countries in regards to the types and variations of the cases, yet at times we notice the terrorist actions, as well as the occasional serial murder cases. Especially during the last three decades various terrorist actions took place and the country needed forensic science more than at any time ever. During this period especially, crime scene investigation became very important (Gulmen *et al.*, 1995).

Our country is very rich in terms of the variation of forensic cases. Although the case distribution is not too complicated, we did start to notice some new cases because of globalization, such as drug use and abuses. Also serial killings and synthetic cannabinoid analyses are very newly known cases for our country. Nation-wide, there are approximately 15,000 autopsy cases per year. Most of those cases are related to accidents and generalized body traumas. Deaths due to systemic pathologies, homicides (mostly due to firearms and stab-bings), suicides, as well as intoxication due to accidents are the ones mostly found in our daily routine practice (İnce, 2013).

26.2 Structure

The main structure of the forensic sciences in our coun-try is summarized below. Especially after the year 2000 forensic sciences became more important and accepted widely by all parties in crime investigations, evidence collection, presentation for the courts, crime prevention and for its value for justice.

The Police and Gendarme Forces are under the authority of the Ministry of the Interior and both of them have their own Criminal Research Laboratories and CSI teams. The Forensic Medicine Council works under the authority of the Ministry of Justice and col-laborates with the forensic departments and institutes of the universities. The courts and the prosecution may ask expertise from all of these units of the forensic sciences (Polat, 2010).

Forensic Sciences in Turkey still lack coordination among the experts and also the divisions. Especially the distinctions between expertise and specialties have not been framed well enough. The main structure of expertise in Turkey is under the umbrella of the Council of Forensic Medicine, which works as a department of the Ministry of Justice. The council holds most of the authority for expertise in the country. The CSI and Criminal Police Laboratories work independently from the council as well as the Gendarme and also the universities.

The Council of Forensic Medicine is structured and centralized in Istanbul with the main office and divi-sions. The Forensic Medicine Council has branches in

major cities of Turkey with divisions of Morgue, Chem-istry and Clinical Legal Medicine expertise. In some branches there can be Biology, Physics or Traffic exper-tise. In spite of all these branches and smaller divi-sions the Council is very much centralized. The Criminal Police or Gendarme Laboratories are also mostly cen-tralized even though they also have branches in var-ious cities. Universities are more diversely organized and usually develop collaborations with each other as well as with the Forensic Medicine Council, Criminal Laboratories and the CSI teams. The main picture in forensic science practices is centralization within a par-ticular institution, mainly the Forensic Medicine Coun-cil, which also is dominated by the Ministry of Justice (İnce, 2013).

The integration of the Forensic Sciences has some difficulties and collaboration problems in the country. Police forces practice in the urban areas while Gen-darmes authorize in the rural regions. Crime Scene Investigations are practiced by the Police or Gendarme CSI teams. These teams analyze the crime scene, collect the evidence and send it to the Criminal Laboratories, mostly with the authorization of the prosecutor. The prosecutor will collect all the data of the cases as a file and collects the reports as well. Reports are in the main separately prepared by different teams and integrated at the prosecutor's office. The main problem seems to be cooperation and collaboration among the teams. The integration of the data at the prosecutor's office also is another disadvantage. The centralized control of the cases also gives the system a cumbersome structure. Control of the integrity of the prosecution still continues to be a problem for the defense in spite of the orders of the new criminal and civil code law (Turkish Police Gen-eral Commandment Center Educational Office, 2003; Gendarme Forensic Organization Law, 1983; Forensic Medicine Council Law, 2003; Turkish Civil Code Law (HMUK), 2011; Turkish Criminal Code Law (CMUK), 2004).

The Forensic Medicine Council, Police and Gendarme are improving their laboratories and divisions and are trying to extend the service to most of the cities of Turkey. The departments are in need of technical equip-ment and technical personnel. Forensic sciences have become more important in Turkey in the last 10 years. This gives the opportunity to hire new scientists to the laboratories and/or divisions because of the increasing demand of the courts as well as the defense. Many new forensic divisions, especially criminal laboratories, have been created during the last decade. All of these laboratories and divisions are equipped with high technology devices and new forensic scientists are hired for these new areas. The Government is the main source to hire the new forensic scientists and also encourages them to become an expert in the forensic sciences, especially with sufficient salaries (İnce, 2013).

26.3 Training

The educational and training period varies within the different forensic sciences.

The forensic medicine specialty is the major area of forensic sciences in Turkey. The forensic medicine specialists are medical doctors and receive four years of training after graduation from the medical school. Six months of pathology and four months of psychiatry (adult and pediatric) mandatory rotations should be completed. The medical doctors perform autopsies all over the country as well as clinical examinations of traumatized people including victims of sexual assaults. Medical doctors complete their specialty training either at the departments of forensic medicine of a university medical school or at the Forensic Medicine Council in Istanbul (Alper *et al.*, 1995, 1999; Salaçin *et al.*, 1994).

There are master and PhD programs available at the university institutes. Graduates of the different colleges may receive a master degree in various areas of the forensic sciences as well as a PhD. Other than that, one can receive a certification as an expert in a certain field by working in the related department for approximately four years at the Police and Gendarme departments and also attend the courses and workshops of the related scientific field. The Forensic Medicine Council designs workshops and courses in the field and gives an expert license afterwards. The main problem is the lack of a board examination and certification system of the forensic sciences. Mostly people become an expert in a field just because of an interest in the area. After the Second World War most of the police and military personnel, as well as the forensic medicine specialist medical doctors, are trained in the United States and received their degrees or certificates from atraining center, such as the FBI, military academies or various institutes. For the last two decades the European Union Erasmus Programs and other opportunities for training courses and

twinning projects became very popular in the forensic sciences as well as in many of the educational areas. Especially the twinning projects of the Turkish Forensic Medicine Council, Criminal Police and Gendarme Departments and also the CSI teams with EU countries improved the educational value of the Turkish forensic experts (Istanbul University Institute of Forensic Sciences, 2014; Ankara University Institute of Forensic Sciences, 2013).

26.4 Funding

The funding of the forensic sciences is mainly supplied by the Central Government. From the early days of the republic until now the budgets are arranged and controlled by the national government. Usually the expert fees are covered by the court budget, which will be collected from the case or, if not, will be covered by the general budget of the Ministry of Justice. The forensic sciences are still not very well funded, yet the government puts serious effort into funding the laboratories, buildings and technical equipment. The European Union projects and United Nations funding gave a serious opportunity in funding, especially in some forensic expertise areas such as city morgues, CSI, criminal laboratories, drugs, etc. The National Government mostly controls the budget of the forensic sciences practice. The priority of the budget depends on the case density of the cities as well as the hinterland and the impact factor of the forensic center. Actually the courts still do not demand forensic scientific expertise as they should, yet it seems to be getting much better. During the 1970s and 1980s there was almost no demand or a minimum demand for scientific expertise from the courts. However, for the last 25 years the effect and demand for the forensic sciences and expertise are rising high. Because of the high demand of the courts and defense attorneys, the inadequacy of the trained and certified number of scientists became apparent. Therefore various programs are now being offered by the National Government for training and are funded. A new source for the institutes and universities is the insurance companies. The insurance companies and private attorneys ask for expertise mainly from the university departments for court expertise in all areas of the forensic sciences. Clinical forensic medicine practice and medical malpractice play important roles in the expertise system nowadays. Especially traffic medicine is very popular besides forensic toxi-cology, forensic hemogenetics, forensic documents and stylistics, remodeling the crime scenes, etc. The univer-sity departments started to fund their own budget with the expertise that they receive and this gives them the opportunity to stand in front of the university board to ask for more funding (İnce, 2013).

26.5 Political issues

Since the Turkish forensic sciences practice has mainly been run by the National Government, sections such as the Forensic Medicine Council and the police and Gend-arme forces, it is affected by the political climate and shifts. The influence of politics is also reported by the European Commission's various reports on the years 2005, 2012 and 2013, as the Forensic Medicine Council under the Ministry of Justice. The reports analyze the situation as:

> Moreover, it is of concern that the Forensic Medical Institute (Forensic Medicine Council) is not fully independent because of its reporting line direct to the Ministry of Justice. Signifi-cant progress has been achieved in the area of the *judiciary* with the adoption and the entry into force of a series of new laws which will contribute to improve its *independence and effi-ciency*. This concerns in particular the new Penal Code, the new Code of Criminal Procedure, the Law on the Courts of Appeal as well as the law on the Enforcement of Sentences and Security Measures. Although higher judicial bodies, such as the Court of Cassation have continued to issue a number of judgments interpreting the reforms in accordance with the standards of the ECtHR, it remains difficult to discern a clear trend in the case law. Intensive training of judges and pros-ecutors has continued, in particular as regards the European Convention for the Protection of Human Rights. Turkey is encouraged to take further steps to strengthen the indepen-dence of the High Council of Judges and Prosecutors and to remove political influence over the appointment of judges and prosecutors. The Turkish authorities have pursued a number of *training programmes on human rights* targeting rele-vant personnel in the Ministry of the Interior, Ministry of Jus-tice, the gendarmerie and the police. Forensic doctors' reports or reports by universities or independent institutions are now recognized as proof by some courts, in addition to the reports of the Forensic Medicine Council under the Ministry of Jus-tice (European Union Turkey 2005 Progress Report, 23 pp.).

However, most of the courts are still taking into consideration the reports of the Forensic Medicine Council centralized in Istanbul and work under the Ministry of Justice. Although the new criminal and civil code laws encourage the independent expertise system, it seems that it is not easy to break the habits of the influence of the 1982 military period legislation on forensic sciences practice. The Forensic Medicine Council still is the main expert for almost all fields of the forensic sciences. The Forensic Medicine Council gives service under the authority of the Ministry of Justice. The president of this council is appointed by the Minister of Justice with the approval of the Prime Min-ister and the President. The presidents of the scientific commissions and the presidents of the branches and all of the other employees of the Council are appointed by the president of the Council, and are also approved by the Minister of Justice. The Forensic Medicine Council is an expert institution that is interested in all fields of the forensic sciences (European Union Turkey 2005 Progress Report, European Union Turkey 2012 Progress Report and European Union Turkey 2013 Progress Report).

26.6 Quality control

The Police and Gendarme forensics teams, such as the criminal laboratories and crime scene investigators, are working as units under the authority of the Ministry of the Interior. There is a planned board certification and examination for the forensic medicine specialists after their training period, yet it is not valid at the moment. There are also no national board or certificate exams for the other fields of the forensic sciences.

The Forensic Sciences Organization in the country is still not well distributed all around the nation with the same quality assurance and quantity (Himberg, 2007; İnce, 2012). The laboratories and the experts are mainly located in Ankara and Istanbul with a few of them in Izmir/Adana and are inadequate to solve the problems of a nation with 80 million people. At times it seems like it is too hard to develop a synergic effect in producing solu-tions for the forensic services and mostly the resources remain unproductive. Although there was a European Union project on standardization and quality assurance in 2007, and a report and suggestions of the Presiden-tial State Supervisory Board for the Nationwide Foren-sic Services, there still is no attempt to reach solutions (Himberg, 2007; State Supervisory Board Report (DDK), 2010; İnce, 2013).

One other serious problem of the country seems to be the centralization of the services and inadequacy of collaboration between the institutes and departments. The three major organizations (Forensic Medicine Council, Police and Gendarme Forensic Sciences Units) and universities are almost having no collaboration with each other and therefore there is a serious lack of institutionalization and process analyzing. The Forensic Medicine Council is in the best position for the collaboration projects with other institutes and universities because of its legal status. The other two major institutes of the Police and Gendarme are not legally capable to either hire any scientist from any other institute or ask for consultation help. This seems to be a serious dilemma, both ethically and legally. In some high profile or problematic cases, the crises are usually solved by the devotion of the scientists and also with the positive volunteer efforts of the experts. Therefore, the good practices between the laboratories are dependent on the volunteer efforts of the individuals, instead of the institutes. This concept is threatening for the Turkish National Forensic Sciences practice in all areas including quality assurance and standardization. Although there are many SWOT analyses for the best forensic practice, it seems that we still have a long way to go (İnce, 2013; Gendarme Forensic Organization Law, 1983).

Forensic science is a very special area that needs to have studies starting from the college level. Therefore, the country needs to develop forensic sciences colleges as well as detailed masters and doctorate programs. Yet, on the other hand, because of the legislation, it is hard for the system to hire those qualified scientists, especially in the three major institutes but also in the university system. This should be changed and the well-educated highly qualified scientist should be a part of the routine daily practices. This can be a fast solution for quality assurance as well as the standardization of the forensic institutes. It seems to be a unique situation for Turkey. We do hope to change the status with a better system in the near future. There is no specific method to keep the active forensic personnel and experts to a common standard and manage to hold the quality assurance today with the current legislation. However, with the personal volunteer efforts, scientists try to keep updated by attending national or international meetings or educational courses, etc. In the year 2006 an unofficial board examination trial had been designed by the National Association of Forensic Medicine Specialists, but it was not repeated. This unsuccessful attempt also shows us that the system should be restructured (Cakici, 2006).

Certification in forensic sciences is an important issue. In all fields of the forensic sciences there should be a well-designed educational module, examination and independent certification. In that way the board of certified forensic experts will start to work in all the fields of the forensic sciences, which will facilitate the courts and the attorneys. Unfortunately today the system tries to solve the absence of this configuration with the European Union Projects and certificate programs. Through the EU Twinning Projects with Turkey and Holland and also with Spain during the years of 2011 and 2013, 1500 experts had been trained and certified from the spectrum of crime scene investigations to forensic pathology. Those experts were all working for the Forensic Medicine Council, Police or Gendarme (İnce, 2013; Gulmen, 2000; Gulmen et al., 1998, 1999).

As a country, our nation and our state had met the quality assurance and standardization issue during the 1990s instead of in the early days of the century such as the USA. The accreditation studies first started in the year 2000 in the forensic sciences with the ISO 17025 Turkish National Standard codes. Accreditations started to be practiced in the forensic laboratories first in 2008 and then began to be extended until they became a part of the Turkish National Forensic Sciences practice. Many laboratories of the Forensic Medicine Council, Police and Gendarme Forensic Institutes are accredited with many methods. New methods are added for the accreditation after follow-ups and inspections. We have been learning about being inspected since 2008 and now understand that inspections are not something to be afraid of but a part of the continuous improvement of ourselves scientifically. As the methods and institutes start to be accredited they become more trustworthy and the judicial system works in a more proper way (İnce, 2013).

The quality assurance and accreditation caused these institutes to use the correct facilities, equipment and technology. Because of the technology resources that these institutes have nationwide, many high profile cases have been solved and the findings were shared with the International Forensic Science Society.

Our country has started many judicial reforms since 2005. Almost every issue such as human rights violations, child abuse and neglect, and violence against women have been completely revised and new laws and legislations have been passed. The Criminal and Civil Code Laws have changed completely and the courts have been redesigned. Most of the judges and attorneys had problems applying the practice according to new legislation but the forensic sciences took an important part in this process. The new attitude of the judicial system is much more evidence based than it used to be and so the forensic sciences and forensic experts became more important than they were previously. The Istanbul Protocol as a United Nations Article took place in our daily clinical forensic medicine practice and training is still going on although examination as mandated by the article still has not been guaranteed nationwide. Evidence collecting, saving and investigation have been redesigned and the police and related officials are still under training. The judges and prosecutors are also under training for better investigation (Criminal Code Law, 2004; Civil Code Law, 2011; Gunay, 2008).

26.7 Research

Unfortunately we are very far behind with scientific research publication, especially in regard to citations and also innovation of new technology devices as well as scientific methods. Scientific publications and their citation ratio are seriously low when we consider the case workload and the country itself. In addition, the daily use of the new scientific methods, which have developed in the publications, is very low. The State Institute and Organizations (Forensic Medicine Council, Police and Gendarme) do not have research funding. The universities have the funding yet they cannot involve and participate as a scientific collaboration in a research project with the government organization because of the legal status. This should be broken and a new pathway should be designed for researches and collaborations between the institutes overall (İnce, 2013).

26.8 Disaster management

Our country has also suffered various disasters, especially earthquakes. In 1999 we had a great Marmara Quake that shook the nation widely. We also had airplane crashes in Diyarbakír, Isparta and Trabzon during the years from 2000 until today. In all of these disasters there was an identification problem. We had a very sad experience with the Marmara Earthquake in which most of the victims were barely identified and we noticed that we were not very well prepared for a disaster of this magnitude. Yet now we have DVI teams that can get ready to go after six hours of the disaster announcement. With the Van city Earthquake in October 2011, the disaster teams were ready in six hours to fly to Van. Many European Union projects had been realized for the education of the forensic scientists. Collaboration projects and educative courses are playing important roles in certifying forensic teams as well as the workshops, with FASE (Forensic Anthropology Society of Europe) and international forensic anthropologists.

The Turkish military, police and government authorities are also getting trained for disaster management as also are the Forensic Medicine Specialists. Yet we have a serious lack of forensic odontologists and the DVI teams are not large enough in number to cover the country. The Forensic Odontology Master degree program and special courses are going on. The DVI teams need to be increased both by number and by qualification (İnce, 2013).

26.9 Legal issues

The forensic sciences are still not very well understood and used by the legal system in Turkey, especially the judges, prosecutors, attorneys and in general the courts. Usually the legal arena still expects to receive expertise reports in the old way and find quick answers so that they can finalize the cases. Especially the new Criminal and Civil Code Laws changed the status of forensic sciences in the legal arena and on the court side too much. The courts are still depending on the Forensic Medicine Council reports as the official one and give the last word to the Council. Of course this is against the spirit of the new code laws, especially when the laws suggest cross examination and independent experts. Of course forensic sciences will improve with the demands of the courts but yet still there is nothing new from the court side. It is not easy and will not be easy to convince the judges to use universities, private Institutes and experts that have quality assurance with an appropriate accreditation and standardization. However, today the conditions are much better than they were 10 years ago. We forensic scientists are hopeful for the future of the forensic sciences in our country.

26.10 New developments

Forensic toxicology is one of the new hit topics in means of research and serious funding and support has been given by the National Science Research Councils. Drug use and abuse have become a serious problem of the country and follow-up cases especially are in important numbers. The forensic sciences in general are also a new interest area.

Forensic sciences are facing new modeling in Turkey. In the year 2009 the Turkish President asked for help from the State Supervisory Board to provide research for our National Forensic Sciences and what should be done in the near future, such as the NAS report of the US (State Supervisory Board Report (DDK), 2010).

The State Supervisory Board worked for more than a year about the Turkish forensic sciences and talked to different academicians, scientists and to the authorities of different government organizations, as well as the universities and also international scientists. The State Supervisory Board presented their report in 2010. The main perspective is to be at the EU standard norms. Turkey can easily adopt the Portugal reforms in the forensic sciences. The next decade will be much brighter for forensic sciences. The courts will start to use the forensic sciences more often and in more detail. The needs of the country will be much more and probably forensic toxicology and hemogenetics will be more important. We probably will practice more autopsies and the autopsy data will be more useful. The European Union projects on forensic sciences and human rights will be more effective. Turkish state institutes and universities as well as independent private forensic institutes will be accredited and Turkish forensic sciences standards and quality assurance will be settled. Many organizations will become a partner of the ENFSI. The system will need a new forensic sciences system over the whole country and new legislation should bring more scientific critics.

A new Academy for the Turkish forensic sciences can be more effective to solve most of the judicial problems in a scientific manner and be much less affected by political influences. The Turkish Academy of Forensic Sciences could then become a Quality Assurance, Accreditation/Standardization scientific umbrella organization. The country has been proud to organize and host international meetings for the last 10 years with the ENFSI Meeting of 2005, the MAFS Meeting of 2009 and the IALM Meeting of 2012. The next 10 years will be much better for the country in terms of forensic sciences, opportunities and development.

References

Alper, B., Salacin, S., Cekin, N., Gulmen, M.K. (1995) *The Curriculum of Forensic Medicine in Cukurova Medical School and the Problems of Forensic Medicine Education. Medical Education in the 21st Century*, Marmara University School of Medicine Press, Istanbul, Turkey.

Alper, B., Altun, A., Gulmen, M.K., Dag, H., Cekin, N. (1999) Forensic serology and haemogenetics in Turkey. Poster presentation in the 15th Triennial Meeting of the International Association of Forensic Sciences, 22–28 August 1999, Los Angeles, California, USA.

Ankara University Institute of Forensic Sciences (2013) Ankara, Turkey. http://www.adlitip.ankara.edu.tr/.

Cakici, M.E. (2006) Forensic Sciences in Turkey: Process Towards European Union; Necessity of New Structures and Solution Proposals. Master Thesis, Cukurova University Publication.

European Union Turkey 2005 Progress Report (2005).

European Union Turkey 2012 Progress Report (2012).

European Union Turkey 2013 Progress Report (2013).

Forensic Medicine Council Law (1982, 2003) Dated April 14, 1982, number 2659; also revised on February 19, 2003, number 4810.

Gendarme Forensic Organization Law (1983) Dated March 10, 1983, number 2803.

Gok, S. (1995) *Forensic Medicine, Yesterday, Today and Tomorrow*, TEMEL Publications, Istanbul, Turkey.

Gok, S., Ozen, C. (1982) *The History and Organization of Forensic Medicine and Sciences in Turkey*, Turkish Ministry of Justice Forensic Medicine Council Publications, Istanbul, Turkey.

Gulmen, M.K. (2000) Double Edged Dilemmas in Forensic Expertise and Ethical Values. IVth National Forensic Sciences Congress Keynote Lecture, 10–13 May 2000, Istanbul University, Istanbul, Turkey.

Gulmen, M.K., Cekin, N., Ozdemir, H., Alper, B., Savran, B., Sen, F., Salaçin, S. (1995) The problems related to the crime scene investigations in Turkey. *Advancement in Science*, 14–16 July 1995, York, UK.

Gulmen, M.K., Cekin, N., Hilal, A., Salacin, S. (1998) Questioning of forensic expertise "Ethical Perspective". *Bulletin of Forensic Medicine* III (2): 57–60.

Gulmen, M.K., Sarica, A.D., Cekin, N., Alper, B. (1999) Forensic Psychology in Turkey. Poster presentation, 15th Triennial Meeting of the International Association of Forensic Sciences, 22–28 August 1999, Los Angeles, California, USA.

Gunay, Y. (2008) How fair the Forensic Medicine Council. *Doctors'* Journal August/September 46. http://www.doktor dergisi.com/default1.asp.

Himberg, O. (2007) European Union and Turkey Progress, Reporter.

İnce, H. (2012, 2013) Reports of the Forensic Medicine Council, as the President of the Forensic Medicine Council between the years 2009 and 2013, Istanbul, Turkey. www.atk.gov.tr.

Istanbul University Institute of Forensic Sciences (2014). http://www.istanbul.edu.tr/enstituler/adli/tarihçe_index.

Polat, O. (2010) *Forensic Medicine*, DER Publishing Co., Istanbul, Turkey.

Salacin, S., Alper, B., Cekin, N., Gulmen, M.K. (1994) The medico-legal system in Turkey, undergraduate and postgraduate curriculum of the forensic sciences. *Acta Medicinae Legalis* XLIV: 372–374.

State Supervisory Board Report (DDK) (2010) Presidential Office, Ankara, Turkey.

Turkish Civil Code Law (HMUK) (2011).

Turkish Criminal Code Law (CMUK) (2004).

Turkish Police General Commandment Center Educational Office (2003) SASEM, Textbook of Crime Scene Investigation, *The Safety and Evidence Collecting*.

CHAPTER 27

Forensic medicine in the United Arab Emirates

Fawzi Benomran

Department of Forensic Medicine, Dubai Police General Headquarters, Dubai, United Arab Emirates

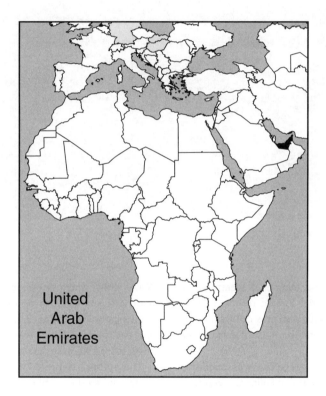

United
Arab
Emirates

27.1 An overview and a historical background

The United Arab Emirates is a federation of seven Emirates, united in 1972, and each of them has a local government as well as being under the umbrella of the Federal State. Forensic Medicine in Dubai is attached to Dubai Police, which is one of the bodies of the local government of Dubai. The other six emirates are served by the Federal Police, but forensic medicine in all of them belongs to the Ministry of Justice.

Investigation into suspicious deaths and crimes as a whole is the responsibility of the police who eventually refer cases to the Public Prosecutor, who refer them to the Courts of Law. The Police in Dubai is delegated by the Public Prosecutor to refer cases to the Department of Forensic Medicine. The warrant of the Police is sufficient for all examinations except dissection of the dead bodies

The Global Practice of Forensic Science, First Edition. Edited by Douglas H. Ubelaker.

© 2015 John Wiley & Sons, Ltd. Published 2015 by John Wiley & Sons, Ltd.

Figure 27.1 The staff entrance of the Department of Forensic Medicine, Dubai Police.

to determine the cause and manner of death. Dubai courts adopt the Inquisitorial System rather than the Adversarial System. The Jury system is not followed in any of the seven Emirates, neither it is followed in any Arab country.

The Department of Forensic Medicine was established in Dubai in 1980, within the Dubai Police General Head Quarters. Initially, the staff consisted of one forensic medical examiner and a few clerking personnel. For two years, the department occupied a temporary building, which has facility for examination of clinical cases, that is injuries, age assessment and sexual crimes. Postmortem examinations were carried out in a basic mortuary at the nearby hospital.

A proper building was erected in 1982 within the perimeter of the Police Headquarters (Figures 27.1 and 27.2). It contained an autopsy room with two autopsy tables, a body store with a capacity of 48 bodies, a clinical examination room, a fixed as well as mobile

X-ray units, and offices for two doctors and clerical staff. A second doctor was appointed at that stage, and a histopathology technician. A mobile body store with a capacity of 32 bodies was supplied, as well as two hearses for body transfer.

The author (Figure 27.3) was appointed in August 1997, and so the number of forensic medical examiners became three. On the author's recommendation, a project of modification and extension of the department was approved for implementation (Figure 27.4). The project was justified by the steady increase of work load. An airplane crash in October 1997 resulted in 59 fatalities and emphasized the need for expansion. The project was concluded in 2001, at which time the author was made Director of the Department.

Until 2011 the Forensic Medical Examiners were non-local and appointed by contract from Egypt, with the exception of the director (author) who comes from Libya. On the author's recommendations, a number of

Figure 27.2 Public entrance of the Department.

local doctors were appointed and sent for postgraduate training abroad. Some of them had finished their training and joined the department.

At present the staff of the department includes seven forensic medical examiners in addition to the director. Amongst these seven are two females and two locals. The addition of new cold storage that can accommodate 80 bodies increased the total capacity to 128 bodies. Two autopsy rooms are available, one with three autopsy and three dissecting tables, and the second is a septic room with one autopsy and one dissecting table. All tables are stainless steel with downdraft air flow and hydraulic height adjustment, and rapid transfer properties. Hydraulic body lifters are also provided. The histopathology laboratory was also modernized.

This department provides medicolegal services in Dubai, which has a population of just over 1.7 million. The Director of Public Prosecution (DPP) and its deputies, as well as the directors of the seven police stations refer cases for examination. Referred cases include

clinical examinations as well as postmortem examinations. The reasons for many deaths are disposed of on the grounds of external examination. Autopsies are only performed by a warrant from the DPP, on a request of the medical examiner. The general aim is to determine the cause and manner of death. It must be emphasized that this study does not represent all deaths that took place in Dubai. Hospital deaths from natural causes and many home deaths are not referred for medicolegal examination.

Clinical examinations constituted of injuries, sexual crimes, age assessments, medical responsibilities, criminal abortions and other miscellaneous cases.

Injured parties are referred by legal authorities to determine the fact of injury or harm, causative agent if possible, duration of treatment and disability incurred if any. Based on that medicolegal assessment the legal authorities determine the degree of culpability involved. Types of cases range from simple fist-fights to attempted homicide. The courts refer victims of road

Figure 27.3 The Director, Professor Fawzi Benomran.

traffic accidents suing for compensation to determine the percentage of disability, which helps the judges in the determination of awarded damages.

Sexual crimes in the UAE are defined in accord with the Islamic tradition (Benomran, 2002a). Any sexual relation outside wedlock is considered unlawful and prosecutable. Obviously, legal authorities do not spy on people in order to prosecute them for consented sexual offenses, but they do investigate when it comes to their attention through an official complaint. The complainant in consented sexual crimes would be a spouse, an employer in cases of servants or a hospital in case of the birth of an illegitimate child. Sometimes the complainant would be the female when her male partner fails to fulfill his promise of payment or marriage, especially consequent on pregnancy. People involved in heterosexual or homosexual indecent behavior in public places are sometimes brought in by the police who are usually called by witnesses. Forcible sexual intercourse, whether hetero- or homosexual, comes to the attention of the legal authorities through a complaint by the victims.

27.2 The General Department of Forensic Science and Criminology

The Department of Forensic Medicine in Dubai Police has been for many years one of the departments of the General Department of Forensic Science and Criminology, which includes several other departments. Of note is the Crime Laboratory, which hosts the Toxicology and Molecular Biology sections, which we rely on extensively in our work. The General Department of Forensic Science and Criminology includes other departments, like Crime Scene Investigation, Digital Crimes Investigation, Development and Training, Criminology and K9 (Canines). Specialists of these departments and sections work as a team in relevant cases, but each furnishes a separate report, which are integrated later in a collective

Figure 27.4 The new extension of the Department with a ramp for a body hearse.

conference. Recruitment of expatriate specialists is based on their postgraduate degrees indicating their qualifications and also their experience attained elsewhere. On the other hand, citizens of the UAE are employed and sent to specialist centers abroad to gain the required qualification and basic experience before they come back and become actively involved in the field. Over 70 young scientists are currently abroad for training and working for postgraduate degrees in different disciplines of Forensic Sciences.

Of note is the ongoing project of building a huge crime laboratory within the Dubai Police General Headquarters. It will be one of the biggest of its kind worldwide. The date of completion will be early 2014, and it will hopefully be opened during the 23rd meeting of the IALM, which will be held in Dubai from 19 to 21 January 2015.

It has been the policy of the institution to achieve international standards. In that direction, we have obtained ISO 90001 and ISO 14000, and worked to obtain ISO 17025 in January 2014. The laboratory undergoes regular proficiency test of CTS (USA) and GTFCh (Germany).

Dubai Police, and hence the General Department of Forensic Science and Criminology, receive their funding from the local government of Dubai. Services are rendered to the governmental legal authorities free of charge, including transferring bodies by hearse to cemeteries, and to and from the airport.

27.2.1 Types of cases handled by the Department

Cases were referred from legal authorities of Dubai (population of 1.7 million) and occasionally the Northern

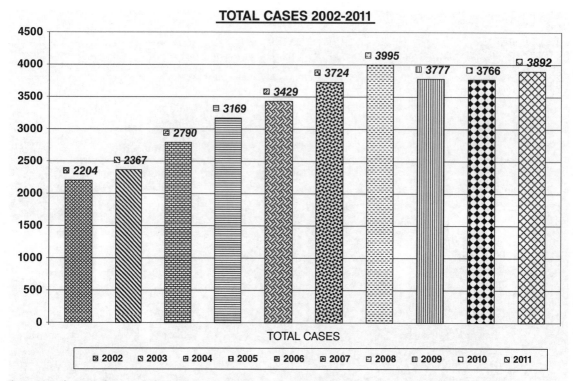

Figure 27.5 The prevailing trend of total cases examined annually in the Department of Forensic Medicine.

Emirates. Local people constitute less than 15% of the total population. Foreign expatriates, being the majority, are largely laborers from the Indian subcontinent. Over 200 nationalities represent the spectrum of foreign inhabitants of Dubai. This mosaic population is reflected by the cases examined in our department.

Prior to 2002, there had been no proper statistical registration in the department. Once made director, the author commenced proper data collection and analysis, in addition to other progressive developments of the department. Information forms were designed to categorize different types of cases, in which doctors are required to fill in information after they have finished writing reports. Information from these forms is transferred to special registers. This procedure was carried out from day to day and results were tabulated at the end of each month. A yearly report was compiled at the end of each year.

During the period extended from January 2002 until the end of 2011, 33,113 cases were examined in the Department of Forensic Medicine of Dubai Police General Headquarters (Figure 27.5). This constituted a yearly average of 3311.3 cases. A steady annual increase was noted up to 2008, with an average annual increment of 8.8%. The percentage of increase from 2002 and 2008 being 81.26%, the latter year count exceeded the former by 1791 cases. The count of 2008 topped that of 2007 by 271 cases, which constituted an annual increase of 7.3%, in accord with the percentage of population growth of Dubai (Centre of Statistical Studies, 2008). A decline was noted during 2009, and less so during 2010, averaging 5.7%, coinciding with a temporary drop of expatriate population due to the global financial crisis (Figure 27.5). A slight increase was noted in 2011, amounting to 126 cases (3.2%).

Cases of death were classified according to variables including sex, age, manner of death, cause of death and anatomical findings at postmortem examination explaining the death. The manner of death is defined as the circumstances of death or how the cause came about, for example natural, accidental, suicide or homicide. The cause of death is defined as the disease or injury that started a train of events or of physiological derangements leading to death.

Cases with an unknown manner of death are fatalities caused by, for example, drowning or blunt injury, but with obscure circumstances. Deaths with an unascertained cause due to decomposition or in cases of bony human remains were included in this category.

It is mandatory for forensic pathologists in Dubai to examine bodies at the locus or crime scene whenever there is a suspicion involving the case. This practice, although painstakingly inconvenient for the doctors, proved to be very useful, especially to ascertain the manner of death in certain irregular suicides that could be suspected to be homicides and vice versa.

Postmortem findings explaining death include anatomical evidence of diseases and lesions by organ, as well as signs of drowning, strangulation, fire burns, electrical burns, aspiration and combined findings. Absence of anatomical findings is also significant as an exclusive measure.

The total number of clinical examinations was 22,518; of these 18,323 were injury cases, 3296 sexual crimes, 577 age assessments, 97 medical responsibilities, 46 criminal abortions, 84 civil actions and the rest ($n = 95$) were miscellaneous cases (Figure 27.5).

Injury cases averaged 1832.3 per year, which constituted 55.33% of the total cases examined annually. Most cases were males (81%), and of these 31% were simple fist-fights. Domestic husband/wife fights constituted 3% of all cases.

Cases of sexual crimes examined averaged 329.6 per annum. It was classified according to the gender and age of the parties involved, whether consented or forcible, and if pregnancy was an issue in the crime.

The assessment of age is required in civil and criminal events. In civil cases, a driver licensing authority refers applicants for the test to ascertain their age of majority. That was needed mainly when expatriates sitting for the driving test lacked an authenticated birth certificate. Ascertaining age of majority is also important in criminal proceedings of the court of law.

Cases of medical responsibility mainly involved live patients suing hospitals for damages. Except for the few cases where the medical facts were so obvious that we were able to reach a decision, we usually acted as an intermediary between the courts and committees of specialist doctors, who were assigned to investigate the case. In 2009, a Law on Medical Responsibility was enacted in the UAE, and consequently a higher committee was

established to investigate such cases and cases gradually ceased to be referred to us (Benomran, 2010).

27.2.2 Statistical information

The total number of cases examined during the period of the study was 33,113. Examinations were carried out by request of the police, the prosecution or the courts and reported to the respective agency. Of these 18,323 (55.33%) were clinical cases of injuries, 10,595 (31.99%) postmortem examinations, 3296 (9.95%) clinical cases of sexual crimes, 577 (1.74%) age estimations, 97 (0.33%) medical responsibility, 46 (0.13%) criminal abortion, 84 (0.25%) civil actions and 95 (0.28%) miscellaneous cases (Figure 27.6).

27.2.2.1 Postmortem examinations

A total of 10,595 deaths were examined; 9434 (89%) of them were males and 1161 (11%) females. The age ranged from 0 to 90 years, with a mean age of 41.2 years. The peak incidence was in the age group 20–50 years, where the extremes of age were least represented (Figure 27.5). Only in 667 cases (6.3% of the grand total) was the deceased a local citizen. Autopsies amounted to 734 cases, which constituted 7% of the total deaths examined.

27.2.2.2 Manner of death

In descending order of frequency, the four manners of death were: natural 6133 (57.88%), accidental 3206 (30.25%), suicidal 947 (8.9%) and homicidal 256 (2.41%). The manner was undetermined in 54 (0.5%) of the cases over the 10 year period (Figure 27.7).

27.2.2.3 Causes of death

The three most predominant causes of natural deaths were coronary artery disease (88%), senility (2%) and malignancies (1.4%).

Accidental deaths were predominantly due to traffic accidents, amounting to 1498 cases (46.72%) of the overall accidental fatalities.

The predominant method of suicide was hanging (81.52%), followed by a fall from height (7.28%), drowning (2.32%), extensive body burns (1.79%), incised wounds (1.5%), ingestion of corrosive liquids (1.4%) and ingestion of insecticides (1.2%). The remaining suicidal methods included drug overdose, stabbing, carbon monoxide poisoning, strangulation, firearm injury, cyanide poisoning, electrocution,

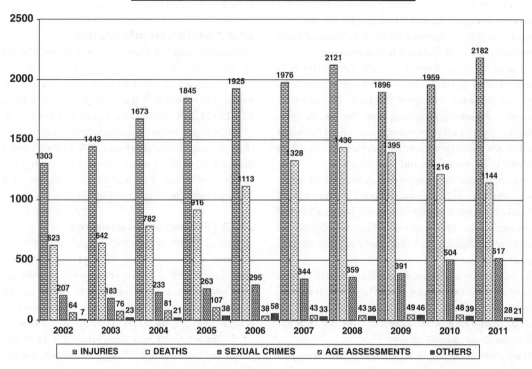

Figure 27.6 The different types of cases examined annually in the Department.

methanol poisoning, electrical saw decapitation and butane gas poisoning.

The most common methods of homicide (see Figure 27.8) were stabbings (37.10%), blunt trauma to the head (25%), ligature strangulation (8.9%), smothering (6.25%), manual strangulation (5.07%) and cut-throat (4%). The rest included firearm injury, run-over by a car, drowning, blunt trauma to the body, torching and battered child syndrome.

27.2.2.4 Autopsy findings explaining the death
Anatomical and/or histological evidence of coronary artery disease, mainly severe atherosclerosis, was the predominant finding of most sudden natural deaths. Other organ pathologies were encountered in other deaths from natural causes according to the underlying disease in each case.

Trauma to the head and multiple injuries due to blunt force impacts were most often encountered in accidental

deaths. In a few cases, we demonstrated that what the police thought to be deaths due to traffic accidents were in fact sudden cardiac deaths of drivers that caused a car to impact another or to get off the road.

Locus examination proved to be indispensable in homicides and suicides. A single case of homicidal strangulation that was staged to simulate suicidal hanging (Benomran, 2002b) and another suicide that the police thought to be a homicide were examples of such importance.

27.2.2.5 Clinical cases of injuries
Live victims of trauma, whether accidental or due to an assault are examined to furnish medicolegal reports to the investigative and legal authorities. To help the lawyers, the doctor must confirm or rule out the occurrence of injury or bodily harm. If an injury is present, the doctor must comment on its causation (blunt or sharp instrument), duration of treatment (whether within

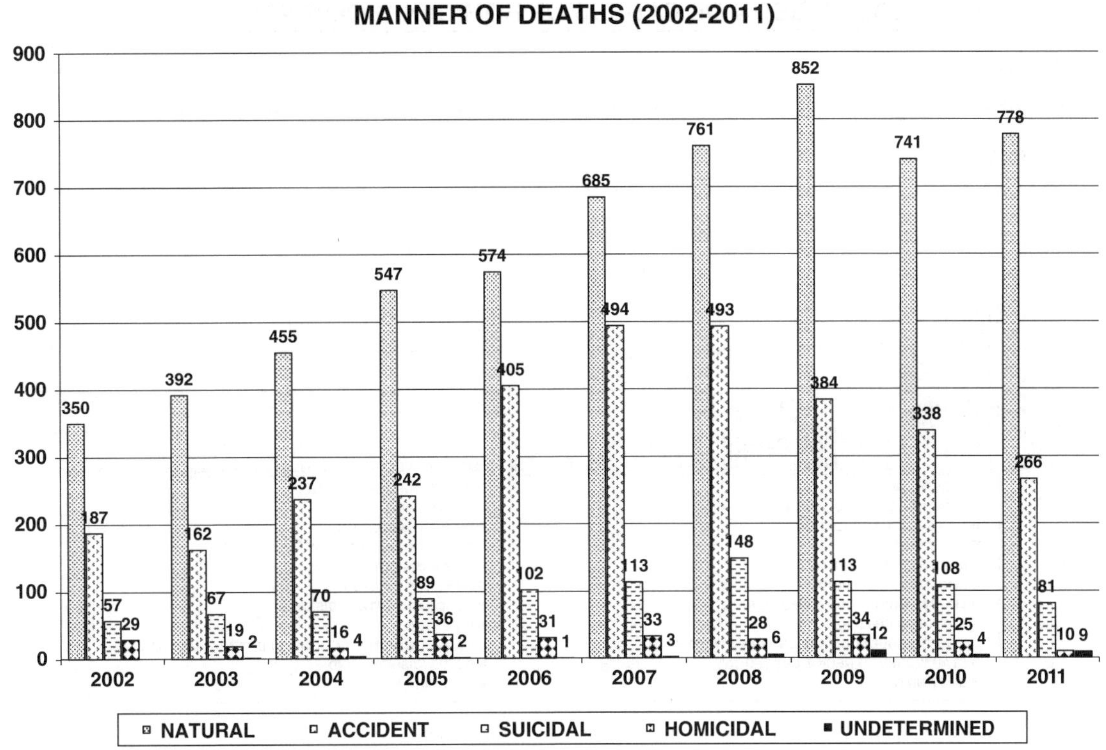

MANNER OF DEATHS (2002-2011)

Figure 27.7 All deaths classified by their different manners.

20 days or more than 20 days) and its outcome (permanent disability or not). The punishment of the perpetrator depends upon the severity of the injury and the weapon used in infliction. In civil cases, where damages may be awarded by the court, the doctor must give an estimate percentage of disability if present.

27.2.2.6 Clinical cases of sexual crimes

The duty of the forensic medical examiner is to find evidence to confirm the occurrence of a sexual crime. Physical injuries may indicate the fact that the sexual act was forceful. The only conclusive material evidence of sexual crimes is the presence of semen from one party on the body of the other party or inside one of the natural orifices. A torn hymen would be strong evidence of sexual intercourse, albeit its interpretation must be considered with great care (Benomran, 2002a).

27.2.2.7 Age estimations

Because of the diversity of the population in the UAE, more often than not people come from countries where

laxity in birth registration and certification lead to doubtful records of passport information. When a person's documented age is thought by the authority to be false, on the grounds of discrepancy with appearance, the help of the forensic medical examiner is sought by the respective authority. This most often arises when applicants for a driver's license are thought to be younger than 18 years (light vehicles) or 21 years (heavy vehicles). Another group of cases are of criminals, where the courts want to confirm the age of majority before passing the sentence.

27.2.2.8 Miscellaneous cases

These constituted cases of medical responsibilities, reports on health in connection with divorce due to harm and examination of nonhuman bones or animal carcasses. From 2009 onwards, the number of medical responsibility cases declined substantially as the law on medical responsibility of the UAE established a special committee to undertake that task (Benomran, 2010).

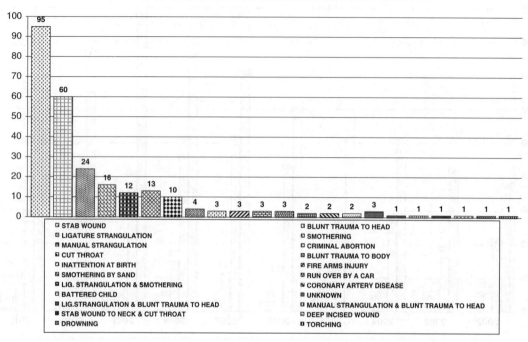

Figure 27.8 A breakdown of homicides by causes of deaths (methods of homicide).

27.3 Discussion

The total number of 33,113 cases examined during the period of the study constituted a yearly average of 3311.3. The average annual increment during the first 7 years was 273.6 cases (8.8%), coinciding with an earlier study (Benomran, 2009). The total cases of 2008 exceeded that of 2002 by 81.26% (Figure 27.5). The relatively high rate of increase of case turnover reflected the population growth of Dubai, which attracts people from all over the world to seek employment and residence in this country with a remarkably booming economy. The count of 2008 topped that of 2007 by 271 cases, which constituted an annual increase of 7.3%, in accord with the percentage of population growth of Dubai during 2005–2007. A decline was noted during 2009, and less so during 2010, averaging 5.7%, coinciding with a temporary recent drop of expatriate population due to the global financial crisis. A slight increase of 126 cases (3.2%) was noted in 2011, reflecting the recent population growth coinciding with the start of the economic recovery.

Examinations are not carried out unless referred by the police, the director of public prosecution or the court. The latter referral is almost exclusive to civil actions, which constituted 84 cases during the period of study (0.25%). Clinical cases included injuries: 18,323 cases (55.33%), sexual crimes: 3296 cases (9.95%), age estimations: 577 cases (1.74%), medical responsibility: 97 cases (0.33%), criminal abortion: 46 cases (0.13%) and other miscellaneous cases, which amounted to 95 or 0.28% of total clinical cases (Figure 27.6).

Of the 10,595 cases of postmortem examinations (31.99% of the grand total), 9434 (89%) were males and 1161 (11%) females. This male:female ratio of approximately 9:1 reflects the predominant male population, where most resident expatriates are single males. The male:female ratios of postmortem examinations in Libya and Scotland were reported to be 3:1 and 3:2 respectively (Benomran, 1993). Other factors common to females in most countries, that is being less prone to violent deaths and less likely to die outdoor and become medicolegal cases, had contributed to that male preponderance.

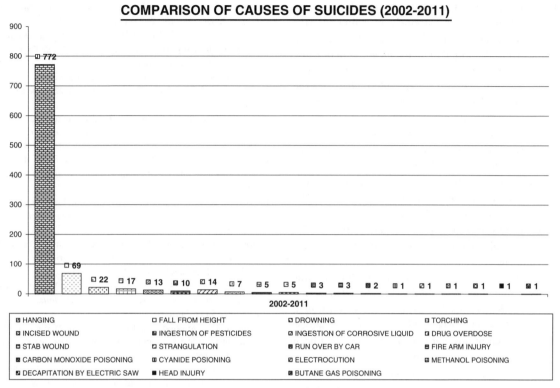

Figure 27.9 A breakdown of suicides by causes of deaths (methods of suicide).

Only in 667 cases (6.29% of total deaths) was the deceased a local citizen, which reflects the fact that citizens are a minority, constituting less than 20% of the population, which is formed largely by noncitizen or expatriate residents.

Autopsies were limited to 734 cases, which constituted 7% of the total deaths examined, and reflected the cultural undesirability of autopsy on the part of the Attorney General and his deputies. In criminal and suspicious circumstances the consent of the relatives is not sought, but the Islamic tradition is strictly observed, where the human body is considered a sacred entity, and quick burial is greatly emphasized.

Accidents and suicides were the two most frequent unnatural manners of death in the present study. The four manners of death in descending order of frequency were natural 6133 (57.88%), accidental 3206 (30.25%), suicidal 947 (8.9%) and homicidal 256 (2.41%). The manner was undetermined in 54 (0.5%) of the cases over the 10 year period, the reason being due to cases being skeletonized remains or decomposing bodies

(Figure 27.7). The most prominent violent manner of death in medicolegal autopsies in other countries were reported to be road traffic accidents and suicides in Norway (Nordrum et al., 1998), suicides in Finland (Saukko, 1995), road traffic and railway accidents in India (Bhattacharjee et al., 1996), road traffic accidents and fire in Scotland (Benomran, 1993) and homicides in Japan (Higuchi and Sukegawa, 1983).

Deaths due to natural causes continue to be the leading manner of death for the overall postmortem examinations. This is due to the current system of death referral in Dubai where many home deaths and all dead-on-arrival to hospitals are referred to the forensic medical examiner.

Stab wounds and blunt trauma to the head are the most frequent causes of death in homicides, making 37% and 25% of homicides, respectively. Next come ligature strangulation (8.9%), where, in this group, a case of homicidal strangulation staged to simulate suicidal hanging was reported (Benomran, 2002b). Homicidal smothering comes next (6.25%), followed by manual strangulation (5%) and cut-throat (4%). Gunshot homicides are extremely rare due to strict firearm legislation in this country (Figure 27.8). Stab wounds were also found to be the most frequent cause of homicidal deaths in other medicolegal practices, namely Norway (Nordrum *et al.*, 1998), New Zealand (Lo, Vuletia and Koelmeyer, 1992) and South Africa (Duflou, Lamont and Knobel, 1988).

Of the homicides, two high profile assassinations had been examined by the author but are yet to be reported awaiting consent issues, although extensively covered by local and international media. A Chechen warlord was shot dead in 2009 (*Gulf News*, 2009), and a Palestinian Resistance Group leader was killed by suffocation in 2010 (*Gulf News*, 2010). In both instances the assassins came to Dubai from abroad specifically to hunt down and eliminate their targets.

Accidental deaths were predominantly due to traffic accidents, amounting to 1498 cases (46.72%) of the overall accidental fatalities. Drug overdose constituted 110 cases, 75% of these being heroin overdose fatalities, where the sign of postmortem sole incisions had been reported in a significant number of cases (Benomran, 2008). Rare and interesting accidental fatalities have been encountered, that is a case of fatal accidental inhalation of sulfuric acid (Benomran, Hassan and Masood, 2008), a few cases of accidental fatal asphyxiation by sand inhalation (Benomran and Hassan, 2008) and one unusual accidental death from positional asphyxia (Benomran and Hassan, 2011).

The predominant method of suicide (Figure 27.9) was hanging (81.52%), followed by a fall from height (7.28%), drowning (2.32%), extensive body burns (1.79%), incised wounds (1.5%), ingestion of corrosive liquids (1.4%) and ingestion of insecticides (1.2%). Many cases of suicidal hangings accompanied by masking and bondage have been encountered (Benomran, Masood and Hassan, 2007). Jumping from a height has been reported to be the method of choice in Singapore (Peng and Choo, 1990), poisoning in Sri Lanka (Hettiarachchi and Kodithuwakku, 1988) and gunshot injuries in Norway (Nordrum *et al.*, 1998).

References

Benomran, F.A. (1993) An objective study of two medico legal systems: Libyan and British. *Medicine, Science and the Law* 33 (4): 315–324.

Benomran, F.A. (2002a) Sexual crimes: perspectives. *Journal of Clinical Forensic Medicine* 9 (1): 1–4.

Benomran, F.A. (2002b) Homicidal strangulation staged to simulate suicidal hanging. *Journale de Medicine Legale* 45 (4–5), Alexandre Lacassagne, Paris: 98.

Benomran, F.A. (2008) Postmortem sole incisions: a new sign of heroin overdose? *Journal of Clinical Forensic Medicine* 15 (1), January: 59–63.

Benomran, F.A. (2009) The medico-legal scene in Dubai 2002–2007. *Journal of Clinical Forensic Medicine* 16, February: 332–337.

Benomran, F.A. (2010) Medical responsibility in the United Arab Emirates, *Journal of Clinical Forensic Medicine* 17: 188–193.

Benomran, F.A., Hassan, A.I. (2008) Accidental fatal asphyxiation by sand inhalation. *Journal of Clinical Forensic Medicine* 15 (6), June: 402–408.

Benomran, F.A., Hassan, A.I. (2011) An unusual accidental death from positional asphyxia. *American Journal for Forensic Medicine and Pathology* 15 (1), March: 31–34.

Benomran, F.A., Hassan, A.I., Masood, S.E. (2008) Fatal accidental inhalation of sulfuric acid. *Journal of Clinical Forensic Medicine* 15 (1), January: 56–58.

Benomran, F.A., Masood, S.E., Hassan, A.I. (2007) Masking and bondage in suicidal hangings. *Medicine, Science and the Law* 47(2): 177–180.

Bhattacharjee, J., Bora, D., Sharma, R.S., Verghese, T. (1996) Unnatural deaths in Delhi during 1991. *Medicine, Science and the Law* 36: 195–198.

Centre of Statistical Studies of Dubai (2008) Report of Social and Demographic Indices, *Albayan Daily Newspaper*, No. 10346, 15 October 2008, p.10.

Duflou, J.A., Lamont, D.L., Knobel, G.J. (1988) Homicide in Cape Town, South Africa. *American Journal of Forensic Medicine and Pathology* 9: 290–294.

Gulf News (2009) A Daily Newspaper of UAE, Issue 30/3.

Gulf News (2010) A Daily Newspaper of UAE, Issue 21/2.

Hettiarachchi, J., Kodithuwakku, G.C.S. (1988) Suicide in Southern Sri Lanka. *Medicine, Science and the Law* 28: 248–251.

Higuchi, T., Sukegawa, Y. (1983) Statistical evaluation in cases of forensic autopsies and the judicial examination in the southern part of Osaka city. *Osaka City Medical Journal* 29: 185–197.

Lo, M., Vuletic, J.C., Koelmeyer, T.D. (1992) Homicides in Auckland, New Zealand, A 14-year study. *American Journal of Forensic Medicine and Pathology* 13: 44–49.

Nordrum, I., Eide, T.J., Jorgrnsen, L. (1998) Medicolegal autopsies of violent deaths in northern Norway 1972–1992. *Forensic Science International* 92: 39–48.

Peng, K.L., Choo, A.S. (1990) Suicide and parasuicide in Singapore 1986. *Medicine, Science and the Law* 30: 225–233.

Saukko, P. (1995) Medicolegal investigative system and sudden death in Scandinavia. *Japan Journal of Legal Medicine* 49: 458–465.

CHAPTER 28

Forensic science practice in the United States

Joseph Peterson[1] & Matthew Hickman[2]

[1] *(Retired) School of Criminal Justice and Criminalistics, California State University, California, USA*
[2] *Department of Criminal Justice, Seattle University, Washington, USA*

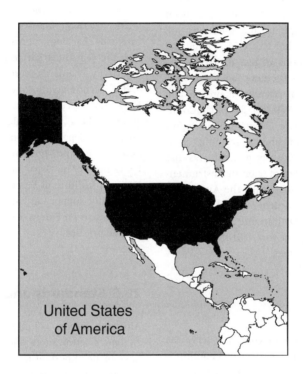

**United States
of America**

28.1 Introduction

There are several important themes that cut across almost all forensic science disciplines in the United States and frame the major issues going forward. These include issues of: scientific progress; key court decisions; practice and policy; standards and methods; education, training and research; national direction and funding; and popular and legal culture. This chapter will begin by briefly describing trends in these areas, how they piece together, and how they overlap. In subsequent sections, this chapter will review forensic science practice in the United States, including discipline-specific histories of forensic services, a review of forensic caseloads, a discussion of the structure of forensic services, integration of forensic sciences, recruitment, training, funding and political influences, certification/accreditation and quality control, disaster preparedness, legal issues, research and technology, and future directions. Although it is necessary to sacrifice some depth for breadth, the goal

The Global Practice of Forensic Science, First Edition. Edited by Douglas H. Ubelaker.
© 2015 John Wiley & Sons, Ltd. Published 2015 by John Wiley & Sons, Ltd.

of the chapter is to provide the reader with an overview of forensic science practice in the United States along with appropriate references for further reading and detail.

28.2 Scientific progress

Good science is at the heart of all forensic examinations and interpretations. Important advances have been made in most forensic disciplines, but questions still persist in certain specialties that lack critical empirical data to support interpretations of test data collected by examiners. DNA testing is the new "gold standard" in the field both in terms of scientific approach and interpretation of data. The National Research Council's (NRC) 2009 *Strengthening Forensic Science* report addressed many of these fundamental scientific questions and limitations. Technologically, great progress has been made in the development of scientific instrumentation and computerized databases like the Automated Fingerprint Identification System (AFIS), Combined DNA Index System (CODIS), and National Integrated Ballistic Information Network (NIBIN) to search and link offenders to their crimes.

28.3 Legal

The central mission of forensic practice is to serve the legal system with accurate and reliable tests and interpretations of data and to assist the trier of fact with timely information. New standards of admissibility for forensic evidence and testimony are guided by the US Supreme Court decision *Daubert v. Merrell Dow Pharmaceuticals* and its progeny (*Joiner* and *Kumho Tire*) that replaced the 1923 *Frye* general acceptance standard in the federal courts and many state courts. Nonetheless, judges still struggle to apply key "scientific practice" criteria articulated in *Daubert*. Other important legal questions include the taking of DNA samples from arrestees (*Maryland v. King*) and if experts are obliged to testify in cases to satisfy the Constitution's confrontation clause (*Melendez-Diaz v. Massachusetts*). Legal "innocence clinics" like the Cardozo Innocence Project have employed DNA testing to exonerate over 300 wrongly convicted and incarcerated persons.

28.4 Policy and practice

Over the decades, forensic laboratories have been chronically underfunded and resources have been strained to meet case demands. Backlogs and untested evidence in such important areas as sexual assault kit and DNA testing plague some laboratories. Many blue ribbon commissions have also questioned the wisdom of locating crime laboratories within law enforcement agencies and if this compromises their objectivity and commitment to science. Periodic forensic laboratory censuses monitor caseloads, backlogs, personnel, and budgets. Scandals over the years have surfaced that indicate scientific and objectivity standards were sacrificed to further police and prosecution ends (for example, the Annie Dookhan, Fred Zain, Joyce Gilchrist, and Arnold Melnikoff cases, among others). The National Research Council proposed an independent Institute of Forensic Science in its 2009 report and, presently, bills are pending in the US Congress. The Department of Justice (DOJ) and the National Institute of Standards and Technology (NIST) are jointly supporting a recently empaneled National Commission on Forensic Science to guide national policy and practice.

28.5 Standards and methods

Although largely voluntary, laboratory accreditation, examiner certification, and quality assurance practices have made important headway to ensure that examiners are qualified and forensic laboratories follow good scientific practice. Crime laboratory accreditation began over thirty years ago and is the centerpiece of the criminalistics profession's commitment to excellence. Most forensic disciplines also have established certification programs that are overseen by the Forensic Specialties Accreditation Board (FSAB) (2013). Beginning with DNA testing procedures, scientific working groups (SWGs) in most forensic specialty areas are developing and setting new testing standards. Efforts to develop uniform codes of ethics across the many forensic specialty areas have been proposed by the National Research Council and other national bodies. Standards and best practices are assuming more prominent positions in the profession with NIST assuming an expanding role.

28.6 Education, training, and research

The quality of education has made significant strides in the forensic field in recent decades, stimulated by guidelines issued by the Technical Working Group on Education (TWGED) in 2004, the formation of the Forensic Science Education Programs Accreditation Commission (FSEPAC), and the accreditation of forensic educational programs around the country. Training opportunities are uneven and remain primarily state-based. Research has grown in most forensic disciplines in recent years and NIJ and NIST have major portfolios of funded research projects addressing forensic problems. A range of laboratory-based research projects is supported and social science research has begun to address the effects of forensic science on case outcomes. Still, research is needed in many forensic disciplines to establish a scientific foundation and guidelines for proper interpretation of examiner data.

28.7 National direction and funding

Given the fact that state and local forensic services dominate scientific input into the nation's criminal justice system, there have been questions over the role of federal oversight and direction. Many federal agencies maintain their own forensic laboratories to serve their agents, and the FBI in particular has provided important leadership on DNA testing and other examination areas. In recent years there have been a number of federal initiatives to support forensic laboratories by expanding DNA testing and reducing case backlogs. There is important national legislation pending in both the US House and Senate that can make significant contributions. Professionally, the Consortium of Forensic Science Organizations (CFSO) has provided important national focus on efforts to influence forensic matters at the national level. The embryonic National Forensic Science Commission, which recently named its members and began holding meetings (US Department of Justice, 2014) should provide important policy guidance, steps to improve quality assurance, and future needs of the field.

28.8 Popular and legal culture

The explosion of forensic science themes on television programs and the popular media has sensitized the lay public and legal practitioners to the tremendous potential of the forensic sciences. Expectations are sometimes raised to unrealistic levels, however, by fictional television dramas, a phenomenon that has become known as the "CSI effect." These dramas have also played a major role in stimulating student interest in this field. The popular media and investigative journalists have also turned a critical eye toward forensic operations and examiners who give inflated and unreliable results. Legal scholars are among the most vocal critics of forensic science practice and standards, but the practicing legal community also often has a poor understanding of the strengths and limitations of forensic science procedures.

28.9 A brief history of forensic services in the United States

28.9.1 Criminalistics

Criminalistics/forensic science laboratories are responsible for the majority of scientific analyses of physical evidence in today's criminal justice system. The first crime laboratories originated in the United States in Los Angeles, CA, in 1923 and Chicago, IL, in 1929 (Thornton, 1975), and many other crime labs resulted from the poor handling and analysis of evidence by the police and independent experts (Dillon, 1977). Fingerprint and latent print examiners actually organized a decade previously in Oakland, California in 1915 forming the International Association for Identification (International Association for Identification, 2012). Chicago Crime Laboratory personnel at Northwestern University founded an early scientific journal (*American Journal of Police Science*) and helped to establish the premier forensic professional association, the American Academy of Forensic Sciences, in 1948.

Thornton (1975) speculates that criminalistics is such a broad area of legal/scientific inquiry that its origins are linked to many diverse fields: legal medicine, toxicology, fingerprinting, document examination, Bertillonage, photography, and even the fictional Sherlock Holmes. Another strong factor in the development of American criminalistics was the belief it could serve as an antidote to the lawlessness and corruption of the police in the 1930s and the "extortion of confessions through brutal methods" (National Commission on Law Observance and Enforcement, 1931, p. 131) and, again, in the 1960s when the US Supreme Court, in decisions like *Miranda* and *Escobedo*, encouraged the police to rely less on coerced confessions and place greater reliance on "extrinsic evidence" and scientific investigations. The European forerunners of American crime laboratories have been addressed by Jurgen Thorwald in his two informative books, *Century of the Detective* (1965) and *Crime and Science* (1967).

The American Academy of Forensic Sciences (AAFS) was founded in 1948 to promote multidisciplinary activities and has grown both in terms of membership (over 6300 members) and member disciplines (11), with criminalistics the largest at about 2800 members (American Academy of Forensic Sciences, n.d. a, n.d. b). The *Journal of Forensic Sciences*, founded in 1956, is the premier scientific journal in the field (Gaensslen, ASTM standardization News, 1975 reprinted in the History of the AAFS; Field, 1998) and promotes the highest scientific standards. In 1965, the President's Commission on Law Enforcement and the Administration of Justice (1967a, 1967b) advocated greater reliance on physical evidence in criminal investigations, and the Omnibus Crime Control Act of 1968 created the Law Enforcement Assistance Administration (LEAA) that channeled federal funds to state and local law enforcement to upgrade their agencies and expand crime laboratories (Omnibus Crime Control and Safe Streets Act, 1968). Parker's (1963) early survey, however, revealed crime laboratories were involved in 2% or less of crime and Joseph's (1968) study found only about 100 crime laboratories nationwide that were severely underfunded. At the same time, The National Advisory Commission on Criminal Justice Standards and Goals found funding was sorely lacking: "Too many police crime laboratories have been set up on budgets that preclude the recruitment of qualified, professional personnel" (National Advisory Commission, 1973, p. 299).

Crime laboratories, nonetheless, expanded in the 1970s and more laboratories were established in closer proximity to local police departments as many states created regional crime laboratory systems (Rehling and Rabren, 1973). Improvements in scientific instrumentation, particularly in the areas of alcohol and drug testing, propelled the scientific capabilities of laboratories. Many new professional organizations were also established as the number of crime laboratories grew. Peterson, Mihajlova and Bedrosian (1985) documented the expansion of crime laboratories in this period, growing to around 300 with about 3000 personnel. About 80% of laboratories were located within law enforcement agencies, budgets remained low, and two-thirds of caseloads were devoted to drug identification and DWI cases. The recent Bureau of Justice Statistics sponsored crime laboratory censuses in the 2000s (Durose *et al.*, 2012) revealed that the number of crime laboratories grew to more than 400.

The 1970s and 1980s witnessed important professional initiatives to engage in proficiency testing, methods development, accreditation and certification that continue today. Poor proficiency testing results (Peterson *et al.*, 1978) and attendant publicity stimulated the field to venture into an array of programs to address laboratory and individual scientist shortcomings. Accreditation of crime laboratories gained traction in the 1980s and remains as one of the most important programs in the field of criminalistics (Presley, 1999). Still, reports of occasional ethical and scientific lapses in the area of criminalistics and crime laboratories revealed a few criminalists to have falsified their qualifications and their results, and to have given biased testimony. An ethics symposium at a 1989 AAFS annual meeting (Peterson, 1989) highlighted the challenges of functioning within an adversarial judicial system and underscored scientists' obligations to be technically competent, not to inflate one's qualifications and results, and to present complete and impartial reports and testimony.

Another very important scientific breakthrough was the development of DNA typing. Important national scientific bodies like the National Research Council evaluated and endorsed DNA typing and stressed the importance of examiner qualifications, standardized laboratory methods and quality assurance procedures (National Research Council, 1996). The leadership of the FBI and establishment of testing standards (TWG-DAM), the development of the Combined DNA Index System (CODIS), and the DNA Identification Act of 1994 were all central to implementation of this technology (Scientific Working Group DNA Analysis Methods, 2013). DNA testing revolutionized the precision and sensitivity of testing biological fluids and stains and has transformed the investigation and prosecution of criminal cases and the identification of unknown individuals. DNA testing also became a powerful technique to reexamine evidence and testimony in older cases that used less specific scientific techniques, to exclude individuals formerly thought to be suspects, and to exonerate those who have been wrongly convicted and incarcerated. (Connors *et al.*, 1996; Innocence Project, 2013).

The modern day march toward higher professional standards in criminalistics began in the 1970s and sharpened the field's ability to identify and potentially individualize physical evidence. National scientific bodies and the recent NRC *Strengthening Forensic Science in the United States* report (2009) have trained their focus on forensic testing and have identified several areas lacking strong scientific foundations. Public and legal scrutiny of the handling and interpretation of scientific evidence has also grown as forensic testing invaded television, newspapers, and popular culture, and expectations have risen. Investigative journalists have published numerous accounts of the reexamination of criminal cases based on questionable forensic findings (Hsu, 2013). Questions have also emerged about the wisdom of placing crime laboratories in police agencies and whether this undermines the goals of scientific excellence and neutrality. The courts have also developed more refined admissibility criteria and procedures to insure that forensic expertise and testimony are grounded in science.

28.9.2 Questioned documents

Worldwide, efforts to determine the authenticity of documents date back centuries and, in the United States, to the mid-1800s. Ordway Hilton provides a brief history of questioned document examination in the U.S. from 1900 to 1979 and notes the work of early examiners (Hilton, 1979). The field advanced as Albert S. Osborn published many articles and gained wide notoriety through his work in the 1930 Lindbergh baby kidnapping case, and through the writings of Professor John Wigmore, a noted Northwestern University law school dean and professor, who was a strong supporter of Osborn and the reliability of questioned document examination (Riordan *et al.*, 2013). Almost all the early document examiners were in private practice, however, as were those who testified at the trial of Bruno Hauptman for the kidnap and murder of the Lindbergh baby. The first document sections of crime laboratories originated in the 1930s with the formation of the Chicago crime laboratory at Northwestern University and at the federal level at the FBI, Treasury, Postal Service, and the National Bureau of Standards. Private examiners continued their research and new methods for examining typewriting, inks, papers, and handwriting were introduced.

After World War II, new procedures and laboratory techniques were needed to examine redesigned typewriters, photocopy machines, new writing instruments, and computer printing devices. As writing materials advanced and were changed, identification features of necessity were modified. Alternative lighting sources, filters, and photographic techniques helped the field progress. The American Society of Questioned Document Examiners was formed in 1942 and the International Association for Identification formed a questioned document section in the 1950s. New examiners were trained through lengthy (two years or more) apprentice style programs principally at state and federal forensic laboratories. Thornton notes, however, how the field was impaired by the errors of examiners in well-known criminal and civil cases (Thornton, 1975, p. 13). While courses in document examination were offered at several academic institutions in the United States, no academic degree programs developed to replace the apprentice method. The American Academy of Forensic Sciences had a questioned document section at its inception, but with only a handful of members in its early years. As of March 11, 2013 this section had grown to 204 members, 42 of whom were fellows (AAFS, n.d. b). In terms of scientific publications, and as noted elsewhere, the *Journal of Forensic Sciences* formed in 1956 and the *Journal of Forensic Document Examination* created in 1986 both served as outlets for questioned document research. Important texts were periodically published and continue to the present day.

28.9.3 Forensic pathology/biology

Medicolegal death investigation is likely the oldest forensic science (Wright and Eckert, 1997) and has its roots in this country in the coroner system introduced by English colonists in the 1600s. Coroners had existed for centuries in England to protect the financial interests of the king and conduct inquests to determine the cause and manner of suspicious deaths. Given the shortage of medically trained personnel in the United States, lay coroners conducted most criminal death investigations until the use of physicians began in Maryland in the 1860s and the formal adoption of a medical examiner system in Massachusetts in 1877 (Davis and Hanzlick, 2013). The use of trained physicians and forensically trained medical examiners were adopted by some jurisdictions, but the use of elected and usually non-physician coroners, who typically contracted for medical advice, prevailed in most others. As with other criminal justice and forensic science delivery systems, a variety of organizations evolved depending upon the preferences and resources of state and local governments.

The debate over the best way to conduct death investigation services has continued for over one hundred years, even though various medical, legal, and governmental commissions have recommended doing away with the coroner system and the adoption of physician medical examiners to determine the cause and manner of death. Preceded by two National Research Council reports in 1928 and 1932, a Model Post-Mortem Examination Act was advanced in 1954 that recommended the abolition of coroners and the adoption of medical examiner systems headed by forensic pathologists in all states (Davis and Hanzlick, 2013). A survey published in 1998 found that while medical examiners served about 50% of the population, few new medical examiner systems have been adopted since 1990 (Hanzlick and Combs, 1998). Several additional groups have addressed this dilemma, including the recent National Research Council report that also called for the replacement of coroner offices with medical examiner systems (National Research Council, 2009, p. 267).

The process of investigating deaths that occur in a violent, sudden, or unusual manner is complex and involves a variety of medicolegal personnel including elected coroners, lay investigators, law enforcement personnel, autopsy technicians and forensic pathologists. While progress has been made over the years, political and legal systems have too often not provided the necessary resources to insure all such deaths are properly recognized and investigated. Professional organizations like the American Academy of Forensic Sciences and the National Association of Medical Examiners are two principal organizations that have been historically in the forefront of efforts to improve the quality of forensic and scientific training of personnel engaged in this effort. The American Academy of Forensic Sciences Pathology/Biology section had 943 members, 229 of whom were fellows, as of March 11, 2013 (AAFS, n.d. b)

28.9.4 Forensic toxicology

Forensic toxicology includes four primary types of casework: death investigation toxicology, human performance, doping control, and workplace drug testing (Logan and Ropero-Miller, 2013). Forensic toxicology examines the harmful effects of drugs and chemicals on living systems. Upon ingestion, the process of absorption, distribution, metabolism, and elimination (Houck and Siegel, 2010) of drugs is a dynamic process affecting their concentration in various regions of the body. The scientific identification and quantitation of drugs and poisons in biological fluids, and the interpretation of those results for medicolegal or administrative purposes, has wide application in society. It is one of the fastest growing of all forensic sciences and rests upon well-established chemical, pharmacological, and instrumental laboratory practices.

Europeans were leaders in the development of techniques to detect arsenic and other poisons in the 1800s, with the Spaniard Matthew Orfila often referred to as the "father of toxicology" as the result of his groundbreaking publications (*Traite des Poisons* ...) and his work in celebrated poisoning cases (Thorwald, 1965). In America, Cornell University Professor Rudolph Witthaus's publications and work in many famous poisoning cases were significant. The office of the New York City Chief Medical Examiner was one of the earliest to establish its own toxicology laboratory in 1918 under the direction of Dr. Alexander Gettler, who was also highly regarded for his teaching and mentorship of professional leaders (Poklis, 1997). Gettler and famed New York City medical examiner Charles Norris are featured in the recent PBS documentary *The Poisoner's Handbook* that was supported by the Forensic Sciences Foundation, Inc. (PBS American Experience, n.d.). Much of the early research was devoted to the detection and measurement of alcohol in blood, breath, and urine, and to determine the equivalency between blood and breath concentrations (Jones, 1996). Work in the mid-1900s by Rolla Harger and Robert Borkenstein focused on the invention of portable devices for law enforcement to measure alcohol breath concentrations of drivers. Much of this work continues to the present (Department for Transport, 2010).

The use of analytical chemistry, gas chromatography, mass spectrometry, and other instrumental techniques for the detection of drugs and poisons found in body fluids and tissue samples at autopsy have increased in sophistication and sensitivity over the years. The introduction of affordable table-top GC-MS units, immunoassay automation, and other instrumentation are significant as well. The interpretation of test results has contributed greatly to understanding the role of alcohol, prescription drugs and controlled substances in the investigation of deaths. Forensic toxicological testing of drugs in the workplace and in the doping of human athletes and animals has grown as well. The reliability of such testing is paramount, as is maintenance of proper records and chain of custody of specimens. Toxicology is one of the original sections of the American Academy of Forensic Sciences (AAFS) and now has 534 members, including 121 fellows (AAFS, n.d. b).

28.9.5 Forensic anthropology

Forensic anthropology is directed to the recovery, examination, and identification of human skeleton remains to resolve legal questions. Through the analysis of skeletal materials, trained physical anthropologists are often able to determine various human characteristics, including the sex, age, stature, and possible ancestry of the victim. Often working with death investigation teams, examination of skeletal remains may also assist in the identification of the victim and the circumstances surrounding their death. Anthropologists make observations on skeletal features, either directly or more commonly through radiographs for identification.

Historically, forensic anthropology is commonly traced to the demise of Harvard professor Dr. George Parkman in 1849, whose dismembered and burned remains were found in the laboratory assay furnace of a faculty colleague, chemist Dr. John Webster. Anatomists testified the remains were consistent with those of a person like Parkman and a dentist identified recovered dentures he had personally made for Parkman. Webster was convicted and executed. Other criminal cases occurred over the decades in which biological anthropologists assisted law enforcement in the identification of skeletal materials. Research by Wilton Krogman leading to his publication of "A guide to the identification of human skeletal material" in the FBI Law Enforcement Bulletin in 1939 (Sorg, 2005), T. Dale Stewart's work at the Smithsonian Institution, and the assessment of Korean War dead also served to develop further the field of forensic anthropology (Newall, 2007).

Health records of soldiers killed in the wars of the 20th century enabled anthropologists to examine remains, establish databases, and, when used in conjunction with fingerprints, dental evidence, and now DNA, enable identifications to be made (Newall, 2007). The work by anthropologists in the Army American Graves Registration Service and the United States Army Central

Identification Laboratory assisted in the identification of war dead from World War II, the Korean War, and the Vietnam War (Burkhart, 1998).

Beginning in the 1980s, physical anthropologists worked in many areas around the world in mass genocide and human rights violation cases to identify the dead. Work continues in four broad categories of forensic anthropology: biological, forensic archaeological, trauma analysis, and taphonomy (Steadman, 2013). The development of the AAFS Physical Anthropology Section in 1972 was a significant step and presently has a total membership of 547 members, 109 of whom are fellows and 245 are student affiliates (reflecting the section's strong academic and teaching orientation). A survey published on the AAFS section website (Agostini and Gomez, n.d.) shows most members hold a PhD and are affiliated with an academic institution. The American Board of Forensic Anthropology (ABFA) lists 99 Diplomates on record as of 2013, including 69 current and 12 retired Diplomates. Nearly half of the current Diplomates have academic affiliations, the remainder are associated with state/local medical examiner offices or forensic science laboratories, military and federal forensic science laboratories, and the private sector.

28.9.6 Forensic odontology

Forensic odontologists help identify deceased persons by examining and comparing the teeth of unknown human remains with premortem dental records. Teeth often survive catastrophic events that make the person unrecognizable, and a detailed examination and X-rays of the remains can be compared with premortem photographs, dental X-rays, and casts that enable a trained forensic dentist to make a positive identification. Forensic odontologists may also examine and interpret dental injuries, neglect, and instances of dental malpractice. Forensic odontologists may also engage in bite mark analysis in criminal investigations of assault, rape, and homicide. Forensic odontologists are primarily general dental practitioners and many maintain affiliations with medical examiner and coroner's offices, military units, as well as federal, state, and local criminal justice agencies.

Teeth have been used for centuries to identify human remains. The celebrated Parkman affair cited earlier is typically referenced as one of the earliest American cases in which a denture was used to identify badly burned remains, and the first case involving a bitemark leading to a conviction dates back to the 1950s (Pretty *et al.*, 2013). Over the years, odontologists have been regularly involved in the identification of victims of various types of mass disasters, ranging from natural disasters, airline crashes, human rights cases, and acts of terrorism. Bitemark cases represent one of the most unusual cases addressed by forensic odontologists, but have become the most controversial due to mistaken identifications, often determined through DNA testing. The assumption is that unique characteristics of the human dentition are transferred by a biter to a victim's skin (or other materials) and that resulting marks and impressions can be properly interpreted and linked to the biter (Bernstein, 1997). Distortion of the skin and lack of detailed tooth markings, however, render many bitemarks unsuitable for comparison.

The Odontology Section of the American Academy of Forensic Sciences was formed in 1969 and the American Society of Forensic Odontology was founded in 1970, as well as other associations worldwide. The American Academy's Odontology Section, meeting annually with the American Society of Forensic Odontology, has been a strong organizational and professional focus for forensic odontologists. The AAFS section grew to 432 members by March,11, 2013, 157 of whom were fellows.

28.9.7 Psychiatry and behavioral science

Forensic psychiatrists and psychologists have historically addressed a range of issues regarding criminal responsibility that arise in criminal and civil law contexts. They address issues such as the mental state of defendants at the time the crime was committed and the competency of defendants to stand trial, to assist with their defense, and to offer predictions of future dangerousness. They address mental health problems within institutions and deliver treatment to those who are incarcerated or under community supervision. They address many civil questions ranging from mandating medical treatment, involuntary commitments, and a host of family and domestic problems; here, forensic psychiatrists and psychologists advise lawyers and judges and often give expert testimony.

Forensic psychology has emerged more prominently in recent years regarding the functioning of the criminal justice system. This might include addressing the accuracy and reliability of police lineups or conditions under which suspects may give false confessions. They may also assist lawyers in selecting members of juries,

in studies of juror behavior, in understanding jury instructions, and in determining the reliability of eyewitnesses. Both psychiatrists and psychologists also assist in determining the fitness of applicants to serve as police officers and to treat and/or counsel criminal justice practitioners.

Billick and Martell (2013) observe that the history of psychiatry in America dates to the founding of the first American hospital by Dr. Benjamin Rush, who also wrote the first psychiatry textbook in 1812, Isaac Ray's monumental treatise on insanity in 1838, and the founding of the American Psychiatric Association in 1844. Significant is a long jurisprudential history to punish only the morally blameworthy, as well as efforts in modern times to define insanity, beginning with the English M'Naghten rule of 1843. Efforts continued with formulation of the "irresistible impulse" doctrine, Judge David Bazelon's "product test" ruling in 1954 in *Durham v. United States* (Curran, 1980), the American Law Institute's Model Penal Code two-pronged definition of criminal responsibility in the 1950s, restrictions to the insanity defense and shifting of the burden of proof to the defense brought on by John Hinckley Jr.'s attempted assassination of President Ronald Reagan in 1981 (Sadoff, 2005), and the Federal Insanity Defense Reform Act.

Clinical psychology in the United States dates to the late 1800s and was stimulated by the demand for psychological treatment of war veterans during and after World War II. In the modern period, forensic psychology was stimulated by the founding of the American Psychology–Law Society in 1969, the creation of the Psychology and Law Division of the American Psychological Association in 1981, and recognition of forensic psychology as a specialty by the Commission for the Recognition of Specialties in Professional Psychology (CRSPP) in 2001. The Psychiatry and Behavioral Science Section of the AAFS was founded in 1948, and was originally composed of forensic psychiatrists, but forensic psychologists were admitted beginning in 1982. The section presently has 160 members, including 29 fellows. Members of the section have maintained active affiliations with the American Academy of Psychiatry and the Law and established the American Board of Forensic Psychiatry in 1976. The American Board of Forensic Psychiatry was discontinued in 1997 when forensic psychiatry was recognized as a specialty by the American Board of Psychiatry and Neurology.

28.9.8 Engineering sciences

The legal responsibility of builders to ensure their structures are safe and well constructed date to Hammurabi's Code from about 1800 B.C. (Noon, 2005). Forensic engineers are commonly engaged in failure analysis, accident reconstruction, determining the cause and origin of fires and explosions, and the evaluation of structures or manufactured products using civil, biomedical, mechanical, electrical, and other engineering principles. Historically, many of the first cases involved bridge and building failure, accident reconstruction involving motor vehicles and airplanes, product liability cases, and the failure of medical devices (Liptai *et al.*, 2013). Fire protection engineering and the investigation of suspicious or incendiary fires also make use of engineers with forensic training. Engineers are involved primarily in civil litigation, but may also lend their expertise to criminal investigations and prosecutions. Many forensic engineers are employed by large companies or are self-employed and engage in forensic work on a part-time and/or on a consultant basis. In addition to engineering training, they must have knowledge of the legal system, rules of testimony, and legal safeguards for handling evidence.

A recent comprehensive forensic science text that covers various forensic specialties breaks forensic engineering into the three areas: structural failures, fire and explosion investigation, and vehicular accident reconstruction (James and Nordby, 2005). Forensic engineers typically have been trained at university in engineering or applied sciences and have obtained graduate degrees. Engineering innovations have been successful in classifying, storing, transmitting, and searching large files of drugs and poisons, fingerprints, bullets and cartridge cases, DNA profiles, and other forensic evidence. Engineering breakthroughs have also made headway in classifying and recognizing handwriting, voices, and facial features. The Engineering Sciences section of the AAFS was founded in 1981 and as of March 11, 2013 had 159 members, 32 of whom were fellows.

28.9.9 Digital and multimedia science

Society has witnessed the rapid growth of new technology, digital devices, and digital evidence in criminal and civil cases in recent decades. With the growth in and transmission of digital information and storage devices, there have been growing instances of computer hacking, crimes against intellectual property, child pornography, and many other examples of Internet crime. New state and federal statutes have been enacted to protect these forms of digital information but violations occur at a rapid pace. Digital and multimedia analysis is an emerging sector of the forensic sciences field dedicated to the examination of computers and other digital devices, the recovery of electronic evidence of crimes, and the analysis of digital video and audio recordings (Baker *et al.*, 2013). Digital examiners examine software, operating systems, hard drives, and other devices to locate deleted, encrypted, or other information from damaged computers.

Since 2002, the FBI has operated a regional computer forensics laboratory system and now has laboratories located in 16 cities throughout the country (Regional Computer Forensic Laboratory (RCFL), n.d.). Each of these sites has about 12 staff examiners (most of whom are officers/technical personnel assigned from local law enforcement agencies) and three administrative staff. The United States Secret Service also operates a network of electronic crimes task forces (ECTF) to combat cyber crime and to protect the integrity of the nation's "financial and critical infrastructures" (United States Secret Service, 2012). Crimes that pose "significant economic or community impact, involvement of organized crime elements, and schemes involving new technology" would qualify. Law enforcement has joined with private industry, private experts, and academia in these task forces. Also, the NCIS maintains a Cyber Crime Unit that uses advanced technologies to examine electronic data of intelligence or evidentiary value (Naval Criminal Investigative Service (NCIS), n.d.). NCIS works with domestic and international law enforcement to address criminal incidents and mitigate threats by using forensic technologies. The AAFS Digital and Multimedia Science Section was formed in 2008 and as of March 11, 2013 had 110 members, 13 of whom were fellows.

28.10 Forensic caseloads

28.10.1 Overview

The US Department of Justice, Bureau of Justice Statistics has sponsored two major data collections that provide periodic information on forensic caseload in the United States: The Census of Publicly Funded

Forensic Crime Laboratories and the Census of Medical Examiner and Coroner Offices. A third annual survey, the National Forensic Laboratory Information System (NFLIS), is sponsored by the Drug Enforcement Administration and is limited to drug chemistry analysis caseloads in the nation's crime laboratories. These three data collections are presently the most systematic and comprehensive sources of information about forensic caseload in the United States. Crime laboratory data are summarized below, and data for the medical examiner and coroner offices are summarized in the "Forensic Pathology/Biology" section. Three BJS crime laboratory censuses have been conducted and published thus far, beginning with the 2002 survey (Peterson and Hickman, 2005) and the most recent data published in 2012 (Durose, 2012). Census results offer some insight into the growth of forensic sciences and the demand for their services. There were 411 crime laboratories identified in 2009, up from 351 laboratories in 2002, or about a 17% increase. These laboratories employed an estimated 13,100 full-time personnel and had combined budgets of about $1.6 billion. More than 50% of these labs were affiliated with state government agencies. The FBI laboratory, with more than 500 employees, is the largest in the nation.

The 411 crime laboratories received about 4.1 million requests for services in 2009 with the great majority of requests being in the areas of DNA analysis (34%), controlled substances (33%), and toxicology (15%). These 4.1 million requests represent more than a 50% increase in submissions since 2002. About 75% of the 1.3 million DNA requests made were convicted offender and arrestee samples for entry into CODIS. One can see the importance of DNA testing in today's modern crime laboratories, with most requests being submitted to state and federal crime labs. Laboratories began and ended the year with more than one million requests backlogged, three-quarters of which were forensic biology requests and 12% were controlled substance requests. As with total DNA requests, most (55%) of the backlogged DNA requests were of convicted offender and arrestee samples. More than half of the backlogged forensic biology requests were reported at the FBI laboratory. Still, between 2008 and 2009, the backlog for actual DNA casework requests increased at a faster rate than for offender and arrestee sample testing.

The NFLIS program collects data from a sample of public laboratories that perform drug chemistry analysis, and generates national estimates regarding the types of drugs being submitted to laboratories. The primary goal of the data collection is to assist the DEA in monitoring illicit drug abuse and trafficking, including the diversion of legally manufactured pharmaceuticals into illegal markets, as well as to support drug scheduling and policy making. NFLIS presently reports 288 participating labs and the most recent data reported are for calendar year 2012 (Drug Enforcement Administration, 2013). NFLIS captures both "drug reports" (i.e., for each drug item analyzed, up to three drugs can be reported to NFLIS) and "drug cases analyzed" (i.e., case-level data, with all drugs identified within a drug-related incident). During 2012, an estimated 1.2 million drug-specific cases were analyzed by State and local forensic laboratories and about 1.6 million drug reports were identified (Drug Enforcement Administration, 2013). The most common drug was cannabis/THC, followed by cocaine, methamphetamine, heroin, and oxycodone.

28.10.2 Questioned documents

There is not detailed information on questioned documents cases being reviewed annually, as many document examiners are in private practice. Only about 16% of crime laboratories in the 2009 Census of Crime Laboratories examined questioned documents. There were about 13,000 requests for examinations of questioned documents in 2009 and 12,000 were completed. Estimates also indicated that the percent change in backlog had increased by more than a third between year end 2008 and year end 2009. A disproportionately large portion of these requests were directed to federal laboratories.

28.10.3 Forensic pathology/biology

There are many forces at play in the area of medicolegal death investigations and this section will give the reader an idea of operations data available in this field, organizations active in professionalizing these services, and the status of efforts to replace coroner offices with medical examination systems. One of the key recommendations of the NRC panel was discontinuance of coroner operations in favor of systems headed by medical examiners. Hanzlick (2007) has observed that although there was movement in this direction between 1960 and 1989, since then it has slowed, almost to a standstill. We begin with a summary of a Bureau of Justice Statistics census of death investigation systems in

2004, followed by a brief discussion of activities of a new scientific working group on medicolegal death investigations and the results of a recent survey of NAME accredited programs.

There were approximately 2000 medical examiner and coroner (ME/C) offices in the United States in 2004, as documented through the 2007 Bureau of Justice Statistics census (Hickman *et al.*, 2007). The offices employed more than 7300 FTE employees and had annual budgets totaling about $718.5 million. Most (80%) of the offices enumerated in 2004 were county coroners' offices and primarily served jurisdictions of fewer than 25,000 persons. Almost one million cases were referred to these offices in 2004, representing about 40% of all 2,398,000 deaths occurring in the United States in that year. ME/C offices accepted about half of the referred cases for further investigation. ME/C offices also reported that they handled about 4400 unidentified persons, 1000 of whom remained unidentified after one year. Most of the unidentified cases were in larger jurisdictions.

The BJS report included additional detailed information from respondents. As noted above, only a minority of these offices served large (500,000 or more persons) jurisdictions, but still employed over half of the ME/C FTE personnel. Forensic pathologists, medical examiners, and coroners made up only 20% of all FTE employees in these offices. Toxicologists, technicians, and other analysts made up 13% of the personnel. Many of these personnel serving large jurisdictions were ancillary (death scene investigators, autopsy technicians, and photographers). Forensic specialists like odontologists and anthropologists made up less than 1% of FTE personnel (discussed in more detail later). Complete autopsies and toxicological examinations were conducted in about half of the cases that offices accepted for further investigation, with larger offices conducting complete autopsies in a higher percentage of cases than smaller jurisdictions.

The Scientific Working Group on Medicolegal Death Investigations (SWGMDI), supported by the National Institute of Justice through an interagency agreement with the FBI, was created in 2011 and has several working committees that have issued a number of recent reports on certification, accreditation, death scene investigation, legal issues, system infrastructure (workload) conditions and needs, research, and organ and tissue procurement. The Group has issued a number of reports on increasing the supply of forensic pathologists, death investigation centers, and autopsy facility needs throughout the United States (SWGMDI, 2013). Available workload data from the SWGMDI indicate an annual postmortem examination caseload (autopsies and external examinations) of nearly 225,000 examinations across 272 reporting facilities (SWGMDI, 2011).

At about the same time as the creation of the SWGMDI, other researchers surveyed about 60 medical examiner and coroner offices that were accredited by the National Association of Medical Examiners (NAME) and that served about one-quarter of the United States population (Weinberg *et al.*, 2013). A key finding was that even these accredited offices varied tremendously in size and that "financial or pathologist efficiency" did not correlate with the size of the jurisdiction, budget per capita, or autopsies per pathologist. This article also commented on another theme addressed in this chapter regarding inquiries by journalists and that such investigators had explored large death investigation systems and the effects of the size, budgets, autopsy rates, and their accreditation status (Schmidt, Shaw, and LaFleur, 2011).

The Armed Forces Medical Examiner System (AFMES) provides "comprehensive and innovative medical legal services worldwide" (Armed Forces Medical Examiner System, 2013) and is composed of the Office of the Armed Forces Medical Examiner, the Armed Forces DNA Identification Laboratory (AFDIL), the Division of Forensic Toxicology, and the Medical Mortality Surveillance Division. This is a large and far-reaching service that operates out of Dover Air Force Base, DE, and works with the investigative units of branches of the military and supports various other federal agencies. It employs forensic pathologists, forensic anthropologists, medicolegal death investigators, DNA examiners, and other technical personnel in the investigation and recovery of evidence and the positive identification of individuals. The AFDIL, in particular, engages in worldwide DNA analysis, research, analytical services and DNA reference specimen collection and storage for US military personnel. The Forensic Toxicology Division performs routine toxicological exams in military air, ground, and sea accidents, medicolegal autopsies, DUI and DWI investigations, blood and urine tests for fitness of duty inquiries, and other cases of national interest.

28.10.4 Forensic toxicology

The recent Census of Publicly Funded Forensic Crime Laboratories 2009 report (Durose *et al.*, 2012) provided limited information on toxicological testing performed in public forensic crime laboratories. (Many private laboratories also provide forensic toxicological testing for medical examiner/coroner offices and crime laboratories but their caseload data are not included.) Forty-two percent of respondents reported performing toxicological testing: 95% of these performed antemortem blood alcohol (BAC) testing; 60% performed testing of antemortem drugs; and 40% performed postmortem testing. Collectively, all crime laboratories reported receiving over 600,000 requests for toxicological services, with backlog decreasing slightly for 2008. The 2004 Census of Medical Examiners reported that forensic toxicologists, lab technicians, and analysts (classified as lab support personnel) made up 13% of FTE in the offices that served communities of 250,000 or more. ME/C offices serving large jurisdictions (250,000 or more) conducted toxicology analyses in a higher percentage of cases (57%) than offices serving smaller (<250,000 population) jurisdictions.

In addition, the Forensic Toxicology Council lists statistics (generated by surveys of the Society of Forensic Toxicologists) on the American Board of Forensic Toxicology website (Forensic Toxicology Council, 2010) indicating that 35% of toxicology laboratories perform postmortem toxicology, that about 6.5 million samples are tested annually under federal regulation, and 50 million nonregulated workload samples are tested. Twenty-four percent of laboratories report that they are accredited by the American Board of Forensic Toxicology and 30% by the College of American Pathologists.

28.10.5 Forensic anthropology and odontology

To a large extent, the workload of forensic anthropologists and odontologists is tied to cases handled in medical examiner and coroner offices because their work (in a forensic context) is primarily focused on the identification of human remains. The BJS census of ME/C offices demonstrated that these specialists are but a small fraction of total full-time employment in ME/C offices and generally limited only to the largest jurisdictions (although they may also provide regional services beyond their "home" jurisdiction). Their services are more often provided on a contractual or consulting basis. Many states, including California, maintain a missing unidentified persons database that relies on dental, fingerprint, and DNA records (State of California, 2013). Dental information is also a key component of rapid and effective victim identification in mass disasters. The Scientific Working Group on Disaster Victim Identification (SWGDVI), sponsored by the FBI and working with domestic and international agencies, is working to set best practices for teams worldwide working in multiple fatality incidents (SWGDVI, 2013). Additional dental charting work is sponsored by the Joint POW/MIA Accounting Council (JPAC) as is the work of the Disaster Mortuary Operational Response Team (DMORT) to aid in assembling and comparing pre- and postmortem information records to aid in disaster victim identification (Pretty *et al.*, 2013). The identification of missing and unidentified persons by the NCIC is yet another area where dental evidence is vital.

28.10.6 Psychiatry and behavioral science

There are little national data available on the caseload of forensic psychiatrists and psychologists, or of other behavioral scientists who may work or provide services in a forensic context. With the exception of forensic psychiatrists and psychologists employed by state prison systems and/or hospitals, persons providing these services are generally self-employed or work on a consulting basis. Available data from the Bureau of Justice Statistics indicate that a substantial proportion of the incarcerated population has mental health problems. Within State prisons, 73% of female and 55% of male inmates in 2004 had mental health problems based upon DSM-IV criteria; in Federal facilities the proportions were lower, 61% of female and 44% of male inmates; and in local jails the proportions were 75% of female and 63% of male inmates (Glaze and James, 2006). At mid year 2000, 1394 of the Nation's 1558 State public and private adult correctional facilities provided mental health services to their inmates, with one in every 8 State prisoners receiving some mental health therapy or counseling services and about 10% receiving psychotropic medications, while 155 State facilities reported specializing in psychiatric confinement during that year (Beck and Maruschak, 2001).

28.10.7 Engineering sciences

In general, public forensic laboratories do not employ forensic engineers as part of their full-time staff. This is essentially a function of low demand relative to cost for such services, but it is also due in part to the fact that their work is primarily in the arena of civil litigation as opposed to criminal matters. Forensic engineers tend to work for private engineering firms or are self-employed, and are generally hired on a consulting basis to provide forensic services in specific cases. Because these services are mostly in the private realm, there are no national data available on forensic workload related to the engineering sciences. A possible exception is with regard to vehicle accident investigations, which may fall under the domain of State and/or local police agencies (and possibly within their laboratory systems), or at the federal level to include aviation, railroad, marine, and other federal transportation and infrastructure accidents investigated by the National Transportation Safety Board (NTSB) with engineering support from their Office of Research and Engineering. However, when an accident involves suspected criminal activity or an NTSB investigation reveals a potential crime, the FBI becomes the lead investigating agency with NTSB operating in a supporting capacity.

28.10.8 Digital and multimedia science

The 2009 BJS crime laboratory census found that 19% of crime laboratories engage in digital evidence examinations, with higher percentages among municipal and federal laboratories. Laboratories estimated they completed 31,000 requests for examinations, which was about 1% of their total examinations. At the end of 2009, they had about 1300 requests backlogged, which was equal to the number they had backlogged at the end of 2008. The FBI Regional Computer Forensics Laboratory (RCFL, discussed earlier) reported receiving a total of 5060 requests for assistance in 2012, which included 8566 digital forensics examinations conducted (Federal Bureau of Investigation, 2013). In addition, law enforcement officers made almost 9000 requests to examine cellular telephones in support of criminal investigations. The FBI Computer Analysis Response Team (CART), which operates within the regional laboratory system but also has six mobile laboratories, conducted more than 13,300 digital forensic examinations

during the fiscal year 2012 (Federal Bureau of Investigation n.d.).

28.11 Structure of major initiatives

Major initiatives in the field have originated from several key areas; details in all the following areas are discussed elsewhere in this chapter:

1. Most programs have originated from the profession itself. While external pressures from the legal system and the scientific community at large are important, most of the major professional initiatives (certification, accreditation, proficiency testing/quality control, scientific working groups, etc.) have originated from one or more of the forensic disciplines or professional organizations.

2. The legal system, through the US Supreme Court or other case law decisions, has served to regulate the collection of physical evidence from criminal suspects and crime scenes, and the admissibility of expert testimony into courts of law.

3. The National Institute of Justice, the National Institute of Standards and Technology, and the Federal Bureau of Investigation have been the primary sources of research funding, efforts to expand DNA testing, reduce laboratory backlogs, and set and enforce standards. The National Science Foundation is becoming involved in funding more basic science research to aid the forensic sciences.

4. Committees of the US Congress have addressed scientific practices, appropriated funds to expand services like DNA testing, and more recently directed national scientific organizations (like the National Academies) to address key scientific questions and, conceivably, to "overhaul" the field of forensic science.

5. The Executive Office of the President's Science and Technology Council, Committee on Science, and Subcommittee on Forensic Science has labored to develop a federal response to the 2009 National Research Council's *Strengthening Forensic Science* report.

6. The United States Congress, the National Institute of Science and Technology (NIST), and the Office of Justice Programs (OJP) have all offered plans to develop a *National Commission (or Institute) on Forensic Science* that would develop standards, improve the

understanding of science by the legal system, forge a uniform code of professional responsibility, and take steps to identify future needs of the field.

28.12 Integration of forensic sciences

The utilization of forensic evidence requires the coordination of various law enforcement, scientific, and judicial agencies. Unfortunately, seamless integration among these agencies and actors is often not the case. Laboratory case management policies, effective communication, case tracking systems, and training and education are areas in need of improvement to support better integration of forensic sciences. One trend to facilitate this integration is having medical examiner/coroner offices and crime laboratories housed in the same forensic facility.

Laboratory submission guidelines establish clear rules outlining what evidence will be accepted for analysis. Research has found clear support for significant reductions in laboratory case workload and turnaround time after the implementation of laboratory acceptance policies (Strom *et al.*, 2011). It is important that all stakeholders (submitting agencies, prosecutors, and defense attorneys) be involved in the development and routine review of these guidelines, as the same study found that most law enforcement officers were only marginally aware of submission policies in their jurisdictions. Frequent and routine communication among submitting law enforcement agencies, laboratories, and prosecutors is essential for effective use of evidence. Prosecutor communication with laboratories in particular has been documented as a significant problem in many US jurisdictions (Strom and Hickman, 2010; Strom *et al.*, 2011). Strom *et al.* (2011) found that prosecutors rarely contacted laboratories to provide updates on case statuses and, in most instances, did not have a standard practice of informing laboratories of cases resolved due to a guilty plea or dismissal. Study participants estimated that 50–75% of the drug case backlog represented cases that had already been pled out or dismissed. Cross-agency information sharing systems should include laboratory staff, prosecutors, defense attorneys, and submitting police agency personnel. Such systems should use barcodes and other unique identifiers in order to track critical information as it moves from one stage of case processing to the next. More short-term approaches towards case reporting include web-based Laboratory Information Management Systems (LIMSs) which provide a secure means for online communication as well as timely updates on laboratory case results (including the ability to print laboratory reports remotely and access to electronic laboratory result litigation packets), and the promotion and use of court-based systems that provide updates on cases.

Training and education to provide a better understanding of the responsibilities, roles, and policies of each stakeholder is a critical need. This should include training for prosecutors, law enforcement officers, and laboratory staff on the judicial system processing including how they charge suspects and conduct plea negotiations. In addition, prosecutors and defense attorneys must educate law enforcement officers about the importance of submitting evidence in a timely fashion to laboratories. Laboratory staff must routinely train law enforcement officers about how the laboratory functions, the appropriate submission process, and the reasons and importance behind particular submission policies. For their parts, laboratory staff should be educated about the issues and needs of the law enforcement officers and for the prosecution. Lastly, prosecutors and law enforcement alike should have a minimal understanding of the capabilities and limitations of forensic science disciplines.

Sexual assault kit (SAK) testing and backlog is another example of labs not coordinating with law enforcement agencies and prosecutors. There is a growing research literature in this area trying to understand the scope of the problem and identify best policies for SAK processing. The benefits of testing are mixed. For example, the NIJ-sponsored New Orleans SAK project, which emerged out of a DOJ civil rights division investigation into the New Orleans Police Department, documented more than 800 untested "old" SAKs and nearly 200 current SAKs that were in need of testing; the project supported testing of all cases, which resulted in 256 DNA profiles being uploaded to CODIS, with 139 CODIS hits (Nelson, 2013). Twenty-four new arrests and six convictions resulted. Peterson *et al.*'s (2011) examination of about 2000 untested SAKs sampled from nearly 11,000 SAKs held in evidence storage by Los Angeles city and county found comparable upload and hit rates, but that 20–30% of the hits were for individuals already in CODIS for that offense. In a smaller sample of 371 backlogged cases, there were no new arrests and two new convictions. It is very difficult to compare the outcomes of such studies because the age and characteristics of backlogged cases may be very different, and follow-up investigations taken by law enforcement agencies are different as well. Both studies, though, concluded that for a full understanding of the value of SAK testing it was essential that computerized systems be implemented to track evidence submission decisions, test results, and investigative actions taken. There is ongoing NIJ-sponsored research in Detroit (which has documented about 8500 untested SAKs) and Houston (which has documented about 4200 untested SAKs). Additional research is needed to understand to what extent these untested kits represent poor coordination between law enforcement and prosecutors, training/education issues, unclear policies, or unclear benefits.

28.13 Recruitment

The forensic sciences have primarily recruited its personnel through government civil service notices, examinations, and procedures, and through notices in professional newsletters and publications. Particular forensic disciplines with a stronger academic basis have also recruited personnel through colleges and universities. The annual meetings and publications of the American Academy of Forensic Sciences have been a long time source of information about job opportunities and a vehicle for employers to recruit new personnel. The growth of regional forensic and discipline specific organizations have increased recruitment efforts at the grassroots, local levels. Organizations like the AAFS have also developed young forensic scientist sections, provide information on their websites about careers and job opportunities, and encourage attendance at professional meetings. There are many other forensic science and criminal justice websites (such as Zeno's Forensic Site, n.d., and Reddy's Forensic Page) that provide information about careers and credentials needed for entry into the field. Television programs with a "CSI" theme have also attracted a growing number of students into forensic science coursework.

Traditionally, students have also learned about potential forensic careers through science-based academic programs and, with a growth of forensic science undergraduate and graduate degree programs, students are able to acquire the knowledge and skills needed to enter the profession. Forensic academic programs may also offer internships in working laboratories that provide agencies with opportunities to evaluate potential new employees. Many universities also have career centers and sponsor criminal justice and forensic science career days at which recruiters provide information. Forensic Science Educational Conferences (American Academy of Forensic Sciences, n.d. c) are also being sponsored at several universities around the country aimed at educating middle school and high school science teachers in developing forensic science high school curricula.

28.14 Education and training

Bachelor's level training in chemistry, biology, or a derivative degree has been the standard academic degree for students wishing to enter the forensic science profession for many decades. Programs begun at such institutions as University of California, Berkeley, Michigan State University, John Jay College of Criminal Justice, and The George Washington University in the 1950s and 1960s started a trend for bachelors, masters, and (limited) doctoral degrees specializing in criminalistics and the forensic sciences (Peterson and De Forest, 1977). Academic programs proliferated in the latter part of the 20th century and forensic laboratories were not always satisfied with graduates. A National Institute of Justice (NIJ) supported technical working group published a "status and needs" report in 1999 (National Institute of Justice, 1999), finding the education and training needs of the field were great. A technical working group on education and training in forensic science (TWGED) was formed and found the need for a system to evaluate and accredit forensic science academic programs (National Institute of Justice, 2004). The Forensic Science Programs Accreditation Commission (FSPAC) was formed and in 2004 began accrediting college and university programs (Presley, Haas and Quarino, 2009). Currently, more than 40 undergraduate and graduate programs in criminalistics/forensic science at 33 colleges and universities have been accredited (Forensic Science Education Program Accreditation Commission, n.d.).

While a bachelor's degree in a natural science has been the traditional educational requirement to practice most forensic science disciplines, many specialties require advanced degrees and training, and graduate degrees increasingly give applicants an edge in competing for entry level positions. Educational programs in forensic disciplines outside the crime laboratory field (e.g., pathology, psychiatry, and anthropology) usually had their origins in older, established parent disciplines. The reader is referred to the AAFS website (aafs.org) for an enumeration of these added education, experience, and other requirements for membership by section (American Academy of Forensic Sciences, n.d. b). To practice particular types of specialties within disciplines (e.g., DNA testing) may require the person to have taken specific coursework. Additional education may also be required to be certified within a specialty, and those added requirements are discussed in a later section under certification.

Added graduate education and training requirements and opportunities are available in other specialties.

28.14.1 Pathology

Forensic pathologists first complete medical school and a residency in anatomic and clinical pathology, followed by an additional year of forensic pathology training, usually at a large coroner or medical examiner's office, investigating natural and traumatic death cases (Wright, 2005). Physicians who complete this training can sit for the Forensic Pathology Board Certification Examination.

28.14.2 Forensic toxicology

Students typically complete an undergraduate degree in chemistry, biochemistry, or pharmaceutical sciences, complete a research-based Master of Science degree, and may proceed to a PhD program in toxicology, with an emphasis in forensic toxicology. Training in this area is often directed to entry level toxicologists who earn certificates and/or preparation for the American Board of Forensic Toxicology exams (following three years of work experience, there are Diplomate (PhD) and Specialist (MS, BS) exams), or the Forensic Toxicology Certification Board Examination (e.g., see Center for Forensic Science Research and Education, 2013).

28.14.3 Forensic anthropology

Graduate training is a common requirement to practice forensic anthropology and there are various educational programs offering graduate degrees (Forensicanthro.com, 2011). Training opportunities in this area

are associated with several forensic anthropology university programs in the United States headed by Diplomates in Forensic Anthropology (American Board of Forensic Anthropology (ABFA), 2008).

28.14.4 Forensic odontology

The initial forensic odontology training course was offered at the Armed Forces Institute of Pathology in 1962 and dental societies (like New York's) have offered training over the decades. The American Academy of Forensic Sciences website lists programs offering degrees and formal courses in forensic odontology approved by the AAFS Odontology Section (American Academy of Forensic Sciences n.d. d). Apprentice training under experienced forensic odontologists is the primary way new dentists gain their forensic expertise.

28.14.5 Psychiatry and behavioral science

Forensic psychiatrists initially must complete medical school and a residency in psychiatry and neurology before they take forensic training. What began as informal sessions at university fellowship training programs in the 1960s (Sadoff, 2005) are now more than 40 fellow training programs in forensic psychiatry accredited by the American Academy of Psychiatry and the Law (American Academy of Psychiatry and the Law, 2013). Upon completion of the training program, students are eligible to take the certification examination. The American Psychology–Law Society (Division 41 of the American Psychological Association) (American Psychology–Law Society, n.d. a) lists 26 clinical doctoral programs, 17 nonclinical PhD programs, and 25 universities that offer masters programs. The site also lists a number of pre- and postdoctoral internship programs and postdoctoral certificate programs offering training in forensic psychology and provides a guide to forensic and legal psychology programs (American Psychology–Law Society, n.d. b).

28.14.6 Engineering sciences

Most forensic engineers begin their professions by obtaining a bachelor's degree in engineering, pursue advanced graduate training in a specialty, and become a registered professional engineer (American Academy of Forensic Sciences, n.d. e). The ASTM Committee E58 on Forensic Engineering was formed in 2008 and is in the process of developing standards to promote awareness of scientific, legal and ethical issues supporting the general practice of forensic engineering investigations, reporting, and testimony (ASTM International, n.d. a).

28.14.7 Digital and multimedia sciences

Experts in this area have a minimum of a bachelor's degree in "computer science, information technology, or engineering" (American Academy of Forensic Science, n.d. f). Computer and digital forensics, and cyber/information security undergraduate and graduate majors at traditional and on-line academic programs are growing in the United States. Graduates of programs may pursue positions in digital forensics, cyber security, and law enforcement positions as forensic analysts, information specialists, and forensic/criminal investigators in public and private agencies.

28.14.8 Questioned documents

While most examiners have bachelor's degrees and some universities offer coursework, there are no university programs in forensic document examination. Examiners receive apprentice style training for a two to three year period under the supervision of a recognized examiner, per the Standard Guide for Training of Document Examiners (ASTM International, n.d. b).

The education and training of police, prosecutor, defense, and judicial personnel in forensic science is at a low level and is a problem. The Federal Judicial Center's Scientific Evidence Manual is one of the notable efforts to provide scientific information for legal personnel (Federal Judicial Center, 2011). The American Academy of Forensic Science designated "Forensic Science Education and Mentorship: Our Path Forward" as its theme for the 2014 annual meeting, which indicates the critical importance of education in the future of the profession (American Academy of Forensic Sciences, n.d. g).

28.15 Funding and political influences

As a field, forensic science has struggled to obtain needed funding since its inception. Funding and politics are, of course, intertwined and it appears some forensic laboratories have lacked the political strength to secure the funds needed to operate top flight scientific operations. The NRC *Strengthening Forensic Science* report cited funding as a problem that limits forensic

laboratories from attracting top scientists, acquiring instrumentation, and undertaking needed research. The SWGMDI Infrastructure Committee survey of medicolegal autopsy facilities in 2011 documented the severe resource constraints facing facilities conducting medicolegal death investigations (SWGMDI, 2011). Limited budgets have resulted in criminalistics operations that can only examine a small fraction of available evidence present at crime scenes, the creation of lengthy evidence backlogs and delays in testing, delaying analyses until cases go to trial, and examining only that evidence needed by prosecutors.

Police and prosecutors have traditionally exercised great control over decisions to collect and examine much forensic evidence. Crime scene investigation units have not been funded adequately and laboratories have not had a strong voice in funding decisions. The crime laboratory has not historically been conceived as a decision stage within the criminal justice process, nor have its personnel been thought of as critical criminal justice decision-makers. However, increasing reliance on forensic evidence has led to the necessary exercise of discretion about the types of cases to accept, the specific evidence to be analyzed, and the prioritization of laboratory workloads. These discretionary decisions, which may be negotiated decisions made in consultation with police and/or prosecutors in some jurisdictions, ultimately impact the administration of justice in substantial ways. In other jurisdictions, written policies are established that clearly define the criteria for case acceptance, with similar impacts.

At the national level, NIJ has nonetheless sponsored many training programs for investigators and examiners across almost all the forensic disciplines in the collection, analysis, interpretation, and standards of practice in various disciplines. This funding has also been instrumental in reducing evidence testing backlogs, enhancing real time and postconviction DNA testing, and using DNA to identify missing persons. It has also supported presentations on utilizing forensic evidence to prosecutors, defense attorneys, and the public at large, using traditional classroom, video, and web-based formats. The NIJ has also been involved in programs to assist and strengthen forensic laboratories, including the Paul Coverdell Improvement Grants Programs, which have distributed over $175 million in grants to forensic laboratories and medical examiner offices from 2002 to 2012 (National Institute of Justice, 2013).

The recent increased federal role in providing direction (and funding) to state and local forensic laboratories also raises some interesting political and policy questions. Increasingly, federal funding has been contingent upon compliance with certain standards (e.g., TWGDAM, NIJ) that has promoted the examination of DNA and to reduce testing backlogs. Two recent national initiatives that are discussed in more detail in later sections (the White House response to recommendations contained in the 2009 NRC Report and the makeup of various SWG groups) reveal that state and local scientists and regional forensic organizations believe they should have a greater voice in the development of national level forensic policy because the vast majority of forensic testing takes place at the state and local levels. The Consortium of Forensic Science Organizations (CFSO, n.d.) and the California Association of Criminalists (CAC Update, 2013) have spoken out on this issue. This also indicates that practitioners are better organized and demanding a greater role in policy, research, and funding decisions than ever before.

28.16 Certification

28.16.1 Criminalistics

The profession was reluctant to implement certification programs when first proposed in the late 1970s, and it was not until the California Association of Criminalists began a regional certification initiative that the idea gained traction. Incorporated in 1989, the American Board of Criminalists (ABC) leads the voluntary certification effort, sets those professional qualifications needed to practice in the field, and is accredited by the Forensic Specialties Accreditation Board (FSAB). ABC certification is a two-tiered process. Applicants must first show they possess a bachelor's degree, have two years of full-time professional experience in criminalistics, and pass a general knowledge examination. To achieve Fellow status applicants need to pass a specialty exam in molecular biology, drug chemistry, fire debris analysis, and trace evidence – hairs and fibers or paints and polymers – and successfully participate in a proficiency testing program (Bashinski and Peterson, 2003). Presently there are more than 900 Diplomates and Fellows (American Board of Criminalistics, 2013).

Within the area of criminalistics, the International Association for Identification certifies bloodstain pattern, crime scene, footwear, forensic art, forensic photography and latent print, and ten print examiners at the AFTE began a certification program in firearms and toolmark examination in 2001. Some state systems of crime laboratories (California and Illinois among them) reimburse examiners for the cost of certification and recertification fees, but most laboratories do not.

28.16.2 Questioned documents

The American Board of Forensic Document Examiners formed in 1977 under the sponsorship of the Forensic Sciences Foundation and is accredited by the Forensic Science Specialties Accreditation Board. Its purpose is to maintain and enhance the standards of qualification for those who practice forensic document examination and to certify applicants who meet ABFDE standards of expertise. It is sponsored by various forensic organizations. Certification is based upon the candidate's personal and professional education, training, experience, and achievement, as well as on the results of a formal examination (written, practicum, and orals board) process, and is valid for a period of five years, after which recertification is required, showing evidence of maintaining currency in the field.

28.16.3 Forensic pathology/biology

There is a severe shortage of board certified forensic pathologists serving jurisdictions around the United States. The Scientific Working Group for Medicolegal Death Investigation (SWGMDI) estimated there were no more than 663 board certified forensic pathologists performing autopsies in the United States in 2012 (System Infrastructure Committee of the Scientific Working Group for Medicolegal Death Investigation, 2013). The American Board of Forensic Pathology began certifying forensic pathologists in 1959 and has certified only about 1300 pathologists in that specialty since then. There are various reasons for this shortage, including the length and cost of medical schooling, the nature and challenges of investigating death cases, high caseloads, and salaries that are typically much lower than average salaries of hospital pathologists.

The American Board of Medical Legal Death Investigators (ABMDI, 2013) certifies individuals to perform the tasks outlined in the 1999 NIJ document *Death Investigation: A Guide for the Scene Investigator*, updated in 2011. The ABMDI's intent is to promote the highest level of professional practice for medicolegal death investigation by certifying individuals who have the proven knowledge and skills necessary to perform these death investigations. It offers both basic and advanced certification of individuals who meet these standards, thereby assisting the courts and the general public in recognizing persons with this expertise. The ABMDI was the first such certification board recognized by the American Academy of Forensic Sciences' Forensic Specialties Accreditation Board in 2005.

28.16.4 Forensic toxicology

The field of forensic toxicology has made significant strides in the past 40 years and is supported by many scientific, research and professional organizations. These include the following.

The American Board of Forensic Toxicology (ABFT) was formed in 1976 primarily to advance the standard of practice in the field and to recognize voluntary applicants who possess the required qualifications and competence to practice forensic toxicology. ABFT certifies both PhD level Diplomates and Forensic Toxicology Specialists (non-PhD level) individuals. Individuals must take and pass a certifying exam and maintain proof of continuing education in the field for recertification. ABFT has certified more than 300 Diplomates who must also maintain high ethical practice and periodically update and renew their qualifications. Beginning in 1996, the Board also accredits forensic toxicology laboratories and, in this way, identifies facilities having the requisite qualifications and competence to engage in this type of scientific testing. Thirty-four laboratories have been accredited by demonstrating compliance with professional standards through inspections and achievement on proficiency tests. Some aspects of toxicological testing (alcohol breath testing) are accredited by ASCLD ISO 17025.

The Forensic Toxicologist Certification Board (FTCB) was formed in 1992 to provide recognition to experienced toxicologists. The FTCB requires only a bachelor's degree in a science and successful completion of a certifying exam.

The Society of Forensic Toxicologists (SOFT) began informally in the 1970s, officially incorporated in 1983, and is open to all individuals engaged in forensic toxicology. SOFT seeks to promote the exchange of information, consensus standards, continuing education and training, and ongoing research. A joint committee of SOFT and the AAFS/Toxicology section developed a set of guidelines in 1991 (which has been updated several

times) for the practice of postmortem and human performance forensic toxicology, ultimately leading to the ABFT accreditation program cited above.

The Forensic Toxicology Council was formed in 2009 and is comprised of representatives from the ABFT, the AAFS Toxicology Section, and SOFT, for the purpose of providing information and guidance to government and policymakers in this field and to promote its advancement.

The Scientific Working Group for Forensic Toxicology (SWGTOX, 2013) was established by the Forensic Toxicology Council in 2009 to develop and disseminate consensus standards for the field of forensic toxicology. SWGTOX has the objective of establishing minimum standards in the following areas: (1) standards, practice and protocols including quality assurance and quality control, (2) educational requirements, (3) accreditation and compliance with standards of practice, and (4) certification standards. SWGTOX has also developed a uniform code of ethics for forensic toxicologists, areas of research and development, and promoting public awareness of the field.

28.16.5 Forensic anthropology

The American Board of Forensic Anthropology (ABFA) was formed in 1977 to serve the interests of science and the public good by recognizing individuals with special expertise in forensic anthropology. Diplomates of the ABFA have distinguished records of education and training, experience and achievement in the field, pass an examination, and adhere to high standards of ethics and practice. To maintain certification, Diplomates must maintain a record of accomplishment and engage in continuing education. The board has certified 99 Diplomates, 70 of whom are active and in good standing.

28.16.6 Forensic odontology

The American Board of Forensic Odontology (ABFO) was organized in 1976 to establish standards of qualifications for those practicing forensic odontology and to certify applicants who meet those standards. Applicants must have earned a DDS, DMD or the equivalent dental degree, had required professional education and case experience (e.g., human identification, dental age estimation, and bitemark cases), other evidence of forensic dental activity (e.g., continuing education, court testimony, academic publications), and written and practicum examinations. Certifications are valid for a period of five years and are renewable via the recertification program. The ABFO also has standing committees to improve the practice, establish standards, and advance specialty areas including bitemarks and pattern injury, human abuse and neglect, and mass disasters. The board has certified 134 Diplomates since the founding of the organization.

28.16.7 Psychiatry and behavioral science

Apart from certification efforts by the American Board of Forensic Psychiatry (ABFP) beginning in 1976, there are various other certification boards in this field. The American Board of Psychiatry and Neurology – which is a Member Board of the American Board of Medical Specialties (ABMS) – offers initial and maintenance of certification in forensic psychiatry (American Board of Medical Specialties, n.d.). Certification in forensic psychiatry by the American Board of Psychiatry and Neurology (ABPN) came about after the American Academy of Psychiatry and the Law was created to provide education in this specialty. Certification in forensic psychiatry was established in 1997 and is only possible after an approved Accreditation Council of Graduate Medical Education (ACGME) residency and passing the ABPN certification examination. Certification is good for ten years and then recertification may be earned for another ten year period to insure the applicant has retained currency in the field.

The American Board of Forensic Psychology was formed in 1978 to offer certification to psychologists passing a written examination, a practice component, and an oral examination (American Board of Forensic Psychology, n.d.).

28.16.8 Engineering sciences

There are various certification programs to which forensic engineers may belong. One of these is the National Academy of Forensic Engineers. To qualify for membership, a candidate must be a member of the National Society of Professional Engineers (NSPE) and must be a registered Professional Engineer (PE) (National Academy of Forensic Engineers, n.d.). The candidate must have appropriate engineering education and experience in practice, including actual experience in forensic engineering. The Society of Forensic Engineers and Scientists was formed in 1980. The purpose of the Society is to share forensic, technical, and business information and to upgrade the standards of the profession. Membership is limited to qualified professionals who are voted on by

the membership, which consists of about 75 members. The International Board of Forensic Engineering Sciences (IBFES) is an independent board formed in 2008 that certifies individuals who are "technically competent, forensically experienced, dedicated to ethical work and professionally correct" with expertise in the forensic engineering sciences. The IBFES originated with support of the Engineering Section of the AAFS and is accredited by the Forensic Specialties Accreditation Board (FSAB). To be certified, individuals must have a minimum of a bachelor's degree in one of the engineering sciences, have professional forensic experience, and competence as demonstrated through written and oral examinations. Members are also bound by the IBFES code of professional practice. Certification is issued for a period of five years and may be renewed by remaining professionally and technically active. The Board has certified approximately 25 individuals.

28.16.9 Digital and multimedia science

The International Association of Computer Investigative Specialists (IACIS, 2013) is dedicated to education in the field of forensic computer science and is approved by the FSAB and offers certification, recertification, and proficiency testing services. Certification involves proceeding through a "practical exercises" phase, and then practical and written examinations based upon core competencies. Recertification is required in the third year following certification.

28.17 Accreditation/quality control

There are various forensic science accreditation programs, with the original (and largest) program instituted by the American Society of Crime Laboratory Directors' Laboratory Accreditation Board (ASCLD/LAB) in 1981 (American Society of Crime Laboratory Directors/Laboratory Accreditation Board, n.d.). While accreditation is also provided by the FQS, a member of the ANSI–ASQ National Accreditation Board (FQS ANSI–ASQ National Accreditation Board, 2014), the American Association for Laboratory Accreditation (A2LA, 2012), as well as programs offered by the American Board of Forensic Toxicology and the National Association of Medical Examiners discussed below, we focus here on ASCLD/LAB. ASCLD/LAB offers a program of accreditation in multiple forensic testing disciplines and breath-alcohol calibration based on ISO/IEC 17025, as well as its "enhanced" ASCLD/LAB–International Supplement Requirements (ASCLD/LAB, 2014). The objective of the accreditation process is to provide an external, independent review of testing procedures and to increase the level of confidence of interested parties in the accredited laboratory's work product. Outside inspectors review the applicant laboratory's operations, management, and physical plant, and ensure analysts have appropriate education and training for the types of evidence they examine, and document training and proficiency testing programs.

A major component of the accreditation is the review of randomly selected case files, analyses and case notes, and data, including interviews with examiners, to ensure that the laboratory conforms to its own written procedures and the ASCLD standards. Accreditation criteria have evolved greatly over the past 30 years and have decidedly moved in an international direction. ASCLD/LAB has received both IAAC regional recognition and ILAC international recognition to offer accreditation under ISO/IEC 17025:2005. The BJS Crime Laboratory Census indicates that 83% of laboratories in the United States are professionally accredited (Durose et al., 2012). Three states, New York, Oklahoma and Texas, require crime laboratories in those jurisdictions to be accredited.

Proficiency testing is another major area of quality assurance. Begun under grants to the Forensic Sciences Foundation, Inc., from LEAA in the 1970s, many fee for service programs (e.g., Collaborative Testing Services, or CTS) are in existence today. Inferior proficiency testing results in the 1970s led to many of the quality assurance programs in today's field. Like accreditation and certification, proficiency testing is also a largely voluntary program except in three states and where laboratories apply for accreditation and individuals apply for certification and the programs require it. The source of most declared proficiency tests is external to laboratories and participants are anonymous. Blind proficiency testing has also been proposed but for cost and other reasons it is infrequently carried out. A study in the 1990s concluded that blind DNA testing was impractical for cost and logistical reasons (Peterson et al., 2003). Random reanalysis is another option for proficiency testing where completed case files are randomly selected and the evidence reexamined anew by another party.

Standardized analysis methods are another aspect to quality control procedures that have been adopted in some, but not all, areas of criminalistics. The ASTM

E-30 forensic science committee (ASTM International, 2013) was one of the earliest groups (1970) advocating the review, evaluation, and standardization of forensic science methods of analysis (criminalistics, questioned documents, forensic engineering, fire debris analysis, drug testing analysis, and collection and preservation of physical evidence). Pioneering work was accomplished under DNA testing beginning in 1988 by the FBI and its technical working group on DNA analysis methods (TWGDAM, 1991). Given the tremendous discriminating power shown by DNA testing, its likely widespread adoption by many laboratories, and a national database that was under development, it became obvious to forensic scientists that testing guidelines and standards were essential. Compliance with TWGDAM is a qualification for laboratories wishing to receive DNA financial assistance and research grants from the federal government.

The NIST (and its predecessor, the National Bureau of Standards) has engaged in research over the decades in developing performance standards and measurement tools, that now has spun off into over 20 Scientific Working Group (SWG) committees under a program administered by various federal agencies including the FBI, NIST, and NIJ (National Institute of Justice, 2012). SWG committees have been formed in questioned documents, controlled substances, DNA, digital evidence, medicolegal death investigation, and others. The NIST has issued a notice in the Federal Register (asking for comment) to replace existing SWGs with a fewer number of "guidance groups" (Federal Register, 2013b). This has stirred some concern among state and local laboratories as to whether these groups operate transparently and with appropriate representation among practicing forensic scientists and professional organizations.

28.17.1 Forensic pathology/biology

The National Association of Medical Examiners (NAME, 2013a) is a key professional organization of physician medical examiners, investigators, and death investigation system administrators. It was founded in 1966 to foster the professional growth of physician death investigators and to disseminate technical and professional information to improve the investigation of violent, suspicious, and unusual deaths. Originally focused on physicians, it has grown to include coroners, medical death investigators, and administrators of modern death investigation systems. NAME maintains contacts with many scientific, medical, and forensic entities and seeks to upgrade the standards of death investigation systems through education and professional activities. In furtherance of its mission to recognize excellence in death investigation systems, NAME operates a voluntary inspection and accreditation program for medicolegal death investigation offices (NAME, 2013a). NAME has also published "Forensic Autopsy Performance Standards" that "address the professional aspects of individual death investigations" and "the fundamental services rendered by a professional forensic pathologist" (NAME, 2013b). Accreditation is conferred for a period of five years and signifies to the public that the office is functioning at a high level of competence. As of the summer of 2012, NAME had accredited approximately 70 offices around the United States. NAME also publishes the journal *Academic Forensic Pathology*. The International Association of Medical Examiners and Coroners (IAMEC) also accredits medical examiner/coroner operations and has accredited 20 (primarily coroner) offices through June 2013 (IAMEC, 2013). The development of TWGs and SWGs by the FBI, beginning with DNA in 1988, the US Supreme Court *Daubert* decision, and the 2009 NRC report recommended the formation of a scientific working group for forensic pathology. At an NIJ sponsored symposium that was held in June 2010 attended by various organizations (AAFS, NAME, IACME, AAFS, and other subject matter experts) it was concluded that the NRC recommendation should be broadened to include a SWG on medicolegal death investigations. The SWGMDI (discussed previously) was created in March 2011 "to advance the scientific basis and quality of medicolegal death investigation (MDI)" (Scientific Working Group for Medicolegal Death Investigation (SWGMDI), n.d.). The group is supported by the NIJ and the FBI and is made up of members from various organizations that support medicolegal death investigations and represent the medical examiner, coroner, medicolegal death investigator, and the forensic community at large. The SWGMDI has issued more than eight standards, guidelines, and best practices, which have been circulated for public comment, reviewed, and approved by its board and published on its website.

28.17.2 Forensic anthropology

The Scientific Working Group for Forensic Anthropology (SWGANTH) was formed in 2008 under the sponsorship of the FBI and the Department of Defense Central Identification Laboratory to develop best-practice guidelines and minimum standards (Scientific Working Group on Forensic Anthropology (SWGANTH), 2013). Guidelines and standards were developed to address forensic analytical methods, protocols, and research, as well as to recommend guidelines for quality assurance and quality control. The group also works to bring organizations and individuals together to exchange information, promote cooperation with domestic and international organizations, and disseminate research.

The Joint POW/MIA Accounting Command (JPAC) Central Identification Laboratory (CIL) was accredited by the ASCLD Laboratory Accreditation Board's International Standards Programs. The CIL employs more than 400 joint military and civilian personnel dedicated to the recovery and identification of US personnel missing from past military conflicts.

28.17.3 Digital and multimedia science

The Scientific Working Group on Digital Evidence (SWGDE, 2013) has various objectives dedicated to foster cooperation, high quality, and consistency in forensic digital examinations. It strives to establish core competencies, best practices, and forensic methodologies. It has drafted a best practices in computer forensics document for "collecting, acquiring, analyzing and documenting the data found in computer forensic examination". It has also drafted a document describing a process for recognizing errors and limitations of tools used in investigations. Lastly, it has published a paper for the use of "electric network frequency" (ENF) to determine the authenticity of audio recording. It lists links to almost 30 agencies involved in digital forensics. It has published various documents that address best practices in digital evidence analysis, mobile phones, GPS examinations, and other electronic devices. In addition, the American Society of Crime Laboratory Directors – Laboratory Accreditation Board offers accreditation in the area of digital multimedia evidence (ASCLD/LAB, n.d.).

Beginning in 1997 at a meeting on imaging technology sponsored by the FBI, the Scientific Working Group on Information Technology (SWGIT) was formed. There are a range of issues that have been addressed by SWGIT, beginning with digital cameras and extending to imaging technology guidance to other forensic groups. It has published more than 20 documents addressing various imaging technology issues, including television security systems, forensic video analysis, photographing various types of evidence, court technology issues, and crime scene videography. ASTM Committee E30.12 addresses standard practice, image processing, and standard terminology.

28.18 Disaster preparedness

The investigation of disasters involving mass fatalities in the United States falls under the jurisdiction of the medical examiner/coroner, but they often lack the resources to respond with the necessary medical, investigative, and ancillary services. Under the US Department of Health and Human Services, the National Disaster Medical System (NDMS) (2013) assists state and local agencies in providing medical services and, in the case of mass fatalities, victim identification and mortuary services through its Disaster Mortuary Operational Response Team (DMORT). The DMORT provides temporary morgue facilities and various private forensic experts to aid in the identification and disposition of deceased victims. The Armed Forces Medical Examiner System (AFMES) mentioned earlier may also be called into such disasters, as well as the National Transportation Safety Board (NTSB), which plays a major role in all transportation mass fatality incidents. Since the attack on the World Trade Center on 9/11/2001, there have been additional grants available to states and localities to prepare for disasters.

The Combatting Terrorism Technical Support Office (CTTSO, 2013) of the US Department of Defense has the objective of sponsoring research that will develop capabilities to aid the Department of Defense and US military in combating terrorism. Through its Technical Support Working Group, research is supported for the investigative and forensic sciences in the areas of crime scene responses, individual identification techniques, and the analysis of electronic evidence.

Along with death investigation operations, criminalistics laboratories may become involved in the identification of persons, explosives, and other hazardous materials associated with mass disaster events. The 2009 NRC *Strengthening Forensic Science* report included an important chapter on the contribution of the forensic sciences to the creation of "effective and timely intelligence and investigative information on terrorists and terrorist groups" (NRC, 2009, pp. 279–286). The identification of bodies and body parts in the aftermath of

the 2001 attack on the World Trade Center focused on the use of DNA technologies – housed within the NYC Office of the Medical Examiner. The FBI crime laboratory was very involved in the identification of strains of anthrax in the same year by persons engaged in terrorist actions against various elected officials and members of the news media. Although conducted after the fact, the investigation of the bombings of the Federal Center in Oklahoma City and Pan Am Flight 103 are examples of investigations into terrorist acts that led to the identification and prosecution of perpetrators.

Refined criminalistics techniques have been employed by federal agencies and the military to reconstruct acts and identify offenders. The NIST is also involved in the development of counterterrorism, response technologies, and communications research. The Scientific Working Group on Disaster and Victim Identification (SWGDVI, 2013) also plays a major role in investigating mass fatality incidents by developing and promoting consensus guidelines and best practices through emphasizing quality assurance and the evaluation of research and innovative technologies. The group works with search and recovery, and many different forensic disciplines including DNA, forensic pathology, odontology, and anthropology, ethics and data management, and other specialties.

28.19 Legal issues

Historically, the forensic sciences received special recognition in the 1960s in such decisions as *Miranda*, *Escobedo*, and others in which the court encouraged the police and legal fact-finders to place less dependence on abusive interrogation practices and place greater reliance on "extrinsic" (physical) evidence and scientific means of fact-finding. The *Brady v. Maryland* decision of 1968 was also significant in that it required the prosecution to share exclusionary evidence with the defense. Perhaps the most significant legal case did not come until the Supreme Court updated the venerable 1923 *Frye* decision in 1993 and emphasized that forensic expert testimony should be based on scientific principles and processes. *Daubert v. Merrell Dow Pharmaceuticals* is a US Supreme Court decision of great importance that has affected all the forensic sciences. The Supreme Court justices challenged judges to think more like scientists, to assume a role of "gatekeeper" in making admissibility decisions, and determine whether the experts seeking to present evidence to the courts used scientific reasoning in reaching their findings.

Four observations were articulated by the justices: (1) if the theory in question had been empirically tested; (2) if the technique had been subjected to peer review and published; (3) if known or potential rates of error were present; and lastly (4) the Court advised that the old "general acceptance" criteria of the *Frye* test could be considered. In two subsequent decisions the Court said that it was not an abuse of discretion by judges to exclude testimony failing these criteria (*Joiner*) and that the criteria applied to all forms of testimony, not just that which was strictly offered by a "scientist" (*Kumho Tire*). Giannelli (Giannelli and Reader, 2006; Giannelli, Imwinkelreid, and Peterson, 2011) has written about the record of courts in reviewing various forensic techniques, including many that belong in the criminalistics domain like firearms identification, fingerprinting, and hair comparison. He noted, too, that even states that have not adopted *Daubert* per se have increasingly asked potential experts to explain the scientific process and reliability of techniques in making admissibility decisions.

Soon after the *Daubert* decision was announced, the Federal Judicial Center published its first *Reference Manual on Scientific Evidence* to assist judges in reviewing complex scientific evidence. The Center recently issued its third edition of the manual (National Academy of Sciences, 2011). The current edition contains chapters on DNA Identification Evidence by Kaye and Sensabaugh and on other types of Forensic Identification Expertise by Giannelli, Imwinkelried, and Peterson, covering fingerprints, handwriting, firearms, microscopic hair comparisons, and bitemark evidence. In the present day, such decisions as *Melendez Diaz v. Massachusetts* addressed whether the Constitution requires forensic scientists examining evidence to appear in court and *Maryland v. Alonzo King*, a 4th amendment search and seizure case, authorized the police to collect DNA samples from felony arrestees. Legal decisions have been (and will always be) key road signs that guide the use and introduction of scientific evidence in courts of law.

28.20 Research, technology, and development

Key research being conducted in the forensic sciences can generally be organized under two large umbrellas:

(1) basic and applied research focused on the tools, techniques, and procedures of the forensic sciences (leaning toward research in the tradition of the physical sciences) and (2) research focused on the role, use, and impact of the forensic sciences in various justice processes (that is more similar to the tradition of the social sciences). As is often the case, this research tends to be driven by the primary funding sources: NIJ, NIST, and NSF. The NIJ's current research foci are in five broad areas: (1) *laboratory operations* (adoption of new technology, addressing laboratory backlogs, capacity enhancement, information systems and databases, standards, and validation); (2) *evidence types* (basic and applied research in all the major areas of evidence); (3) *investigations* (the use of forensic evidence from the crime scene up to adjudication); (4) *postconviction testing* (the role and use of DNA in postconviction testing to discover wrongful convictions); and (5) *social science research on forensic science* (how evidence finds its way to the laboratory, how "context" can affect evidence processing, and how forensic scientists interpret evidence, their findings, and report their conclusions). In addition, large funding streams are available for training and laboratory enhancement (discussed earlier in the Funding section).

Consistent with their core missions, NIST research has tended to focus on the development of standards and measurement in the forensic sciences and NSF research has tended to focus on basic scientific research. NIST has published an archive of nearly 600 active interagency research and development projects reported by nine federal agencies, including DoD, DHS, FBI, NIJ, the Ames National Lab (with NIJ funding), NIST, NSF, US Geological Survey (USGS), and the US Secret Service (USSS) (NIST, n.d.). More than 200 NSF awards for basic research that "will have future impact on various forensic science disciplines" are listed in the archive. Of the 591 projects listed in the NIST archive as of October, 2013, the most frequent specific category of research listed was the area of forensic DNA (91 projects, or 15% of all projects). Other frequent categories of research, collectively accounting for about one-third of all listed projects, include: medicolegal death investigation (41 projects, including 19 in forensic anthropology, 12 in forensic toxicology, 9 in forensic pathology, and 1 in forensic entomology), trace evidence (37), impressions evidence (29), fingerprint evidence (28), biometrics (24), digital/multimedia forensics (21), and crime scene investigation (19). Additional projects were in the areas of controlled substances analysis (14), explosives/fire/arson investigation (11), questioned documents (9), nuclear forensics (8), environmental forensics (8), and pattern evidence (7). It should be noted that several awards were listed as "general forensics" (30), and many NSF awards were in generic categories of "NSF Education" or "Research and Education" (92), "NSF research" (82), and "NSF Instrumentation" or "Instrumentation Development and Education" (19). Much of the research is funded internally, represent continuing projects, or funding has not been disclosed, but the reported grant awards to external entities total nearly $252 million. It should also be noted that the NSF recently issued a call for proposals to existing programs on "fundamental research questions which might simultaneously advance activities related to research and education in forensic sciences" (National Science Foundation, 2013). An emphasis of the program is collaboration between forensic scientists and basic science researchers on far reaching topics, including: cognitive bias, remote measurement and imaging, storage and manipulation of large data sets (including biological data), studying how jurors understand forensic evidence, determining the provenance of forensic samples including the use of Geographic Information Systems, and integrating forensics into STEM curricula.

28.20.1 Criminalistics

There has been limited support for criminalistics research over the years. Ballou *et al.* (2013) provide an interesting overview of key problems as well as important future directions in the areas of illicit drugs, DNA analysis, fire investigation, and trace evidence. Research has been published in academic journals and textbooks for decades, but it was with the formation of the National Institute of Justice that funding in all areas of forensic science became available and the field started to make major advancements. Applied research has been supported in many areas.

NIST Programs have emerged in more recent years in developing performance standards, guidelines, and related publications. Recent and new publications include: *Latent Print Examination and Human Factors* (February 2012), a *Biological Evidence Preservation Handbook*, and an updated *Crime Scene Investigation: A Guide for Law Enforcement* handbook just published in September 2013, and future work in questioned documents in

2013. Other workshops are being held in DNA mixtures, synthetic drugs, handwriting, and firearms. An updated forensic laboratory facilities guide (last edition in 1998) is due, and a new report on standardizing quantitative and qualitative terminology in forensic reports to law enforcement, legal practitioners, and jurors is anticipated.

Fingerprints were one of the first areas of pattern evidence where advances in technology in the 1980s permitted the digitization of large databases of known 10 print and latent print files. The advent of Automated Fingerprint Identification Systems (AFIS) has greatly improved the efficiency of both 10 print and latent searches. However, substantial problems of interoperability between standalone AFIS databases remain, and in the absence of any federal mandate regarding interoperability, and with thin resources to support interoperable AFIS, nationwide interoperability remains an important but elusive goal (NRC, 2009). The Combined DNA Index System (CODIS) was formed by the FBI in 1990 and the DNA Identification Act of 1994 authorized the FBI to implement a national index that went online in 1998. In rapid succession, funding was authorized to establish state and local testing capabilities. State legislatures authorized officials to take DNA from convicted offenders and to enter it into these databases. Many states have now authorized (and the US Supreme Court has approved) the police to collect DNA from arrestees to enter their profiles into CODIS. As of August 2013, the National DNA Index (NDIS) contains over 10,535,300 offender profiles, 1,613,100 arrestee profiles, and 509,900 forensic profiles (Federal Bureau of Investigation, Lab Services, n.d.).

NIBIN is one additional area of criminalistics evidence where databases of bullet and cartridge characteristics have been created. All the above areas, latent fingerprints, DNA, and firearms information, allow investigators to take questioned evidence found at a crime scene and to search these files against known standards. This has been a revolutionary form of determining the origin of crime scene evidence that has changed the face of investigations.

28.20.2 Questioned documents

As noted in the NIST archive of current research, there were nine projects in the specific category of questioned documents. The projects deal with counterfeit identity and travel documents, ink analysis, four projects on handwriting analysis (largely focused on the statistical analysis of handwriting), thermal ribbon analysis, human factors in handwriting analysis, and secure document component analysis and sourcing. These projects were funded by the DoD, NIJ, NIST, and the USSS. Aside from one internal NIST study, the eight external research awards totaled $3.7 million.

28.20.3 Forensic pathology/biology

Gill *et al.* (2013) discuss two primary initiatives, among them radiography (particularly of infants, charred remains, and for the detection of foreign bodies and projectiles) and the use of "whole body digital scanning" and computerized tomography (CT). CT can be used in "triage autopsies" or "virtual autopsies" in situations where dissection autopsies are not possible or as a triage tool to determine which individuals need a complete autopsy, but additional training and research are needed to determine the range of possible applications. Also, research is needed in the area of molecular testing, including genetic cardiac diseases, inheritable thrombosis, pharmacogenetics, and the detection of infectious agents (Gill *et al.*, 2013). The National Research Council noted a need for research to promote greater use of computerized case records and information systems, as well as greater funding from a national level, increased interaction between medical examiner offices and university pathology departments, more coordinated research through forensic pathology residency programs, and better collection of information from routine autopsies. The NIST archive of current research lists nine projects in the area of forensic pathology, including the use of CT to supplement autopsies, applications of molecular autopsies, statistical analysis of pediatric fractures, development of pediatric head injury assessment tools, new methods for characterizing bacterial and fungal communities associated with corpse decomposition, interpretation of patterned injuries, and impact of body temperature and postmortem interval on magnetic resonance imaging (MRI) of unfixed tissues. All of these projects were funded by the NIJ, and awards totaled $5.6 million.

28.20.4 Forensic toxicology

Logan and Ropero-Miller (2013) identified a number of research needs in forensic toxicology, including the interpretation of extremely low levels of drug concentrations, improved databases to aid in interpreting drug

levels in multiple biological matrices, the development of assays for new designer drugs of abuse, additional research data to improve interpretive toxicology, the need for greater standardization in toxicological testing and reports (see SWGTOX above), better access to the scientific literature by practicing toxicologists, and more international collaboration and development.

The NIST archive of current research lists 12 projects in the area of forensic toxicology, dealing with the detection of cocaine in hair samples, GHB metabolites in urine samples, three projects on designer and synthetic drugs, expansion of cheminformatic databases of spectral data, and improved separation techniques. These projects were funded by the FBI, NIJ, and NIST, and external awards totaled $3.9 million.

28.20.5 Forensic anthropology

The NIST archive of current research lists 19 projects in the area of forensic anthropology, including three projects focused on improved methods of sex estimation (one using CT scans), facial reconstruction, ethnicity determination, reconstruction of fragmentary skeletal remains, computer assisted age at death estimation, radiographic databases, and entomology. These projects were funded by the FBI and NIJ, with external awards totaling $5.6 million.

28.20.6 Forensic odontology

Pretty *et al.* (2013, p. 198) call for research in three primary areas: victim identification, age estimation, and bitemark analysis. The NRC study did not mention either of the first two areas in need of research. Still, in the first area, work must continue on refining procedures and criteria for victim identification, the use of better dental materials, and use of digital radiography and computerized matching systems. Age estimation still requires research involving large population studies and data to support placing a subject within a certain age range. As noted above, it was the third area that has the greatest need for research. Pretty *et al.* (2013) point out the serious human subject problems in developing databases of various forms of bitemarks on live subjects. This problem may be insurmountable. Using media other than "live" skin have been suggested including materials such as Styrofoam, pigskin, and human cadavers. Hypothesis driven studies, and development of models that can identify and control necessary variables, are necessary but require funding. There was only one project in the

NIST archive of current research focused on replication of known dental characteristics in pigskin and new technologies for imaging specialists. This research was funded by the NIJ for $700,000.

28.20.7 Psychiatry and behavioral science

There are many contemporary areas of research in forensic psychiatry and psychology. Forensic neuroscience has many applications in both the civil and criminal areas, ranging from documentation of head injuries to establishment of criminal responsibility, to lie detection, and the study of psychopathy and the prediction of dangerousness. Other areas include tests and measures or detection of malingering and deception and have both criminal and civil applications. Research indicates, however, that the prediction of dangerousness of the mentally ill is a very problematic area, with the odds of correctly predicting that a mentally ill prisoner will recidivate upon release is no better than chance (50:50). Research predicting the causes of violent criminal behavior and determining the role played by genetics, advances in neuroscience, and a variety of social, psychological, and environmental factors continues as well and represents a fertile area for important research.

28.20.8 Engineering sciences

Forensic engineering is a very broad area encompassing civil, mechanical, electrical, biomedical engineering, as well as accident reconstruction, making it difficult to identify key research, technology, and development relevant to forensic applications. Basic research being conducted in a wide variety of disciplines may ultimately impact forensic engineering. However, as noted earlier, the major areas of focus in forensic engineering are structural failures, fire and explosion investigation, and accident reconstruction. There were 11 projects in the NIST archive that were focused on explosives/fire/arson investigation, mostly dealing with the detection of ignitable liquids and totaling more than $3.2 million. In addition, there are current projects in the area of trace evidence relevant to accident investigations (such as automotive paint analysis) and crime scene investigation (such as tire track analysis). There was only one project in the NIST archive in the specific area of engineering forensics, funded by NIST and dealing with materials fatigue and failure analysis.

28.20.9 Digital and multimedia sciences

The NIST archive of current research lists 21 projects in the area of digital/multimedia forensics. Several of these projects are related to the use of software that can assist with the extraction of information from smartphone backups and networked computers. There are also three projects on tools for "cloud forensics." Additional projects are focused on software reference libraries, the use of internet anonymizers, automated human image detection, detection of digital forgery, hard drive recovery, and the identification and resolution of forensic image bottlenecks. These projects were funded by the NIJ, NIST, and DHS, and external awards totaled $10.1 million.

28.20.10 Social science research on the forensic sciences

Finally, in discussing research, technology, and development in the forensic sciences, it is important to discuss the growing area of social science research on the forensic sciences. Within this area are important studies of crime laboratory functions, workloads, and policies/procedures (including the BJS censuses of crime laboratories and offices of medicolegal death investigation), the function and role of forensic science in the administration of justice (including case processing studies that examine the processes and impact of forensic evidence on criminal case outcomes, and how law enforcement agencies and prosecutors use forensic evidence), quality issues (such as cognitive biases in the processing of evidence), the adoption of business models for forensic laboratory services, ethics in the forensic sciences, jury decision-making with regard to forensic evidence, and popular media effects such as the "CSI effect." Although this type of research can be found in the venerable *Journal of Forensic Sciences*, it is also found in a wide variety of other outlets, including journals in criminal justice, psychology, sociology, and law reviews. Relatively new journals such as *Forensic Science Policy and Management* are becoming an important means of disseminating social science research on the forensic sciences.

28.21 Future directions

There are three major areas that have long-term bearing on the future of forensic science in the United States.

The first is the landmark NRC report, *Strengthening Forensic Science in the United States*. Moving forward, it is important to consider what has happened (or what needs to happen) in the wake of the NRC study. Second, and related, is the issue of federal funding and policy, which have been significantly stimulated by the NRC report. The receipt of federal funding is the most powerful national leverage, short of specific legislation, to effect change in the forensic sciences. The recently appointed National Commission on Forensic Science holds great promise in shaping the future direction of the field of forensic science.

28.21.1 Follow-up on the national research council report

The NRC Study had several pointed criticisms and suggestions for research in various forensic disciplines:

Questioned documents. The report discussed the comparison and analysis of documents, inks, and writing instruments, and understanding their history. Examination of handwriting is particularly challenging as examiners must distinguish among intrapersonal and interpersonal variations of writing samples. ASTM has a long history in working with questioned document examiners and has promoted standards, including various scales used for expressing examiners' certainty of identification. Proficiency testing research has shown that questioned document examiners fare much better than lay persons in determining if writing samples "match" and if signatures are genuine, but still err by 3.4% to 6.5% of the time (NRC, 2009). The Committee concluded that the "scientific basis of handwriting comparisons" must be "strengthened" but that there "may be a scientific basis for handwriting comparison."

Forensic toxicology. The NRC Report was unfavorable toward many of the forensic disciplines, and did not devote significant attention to forensic toxicology, but did acknowledge that the field needed added equipment, staffing, and greater automation. Logan and Ropero-Miller (2013) highlighted areas of general forensic concern cited in the NRC report that pertained to toxicology. The NRC report stressed the importance of uniform reports, the need for precision and accuracy of lab results, and estimates of uncertainty of quantitative analyses. The adoption of routine quality assurance programs

and quality control procedures are needed, as are proficiency testing, certification of personnel and accreditation of laboratories. Expanded graduate education and research endeavors are necessary and continuing professional education and training of attorneys and judges are needed.

Forensic odontology. The Committee was highly critical of bitemark analysis because of the "elasticity of the skin, unevenness of the surface bite, and swelling and healing" (NRC, 2009, p. 174). While the ABFO guidelines list various methods for examining bitemarks, they do not issue criteria for interpreting results and associating a bitemark to a person's dentition, and with a specified degree of probability. The Committee noted research had shown a "high probability of false positive matches" (NRC, 2009, p. 174). The Committee summarized its findings as follows: (1) the lack of scientific data supporting the uniqueness of human dentition; (2) distortion problems associated with transferring these patterns to human skin; and (3) the lack of a standard for the number of individual characteristics required to conclude an identity has been reached. The Committee feared there was potential for serious bias among bitemark examiners when comparing a suspect's dentition with a bitemark. The Committee called for large studies to evaluate the uniqueness of bitemarks, the ability of skin to register necessary detail, and criteria necessary to associate bitemarks to a particular person, to the exclusion of all others, with known degree of probability.

28.21.2 Federal funding and policy activity

The 2009 NRC *Strengthening Forensic Science* report has stimulated significant activity at the federal level. There is both general legislation, described below, and specific activities of the Office of the White House concerning this response:

Congressional. Both the US Senate and the US House of Representatives have bills pending: Senator Patrick Leahy's Criminal Justice and Forensic Science Reform Act (S. 2177) to establish an Office of Forensic Science and a Forensic Science Board and to strengthen and promote confidence in the criminal justice system by ensuring scientific validity in forensic testing and Senator Jay Rockefeller's Forensic Science and Standards Act of 2014

(S. 2022) that would shift funding and decision-making (away from the DOJ) to NIST and NSF. Leahy introduced this bill for the first time in 2012 and reintroduced it in March 2014. In addition, other bills are being put forth to continue funding of laws to improve the quality and timeliness of forensic services involving violent crimes against women, elimination of DNA backlogs, and other crimes. The Violence Against Women Act (VAWA), including the Sexual Assault Forensic Evidence Reporting (SAFER) Act, which provides grants to combat violent sex crimes and domestic violence and to provide audits of untested sexual assault evidence, was passed by the House and Senate in February, 2013. The Justice for All Act, originally passed in 2004, is also up for reauthorization. Funds to assist in eliminating DNA backlogs and Coverdell Improvement Grants to improve the "quality and timeliness" of crime lab and medical examiner services are provided. Among other requirements, grantees must have in place a "process to conduct investigations into allegations of negligence or misconduct affecting forensic results." This is in large part the result of revelations from the Innocence Project and other crime laboratory scandals. Nominal funds are also provided to support the proposed National Forensic Science Commission.

Also, in direct response to the NRC study, the Office of the White House Subcommittee on Forensic Science, Committee on Science, National Science and Technology Council (which terminated at the end of 2012), set out to develop a federal response to issues raised in the NRC study by creating a "prioritized national research agenda." Interagency Working Groups (IWG) of federal, state, and local scientists, researchers, and lawyers were formed to produce recommendations in the following areas: accreditation and certification, education, ethics and terminology, standards, practices and protocols, outreach and communications, and research, development, testing, and evaluation. There were frustrations felt by many over the process followed including the "closed" meetings, limited funding and face to face meetings, no provisions for professional comment and feedback on draft recommendations, and that the final "White Paper" still has not been published. A recent report in *Chemical and Engineering News* sums up the criticisms (Widener, 2013). At this stage it is unclear what the White House response to the NRC recommendations will be.

28.21.3 National Commission on Forensic Science

Probably the most significant response is the joint DOJ/NIST National Commission on Forensic Science intended to "strengthen and enhance" the future of forensic science (Federal Register, 2013a). This bodes well for the field. It should also be noted that the NRC report called for the creation of an independent National Institute of Forensic Science (NRC) (2009), the status of which remains unclear. The recently appointed Commission is made up of distinguished practitioners, academic researchers, prosecutors, defense attorneys, judges, and other stakeholders to help standardize national guidance for forensic science practitioners (US Department of Justice, 2014). A website for the Commission (www.justice.gov/ncfs) provides meeting agendas, materials, webcasts, and other information. The Commission will work with the DOJ in the development of policy recommendations and with NIST administered guidance groups to propose discipline-specific procedures. Outcomes should include standards, priorities, guidance in the law–science courtroom interface, development of a uniform code of professional responsibility, and minimum standards for training, certification, and accreditation. As of this writing, the Commission has met three times, and formed six subcommittees (Accreditation and Proficiency Testing; Interim Solutions; Medico-legal Death Investigation; Reporting and Testimony; Scientific Inquiry and Research; and Training on Science and Law). The work of the Commission will be shared with the professional community in the months and years to come.

Acknowledgements

The authors wish to acknowledge and thank Victor Weedn, Barry Fisher, and Jeri Ropero-Miller for their helpful comments on an earlier draft of this chapter.

Cases cited

Brady v. Maryland, 373 U.S. 83 (1963).
Daubert v. Merrell Dow Pharmaceuticals, Inc., 509 U.S. 579 (1993).
Durham v. United States, 214 F.2d 862 (1954).
Escobedo v. Illinois, 378 U.S. 478 (1964).

Frye v. United States, 293 F. 1013 (D.C. Cir. 1923).
General Electric Co. v Joiner, 522 U.S. 136 (1997).
Kumho Tire Co., Ltd. v Carmichael, 526 U.S. 137 (1999).
Maryland v. King, 569 U.S. _____ (2013).
Melendez-Diaz v. Massachusetts, 557 U.S. 305 (2009).
Miranda v. Arizona, 384 U.S. 436 (1966).

References

Agostini, G., Gomez, E. (n.d.) *Forensic Anthropology Academic and Employment Trends*, American Academy of Forensic Sciences, viewed 15 November 2013, http://aafs.org/sites/default/files/pdf/PAEmploymentTrends.pdf.

American Academy of Forensic Sciences (n.d. a) *American Academy of Forensic Sciences*, Colorado Springs, viewed 15 November 2013, aafs.org.

American Academy of Forensic Sciences (n.d. b) *Membership*, Colorado Springs, viewed 17 November 2013, http://aafs.org/membership.

American Academy of Forensic Sciences (n.d. c) *Forensic Science Educational Conferences*, Colorado Springs, viewed 17 November 2013, http://aafs.org/forensic-science-educational-conferences.

American Academy of Forensic Sciences (n.d. d) *Approved Courses in Forensic Odontology*, Colorado Springs, viewed 17 November 2013, http://www.aafs.org/undergraduate-and-graduate-degrees-dentistry.

American Academy of Forensic Sciences (n.d. e) *Engineering Sciences*, Colorado Springs, viewed 17 November 2013, http://aafs.org/career-engineering-sciences.

American Academy of Forensic Sciences (n.d. f) *Digital and Multimedia Sciences*, Colorado Springs, viewed 17 November 2013, http://aafs.org/career-digital-multimedia-sciences.

American Academy of Forensic Sciences (n.d. g) *2014 AAFS 66th Annual Scientific Meeting*, viewed 22 November 2013, http://aafs.org/aafs-66th-annual-scientific-meeting-seattle-wa-2014.

American Academy of Psychiatry and the Law (2013) *Directory of Forensic Psychiatry Fellowships 2013*, Bloomfield, CT, viewed 17 November 2013, http://www.aapl.org/fellow.php.

American Association for Laboratory Accreditation (A2LA) (2012) *Forensic Examination Accreditation Program*, viewed 11 January 2014, http://www.a2la.org/appsweb/forensics.cfm.

American Board of Criminalistics (2013) *About Us – History*, viewed 24 September 2013, http://www.criminalistics.com/.

American Board of Forensic Anthropology (ABFA) (2008) *What is Forensic Anthropology?*, viewed 17 November 2013, http://www.theabfa.org/forstudents.html.

American Board of Forensic Psychology (n.d.) *American Board of Forensic Psychology*, Chapel Hill, NC, viewed 18 November 2013, http://www.abfp.com/.

American Board of Medical Specialties (n.d.) *American Board of Psychiatry and Neurology, Inc.*, Buffalo Grove, IL, viewed 18 November 2013, http://www.abpn.com/candidates_fp.html.

American Board of Medicolegal Death Investigators (2013) *American Board of Medicolegal Death Investigators*, Baltimore, MD, viewed 18 November 2013, http://abmdi.org/.

American Board of Forensic Toxicology (n.d.) *What is Forensic Toxicology? Forensic Toxicology Statistics*, p. 6, viewed 15 November 2013, http://www.abft.org/files/WHAT%20IS%20FORENSIC%20TOXICOLOGY.pdf.

American Psychology–Law Society (n.d. a) *Division 41 of the American Psychology Association*, viewed 17 November 2013, http://www.ap-ls.org/education/GraduatePrograms.php.

American Psychology–Law Society (n.d. b) *Guide to Graduate Programs in Forensic and Legal Psychology 2010–2011*, 2nd edn, Omaha, NE, viewed 17 November 2013, http://www.apls.org/education/Guide%20to%20Graduate%20Programs%20in%20Forensic%20and%20Legal%20Psychology%204-9-12.pdf.

American Society of Crime Laboratory Directors/Laboratory Accreditation Board (n.d.) *About ASCLD/Lab – History*, Garner, NC, viewed 24 September 2013, http://www.ascld-lab.org/.

Armed Forces Medical Examiner System (2013) Viewed 22 November 2013, http://www.afmes.mil/.

ASTM International (2013) *Committee E30 on Forensic Sciences*, West Conshohocken, PA, viewed 24 September 2013, http://www.astm.org/COMMITTEE/E30.htm.

ASTM International (n.d. a) *Committee E58 on Forensic Engineering*, West Conshohocken, PA, viewed 17 November 2013, http://www.astm.org/Standards/E2388.htm.

ASTM International (n.d. b) *Committee E2388-11 Standard Guide for Minimum Training Requirements for Forensic Document Examiners*, West Conshohocken, PA, viewed 17 November 2013, http://www.astm.org/Standards/E2388.htm.

Baker, D., Brothers, S., Geradts, Z., Lacey, D., Nance, K., Ryan, D., Sammons, J., Stephenson, P. (2013) Digital evolution: history, challenges and future directions for the digital and multimedia section. In: *Forensic Science: Current Issues, Future Directions*, Ed. D.H. Ubelaker, 1st edn, Wiley-Blackwell, West Sussex, UK.

Ballou, S., Houck, M., Siegel, J., Crouse, C., Lentini, J., Palenik, S. (2013) Criminalistics: the bedrock of forensic science. In: *Forensic Science: Current Issues, Future Directions*, Ed. D.H, Ubelaker, 1st edn, Wiley-Blackwell, West Sussex, UK.

Bashinski, J., Peterson, J. (2003) Forensic sciences. In: *Local Government Police Management*, Eds W. Geller and D. Stephens, 4th edn, ICMA, Washington, DC.

Beck, A., Maruschak, L. (2001) *Mental Health Treatment in State Prisons, 2000*, Bureau of Justice Statistics, Washington, DC.

Bernstein, M. (1997) Forensic odontology. In: *Introduction to Forensic Sciences*, Ed. W.G. Eckert, 2nd edn, CRC Press, Boca Raton, FL.

Billick, S., Martell, D. (2013) Forensic psychiatry and forensic psychology. In: *Forensic Science: Current Issues, Future Directions*, Ed. D.H. Udebaker, 1st edn, Wiley-Blackwell, West Sussex, UK.

Burkhart, F. (1998) *Ellis R. Kerley is Dead at 74: A Forensic Sherlock Holmes*, New York, viewed 15 November 2013, http://www.nytimes.com/1998/09/12/us/ellis-r-kerley-is-dead-at-74-a-forensic-sherlock-holmes.html.

CAC Update (2013) *CAC Position on NIST Guidance Groups*, viewed 18 November 2013, cac@memberlodge.org.

Center for Forensic Science Research and Education (2013) *Center for Forensic Science Research and Education*, Willow Grove, PA, viewed 15 October 2103, http://forensicscienceeducation.org.

Combatting Terrorism Technical Support Office (2013) US Department of Defense, http://www.cttso.gov/?q=ifs.

Connors, E., LundgrenT., Miller, N., McEwen, T. (1996) *Convicted by Juries, Exonerated by Science: Case Studies in the Use of DNA Evidence to Establish Innocence after Trial*, National Institute of Justice, Washington, DC.

Consortium of Forensic Science Organizations (CFSO) (n.d.) *Advocacy Newsletters*, viewed 18 November 2013, http://www.thecfso.org/advocacy/.

Curran, W. (1980) History and development. In *Modern Legal Medicine, Psychiatry and Forensic Science*, Eds C.S. Petty, W.F. Curran, and L. McGarry, F.A. Davis Company, Philadelphia, PA.

Davis, G., Hanzlick, R. (2013) *The Medical Examiner and Coroner Systems, Medscape Reference – Drugs, Diseases and Procedures*, viewed 15 October 2013, WebMD, LLC, http://emedicine.medscape.com/article/1785357-overview.

Department for Transport (2010) *The Relationship between Blood Alcohol Concentration (BAC) and Breath Alcohol Concentration (BrAC): A Review of the Evidence*, report prepared by A. Jones, Department for Transport, London, viewed 21 November 2013, http://assets.dft.gov.uk/publications/research-and-statistical-reports/report15.pdf.

Dillon, D. (1977) *A History of Criminalistics in the United States, 1850–1950*, Doctoral Dissertation, University of California, Berkeley, CA.

Drug Enforcement Administration (2013) *NFLIS National Forensic Laboratory Information System 2012 Annual Report*, US Department of Justice, Drug Enforcement Administration, Office of Diversion Control, Washington, DC, viewed 15 November 2013, http://www.deadiversion.usdoj.gov/nflis/.

Durose, M., Walsh, K., Burch, A. (2012) *Census of Publicly Funded Forensic Crime Laboratories, 2009*, Bureau of Justice Statistics, Washington, DC.

Federal Bureau of Investigation (2013) *Fiscal Year 2012 Regional Computer Forensics Laboratory Program Annual Report*, US Department of Justice, Washington, DC.

Federal Bureau of Investigation (n.d.) *Computer Analysis Response Team*, Washington, DC, viewed 15 November 2013, http://www.fbi.gov/news/stories/2013/january/piecing-together-digital-evidence.

Federal Bureau of Investigation, Laboratory Services (n.d.) *Combined DNA Index System (CODIS) The FBI Federal Bureau of Investigation*, Washington, DC, viewed 24 September 2013, http://www.fbi.gov/about-us/lab/biometric-analysis/codis.

Federal Judicial Center (2011) *Reference Manual on Scientific Evidence*, 3rd edn, The National Academies Press, Washington, DC, viewed 22 November 2013, http://www.fjc.gov/public/pdf.nsf/lookup/SciMan3D01.pdf/$file/SciMan3D01.pdf.

Federal Register (2013a) *Notice of Establishment of the National Commission on Forensic Science*, Vol. 78, no. 36, February 22, Government Printing Office, Washington, DC.

Federal Register (2013b) *Possible Models for the Administration and Support of Discipline-Specific Guidance Groups for Forensic Science*, Vol. 78, No. 188, September 27, Government Printing Office, Washington, DC.

Field, K. (1998) *History of the American Academy of Forensic Science*, American Society for Testing and Materials, West Conshohocken, PA.

Forensicanthro.com (2011) *Forensic Anthropology Programs*, viewed 15 November 2013, http://www.forensicanthro.com/index.html.

Forensic Science Education Program Accreditation Commission (n.d.) *Accredited Universities*, viewed 23 October 2013, http://fepac-edu.org/.

Forensic Specialties Accreditation Board (2013) *Accredited Organizations*, viewed 17 December 2013, http://thefsab.org/accredited.htm.

Forensic Toxicology Council (2010) *Briefing: What is Forensic Toxicology*, Forensic Toxicology Statistics, p. 6, reviewed 26 October 2013, http://www.abft.org/files/WHAT%20IS%20FORENSIC%20TOXICOLOGY.pdf.

FQS ANSI-ASQ National Accreditation Board (2014) *FQS Forensic Accreditation*, viewed 11 January 2014, http://fqsforensics.org/accreditation.aspx.

Giannelli, P., Imwinkelreid, E., Peterson, J. (2011) Reference guide on forensic identification expertise. In: *Reference Manual on Scientific Evidence*, 3rd edn, National Academies Press, Washington, DC.

Giannelli, P., Reader, M. (eds) (2006) Forensic evidence. In: *Achieving Justice: Freeing the Innocent, Convicting the Guilty*, Report of the ABA Criminal Justice Section's ad hoc Innocence Committee to Ensure the Integrity of the Criminal Process, Washington, DC.

Gill, J., Tang, Y., Davis, G., Harcke, H., and Mazuchowski, E. (2013) Forensic pathology – the roles of molecular diagnostics and radiology at autopsy. In *Forensic Science: Current Issues, Future Directions*, Ed. D.H. Ubelaker, 1st edn, Wiley-Blackwell, West Sussex, UK.

Glaze, L., James, D. (2006) *Mental Health Problems of Prison and Jail Inmates*, Bureau of Justice Statistics, Washington, DC.

Hanzlick, R., Combs, D. (1998) Medical examiner and coroner systems: history and trends. *Journal of the American Medical Association* 279 (11): 870–874.

Hanzlick, R. (2007) The conversion of coroner systems to medical examiner systems in the United States: a lull in the action. *American Journal of Forensic Medicine and Pathology* 28 (4): 279–283.

Hickman, M., Hughes, K., Strom, K., Ropero-Miller, J. (2007) *Medical Examiners and Coroners' Offices, 2004*, Bureau of Justice Statistics, Washington, DC.

Hilton, O. (1979) History of questioned document examination in the United States. *Journal of Forensic Sciences* 24 (4): 890–897.

Houck, M., Siegel, J. (2010) *Fundamentals of Forensic Science*, 2nd edn, Academic Press, Burlington, MA.

Hsu, S. (2013) U.S. reviewing 27 death penalty convictions for FBI forensic testimony errors, *Washington Post*, 17 July 2013, viewed 24 September 2013, http://articles.washingtonpost.com/2013-07-17/local/40632927_1_convictions-death-row-cases-capital-cases.

Innocence Project (2013) Innocence Project of Cardozo School of Law at Yeshiva University, New York, NY, http://www.innocenceproject.org.

International Association for Identification (2012) IAI History, viewed 11 January 2014, http://www.theiai.org/history/.

International Association of Computer Investigative Specialists (IACIS) (2013) Leesburg, VA, http://www.iacis.com/.

International Association of Medical Examiners and Coroners (IAMEC) (2013) *Accreditation*, viewed 19 December 2013, http://theiacme.com/accreditation.html.

James, S., Nordby, J. (eds) (2005) *Forensic Science: An Introduction to Scientific and Investigative Techniques*, Taylor & Francis, Boca Raton, FL.

Jones, A. (1996) Measuring alcohol in blood and breath for forensic purposes – a historical review. *Forensic Science Review* 8: 13–44.

Joseph, A. (1968) *Study of Needs and The Development of Curricula in the Field of Forensic Science: A Survey of Crime Laboratories*, John Jay College of Criminal Justice, New York, NY.

Liptai, L., Aleksander, A., Grainger, S., Hainsworth, S., Loomba, R., Unarski, J. (2013) Global thinking and methodologies in evidence-based forensic engineering science. In: *Forensic Science: Current Issues, Future Directions*, Ed. D.H. Ubelaker, 1st edn, Wiley-Blackwell, West Sussex, UK.

Logan, B., Ropero-Miller, J. (2013) Forensic toxicology: scope, challenges, future directions and needs, In: *Forensic Science: Current Issues, Future Directions*, Ed. D.H. Ubelaker, 1st edn, Wiley-Blackwell, West Sussex, UK.

National Academy of Forensic Engineers (n.d.) Hawthorne, NY, < http://www.nafe.org/>.

National Academy of Sciences (2011) *Reference Manual on Scientific Evidence*, 3rd edn, National Academies Press, Washington, DC.

National Advisory Commission on Criminal Justice Standards and Goals (1973) *Task Force Report on Police*, US Government Printing Office, Washington, DC.

National Association of Medical Examiners (2013a) *Accreditation Standards*, Marceline, MO, viewed 18 November 2013, thename.org.

National Association of Medical Examiners (2013b) *Forensic Autopsy Performance Standards*, Marceline, MO, viewed 17 December 2013, thename.org.

National Commission on Law Observance and Enforcement (1931) *Report on Lawlessness in Law Enforcement*, No. 11, US Government Printing Office, Washington, D.C.

National Disaster Medical System (2013) US Department of Health and Human Services, Public Health Emergency, January 2013, viewed 19 December 2013, https://www.phe.gov/preparedness/responders/ndms/Pages/default.aspx.

National Institute of Justice (1999) *Forensic Sciences: Review of Status and Needs*, Washington, DC.

National Institute of Justice (2004) *Education and Training in Forensic Science: A Guide for Forensic Science Laboratories, Education Institutions, and Students*, Washington, DC.

National Institute of Justice (2012) *Scientific Working Groups*, Washington, DC, viewed 24 September 2013, http://www.nij.gov/topics/forensics/lab-operations/standards/scientific-working-groups.htm.

National Institute of Justice (2013) *Forensic Sciences*, Washington, DC, viewed 24 September 2013, http://www.nij.gov/topics/forensics/.

National Institute of Standards and Technology (n.d.) *Consolidated Active Federal Forensic Science RD Projects List*, viewed 31 October 2013, http://collaborate.nist.gov/twiki-fs/bin/view/ForensicScience/ResearchDevelopmentList.

National Research Council (1996) *The Evaluation of Forensic DNA Evidence*, National Academies Press, Washington, DC.

National Research Council (2009) *Strengthening Forensic Science in the United States: A Path Forward*, National Academies Press, Washington, DC.

National Science Foundation (2013) *Dear Colleague Letter: Forensic Science – Opportunity for Breakthroughs in Fundamental and Basic Research and Education*, viewed 13 January 2014, http://www.nsf.gov/pubs/2013/nsf13120/nsf13120.jsp.

Naval Criminal Investigative Service (NCIS) (n.d.) *Cyber Department*, Quantico, VA, viewed 15 November 2013, http://www.ncis.navy.mil/CoreMissions/cyber/Pages/default.aspx.

Nelson, M. (2013) *Analysis of Untested Sexual Assault Kits in New Orleans*, National Institute of Justice, Washington, DC.

Newall, G. (2007) *Subdisciplines: Forensic Anthropology*, Indiana University, Bloomington, viewed 16 October 2013, http://www.indiana.edu/~wanthro/theory_pages/forensic.htm.

Noon, R. (2005) Structural failures. In: *Forensic Science: An Introduction to Scientific and Investigative Techniques*, Eds S. Jones and J. Nordby, Taylor & Francis, Boca Raton, FL.

Omnibus Crime Control and Safe Streets Act (1968) Public Law 90-351, 82 Stat 197.

Parker, B. (1963) Status of forensic science in the administration of criminal justice. *Revista Juridica de la Universidad de Puerto Pico* 32: 405.

PBS American Experience (n.d.) *Tales from the Poisoner's Handbook*, viewed 18 January 2014, http://www.pbs.org/wgbh/americanexperience/features/interactive/poisoner's-tales/.

Peterson, J. (1989) Symposium on ethical conflicts in the forensic sciences. *Journal of Forensic Sciences*, 33 (4): 717–718.

Peterson, J., De Forest, P. (1977) The status of forensic science degree programs in the United States. *Journal of Forensic Sciences* 22 (1): 17–33.

Peterson, J., Hickman, M. (2005) *Census of Publicly Funded Forensic Crime Laboratories 2002*, Bureau of Justice Statistics, Washington, DC.

Peterson, J., Mihajlovic, S., Bedrosian, J (1985) The capabilities, uses and effects of the nation's criminalistics laboratories. *Journal of Forensic Sciences* 30: 10–23.

Peterson, J., Fabricant, E., Field, K., Thornton, J. (1978) *Crime Laboratory Proficiency Testing Research Program*, US Government Printing Office, Washington, DC.

Peterson, J., Lin, G., Ho, M., Gaensslen, R. (2003) The feasibility of external blind DNA proficiency testing. *Journal of Forensic Sciences* 48 (1): 21–31.

Peterson, J., Johnson, D., Herz, D., Graziano, L., Oehler, T. (2011) *Sexual Assault Kit Backlog Study Final Report*, National Institute of Justice, Washington, DC.

Poklis, A. (1997) Forensic toxicology. In: *Introduction to Forensic Sciences*, Ed. W.G. Eckert, 2nd edn, CRC Press, Boca Raton, FL.

President's Commission on Law Enforcement and Administration of Justice (1967a) *The Challenge of Crime in a Free Society*, US Government Printing Office, Washington, DC.

President's Commission on Law Enforcement and Administration of Justice (1967b) *Task Force Reports: The Police and Science and Technology*, US Government Printing Office, Washington, DC.

Presley, L. (1999) The FBI laboratory and ASCLD/LAB accreditation. *Forensic Science Communications* 1 (1), viewed 14 November, 2013, http://www.fbi.gov/about-us/lab/forensic-science-communications/fsc/april1999/index.htm/presley.htm.

Presley, L., Haas, M., Quarino, L. (2009) The forensic science assessment test (FSAT): a potential tool for the academic assessment of forensic science programs. *Forensic Science Policy and Management* 1: 74–84.

Pretty, I., Barsley, R., Bowers, M., Bush, M., Bush, P., Clement, J., Dorion, R., Freeman, A., Lewis, J., Senn, D., Wright, F. (2013) Odontology – dentistry's contribution to truth and justice. In: *Forensic Science: Current Issues, Future Directions*, Ed. D.H. Ubelaker, 1st edn, Wiley-Blackwell, West Sussex, UK.

Reddy's Forensic Page (n.d.) Viewed 17 November 2013, http://www.forensicpage.com/.

Regional Computer Forensics Laboratory (RCFL) National Program Office (n.d.) Quantico, VA, viewed 16 October 2013, http://www.rcfl.gov/index.cfm.

Rehling, C., Rabren, C. (1973) *Alabama's Master Plan for a Crime Laboratory Delivery System*, US Government Printing Office, Washington, DC.

Riordan, W., Gustafson, J., Fitzgerald, M., Lewis, J. (2013) Forensic document examination. In: *Forensic Science: Current Issues, Future Directions*, Ed. D.H. Ubelaker, 1st edn, Wiley-Blackwell, West Sussex, UK.

Sadoff, R. (2005) Forensic psychiatry. In: *Forensic Science: An Introduction to Scientific and Investigative Techniques*, Eds. S. James and J. Nordby, Taylor & Francis, Boca Raton, FL.

Schmidt, K., Shaw, A., LaFleur, J. (2011) *Autopsies in the U.S.A., Post Mortem: Death Investigation in America*, Pro Publica, 31 January 2011, viewed 16 December 2013, http://projects.propublica.org/forensics/.

Scientific Working Group DNA Analysis Methods (2013) *History of DNA QA Standards & SWDDAM*, viewed 15 November 2013, http://www.swgdam.org/History%20of%20QA%20%20SWGDAM%20Jan%202013.pdf.

Scientific Working Group on Digital Evidence (SWGDE) (2013) Viewed 18 November 2013, https://www.swgde.org/.

Scientific Working Group on Disaster Victim Identification (SWGDVI) (2013) Viewed 15 November 2013, http://www.swgdvi.org/index.html.

Scientific Working Group on Forensic Anthropology (SWGANTH) (2013) Viewed 22 November 2013, http://swganth.org/.

Scientific Working Group on Forensic Toxicology (SWGTOX) (2013, viewed 18 November 2013, <http://www.swgtox.org/>.

Scientific Working Group for Medicolegal Death Investigation (SWGMDI) (2011) *Infrastructure Committee Report 3, Medicolegal Autopsy Facilities in the United States, May 26, 2011*, http://swgmdi.org/images/iscomrpt3-facilities2011.pdf.

Scientific Working Group for Medicolegal Death Investigation (SWGMDI) (2013) Articles, viewed 29 October, 2013, http://swgmdi.org/.

Sorg, M. (2005) Forensic anthropology. In: *Forensic Science: An Introduction to Scientific and Investigative Techniques*, Eds S. James and J. Nordby, Taylor & Francis, Boca Raton, FL.

State of California Department of Justice, Missing and Unidentified Persons Unit (2013) Viewed 15 November 2013, http://oag.ca.gov/missing/mups.

Steadman, D. (2013) The places we will go: paths forward in forensic anthropology. In: *Forensic Science: Current Issues, Future Directions*, Ed. D.H. Ubelaker, 1st edn, Wiley-Blackwell, West Sussex, UK.

Strom, K., Hickman, M. (2010) Unanalyzed evidence in law enforcement agencies: a national examination of forensic processing in police departments. *Criminology and Public Policy* 9: 381–404.

Strom, K., Hickman, M., Smiley-MacDonald, H., Ropero-Miller, J., Stout, P. (2011) Crime laboratory personnel as criminal justice decision makers: a study of controlled substance processing in ten jurisdictions. *Forensic Science Policy and Management* 2: 57–69.

System Infrastructure Committee of the Scientific Working Group for Medicolegal Death Investigation (2013) *Workplace Locations of Board Certified Forensic Pathologists in the United States Who Perform Medicolegal Autopsies for Medical Examiner/Coroner Systems: 2012 – Draft*, viewed 29 October 2013, http://swgmdi.org/images/si7.workplacelocationsprcdraft.9.17.13.pdf.

Technical Working Group on DNA Analysis Methods (TWG-DAM) (1991) Guidelines for a Quality Assurance Program for DNA Analysis. *Crime Laboratory Digest*, Vol. 18, No. 2, US Department of Justice, Federal Bureau of Investigation, Washington, DC.

Thornton, J. (1975) Criminalistics: past, present and future. *Lex et Scientia* 11: 1–44.

Thorwald, J. (1965) *The Century of the Detective*, trans. by Richard and Clara Winston, Harcourt, Brace and World, Inc., New York.

Thorwald, J. (1967) *Crime and Science*, trans. by Richard and Clara Winston, Harcourt Brace and World, Inc., New York.

United States Department of Justice, Office of Pubic Affairs (2014) *U.S. Departments of Justice and Commerce Name Experts to First-ever National Commission on Forensic Science*, Washington, DC, viewed 11 January 2004, http://www.justice.gov/opa/pr/2014/January/14-at-029.html.

United States Secret Service (2012) *Electronic Crimes Task Forces and Working Groups*, Washington, DC, viewed 15 November 2013, http://www.secretservice.gov/ectf.shtml.

Weinberg, M., Weedm, V., Weinberg, S., Fowler, D. (2013) Characteristics of Medical Examiner/Coroner Offices Accredited by the National Association of Medical Examiners. *Journal of Forensic Sciences* 58 (5), 1193–1199.

Widener, A. (2013) First steps toward forensic reform. *Chemical and Engineering News* 91 (11): 27–29.

Wright, R. (2005) The role of the forensic pathologist. In: *Forensic Science: An Introduction to Scientific and Investigative Techniques*, Eds S. James and J. Nordby, Taylor & Francis, Boca Raton, FL.

Wright, R, Eckert, W. (1997) Forensic pathology. In: *Introduction to Forensic Sciences*, Ed. W.G. Eckert, 2nd edn, CRC Press, Boca Raton, FL.

Zeno's Forensic Site (n.d.) Viewed 17 November 2013, http://forensic.to/.

CHAPTER 29

Legal medicine and forensic science in Uruguay

Hugo Rodríguez Almada

Department of Legal Medicine of the School of Medicine in the University of the Republic, Montevideo, Uruguay

Uruguay

29.1 Introduction

Uruguay is a small country in South America with a surface area of 176,215 square kilometers. Its 3,290,000 inhabitants are highly concentrated in Montevideo, the capital city, and the metropolitan area, which accounts for over half of the country's population.

The relief is characterized by a soft and wavy profile, 514 meters being its maximum height. A temperate climate prevents the country from experiencing extreme temperatures. Uruguay evidences good social and health indicators when compared to other countries in Latin America (low illiteracy and infant mortality rates, high human development and life expectancy rates and the most just distribution of wealth in the region).

Historically, the country has relied on a strong public education system characterized by its being free and universal, including college education.

In 1825 Uruguay declared its Independence after a number of emancipating battles and in 1830 it passed the

The Global Practice of Forensic Science, First Edition. Edited by Douglas H. Ubelaker.
© 2015 John Wiley & Sons, Ltd. Published 2015 by John Wiley & Sons, Ltd.

country's first Constitution. In terms of its political and institutional structure, Uruguay is a democratic republic. However, between 1973 and 1985 the democratic form of government was substituted by a civic–military dictatorship that dissolved parliament and ruled under a state terrorist regime that ran over human rights, the forensic research of which is still incipient.

The development of forensic sciences in Uruguay has been largely determined by these unique geographic, demographic, social and political characteristics of the country, which differ from those present in most of the region.

29.2 Legal medicine and forensic sciences historical review

Medicolegal expert examinations in the times of colonies under Spanish rule (1724–1811) were performed by surgeons. They identified the wounded bodies and dissected the corpses. The first forensic autopsy recorded took place in 1760 and the first forensic accounting on skeletal remains was done in 1797 (Soiza Larrosa, 1985).

Considering independent times, the creation of "police doctors" in 1827 constituted a milestone in the field. These doctors were responsible for providing assistance to police officers and prisoners, although they also prepared the expert reports requested by the authorities. The first reference to "medical doctors" is found in the Health Regulations of 1883, which also accounts for the position of "court chemical expert" (Soiza Larrosa, 2002).

In 1851 the first research process due to a supposed malpractice case took place after the death of General Eugenio Garzón, a politician who played a key role in the country's political arena and who would have become the next president of the republic. The autopsy on Garzón's corpse and the case report was performed by eight of the most renowned doctors of those times, and they concluded that Pedro Capdehourat, the treating physician, was responsible for Garzón's death. As a result, he was not authorized to practice medicine. One hundred and fifty years after, upon a review of the case it was found there had been no malpractice case and that health care assistance for General Garzón had been provided according to medical knowledge of the time (Riveiro and Roó, 2007).

In 1877 the Chair in Legal Medicine was established at the University's School of Medicine (the current University of the Republic), which would exert an essential influence on the development of legal medicine and forensic science until today.

Autopsies were performed in cemeteries until 1914. As from that date, according to the provisions in an agreement signed by the Judiciary and the School of Medicine, the Court Morgue was found in the Legal Medicine Department's premises. Sixty years later, the current Court Morgue was established, which comprises Chemical and Toxicology as well as Anatomic Pathology and Anthropology Laboratories (Soiza Larrosa, 1992). However, in faraway areas in the country's provinces, autopsies are still performed in cemeteries or public hospitals.

Act N° 5,217 of 1915 provided that medicolegal actions were to be performed by "public service doctors", except for judicial autopsies that were under the scope of the Anatomic Pathology Department of the School of Medicine. It was Martin Martinez Pueta, Chair of Legal Medicine, who in 1916 prepared a draft project for the organization of forensic actions, emphasizing the need for a specialization in legal medicine. Among other supporting comments, Dr. Martinez Pueta questioned the quality of expert reports prepared by the Anatomic Pathology Department, the members of which lacked medicolegal training. The project advocated the creation of a forensic physicians body and the Forensic Technical Institute (Martínez Pueta, 1917).

Both initiatives by Martínez Pueta came true. Thus, Act N° 5,635 of 1918 derogated the previous norm, creating the forensic doctor position as such, who would report to criminal judges. The law provided that forensic doctors would perform all expert tasks and actions, including autopsies.

Likewise, the creation of the judiciary's Forensic Technical Institute only took place in 1937. The new institute gradually took over expert examinations of lesions, violent deaths, toxicology, and assessment of criminal responsibility, filiations, determination of age, ballistic and study of documents. The titles issued are registered at the Ministry of Public Health (Soiza Larrosa, 2005).

In 1972, Legal Medicine was recognized as a specialization in Uruguay, and from that date and until today the School of Medicine of the University of the Republic is responsible for certifying it. Titles issued are registered at the Ministry of Public Health. This is the only discipline among the forensic sciences that entails such a degree of academic formality and acknowledgment by public authorities.

29.3 Education and training of human resources in forensic science

Education and training of forensic science in Uruguay is rather heterogeneous. This assertion does not refer to training in the "primary discipline" – that is anthropology, dentistry, medicine, chemistry, among others, but rather to its specialization applied to the forensic field.

In this respect, the situation of Legal Medicine is clearly different from the rest of the forensic disciplines.

29.3.1 Training in legal medicine

In Uruguay there is a long tradition of training specialized physicians in legal medicine at the Department of Legal Medicine of the School of Medicine in the University of the Republic. The University of the Republic is the only public university in the country. Simultaneously, the School of Medicine has a Graduate School that is authorized to issue certifications for all medical specializations, including legal medicine.

The Department of Legal Medicine was established in 1877 and all medical students attend its courses in the specialization. Also, the Department is responsible for postgraduate courses and since 1972 the country has trained specialists in Legal Medicine, whose title is recognized by health authorities.

The title of specialist in Legal Medicine is obtained after attending classes and courses, approving and meeting all academic requirements for postgraduate in the field of expertise. It comprises three years of theoretical courses and practical training (performance of autopsies, assessment of lesions and study of judicial files).

The higher teaching staff of the Department of Legal Medicine are responsible for all educational issues. Practical training takes place within judicial premises, authorized by the judicial authorities and forensic doctors on duty, under the supervision of university teaching staff, who sometimes play two roles.

The theoretical content of the specialization courses aims to train experts with a holistic perspective, who can adequately handle the different aspects of legal medicine: thanatology, lesionology, forensic sexology, forensic dentistry, forensic anthropology, forensic

psychiatry, forensic toxicology, forensic genetics, criminal, civil and labor law. This theoretical training is complemented with theoretical–practical activities at the court morgue, the forensic clinic and the molecular genetics laboratory. Moreover, training includes working in polyclinics and hospitals, assessing victims of different forms of violence. This part of the training in the health system often takes place in the pediatrics services, and aims to train doctors in the early diagnosis of different forms of child abuse.

Academic requirements to obtain the specialist title include mandatory attendance of courses, approving written tests and/or practices every semester, presenting case reports or reviews of topics in each one of the first years, a final thesis, a practical test consisting of performing a complete autopsy and writing the corresponding case report.

Since 2009, training in the specialization underwent a positive change, when legal medicine became part of the national system of medical residences. This system established by Act N° 18,438 is a learning and training regime in a medical specialization for professionals who have recently graduated and takes place in a certified teaching health care center, where students intensively act under the guidance and supervision of established higher staff of the institution and higher teaching staff. The syllabus for training in the specialization is covered under such conditions in order to obtain the corresponding title. To enter such a regime, students need to take part in an exam and merit-based selection process that is open and anonymous, providing education and training through 48 weekly and remunerated hours of supervised practical work.

The Residence in Legal Medicine lasts three years. Resident physicians need to observe the number of hours agreed (48 hours a week), apart from the rest of the regular academic requirements of students attending conventional postgraduate courses (attending academic activities, evaluation tests twice a year, preparing three scientific studies and the final practical exam).

The evaluation of the first years of the Residence in Legal Medicine proved the advantages of this kind of training for specialists. In fact, residents complete their training with significant experience after having practiced, on average, around six hundred autopsies and around three hundred assessments of child physical or sexual abuse or battered women. Thus, the first generations of Residents in Legal Medicine rapidly blended into the labor market as forensics for the Judiciary and/or university professors in this area of specialty.

29.3.2 Training in other forensic sciences

As has already been pointed out, in Uruguay there is no systematic professional training in forensic sciences post-graduates other than Legal Medicine. However, there are a number of professionals who work in the forensic context, such as chemists, physical anthropologists and biologists.

In other cases, professionals have been empirically trained through their own work experience. Also, a number of people were trained abroad by taking diploma courses, Masters or PhDs in other countries. The online education offer existing, thanks to ICT progress, has contributed to these processes. Such is the case of the remote Masters in Forensic Medicine and Forensic Sciences offered by the University of Valencia, led by Professors Fernando Verdú Pascual and Ana Castelló Ponce, respectively, which have included Uruguayan professors since they were launched. Indeed, several Uruguayan professionals have taken advantage of these virtual masters. In other cases professionals have taken courses or completed internships.

In spite of there being no systematic training in forensic sciences, the University of the Republic has led positive efforts to that end for over two decades. The School of Humanities and Educational Sciences has developed postgraduate courses for anthropologists or doctors. Among them are those developed in 1995 by Professor Hector Soto Izquierdo (Institute of Legal Medicine, Havana, University of Havana) on forensic anthropology and in 1997 by Professor Ranajit Chakraborty (Houston Univesity). The School of Medicine has offered updating courses on forensic anthropology, those taught by Professors Douglas Ubelaker (Smithsonian Institution; The George Washington University; Consultant in Forensic Anthropology to the FBI) and Valeria Silva Braz (Universidade Federal do Rio de Janeiro) being worth mentioning. Likewise, the School of Dentistry has organized courses on legal and forensic dentistry, with the collaboration of Professor Jorge Paulete Vanrell (Paulista University).

Today, efforts are being made to consolidate a space for graduate and postgraduate training spaces in forensic dentistry.

For the continuing training of professionals, the Department of Legal Medicine of the School of Medicine collaborates with the Forensic Technical Institute to offer updating courses for forensic doctors around the country, despite not all of them having their specialist degree.

Apart from university training, in the field of criminalistics the National Bureau of Technical Police (police scientists) is responsible for training experts at the same work sites. The School of Criminalistics operates within the headquarters of the National Bureau of Technical Police, and both low rank staff and officials receive specific training on criminalistics, apart from their general training in police issues. Courses cover 340 hours (280 theoretical and 60 hours of practice) along the following thematic axis: papilloscopy, photography, planimetry, applied chemistry, accidentology, documentoscopy, graphoscopy, ballistics, legal medicine, applied biology, applied legislation and criminology ICT (Camejo, 2008). The police graduating from the School of Criminalistics obtain an Expert Assistant Degree. These Expert Assistants may practice in the different areas of criminalistics, such as crime scene investigation, ballistics, accidentology, documentology, dactilloscopy or ICT. The most experienced staff at the National Bureau of Technical Police is responsible for their training and they have historically profited from the collaboration of the staff from the Legal Medicine Department of the School of Medicine of the University of the Republic. This collaboration has been mutual and criminalistic experts from the Police Scientists have also contributed to training doctors specialized in legal medicine.

29.4 Organization of forensic sciences

Describing the organization of the forensic sciences in Uruguay implies mentioning its three hierarchies: the Forensic Technical Institute of the Judiciary, the National Bureau of Police Investigation and the academic services associated with the University of the Republic.

29.4.1 Forensic Technical Institute (ITF)

The Forensic Technical Institute is the technical counseling body belonging to the judiciary, whose human and material resources report to the judges who decide on different fields, although in particular in the area of criminal law. Its organizational chart is rather complex.

The highest authorities, both the Director and Deputy Director, have historically been professionals from the field of law (lawyers or notary publics) rather than professionals from the field of forensic science.

With the purpose of illustrating the organization and development of the Forensic Technical Institute four main divisions will be considered: the Department of Forensic Medicine, the Department of Medical Criminology, the Chemistry and Toxicology Department and the Identification Department. Likewise, it comprises other areas that are not relevant to this overview, such as accounting expert examination or social services.

29.4.1.1 Department of Forensic Medicine

The Department of Forensic Medicine is responsible for conducting expert examinations in connection with all kinds of violent events and/or events that seem to have a criminal aspect (car accidents, domestic violence, sexual violence, self-aggression, medical malpractice, among others), both in individuals who are alive or are corpses. This task is carried out by forensic doctors from the competent courts who report to the criminal judges on duty. The forensic doctors carry out the entire expert examination: they go to the crime scene, perform the autopsy, assess the lesions of individuals who are alive, whether victims or aggressors and prepare the corresponding reports.

In Montevideo, the capital city, apart from forensic doctors on duty who participate in expert examinations in their different stages, there are those who work exclusively at the Forensic Clinic, where they assess lesions, and others who practice in the Adolescence or Family Courts specialized in domestic violence. They are not responsible for performing autopsies.

Forensic doctors may request complementary studies, such as those provided by the Chemistry and Toxicology Laboratories, Anatomic Pathology and Anthropology Departments. All of these services are centralized in the country's capital city, and thus samples need to be sent to Montevideo from anywhere around the country.

Forensic doctors of Montevideo may also request radiographic studies and a photographer to record the findings. In the rest of the country the Scientific Police are responsible for taking pictures but there are no X-ray resources available.

Table 29.1 presents the budgeted technical human resources allocated to the Forensic Medicine

Table 29.1 Technical human resources in the Department of Forensic Medicine of the Forensic Technical Institute

Position	Number
Director (Forensic Doctor)	1
General Counseling Physician	1
Forensic Doctors for the capital city	8
Autopsy Doctors for the capital city	3
Forensic Doctors for the provinces	39
Doctors for the Anatomic Pathology Laboratory	2
Anthropologist	1
Radiologist	1
Photographer	1
Forensic Doctors for Domestic Violence Courts in the capital city	2
Forensic Doctors for Adolescent Courts in the capital city	3
Forensic Clinic Doctors	4
Forensic Doctors to Assess hospitalized individuals	2
Forensic Clinic Nurses	1

Department, although administrative and service staff are not included.

As to the activity at the Court Morgue of Montevideo, statistics have remained the same in the last five years, there being around 2300 autopsies per year. Of these, over half (55%) correspond to external examination in the case of natural deaths, 44% are complete autopsies and 1% are examinations on bone remains (Instituto Técnico Forense, 2009).

The Sudden Unexpected Death of an Infant Program, led by the Ministry of Public Health and the Judiciary constitutes a peculiar situation in the forensic field in Uruguay. With the purpose of improving diagnosis of children's sudden death, Act N° 18,537 of 2009, regulated by Decree 07/010, provides that autopsies on children under one year old who died of apparently natural causes are to be performed jointly by the forensic doctor on duty and a doctor who is specialized in anatomic pathology, at the country's reference Pediatrics Hospital Morgue. Also, a Sudden Death of an Infant Committee was created to supervise these autopsies, to prepare protocols for actions, to design and suggest preventive measures and to prepare an annual report on deaths and their causes. The regulation of the law established a gradual application process, starting at the capital city and nearby areas.

29.4.1.2 The Chemical and Toxicology Laboratory

The Chemical and Toxicology Laboratory Department is an administrative structure that is independent from the Forensic Medicine Department, although it is closely related to it both technically and geographically, since it is located in the same building of the judicial morgue of Montevideo. In spite of it being in the capital city, it receives samples from around the country.

Its technical staff is made up of professionals with a pharmaceutical chemist's profile: a Director (chemist), four forensic chemists and four assistant chemists (advanced students of chemistry and graduates in clinical laboratory).

This laboratory has been a pioneer in the region ever since 1995, when it started implementing a systematic toxicology analysis for the purpose of searching for toxicologically interesting substances in general. To that end it initially used thin layer chromatography (TLC) and gas chromatography with a nitrogen–phosphorus detector (GC-NPD). Later on, other techniques such as high-performance liquid chromatography (HPLC-UV) and the mass spectometry detector (GC-MSD) were also adopted.

Today, the laboratory has the following analytical equipment: three gas chromatographs with a nitrogen–phosphorus detector and an electron capture detector (GC-NPD/ECD), a gas chromatograph with a flame ionization detector (GC-FID) coupled with a head space autosampler, a gas chromatograph detector with an ion trap mass spectrometer (GC-MSD) and a liquid chromatograph with a diode arrangement detector (HPLC-DAD). In addition to this, a liquid chromatograph with a mass spectrometry detector has been recently added to this equipment.

The quality control of the methods is carried out by means of internally adapted and controlled methodologies, the results being validated by two different analytical methods. The interpretation of results is done according to the international bibliography of reference (Instituto Técnico Forense, 2009).

The work done in the Chemical and Toxicology Laboratory is divided into four main headings: thanatological cases, studies of people who are alive, analysis and custody of confiscated drugs and other expert examinations.

The thanatological cases correspond to samples obtained from corpses when the forensic doctor requests a certain substance to be determined. There is a protocol

Table 29.2 Biological sample to be sent to the Chemical and Toxicology Laboratory, depending on the suspected toxic substance

Suspected toxic	Biological sample required
Toxicology screening	Blood, gastric contents, liver, urine: > 10 ml
Ethyl alcohol	Blood: > 10 ml; humor vitreous: > 2 ml
Drug abuse	Blood, urine: > 10 ml
Psychotropic drugs	Blood, gastric contents, liver, urine: > 10 ml
Pesticides	Blood, gastric contents, urine: > 10 ml
Carbon monoxide	Blood: > 10 ml
Other toxic	Call the Lab

established by the laboratory stating how to take, preserve and send samples by forensic doctors. Table 29.2 presents the sample and the number needed for the most frequently requested toxic substances. The alcohol level of the blood, general toxicological screening, psychiatric drugs, abuse drugs, carboxyhemoglobin and pesticides are the most often requested analyses. Similarly, other substances such as cyanide, abortifacients, metal and organic solvents such as arsenic, among others, are requested to be determined.

Examinations while a person is alive aim to determine the alcohol level of the blood. Of the 1800 alcohol analyses done every year in the laboratory, 50% relate to people who are alive.

A significant amount of the work done in the laboratory has to do with the analysis and custody of illegal drugs confiscated by the judiciary. Since 1998 and according to the provisions under Act N° 17,016, confiscated substances are sent to the Forensic Technical Institute in order to be analysed and subsequently destroyed upon the decision by the relevant authorities.

When Law N° 17,016 was passed, the workload at the laboratory was multiplied by six and also analyses of confiscated drugs rose from 14% in 1999 to 54% in 2012.

Last, several different expert examinations are grouped under the "other examinations" heading and include the following: request for technical reports on technical products, adulterated products, illegal sale of medicines, domestic and farm animal deaths, products that are not registered in the country, as well as

Table 29.3 Technical human resources in the Criminology Department of the Forensic Technical Institute

Position	Number
Director (Psychiatrist)	1
Psychiatrists for the capital city	8
Pediatric Psychiatrists for the capital city	8
Psychiatrist for Domestic Violence Courts in the capital city	8
Psychiatrists for the provinces	15
Deputy-Director of the Psychology Department	1
Psychologists for Adolescent Courts in the capital city	2
Psychologists for Domestic Violence Courts in the capital city	2
Social Workers for the capital city	3
Forensic Clinic Nurses	1

extension and replication of reports and assessment of several cases involving chemical substances, drug abuse and technical opinions on analytical determinations done by other laboratories (Mañay, 2005).

29.4.1.3 Criminology Medical Department

The Criminology Medical Department directly reports to the authorities of the Forensic Technical Institute and its technical staff is made up of psychiatrists, psychologists and social workers (see Table 29.3). As with other departments, it is highly concentrated in the capital city. Examinations carried out by this department may involve a technical member of the staff or a group of experts, which in most cases is a multidisciplinary committee.

In terms of psychiatric examinations, most are ordered by criminal judges and may assess the alleged criminal, the victim or a witness. The purpose of an examination performed to assess the criminal is to enable experts to inform the relevant judges about the psychiatric condition of the individual, in order to determine whether the defendant is chargeable or not. In other cases, this kind of examination focuses on the defendant's personality and aims to determine how dangerous they may be. These expert examinations are often accompanied by the Forensic Psychological Report, issued after a number of interviews and several tests (Instituto Técnico Forense, 2009).

For Family Law, psychiatric and psychological reports are requested to solve several conflicts. In this respect

it is worth mentioning that in Uruguay there are Family Courts specialized in domestic violence that include multidisciplinary technical teams who perform the requested expert examination. In 2010, a total of 15,006 cases of domestic violence were reported, 6,003 of which took place Montevideo.

Assessment of defendants less than 15 years of age is done by Pediatrics Psychiatrists, without prejudice to the participation of psychologists, as applicable. Also, a few reports are prepared for civil or labor cases, the object of which is to determine and assess psychological harm.

In particular, in adolescent and family law, a social examination is often requested by social workers.

29.4.1.4 Identification Department

The Identification Department is responsible for the National Registry of Criminal Records. The department does not participate in criminal investigation, although it plays an important role by informing the courts about the criminal record of the people accused of a crime, which results in a mitigating or aggravating factor in the sentencing phase, as applicable.

The history of this department begins earlier than the creation of the Forensic Technical Institute. Originally, it started being an "Anthropometric Identification and Criminal Anthropology Office" (1896) and later turned into an "Identification and Medico-Legal Studies Office" (1907). The Alphonse Bertillon (1853—1914) anthropometric system, extended in those days, was used throughout the initial phase. In 1927 the office became a registry of the prosecuted and the Dactiloscopy File was created, following the system created by Juan Vaucetich (1858–1925).

Today, the National Registry of Criminal Records uses the SiCo computer system that allows for the database to be updated, criminal record spreadsheets to be issued, the interface with all the courts in the country through a modem enables dactylograms and photographs to be sent, as well as prosecution statistics to be prepared and different variables to be combined.

The number of prosecutions ranged between 10,000 and 112,000 a year in the last decade (Instituto Técnico Forense, 2009).

29.4.2 Police Scientists (DNPT)

In Uruguay, the work done by police scientists is controlled by the National Bureau of the Technical Police, the institution responsible for criminal investigation that involves criminology. While forensic doctors are responsible for assessing injured people and the victim's corpses in violent or apparently criminal events, the Technical Police is responsible for examining the evidence in the crime scene and processing them in the laboratory. Within the Uruguayan system, the police serve as an auxiliary to justice, and it is the criminal judges who lead the investigation.

The National Bureau of Technical Police comprises a number of departments that are specialized in different disciplines and activities involving examinations, as recently restructured. They are organized under the following divisions: Criminology Department and Criminal Identification Department. All in all, 190 experts work in this body, including administrative staff and assistant experts (De Los Santos, 2000).

29.4.2.1 Criminalist Department

This Department includes the following divisions and offices, the objectives of which are outlined below.

Examinations Inspection, Photography and Planimetrics Units

The Examinations Inspection Department reports to the Crime Scene Investigation Department. It carries out its duty through teams of experts who perform the photographic and planimetric survey of the site, apart from other experts as the case requires (e.g. ballistics, accidentology, etc.).

The experts aim to secure the scene, to document it and to collect the necessary evidence for the investigation, after packing and labeling each item. This task includes looking for subevidence or signs and latent prints, with the aid of the appropriate light, metal detection devices and the collection of prints with cast or silicone molds.

As previously pointed out, the photographers in the experts team of the Crime Scene Investigation Department record the findings by means of pictures or videos. Since 2000 the digital technology caused the gradual introduction of different software for the treatment of images.

The Planimetrics Unit is responsible for preparing the sketches at the crime scene, which are later processed by computers to obtain plans to a scale. Also, the experts in this division compose "spoken portraits" or "facial identification" based on information provided by witnesses.

The data provided by witnesses are processed with a software and result in an electronic portrait (Grupo Iberoamericano de Trabajo en la Escena del Crimen, 2010).

Ballistics Unit

The Ballistics Unit is responsible for examining the firearms, as well as ammunition, projectiles and cartridges, in order to determine whether a certain projectile was fired by a certain person. In the last 20 years the Ballistic Unit has examined 50,000 firearms confiscated by the police, the vast majority of which were small arms of civilian use, 22 calibers being the most common ones (Rodríguez, 2009).

For external ballistics, experts study the trajectory of the projectile and its effects. The department has a ballistics comparison microscope that enables the comparison between cartridges and projectiles in sample shots and dubious material. The equipment includes a video camera that is connected to a computer to digitalize images and incorporate them into the examination report.

Additionally, the unit houses a 4,500 liter recovery tank to shoot the projectiles into the water, slowing them down and preserving the marks in the barrel bore. This enables the examination and testing of witness projectiles with no accidental deformation to perform comparisons. A proving ground is also used to test firearms (Figure 29.1).

Chemical and Biological Laboratories

The Biological Laboratory focuses on the identification of spots and evidence, cadaveric specimens and filiation in criminal cases, through molecular genetics techniques, in particular polymorphic DNA typification. The material received at the Biological Laboratory is processed according to a protocol to determine whether it is a biological substance by means of gradually increasing specificity (probability, certainty and species). Subsequently it is amplified and then compared to a conclusive sample collected by a buccal swab and preserved in an FTA card. Mitochondrial DNA analyses are also done in this laboratory when biological samples are too small.

In 2003, the Biological Laboratory completed 800 reports corresponding to DNA analysis, most of which corresponded to criminal events in Montevideo (59% of all analysis performed). The most frequent crimes whose investigation required the support of the Biological Laboratory were the following: homicides (23%), crimes

Figure 29.1 Ballistics Unit of Police Scientists (DNPT) is responsible for examining the firearms, as well as ammunitions, projectiles and cartridges (Courtesy of Ballistics Unit of DNPT).

against property (theft and burglary) (22%) and rapes (16%).

Simultaneously, the Chemical Laboratory is responsible for the analysis of toxic substances requiring criminal investigation, usually abuse drugs or several inorganic toxics (such as arsenic, cyanide and chromium), or organic toxics (such as pesticides, organochlorines and organophosphates) (Linder, 2008).

Last, the laboratory collaborates in traffic accident investigations, comparing glass fragments, earth, fibers and paint and other signs left in the other vehicle, the pavement, garments or the victim's body. In terms of dactyloscopic identification, it examines latent prints.

Road Accidentology Unit

This unit has been operative since 2000 and is responsible for accidentology examinations, mainly focusing on traffic accidents, as requested by courts around the country.

This kind of expert investigation implies a complete examination of the vehicles that took part in the event, including the brake system, the condition of tires, the light system, the horns, the windshield wipers, the mirrors, the safety belts and load in the vehicle. It is also essential to survey the site, as well as to collect fingerprints and signs both in the inner and outer surfaces of the vehicles. Likewise the report includes a reference to the weather, the lighting conditions, the road, traffic signs and elements that, in spite of not belonging to the scene, could have had an impact on the accident, such as skid marks and speed calculations, among others.

The accident criminology examination involves on-site work, the subsequent study of vehicles in a sheltered area and eventually the participation in the reconstruction of the event ordered by the judge.

Forensic ICT Unit

This unit became part of the National Bureau of Technical Police in 2005. It provides counseling to the judiciary and any other public entity needing assistance in terms of hardware, software, operative systems and the possibility of committing crimes with such equipments, as well as the participation of certain equipment in the violation of the law, within a local network or the Internet.

The Forensic ICT Unit participates in cases of traditional crimes committed with the computing equipment (as in the case of document forgery, crime against property through the Internet, child pornography and other sex crimes) (Royes, 2008).

Documentology, Graphoscopy, Currency and Trademarks Unit

This Unit is responsible for a number of tasks such as the examination of local and foreign currency, the study of signatures and several documents (passports, ID cards, checks, credit cards) or the prints left by trademarks and labels. The reports issued by this Unit are used in criminal and administrative investigations by public entities.

To that end, it houses the necessary equipment and devices such as a video spectral comparator (VSC) featured with ultraviolet, infrared and blue illumination, capable of identifying physical or chemical alterations in the documents. It is also equipped with a microscope magnifying glass and a documentoscopy, which are used to detect alterations and forgery of currency and other documents.

29.4.2.2 Criminal Identification Department

The Criminal Identification Department comprises two divisions: the Criminal Investigation ICT and the National Registry of Genetic Prints.

Criminal Indentification ICT

This division is responsible for identification through fingerprints. In the past, this task was under the scope of the Dactyloscopy Decadactlilar Department, where the fingerprints of all prosecuted and charged people in the country were classified and filed, as well as those belonging to foreigners, together with the information provided by Interpol. The registry included around 300,000 files with the prints of the ten fingers of the hands of the people with criminal records, as well as congenital or acquired abnormalities in their hands.

Today, the manual search and identification has been substituted by a computer automatized search, assisted by the AFIS (Automated Fingerprint Identification System). In fact, in 2013, 300 cases were clarified thanks to this identification system.

Genetic Prints National Registry

Act N° 18,849 of 2011 provided for the creation of this registry, which reports to the National Bureau of Technical Police with the following objectives: (1) to contribute to the clarification of events under criminal investigation, in particular those in connection with the differentiation of responsible individuals, based on the identification of the noncodifying genetic profile of the DNA component; (2) to identify and contribute to finding people who are lost, missing or dead; (3) to assist in the resolution of court disputes or in connection with the identity of actors or alleged actors in criminal events.

The law guarantees the confidentiality of information and states that the registry is not authorized to keep DNA samples (codifiable or noncodifiable). It further establishes that the department must dispose of all genetic material. Information used for identification purposes may only be requested by competent judges.

As provided by law, the National Registry of Genetic Prints shall comprise the following three divisions:

a. Latents Genetic File Division: this division deals with unidentified material obtained from signs and evidence collected in the crime scene.

b. Criminal Identification Genetic File Division: the genetic profiles of the prosecuted by the competent authorities are systematically filed in this division under a codes system (anonymously).

c. Genetic File Division: this contains the identification of staff belonging to the Ministry of the Interior and the Ministry of Defense.

The National Registry of Genetic Prints uses the CODIS (Combined DNA Index System) developed by the FBI.

29.4.3 University services

The University of the Republic has taken an active part in the origin and development of Forensic Sciences in Uruguay, not only in the training of human resources, but also in developing expert examination.

29.4.3.1 Legal Medicine Department

The School of Medicine of the University of the Republic receives an average of 1,000 cases a year, being requested to issue an examination statement for each one of them. Judges in the various fields of law and different public institutions, in particular the health authorities, refer these cases to the University, seeking expert support. As for casuistics, alleged medical malpractice cases lead the requests for examination, followed by traffic accidents.

Within this universe, a large amount of the work corresponds to the facilities offered by the Legal Medicine Department. In medical malpractice cases, a Medical Committee made up of doctors from the different fields of medicine (legal medicine and the relevant specialization) issues the examination report, and in other cases, assessment of body harm caused by traffic or work accidents – among other circumstances – is made.

Without prejudice of the work done by professionals at the Forensic Technical Institute of the judiciary, Criminal Law refers to the Legal Medicine Department seeking judges' technical counseling to solve complex cases, such as serial crimes (as in the case of the " nurse murderers") or cases with a historical interest (the Leandro Gomez case).

The Legal Medicine Department has participated in the investigation of several cases of violation of human rights during the civilian–military dictatorship (1973–1985) at the request of public prosecutors, judges or plaintiffs. Many of the cases were clarified and the cause of death of political prisoners was found through the "historical autopsy" method, described in a collaborative study of the University of the Republic (Uruguay) and the University of Valencia (Spain) (Rodríguez Almada and Verdú Pascual, 2003). In this way, the death of three political prisoners that had occurred within the context of torture forty years before was clarified (the Nibia Sabalsagary, Aldo Perrini and Iván Morales cases). In another very notorious case of an unusual political homicide with a poisoned bottle of wine, the historical autopsy failed to provide information on the evident cause of death, although it enabled two lines of investigation to clarify the case to be suggested (the Cecilia Fontana case).

Similarly, the Legal Medicine Department was called to be part of a Medical Committee to clarify the case of the first political murder by the civilian–military dictatorship (the Ramón Peré case). In this case, the assessment by experts at the Forensic Technical Institute and that performed by two experts hired by the defense for the accused militaries were contradictory.

The Medical Committee, through the exhumation of the victim's skeletal remains, managed to determine the circumstances of death (a shot in the back, the bullet entering the body through a vertebrae), which implied the resolution of the case. Also, at the request of the Commission for Peace, an experimental study was conducted on the cremation of the skeletal remains.

The Legal Medicine Department also collaborates with other public agencies in expert examinations in connection with human rights. In that sense, it provides counseling to the National Institute of Human Rights and the Ombudsman, in particular to assess the situation of adolescents who violated the law and are deprived of liberty. It also works with the Ministry of Education and Culture deciding on the harm caused to former political prisoners during the dictatorship by the state terrorism regime, with the purpose of compensating them, as per the provisions given in Act N° 18,596.

A further contribution of the Legal Medicine Department occurs within the framework of medicolegal consultations arising from the public sector health system, both in primary healthcare centers and in reference hospitals.

In Uruguay, a great deal of scientific investigation is conducted by the University of the Republic, and the Forensic Sciences is no exception. Although the Forensic Sciences are not the first priority for the funding agencies, a few lines of investigation have been defined. The investigation on the sudden unexpected death of infants carried out for over ten years constitutes an example (Rodríguez Almada et al., 1998, 1999, 2007, 2009; Mederos et al., 1998).

29.4.3.2 Donation and Transplant National Institute (INDT)

The Cells, Organs and Tissues Donation and Transplant National Institute is a combined public service (Ministry of Public Health and University of the Republic), which, given the specific nature of its activity, houses a qualified Immunogenetics and Histocompatibility Laboratory to perform filiation studies. Since 2011, and thanks to an agreement with the National Institute of Donation and Transplant and the Legal Medicine Department, the Genetic Forensic Unit was created in the facility of the Immunogenetic Laboratory (Figure 29.2).

The specific unit is divided into pre-PCR, PCR and post-PCR and is controlled by a video surveillance system. The work has been focused on several topics:

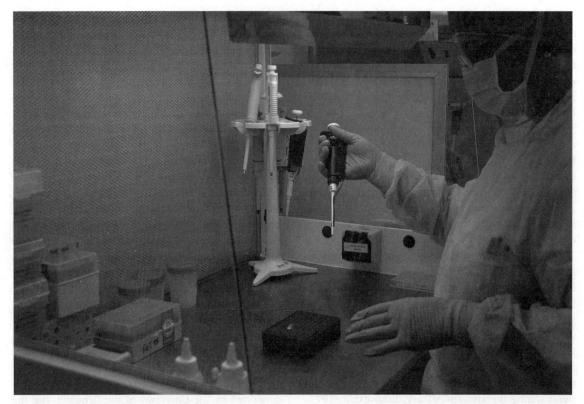

Figure 29.2 Since 2011, and thanks to an agreement with the National Institute of Donation and Transplant and the Legal Medicine Department, the Genetic Forensic Unit was created. *Source:* Courtesy of National Institute of Donation and Transplant (INDT). Creative Commons – By Non-commercial Share Alike.

a. Paternity and kinship cases with blood samples. The National Institute of Donation and Transplant Laboratory has resolved more than 9000 paternity cases (more than 27,000 persons were tested). The number of blood samples studied in the last five years are the following: 2013 – 1263 cases, 2012 – 899 cases, 2011 – 906 cases, 2012 – 1107 cases, 2009 – 901 cases.

b. Paternity and kinship cases, with skeletal remains – 15 cases.

c. Forensic cases related to identification – 14 cases.

d. Genetic Samples Bank to solve cases of the missing – samples from 213 families.

The Unit is formed by staff who are specialized in clinical laboratory procedures and also have specific training in forensic sciences. Table 29.4 presents the laboratory equipment and software available. The Laboratory periodically participates in quality control

processes of the SLAGF (Sociedad Latinoamericana de Genetica Forense – Latin American Society of Forensic Genetics) and ISFG-GE (Grupo Español y Portugués de la Sociedad Internacional de Genética Forense – Spanish and Portuguese Group of the International Society of Forensic Genetics).

29.4.3.3 Other university services

According to the Uruguayan legislation, courts may request counseling from the different public agencies, and thus the different services belonging to the University of the Republic are called on to provide information on technical issues and are asked to prepare expert reports.

With the purpose of this outline to be complete, the work done by the School of Humanities and Educational Sciences is worth mentioning, whose work supported the investigation of the crimes committed under

Table 29.4 Genetic Forensic Unit: Laboratory Equipment and software available

Sequencer and Fragment Genetic Analyzer – ABI 3130 XL, 4
    capillaries
Real-Time Thermal Cycler – 7500 Real Time PCR System
Automatic Thermal Cyclers – 2 units Gene Amp 2700, 1 unit
    Master Cycler Nexus Gradient Eppendorf, 1 unit Genius, and
    1 unit Perkin Elmer 2400
Genetic Data Analysis software – Gene Mapper 3.2 software
An integrated software package for DNA identification – DNA
    view and Pater (Charles Brenner)
Spectrophotometer for nucleic acid – Nanodrop 1000
Automated equipment for DNA extraction – 6100 Nucleic Acid
    Prep Station
Laminar flow chambers
Other equipment: Freezer – 80–20 °C, refrigerators,
    microcentrifugals, vortex, scales, thermal baths, magnetic
    stirrers, reverse osmosis equipment, phmeters, microwave
    oven, electroforesis equipment, transilluminator, automatic
    pipettes and other accessories for molecular biology
    techniques

the state terrorist regime. In fact, in 2005 the Presidency of the Republic and the University of the Republic entered an agreement to investigate the violations of human rights in the recent past and to learn about the final destination of the missing prisoners. Within this agreement, the University of the Republic was responsible for contributing the work teams needed to cover the objectives set. In this way, two work teams, a historical and an anthropological one were formed at the School of Humanities and Educational Sciences.

The historical compilation work by Rico and collaborators (Rico, 2008) constitutes a milestone in the investigation of these topics, in particular in connection with the final destination of the victims who were forced to disappear and political murders. The same historical investigators had conducted a compilation work that resulted in an official reports on the missing prisoners (Presidencia de la República, 2007).

The archaeological group focused on finding the burial sites (López Mazz, 2006). Until now, there are records of 175 Uruguayan people missing, who disappeared in Uruguay. So far, the archaeological search managed to find the remains of four of them: Fernando Miranda (2006), Ubagesner Chávez Sosa (2009), Julio Castro (2011) and Ricardo Blanco (2012). Their identification was confirmed by DNA tests done

in national and Argentine laboratories. The reports on the causes and circumstances of death were prepared by forensic doctors appointed to work on the cases.

29.5 Future directions: reflections on the challenges of the forensic sciences in Uruguay

This outline shows that forensic science in Uruguay lacks both human and material resources and that these are concentrated in the capital city. However, the main challenge lies in the training and education of staff rather than in acquiring special equipment. The experience in Uruguay proved that when sophisticated technology is handled by staff who are not sufficiently trained there may be mistakes in interpretation. Likewise, a large majority of cases may be adequately solved with basic equipment, provided there are well informed and trained forensic professionals. Therefore, it is understood that a great goal in Forensic Sciences in Uruguay is for all forensic doctors in the country to be specialists in legal medicine, and for other professionals to receive specific training in forensic methodology.

Without underestimating the negative effect of bureaucratic and cultural obstacles, or the impact of institutional inertia, countries like Uruguay have a limited budget. In fact, the budgets of the judiciary, the Technical Police and university services are defined every five years, once they are approved by the two chambers in the Congress. Forensic science is not seen as a priority by the public powers.

A further weakness that has already been addressed and is gradually improving is the need for an appropriate and well articulated national plan for disaster management. The forensic area of disaster and the management of corpses are still under development in spite of there being a National Emergency System in the country in order to plan and organize a response to disasters and perform drills. In 2012 the Forensic Technical Institute created a work team to make progress on protocols for action, which are to be articulated with the National Bureau of Technical Police. In addition to this, ever since it was created, the Legal Medicine Department of the School of Medicine at the University of the Republic is a member of the Iberoamerican Network of Legal Medicine and Forensic Science Institutions,

Figure 29.3 The Legal Medicine Department of the School of Medicine at the University of the Republic is a member of the Spanish and Iberoamerican American Network of Legal Medicine and Forensic Science Institutions. The photograph shows a simulacrum of an identification in a mass disaster in Bogotá, Colombia, in 2009. *Source:* Courtesy of Hugo Rodriguez Almada.

which, along with the Red Cross aims to encourage the articulation and cooperation in the region in the event of mass disasters (Figure 29.3).

Acknowledgments

José Azambuya (DNPT), Milka Bengochea (INDT), Jorge Echeverry (DNPT), Williams García Lafont (DNPT), Mónica Etcheverry (ITF), Grisel Fernández (DNPT), Noriko Hikichi (ITF), Nelly Mañay (ITF), Domingo Perona (ITF) and Patricia Porley (ITF).

References

Camejo, B. (2008) Escuela de Criminalística. *CPC* 1: 19–21.

De Los Santos, R. (2000) *Manual de Criminalística de campo.* Dirección Nacional de Policía Técnica, Montevideo.

Grupo Iberoamericano de Trabajo en la Escena del Crimen (GITEC) (2010) *Manual de buenas prácticas en la escena del crimen.* Viewed 7 January 2014. http://www.aicef.net/index. php/manuales-de-buenas-practicas.

Instituto Técnico Forense (2009) *Manual de Procedimientos,* Poder Judicial, Montevideo.

Linder, M. (2008) Laboratorio Químico. *CPC* 1: 22–25.

López Mazz, J. (2007) Informe Final 2005–2006. Investigaciónes arquelógicas sobre detenidos-desaparecidos. In: *Presidencia de la República: Investigación Histórica sobre Detenidos Desaparecidos,* Vol. V, En cumplimiento del artículo 4° de la Ley N° 15.848. IMPO, Montevideo.

Mañay, N. (2005) Casuística del Laboratorio de Toxicología Forense de Uruguay. In: *1er. Congreso Regional Sudamericano,* The Internantional Association of Forensic Toxicolgist, Buenos Aires-La Plata, Argentina.

Martínez Pueta, M. (1917) Sobre organización médico forense en Uruguay. In: *I Congreso Médico Nacional,* Vol. 4, Montevideo, pp. 180–201.

Mederos, D., Rodríguez Almada, H., Díaz, J.L., Ferrari, A. (1998) Peritajes judiciales en menores de un año. *Review of Medicine in Uruguay* 14: 28–33.

Presidencia de la República (2007) *Investigación Histórica sobre Detenidos Desaparecidos*, En cumplimiento del artículo 4° de la Ley N° 15.848, IMPO, Montevideo.

Rico, A. (2008) *Investigación Histórica sobre Dictadura y Terrorismo de Estado en Uruguay (1973–1985)*, 3 volumes, UDELAR, Montevideo.

Riveiro, G., Roó, R. (2007) Análisis médico-legal del primer caso de responsabilidad médica en Uruguay. *Review of Medicine in Uruguay* 23: 179–186.

Rodríguez, J. (2009) Balística. *CPC* 2: 28–30.

Rodríguez Almada, H., Verdú Pascual, F. (2003) La autopsia histórica: presentación del método y su aplicación al estudio de un hecho violento ocurrido en Uruguay en el año 1972. *Review of Medicine in Uruguay* 19: 126–139.

Rodríguez Almada, H., Mederos, M., Díaz, J.L., Ferrari, A. (1998) Muerte en domicilio en el período posneonatal: Montevideo 1996. *Review of Medicine in Uruguay* 14: 147–153.

Rodríguez Almada, H., Mederos, D., Echenique, M., Vilas, R., Ferrari, A. (1999) Muerte posneonatal en domicilio y accesibilidad a los servicios de salud. Las Piedras, La Paz, Progreso; 1/7/96-30/6/98. *Review of Medicine in Uruguay* 15: 221–229.

Rodríguez Almada, H., Ferrari, A., Arzuaga, L., Echenique, M., Mederos, D. (2007) La muerte posneonatal en domicilio diez años después. *Review of Medicine in Uruguay* 23: 242–250.

Rodríguez Almada, H., Ciríacos, C., Arzuaga, L., Ferrari, A. (2009) Muerte en domicilio versus muerte en un centro asistencial: estudio comparativo. Montevideo, 2006. *Review of Medicine in Uruguay* 23: 242–250.

Royes, G. (2008) Laboratorio informático. Abusos sexuales infantiles. *CPC* 1: 5–11.

Soiza Larrosa, A. (1985) Historia de la Medicina Legal y los peritajes médico-forenses en el Uruguay (1724-1883). In: *Psiquatría Forense*, Eds. H. Puppo Touriz, D. Murguía and D. Puppo Bosch, Librería Médica Editorial, Montevideo, pp. 1–46.

Soiza Larrosa, A. (1992) Historia de la Cátedra de Medicina Legal de la Facultad de Medicina de Montevideo. *Sesiones Sociedad Uruguaya de Historia de la Medicina* IX–X: 250.

Soiza Larrosa, A. (2002) Médicos al servicio de la verdad jurídica. Historia de los médicos de Policía y los médicos forenses en el Uruguay (1826–1918). *Rev. Uruguaya de Derecho Penal,* Special Issue: 633–677.

Soiza Larrosa, A. (2005) *Historia de la Cátedra de Medicina Legal Historia de la Cátedra de Medicina Legal de la Facultad de Medicina de Montevideo. 1877–1974.* Departamento de Medicina Legal. Viewed 18 December 2013, http://www.medicinalegal.edu.uy/depto/dml-hist.pdf.

CHAPTER 30

Conclusions: global common themes and variations

Douglas H. Ubelaker

Department of Anthropology, National Museum of Natural History, Smithsonian Institution, Washington, DC, USA

This volume provides perspective on the Global Practice of Forensic Science from a sample of 28 countries located within the continental areas of Africa, the Americas, Asia, Australia and Europe. I express my gratitude to the 63 authors working in these countries who took time from their busy schedules to synthesize key information related to the practice of the forensic sciences in their geographic areas. Although they all have demanding work schedules and responsibilities and are well respected and productive scholars, they found the time to meet the deadlines required to produce this volume. As a result of their professional, enthusiastic response and effort, key information is now available on the global practice of forensic science.

Of course, it was not possible to assemble in one book perspectives from all countries of the world. The selection provided here was designed to sample the practice of forensic science from different continental areas and from a variety of countries with distinct histories and forensic academic traditions. In each case, however, authors were selected who have demonstrated remarkable professional productivity and awareness of the breadth of forensic activity in their countries. The chapters represent a case in point of their scholarly abilities and perspective.

As indicated in the introduction, authors were provided with suggested guidelines on the structuring of their chapters and topics to consider for inclusion. Some authors closely followed these suggestions while others chose alternative organization. Likewise authors varied in the extent to which they attempted to provide overviews of all areas of the forensic sciences versus those areas closest to their own expertise. The collective

result of their efforts, however, is a remarkable assemblage of information related to the theme of the volume. Their work reveals patterns that are shared globally in both history and current practice. The chapters also indicate considerable variation in the structure, integration, processes of training and certification and funding issues.

30.1 History

30.1.1 Deep roots

Scholars in some countries detect very deep roots to the practice of forensic science. In Egypt, forensic expertise is identified in Imhotep (2667–2648 BC) who served as physician to the Pharaoh Zoser. References to forensic science can be found in ancient texts in India and in the Middle Ages in Switzerland. The first reference to medicolegal issues in Spain has been detected at 642 AD. In Korea, a text on forensic medicine was published in 1438 through annotation of an even earlier Chinese document. The first autopsies were recorded in Mexico in 1576, Uruguay in 1760 and Turkey in 1768.

30.1.2 Political history

It can be argued that forensic development in all countries relates to their particular political history and related global influences. Political history plays an especially prominent role in the advancement of forensic science in Estonia, Hong Kong, South Africa, Turkey and Singapore. Both Hong Kong and Singapore represent former British colonies, with the latter gaining independence in 1965. As such, both countries reveal strong linkages with the United Kingdom in training

The Global Practice of Forensic Science, First Edition. Edited by Douglas H. Ubelaker.

© 2015 John Wiley & Sons, Ltd. Published 2015 by John Wiley & Sons, Ltd.

and forensic practice. South African history includes Dutch colonization but also with strong English influences. Turkey's geopolitical global positioning allowed for French, German and recent United States influence. Until 1944, Estonia was part of the Soviet Union and relied heavily on Soviet training and forensic practice organization.

30.1.3 Academic linkages

Many of the scholars in this volume trace the origins of forensic science in their countries to academic developments, especially focused university instruction. As early as 1532, Germany established a legal code calling for consultation of specialist doctors with specific university training. In Hungary, creation of the first faculty of forensic medicine extends back to 1793. In the early 19th century, forensic-related university coursework and faculties were established in Argentina, Chile, Denmark, Egypt and Germany. Also in the 19th century, Japan, Mexico, and Uruguay established university-based forensic programs.

Many of the chapters cite scholarly publication as an early stimulus for the development of forensic science (e.g., the Royas 1936 publication on Legal Medicine in Argentina). Also the linkage between academia and the practice of forensic science has been a significant factor throughout the global development of the discipline. In Australia, such linkage has been a specific target of Royal Commission decisions. In the United States, it has been a key factor in recent discussions related to the critical report of the National Research Council.

30.1.4 Case influences

Throughout the global history of forensic science, individual cases, especially controversial, high profile cases have played significant roles in stimulating progress. To a large extent successful case applications have proven to be a powerful stimulus for advancement in demonstrating how science applications can contribute in positive ways.

Advancement has also been stimulated by problems in forensic science that have emerged and been recognized through case applications. In many countries, efforts to fix recognized problems in forensic science have led to positive advances. In Australia, examples of the Gun Ally Murder in 1921, the Edward Splatt case in 1978 and the Chamberlin convictions in 1980 all revealed shortcomings in forensic science that stimulated corrections in

the form of major advances. In Chile, forensic problems related to the 1909 German Legation developments and the Patio 29 analyses subsequent to the 1973 military coup all stimulated considerable reform in forensic procedure and training. Also noteworthy in this regard is the 1727 fatal shooting case in Denmark and case development discussed in the Hong Kong chapter. Much of the current discussion in the United States results from perceived shortcomings of some areas of forensic science related to specific case applications.

30.1.5 Facility development

Nearly all of the country chapters relate the historical development of forensic science to the establishment of specific facilities. Clearly, progress and development of global forensic science is historically linked to the establishment of organizational structure, laboratories and related central facilities. The following is a listing of the chronological development of key institutions/facilities in different countries. The dates reflect the year of establishment.

1827 Police Doctors, Uruguay
1849 Chemical Examiner's Laboratory, Madras, India
1886 National Institute of Toxicology and Forensic Sciences, Spain
1896 Judicial Morgue, Argentina
1902 Scientific Section of the Police, Italy
1903 Creation of the Forensic Service, Mexico
1904 Toxicology Laboratory, Japan
1908 Anthropometric Office, Finland
1909 Forensic Medical Institute, Chile
1913 Forensic Medicine and Sciences Institute, Turkey
1913 Forensic Laboratory, Montreal, Canada
1914 Central Bureau of Legal Medicine, Bogotá, Colombia
1921 Cabinet of Forensic Science, Estonia
1922 Police Technical Laboratory, Denmark
1923 Los Angeles Crime Laboratory, United States
1926 Crime Investigation Centre, Finland
1929 Chicago Crime Laboratory, United States
1945 National Forensic Laboratory, The Netherlands
1948 American Academy of Forensic Sciences, United States
1948 Building constructed to support forensic work in Bogotá, Colombia
1955 National Forensic Service established as an independent unit, Korea

1980 Department of Forensic Medicine, Dubai

1982 Building Construction for the Department of Forensic Medicine, Dubai

1991 National Institute of Forensic Science, Australia

1991 National Institute of Legal Medicine and Forensic Sciences, Colombia

2008 Forensic Science Institute, Estonia

The above list represents key historical developments related to structure expressed in the country chapters in this volume. Of course, each country has a long list of historical developments that influenced the development of forensic science. The formation of specific central forensic units and the physical structures to house them represent important global elements in the progress of forensic science.

The country chapters also reveal that while each country has its own particular forensic history, global connections are apparent throughout. These connections reflect geopolitics and general developments in forensic science, as well as personal contacts and relationships of individual forensic scientists.

30.2 Types of cases

In general, the country chapters reveal that the types of cases investigated relate closely to the individual forensic specialties. The major areas of case investigation are shared globally with a particular increase in demand for analyses related to DNA, controlled substances, toxicology and digital evidence.

Comparison of statistics by country is complicated by variation in reporting styles. Variation is noted, however, in information provided by some countries in the nature of autopsies and general forensic investigation of criminal activity. For example, Argentina reports that the major focus of autopsies is accidental (54%) followed by suicides (24%) and homicides (22%). Further north in Latin America, Colombia reports that of violent deaths, most (56%) are attributed to homicide, followed by traffic accidents (22%), accidental (10%) and suicide (7%), with access to firearms cited as a major contributing factor in the high rate of homicide. Nonfatal injuries in Colombia mostly resulted from interpersonal violence, followed by domestic violence, transportation incidents, sexual incidents and accidents. In contrast, Denmark statistics reveal that most autopsies focus on accidental deaths, followed by natural, suicide

and homicide, with rape investigation also a major initiative.

Australia reports that breaking and entering represents the primary focus of forensic case investigation, followed by motor vehicle theft, robbery, sexual assault, kidnapping/abduction, murder, attempted murder and manslaughter.

In Dubai, forensic clinical examinations most assessed individual injury, followed by sexual crimes, age assessment, various medical issues and criminal abortions. Most injuries involved interpersonal violence followed by domestic issues. The most common manner of death was natural followed by accidental, suicidal and homicide.

In Estonia forensic investigation most commonly involved toxicology followed by criminalistics, medical and psychiatric evaluations.

The Finland chapter relates primary forensic investigation into issues of drunken driving followed by drugs, fingerprint analysis, document examination and arson investigation.

Statistics from the United States reveal that crime laboratories mostly conducted DNA analysis, followed by the investigation of controlled substances and toxicology.

30.3 Structure

Organizational structure represents a key element in the practice of forensic science globally. Most countries represented in this volume trace important elements of their history in forensic science to the formation of organizational structure and the facilities to house them. Such organizations are needed to provide centralized equipment and qualified staff to meet the casework requirements in their areas. Variation in structure relates to the particular histories of forensic development in individual countries, as well as their relative size.

A common model, especially in larger countries, consists of large central facilities with regional branches where needed. Examples consist of the Chilean Forensic Medical Service, the Instituto Nacional de Medicina Legal y Ciencias Forenses in Colombia, the Department of Forensic Science and Criminology associated with the Dubai Police in Dubai, United Arab Emirates, the Estonian Forensic Science Institute, the Hong Kong

Government Laboratory and the Health Sciences Authority in Singapore. Such central units offer the equipment and expertise to address specialized forensic problems and regional applications as needed.

Somewhat more complex models consist of multiple central facilities divided along discipline lines. Such division is especially common between legal medicine practice and that involving application more closely allied with police activities. For example, in Argentina the activity of forensic doctors of the Judiciary are separate from specialists of the police and security units. In Denmark, pathology-related activity is centered at university institutes while other forensic work is associated with police units. Egypt features three government structures, the Egyptian Medicolegal Authority, the departments of Forensic Medicine and Toxicology and the General Administration for Criminal Evidence Investigations. In Finland, structures consist of the Central National Bureau of Investigation and the Forensic Medicine Unit of the National Institute for Health and Welfare (associated with university medical schools in five cities). Hungary forensic structure includes five types of institutions: the National Institute of Forensic Medicine, medical universities, a network of forensic science institutes, police criminal forensic medical services and a Board of Forensic Medicine Experts of the Health Scientific Council. Structures in India consist of the Central Forensic Science Laboratories in different regions and the departments of forensic medicine in the Ministry of Health and Family Welfare. Forensic science in Korea is centered in the National Forensic Service, the Prosecutor's Office, the military and the Coast Guard. The Netherlands has the National Forensic Institute with related activities in the Dutch National Police, universities and commercial forensic institutes. Switzerland lists five Institutes of Legal Medicine with units of forensic medicine, traffic medicine, toxicology, chemistry and genetics coupled with two Institutes of Forensic Science. Forensic science in Uruguay is centered in the Forensic Technical Institute of the Judiciary, National Bureau of Police Investigation and university-based academic services.

More decentralized forensic activity seems to prevail in most other countries represented in the volume. Distribution of forensic services in regions within the country is featured in Australia, Canada, France, Italy, Japan, Mexico, Spain and South Africa. In Turkey, laboratories are associated with the police and Gendarme forces and legal medicine is concentrated in the Forensic Medicine Council with its regional branches. The United States has the Federal Bureau of Investigation forensic laboratory and the forensic facilities of the Bureau of Alcohol, Tobacco, Firearms and Explosives, but most forensic work is distributed through state facilities supplemented with many private experts. German forensic science is associated with universities and public health organizations.

30.4 Integration of forensic science

Relatively few of the chapters directly addressed the issue of the integration of information in forensic casework. Presumably, integration is provided by the legal process, especially by the office of the prosecutor in most countries, as noted specifically in Japan. The Netherlands chapter also notes the key role of the prosecutor in integration of evidence, also citing the police. In Spain, integration is generally lacking until court proceedings. Turkey also notes the role of the prosecutor and adds that this structure creates a problem for the defense. The Australia chapter notes limited integration of forensic evidence prior to court proceedings, with the exception of some homicide cases in which conferences may be held to make decisions on needed analysis.

In Colombia, the various forensic functions are centralized in the National Institute of Legal Medicine and Forensic Science. However, even there, major responsibility for integration of reports and evidence within an individual case rests with the office of the prosecutor.

The most comprehensive approach to integration of diverse forensic analyses in report writing comes from Chile. The Chilean system uses a model integrated investigation report highlighted in both the human rights division and the special forensic identification units of the Forensic Medical Service. Analyses are independently conducted by specialists but then results are compared, discussed and integrated into a final report.

30.5 Recruitment/training

The extent and types of recruitment and training correlate closely with specific disciplines. For laboratory positions, most countries report a mix of in-house training and recruitment from local universities. In

Australia, a minimum requirement is the Bachelor of Science degree. In Columbia, education requirements are supplemented with a rigorous process of resume review and verification, interviews and testing. In Hong Kong, applicants must pass the civil service examination and meet language requirements in both Cantonese and Chinese. In The Netherlands, knowledge of the Dutch language and a certificate of good conduct supplement the hiring requirements.

In the fields of forensic pathology, forensic medicine, and odontology forensic training to supplement the standard degrees is required in most countries. For forensic medicine/pathology postdegree training in forensic applications is six months in Egypt, two years in Mexico, three years in Columbia and Uruguay, four years in Turkey and five years in Australia and Hungary. Medical school training in forensic medicine is required in France, Hungary and Switzerland.

Linkages with training and degree programs vary considerably both among disciplines and among countries. University training is most common in the fields of forensic medicine, odontology, anthropology, toxicology, DNA analysis and entomology. In other fields of forensic sciences training may also be provided by the hiring organization with recruitment from within existing personnel.

In most larger countries, programs in forensic science are reported within major universities. This is especially noted in Australia, Colombia, Germany, Hungary, Japan, Korea, The Netherlands, Spain, South Africa, Switzerland, Turkey and the United States.

The global trend seems to involve an increase in university-based graduate programs in forensic science. With the increase in these programs, forensic institutions rely more heavily on them for recruitment and training purposes. This university-based growth in forensic education reflects increasing awareness of the value and employment opportunities of forensic science as well as strong student interest in this area of science application.

30.6 Funding

Sufficient funding for forensic science represents a global issue. All countries represented in this volume face major challenges in securing adequate funds for personnel, equipment, structures, research, training and related areas of forensic science. Government funding of major units of forensic science is nearly universal; thus forensic budgets are in competition with other priorities. Core central budgets are supplemented with service fees in Colombia, Estonia, Germany, Hungary, Japan, The Netherlands and Singapore. Turkey reports significant income additions from insurance companies and private attorneys.

In some countries, specific events or developments have triggered funding largely designed to correct apparent deficiencies in forensic science. For example, Argentina reports that a 1992 terrorist attack resulting in 85 casualties brought to light problems in forensic science that stimulated funding increases.

The Patio 29 incident and related developments in Chile revealed a need for forensic science reform, especially in the identification process. Funds were subsequently appropriated to substantially modernize facilities, train personnel and institute other reforms.

Australia reports that budget concerns have led to outsourcing of some services. This practice represents a global concern as those in administrative control assume more of the business model in the practice of forensic science. Research is especially at risk with budget reductions and increased emphasis on a fee for service approach.

30.7 Political influences

Practitioners globally agree that forensic scientists apply their science to evidence and cases in an independent fashion. Generally, there is a lack of political influence in direct forensic analysis and interpretation. Forensic scientists are conscious of the need to do their work in an independent fashion and strive to limit bias factors. This point of view is articulated especially in the chapter from Hungary.

However, it is clear from the history sections of many chapters that the practice of forensic science today, especially relating to training and structure, reflects to a large extent geopolitical history. Even today, as noted in the chapter on the United States, politics and funding for forensic science are closely connected. The indirect influence of politics on the practice of forensic science relates to decisions on priorities of service and budget, as articulated in chapters on Japan and Turkey. In Australia and Chile, political decisions for funding were made to effect forensic reform and change in the aftermath of perceived problems. Since funding in most forensic units globally is channeled through budgets of governments, police units and universities, they are vulnerable to political influences affecting administration and governing.

The dynamic interplay of politics and forensic science perhaps can be viewed most clearly in Latin America, especially in the chapters from Argentina and Colombia. The Argentina chapter reports that since 1930 the country's democratic system has been replaced six times through military coups d'états. The period between 1976 and 1983 was especially challenging with apparent compromise of the independence of aspects of the legal system and also elements within the practice of forensic science. The Argentine chapter relates the sad account of the many citizens who experienced forced disappearance at that time and how the work of some forensic scientists likely was compromised as well. These events led to the formation of the Argentine Forensic Anthropology Team with a nongovernment, independent affiliation.

The Colombia chapter notes that in that country continuous armed conflict has been present for over 50 years. Such strife has involved the government in different ways over that period, providing a very challenging context for the practice of forensic science. Our Colombian colleagues relate how forensic science has attempted courageously to maintain independence throughout that period. The challenges have even involved direct security issues, especially for those working in remote areas.

30.8 Certification, accreditation, and quality control

Quality control represents a global concern in the practice of forensic science. All countries strive in their own ways to ensure that those handling and interpreting evidence are qualified to do so and the work is done in an adequate facility. However, structural approaches to these issues vary greatly within countries and within disciplines.

Australia reports certification procedures for those working in crime scene investigation, fingerprint identification and firearms. Certification includes examination followed by recertification procedures. Laboratory accreditation is in place with procedures following those outlined in ISO/IEC 17025.

Such procedures are not required in Canada, but accreditation is accomplished also by the ISO/IEC 17025 provided by the Standards Council of Canada and ASCLD/LAB.

In Hungary, all forensic experts need to be certified. All laboratories of DNA and toxicology are accredited.

Accreditation is noted to be in place in Germany, Turkey and The Netherlands but only for two laboratories in South Africa and only for laboratories of DNA and forensic medicine in Spain. Colombia reports that 17 laboratories are accredited in the country.

In Korea, accreditation is also based on the ISO 17025 standards.

The Singapore chapter relates that certification procedures are in place and laboratory accreditation is accomplished by ASCLAD/LAB.

Processes for certification and accreditation and related quality control measures are in place in Chile, Dubai and Estonia.

Mexico cites certification procedures for Legal and Forensic Medicine practitioners.

In the United States, most disciplines offer certification procedures and extensive efforts of laboratory accreditation have been made. Nevertheless concerns of quality control and bias factors persist. Discussions continue on structural and procedural mechanisms for advancement.

30.9 Technology

Along with trained personnel, technology represents a key measure of forensic progress in many countries. The Finland chapter notes that when its Anthropometric Office began in 1908 it contained only one expert whose "only tool was a light microscope." It is likely that this account could be repeated in many countries and serves to contrast the technology available in the early days with the forensic science of today. Many of the major historical advances in the forensic sciences are technological in nature. Accordingly, many of the country chapters mention key technological acquisitions in their accounts of historical progress.

Technology also represents an issue that shows considerable global variation and closely relates to the size and resources of particular countries and institutions within them. Technology is very much about expensive equipment. However, it also involves costly maintenance and the necessary personnel training for successful operation. For example, India reports success with technological acquisition but deficiencies in trained personnel for operation and maintenance. These issues are articulated in various ways in the other country chapters and reveal close linkages with funding and structure.

The Australia chapter also notes the related issue of information technology and data management. There, a trend is noted toward miniaturization and mobility of equipment, as well as the need for electronic communication. The Finland chapter reminds us that technology also concerns laboratory automation, data systems and electronic archiving.

The mobility factor is also discussed in the Colombia chapter. In Colombia, as in some other countries, major equipment is concentrated in the central facilities, complicating access to those working at long distances.

The Spain chapter notes that technology access varies in different institutions within the country. In countries and institutions lacking resources for acquisition of key equipment, collaboration with others can prove to be helpful. This approach is addressed particularly in the Netherlands and Singapore chapters.

30.10 Disaster preparedness

Many countries report either existing disaster preparedness plans or efforts in place to form them (e.g., Hungary). The following presents a partial listing of the plans outlined for some of the countries in this volume:

Argentina: the Emergency Master Plan for Buenos Aires.

Australia: the Disaster Victim Identification Committee. National training classes are conducted regularly and Interpol guidelines are followed. The Chemical Warfare Agent Laboratory Network is also in place in case of chemical attack.

Colombia: A National Disaster Plan is in place with regular training. Implementation is decentralized with units in eight regions.

Denmark: the Disaster Victim Identification Team is in place.

France: A disaster victim identification unit exists within the Gendarmerie.

Italy: A unit exists for the Identification of Victims of Great Disasters within the Carabinieri.

Japan: In 1997 the Japanese Society of Legal Medicine formed the postmortem examination supporting system.

Mexico: The National Center for Disasters Prevention is available to assist.

The Netherlands: a plan for disaster preparedness has been in place since 2005.

Singapore: units have been formed and include periodic training.

Spain: in 2009 professional roles were defined by law.

South Africa: in 2002 the National Disaster Management Act was passed.

Turkey: teams have been organized and need only six hours of preparation for availability.

United States: units available include those of the Disaster Mortuary Operational Response Team, Armed Forces Medical Examiner System, National Transportation Safety Board, and the Federal Bureau of Investigation.

The efforts and teams listed above are available as needed within their countries. Teams in many countries also have assisted in the aftermath of disaster events in other countries as well. Such international cooperation was especially noted in the chapters on Chile, Denmark, Italy and Singapore.

30.11 Legal issues

Since the important work of the forensic sciences is conducted in a legal context it can be argued that all aspects present legal issues. However, those singled out for discussion in the country chapters primarily relate to the general model for testimony, rules relating to the admission of evidence and expert qualifications.

In all chapters both the judge and prosecutor are cited as key figures in the legal process. In general, the prosecutor has the responsibility to assemble the forensic evidence used against the accused and to organize the presentation of that evidence in the court. The judge regulates this process and makes decisions that directly impact the course of court events. Variance can be seen globally in the role of the defense. Most countries in North America and Europe, as well as Australia, Japan and Singapore, employ an adversarial system that allows for witness cross-examination, defense presentation of experts and independent analysis by defense experts.

In contrast, the United Arab Emirates and other Arab countries employ the inquisitorial system. This system places responsibility for the organization and presentation of evidence in the hands of the prosecutor. The jury system is not employed in any of the Arab countries.

The countries from Latin America represented in the volume report that a transition is generally underway from an inquisitorial model toward elements of an adversarial system. The Argentina chapter describes the current process as "a mixed, semi-adversarial system." The Chile chapter notes that since 2000 AD a shift has been underway to allow a public defense entity. Mexico indicates control by the judge but that the system is moving toward an adversarial jury system. In Colombia, court proceedings relating to forensic testimony can include expert cross-examination with technical support provided to both the prosecution and the accused.

Considerable variation exists in the extent to which rules are defined regarding expert testimony and the admission of evidence. In Germany, the emphasis is upon oral debate in the courts and expert independence. Italy features court (judge) appointed experts. In The Netherlands, the role of the expert is carefully defined, with the judge deciding if the appointment of experts is appropriate in each case. In the United States, court decisions have been registered that relate to scientific testimony and the introduction of evidence but the different states vary in the extent to which they rely upon those decisions.

30.12 Research

Most topics of research interest are of global concern and involve many international teams and projects. Research remains a strong activity of individual scientists who work in both academic and applied institutions. Research sponsored by particular institutions tends to follow the casework needs and priorities of those units. The limiting issues are articulated in the Australia chapter: lack of funds, lack of time and lack of research experience. While these general features are shared globally, most countries report specific factors in relation to research. These are generally summarized in the following discussion.

In Australia, recognized research categories consist of validation of new methods, bringing technology from other science areas to focus on forensic applications and new knowledge. Recent grant history includes attention to specific issues.

Canada reports no central funding source for research. Research reflects individual initiatives, frequently with university or grant funding from a variety of sources.

In Chile, most research in the forensic sciences is conducted within police units. The laboratory units of the police organization employ forensic scientists who conduct research to strengthen their scientific methodology.

Colombia reports a formal program for research including a key publication outlet. Eight areas of research are featured for funding.

In Estonia, research structure and defined topics of interest are listed within the Estonian Forensic Science Institute.

The National Bureau of Investigation in Finland lists a program of research and development but indicates that minimal basic research is conducted there. Most forensic research in Finland is international in scope and conducted through participation in collaborative projects.

The pattern in Hungary consists of a mix of both national and international projects. As in most countries, a variety of institutions are involved.

India reports that most research is concentrated in universities. As in most universities, professors are evaluated on the extent of their research publications.

In Italy, research is conducted in diverse institutions. Recent years have witnessed an increase in research activity and publication.

Japanese research is concentrated in both the universities and police units. Institutional research is closely related to their particular missions.

Research and development in Korea recently has been augmented by funds supplied directly by the Korean government.

In The Netherlands a research and development program is featured in the Nederlands Forensisch Institut. This program targets seven major research issues.

Singapore reports considerable research activity broadly focused in various institutions within the country.

Research is predominately university-based in Spain.

South Africa indicates that many discipline-specific research projects are underway.

In Switzerland, research is largely concentrated within university institutes.

In the United States, research is a robust and diverse activity involving many individuals and institutions. The major funding source of forensic science research has been the National Institute of Justice, located within the Justice Department at the federal level. Like central funding organizations in other countries, they target general areas of research need that have been defined by the forensic science community of scholars and practitioners.

30.13 Future directions

Our chapter authors varied considerably in their responses to the suggestion provided to address key challenges and apparent trends. Those who responded generally presented a mix of major needs and existing problems coupled with some assessment of developments likely to be sustained in the future. As noted in the Germany chapter "predicting the future is no easy matter." Nevertheless, many concerns, developments and wish lists are shared by many countries and offer some grounds for hopeful prediction.

The major issue listed in most countries involved some aspect of laboratory accreditation, quality control, and protecting the security of evidence. These issues were particularly cited in Colombia, Egypt, Estonia, The Netherlands, Japan, South Africa and the United States. Accreditation was a concern even in some countries that currently have it for major laboratories. The apparent goal is to expand accreditation to smaller units or to disciplines that currently lack it. Colombia, Estonia and The Netherlands also list improved certification as a related goal. These countries note the need to establish minimum standards for individual practitioners in a variety of forensic disciplines.

Improved training represents another global concern and likely area for future improvement. Enhanced training is desired by forensic specialists in Finland, Hungary, Korea, The Netherlands, South Africa and Uruguay. These chapters generally note the shortage of trained specialists in some forensic fields and the need to make forensic science sufficiently attractive to entice and maintain key personnel. Authors relate that technology acquisitions must be accompanied by personnel trained to maintain and use them.

Training is also needed for nonforensic specialists in law enforcement and the justice system. Such training is needed to improve how forensic science is utilized in the justice process (Turkey and Japan). Education relates not only to the many positive ways that forensic science can contribute but also its limitations. This general educational initiative was especially apparent in the chapters

from Estonia, Hungary, Japan, Korea, The Netherlands and the United States.

Integration represents another area of major concern. Discussions of the need for enhanced integration related both to activity within the practice of forensic science (note the Italy chapter) and between forensic practitioners and academics in the university system (Egypt, Japan, Korea and Spain). Many countries note a hiring trend in forensic science laboratories and disciplines to utilize those trained in universities. This positive trend requires that university professors are cognitive of laboratory needs and the actual applications of the science being taught. Improved linkages between universities and forensic laboratories are also likely to enhance research initiatives related to forensic applications.

Predicted future directions in the United States closely follow the recommendations of the frequently cited 2009 report of the National Research Council. Basically, the report calls for a national plan for forensic science with augmented federal organization and funding. The need for a similar plan and commitment also was noted in the chapters on Argentina and Australia.

Many of the country chapters noted that technology, trained personnel and general forensic capability were concentrated in major urban centers. A current need and likely future direction is to augment this central resource in ways that better meet needs throughout the country. This development involves regional centers, more rapid response and quality work in rural areas and more mobile use of technology. Such issues are especially noted in the chapters from Australia, Chile and Colombia.

Disaster management and resources to address mass fatalities represents a concern facing many countries. While many regions have disaster preparedness plans in place, it remains an area in need of attention. Future developments in augmenting capability to respond to disaster events were noted especially in Chile, Colombia and Egypt.

Needs and likely future directions related to many other aspects of forensic science. Examples include enhanced molecular and virtual autopsy (Australia and Colombia), improved and more regular international cooperation (Chile and The Netherlands), more forensic resources directed toward child abuse and sexual crimes (Chile and Colombia), improved use of statistics (The Netherlands and South Africa) with enhanced studies of validation and error rates (Australia and the United States), improved infrastructure and facilities (Estonia, The Netherlands and South Africa) and more rapid reporting of results (The Netherlands). The chapters from Singapore and Spain call attention to the need for both research and publication for the advancement of forensic science.

Other issues discussed include improved technology and databases (Japan), the need to protect privacy (Japan) and the assessment of cognitive bias in forensic science (Australia and the United States). The Australia chapter also notes the high cost for training and limited availability of some key personnel that argues for more selective use.

This volume reveals that major issues in the forensic sciences are shared globally. While the key problems are well known to all, each country tries to find its own solutions. These solutions are rooted in the history and culture of the region. Increasingly, new directions call for international cooperation and the global sharing of information. The electronic age greatly improves the potential for such sharing, especially with research publication, development of protocols and technology information. International meetings, workshops and associations now put global practitioners in contact, enhancing training opportunities and information sharing. The global practice of forensic science continues its dynamic evolution.

Index

The Global Practice of Forensic Science, First Edition. Edited by Douglas H. Ubelaker.

© 2015 John Wiley & Sons, Ltd. Published 2015 by John Wiley & Sons, Ltd.